The Guardian
Guide to the UK's Top Companies
1995

The Guardian
Guide to the UK's Top Companies 1995

EDITED BY ROGER COWE

INTRODUCED BY ALEX BRUMMER

FOURTH ESTATE · *London*

First published in Great Britain in 1993 by
Fourth Estate Limited
289 Westbourne Grove
London W11 2QA

This revised edition first published 1994

Copyright © 1993, 1994 by Guardian Newspapers Ltd

The right of Roger Cowe to be identified as the editor of
this work has been asserted by him in accordance with the
Copyright, Designs and Patents Act 1988.

A catalogue record for this book is available from the
British Library.

ISBN 1-85702-239-4

All rights reserved. No part of this publication may be
reproduced, transmitted, or stored in a retrieval system,
in any form or by any means, without permission in writing
from Fourth Estate Limited.

Typeset by Type Technique, London
Printed in Great Britain by The Bath Press, Avon

Contents

Acknowledgements viii

Introduction *by Alex Brummer* ix

Commentary and key xv

BANKS 1

Abbey National
Bank of Scotland
Barclays
HSBC Holdings
Lloyds Bank
National Westminster Bank
Royal Bank of Scotland
Standard Chartered
TSB Group

DRINKS COMPANIES 24

Allied Domecq
Bass
Grand Metropolitan
Guinness
Scottish & Newcastle
Whitbread

DRUG COMPANIES 40

Fisons
Glaxo Holdings
SmithKline Beecham
Wellcome
Zeneca

ELECTRICITY COMPANIES 54

Electricity Generators
National Power
PowerGen
Northern Ireland Electricity
Scottish Hydro-Electric
Scottish Power

Regional Electricity Companies
Eastern Electricity
East Midlands Electricity
London Electricity
MANWEB
Midlands Electricity
Northern Electric
NORWEB
Seeboard
Southern Electric
South Wales Electricity
South Western Electricity
Yorkshire Electricity

INSURANCE COMPANIES 92

Commercial Union
General Accident
Guardian
Legal & General Group
Prudential Corporation
Royal Insurance
Sun Alliance

SUPERMARKET GROUPS 110

Argyll Group
Asda Group
Kwik Save Group
Wm Morrison Supermarkets
J Sainsbury
Tesco

vi CONTENTS

WATER COMPANIES 127

Anglian Water
Northumbrian Water Group
North West Water Group
Severn Trent
Southern Water
South West Water
Thames Water
Welsh Water
Wessex Water
Yorkshire Water

INDIVIDUAL COMPANIES 151

Argos 151
Arjo Wiggins Appleton 154
Associated British Foods 157
BAA 160
BAT Industries 163
BET 167
BICC 170
Blue Circle Industries 173
BOC Group 176
Body Shop International 180
The Boots Company 183
Bowater Industries 186
BPB 189
British Aerospace 192
British Airways 195
British Gas 199
British Petroleum Co 202
British Steel 206
British Telecommunications 209
BTR 213
Burmah Castrol 216
Burton Group 219
Cable & Wireless 222
Cadbury Schweppes 225
Caradon 229
Carlton Communications 232
Coats Viyella 235
Courtaulds 238

De La Rue 241
Dixons Group 244
Enterprise Oil 247
Eurotunnel 250
Forte 253
General Electric Company 256
GKN 260
Granada Group 263
Great Universal Stores 266
Hanson 269
ICI 274
Inchcape 278
Kingfisher 281
Ladbroke Group 284
Land Securities 287
Lonrho 290
Lucas Industries 294
MAI 297
Marks & Spencer 300
MEPC 304
MFI 306
Next 309
NFC 312
Northern Foods 315
P&O 318
Pearson 322
Pilkington 325
The Rank Organisation 328
Reckitt & Colman 332
Redland 335
Reed Elsevier 338
Rentokil Group 341
Reuters Holdings 344
RMC Group 348
Rolls-Royce 351
Rothmans International 355
The RTZ Corporation 358
Saatchi & Saatchi Company 361
Sears 365
Shell Transport & Trading Co 368
Siebe 371
Smith & Nephew 375

W H Smith Group   378
Smiths Industries   381
Storehouse   384
Tarmac   387
Tate & Lyle   390
Taylor Woodrow   393
Thorn-EMI   396
TI Group   399
Tomkins   403
Trafalgar House   406
Unilever   410
United Biscuits (Holdings)   414
United Newspapers   417
Vodafone Group   420
S C Warburg Group   423
Williams Holdings   427
George Wimpey   430
Wolseley   433
WPP Group   436

Analysis and tables   441
Index of brands and subsidiaries, and their parent companies   447
Glossary   451

Acknowledgements

I had always regarded authors' acknowledgements to their families to be rather tokenist, but now I know otherwise. Following completion of this book, I am looking forward to spending more time with my family, as so many government ministers have said at one time or another, although in their case they were preparing to write their books, not to finish them. I owe a huge debt to my family for putting up with my absences, and to my short temper during presences.

Many other people and organisations must also be thanked. Beginning at the beginning, Giles O'Bryen, then editorial director of Fourth Estate, came up with the idea of a book along these lines. *Guardian* financial editor Alex Brummer honed that idea and encouraged me, firstly to develop the idea, and subsequently to edit the book. Alex has also contributed the valuable Introduction. Other members of the *Guardian* business team are also owed thanks, partly for bearing with my distraction during the book's preparation, and secondly for contributing, as follows: Nicholas Bannister, for Outlooks on BT, Cable & Wireless and Vodafone; Simon Beavis, for the Outlook sections on the electricity industry and British Gas; Lisa Buckingham and Ben Laurance, for sharing with me the task of updating the bulk of the company commentaries; Nick Pandya, for verifying the key reference data; Rebecca Smithers, for Outlooks on British Airways, Eurotunnel and NFC; Pauline Springett, for the building and property companies.

Two other individuals have played an important part in this book: Kate Parker, the copy-editor, whose meticulous attention to detail has prevented many errors appearing and whose questioning has helped to clarify the text at various points; and Clive Priddle of Fourth Estate, whose ideas, observations and overall management of the project has ensured that it reached its conclusion more or less on time and in good shape.

I must also acknowledge major sources of information. EIRIS has contributed directly, because its research forms the basis for the section on corporate conscience. Corporate governance details stem from information provided by PIRC for the first edition. Also Datastream whose database has provided the financial records, share price statistics and the graphs. Others have helped indirectly: New Consumer, whose publications *Changing Corporate Values* and *Britain's Best Employers* include valuable ideas as well as information. Both these books were published by Kogan Page. The Ethical Consumer publication was also a useful reference. More broadly, I owe thanks to all the stockbrokers' analysts who have shared their views with me since 1987, when the Outlook column commenced in its present form in the *Guardian*, and who regularly provide their research material.

Finally, and in another statement which is far from tokenist, any errors and omissions remain my responsibility.

Roger Cowe
London, July 1994

Introduction

The corporation, or 'company' as we have come to know it, is going through profound change. Two major themes are evident – organisational or struc- tural change, and a shift in the underlying values which guide companies' operations.

These developments are altering dramatically the concept of major companies as national champions – an attitude which has been with us since the Second World War and which was best summed up by the one-time General Motors chairman Charles E Wilson, speaking before the US Congress in 1952: 'What is good for the country, is good for General Motors, and what's good for General Motors is good for the country.' This philosophy, which could have been applied equally to British Petroleum or to ICI in Britain, is looking increasingly dated. Companies are now global organisations in which the centre of management and production is often much less powerful and important than some of the parts. The split in 1993 of Britain's bellwether industrial corporation ICI into two parts (ICI, the bulk chemical group, and Zeneca, the bioscience and pharmaceutical business) is part of this trend, as is the rationalisation of IBM as a computer superpower and the decision of foreign-owned transnationals, like Nissan and Hoover, to move production to the United Kingdom.

In much the same way as the organisation, span and range of the company has changed, so has the ethical framework in which it operates, and consequently the objectives and constraints which guide the business world. The earliest joint stock companies of the 16th and 17th centuries, like the Muscovy Company and the East India Company, were largely exploitative: they would deal in anything from opium to slaves so long as it turned a profit. Similarly, at the coal mines and textile mills on which the industrial revolution was built, profit was king. Child labour and life on the factory floor were cheap. It was only with the great social reforms of the 19th and 20th centuries and with the rise of trade unionism that corporations began to acknowledge that they had responsibilities other than delivering profits to the owners, prosperity to the managers and dividends to the shareholders. The growing strength of the labour movement, together with health and safety legislation and the welfare state, required the corporation to take on new social responsibilities as part of the business of making profits and dividends. However, despite all the legal requirements, from the Companies Acts (which govern the way in which companies are run) to modern environmental legislation, most corporate behaviour can be justified in one phrase – the interests of the shareholder. It is in the name of the shareholder that a variety of corporate transgressions from carelessness in the treatment of the consumer, to fraud and environmental despoilation, have been justified.

In the mid-1990s this is no longer acceptable behaviour. It is no longer relevant to see corporations simply in terms of quarterly or half-yearly dividends. Companies have to be seen to have medium- to long-term horizons. It is not sensible to pay dividends this year and ask shareholders for more funds to expand next year; it makes no corporate sense, no industrial sense, no economic sense. The modern corporation, to be successful, has to be attentive to a wide range of different groups in addition to the shareholder. These other stakeholders have as large a share in the survival, prosperity and integrity of the corporation as the shareholders themselves. Indeed, in an era of increasingly blurred ownership lines – in which the largest shareholders are often pension funds representing groups of retirees and future retirees – they are, in effect, one and the same.

Who are these other stakeholders? They are the consumers who buy a product or a service; the em-ployees who make the product and provide the service; the environment which is touched by the process of production and distribution – both the local environment, for instance in the case of a new terminal at Heathrow Airport, and the national and global environment in terms of chlorofluorocarbon levels, global warming and the greenhouse effect. Then there are the suppliers. These are not just the firms providing the components. In an era of out-sourcing and increasing specialisation many companies are no longer unitary but modular – a global network of interconnecting units. Perhaps, however, the most important stakeholder of all is a nation's industrial base and its economy. A good company leads by example. A firm which pays its executives 30 per cent extra per annum when a country is in recession is neither leading by example, using its shareholders' funds wisely or contributing sensibly to the nation's economy. Similarly, a firm which puts dividends above strategic investment in research and development is also doing the shareholders and the economy a disservice.

Indeed, the purpose of the non-financial analysis in this book is to show that there are many other ways of looking at companies other than in terms of share price, dividend, earnings per share, debt/equity ratios, cash flow and the yields on the warrants. These are important and recognisable measures of corporate success, but not the only ones. Marks & Spencer has for decades recognised that looking after other stakeholders, notably its workforce and the consumer, produces handsome dividends in the shape of employee loyalty, a skilled workforce, consumer preference and a higher rating for its shares than others in the retail sector. It has also recognised that there is better quality to be obtained as well as kudos from buying British, wherever possible, and by forming close links with suppliers.

Many corporations, particularly in the Anglo-Saxon economies, have failed to respond quickly enough to worldwide changes in business practice. These changes include the globalisation of production; a less centralised and more mobile style of management; the impact of technology (and particularly the microprocessor) on the way that companies operate, communicate and process information. The nature of these changes, as they apply to the United States, is outlined by Robert B Reich in his influential book *The Work of Nations* (Simon & Schuster, 1992). However, the principles he espouses are common to most of the larger Group of Seven industrial countries, and to Britain in particular because it shares a common style of capitalism with the US. It is argued that national champions everywhere, from IBM to ICI and Daimler-Benz, are being supplanted by 'global webs' which have no particular connection to any single nation. In much the same way as British companies increasingly produce and buy from abroad, so it is that overseas firms increasingly produce and buy in Britain. Nissan, in many respects, is now a British car maker in much the same way as Rover – now owned by the German manufacturer BMW – which in turn has production and licensing agreements with another Japanese company, Honda. GEC and its French counterpart, Alstrom, have pooled technology and production to engineer and market trains, such as the TGV, and power stations. The British computer manufacturer ICL has become a UK outpost of its Japanese owners, Fujitsu. The global networks owe nothing to particular nations, but they do conform to certain patterns. There is a cost arbitrage which basically puts mass production into the lower-wage economies (such as Britain) close to a high-volume, high-wage economy such as that in much of Continental Europe. This was the French complaint against Scotland's capture of Dijon's Hoover production.

With this different style of manufacturing comes a different style of organisation. Regional or local management has much more autonomy. Instead of looking towards the centre for specialist services, it brokers them locally. Companies buy in a series of services, from management consultancy to advanced research, public relations, engineering, investment banking and software engineering. It is this decentralisation together with technological advances – such as fascimile, electronic messaging, satellite communications and video conferencing – which have rendered the huge corporate headquarters, of the likes of IBM or ICI, obsolete. The world recession of 1989–92 was as much about shedding what the army would call staff jobs, as it was about firing the 'poor bloody infantry'. Indeed, modern corporations have become a little like modern armies: the stress is on a small centre and on a great deal of rapid-deployment capability.

Accompanying these structural changes has been a change of mood in the world's boardrooms. The buccaneering entrepreneur is no longer so fashionable. Powerful institutional shareholders, representing the major investment funds, have become more fastid-ious about corporate behaviour. These shareholders have become less tolerant of management mistakes and less trusting of executives who demand to take too much of the decision-making unto themselves. In the first category one must include the dramatic departures of John Akers as chief executive of IBM early in 1993; James Robinson at American Express; Paul Lego at Westinghouse; Bob Horton at BP in 1992; and Ernest Scroggs, chief executive of drugs group Fisons, in late 1993. The activism of institutional shareholders and non-executives in fact cost some 25 UK chief executives their jobs during 1992. And chieftains who once thought they were invincible, like Lord King of British Airways and Lords Hanson and White of the Hanson group, have felt the hot breath of corporate governance upon their necks.

Much of the pressure currently being exerted on Britain's boardrooms stems from the Robert Maxwell affair. When the late boss of two public companies (Mirror Group Newspapers and Maxwell Communications Corporation) tipped overboard off the Canary Islands in 1991, a huge financial chasm opened up. But, just as significantly, the 'tycoon factor' – too much power vested in a single corporate executive – became a downside for any quoted company. Those around Robert Maxwell were shown to be ciphers with no power to hold the persuasive entrepreneur in check. After that experience and amid a great deal of dissatisfaction over other aspects of boardroom behaviour, from the exaggerated amounts that executives paid themselves to the accounting devices adopted to make profits figures look better, the Cadbury Committee was formed with the aim of providing UK companies with a framework to govern themselves better.

The Cadbury Code, which was eventually adopted in the autumn of 1992, seeks to make company boards sensitive to the broader range of governance and other social issues which confront corporations in the 1990s. The Code's central theme was that no longer could major corporations (there are questions in terms of a company's size as to how far the structures of corporate governance can be applied) be run like personal fiefdoms. Boardrooms, like democratic governments, need checks and balances if the all-powerful executive is not to trample over the interests of stakeholders.

John Thompson, a senior executive at insurance group Standard Life, and regarded as a guru in the important Edinburgh fund management community, quotes Lord Acton to make the case for broader distribution of authority and responsibility in the boardroom: 'Power tends to corrupt and absolute power corrupts absolutely.' Mr Thompson believes that the same principles must apply to businessmen, and none should be excluded. He has insisted, for instance, that a corporate chairman as powerful as Lord Hanson appear before his investment committee to explain various aspects of its profits statements and governance.

The Cadbury Report laid down several basic rules for improving the power structure in Britain's boardrooms. At the very pinnacle of the company' author-ity should be split between an experienced chairman and an effective chief executive. It is no longer satisfactory for the power to be vested in a single individual. The Cadbury rule has already begun to prevail. At BAT Industries, for instance, the driving force in recent years, Sir Patrick Sheehy, announced in 1993 that he would be sharing power with a new chief executive, Martin Broughton. Barclays, after a long internal debate, split the roles of chairman and chief executive once invested in a single individual – Andrew Buxton – between him and a new chief executive, Martin Taylor. At British Airways, where an ethical breach in the shape of the alleged dirty-tricks campaign against Virgin cost the company dearly, Lord King paid with his job, and his successor, Sir Colin Marshall, is required to share boardroom responsibilities with group managing director Robert Ayling.

But simply splitting the role of chairman and chief executive and adding non-executive/independent directors will not change delinquent behaviour in Britain's boardrooms. That requires a new boardroom culture, a greater sensitivity to shareholders and a willingness to listen and respond to other stakeholders: in other words, a fresh value system. Some of the Cadbury Code attempts to address this. The recommendations for non-executive remuneration committees were designed to curb some of the worst excesses of overpayment in the boardrooms, but the system has not worked as expected. Directors' salaries have increased sharply, at a time of wage restraint elsewhere in the economy, as the remuneration committees have rounded up wage increases and constructed over-generous performance-related pay schemes. Similarly, the three-year limit on service contracts was intended to bring an end to large-scale pay-offs such as those seen at the retailing group Burton, at British Aerospace and at the pharmaceuticals group Glaxo. The Association of British Insurers, one of the largest institutional investor groups, now recommends a one-year limit on service contracts and pay-offs. In addition, the introduction of audit committees should ensure that 'independent' auditors are protected from the interference of top executives who have the power to dismiss them.

Far less clearly defined in the Cadbury Report is the company's relationship with other stakeholders and its role in a broader society. In much the same way as there should be a remuneration committee and an audit committee, there must be a case in the 1990s and beyond for a strategic panel and an environmental panel. The strategic committee would be looking at the long-range change in corporate organisations and helping directors make staffing decisions to adjust to that. It would also need to look over the horizon: many boards cannot see beyond the next dividend payment. The strategic committee would need to look at future investment, research and development, and carry out cost-benefit analysis on new projects. But most important of all, it would need to accept that in the successful modern corporation, in which the skill base, expertise and technological edge are be all important, there must be a willingness to look beyond two or three years of losses towards profits in seven years' time. Britain's most prosperous corporations, like Glaxo and Wellcome, have done just that and have become the centre of hugely successful global networks. Britain's retailing chains such as Marks & Spencer, Tesco and Sainsbury have invested heavily in new-concept stores, fresh technologies and new products, and it has paid off handsomely. But those companies without strategic vision, including many which were once part of our manufacturing base, have failed on this front, putting short-term gains ahead of longer-term growth.

Similarly, Britain's directors need to pay as much attention to the welfare of employees as to their own. At a time when government training and retraining budgets are under stress, if existent at all, the new corporation has a role to play in finding its surplus employees new skills and redeploying them humanely. It must recognise that pension funds are not simply a pot of cash, for the use of management, but are a form of deferred wages which become even more important at a time of a more mobile labour market and corporate structures that are perpetually changing.

It is the ability of companies to adapt to fast-changing economic structures and new social and environmental responsibilities which will ensure their success in future generations. Those companies which have ignored their environmental responsibil-ities are now being forced to meet the costs through tougher regulation. Far better to incorporate the 'green' factor into investment decisions. This is among the many fresh ways in which companies will be assessed in the 1990s and beyond the year 2000. In this guide we seek to analyse companies by looking at them through a high-powered, multifaceted telescope – moving beyond the cult of the dividend.

Alex Brummer
Editor *Guardian* Finance & Economics section

Commentary and key

This book builds a picture of big business in Britain, through profiles of almost 150 leading companies. It charts the couplings and uncouplings, the diversifications and disposals, the follies and the fashions of the 1980s, and the effect that these had upon Britain's top companies as they emerged from the recession into the mid-1990s. Financial statistics and share price movements are part of the picture, but it is based, above all, on the premise that business is about much more than sales and profits, earnings per share and price/earnings ratios. Business is more complex than is often supposed, and the Outlook sections on these companies explore those complexities, explain strategies and histories and analyse the business issues. The major companies are also viewed as important members of society, and their impact on society is reported, using a number of environmental, social and ethical criteria. In the belief that how companies are run is as important as how large their profits are, how they measure up to the new standards of corporate governance is also covered. This approach to business provides a uniquely rounded view of Britain's most significant companies, which this book has attempted to capture for the benefit of existing and potential investors, employees, suppliers, customers and the communities in which these companies operate.

Such a project has involved some difficult decisions about what material to include – which this foreword explains, as well as clarifying the criteria used and describing specific items referred to in each section of the profiles.

Coverage

The first decision concerned which companies to include. The members of the FTSE 100 index in the first quarter of 1993 – the 100 largest companies quoted on the Stock Exchange, measured by their stock market value – form the core of the book. To them have been added those privatised utilities which are not in the FTSE 100; large and important companies such as Storehouse, Lucas and Trafalgar House, which were not in the index at the time of writing because of the impact of recession or of excesses during the 1980s; and smaller companies which are sufficiently interesting and important, or potential FTSE members of the future, such as Body Shop and Argos.

Inevitably, there were some companies which would have merited inclusion had there been more space, but the line had to be drawn somewhere. Hence such companies as EMAP, Unigate and Lloyds Chemists had to be excluded. Perhaps they will find a place in future editions.

There are a number of changes from the first edition. Out have gone the smaller building and property companies and others which have shrunk or were just above the cut-off in the first edition but fell just below this year. They are Signet, which was Ratners; Dalgety; English China Clays; Hillsdown; Racal; Vickers and – despite its victory against Enterprise – Lasmo.

In their place are the building-materials companies BPB and RMC, retailers MFI and Next, media groups MAI and United Newspapers, plus S G Warburg and Wolseley.

Timing

Another key decision concerned timing. There is no close season for business; no point at which companies records can be added up and compared on an identical basis. Companies' can and do choose any point in the calendar year as the end of their financial year, which means that whatever the publication date for this book, there would be some companies with recently published new financial information which could not be included. December is the most popular year-end date, however, so publication has been timed to include as far as possible the latest figures for those companies with December year-ends. Unfortunately this means that some 1994 figures for those companies with March year-ends (which report their results in June) could not be included.

It is not just the cut-off date for the financial records that needed to be taken into account. Brands and subsidiaries change hands, directors are appointed and resign, regardless of the time of year. This particularly affects the Corporate Governance section on each company, since in the wake of the Cadbury Report, published in December 1992, many companies have been making changes to their boardroom arrangements, details of which were not revealed until the publication of annual reports in the spring and summer. I have endeavoured to ensure that such details are correct as at 30 June 1994. Likewise the stock market values quoted are as at July 1994, while share price data cover periods up to the same date. The date of the latest financial data is shown at the top of the final column in the Financial Record.

Organisation

Those companies which are sufficiently similar have been grouped together in homogeneous sectors: banks and insurers, the supermarket groups, the electricity and water companies, drinks and drug companies. But over half the companies covered by this book cannot easily be categorised in this way, even though they operate in the same industry and might be members of the same Stock Exchange sector. There are many similarities between Storehouse and Marks & Spencer, for example, but there are also many differences, so that these and other stores companies have individual entries. Likewise, Smith & Nephew, while officially a member of the same stock market sector as Glaxo and Wellcome, is treated separately here because it is not primarily a drug company.

The main textual part of each entry, whether it concerns an individual company or a sector, consists of an Outlook, modelled on the column of the same name which appears daily in the *Guardian*'s financial pages. This offers a commentary on the company or sector, highlighting what could be considered to be most important and interesting about its past, present and possible future. Together, these commentaries offer an insight into the recent history of British business: the successes and failures, the swings in strategy from diversification to concentration, the 1980s takeover boom, fuelled by excesses of ambition and debt, and followed by recuperation.

This discursive section is preceded by a collection of key reference data giving a snapshot of what each company is and does, its size, growth and solvency, and the major developments in its history. Principal brands and subsidiaries are listed, with the emphasis on those most relevant to UK readers and those not carrying the company name. This information is supplemented by an index of the most significant brands and subsidiaries, together with the companies that own them. These individual sections are supplemented and analysed by a review of the whole, including a collection of useful tables providing unique snapshots of British industry from 1989 to 1994. A glossary of financial and business terms is also provided at the back of the book.

On the basis that fluctuations in the share price are often only loosely related to the key events in a company's life, a separate section charts movements in the share price, over the last five years for most companies, but less than that for those which have not been public companies for that period, and occasionally for a longer period where that is necessary to illustrate a long-term trend.

Based on the belief that large companies have an importance to society beyond their mere financial impact, a section labelled Corporate Conscience has also been included, which reports upon a company's ethical and environmental stand. This section is based on the extensive research material supplied by the ethical information service EIRIS. Likewise, the pensions research group PIRC has supplied the detailed boardroom data which forms the basis of the section examining how each company governs itself.

The remainder of this foreword explains the main items referred to in each of these sections, as well as the accounting measures included in the Financial Record.

Key reference data

Substantial shareholdings have been included only where the holder is or could be significant for the company – routine holdings by institutions such as Prudential or other insurance companies have not been included.

Brands and subsidiaries have only been included if there is no obvious connection with the parent company, and if they are likely to be known to a British audience. Thus those bearing the name of the holding company (such as Granada TV under Granada), or foreign subsidiaries, have not normally been included.

Financial record

There are many ways of assessing businesses financially. None are perfect. Indeed, as explained later, accounting information in the late 1980s was seriously flawed, making financial analysis even more difficult. The Financial Record section presents a concise, comprehensive picture of the finances of each company. It covers key profit and loss figures such as sales, profits, earnings and dividends, cash flow and balance sheet data, and key ratios. The information is drawn from the Datastream database (as are the graphs which amplify this financial analysis). The figures may not correspond with those published in companies' official accounts, because Datastream adjusts the published accounts in several ways: to aid comparability between companies and over time; and to minimise the impact of companies' creative accounting. (We have also followed the Datastream convention of using an 'M' at the end of a figure to indicate that it is expressed in millions rather than the usual hundreds of thousands.)

The first group of figures concentrates on profits and the distribution of profits. *Total sales* gives an indication of the size of a company, and its growth. *Pre-tax profit* is the main measure of profit. It refers to profits after all routine costs and charges, including interest costs, have been taken into account, but before tax and dividends. (Unlike interest payments, dividends are considered to be a distribution of profits to shareholders, rather than a cost of capital.) Until a new accounting standard came into force in 1993, however, one crucial omission from pre-tax profit was a group of costs or charges described as 'extraordinary items'. This term was intended to be used rarely, for items (costs or profits) which were truly beyond the normal scope of the business. In practice, though, many companies routinely categorised redundancy and reorganisation costs as extraordinary. This had the effect of inflating pre-tax profits, so *published retentions* are also shown – i.e. net profit after all costs or income, tax and dividends. This is the final profit which is added to shareholders' funds to increase the net wealth of the company (or deducted, in the case of losses).

Significant takeovers financed by issuing shares distort the profits trend, since the profit of the acquired company is added to the existing company's profits. For this reason *earnings per share* became a popular measure of profits during the 1980s. This represents the profits (after tax) available for shareholders, expressed as an amount per share rather than an absolute figure. Thus a share-based acquisition would add to pre-tax profits, but not to earnings per share, unless the acquired profits represented a higher earnings figure in relation to the shares issued to make the acquisition (see below, under Takeover Accounting, for a fuller explanation). Earnings per share is also important because it is the basis for the price/earnings ratio, commonly used to assess share price levels. Until 1993 extraordinary items were excluded from the earnings figure, which in that respect was as flawed an indicator as pre-tax profit. And the nature of the calculation means that a suitably priced, share-based takeover will increase earnings per share even if performance does not change. Together with the ratios explained later, however, these are the best available measures of profit.

Dividend per share is the amount actually paid out to shareholders (earnings being the amount of profit the company has made on their behalf – the relationship between the two is expressed as *dividend cover*, which is explained later.) The dividend is the only item so far which represents actual cash. Even the sales figure is an accounting number which represents the value of goods sold rather than the amount of cash received during the year. Profit and cash flow can deviate widely, mainly because of the impact of capital investment (for accounting purposes the cash outflow is spread over a number of years and charged against profits as depreciation), but also because of changes in working capital (stocks, debtors and creditors). Cash flow is particularly important in times of financial crisis, since heavy cash outflows can cause trouble for expanding companies with limited resources, while companies in financial trouble can ease their plight by squeezing working capital and cutting capital investment, even if they are making losses. The *operating cash flow* figure represents net cash from the company's operations, after tax, dividends and all other costs or profits; after net capital investment, but before acquisitions or disposals and the raising or repayment of capital. It is roughly analogous to what is sometimes described as 'free cash flow' and indicates (over a period such as five years) whether a company is generating spare funds which will finance expansion.

For most companies, profits are more important than assets, but the value of a company's assets are nevertheless significant. When (before stricter accounting standards were introduced in 1993) huge provisions or write-offs could be slipped past the reported profit figures, examining the change in assets might have given a better indication of progress. This type of analysis is most applicable to asset-based business such as hotels, and is expressed as *net assets per share*, in the same way as earnings per share, to cope with distortions from share-based takeovers.

The other balance sheet figures quoted are the *net debt/(cash)* position at the end of each year, and the total of *shareholders' funds*. Shareholders' funds represent a company's net wealth, which technically belongs to the shareholders. It is the total of capital contributed by shareholders, plus the accumulation of those net profits which have not been distributed as dividends, and any other increases in wealth such as a rise in the value of property. In the early 1990s, of course, property values were plunging, and this hit shareholders' funds in many asset-based companies, notably the builders, brewers and property companies. Because such reductions in wealth do not pass through the profit and loss account, even as extraordinary items, shareholders' funds sometimes fall even when the company is showing positive retained profit. The same applies when a company makes a big takeover involving large write-offs of goodwill (see below under Takeover Accounting).

In addition, shareholders' funds are important in combination with other figures. The level of debt, for example, is usually assessed by comparison with the level of shareholders' funds. The relationship of debt to equity (expressed as a percentage) is known as 'gearing' – shown in the key reference data for each company as a measure of *solvency*. Bankers generally like to see significantly more equity (shareholders' capital) in a company than debt – in other words, gearing should be well below 100 per cent. Most companies, in most circumstances, aim to keep gearing below 70 per cent. Otherwise, room for financial manoeuvre becomes severely limited, but also interest costs are likely to mount alarmingly.

The level of debt is an imperfect guide to the level of interest costs, however, especially in these days of financial instruments which fix interest at low levels even in times of high interest rates. Also, what matters is a company's ability to pay the interest bill, which depends on available profits rather than capital employed. Thus *interest cover* has become popular as a measure of financial viability, being the number of times the interest bill is 'covered' by the available profits. Most companies aim to keep interest above three times, and would be happier with five times. (Under the Datastream convention, interest cover is shown as negative if the interest figure is income rather than a cost.)

Interest cover is one of the collection of ratios included in the Financial Record. These help to compare companies of different sizes, where the relationship between the absolute figures might be less obvious, but, more importantly, the ratios help to assess performance by relating one figure to another.

Return on capital, for example, shows profits in relation to the capital employed in the business. In this case the ratio links profits before interest to the total capital employed: loan capital and equity. This is the most common measure of profitability, and is useful because it includes a measure of the efficiency with which a company uses its capital, as well as the efficiency of its operations.

The latter is reflected in the *profit margin*, expressing pre-tax profits as a percentage of sales. This is particularly relevant to trading businesses such as retailers, but also applies to other companies. Care must be taken in interpreting movements in the margin: they may not relate directly to the direct margin between cost and selling price. Margins change because of the changing nature of a company, and because of changes in sales volumes, which spread overhead costs more, or less, thinly and thus affect the profit margin percentage even if costs and selling prices have not altered.

Sales per employee is also particularly relevant for retailers, as well as being a rough measure of profitability for any company.

Dividend cover is a similar concept to interest cover, showing the number of times the dividend is 'covered' by available earnings. In the UK up to half of post-tax profits are normally paid out to shareholders, so that a dividend cover of two times would be acceptable. Anything below that level begins to put the maintenance of the dividend in doubt, however, unless profits are expected to rise swiftly.

Ratios showing the percentage increase in sales and earnings help to interpret the absolute figures shown at the top of the table. The percentages show whether growth (or decline) is accelerating or decelerating, which is unlikely to be obvious from the absolute figures.

The final two ratios refer to investment. Since depreciation spreads the capital investment across the expected life of the equipment of a company, maintaining that company's capital base should require investment at least equal to the amount of depreciation (not necessarily in each year, but taking several years together). Allowing for the fact that depreciation is based on historical costs, which might be assumed to be an average of five years out of date, investment should exceed depreciation by the level of inflation over the previous five years (a total of 33 per cent between 1988 and 1993). *Investment x depreciation* helps to assess the level of investment, but more importantly the trend, and is supplemented by the other investment ratio, expressing *investment as a percentage of assets*.

Finally, the *number of employees* helps to remind readers that businesses are about people as well as capital and inanimate assets, and this measure indicates how a company has been growing or shrinking. This number is complicated by the growing use of part-time employees, especially in retailing. In general, the number quoted is the total number of people, not the equivalent number of full-time employees.

This collection of figures should give a reasonable interpretation of the position and performance of most companies. But there are a number of caveats.

First, numerical analysis can generally only raise questions rather than provide answers. The answers come from the business itself – from what the company is doing or is planning to do, and what is happening in its markets. Second, figures can be misleading. For example, a five-year growth trend can seem impressive, until inflation is taken into account. Cumulative inflation from mid-1989 to mid-1993 amounted to 22 per cent, so that sales, earnings or similar growth of less than that over the period actually represent real decline.

Third, some companies are less susceptible to the standard accounting treatment and analysis which applies to the mass of manufacturers and retailers. Oil companies, for example, have rather different characteristics to most, although they are sufficiently similar to fit the standard analysis. Property and financial companies (banks and insurers) are so different that the Financial Record for these companies has been tailored specifically to suit them. For example, *sales* has been replaced by *rental income* for the property sector, *net interest* for banks, and *premiums* for insurance companies. Many of the ratios are also different, although where possible ratios have been used to address similar issues to those of the mainstream companies.

Takeover accounting

The integrity of accounting figures was severely damaged during the 1980s by lax reporting rules. These have been tightened up in the early 1990s, with a number of Financial Reporting Standards, issued by the Accounting Standards Board, that strictly limit the scope for choice in presenting the accounts, and have forced greater and clearer disclosure. One consequence has been that profits and earnings per share are likely to show a much less even progression from 1993 onwards than they have in the past.

The worst examples of lax accounting were in the area of takeovers, which has meant that it is essential to treat with extreme caution the accounting figures from any company which indulged in frequent takeovers in the 1980s. A number of factors muddied the waters:

● Goodwill. After a takeover the acquirer determines what is called the 'fair value' of the assets which have been bought, and adds this amount to its balance sheet. The difference between this and the actual amount paid for the acquisition (often a very large sum, especially in takeovers of service companies or others with a low level of assets) is described as 'goodwill' and is immediately written out of the balance sheet. This has the effect of reducing shareholders' funds, in extreme cases such as Saatchi & Satchi and WPP actually turning the figure negative. This clearly disturbs any ratio (such as gearing or return on capital) which uses the shareholders' funds figure.

● Fair value. Determining the 'fair value' of assets is fraught with difficulty and can have a significant impact on subsequent profits. A company which

undervalues the acquired assets benefits from an immediate bonus when assets such as stocks or debtors are realised, and if fixed assets are undervalued, this reduces the subsequent depreciation charge.
● Reorganisation provisions. Companies making acquisitions have also been allowed at the time of the takeover to make provisions for the cost of planned reorganisation. This has the effect of removing those costs from the profit calculation in subsequent years when the reorganisation is carried out. Companies making acquisitions therefore have an automatic profits advantage over non-acquirers, which have to set such reorganisation costs against profits – especially now that such costs cannot be treated as extraordinary, as they could until 1993.
● The takeover price effect. Even without manipulating the accounting figures, the price of a takeover will affect the group's subsequent earnings per share. If the price/earnings ratio of the acquisition is lower than that of the acquirer's shares, earnings will rise, merely as an arithmetical result of the deal and even if there is absolutely no change in the performance of the two companies. This was one of the key factors in the 1980s takeover boom: high p/e ratios enabled companies to make share-based takeovers, which automatically increased earnings per share, thus sustaining the high share price and enabling further takeovers, even if the underlying business was in decline, as it often was.

Analysis of such acquisitive companies is therefore extremely dangerous, but operating ratios, such as sales per employee and profit margins, can help to pierce the fog enveloping their accounts.

Share price graph
Movements in a company's share price reflect investors' views about the company itself, but also movements of the market as a whole, based on investors' feelings about general economic prospects. The share graphs therefore show two lines: one of the actual share price; the second showing the movement of the share price relative to the stock market as a whole (as represented by the all-share index). This second line merely indicates relative movement – the scale on the axis does not apply to it. If a share price had moved exactly in line with the all-share index, this second line would be flat. If the line rises, this indicates that the share price has performed better than the market (it might have fallen in absolute terms, but by a smaller proportion than the whole market). If the relative line falls, this shows that the share price has performed worse than the all-share index.

Share record
The statistics that accompany the graphs show the main indicators of share price performance, adding to the information on share price provided by the graphs. The figures show the position in July 1994, plus the high and low over the previous five years.

Return on shareholders' equity is a return on capital figure, which relates specifically to the returns for shareholders. Unlike the return on capital shown in the Financial Record, it relates profits after interest payments to shareholders' capital alone, rather than to total capital employed

The *price/earnings ratio* is the main means of assessing the relative price of a share. Prices cannot be compared directly, because a share in one company represents a different entitlement to that in another. Prices can only be compared by reference to the wealth or earnings which the shares offer. This is what the p/e ratio does: relating the price of a share to the earnings (not dividends) attached to it. It is calculated as share price divided by earnings per share.

Dividend yield relates shareholders' income from the dividend (as opposed to notional earnings) to the share price. It is analagous to an interest rate, although it must be remembered that for most shareholders the main benefit of holding shares is the capital growth, not the dividend income.

Corporate conscience
This section of each entry reports upon each company's or sector's ethical, social and environmental performance. The information is based on research by EIRIS, the Ethical Investment Research Service, which uses a wide-ranging checklist and reports the involvement of any part of a company in each item on the list. EIRIS makes no judgements about the morality of these activities: it merely indicates their presence in or absence from a company. This is particularly important for an issue such as involvement in South Africa, which has swung from being a negative to a positive factor since transition to a democratically elected government. EIRIS's main findings for each company have been detailed, with an indication of the scale and importance of a company's involvement, where appropriate. As in other sections, a flavour of a company's attitude has been given, as well as the bald facts. There has been no attempt to replicate EIRIS's checklist for each company: only what is most significant for each has been reported. These judgements have been made using other material in addition to the EIRIS research, including publications from New Consumer. It is possible that the involvement of a subsidiary in an area of ethical concern took place before that company was acquired by its present owner; such involvements are deemed to have been transferred with the acquisition.

The following explains some of the ethical criteria employed by EIRIS and used in the Corporate Conscience section:
● Advertising. Complaints from the public upheld by the Advertising Standards Authority (ASA) in the two-year period to the start of 1993.
● Animal testing. Companies are reported if they make or sell drugs, cosmetics, toiletries or other products which have been (or ingredients of which have been) normally tested on animals, unless it is clear that these products have not been tested on

animals. Reference is made to companies which support research into alternatives through the British Union for the Abolition of Vivisection (BUAV) and the Fund for the Replacement of Animals in Medical Experiments (FRAME).

● Community involvement. Membership of Business in the Community (BITC) and the Per Cent Club (set up by members of BITC) is reported, and an indication given of the extent of a company's community and charitable support by way of donations and secondment of staff, or by other means such as payroll-giving schemes, which encourage employees to make regular donations where companies have provided EIRIS with this information.

● Electricity service. Measures of complaints, disconnections and failures, as reported by the electricity industry's regulator, Offer. The period covered is April 1991 to March 1992, except for failure to comply with the specific standards of performance laid down by the regulator, which only became effective in July 1991 – in this instance the period covered is July 1991 to March 1992.

● Environment. EIRIS reports companies which have a publicly stated environmental policy that meets at least two of the following criteria: it is comprehensive, dealing with all aspects of the group's environmental impact; it includes measurable goals and target dates; it includes specific rules, guidelines or responsibilities for implementation; it includes regular monitoring and review. Companies which have had an independent environmental audit are also reported, where they have reported this to EIRIS.

● Equal opportunities. Formal policy for recruitment, training and monitoring of women and ethnic minorities; the proportions of these groups constituted by management staff; carers' benefits (i.e. flexitime, job sharing, career breaks, childcare facilities, maternity and paternity leave).

● Health and safety. EIRIS reports groups which have been successfully prosecuted by the Health and Safety Executive, (not by local authorities). The period covered in this book is 1988–92.

● Human rights. EIRIS uses four lists of countries which might be considered to infringe human rights (referred to in this book as countries with oppressive regimes): 39 countries in which Amnesty International (AI) has reported extra-judicial executions or disappearances; 65 countries where AI has reported incidences of torture; 51 countries where AI has identified prisoners of conscience; 40 countries which have committed frequent official acts of violence against citizens, according to the latest edition of *World Military and Social Expenditures*.

● Military involvement. Contracts with the Ministry of Defence in the three years to spring 1992; the production or sale of civilian or non-civilian goods for military use; exports to military users; taking part in defence exhibitions.

● Ozone-depleting chemicals (ODCs). EIRIS identifies those companies which supply or use ODCs, including chlorofluorocarbons (CFCs). It also reports companies which are committed to phasing out ODCs by the end of 1995.

● Pesticides. Any manufacture of pesticide products; marketing of products thought by the Health and Safety Executive to be implicated in incidents investigated by them, or including ingredients banned or restricted in at least five countries, or on the UK government's Red List. The Red List covers 23 toxic substances which the Department of the Environment believes to present the greatest danger to the aquatic environment.

● South Africa. Reported separately from countries which infringe human rights. EIRIS monitors wage levels of black South African workers as recorded by companies in their annual filings with the Department of Trade and Industry. It compares these with two standards of minimum pay: 50 per cent higher than the minimum living level (MLL) for a family of six people (as recommended by the 1977 European Commission Code of Conduct); and the supplemented living level (SLL) for a family of five people (described as the 'absolute minimum' by the 1985 revision of the Code). These required wage levels are calculated by the University of South Africa, and the SLL (described in this book as the absolute minimum) is approximately 15 per cent lower than MLL + 50 per cent (described as a reasonable minimum level).

● Trade union representation. EIRIS reports companies which have shown that at least a quarter of their employees are represented by trade unions.

● Water pollution. Companies which discharge trade effluent into water must obtain consent from the National Rivers Authority or one of the River Purification Boards. Such discharge consents set permitted limits based on a number of parameters: for example, the level of acidity or alkalinility of the discharge, or the amount of specific substances in the effluent, such as mercury or zinc. EIRIS reports the number of occasions on which samples showed that the consent level for each parameter has been exceeded over a particular period.

● Water service. As for the electricity companies, EIRIS reports statistics published by the industry regulator, Ofwat. These cover the rate of complaints and disconnections; the number of health-threatening incidents formally reported by the water companies to the Drinking Water Inspectorate; and the number of times that sewage treatment works did not comply with discharge consent limits.

Corporate governance

The Cadbury Committee (whose influence on company boardrooms is described by Alex Brummer in his Introduction), chaired by Sir Adrian Cadbury, was set up in May 1991 to examine the financial aspects of corporate governance in the wake of the scandals of the late 1980s and 1990. A draft report was published in May 1992 and the final report in December. The Stock Exchange (which had helped set up the Cadbury Committee) agreed that listed companies should be required to report in their annual accounts whether or not they complied with the Cadbury Code. The key requirements of the Code are as follows:

● Division of responsibility at the head of the company. The Code does not prohibit the existence of a joint chairman/chief executive, but says that in such cases it is essential there should be a strong, independent element on the board with a recognised senior member.

● A strong, non-executive contingent, normally a minimum of three non-executive directors, usually with no links to the company's management or other relationships that may impair their independence, and normally recruited through a formal process by a nominations comittee that has a majority of non-executives.

● Executive directors' pay should be shown clearly, with separate figures for bonuses plus an explanation of their basis, and including pension contributions and share options. Service contracts should not exceed three years and these matters should be supervised by a remuneration committee consisting mainly of non-executives.

● The board should include an audit committee consisting of at least three non-executive directors.

The criteria used in this section are based on these recommendations, as applied by PIRC. PIRC's criteria for the independence of non-executive directors are that they should not have been employed as executives in the company during the previous three years, should not be professional advisers to the company, should not represent a shareholder with a notifiable interest (3 per cent or over), and should not be a director of a company in which the group has a notifiable interest.

In addition to these specifications of the Cadbury Code, PIRC reports on whether certain posts on the board are insulated from periodic election. The constitution (articles of association) of many companies provides that some or all of the executive directors do not need to stand for re-election by shareholders. The PIRC data reports such provisions using the following code for the position so insulated: Ch = chairman; DCh = deputy chairman; CE = chief executive; JCE = joint chief executives; MD = managing director; JMD = joint managing directors; FinD = financial director; All execs = all executive directors. In some cases a position may be defined in the articles as insulated, and therefore reported, but such a post may no longer exist: managing director, for example.

BANKS

Outlook
Like the insurance sector, the banks have repeatedly belied their reputation for being cautious, losing money on one grand fling after another. There was the 1970s property fiasco, which would have brought down the whole financial system but for the intervention of the Bank of England. Then the banks made the doomed decision to lend money to developing countries (admittedly with official encouragement from the government), which entailed huge losses. The next move was to become financial conglomerates: vast sums of money were poured into stockbroking and investment banking in the run-up to the London stock market's Big Bang in 1986. And after this strategy went awry, there was a return to property again, just in time for the 1990s property crash.

Until the mid-1980s these disastrous escapades were financed by the domestic banking oligopoly. But that all changed in the 1980s with liberalisation of the financial system which brought building societies into direct competition with the banks. There used to be the Big Four – Barclays, National Westminster, Midland and Lloyds. Midland had for a time between the wars been the largest bank in the world, but was overtaken internationally following expansion of the US leaders, and in the UK as a consequence of the final round of bank mergers in the 1960s which brought Barclays and National Westminster to the top of the UK league. Up until the late 1980s the Big Four had the great advantage of free 'raw materials': most customers kept most of their money in current accounts, which of course did not pay interest – even deposit accounts paid meagre interest rates – and charges were more or less at the discretion of the bank manager. This position was exacerbated by the growth of credit cards which, in return for easy credit, charged extortionate rates to those who failed, often through inertia, to pay off the monthly bill.

In the 1980s this cosy banking cartel was rudely invaded by the building societies. They had always been competitors for deposits, but not for regular banking services. And even on the savings front, because mortgages had been rationed, building societies were able to offer deposits with low interest rates, reducing the competitive pressure on banks to provide attractive interest rates. When building societies started offering current accounts, and especially when they started paying interest on current-account balances, the banks were faced with the loss of their safe, protected source of domestic profits which had supported the rest of the business for so long. Building societies, and the second-tier banks, also began to compete on credit cards, and when recession began to force up bad debts in this business, the banks lost another source of easy revenue, even after they had introduced charges. Of course the banks also competed more forcefully on building society ground by offering mortgages, but that proved to be a mixed blessing during the housing slump of the late 1980s.

The general trend of the late 1980s and early 1990s was a desperate bid to drive down costs faster than bad debts could rise upwards. The battle was futile in the depth of the recession, when the banks collectively wrote off £6 billion (in 1992) as a consequence of rash lending in the 1980s boom, and as the recession took its toll even of seemingly secure companies. The banks came out of the recession committed to making further cost savings, which were achieved partly by the huge investments in new technology, and partly by the need for less staff as a result of fewer customers needing to come in person, and less frequently, to the bank branches. There seemed little prospect of escape from competitive pressures in retail banking, however, since the emergence of the building soocieties as quasi banks had left Britain with far too many bank branches.

One popular escape route from this unpleasant fact, and from the continuing controversy over charging for basic banking services, was to shift more of their income to fee- or commission-based business: in other words, moving into closer competition with insurance companies as well as building societies. It remains to be seen whether this will prove any more lucrative in the long run, since the UK must surely have too many insurance companies as well as too many bank branches.

Abbey National is now a bank, but because of its building society past it has a markedly different business and cost structure compared with the traditional banks. Building society branches are smaller and the business is concentrated on fewer areas: indeed it is dominated by savings and mortgage lending. Abbey National showed TSB where it went wrong by sticking closely to this core business even once it had converted itself into a bank. It has moved into mainstream retail banking, but made a success of its current-account operation (in operational terms, even if financial returns have not met expectations) and its losses on mortgage defaults were containable. It has also copied the banks' move into insurance – it acquired Scottish Mutual in 1992 – which, it could be argued, is a natural extension of the company's savings activities. The one area in which Abbey National met with complete failure was in following the trend to estate agency in the mid-1980s. The Cornerstone agency was eventually put up for sale in 1993, as Abbey realised, in common with insurance companies such as Prudential, that estate agencies do not bring in the extra business in mortgage or insurance that is necessary to justify the investment.

Bank of Scotland (BoS) should not to be confused with the Royal Bank of Scotland, although inevitably it is. BoS is the conservative one: it has carefully moved beyond the confines of its national borders, but without splashing out on acquisitions or making rash bids for market share by lending to customers with poor prospects. Caution has been its watchword, and this is evinced in its relatively steady results (though not entirely untainted by bad debts). Yet caution has not prevented the bank from expanding: more than half its lending is in England, but through a small network of business-oriented regional offices, and through the retail distribution networks of others such as the Automobile Association and the National Farmers Union. BoS has also sometimes taken a lead, for example with its home banking service, delivered via television or computer screen. For a conservative bank, it has been very good at not standing still.

Barclays regained from Nat West in the late 1980s the title of Britain's biggest bank. But that was before both banks paid the price of worrying too much about market share and too little about profitability. During the recession all the banks suffered, as the chickens of over-optimistic lending came home to roost in the form of huge bad debt provisions. Barclays seemed to have been more reckless than most in its lending to the property sector. In 1991 and 1992 its total provisions against bad debts from UK lending amounted to £3.3 billion, turning relatively healthy operating profits into a heavy loss in 1992 – the first in its 300-year history.

As if this was not bad enough, Barclays compounded its troubles by mishandling changes in top management. Following the early departure of Sir John Quinton from the chairmanship of the bank, Andrew Buxton took over as chairman and chief executive, despite the widespread belief that, in general, these two roles should be split, and that, specifically, Mr Buxton should share some of the blame for the bank's appalling lending record in the late 1980s. Pressure from shareholders, following the loss, led to the appointment of Martin Taylor – from Courtaulds Textiles – as chief executive. Having returned to profit in 1993, the bank, under Mr Taylor's leadership, embarked on an attempt to break the mould of traditional banking. He insisted that Barclays should be run like any other business.

Lloyds was in most respects the most successful bank of the 1980s, but only because it did not succeed in its endeavours to match the scale of the others. Having failed in its attempt to take over first Royal Bank of Scotland and then Standard Chartered (rather fortunately, given their subsequent performance), Lloyds took on more modest, though more pertinent, ambitions. It pursued them with vigour, determination and clarity of vision, thanks to the dual leadership of Sir Jeremy Morse and Brian Pitman. They avoided the worst excesses of Big Bang, and quickly pulled out of trading in government stocks (gilts) when this proved to be an unpromising activity. They concentrated on keeping costs down, long before their rivals felt the need to do so. And an innovative deal with insurance company Abbey Life brought them into this apparently promising area much earlier than the other major banks. The result was a performance which looked good by comparison with most of the sector, although inevitably Lloyds could not escape the bad debts that came with recession. The only problem was that by the start of the 1990s it was difficult to see how or where Lloyds could advance. Despite cutting costs and taking care with the balance sheet, the bank appeared to lack purpose, hence a desperate bid to snatch Midland from under the nose of Hong Kong and Shanghai Banking Corporation (HSBC). At the end of April 1994, however, Lloyds unveiled its strategy for the future. A £1.8 billion bid for the Cheltenham & Gloucester Building Society was aimed at beefing up Lloyds's share of the UK mortgage market, at a time when lending was slack.

Midland's fall from grace was completed when it was taken over by HSBC in 1992. The fall began when, attempting to further its international standing, it bought Crocker National Bank in California. Eventually Midland was forced to sell the bank, having signally failed to earn an adequate return on its investment. But its problems were far from over. Crocker could only be sold if Midland kept its semi-worthless loans to Latin-American countries – loans which subsequently required enormous provisions because of the economic collapse of those countries. Added to Midland's own debt provisions for Third World countries, these charges enfeebled the group in the late 1980s.

Bank of England deputy governor Sir Kit McMahon was drafted in as chairman and chief executive to knock Midland into shape. But he could not prevent one expensive accident after another (such as the treasury operations losing millions by betting the wrong way on interest rates in 1989). And his grand strategy – to merge with HSBC – came to nought in 1990 when HSBC pulled out after lengthy exploratory talks and a share swap. The departure was temporary, however. HSBC returned with a full takeover offer in 1992, and finally achieved its ambition of not only having a UK stock market quotation, but also a UK banking base.

Midland's main legacy to the banking world may be First Direct, the telephone banking service. It has never been clear how much this operation cost to set up and promote, nor whether the business has come near to repaying that investment. But in principle at least, First Direct seems to be the kind of low-cost, high-service retail banking operation which all banks are trying to move towards.

National Westminster marred its record with an expensive foray into the US, and its even more expensive and embarrassing involvement with UK stock market operations. Nat West paid $820 million for First Jersey National in 1987, only to see the bank (now renamed NatWest Bancorp) plunge into loss as recession hit New England. By 1992 the figures were improving, however, and the bank made a further foray into the US with the acquisition of Citizens First Bancorp in early 1994.

Events back home were more significant, however. First, Nat West plunged wholeheartedly into Big Bang, trying to build an integrated investment bank around its existing, though tiny, merchant bank, County. If the result had merely been the substantial losses from stock market operations, the move would soon have been forgotten. But Nat West became involved in a huge fraud trial over its handling of a rights issue for the employment agency group Blue Arrow, when it was acquiring US rival Manpower at the height of the 1987 bull market. Eventually an inquiry by the Department of Trade and Industry exonerated Nat West, but the affair cost the bank's chairman and several senior executives their jobs, and tarnished the name of County Nat West. (Its name was changed to NatWest Markets in 1993, and is now a major source of Nat West's profits.)

Royal Bank of Scotland (RBS) has, like its English brethren, lost vast sums of money on property lending, and on merchant banking though its Charterhouse subsidiary (which was sold in 1993). But having twice beaten off unwelcome predators in the 1980s, RBS must feel reasonably secure for the time being. Yet the bank seems to have done little to distinguish itself. It attempted to expand in England through a traditional branch network (originally as Williams and Glyn's) and through the aggressive corporate lending of Charterhouse. Neither operation proved particularly fruitful. It has also attempted to expand abroad, notably through links with Banco Santander in Spain and several other European institutions, but also with purchases in the US. The most successful diversification was into insurance, however, in the form of Direct Line, although this brought opprobrium upon the bank because of the huge performance-related payments made to the insurance business's founder, Peter Wood. So successful was Direct Line, however, that it could become a candidate for separate flotation – which would leave RBS still looking for a role.

Standard Chartered is probably most famous for having once been the employer of prime minister John Major. It is certainly a more notable aspect than its recent business record. Like Midland, this bank has had the attentions of a senior Bank of England figure, Rodney Galpin, who was drafted in as chairman and chief executive to try and sort out a dismal legacy. Like Sir Kit McMahon at Midland, Mr Galpin found that the task was not easy. Like Midland, Standard Chartered suffered from bad debts in Third World countries, but in most other respects the bank is very different from its UK peer group – except for HSBC.

This bank is a relic of empire, arising in 1969 from the combination of Standard Bank of Africa and the Chartered Bank of India, Australia and China. The merger gave the group a huge international network, but (like HSBC) a lack of business in the UK. The natural response was to try and buy a UK bank, but Standard Chartered's bid for Royal Bank of Scotland was prevented by the Monopolies Commission. The next best alternative might have been to accept the bid from Lloyds in 1986, but the resulting loss of independence did not seem so appealing and Standard Chartered managed to beat off the attentions of Lloyds with the aid of a collection of foreign investors.

Subsequent attempts to build up UK lending led to some spectacular collapses when recession caught up with over-optimistic debt levels, which led to huge bad debt provisions in 1991 and 1992: Brent Walker was the most prominent case, which was propped up by the banks who were seeking to salvage something from the mess. In the early 1990s Standard Chartered was very much as it had been when Mr Major left the bank on his election to Parliament in 1979 – still looking for a UK base to balance its international network, and still trying to escape from a series of accidents. For example, massive provisions were forced by a banking scandal in India in 1993. Standard Chartered looked set to be embroiled in the affair – which led to the departure of Mr Galpin and his boardroom colleagues – for many years.

TSB was once a loose collection of savings banks which the Thatcher government of the 1980s decided to privatise: 'privatisation' is not strictly accurate in this instance, since TSB was not owned by the government, but the flotation on the stock market was handled in just the same way as that of British Gas or any of the other privatisations. Its new status went to TSB's head: it splashed money around like a reckless teenager come into an inheritance, even refusing to cut the price offered for Hill Samuel despite the fact that the stock market crash intervened, slashing the value of every public company at a stroke.

Hill Samuel proved to be a disastrous investment, as did the other major acquisition, the Target insurance group. Former stock exchange chairman Sir Nicholas Goodison was drafted in to sort out the mess, but it took years to try and convert the decentralised, savings-oriented, working-class-dominated Trustee Savings Banks into a financial conglomerate like all the others. And having achieved this, it was difficult not to wonder whether it would not have been better to leave it as a specialist savings bank. After all, Britain is not short of conventional retail banks.

Shares

The banking sector has proved a weak performer against the stock market as a whole since the boom days of 1986, although it picked up in 1992–3 as the shares began to be bought for their potential during economic recovery.

In 1986 Nat West took over from Barclays as the biggest UK bank and its shares outperformed the banking sector until the crash of 1987. A steady decline then set in as the stock market crash, plus the Blue Arrow affair which stemmed from it, raised doubts about the group's expansion into the securities business which proved a drain on profit in 1988–9. After 1990 the shares dropped steadily against the sector as the group's exposure to bad debts came into sharper focus, and while the price soared in the bull market of 1992–3, the shares remained weak.

The rating of Barclays against the sector fell away from 1986 until the market crash of 1987 but then slowly gained ground – only to drop steeply in 1991 when the bank regained its lead over Nat West but revealed poor cost control. Lloyds came through like a dark horse to outperform its bigger rivals. It too made mistakes, but it also set out to be more efficient than its competitors, and the shares outperformed the banking sector from the time of the market crash onwards. Midland was the weakest of the big banks in 1986 and the shares were supported by hopes of a bid through the late 1980s. But profits shrank to nothing in the early 1990s, the dividend was cut and the board was shaken up. The shares rallied strongly when Hong Kong and Shanghai Bank came to the rescue with a bid, and the combined bank was seen as having good potential to benefit from the UK economic recovery.

As far as share price is concerned, TSB alternates with Standard Chartered to occupy the bottom of the league in this sector. TSB's reputation was at its zenith when the group was floated in 1986, but its diversification policy played havoc with its performance, and the share price suffered. It slipped until 1989 when the group changed strategy, but fell even more steeply after the merchant banking problems of its subsidiary Hill Samuel came to light in 1991. The nadir of the share rating was reached in 1992, but in the strong market rally that ensued, TSB was seen as a recovery play. Standard Chartered has been a volatile stock, with a reputation for being disaster-prone. Its rating against the sector fell until 1990 when analysts recognised that the strength of its Far Eastern operation was at the centre of the group's strategy, and the shares were re-rated accordingly.

Among the top players, Bank of Scotland has been a steady performer, but problems with bad debts surfaced later than in the case of the English banks affected its rating in 1992–3. Royal Bank of Scotland's performance has been more like that of the English banks, with plenty of mistakes and losses, but with bid speculation thrown in.

Abbey National burst upon the sector in 1989 when it changed into a public company from a traditional building society. It immediately became a star turn because it clearly refused to copy TSB's acquisition path. Its low costs and strong balance sheet caused the rating to soar until 1991 when worries over bad debt brought progress to a halt. In late 1992 the rating was hit as the company's results were below expectation and the market concluded that the level of debt provisions would fall only slowly. Overall, bank share prices in the spring of 1994 reflected an anticipated growth in profits, although the City was not expecting the continuing recovery to benefit bank shares significantly.

Corporate conscience

Third World debt has been central to the business of British banks, and as an issue of conscience it should be of equal concern to them as the environment is to chemical companies. But most bankers seem to regard the matter as one of those troublesome problems which has damaged profits, and therefore their reputation in the City, yet which is a natural consequence of the business and not something that raises moral issues. Some major banks believe that they have solved the problem of 'problem country debt', as they like to sanitise it, by selling the debt. Abbey National and TSB were fortunate in avoiding the whole episode because they were still essentially trading as respectively a building society and a savings bank during the late 1970s and early 1980s when lending to the Third World took place. And the Scottish banks were not at the forefront of this particular loss-making fashion.

Turning to other matters of conscience: banks are prodigious advertisers, for example, and suffer complaints as a result. Only Bank of Scotland and Standard Chartered escape on this issue.

Apart from Barclays, the Big Four are more implicated in military matters. Nat West in particular has a heavy involvement, not only in the provision of financial services. Through various of its associate companies it is involved in manufacturing, among other things, military support and communications systems, and military trucks. Likewise both Nat West and Lloyds have connections with the nuclear industry.

On a positive note, Barclays, Lloyds, Nat West, Royal Bank of Scotland and TSB all have environmental policies, including independent audit in the case of Lloyds. But it is Nat West that has shown greater willingness to carry its policy into its mainstream business as well, rather than restricting it to the use of recycled paper and a 'greener' company car policy.

All the banks are members of BITC, except Bank of Scotland, which is nevertheless a member of the Per Cent Club. In its annual report Bank of Scotland has a lengthy section on what it describes as 'other operational issues'. In the 1993 annual report this included news of work with homeless people, justified because 'the Bank, as a significant institution in Scottish society, feels a moral and social obligation to play a part in helping homeless individuals become more self-reliant'. All except Standard Chartered support Opportunity 2000. However, all of the major banks have suffered considerable criticism recently over their treatment of staff. In response to the introduction of new technology and to the changing face of banking, thousands of jobs are being cut, with the loss of hundreds of banks. While recognising that this policy reduces overheads, bank staff maintain that it will undermine customer relations.

Corporate governance

Because of the need to exhibit their corporate probity more publicly than most companies, banks generally have huge boards with a much higher proportion of non-executive directors than ususal. However, they are also embracing the trend of publishing a separate annual review (with summary financial information) to the formal report and accounts, which can mean that important information, e.g. on directors' pay, is not communicated to many shareholders.

Abbey National has a majority of non-executives in its 16-strong board. Membership of board committees is clearly indicated and deputy chairman Peter Davis reported fully on their working in the 1992 annual report. Bonus arrangements are referred to in the accounts, though they appear to be largely discretionary, rather than based on clear formulae. But the profit-sharing scheme pays out a maximum of only 10 per cent of salary – more reasonable than many such schemes. Abbey National also appears not to indulge in lengthy service contracts even for prized executives, and has abandoned the practice of paying pensions to long-serving non-executives, including the chairman.

Bank of Scotland retains the character of a central bank, with a board consisting entirely of non-executives except for group chief executive Bruce Patullo, who also glories in the title of 'Governor'. However, the fact that there are no top executives on the board means that payments to the key executives are not reported at all. The directors' report on 1992 mentioned membership of audit and remuneration committees, and the fact that the position of governor was accompanied by only a 12-month service contract.

Barclays appointed Andrew Buxton to take over as as chairman and chief executive, following the retirement of Sir John Quinton in 1992. This was despite disquiet on the part of investors, and despite eventually having to accept that a separate chief executive should be recruited. The 1992 report included a statement on corporate governance which said that the group complied with the Cadbury Code, and went on to argue that Mr Buxton's joint roles did not conflict with the Code. In the end, however, the bank appointed Martin Taylor as chief executive. The 1993 report revealed huge bonus payments to BZW executives, justified by Barclays on the basis that pay should be kept competitive, although this should not be the reason for awarding a bonus. At least service contracts are for no longer than 12 months.

HSBC has set up audit and remuneration committees, but does not seem to see this as a significant issue. It retains the curious post of 'adviser to the board', a person whose purpose is not at all clear, but who none the less sits on the audit committee. Nor does the company elaborate upon 'expatriate benefits in kind', which apparently constitute a large part of directors' pay, and which are considered 'normal within the locations in which they are employed'.

Lloyds Bank clearly does not give a high priority to corporate governance. The 17-strong board contains 11 non-executives but communication on these matters is minimal. The annual report mentions only an audit committee, with no reference to executive pay. The accounts provide only the sketchiest details of executive remuneration, which are not included in the new-style short report to shareholders.

National Westminster seems to take governance issues rather more seriously than the other banks. The boardroom has been slimmed since Lord Alexander took the chair, but it still contains 20 people, 13 of whom are non-executives. The 1992 annual review (separated from the formal report and accounts, and containing only summary financial information) included a two-page corporate governance report by deputy chairman Sir Edwin Nixon which indicated that there is a 'public and social policy committee' as well as committees for nominations, remuneration, audit and compliance. Unlike some summary reports, Nat West included a note on directors' pay, giving details of bonus schemes. The highest-paid director, Richard Goeltz, was reported as receiving a 'once-only, guaranteed bonus' of £100,000, but there was no explanation why.

Royal Bank of Scotland merely notes the (entirely non-executive) membership of audit and remuneration committees in its annual report. The same reticence applies to directors' pay. Despite the public controversy over the £6 million bonus paid to Direct Line founder Peter Wood, the accounts make the briefest reference to this being 'his share of the growth of that company'.

Standard Chartered has split the roles of chairman and chief executive following the retirement of Rodney Galpin. Patrick Gillam, in one of his final tasks as deputy chairman, made a full statement on corporate governance in the 1992 annual report, describing the separation of the previously unified 'remuneration and personnel strategy committee', as well as the membership and working of audit, risk review, and donations committees. The company gave only outline information on bonus schemes, however.

TSB has had plenty problems since it became a public company, but they cannot all be blamed on poor governance structures. As one of his reforms to the company Sir Nicholas Goodison has now established the right balance in the boardroom and put appropriate committees in place. But the main problem was not the make-up of the board: it simply made the wrong decisions. The accounts give only partial explanation of directors' bonuses, but do explain that the pay-off to departed chief executive Don McCrickard was negotiated 'through external advisers' following termination of his contract.

6 BANKS

ABBEY NATIONAL

Share record

Return on shareholders' equity	%	11.54
5-year price high	p	522.0
5-year price low	p	141.0
Dividend yield	%	4.26
5-year high	%	7.28
5-year low	%	2.84
Price/earnings ratio		12.1
5-year high		17.8
5-year low		5.8

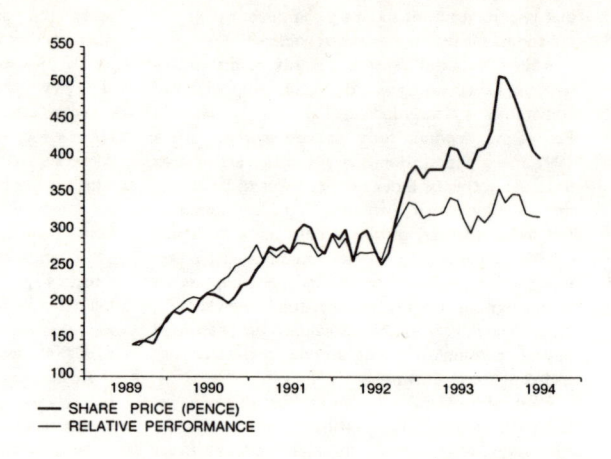

Share price performance (in pence)

— SHARE PRICE (PENCE)
— RELATIVE PERFORMANCE

Financial record

		31/12/89	31/12/90	31/12/91	31/12/92	31/12/93
Gross profit	£	3,475M	4,563M	4,234M	3,963M	3,424M
Bad debt provision	£'000	14,000	55,000	155,000	322,000	218,000
Pre-tax profit	£'000	501,000	582,000	624,000	601,000	735,000
Published retentions	£'000	248,000	252,000	276,000	166,000	206,000
Earnings per share	p	24.66	29.11	31.45	27.92	32.42
Dividend per share	p	5.70	9.50	10.50	11.50	14.00
Net assets per share	p	207.71	224.66	261.15	305.00	932.80
Shareholders' funds	£	2,451M	2,699M	2,971M	3,184M	3,386M
Return on long term capital	%	18.41	19.78	18.24	15.03	3.11
Return on shareholders' equity	%	13.07	13.94	13.59	10.93	11.54 1.09
Pre-tax margin	%	1.47	1.36	1.17	0.93	n/a
Operating profit per employee	£	n/a	n/a	n/a	n/a	14.91
Free resources ratio		6.09	4.87	3.78	0.35	2.32
Dividend cover		4.33	3.06	2.99	2.43	-13.60
Net income growth	%		31.31	-7.21	-6.40	16.10
Earnings growth	%		18.05	8.04	-11.20	
Total advances	£	29,747M	35,014M	38,975M	41,035M	48,605M
Customer deposits	£	33,675M	42,175M	52,353M	62,946M	52,511M
Number of employees		14,903	16,671	18,153	19,986	19,046

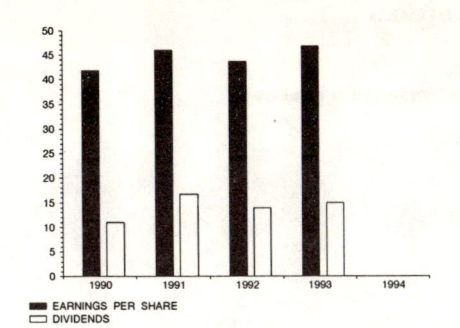

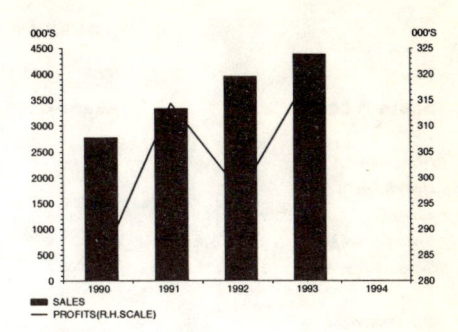

Earnings and dividends

Sales and profits

ABBEY NATIONAL plc

Abbey House, Baker Street, London NW1 6XL
Tel: 0171 612 4000
Chairman Sir Christopher Tugendhat
Chief executive Peter Birch
Size net interest £1.7 billion, £5.3 billion stock market value, 19,000 employees
5-year growth net interest n/a, earnings per share 31%, employment 28%
Solvency n/a
Political donations 0
Charitable donations £420,000

Major developments
1944 formed from a merger of Abbey Road and National building societies
1988 launched interest-bearing current account
1989 converted from a building society to a plc
1992 bought The Scottish Mutual Assurance Society
1993 launched Abbey National Life

Corporate governance

Separate Chairman and Chief Executive Y
Number of Directors 16
Number of Non-Executive Directors 8
(8 Independent Directors)
Insulated Directors None

Board Committees
Audit: Y   Remuneration: Y

Remuneration

Year end	31.12.91	31.12.92	31.12.93
Total board £M	1.47	1.87	2.26
% change	36	28	21
Highest paid £	261,906	257,566	329,179
% change	37	-2	28

Board
Birch, Peter G *Chief Executive*
Fry, John *Executive Director*
Jones, Gareth *Executive Director*
Knighton, Robert *Executive Director*
Patrick, Douglas *Executive Director*
Toner, Charles *Executive Director*
Villiers, Charles *Executive Director*
Harley, Ian *Finance Director*
Barnes, Mair *Independent Non-Executive*
Denholm, Allan *Independent Non-Executive*
Heiser, Sir Terry *Independent Non-Executive*
Llowarch, Martin E *Independent Non-Executive*
Lord Rockley *Independent Non-Executive*
Morrison, Sara *Independent Non-Executive*
Tuckey, James L *Independent Non-Executive*
Lord Tugendhat *Non-Executive Chairman*

BANK OF SCOTLAND

Share record

Return on shareholders' equity	%	11.38
5-year price high	p	246.0
5-year price low	p	75.0
Dividend yield	%	3.30
5-year high	%	6.73
5-year low	%	2.37
Price/earnings ratio		15.2
5-year high		37.3
5-year low		5.9

Share price performance (in pence)

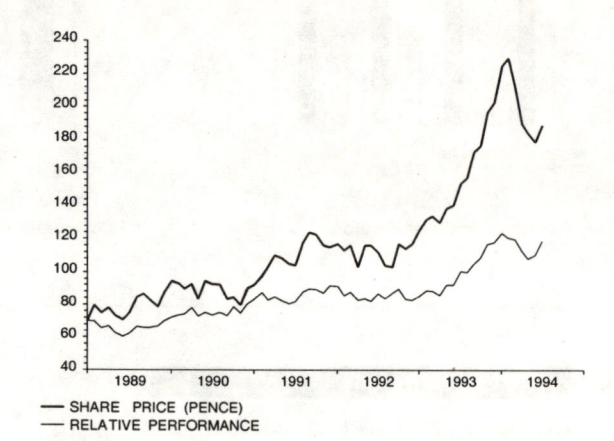

— SHARE PRICE (PENCE)
— RELATIVE PERFORMANCE

Financial record

		28/2/90	28/2/91	29/2/92	28/2/93	28/2/94
Gross profit	£	2,022M	2,588M	2,493M	2,382M	1,895M
Bad debt provision	£'000	90,400	202,300	252,800	371,700	313,900
Pre-tax profit	£'000	202,400	129,400	128,200	119,100	281,000
Published retentions	£'000	73,600	33,000	20,500	4,900	83,200
Earnings per share	p	12.19	6.84	5.27	4.48	12.61
Dividend per share	p	3.58	4.01	4.05	4.57	5.05
Net assets per share	p	177.29	199.79	212.94	221.91	249.49
Shareholders' funds	£	895,800	1,049M	1,261M	1,251M	1,304M
Return on long term capital	%	14.99	9.53	7.54	6.60	5.78
Return on shareholders' equity	%	12.86	6.60	3.98	4.15	11.38
Pre-tax margin	%	1.18	0.64	0.55	0.42	0.96
Operating profit per employee	£	14.95	9.91	9.14	7.53	19.02
Free resources ratio		7.42	6.65	7.61	7.17	7.63
Dividend cover		3.41	1.70	1.30	0.98	2.50
Net income growth	%	62.90	28.01	-3.67	-4.46	-20.42
Earnings growth	%	12.56	-43.94	-22.86	-15.10	181.60
Total advances	£	11,548M	13,528M	15,179M	18,049M	25,342M
Customer deposits	£	16,298M	19,809M	21,946M	25,753M	23,437M
Number of employees		15,200	16,100	16,300	17,150	16,595

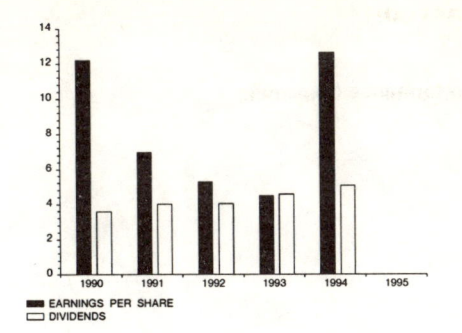

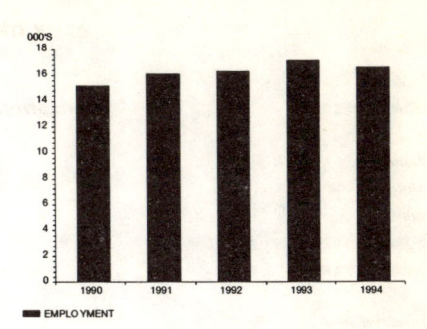

Earnings and dividends

Employment

BANK OF SCOTLAND plc

P O Box 5, The Mound, Edinburgh EH1 1YZ
Tel: 0131 442 7777
Governor and group chief executive Bruce Patullo
Main subsidiaries Bank of Wales, British Linen Bank, Kellock Holdings, NWS Bank
Size £1.1 billion net interest, £2.3 billion stock market value, 16,600 employees
5-year growth net interest n/a, earnings per share 3%, employment 9%
Solvency n/a
Political donations 0
Charitable donations £527,000

Major developments
1695 constituted by Act of Parliament
1907 bought Caledonian Banking Co
1955 bought The Union Bank of Scotland
1971 merged with the British Linen Bank
1985 bought Commercial Bank of Wales; set up first home banking service
1992 bought New Zealand bank Countrywide

Corporate governance
Separate Chairman and Chief Executive N
Number of Directors 15
Number of Non-Executive Directors 14
(11 Independent Directors)
Insulated Directors Not known

Board Committees
Audit: Y Remuneration: Y

Remuneration

Year end	29.02.92	28.02.93	28.02.94
Total board £M	0.93	0.64	0.81
% change	15	-31	26
Highest paid £	216,000	221,000	326,000
% change	5	2	48

Board
Patullo, D Bruce *Chairman & Chief Executive*
Boyd, J Edward *Independent Non-Executive*
Grant, Sir Alistair *Independent Non-Executive*
Hutchison, Thomas O *Independent Non-Executive*
Jack, Professor Robert B *Independent Non-Executive*
Knox, Lesley M S *Ind. Non-Executive*
Lord Remnant *Independent Non-Executive*
Menzies, John Maxwell *Ind. Non-Executive*
Pelham Burn, Angus M *Independent Non-Executive*
Rankin, Sir Alick Michael *Ind. Non-Executive*
Reid, Sir Bob *Independent Non-Executive*
Shaw, Professor Jack C *Independent Non-Executive*
Bell, A Scott *Non-Executive*
Lessels, Norman *Non-Executive*
Smith, Sir Robert Courtney *Non-Executive*

10 BANKS

BARCLAYS

Share record

Return on shareholders' equity	%	5.61
5-year price high	p	644.0
5-year price low	p	280.0
Dividend yield	%	3.42
5-year high	%	10.07
5-year low	%	2.43
Price/earnings ratio		28.6
5-year high		36.8
5-year low		5.6

Share price performance (in pence)

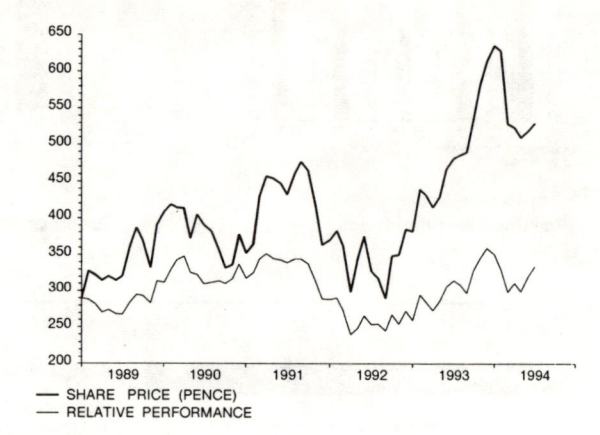

— SHARE PRICE (PENCE)
— RELATIVE PERFORMANCE

Financial record

		31/12/89	31/12/90	31/12/91	31/12/92	31/12/93
Gross profit	£	12,041M	13,740M	12,331M	10,782M	7,034M
Bad debt provision	£'000	1,397M	1,233M	1,547M	2,534M	1,869M
Pre-tax profit	£'000	692,000	760,000	533,000	-100,000	672,000
Published retentions	£'000	144,000	254,000	-96,000	-586,000	67,000
Earnings per share	p	28.85	25.01	15.21	0.00	19.86
Dividend per share	p	19.57	21.15	21.15	15.15	15.15
Net assets per share	p	695.52	656.71	671.28	678.35	788.61
Shareholders' funds	£	6,225M	6,105M	5,740M	5,279M	5,312M
Return on long term capital	%	9.48	10.31	8.21	2.19	7.26
Return on shareholders' equity	%	6.77	5.95	3.86	-3.47	5.61
Pre-tax margin	%	0.55	0.63	0.41	-0.10	0.43
Operating profit per employee	£	n/a	n/a	n/a	n/a	9.52
Free resources ratio		6.66	5.48	5.90	5.44	-0.42
Dividend cover		1.47	1.18	0.72	0.00	1.31
Net income growth	%	55.99	14.11	-10.25	-12.56	-34.76
Earnings growth	%	-54.01	-13.31	-39.20	-100.00	0.00
Total advances	£	89,861M	92,793M	92,269M	95,748M	117,081M
Customer deposits	£	108,266M	116,084M	117,245M	121,336M	122,472M
Number of employees		116,500	116,800	111,400	105,000	99,000

BANKS 11

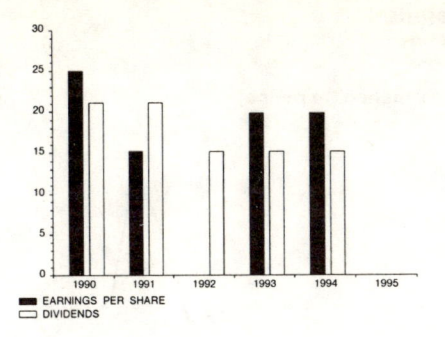

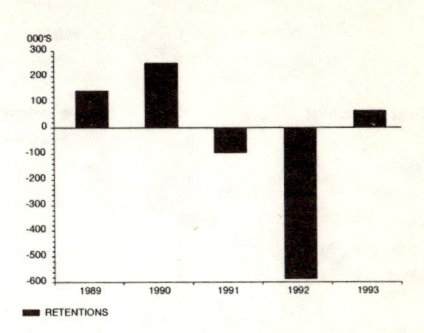

Earnings and dividends

Retentions

BARCLAYS plc

54 Lombard St, London EC3P 3AH
Tel: 0171 626 1567
Chairman Andrew Buxton
Chief executive Martin Taylor
Main subsidiaries Barclays de Zoete Wedd, Mercantile Credit
Size £7.4 billion net interest, £9.0 billion stock market value, 99,000 employees
5-year growth net interest n/a, earnings per share -31%, employment -15%
Solvency n/a
Political donations 0
Charitable donations £1 million

Major developments
1836 formed by Royal Charter
1925 re-incorporated under the Colonial Bank Act
1954 name changed to Barclays Bank International
1966 launched UK's first credit card Barclaycard
1967 first hole-in-wall cash machine
1984 acquired Mercantile Credit Company
1985 bought stockbrokers de Zoete & Bevan, Wedd Durlacher to form BZW
1986 disinvested from South Africa
1987 sponsored Football League
1989 launched interest-bearing current account
1990 bought 51% stake in L'Européene de Banque
1991 bought the remaining 49% of L'Européene de Banque
1993 made first loss in 300 years
1994 Martin Taylor appointed chief executive

Corporate governance
Separate Chairman and Chief Executive Y
Number of Directors 14
Number of Non-Executive Directors 8
(8 Independent Directors)
Insulated Directors None

Board Committees
Audit: Y   Remuneration: Y

Remuneration

Year end	31.12.91	31.12.92	31.12.93
Total board £M	3.02	2.88	4.55
% change		-3	-5	58
Highest paid £M	0.45	0.52	1.44
% change	33	17	174

Board
Taylor, J Martin *Chief Executive*
Buxton, Andrew R *Executive Chairman*
Band, David *Executive Director*
Middleton, Sir Peter *Executive Director*
Robinson, Francis Alastair *Executive Director*
Stocken, Oliver H J *Finance Director*
Baker, Mary Elizabeth *Independent Non-Executive*
Birkin, Sir Derek *Independent Non-Executive*
Henderson, Sir Denys *Independent Non-Executive*
Lord Lawson of Blaby *Independent Non-Executive*
Mobbs, Sir Nigel *Independent Non-Executive*
Ogata, Shijuro *Independent Non-Executive*
Peelen, Jan *Independent Non-Executive*
Lord Wright, *Independent Non-Executive*

12   BANKS

HSBC HOLDINGS

Share record

Return on shareholders' equity	%	16.97
5-year price high	p	1099.0
5-year price low	p	305.0
Dividend yield	%	4.04
5-year high	%	6.34
5-year low	%	2.41
Price/earnings ratio		11.3
5-year high		30.7
5-year low		10.3

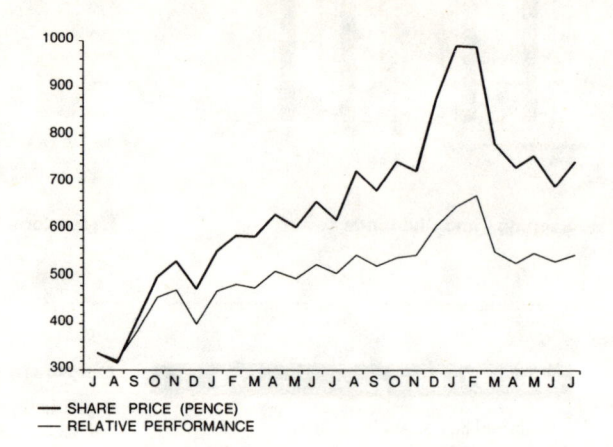

Share price performance (in pence)

— SHARE PRICE (PENCE)
— RELATIVE PERFORMANCE

Financial record

		31/12/92	31/12/93
Gross profit	£	12,075M	9,921M
Bad debt provision	£'000	1,185M	1,158M
Pre-tax profit	£'000	1,440M	2,297M
Published retentions	£'000	749,000	1,212M
Earnings per share	p	48.35	64.39
Dividend per share	p	19.00	23.50
Net assets per share	p	723.13	1,230
Shareholders' funds	£	8,076M	9,334M
Return on long term capital	%		
Return on shareholders' equity	%	11.51	16.97
Pre-tax margin	%	0.93	1.30
Operating profit per employee	£	21.52	21.17
Free resources ratio		5.80	0.11
Dividend cover		2.54	2.74
Net income growth	%		-17.84
Earnings growth	%		33.18
Total advances	£	90,481M	137,020M
Customer deposits	£	151,516M	157,731M
Number of employees		79,470	104,027

BANKS

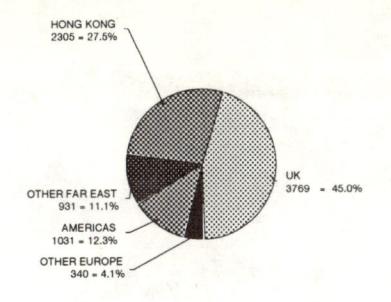

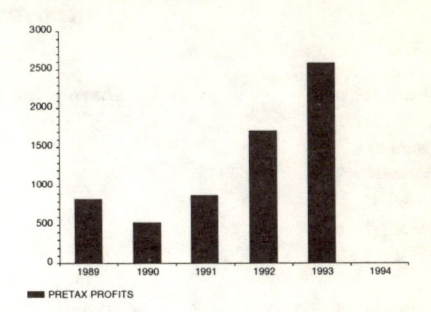

Sales analysis

HONG KONG 2305 = 27.5%
OTHER FAR EAST 931 = 11.1%
AMERICAS 1031 = 12.3%
OTHER EUROPE 340 = 4.1%
UK 3769 = 45.0%

Profits

PRETAX PROFITS (1989–1994)

HSBC HOLDINGS plc

10 Lower Thames Street, London EC3R 6AE
Tel: 0171 260 0500
Chairman Sir Willie Purves
Chief executive John Bond
Main subsidiaries Forward Trust, Hongkong Bank, Marine Midland, Midland Bank, Samuel Montagu
Size £8.0 billion net interest, £19.5 billion stock market value, 104,00 employees
Growth figures are not applicable because of the transformation in the group following the acquisition of Midland Bank.
Solvency n/a
Political donations 0
Charitable donations £5.4 million

Major developments
1836 Midland bank first established as Birmingham & Midland Bank
1865 Hongkong Bank founded
1965 HSBC rescued Hang Seng Bank
1972 Midland bought Thomas Cook; HSBC formed merchant banking subsidiary
1980 HSBC bought 51% of Marine Midland; Midland bought 51% of Crocker National Bank
1981 HSBC bid for Royal Bank of Scotland blocked by Monopolies Commission
1985 Midland bought stockbrokers W Greenwell to form Midland Montagu
1986 Midland sold Crocker at a loss of $1 billion; HSBC bought James Capel stockbrokers
1988 HSBC bought 14.9% stake in Midland
1989 Midland launched First Direct remote banking
1992 HSBC acquired Midland; sold Thomas Cook
1993 head office moved to London

Corporate governance

Separate Chairman and Chief Executive Y
Number of Directors 19
Number of Non-Executive Directors 11
(9 Independent Directors)
Insulated Directors None

Board Committees
Audit: Y   Remuneration: Y

Remuneration

Year end	31.12.91	31.12.92	31.12.93
Total board £M	3.83	3.81	4.82
% change	30	-1	27
Highest paid £	n/a	890,000	965,000
% change			8

Board
Bond, J R H *Chief Executive*
Purves, Sir W *Executive Chairman*
Asher, B H *Executive Director*
Gray, J M *Executive Director*
Knox, N R *Executive Director*
Strickland, J E *Executive Director*
Whitson, Keith *Executive Director*
Delbridge, Richard *Finance Director*
Connolly, D E *Independent Non-Executive*
Hotung, Sir Joseph *Independent Non-Executive*
Liao, D P H *Independent Non-Executive*
Mackay, Charles D *Independent Non-Executive*
Maitland Smith, Geoffrey *Ind. Non-Executive*
Marshall, Sir Colin *Independent Non-Executive*
Murufushi, M *Independent Non-Executive*
Newton, Sir Wilfred *Independent Non-Executive*
Sohmen, H *Independent Non-Executive*
Baroness Dunn *Non-Executive*
Walters, Sir Peter *Non-Executive*

LLOYDS BANK

Share record

Return on shareholders' equity   %   19.13
5-year price high   p   684.0
5-year price low   p   229.3

Dividend yield   %   4.96
5-year high   %   7.94
5-year low   %   3.49

Price/earnings ratio   11.9
5-year high   21.0
5-year low   6.8

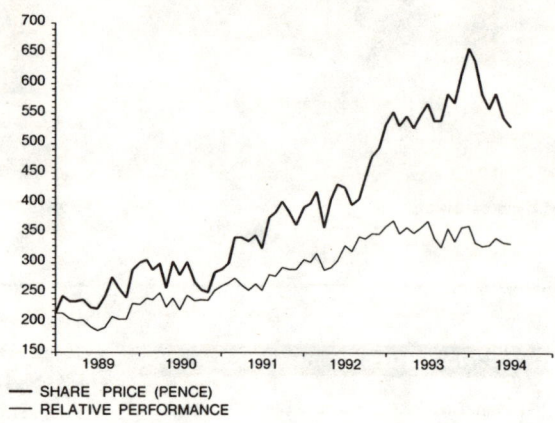

Share price performance (in pence)

— SHARE PRICE (PENCE)
— RELATIVE PERFORMANCE

Financial record

		31/12/89	31/12/90	31/12/91	31/12/92	31/12/93
Gross profit	£	6,982M	7,252M	6,315M	5,968M	4,041M
Bad debt provision	£'000	2,108M	778,000	918,000	736,000	503,000
Pre-tax profit	£'000	-715M	606,000	616,000	830,000	1,031M
Published retentions	£'000	-808M	170,000	150,000	208,000	321,000
Earnings per share	p	0.00	25.04	26.30	37.27	47.38
Dividend per share	p	13.30	15.30	16.70	18.40	22.10
Net assets per share	p	405.79	372.57	392.14	441.79	544.48
Shareholders' funds	£	2,365M	2,271M	2,476M	2,730M	3,063M
Return on long term capital	%	-9.49	17.74	16.13	17.45	8.72
Return on shareholders' equity	%	-25.19	13.74	13.41	16.94	19.13
Pre-tax margin	%	-1.50	1.16	1.31	1.63	1.56
Operating profit per employee	£	-9.36	6.98	10.53	12.19	12.71
Free resources ratio		4.17	3.83	4.49	4.31	-0.50
Dividend cover		0.00	1.64	1.57	2.03	2.14
Net income growth	%	47.61	3.87	-12.92	-5.49	-32.29
Earnings growth	%	-100.00	0.00	5.03	41.71	27.11
Total advances	£	42,494M	40,625M	36,995M	37,804M	52,376M
Customer deposits	£	52,395M	50,388M	46,223M	49,051M	51,003M
Number of employees		84,679	79,890	71,803	67,083	67,182

BANKS 15

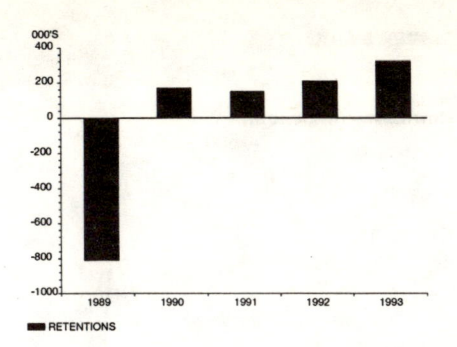

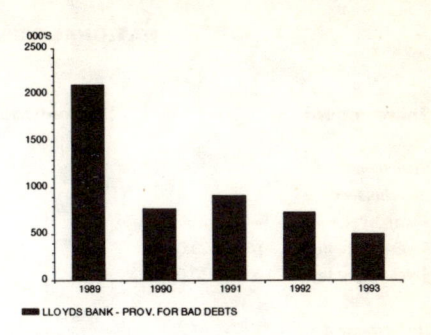

Retentions

'Problem country' debt

LLOYDS BANK plc

71 Lombard Street, London EC3P 3BS
Tel: 0171 626 1500
Chairman Sir Robin Ibbs
Chief executive Brian Pitman
Main subsidiaries Lloyds Abbey Life (60%), Black Horse Financial Services, Lloyds Bowmaker
Size £4.0 billion net interest, £7.3 billion stock market value, 67,200 employees
5-year growth net interest n/a, earnings per share nil, employment -21%
Solvency n/a
Political donations 0
Charitable donations £1.3 million

Major developments
1865 formed as Lloyds Banking Co Ltd
1884 name changed to Lloyds Barnetts & Bosanquets Bank Ltd
1889 name changed to Lloyds Bank Ltd
1984 built temporary 21% share stake in Royal Bank of Scotland
1986 bid for Standard Chartered failed
1989 merger with Abbey Life Group to form Lloyds Abbey Life
1992 announced plans to wind down Lloyds Merchant Bank
1994 announced £1.8 billion bid to take over Cheltenham & Gloucester Building Society

Corporate governance

Separate Chairman and Chief Executive Y
Number of Directors 18
Number of Non-Executive Directors 11
(9 Independent Directors)
Insulated Directors Ch, MD, JMD

Board Committees
Audit: N   Remuneration: Y

Remuneration
Year end	31.12.91	31.12.92	31.12.93
Total board £M	2.70	2.74	2.61
% change	7	2	-5
Highest paid £	420,112	419,581	446,513
% change	7	-0.1	6

Board
Pitman, Brian I *Chief Executive*
Ibbs, Sir Robin *Executive Chairman*
Brown, Paul G *Executive Director*
Davies, John *Executive Director*
Maran, Stephen A *Executive Director*
Moore, Alan E *Executive Director*
Pirrie, David B *Executive Director*
Greenbury, Sir Richard *Independent Non-Executive*
Lord Plumb *Independent Non-Executive*
Nicholson, Peter C *Independent Non-Executive*
Prosser, Ian M G *Independent Non-Executive*
Quinlan, Sir Michael *Independent Non-Executive*
Raisman, John M *Independent Non-Executive*
Smith, C Russell *Independent Non-Executive*
Swainson, Eric *Independent Non-Executive*
Walker, Sir David *Independent Non-Executive*
Hornby, Sir Simon *Non-Executive*
Thompson, Michael H R *Non-Executive*

16 BANKS

NATIONAL WESTMINSTER BANK

Share record

Return on shareholders' equity % 12.66
5-year price high p 628.0
5-year price low p 230.0

Dividend yield % 4.92
5-year high % 10.14
5-year low % 3.54

Price/earnings ratio 11.8
5-year high 49.7
5-year low 5.0

Share price performance (in pence)

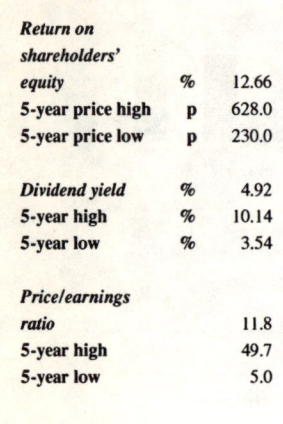

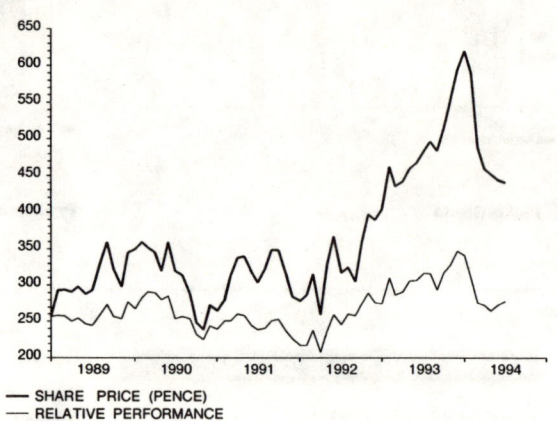

— SHARE PRICE (PENCE)
— RELATIVE PERFORMANCE

Financial record

		31/12/89	31/12/90	30/12/91	31/12/92	31/12/93
Gross profit	£	10,961M	12,251M	11,133M	10,556M	8,550M
Bad debt provision	£'000	1,435M	1,153M	1,875M	1,903M	1,262M
Pre-tax profit	£'000	454,000	509,000	199,000	540,000	1,170M
Published retentions	£'000	-65,000	86,000	-220M	-103M	276,000
Earnings per share	p	18.09	13.55	8.04	19.94	46.22
Dividend per share	p	16.70	17.50	17.50	17.50	18.50
Net assets per share	p	703.26	666.00	660.82	701.10	917.60
Shareholders' funds	£	5,948M	5,908M	5,544M	5,540M	5,726M
Return on long term capital	%	7.39	8.31	5.32	7.74	5.36
Return on shareholders' equity	%	4.27	3.20	2.19	5.56	12.66
Pre-tax margin	%	0.34	0.44	0.14	0.40	0.84
Operating profit per employee	£	n/a	n/a	n/a	n/a	9.00
		5.27	4.58	4.19	4.18	-0.27
Free resources ratio		1.08	0.77	0.46	1.14	2.50
Dividend cover	%	48.30	11.77	-9.13	-5.18	-19.00
Net income growth	%	-70.65	-25.11	-40.70	148.15	131.80
Earnings growth						
Total advances	£	83,351M	87,407M	83,665M	94,876M	110,830M
Customer deposits	£	101,251M	106,332M	107,494M	126,224M	83,973M
Number of employees		113,000	113,000	102,000	99,800	96,700

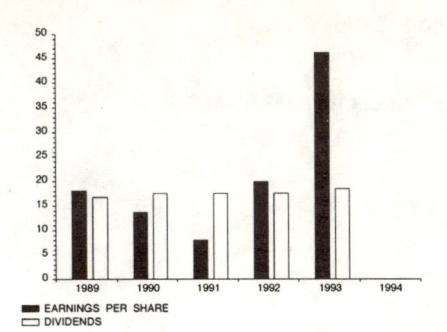

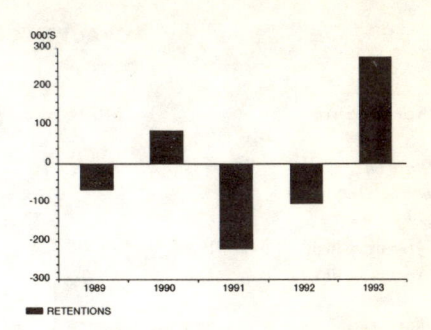

Earnings and dividends

Retentions

NATIONAL WESTMINSTER BANK plc

41 Lothbury, London EC2P 2BP
Tel: 0171 726 1000
Chairman Lord Alexander of Weedon
Chief executive Derek Wanless
Main subsidiaries 3i (23%), Coutts, Lex Vehicle Leasing (50%), Isle of Man Bank, Lombard, Rover Finance (50%), Switch card services (33%), Ulster Bank
Size £7.0 billion net interest, £7.9 billion stock market value, 98,000 employees
5-year growth net interest n/a, earnings per share n/a, employment -14%
Solvency n/a
Political donations 0
Charitable donations £1.6 million

Major developments

1833 National Provincial Bank established
1836 Westminster Bank established
1968 merger to create National Westminster
1985 bought stockbrokers Fielding Newson-Smith, Bisgood Bishop
1988 bought stockbroker Wood Mackenzie
1991 joint insurance venture with Clerical Medical
1993 set up Nat West Life
1994 bought Citizens First Bancorp

Corporate governance

Separate Chairman and Chief Executive Y
Number of Directors 20
Number of Non-Executive Directors 12
(12 Independent Directors)
Insulated Directors Ch, DCh

Board Committees
Audit: Y   Remuneration: Y

Remuneration

Year end	31.12.91	31.12.92	31.12.93
Total board £M	3.88	4.85	6.04
% change	2	25	25
Highest paid £	385,155	383,900	554,238
% change	-23	-0.3	44

Board

Wanless, Derek *Chief Executive*
Lord Alexander of Weedon *Executive Chairman*
Gray, Martin *Executive Director*
Melbourn, John William *Executive Director*
Morris, Albert *Executive Director*
Owen, Martin *Executive Director*
Tugwell, John *Executive Director*
Goeltz, Richard *Finance Director*
Angus, Sir Michael R *Independent Non-Executive*
Banham, Sir John *Independent Non-Executive*
Baroness Young *Independent Non-Executive*
Butler, Sir Richard Clive *Ind. Non-Executive*
Child, Denis Marsden *Independent Non-Executive*
Lipworth, Sir Sydney *Independent Non-Executive*
MacLaurin, Sir Ian Charter *Ind. Non-Executive*
Nixon, Sir Edwin Ronald *Ind. Non-Executive*
Pilkington, Sir Antony R *Ind. Non-Executive*
Powell, Sir Charles David *Ind Non-Executive*
Quigley, Sir George *Independent Non-Executive*
Taylor, Martin Gibbeson *Ind. Non-Executive*

ROYAL BANK OF SCOTLAND

Share record

Return on shareholders' equity	%	8.22
5-year price high	p	519.0
5-year price low	p	121.0
Dividend yield	%	3.74
5-year high	%	8.37
5-year low	%	2.65
Price/earnings ratio		13.2
5-year high		111.3
5-year low		5.3

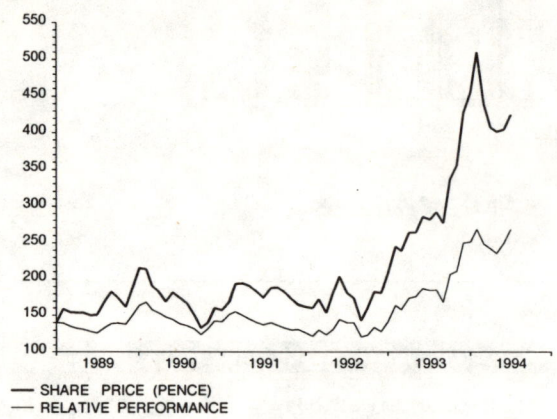

Share price performance (in pence)

Financial record

		30/9/89	30/9/90	30/9/91	30/9/92	30/9/93
Gross profit	£	2,504M	3,142M	3,022M	2,693M	2,160M
Bad debt provision	£'000	194,100	173,000	351,100	400,800	293,300
Pre-tax profit	£'000	215,300	238,800	62,800	41,700	272,800
Published retentions	£'000	92,400	130,200	5,000	-58,000	51,500
Earnings per share	p	17.48	18.31	5.39	2.44	18.86
Dividend per share	p	7.20	8.40	8.80	8.80	11.00
Net assets per share	p	380.55	373.08	381.53	391.30	450.48
Shareholders' funds	£	1,411M	1,508M	1,601M	1,780M	1,897M
Return on long term capital	%	11.22	12.71	5.73	4.00	9.81
Return on shareholders' equity	%	9.01	8.63	2.69	1.12	8.22
Pre-tax margin	%	0.76	0.78	0.14	0.09	0.81
Operating profit per employee	£	8.10	9.65	n/a	n/a	n/a
Free resources ratio		7.75	6.79	6.66	6.42	7.89
Dividend cover	%	2.43	2.18	0.61	0.28	1.71
Net income growth	%	60.03	25.47	-3.83	-10.86	-19.80
Earnings growth		-31.25	4.73	-70.55	-54.82	674.35
Total advances	£	17,397M	19,464M	20,903M	22,488M	23,232M
Customer deposits	£	23,219M	25,730M	27,782M	29,464M	30,301M
Number of employees		26,530	25,803	24,616	24,116	23,299

BANKS 19

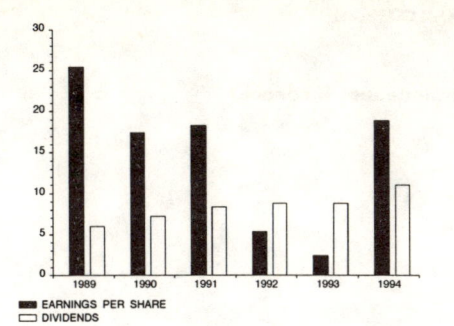

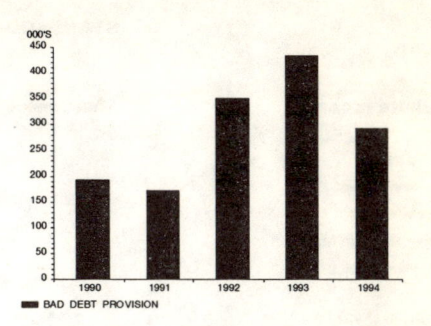

Earnings and dividends

'Problem country' debt

ROYAL BANK OF SCOTLAND GROUP plc

36 St Andrew Square, Edinburgh EH2 2YB
Tel: 0131 556 8555
Chairman Lord Younger
Chief executive Dr George Mathewson
Main subsidiaries Capital House, Direct Line Insurance, RoyScot
Size £1.4 billion net interest, £3.2 billion stock market value, employees 23,300
5-year growth net interest n/a, earnings per share -8%, employment -12%
Solvency n/a
Political donations 0
Charitable donations £1.7 million

Major developments
1968 merger of RBS and National Commercial Bank of Scotland
1981 bids from Standard Chartered and HSBC blocked by Monopolies Commission
1984 Lloyds Bank built 21% stake
1985 Lloyds sold stake bought merchant bank Charterhouse Japhet merged Williams & Glyn's into branch operation
1986 bought stockbroker Tilney & Co
1987 bought travel agent A T Mays Group
1988 bought out the remaining 25% of Direct Line Insurance; bought Citizens Financial (US); linked with Banco Santander of Spain
1989 sold 76% interest in A T Mays Group
1993 sold Charterhouse

Corporate governance

Separate Chairman and Chief Executive Y
Number of Directors 21

Number of Non-Executive Directors 12 (10 Independent Directors)
Insulated Directors CE, MD
Board Committees
Audit: Y   Remuneration: Y

Remuneration

Year end	30.09.91	30.09.92	30.09.93
Total board £M	2.65	8.81	22.57
% change	20	233	152
Highest paid £M	0.49	6.12	18.47
% change	2	1,247	202

Board
Lord Younger *Executive Chairman*
Mathewson, Dr George R *Chief Executive*
Barclay, John Alistair *Executive Director*
Fish, Lawrence K *Executive Director*
McLuskie, Norman C *Executive Director*
Robertson, Iain S *Executive Director*
Schofield, G Anthony *Executive Director*
Speirs, Robert *Executive Director*
Wood, Peter J *Executive Director*
Channon, Prof. Derek F *Ind. Non-Executive*
Duthie, Sir Robin G *Ind. Non-Executive*
Grant, Ian *Ind. Non-Executive*
Greig, Henry *Ind. Non-Executive*
Grossart, Angus McFarlane *Ind. Non-Executive*
Hamilton, Alexander M *Ind. Non-Executive*
Nelson, Dr Elizabeth *Ind. Non-Executive*
Vallance, Sir Iain D T *Ind. Non-Executive*
Wilson, William M *Ind. Non-Executive*
Wood, Sir Ian Clark *Ind. Non-Executive*
Botin-Sanz, Emilio *Non-Executive*
Botin-Sanz, Jaime *Non-Executive*

STANDARD CHARTERED

Share record

Return on shareholders' equity	%	17.0
5-year price high	p	357.7
5-year price low	p	52.0
Dividend yield	%	2.80
5-year high	%	22.44
5-year low	%	1.79
Price/earnings ratio		11.1
5-year high		35.7
5-year low		4.8

Share price performance (in pence)

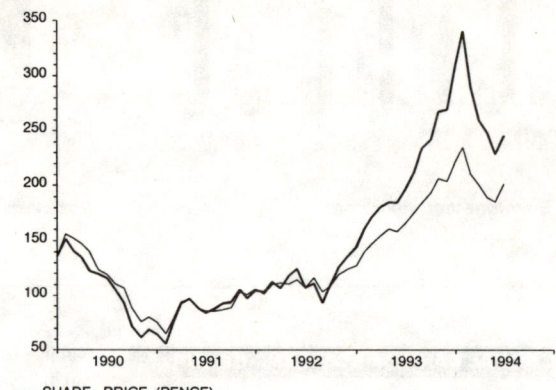

— SHARE PRICE (PENCE)
— RELATIVE PERFORMANCE

Financial record

		31/12/89	31/12/90	31/12/91	31/12/92	31/12/93
Gross profit	£	915,700	902,900	938,100	1,184M	1,786M
Bad debt provision	£'000	594,900	174,700	159,400	366,200	233,000
Pre-tax profit	£'000	-195,000	150,000	205,700	91,000	371,000
Published retentions	£'000	-113,000	-13,200	12,600	21,100	171,000
Earnings per share	p	0.00	3.25	11.12	0.00	21.43
Dividend per share	p	8.75	5.00	5.00	5.00	6.00
Net assets per share	p	262.83	240.52	236.18	258.80	422.79
Shareholders' funds	£	963,900	989,900	967,000	1,004M	1,297M
Return on long term capital	%	-1.68	12.50	14.04	7.50	n/a
Return on shareholders' equity	%	-30.83	3.07	10.75	-4.24	17.00
Pre-tax margin	%	-0.93	0.70	0.89	0.29	1.29
Operating profit per employee	£	n/a	n/a	n/a	n/a	11.76
Free resources ratio		9.53	9.23	8.36	8.26	-3.50
Dividend cover		0.00	0.65	2.22	0.00	3.57
Net income growth	%	-12.52	-1.40	3.90	26.22	50.83
Earnings growth	%	-100.00	0.00	242.14	-100.00	0.00
Total advances	£	18,124M	15,240M	16,905M	20,067M	22,283M
Customer deposits	£	22,084M	19,819M	21,170M	24,794M	24,365M
Number of employees		30,000	30,000	30,000	30,000	30,432

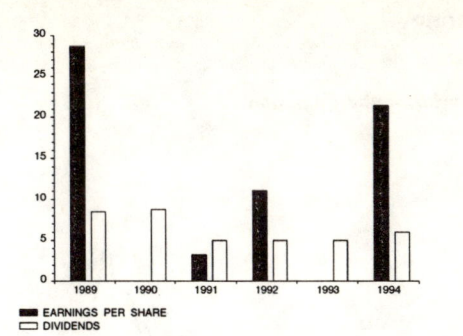

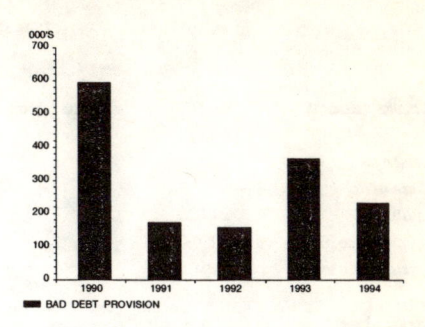

Earnings and dividends

'Problem country' debts

STANDARD CHARTERED plc

1 Aldermanbury Square, London EC2V 7SB
Tel: 0171 280 7500
Chairman Patrick Gillam
Chief executive Malcolm Williamson
Size £1.7 billion net interest, £2.6 billion stock market value, employees 30,400
5-year growth net interest n/a, earnings per share n/a, employment 1%
Solvency n/a
Political donations 0
Charitable donations £1 million

Major developments
1969 formed on merger of Standard Bank and Chartered Bank
1981 bid for Royal Bank of Scotland blocked by Monopolies Commission
1986 bid from Lloyds Bank failed

Corporate governance

Separate Chairman and Chief Executive Y
Number of Directors 16
Number of Non-Executive Directors 9
(7 Independent Directors)
Insulated Directors All execs

Board Committees
Audit: Y   Remuneration: Y

Remuneration

Year end	31.12.91	31.12.92	31.12.93
Total board £M	2.60	2.20	3.73
% change	37	-15	69
Highest paid £	303,815	393,093	529,000
% change	16	29	35

Board
Williamson, G Malcolm *Chief Executive*
Gillam, Patrick J *Executive Chairman*
Brougham, David P *Executive Director*
Castleman, Christopher *Executive Director*
McFarlane, John *Executive Director*
Moir, David G *Executive Director*
Wood, Peter *Finance Director*
Agnew, Rudolf I J *Independent Non-Executive*
Baillie, Robin A M *Independent Non-Executive*
Craig, John E *Independent Non-Executive*
Lord Stewartby *Independent Non-Executive*
Mackrell, Keith A V *Independent Non-Executive*
Robins, Sir Ralph H *Independent Non-Executive*
Stenham, Anthony W P *Independent Non-Executive*
Brown, William C L *Non-Executive*
Williams, Geoffrey *Non-Executive*

22 BANKS

TSB GROUP

Share record

Return on shareholders' equity   %   14.28
5-year price high   p   289.0
5-year price low   p   101.5

Dividend yield   %   5.00
5-year high   %   7.62
5-year low   %   3.09

Price/earnings ratio   9.3
5-year high   206.0
5-year low   7.0

Share price performance (in pence)

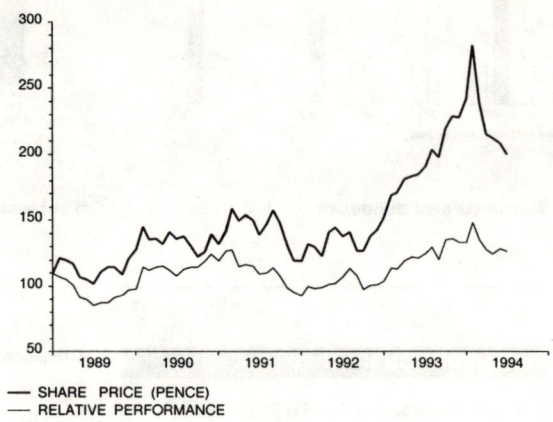

— SHARE PRICE (PENCE)
— RELATIVE PERFORMANCE

Financial record

		31/10/89	31/10/90	31/10/91	31/10/92	31/10/93
Gross profit	£	2,294M	3,117M	2,832M	2,291M	1,926M
Bad debt provision	£'000	92,000	261,000	654,000	597,000	343,000
Pre-tax profit	£'000	356,221	312,471	-46,718	43,763	366,000
Published retentions	£'000	14,000	21,000	-73,000	-177,000	73,000
Earnings per share	p	20.63	13.58	0.00	1.16	17.22
Dividend per share	p	5.80	6.40	6.40	6.40	7.68
Net assets per share	p	180.15	177.86	175.73	162.38	170.40
Shareholders' funds	£	1,853M	1,814M	1,742M	1,638M	1,740M
Return on long term capital	%	16.92	15.11	1.16	5.19	17.13
Return on shareholders' equity	%	11.57	10.03	-2.75	0.53	14.28
Pre-tax margin	%	1.56	1.26	-0.20	0.21	1.60
Operating profit per employee	£	4.54	4.21	-2.68	0.41	12.63
		5.82	5.26	5.81	4.74	5.70
Free resources ratio		3.56	2.12	0.00	0.18	2.24
Dividend cover	%	47.91	35.88	-9.15	-19.12	-15.92
Net income growth	%	12.89	-34.17	-100.00	0.00	1,382
Earnings growth						
Total advances	£	18,683M	20,758M	18,809M	20,404M	19.143M
Customer deposits	£	21,509M	23,047M	21,727M	23,403M	21,438M
Number of employees		43,640	42,818	39,773	36,715	33,484

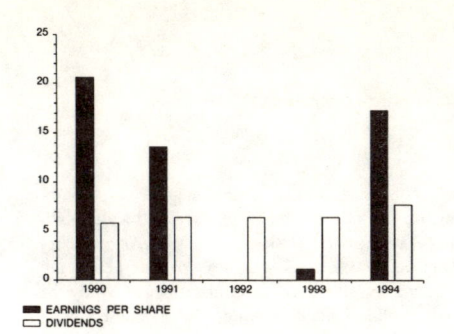

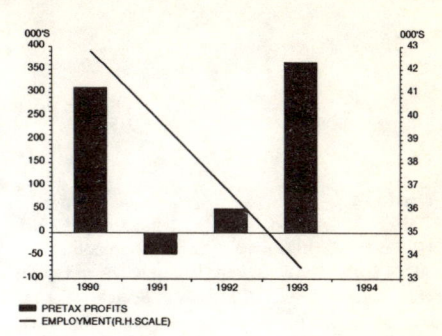

Earnings and dividends

Profits and employment

TSB GROUP plc

25 Milk Street, London EC2V 8LU
Tel: 0171 398 3712
Chairman Sir Nicholas Goodison
Chief executive Peter Ellwood
Size £1.4 billion net income, £3.2 billion stock market value, 33,500 employees
5-year growth net interest n/a, earnings per share -17%, employment -23%
Solvency n/a
Political donations 0
Charitable donations £1.1 million

Major developments
1810 first thrift institution founded which eventually formed basis of nationwide federation of mutual Trustees Savings Banks
1981 bought finance house United Dominion Trust; bought Swan National car hire business
1986 floated on the stock exchange
1987 bought merchant bank Hill Samuel; bought Target pensions and life insurance group
1989 Sir Nicholas Goodison took over as chairman; abolition of regional boards
1991 sold Target to Equity & Law; sold Northern Ireland branch network to Allied Irish Bank
1993 sold estate agency network

Corporate governance

Separate Chairman and Chief Executive Y
Number of Directors 15
Number of Non-Executive Directors 9
(9 Independent Directors)
Insulated Directors None

Board Committees
Audit: Y   Remuneration: Y

Remuneration

Year end	31.10.91	31.10.92	31.10.93
Total board £M	2.04	2.34	1.99
% change	-6	15	-15
Highest paid £	300,700	373,407	516,819
% change		17	24	38

Board
Ellwood, Peter B *Chief Executive*
Goodison, Sir Nicholas *Executive Chairman*
Elbourne, J K *Executive Director*
Fairey, M E *Executive Director*
Freeberg, H R *Executive Director*
Burns, J A *Finance Director*
Anderson, G A *Independent Non-Executive*
Bolton, L *Independent Non-Executive*
Bosel, Hans-Detlef *Independent Non-Executive*
Field, M H *Independent Non-Executive*
Harwood, P A *Independent Non-Executive*
Lady Prior *Independent Non-Executive*
McCracken, P G *Independent Non-Executive*
Mcpherson, J H F *Independent Non-Executive*
Plastow, Sir David *Independent Non-Executive*

DRINKS COMPANIES

Outlook

The drinks business is a global industry in which Britain excels. In Guinness, Grand Metropolitan and Allied-Lyons, it has the three largest wines and spirits companies in the world. Moreover, Scotch whisky is one of Britain's five largest export earners: the Japanese drink it, the Americans drink it, and to an increasing degree, people in the southern half of Europe are developing a taste for it. Where beer is concerned, however, the story is rather different. Since 1989 the brewing industry has been going through the most enormous upheavals: it has become concentrated in fewer and fewer hands and those brewers who are left have had to contend with a declining market for their product.

If one looks first of all at wines and spirits: in 1989 there were four British brewers with heavy investment in this area – Guinness (parent of United Distillers after the extraordinary tussle for control of the old Distillers group in 1986); Grand Metropolitan (parent of International Distillers and Vintners, or 'IDV'); Allied-Lyons (which owned Hiram Walker); and Whitbread (parent of James Burroughs). By the end of 1989 Whitbread had sold James Burroughs – best known for Beefeater gin – to Allied-Lyons. And so there were three. But those three have prospered mightily. In the latter half of the 1980s, the British drinks industry woke up to two things. First, they realised that it was no good just manufacturing the product and then shipping it off to foreign shores: you had to control the distribution and marketing when it arrived in overseas markets. So the producers have endeavoured – often by takeovers of other national drinks companies abroad – to increase their involvement in the markets where their goods are sold. In 1986 IDV bought Heublein, the company which makes Smirnoff vodka. Guinness engineered a share swap in 1988 with LVMH, parent of Louis Vuitson and maker of Moët champagne and Hennessey cognac, so that each company ended up owning rather more than one-quarter of the other. (Guinness rejigged the arrangement in 1994: it now holds a stake only in Moët Hennessey, the drinks part of LVMH.) In 1994 Allied-Lyons bought the Spanish company Pedro Domecq, and signalled its intention to quit food manufacturing and brewing.

Second, the producers cottoned on to the idea that making money out of spirits is not primarily about producing large volumes; it is about using every marketing tool at your disposal – notably advertising and packaging – to make consumers crave products which are up-market and on which you earn higher margins. (The Japanese, in particular, showed themselves to be susceptible to this approach, succumbing, for instance, to the élitism associated with imbibing 12-year-old whiskies.) The drinks industry summed up this trend in its own phrase: people are drinking less, but they are drinking better. So by the early 1990s, United Distillers, for example, found itself making nearly 30p for every £1 of spirits it sold: a handsome and enviable profit margin.

The recession of the early 1990s brought its problems. In Japan falls in company profitability necessitated cuts in executive expense accounts – which had previously been a major vehicle through which conspicuous consumption of ridiculously expensive spirits had been expressed. And in 1993, a decade after the Scotch whisky industry realised that it had to start cutting production to prevent the growth of a whisky loch to match the EC wine lake, the distillers went through the same agonies. Whisky drinking in Britain has fallen sharply and in the US it is in modest decline; only the emerging markets in countries like Greece, Spain, France and South America are helping to take up some of the slack.

All this is nothing compared with the travails that have been afflicting brewing. The pace of recent change has been extraordinary. Five years ago there were six large brewing groups in Britain – Bass, Grand Metropolitan, Allied-Lyons, Whitbread, Courage (now owned by Foster's of Australia) and Scottish & Newcastle. (Purists would point out that Guinness is also a large brewer – particularly now that it owns Cruzcampo in Spain – but somehow this company tends to be overlooked because it owns no pubs.)

In 1989 the Monopolies Commission declared that the government should try to weaken the large companies' grip on the market by telling them to free thousands of pubs from the obligation to sell their beer. The recommendations were watered down after some heavy and effective lobbying by the brewers. Nevertheless, the report provoked upheaval in the industry. Grand Metropolitan sold its breweries to Courage. Courage handed control of thousands of its pubs to Grand Metropolitan. Whitbread and Allied-Lyons flirted with – but eventually rejected – the idea of merging their brewing operations. Allied-Lyons eventually pooled its breweries with the UK operation of the Danish lager company Carlsberg. Whitbread, Scottish & Newcastle and Bass fell into line with the new rules by selling or leasing pubs to independent operators. In many cases, the brewers tied up supply deals with this new breed of pub operator, so that although control of the outlets had changed, the brewers were still guaranteed regular orders to keep their plants running at high capacity.

Some of Britain's smaller, regional brewing groups decided to pull out of beer production altogether: Greenall Whitley, for example, contracted out its brewing to Allied-Lyons so that it could concentrate on running pubs; and Boddingtons sold its breweries to Whitbread so that it, too, could become a retail-only company. The big brewers felt particularly resentful that they were being asked to sell or lease properties just as the property market was declining. But by autumn 1992 – the government's deadline for complying with the new regulations – all the brewers had fallen into line in one way or another.

The recession exposed a curious irony in the way some of these companies had expanded during the late 1980s. Bass had become the largest hotelier in the world by buying Holiday Inns; Whitbread spent heavily on expanding its restaurant chains, including Beefeater and Pizza Hut; while Grand Metropolitan followed Allied-Lyons into foods with the purchase of Pillsbury. When the downturn came, it was those newer, supposedly more attractive businesses which suffered even more than the basic beer and pubs operations.

Just as Guinness prospered when the prices of premium drinks were soaring, it has suffered as consumers have become more price conscious. In spring 1994 the company accepted that its Bells brand, still the most popular Scotch whisky in Britain, could not carry on as before: it was losing sales to cheaper brands and the supermarkets' own-label products. Bells was relaunched as an eight-year-old blend but at the same price as the old Bells – a real sign of Guinness's acknowledgement that in a fiercely competitive environment prices cannot defy gravity for ever.

Allied-Lyons is transforming itself into Allied Domecq, with the purchase in 1994 of Pedro Domecq – a deal that was funded through a £650 million rights issue. The takeover will put the group into the big three of the world drinks industry, alongside its British rivals. Allied-Lyons is due to sell its food operations, and by the end of 1995 it is expected to have sold its half share in the Carlsberg-Tetley brewing operation to its Danish partner.

Grand Metropolitan appears eager to extricate itself from pub ownership, the company's legacy of the deal with Foster's, under which it pulled out of brewing. The group's previously sure-footed progress in the wines and spirits business began to be questioned in early 1994 when the group lost the distribution rights to two important brands in the US – Grand Marnier and Absolut vodka. In 1993 Grand Metropolitan set aside £175 million to cover the cost of expected cutbacks across all its businesses: in particular, the group's Pearle opticians company in the US was to be slimmed down and proposed job cuts were unveiled at Green Giant, part of its Pillsbury foods arm.

Whitbread is keen to continue developing its retail operations in pubs and restaurants. The company has dismantled a complex cross-ownership share structure linking itself and Whitbread Investment Company, which makes it easier for Whitbread to raise money from shareholders if it needs to finance a large acquisition.

Scottish & Newcastle underlined its commitment to its core beer and pubs businesses in September 1993 by paying Grand Met £700 million for more than 1,650 Chef & Brewer pubs. The takeover was financed in part by a £405 million rights issue and gave Scottish & Newcastle a foothold in the south of England; before, it had operated only in the Midlands, the North and Scotland.

Bass remains the largest brewer in Britain, with nearly a quarter of the market. It has shown itself determined to match the rock-bottom prices being offered to free-trade publicans by its rivals. Hence in 1993 profit margins fell, but the company's market share went up. The troublesome Holiday Inns acquisition, which appeared to have been disastrously ill-timed, showed some signs of revival in 1993.

Shares

The drinks sector has been extremely popular with investors for most of the period since the mid-1980s, despite the persistent threats from the Monopolies Commission to the companies' UK brewing base. Part of this popularity stems from the steady movement by most companies away from that threatened base, both geographically and by product. As a result of such diversification, investors have regarded drinks companies as moving from mature, even declining markets, with severe regulatory pressure, into areas with greater potential for growth, such as hotels, leisure and food.

To this general trend must be added a realisation in the late 1980s that these well-established companies had discovered a major new opportunity for profits growth by taking control of distribution of their spirits products. The Scotch whisky industry is a classic case: down on its knees in the mid-1980s, but suddenly, just a few years later, looking very promising as it began to concentrate on margins, not volumes.

As a result of these changes in the industry, the sector index moved up fairly steadily from the time of the market crash in 1987 to the beginning of 1992. It had been slipping during the pre-crash boom, as the sector lost out to what were then regarded as the more glamorous areas. There was only one serious setback on this upward road: at the beginning of 1991 it suddenly emerged that pubs were not immune from recession. Bass warned that beer sales were 1.5 per cent lower in the first quarter, and profits would be 10 per cent lower than in the previous year. The warning affected the whole sector, which had previously been seen as 'defensive' on the grounds that the numbers of people unable to afford a drink would be balanced by the numbers of those who were drowning their sorrows because they could not afford to go anywhere other than the local.

By the end of 1991 shares in the sector were rising again, but not for long. Their performance relative to the stock market as a whole levelled out at the beginning of 1992, and by the autumn had begun to fall sharply, only steadying again in the spring of 1993. The reasons were various: the UK brewing businesses faced heavy property write-offs and bad debts on their pub estates; the end of margin growth in the spirits industry appeared to have arrived, together with pressure on volumes as the important Japanese buyers, suffering their own recession, began to trade down from the extortionately priced gift bottles which had been so much in favour.

Individual companies fared quite differently both in the good times and the bad. Allied-Lyons was long seen as the Aunt Sally of the sector, but, precisely because of this dim view of its performance and its management, it was also regarded as a bid target and on occasions its shares soared (especially at the end of 1988). More recently, the group was boosted by the warm reception given to its Pedro Domecq deal. Scottish & Newcastle did not have the same image, but it too had received unwelcome approaches from Australian John Elliott, of Elders, causing a similar surge in the company's share price – although this came crashing down again when the Monopolies Commission ruled out the bid from Elders. Both companies' shares remained remarkably steady in the 1990s, compared to their rivals', despite the renaissance of Allied-Lyons under new management, and Scottish & Newcastle's move into the holiday business with Center Parcs.

Guinness was the star of the sector for most of the period, after it had recovered from the scandal over its bid for Distillers. Ironically its success in the bid was the cause of it subsequently being in favour with investors, because of the policy of restricting output but boosting margins through the acquired Scotch whisky business. Guinness therefore suffered in 1992 and 1993 when the high-margin era appeared to be ending. But when the group rejigged its relationship with LVMH, this resulted in a net cash inflow for the UK company, which lifted the shares in early 1994.

Grand Metropolitan also benefited from involvement with spirits, as it applied a similar philosophy of reaping margin and distribution rewards. Shares in the company were helped by Grand Met's departure from brewing (following a ground-breaking deal with Courage) and hotels and into food (following the gigantic takeover of Pillsbury). The group suffered some ups and downs during this transition, especially when the stock market felt that the group was deal-obsessed, but its shares rose fairly steadily once the period of acquisitions came to an end.

Bass had long been regarded as one of the best in the sector, but as the largest UK brewer it possibly had most to lose from the UK Beer Orders. It also suffered as a result of its expensive and ill-timed move into hotels, just ahead of the recession. The squeeze on beer margins pushed the shares down throughout most of 1993. Whitbread, on the other hand, remained wedded to UK brewing. Recession hit its attempt to diversify into restaurants, however, and the group seemed to be worse affected than most in its core UK pub operations. By contrast, Scottish & Newcastle shares were boosted by the Chef & Brewer deal.

Throughout 1993 there was little widespread enthusiasm, however, either for the sector or for its components. Recovery was expected to be slow for these companies, and for their shares.

Corporate conscience

If you can forgive them the 'sins' of their core business – alcohol and the sale of tobacco as a sideline to drinks retailing – the record of these companies is not bad, although their consciences are probably slightly less clear than most of the companies in this book.

With regard to employment, their performance tends to be below average, especially if the treatment of pub tenants is taken into account, but all except Bass have adequate equal opportunities policies. Almost all have a reasonable record for community involvement and support, however, and they are generally less involved than most in countries with oppressive regimes. Only Bass and Guinness have escaped recent advertising complaints, while all except Bass and Scottish & Newcastle have caused water pollution in recent years. Scottish & Newcastle is the only drinks company not to be a member of BITC.

Guinness earns more black marks than all except Grand Metropolitan, because of a presence in the oppressive regimes of Cameroon and Nigeria, an association with animal testing through LVMH cosmetics, and because of an obscure associate company (Hardwood Dimensions) which imports and wholesales tropical hardwoods for use in musical instruments, sports goods, furniture and tool handles. These negative aspects are balanced by membership of the Per Cent Club as well as BITC, and a record of donating more than one per cent of profits to charity, plus a high level of unionisation among employees. (The employment record is marred by a £12,000 fine under health and safety laws.)

Grand Metropolitan is the only one of the drinks companies to be involved in intensive farming (through its food interests) and low pay in South Africa. These aspects are balanced by the group's strong commitment to community involvement, exhibited not only by membership of BITC and the Per Cent Club, but also through the personal commitment of chairman Lord Sheppard. Grand Met joins Whitbread in supporting Opportunity 2000.

Whitbread has been convicted twice of water pollution, despite having no examples of exceeding consent levels; while Allied-Lyons has a record of 7 excesses but only one conviction. In addition, Allied-Lyons has two health and safety convictions, where Whitbread, like Bass, has none. Allied-Lyons is the only drinks company committed to phasing out CFCs by the end of 1995.

Corporate governance

The drinks companies do not have a very good record on governance, although Grand Metropolitan has a powerful team of non-executives on the board. This sector also includes some of the most regular and generous donors to the Conservative Party, although Allied-Lyons stopped making contributions in 1993. Neither Scottish & Newcastle nor Whitbread, which have continued contributing, have deemed it necessary to ask shareholders for approval for these payments.

Allied-Lyons's boardroom was rather light on non-executives, but in his first annual report new chairman Michael Jackaman promised to boost the non-executive team, which he quickly did. The company set up a remuneration committee in 1992, although it is a pity that this has not been followed by fuller disclosure on executive pay, such as the criteria for performance bonuses.

Bass is one of the declining number of recalcitrants which continues to combine the two top jobs of chairman and chief executive, in the hands of Ian Prosser. Deputy chairman Kenneth Dixon pointed this out in his commentary on the board in the 1992 annual report, and in 1993 the report justified this by reference to the strong non-executive team, which is selected through a formal process. The overall level of disclosure is generous, although it is possible to deduce from the annual report that executive directors enjoy three-year rolling service contracts.

Grand Metropolitan provides an above-average level of disclosure and governance, and in 1993 finally split the roles of chairman and chief executive. It has one of the strongest non-executive teams among the companies in this book.

At **Guinness** standards of corporate governance are high, as befits a company whose boardroom performance fell so far short of an acceptable standard during the infamous Distillers takeover. The non-executives' ability to appoint and remove the chairman, fix executive remuneration and form the audit committee are detailed in the annual report, although departures of senior executives and rumours of boardroom rifts suggest all is not rosy. Succession at the top of the company appears to be well planned. There is also a comparatively high level of disclosure on executive remuneration and the basis on which performance pay is calculated.

Scottish & Newcastle chairman Sir Alick Rankin showed some scepticism about the Cadbury Report in his 1993 statement, suggesting that its proposals could cramp the company's style. The report did include a full statement of compliance, however. Only limited information is given on directors' pay.

Whitbread The non-executive component of the board has been strengthened in a further step away from family control. Reorganisation of the shares has removed another source of discontent. Whitbread could make an additional improvement by providing greater disclosure of directors' pay and bonuses.

ALLIED DOMECQ

Share record

Return on shareholders' equity | % | 14.77
5-year price high | p | 684.4
5-year price low | p | 406.9

Dividend yield | % | 4.83
5-year high | % | 5.32
5-year low | % | 3.50

Price/earnings ratio | | 15.1
5-year high | | 17.2
5-year low | | 9.7

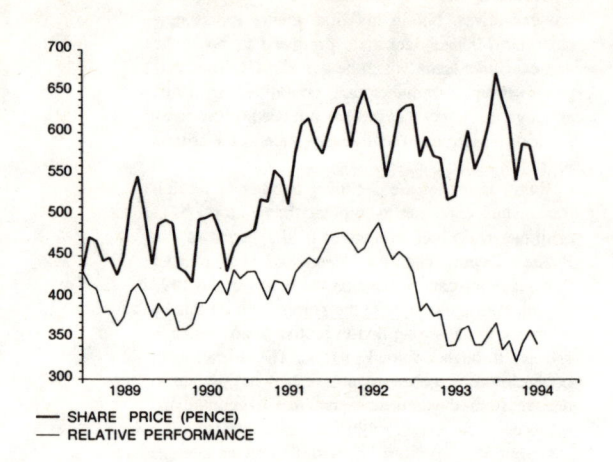

Share price performance (in pence)

— SHARE PRICE (PENCE)
— RELATIVE PERFORMANCE

Financial record

		28/2/89	28/2/90	28/2/91	29/2/92	28/2/93
Total sales	£	4,504M	4,731M	5,133M	5,360M	5,266M
Pre-tax profit	£'000	459,000	501,000	566,000	597,000	608,000
Published retentions	£'000	201,000	222,000	146,000	124,000	74,000
Earnings per share	p	37.27	38.77	41.85	41.44	36.45
Dividend per share	p	14.81	16.74	18.58	19.75	20.74
Operating cash flow	£'000	161,000	-134M	239,000	-49,000	137,000
Net assets per share	p	553.25	583.00	558.33	522.29	504.50
Net debt/(cash)	£	1,077M	2,033M	1,910M	1,930M	1,818M
Shareholders' funds	£	2,969M	2,517M	2,624M	2,680M	2,382M
Return on capital	%	16.77	15.54	18.62	18.29	17.76
Profit margin	%	9.21	9.36	9.51	9.42	9.67
Sales per employee	£	55.30	54.21	61.66	68.07	73.43
Interest cover		4.25	3.90	3.08	3.31	3.71
Dividend cover		2.52	2.32	2.25	2.10	1.90
Sales increase	%	6.33	5.04	8.50	4.42	-1.75
Earnings growth	%	14.30	4.04	7.94	-0.98	-5.00
Investment x depreciation		0.79	1.86	0.60	1.14	0.94
Investment as % assets		3.13	6.98	2.61	5.26	4.74
Number of employees		81,440	87,273	83,243	78,743	71,713

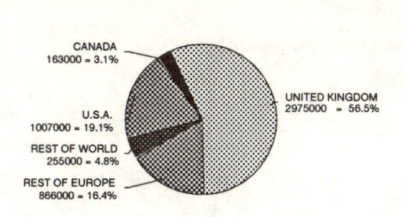

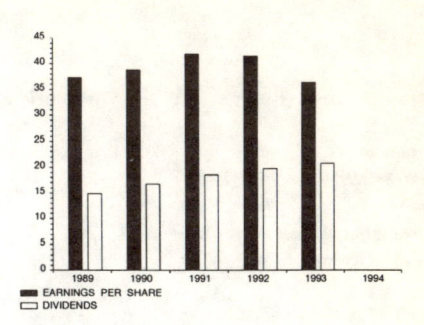

Sales analysis

Earnings and dividends

ALLIED DOMECQ plc

24 Portland Place, London W1N 4BB
Tel: 0171 323 9000
Chairman Michael Jackaman
Chief executive Tony Hales
Substantial interests Suntory 4.3%
Main brands and subsidiaries Ansells, Augustus Barnett, Ballantine's, Ballygowan, Baskin-Robbins, Beefeater gin, Benskins, John Bull, Burton, Canadian Club, Carlsberg-Tetley, Castlemaine, Cockburn's, Courvoisier, Lamb's, Lowenbrau, Maryland Cookies, Skol, Swan Lager, Taylor Walker, Teacher's, Tetley tea, Tetley bitter, Tia Maria, Victoria Wine
Size £5.3 billion sales, £6.0 billion stock market value, 71,700 employees
5-year growth sales 17%, earnings per share -2%, employment -12%
Solvency debt = 76% shareholders' funds, interest cover 4 times
Political donations 0
Charitable donations £1.3 million

Major developments
1960 merger of Joshua Tetley and Walker Cain
1961 merger of Ind Coope, Tetley Walker and Ansells
1963 name changed to Allied Breweries
1968 bought Showerings
1976 bought Teacher's
1978 bought J Lyons
1981 name changed to Allied-Lyons
1986 bought Hiram Walker; Elders' bid lapsed after reference to Monopolies Commission
1988 link with Suntory
1989 bought 69% stake in Château Latour; bought Dunkin Donuts Inc; bought James Burrough
1991 bought 24% Champagne Lanson; £150 million currency loss led to top management shake-up
1992 leased over 700 pubs to Brent Walker; Showerings sold to management; Lyons Maid sold; breweries merged with Carlsberg UK
1993 bought Augustus Barnett
1994 sold Lyons coffee; bought Pedro Domecq; change of name to Allied Domecq

Corporate governance

Separate Chairman and Chief Executive Y
Number of Directors 11
Number of Non-Executive Directors 5
(5 Independent Directors)
Insulated Directors None

Board Committees
Audit: Y   Remuneration: Y

Remuneration

Year end	7.03.92	6.03.92	6.03.93
Total board £M	3.22	3.23	2.39
% change	2	0.4	-26
Highest paid £	369,319	390,847	404,000
% change	3	6	3

Board
Hales, Anthony J *Chief Executive*
Jackaman, Michael C J *Executive Chairman*
Jarvis, D W *Executive Director*
Moss, R *Executive Director*
Trigg, J A *Executive Director*
Macfarlane, P *Finance Director*
Mason, W E *Independent Non-Executive*
Rivett-Carnac, Miles *Independent Non-Executive*
Robb, John Weddell *Independent Non-Executive*
Stapleton, N J *Independent Non-Executive*

BASS

Share record

Return on shareholders' equity   %   9.64
5-year price high   p   653.0
5-year price low   p   437.6

Dividend yield   %   4.81
5-year high   %   5.40
5-year low   %   2.92

Price/earnings ratio   15.1
5-year high   17.6
5-year low   9.3

Share price performance (in pence)

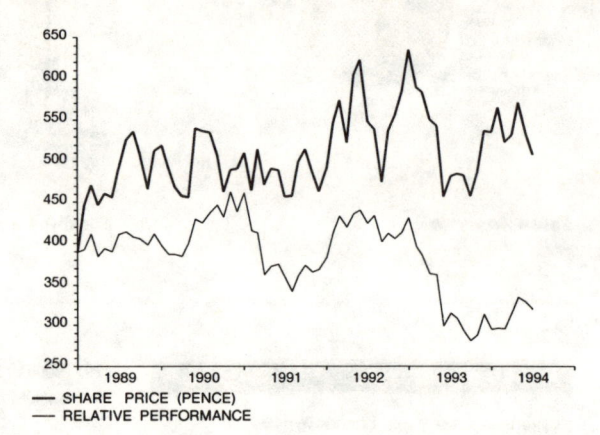

— SHARE PRICE (PENCE)
— RELATIVE PERFORMANCE

Financial record

		30/9/89	30/9/90	30/9/91	30/9/92	30/9/93
Total sales	£	4,063M	4,461M	4,383M	4,307M	4,451M
Pre-tax profit	£'000	470,000	494,000	521,000	581,000	521,000
Published retentions	£'000	285,000	359,000	306,000	270,000	142,000
Earnings per share	p	44.66	48.48	48.07	49.64	37.53
Dividend per share	p	13.77	15.82	17.68	18.90	19.80
Operating cash flow	£'000	137,000	166,000	281,000	157,000	24,000
Net assets per share	p	479.81	651.29	658.19	574.48	574.36
Net debt/(cash)	£'000	671,000	1,368M	719,000	623,000	787,000
Shareholders' funds	£	2,736M	2,935M	3,622M	3,343M	3,413M
Return on capital	%	16.83	16.79	13.59	13.87	13.10
Profit margin	%	11.65	11.07	11.89	13.49	11.71
Sales per employee	£	44.78	45.36	48.64	51.22	54.88
Interest cover		8.44	4.43	5.66	13.26	7.11
Dividend cover		3.24	3.06	2.72	2.63	1.90
Sales increase	%	8.08	10.53	-1.75	-1.73	3.34
Earnings growth	%	21.56	8.55	-0.86	3.27	-24.40
Investment x depreciation		2.14	1.57	0.46	0.80	1.97
Investment as % assets		8.15	5.31	1.78	3.38	8.53
Number of employees		90,138	98,345	90,104	84,095	81,105

DRINKS COMPANIES

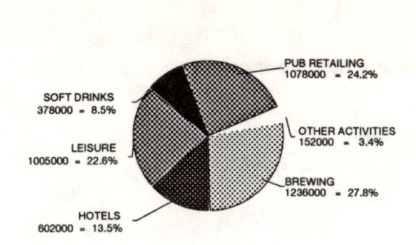

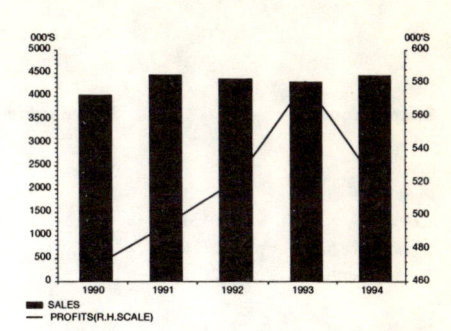

Profit analysis

Profits and sales

BASS plc

20 North Audley Street, London W14 1WE
Tel: 0171 409 1919
Chairman and chief executive Ian Prosser
Main brands and subsidiaries Bass, Britvic, Carling Black Label, Charrington, Coral Bookmakers, Gala bingo clubs, Holiday Inn, Stones, Tango, Tennent's lager, Toby, R Whites, Worthington Bitter
Size £4.5 billion sales, £4.8 billion stock market value, 81,100 employees
5-year growth sales 10%, earnings per share -16%, employment -10%
Solvency debt = 23% shareholders' funds, interest cover 7 times
Political donations 0
Charitable donations £870,000

Major developments
1967 merger of Bass, Mitchells & Butlers and Charrington breweries
1980 bought Coral Leisure
1983 bought Augustus Barnett
1985 bought Horizon Travel; bought 12 Holiday Inns in USA; bought wine and spirit business of Reckitt & Colman
1987 bought Horizon Holidays; bought Wings holiday company from Rank; sold Pontin's to management
1988 bought Holiday Inn outside USA, Mexico and Canada; bought Zetters Leisure; sold Horizon Holidays to Thomson
1990 bought remainder of Holiday Inn; sold Crest hotels to Forte
1991 bought Granada bingo clubs; merged chain named Gala
1993 sold Augustus Barnett to Allied-Lyons

Corporate governance

Separate Chairman and Chief Executive N
Number of Directors 9
Number of Non-Executive Directors 4
(4 Independent Directors)
Insulated Directors Ch, CE, MD

Board Committees
Audit: Y   Remuneration: Y

Remuneration

Year end	30.09.91	30.09.92	30.09.93
Total board £M	2.79	2.72	2.81
% change	7	-2	3
Highest paid £	427,485	452,000	531,000
% change	3	6	17

Board
Prosser, Ian M G *Chairman & Chief Executive*
Bowman, P *Executive Director*
Langton, B D *Executive Director*
Portno, A D *Executive Director*
Swan, J R D *Executive Director*
Middleton, Sir Peter *Independent Non-Executive*
Mulcahy, Sir Geoffrey J *Independent Non-Executive*
Perry, Sir Michael Sydney *Ind. Non-Executive*
Dixon, Kenneth H M *Non-Executive Deputy Chairman*

GRAND METROPOLITAN

Share record

Return on shareholders' equity   %   83.31
5-year price high   p   512.0
5-year price low   p   249.0

Dividend yield   %   3.92
5-year high   %   4.73
5-year low   %   2.97

Price/earnings ratio   12.4
5-year high   22.5
5-year low   9.5

Share price performance (in pence)

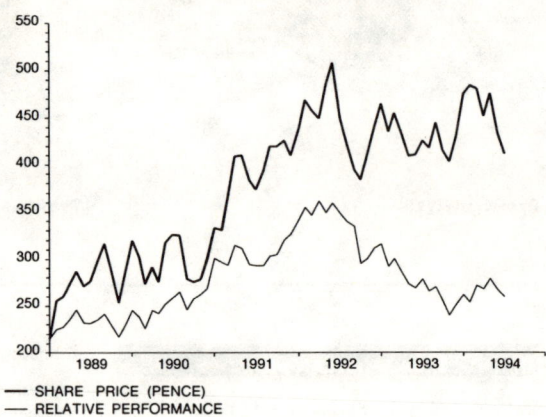

— SHARE PRICE (PENCE)
— RELATIVE PERFORMANCE

Financial record

		30/9/89	30/9/90	30/9/91	30/9/92	30/9/93
Total sales	£	9,298M	9,394M	8,748M	7,913M	8,120M
Pre-tax profit	£'000	708,000	843,000	907,000	897,000	919,000
Published retentions	£'000	901,000	871,000	214,000	378,000	164,000
Earnings per share	p	24.82	29.17	31.10	28.78	33.20
Dividend per share	p	8.83	10.20	11.35	12.30	13.00
Operating cash flow	£'000	557,000	308,000	257,000	40,000	382,000
Net assets per share	p	210.79	222.20	216.14	215.03	215.17
Net debt/(cash)	£	3,696M	2,938M	2,642M	2,485M	2,872M
Shareholders' funds	£	2,810M	3,401M	5,658M	5,964M	6,367M
Return on capital	%	27.43	28.56	27.64	26.20	26.79
Profit margin	%	7.42	8.73	10.29	11.22	11.07
Sales per employee	£	61.10	68.00	71.60	77.27	93.16
Interest cover		3.66	4.43	6.26	10.45	7.29
Dividend cover		2.81	2.86	2.74	2.34	2.55
Sales increase	%	54.23	1.03	-6.88	-9.55	2.62
Earnings growth	%	14.87	16.03	6.64	-4.31	15.36
Investment x depreciation		0.83	0.42	1.69	1.30	1.05
Investment as % assets		4.12	2.42	12.48	10.16	8.73
Number of employees		152,175	138,149	122,178	102,405	87,163

DRINKS COMPANIES

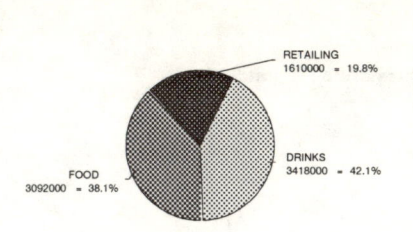

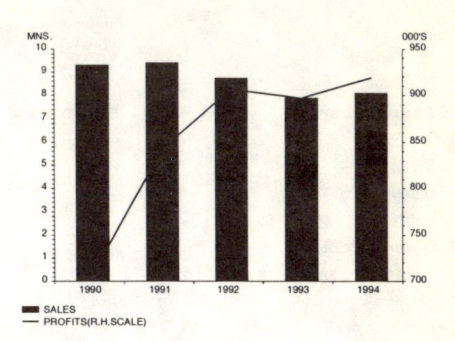

Profit analysis

RETAILING 1610000 = 19.8%
FOOD 3092000 = 38.1%
DRINKS 3418000 = 42.1%

Sales and profits

GRAND METROPOLITAN plc

20 St James's Square, London SW1Y 4RR
Tel: 0171 321 6000
Chairman and chief executive Lord Sheppard
Chief executive George Bull
Main brands Aqua Libra, Baileys, Burger King, Cinzano, Croft Original, Gilbey's, Green Giant, Häagen-Dazs, Heublein, J & B, Malibu, Metaxa, Old Orleans, Pearle Vision, Le Piat D'Or, Pillsbury Smirnoff
Main subsidiaries Cinzano, W & A Gilbey, Heublein, Inntrepreneur, International Distillers and Vintners, Justerini & Brooks, Metaxa, Pillsbury
Size £8.1 billion sales, £9 billion stock market value, 87,200 employees
5-year growth sales -13%, earnings per share 34%, employment -43%
Solvency debt = 45% shareholders' funds, interest cover 7 times
Political donations 0
Charitable donations £10.5 million

Major developments
1961 became public
1962 name changed to Grand Metropolitan Hotels
1969 bought Express Dairies
1970 bought Berni Inns; bought Mecca Group
1971 bought Watney Mann
1973 name changed to Grand Metropolitan Ltd
1985 bought Quality Care Inc; sold Mecca Leisure
1987 bought Heublein (US); sold Compass group
1988 sold Inter-Continental hotels; bought Vision Express Superstores; bought William Hill from Sears
1989 sold London Clubs casinos; bought Pillsbury including Burger King; bought Metaxa; sold William Hill and Mecca betting to Brent Walker; bought UB

Restaurants
1990 bought Jus-rol Ltd; sold Berni
1991 sold Pizzaland/Wimpy restaurants not converted to Burger King; swapped breweries for pubs with Courage; sold Peter Dominic
1992 sold Express Dairies to Northern Foods; sold Express Foods to management; bought Cinzano
1993 sold Chef & Brewer to Scottish & Newcastle

Corporate governance

Separate Chairman and Chief Executive Y
Number of Directors 12
Number of Non-Executive Directors 5
(5 Independent Directors)
Insulated Directors None

Board Committees
Audit: Y Remuneration: Y

Remuneration

Year end	30.09.91	30.09.92	30.09.93
Total board £M	3.79	3.68	3.60
% change	-5	-3	-3
Highest paid £	713,391	770,682	771,884
% change	12	8	0.2

Board
Lord Sheppard *Executive Chairman*
Bull, George J *Chief Executive*
Cawdron, Peter *Executive Director*
McGrath, John *Executive Director*
Nash, David P *Executive Director*
Tagg, David E *Executive Director*
Corbett, Gerald *Finance Director*
Giordano, Richard V *Independent Non-Executive*
Harvey Jones, Sir John *Independent Non-Executive*
Höhler, Prof. Gertrud *Independent Non-Executive*
Marshall, Sir Colin *Independent Non-Executive*

34 DRINKS COMPANIES

GUINNESS

Share record

Return on shareholders' equity	%	25.64
5-year price high	p	635.0
5-year price low	p	262.5
Dividend yield	%	3.65
5-year high	%	3.83
5-year low	%	2.07
Price/earnings ratio		16.0
5-year high		21.5
5-year low		13.0

Share price performance (in pence)

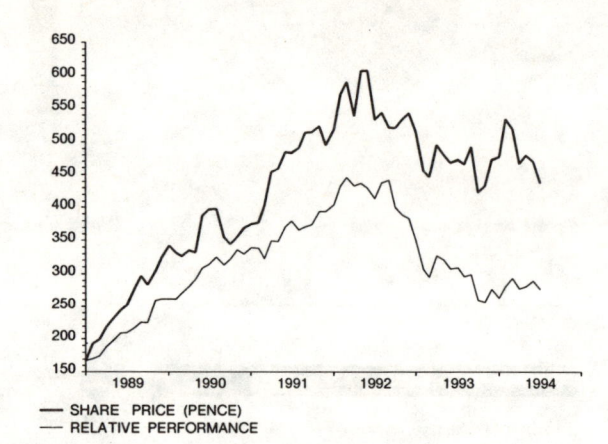

— SHARE PRICE (PENCE)
— RELATIVE PERFORMANCE

Financial record

		31/12/89	31/12/90	31/12/91	31/12/92	31/12/93
Total sales	£	3,076M	3,511M	4,067M	4,363M	4,663M
Pre-tax profit	£'000	691,000	847,000	956,000	920,000	875,000
Published retentions	£'000	249,000	372,000	377,000	287,000	175,000
Earnings per share	p	25.67	27.73	35.32	32.55	29.33
Dividend per share	p	7.65	9.38	10.80	11.85	12.80
Operating cash flow	£'000	-18,000	361,000	182,000	205,000	197,000
Net assets per share	£'000	170.54	201.71	230.93	229.92	225.62
Net debt/(cash)	£	1,323M	1,106M	1,797M	2,029M	1,874M
Shareholders' funds	£	3,962M	4,281M	4,759M	4,898M	4,958M
Return on capital	%	30.87	31.95	31.12	29.85	25.68
Profit margin	%	18.34	19.54	19.23	17.72	15.14
Sales per employee	£	172.33	188.79	176.62	177.81	200.34
Interest cover		7.27	6.81	5.83	4.79	4.76
Dividend cover		3.36	2.96	3.27	2.75	2.29
Sales increase	%	10.81	14.14	15.84	7.28	6.88
Earnings growth	%	40.40	8.04	27.34	-7.85	-9.89
Investment x depreciation		1.32	1.48	1.72	1.57	1.25
Investment as % assets		7.83	10.52	12.20	11.63	10.03
Number of employees		17,849	18,597	23,027	24,538	23,275

DRINKS COMPANIES   35

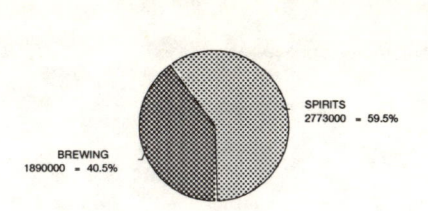

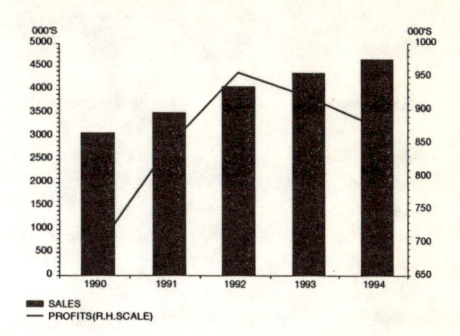

Profit analysis

BREWING 1890000 = 40.5%
SPIRITS 2773000 = 59.5%

Sales and profits

■ SALES
— PROFITS(R.H.SCALE)

GUINNESS plc

39 Portman Square, London W1H 9HB
Tel: 0171 486 0288
Chairman Tony Greener
Chief executive Brian Baldock
Substantial shareholding LVMH 24%
Main brands Bells, Dewars, Gordon's gin, Guinness, Harp Lager, Hennessy, Johnnie Walker, Kaliber, Rebel Yell, Red Stripe, Smithwicks Ale, Tanqueray gin, White Horse,
Main subsidiaries Christian Dior (17%), Gleneagles Hotel, United Distillers
Size £4.7 billion sales, £8.9 billion stock market value, 23,300 employees
5-year growth sales 52%, earnings per share 14%, employment 30%
Solvency debt = 39% shareholders' funds, interest cover 5 times
Political donations 0
Charitable donations £2.2 million

Major developments

1886 formed to buy a brewery business founded in 1759
1984 acquired Martin the Newsagent; acquired Champneys health club
1985 acquisition of Arthur Bell
1986 beat Argyll to acquisition of Distillers; Department of Trade and Industry inspection
1988 share swap with LVMH Moët Hennessy
1989 increased stake in LVMH Moët Hennessy
1990 bought outstanding 25% of Harp Lager Co; bought Cruzcampo brewer (Spain)
1991 Guinness agrees to pay Argyll £100 million compensation
1992 sold Champneys
1994 LVMH shareholding restructured

Corporate governance

Separate Chairman and Chief Executive Y
Number of Directors 10
Number of Non-Executive Directors 6
(4 Independent Directors)
Insulated Directors None

Board Committees
Audit: Y   Remuneration: Y

Remuneration

Year end	31.12.91	31.12.92	31.12.93
Total board £M	2.29	2.36	2.36
% change	8	3	0
Highest paid £	781,000	777,000	648,000
% change	19	-0.5	-17

Board
Greener, Anthony   *Executive Chairman*
Baldock, Brian   *Chief Executive*
O'Neill, Brendan R   *Executive Director*
Yea, Philip E   *Finance Director*
Cadbury, N Dominic   *Independent Non-Executive*
MacLaurin, Sir Ian Charter   *Ind. Non-Executive*
Plastow, Sir David   *Independent Non-Executive*
Sihler, Dr Helmut   *Independent Non-Executive*
Arnault, Bernard   *Non-Executive*
Julien, Michael   *Non-Executive*

SCOTTISH & NEWCASTLE

Share record

Return on shareholders' equity	%	10.06
5-year price high	p	583.0
5-year price low	p	270.0
Dividend yield	%	4.11
5-year high	%	5.79
5-year low	%	3.50
Price/earnings ratio		17.1
5-year high		19.0
5-year low		10.2

Share price performance (in pence)

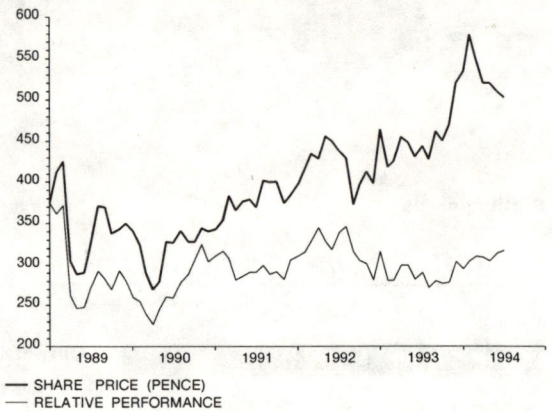

— SHARE PRICE (PENCE)
— RELATIVE PERFORMANCE

Financial record

		30/4/89	30/4/90	30/4/91	30/4/92	30/4/93
Total sales	£	1,028M	1,240M	1,378M	1,487M	1,514M
Pre-tax profit	£'000	133,000	173,200	202,900	210,800	200,500
Published retentions	£'000	40,900	483,100	59,300	81,600	60,800
Earnings per share	p	22.20	26.71	31.46	34.64	34.48
Dividend per share	p	10.44	12.53	14.46	15.52	16.23
Operating cash flow	£'000	-14,700	647,000	96,300	-6,900	-31,400
Net assets per share	p	343.08	433.41	379.02	385.60	399.79
Net debt/(cash)	£'000	271,800	285,600	296,000	307,300	411,000
Shareholders' funds	£	1,160M	1,240M	1,253M	1,331M	1,423M
Return on capital	%	14.91	14.42	14.47	15.92	14.79
Profit margin	%	12.77	13.85	14.72	14.18	13.24
Sales per employee	£	41.90	40.25	45.32	50.55	53.16
Interest cover		6.89	6.51	14.07	11.27	8.48
Dividend cover		2.14	2.14	2.18	2.23	2.12
Sales increase	%	12.78	20.63	11.13	7.90	1.84
Earnings growth	%	14.07	20.16	17.25	10.12	-0.48
Investment x depreciation		2.43	-10.02	1.57	2.35	2.55
Investment as % assets		7.00	-34.19	5.84	8.30	8.64
Number of employees		24,536	30,812	30,411	29,414	28,487

DRINKS COMPANIES

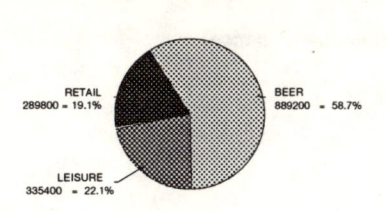

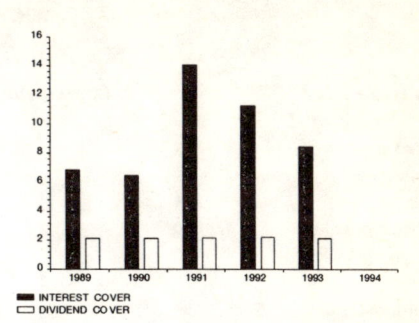

Profit analysis

RETAIL 289800 = 19.1%
BEER 889200 = 58.7%
LEISURE 335400 = 22.1%

Interest and dividends

■ INTEREST COVER
□ DIVIDEND COVER

SCOTTISH & NEWCASTLE plc

Abbey Brewery, 111 Holyrood Road,
Edinburgh EH8 8YS
Tel: 0131 556 2591
Chairman Sir Alick Rankin
Chief executive Brian Stewart
Main brands Beck's, Kestrel, McEwan's, Newcastle Brown, Tartan, Theakston's, Welcome Inns, Pontin's, Center Parcs, Youngers
Main subsidiaries Matthew Brown, Center Parcs, Home Brewery, Pontin's, Theakston's, William Younger
Size £1.5 billion sales, £2.8 billion stock market value, 28,500 employees
5-year growth sales 47%, earnings per share 55%, employment 16%
Solvency debt = 29% shareholders' funds, interest cover 8 times
Political donations £50,000 Conservative Party
Charitable donations £339,000

Major developments
1931 merger of William Younger and William McEwan to form Scottish Brewers
1960 merged with Newcastle Breweries to become Scottish & Newcastle Breweries
1986 acquired Home Brewery
1987 acquired Matthew Brown
1988 acquired 50% stake in Pontin's; bid from Australian brewer Elders blocked by Monopolies Commission
1989 bought the remaining 50% stake of Pontin's bought 75% of Center Parcs; sold Thistle Hotels
1990 bought balance of interest in Center Parcs
1993 bought Chef & Brewer from Grand Metropolitan

Corporate governance

Separate Chairman and Chief Executive Y
Number of Directors 12
Number of Non-Executive Directors 3
(2 Independent Directors)
Insulated Directors Ch, CE

Board Committees
Audit: Y   Remuneration: Y

Remuneration

Year end	28.04.91	3.05.92	2.05.93
Total board £M	1.54	1.70	1.78
% change		10	5
Highest paid £	269,296	271,019	286,135
% change		1	6

Board
Stewart, Brian   *Chief Executive*
Dickson, Guy   *Executive Director*
Fairweather, Henry   *Executive Director*
Hannah, Ian   *Executive Director*
Hemmings, Trevor   *Executive Director*
Mowat, Alastair   *Executive Director*
Reed, Gavin   *Executive Director*
Summers, Roy   *Executive Director*
Wilkinson, Derek   *Finance Director*
Field, Sir Malcolm   *Independent Non-Executive*
Lord Nickson   *Independent Non-Executive*
Rankin, Sir Alick Michael   *Non-Executive Chairman*

38 DRINKS COMPANIES

WHITBREAD

Share record

Return on shareholders' equity	%	7.61
5-year price high	p	614.0
5-year price low	p	343.0
Dividend yield	%	4.34
5-year high	%	6.16
5-year low	%	3.66
Price/earnings ratio		17.6
5-year high		20.2
5-year low		10.4

Share price performance (in pence)

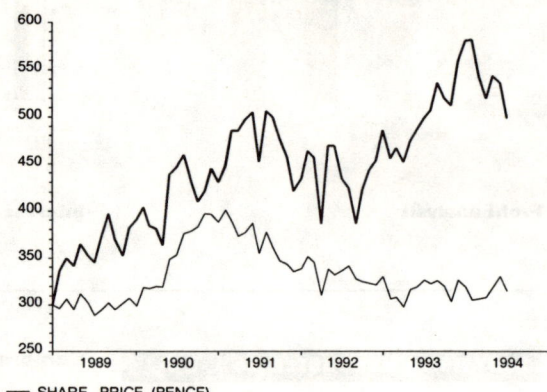

— SHARE PRICE (PENCE)
— RELATIVE PERFORMANCE

Financial record

		28/2/89	28/2/90	28/2/91	29/2/92	28/2/93
Total sales	£	1,845M	2,048M	2,060M	2,191M	2,346M
Pre-tax profit	£'000	193,800	223,500	251,500	183,300	222,900
Published retentions	£'000	106,700	461,700	78,800	51,300	27,000
Earnings per share	p	30.43	35.85	39.78	28.10	33.16
Dividend per share	p	12.55	14.80	16.30	16.95	17.75
Operating cash flow	£'000	-31,900	97,300	42,400	16,700	70,800
Net assets per share	p	624.51	653.86	701.49	711.94	538.24
Net debt/(cash)	£'000	516,700	171,300	329,900	453,300	399,500
Shareholders' funds	£	2,177M	2,558M	2,597M	2,533M	2,003M
Return on capital	%	11.15	10.43	10.06	7.51	10.14
Profit margin	%	9.60	10.18	11.77	7.95	9.04
Sales per employee	£	34.05	32.72	31.38	32.28	36.29
Interest cover		5.17	4.80	22.57	4.83	4.81
Dividend cover		2.43	2.42	2.44	1.66	1.87
Sales increase	%	9.27	11.00	0.57	6.38	7.08
Earnings growth	%	12.80	17.79	10.98	-29.36	17.97
Investment x depreciation		3.07	2.34	2.69	1.82	0.76
Investment as % assets		7.01	5.72	6.58	5.02	2.85
Number of employees		54,192	62,604	65,648	67,886	64,665

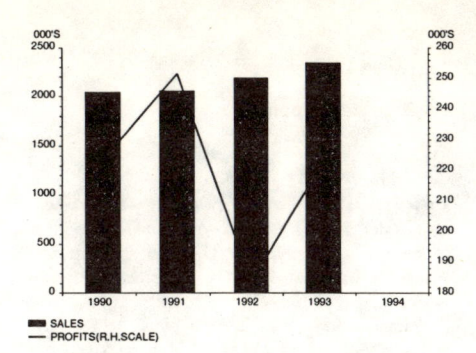

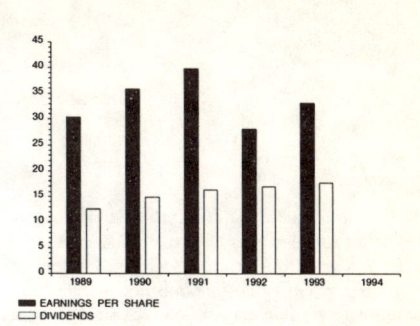

Profit analysis

Shareholders' funds

WHITBREAD plc

Brewery, Chiswell Street, London EC1Y 4SD
Tel: 0171 606 4455
Chairman Sir Michael Angus
Chief executive Peter Jarvis
Substantial shareholdings Whitbread Investment Company 8%
Main brands and subsidiaries Beefeater restaurants, Boddington, Country Club Hotels, Flowers, Heineken, Lansbury Hotels, Mackeson, Mulligan's, Murphy's Irish Stout, Pizza Hut, Stella Artois, TGI Friday's, Thresher, Travel Inns, Trophy Bitter, Wayside Inns
Size £2.3 billion sales, £2.9 billion stock market value, 64,700 employees
5-year growth sales 27%, earnings per share 9%, employment 19%
Solvency debt = 20% shareholders' funds, interest cover 5 times
Political donations £30,000 Conservative Party
Charitable donations £564,525

Major developments
1986 licensing agreement with Heineken NV; bought Wendy burger chain
1987 bought James Burrough
1989 bought Boddington brewery
1990 sold James Burrough to Allied-Lyons; bought Berni Inns from Grand Met
1991 bought Peter Dominic from Grand Met
1992 celebrated 250th anniversary
1993 share structure reorganised; takeover of Whitbread Investment Co.

Corporate governance
Separate Chairman and Chief Executive Y
Number of Directors 11
Number of Non-Executive Directors 6
(2 Independent Directors)
Insulated Directors MD

Board Committees
Audit: Y   Remuneration: Y

Remuneration

Year end	29.02.92	27.02.93	26.02.94
Total board £M	1.60	1.80	1.77
% change	-6	13	-2
Highest paid £	330,428	412,210	470,413
% change	-2	25	14

Board
Jarvis, Peter   *Chief Executive*
Templeman, Miles   *Executive Director*
Thomas, David   *Executive Director*
van Riemsdijk, Wess   *Executive Director*
Perelman, Alan   *Finance Director*
Broughton, Martin F   *Independent Non-Executive*
Franklin, Sir Michael   *Non-Executive*
Padovan, John   *Non-Executive*
Vuursteen, Karel   *Non-Executive*
Whitbread, Samuel C   *Non-Executive*
Angus, Sir Michael R   *Non-Executive Chairman*

DRUG COMPANIES

Outlook

The most important event to occur in the pharmaceutical sector for years was the arrival of Zeneca – the drugs arm of ICI which was demerged from the chemical group in 1993. Zeneca is not entirely comparable with the drug majors, however, since it is not only a drug company, but it comprises ICI's agrochemical and biochemical businesses, including the food product Quorn and a new, biodegradable plastic. Drugs form its major profits source, however, and are likely to be the determinant of its success. As Zeneca became a public company, there were serious question marks about the prospects for its main products. The heart drug Tenormin had been its blockbuster (the equivalent of Glaxo's Zantac or Wellcome's Zovirax, though not as big) but its US sales plummeted in 1992 when the US patent expired. Zeneca proudly pointed to a clutch of new products which it claimed could more than compensate for the continuing decline of Tenormin: alternative heart drug Zestril, cancer treatments Nolvadex and Zoladex, the anaesthetic Diprivan, and (just emerging from the development pipeline) Accolate, an asthma drug.

Zeneca's experience with Tenormin sent shivers through the industry, because of the importance of one or two key products to most of the major groups, and the impending expiry of patents on many of them in key markets. The dependence on a single product by huge companies such as Glaxo is one of many peculiarities of the drugs business. A more fundamental idiosyncrasy is that this is an industry which rests on its reputation for healing, yet makes money primarily from ailments which require continuous treatment. Recurring or persistent problems of the overdeveloped world, such as cancer, ulcers and migraine, are the ideal subjects for commercial exploitation; not illnesses which get better, nor the common and treatable problems of developing nations.

Products such as Zantac (Glaxo's ulcer treatment) have made their owners immensely wealthy by most standards, partly because such drugs are used for illnesses needing a course of treatment, and partly because this is a global industry. The barriers to selling drugs in Japan have been difficult to surmount, but the drug companies have nevertheless built large businesses there, as they have all over the world. Yet this global business is still highly fragmented. Glaxo is neck and neck as world leader with US company Merck, and was Britain's most valuable company according to the stock market's assessment for a period in the early 1990s. But Glaxo and Merck between them account for less than a tenth of the world market for drugs. Big though they are, they are nowhere near as dominant as Guinness or Grand Metropolitan in the drinks industry, ICI or Du Pont in chemicals, British Airways, American or United in the airline business.

Fragmentation means there is plenty to play for, and plenty of scope for the kind of mergers between leaders which created SmithKline Beecham, as well as Bristol-Myers Squibb in the US. It also means that small companies such as Fisons, or the drugs arms of Boots and Reckitt & Colman, can still occasionally make it big. Indeed, that is how Glaxo climbed quickly from relative obscurity at the start of the 1980s. Much is made of the need for huge research labs to develop the compounds which will be tomorrow's world beaters, and of the need for powerful marketing teams to persuade doctors to prescribe them. But marketing can be bought through licensing deals, and many blockbusters have come from small research labs – as evidenced by Zantac.

Zantac is an interesting illustration of the relationship between, and relative importance of, the 'development' end of R&D and the upstream end of marketing. Zantac was essentially just a more effective formulation of SmithKline's Tagamet, the original compound made by a breakthrough in research into ulcer treatment, but it was Glaxo who gained by developing the drug. The other important aspect of research and development is its all-or-nothing financial characteristic. A blockbuster product such as Zantac is a bonanza for its owner. Alternatively, millions can be poured into a compound which stumbles at the final hurdle, as Boots found with Manoplax.

Zantac still accounts for almost half Glaxo's sales, explaining why this is sometimes described as a one-product company. The 'one product' tag is a little unfair since the company has many smaller products such as Beconase, and has launched a series of new drugs that include the migraine product Imigran, the asthma drug Serevent, and Zofran, which acts against nausea. But Zantac is still hugely important to Glaxo, and the imminent expiry of the drug's patent protection in many markets is a cause for concern about the company's future profitability.

Most leading companies similarly owe much of their growth to one or two compounds. Wellcome is highly dependent on Aids therapy Retrovir, and Zovirax, the anti-Herpes product which is valued increasingly for its action against shingles. Wellcome, like most of the other companies in this sector, is more than just a drug company. It is also well represented in the grocery end of the business, with 'over-the-counter' (OTC) products such as the cough 'treatments' Actifed and Sudafed, now marketed through a joint venture with Warner Lambert – Warner Wellcome. These provide a cushion of profits and cash flow to offset the volatility of business in patented drugs. The attraction of OTC products led to upheaval at Glaxo in 1993, when chief executive Ernest Mario departed, apparently after disagreement with chairman Sir Paul Girolami regarding Glaxo's strategy for OTC sales.

SmithKline also has a substantial consumer products element, with Beecham's famous 'health' products such as Lucozade, Ribena, Tums and Macleans toothpaste. Pharmaceuticals are easily its biggest profit-earner, however, Tagamet being important, in addition to the oral antibiotic Augmentin.

The balance of business at Fisons is a little different. It is probably best known for its peat, much to the company's annoyance since the group's survival strategy, following a series of disasters, involved selling off this business, as well as its consumer healthcare operations. It aims to retain the scientific instrument and laboratory supplies businesses and its pharmaceutical activities, which concentrate on anti-asthmatic and anti-allergic products such as Intal and Tilade. But repeated problems with US approval for Tilade have cast doubt on how long Fisons will remain independent. This has not been helped by the bungled appointment in 1991 of Cedric Scroggs as chief executive. He lasted only 20 months in the post.

On the surface, the future for the drug industry looks exciting. The world population is ageing, which implies increasing use of medicinal drugs. Economic development is usually accompanied by greater spending on drugs, suggesting that whole new markets will open up for these companies in Africa and elsewhere. In the developed world Japan still offers an enticing opportunity for most Western drug companies.

All is not rosy, however. First, the long-term prospect of genetic treatments, and even alternatives such as acupuncture, herbal and other remedies, poses some threat to the share of the total market of conventional drugs. More significantly, especially in the short term, is pricing pressure. Faced with growing healthcare costs, Western governments have acted to stem the rising costs of the drug component of government health budgets. This applies especially in the US, the world's largest drug market, where one of President Clinton's first acts was to set up an inquiry into healthcare costs. Pressure on pricing means that companies must rely on the development of new (higher-margin) products and/or growing volumes of sales rather than increased prices.

This brings us back to research and marketing. In the past the most successful companies combined innovative products with forceful marketing. In the US especially, the sheer size of a sales force behind a product was crucial to its success in the market. The nature of the game has changed, however. In the US – the biggest single market – the emergence of healthcare organisations which take total responsibility for large groups of insured people has altered the focus of drug sales, and spawned a number of mergers with medical service providers, as exemplified by Merck's merger with Medeo, and SmithKline's with Diversified Pharmaceutical Services. In the spring of 1994 Glaxo seemed about to follow suit by doing a deal with McKesson, although a full merger was doubtful, partly as a result of chairman Sir Paul Girolami's well-known aversion to takeovers. The announcement in June 1994 of his intention to retire after the AGM in November 1994 raised speculation that Glaxo might subsequently become more aggressive in this field. In all, there certainly appears to be no danger that the drug industry will cease to be an exciting sector.

Shares

The drug sector experienced a huge surge at the start of the 1990s, but fell back rapidly from the beginning of 1992. Recession partly accounted for the dramatic rise and fall: drug shares were initially seen as recession-proof while those in other sectors slumped, but then became less attractive as prospects for the other sectors improved. The soaring rating from the beginning of 1989 was also based on a belief that the industry was entering a period of long-term growth, because of the developed world's ageing population and the growth of diseases such as Aids. The downturn was prompted largely because of the pricing pressures facing the industry, especially in the US since the election of Bill Clinton.

Within the sector there have been some wide variations from the average. Fisons fell from grace during 1991 and 1992 as its troubles with US regulators mounted, and SmithKline Beecham's rise gathered pace from the start of 1992, reflecting the perceived benefits of the merger and corresponding to growing disillusionment with Glaxo. Previously SmithKline's share performance had been relatively modest, especially by comparison with Glaxo and Wellcome, which soared from their mid-1980s ratings, in Glaxo's case making it the most valuable company on the British stock market for a spell.

Drug company share prices are much more closely linked to individual products than they are in most sectors, because of the significance of individual products in a company's portfolio. Much of Wellcome's extreme volatility is due to the development history of Retrovir. The huge surge in the share price in 1989 accompanied the first major acceptance of the compound as a treatment (though not a cure) for Aids. The subsequent plunge reflected the campaign to cut the price of the drug, while the next leap of the shares matched the widening uses of the drug. The return of the company's rating to more normal levels followed reductions in Retrovir's dosage and price, but Wellcome's shares remained very highly valued in relation to its likely earnings, indicating continued faith in the group's prospects for growth.

The fall of both Glaxo and Wellcome in the first half of 1992 corresponds to the industry's fall from grace. The public offering of almost £300 million Wellcome shares, as the Wellcome Trust (once the outright owner) reduced its stake to 40 per cent, did not help the rating of this company, or the sector as a whole. SmithKline largely escaped this downrating, however, although it did suffer a little towards the end of 1991. The shares' recovery after this period was as a result of the company's growing standing within the investment community. That in turn was based on the perceived prospects of drugs like Augmentin, Relafen, Kytril and Paroxetine, together with the widening belief that the merger between SmithKline and Beecham had been a success.

On the other hand, during 1991 and 1992 the share price of Fisons moved downwards, reflecting growing dissatisfaction with the old management, and the period of turmoil following the departure of former chairman and chief executive John Kerridge. The shares continued to struggle as Fisons's problems proved difficult to overcome.

Corporate conscience

The ethics of the drug business hang upon the nature of their research and the prices charged for the resulting products. Drug companies must satisfy their shareholders, like any other company, and so must concentrate their efforts on therapeutic areas which offer the most promising financial returns, not the areas which might bring most relief to most people – that is the job of governments or charitable foundations. Having launched a product, a company must then charge a price which brings the best long-term returns, and which pays for the research on compounds that never make it to the market.

Wellcome has caused controversy on both these fronts. First, the Wellcome Trust was accused of treachery when it turned the operating business into a public company, although the courts agreed that this did not contravene the last wishes of the group's founder. Second, the public company has been fiercely criticised for the prices at which it has sold Retrovir, with Aids campaigners alleging that the company has profiteered at their expense, and arguing (unsuccessfully) that a cut in the price of Retrovir could be compensated by a cut in the dividend payment to shareholders.

Other companies have not been in the firing line as much as Wellcome, mainly because they do not have major drugs in areas as sensitive as Aids. But the issue of pricing does not just apply to prescribed drugs; it also concerns OTC medicines. Consumer organisations have pointed out that companies such as Wellcome and SmithKline Beecham profit from selling branded products for the treatment of coughs and colds at much higher prices than the equivalent generic drugs such as paracetamol, and with no added medical benefit for sufferers. There seems little difference, however, between this example of consumer product branding and the activities of companies such as Unilever, which sell branded products for higher prices than equivalent 'own label' or 'tertiary' brands.

Drug companies are no strangers to ethical issues, but they do not normally attract the wrath of environmentalists, since their products and production processes are normally fairly innocuous from an environmental point of view: necessarily 'clean' in a technical sense, and with industrial waste less likely to be an issue than in other sectors. However, Fisons has suffered fierce criticism from environmentalists over its horticultural activities, notably peat extraction – although it has endeavoured to pacify the critics by handing over a portion of its peat bogs to English Land, the remainder to follow early next century.

The five companies covered in this section are also exposed in many of the areas monitored by EIRIS. SmithKline has one adverse advertising judgement on the record, for example. All are represented in countries with poor human rights records.

Their business exposes these companies on the issue of animal testing. Fisons and Zeneca are also involved in making pesticides, and all except SmithKline use ozone-destroying chemicals – for example, Glaxo in its Becotide and Ventolin inhalers – but they are working on replacements. Fisons has military and nuclear connections through its VG instrument subsidiary, and all of these companies have been accused of breaking the code of drug marketing in the Third World, mainly in Pakistan, at least once in the last few years. In addition, Zeneca has infringed Third World codes on pesticides, according to the Pesticides Trust.

Offsetting this record, all except Zeneca are members of BITC, and only SmithKline and Zeneca are not members of the Per Cent Club. Glaxo, as befits its status as one of the country's most significant companies, has a particularly strong record of helping charities and the community. It also has a thriving equal opportunities policy, including support for Opportunity 2000. Likewise, Wellcome is strong on equal opportunities, and is also more unionised than the other companies.

Fisons does not appear to have an adequate environmental policy, and nor does SmithKline. SmithKline exceeded its water pollution consent levels on 7 occasions in 1990/91, and its plant at Irvine in Scotland has merited particular criticism from Greenpeace. Glaxo and Zeneca also figure on this issue. In addition, SmithKline also received a £750 fine in 1991 under health and safety laws. Zeneca has not yet responded to EIRIS on these matters.

Corporate governance

The drug companies provide contrasting examples of autocracy and collegiate professionalism. With some of the highest pay packets among companies in this book, they have much to disclose on this subject, although most fail to do so.

Fisons's non-executives were put on their mettle in 1992 when the company and its then chairman and chief executive, John Kerridge, began to lose credibility. Mr Kerridge retired suddenly through ill health, and the job of chairman was taken by non-executive Patrick Egan. Mr Egan has opened up the group to outside scrutiny, but business matters have been higher on his agenda than has corporate governance. The roles of chairman and chief executive have been split, but the annual report goes little further than the legal minimum on disclosure.

Glaxo's boardroom has a fair proportion of non-executives, although the independence of Donald Derx is minimal as he was formerly head of the group's corporate affairs and there is a preponderance of 'the great and the good' rather than the experienced and powerful. The power of the independent contingent was also questioned in 1993 when chairman Sir Paul Girolami reasserted control, leading to the departure of chief executive Dr Ernest Mario. The annual report for 1993 included much greater detail than before on directors' pay, and on corporate governance generally.

SmithKline Beecham has attracted attention because of the huge salaries commanded by top executives. But the company does things by the book – half the directors are non-executive and the annual report provides details of the remuneration packages as well as saying what it expects from its senior executives. The two vice-chairmen provided a full commentary on governance in the 1992 annual report.

Wellcome adopted many of the interim recommendations of the Cadbury Report early, but not with great vigour. For example, the remuneration committee does not explain how directors' bonuses are awarded, saying they are based on financial objectives, but not what those objectives are. In addition, the non-executives are in a minority on the board, and, as with Glaxo, tend to be short on powerful business people, although the addition of Rentokil's Clive Thompson in February 1993 has helped to redress the balance to a small extent. More significantly, chief executive John Robb assumed the additional role of chairman in 1993, after the retirement of Sir Alastair Frame, and shows no sign of relinquishing the post. The need for a separate chairman was emphasised by a number of changes on the board, including the departure of finance director John Precious in June 1994, expected to be followed shortly by former research director Dr Trevor Jones.

Zeneca as one of the newest drug companies in the public arena, has been created with all the right structures in place: there are five strong non-executives on the board, while chairman Sir Denys Henderson shares this job with the same post at ICI. Non-executive audit and remuneration committees exist, and the company's first annual report in 1993 was reasonably informative.

FISONS

Share record

Return on shareholders' equity	%	0.00
5-year price high	p	513.0
5-year price low	p	107.0
Dividend yield	%	3.79
5-year high	%	10.16
5-year low	%	1.82
Price/earnings ratio		64.1
5-year high		70.9
5-year low		8.7

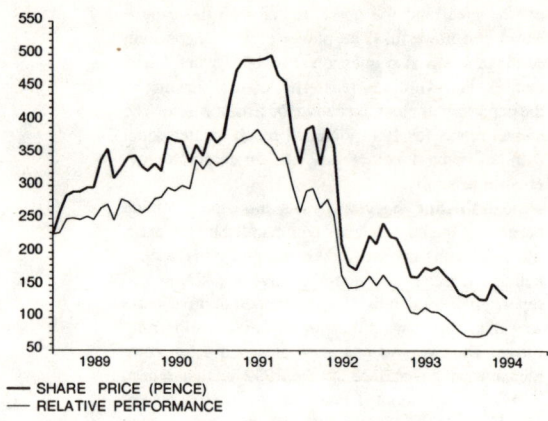

Share price performance (in pence)

― SHARE PRICE (PENCE)
― RELATIVE PERFORMANCE

Financial record

		31/12/89	31/12/90	31/12/91	31/12/92	31/12/93
Total sales	£'000	979,400	1,164M	1,225M	1,284M	1,324M
Pre-tax profit	£'000	169,000	230,200	190,500	100,300	25,700
Published retentions	£'000	79,700	117,500	65,000	35,500	-52,500
Earnings per share	p	22.26	26.37	20.80	10.17	0.00
Dividend per share	p	6.20	7.50	8.70	8.70	4.30
Operating cash flow	£'000		61,500	5,500	-58,000	-69,500
Net assets per share	p	83.98	72.58	73.55	87.12	101.52
Net debt/(cash)	£'000	114,500	117,000	171,300	349,000	200,000
Shareholders' funds	£'000	370,600	414,700	445,900	522,300	494,600
Return on capital	%	43.50	51.71	45.33	25.37	8.45
Profit margin	%	16.83	19.48	15.55	7.81	1.94
Sales per employee	£	80.88	81.89	85.47	88.71	99.10
Interest cover		-81.40	-250.89	19.68	6.87	3.20
Dividend cover		3.59	3.52	2.39	1.17	0.00
Sales increase	%	25.19	18.85	5.27	4.81	3.13
Earnings growth	%	22.29	18.49	-21.12	-51.10	-100.00
Investment x depreciation			2.01	1.92	2.16	1.78
Investment as % assets			22.83	22.04	23.71	21.35
Number of employees		12,109	14,214	14,336	14,477	13,364

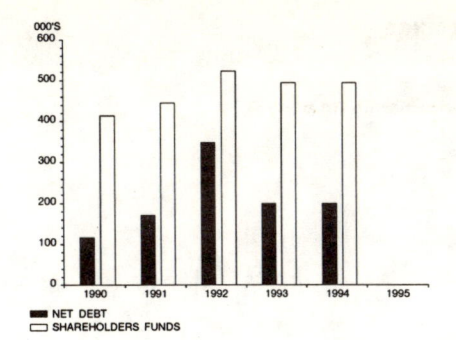

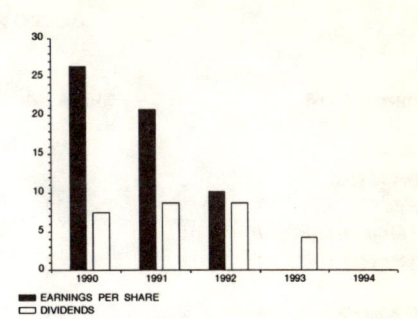

Net debt and shareholders' funds

Earnings and dividends

FISONS plc

Fison House, Princes Street, Ipswich,
Suffolk IP1 1QH
Tel: 01473 232525
Chairman Patrick Egan
Chief executive vacant
Main brands and subsidiaries Gallenkamp, Intal, Opticrom, Pentamidine, Rynacrom, Tilade, VG, Weedex weedkiller
Size £1.3 billion sales, £1.0 billion stock market value, 13,400 employees
5-year growth sales 35%, earnings per share -100%, employment 10%
Solvency debt = 40% shareholders' funds, interest cover 3 times
Political donations 0
Charitable donations £110,000

Major developments
1981 agrochemical business put into joint venture with Boots
1982 sold fertiliser business
1986 Tilade launched in UK
1988 bought pharmaceutical division of Pennwalt Corporation
1989 bought VG Instruments
1991 US Food and Drugs Administration criticised Fisons production methods; Inferon and Opticrom withdrawn from the US market
1992 management shake-up; sold UK consumer healthcare business (Sanatogen); sold US consumer healthcare business to Ciba-Geigy
1993 development of Tipredane abandoned

Corporate governance

Separate Chairman and Chief Executive Y
Number of Directors 11
Number of Non-Executive Directors 4
(4 Independent Directors)
Insulated Directors None

Board Committees
Audit: Y   Remuneration: Y

Remuneration

Year end	31.12.91	31.12.92	31.12.93
Total board £M	1.40	1.24	2.14
% change	2	-11	72
Highest paid £	343,356	256,743	314,847
% change	-22	-25	23

Board
Egan, Patrick V M *Executive Chairman*
Bailey, John *Executive Director*
Cocca, Maurice *Executive Director*
Johnson, Dr Peter *Executive Director*
Redmond, Michael *Executive Director*
Richardson, David *Executive Director*
Hankinson, David *Finance Director*
Bodmer, Sir Walter *Independent Non-Executive*
Harris, Sir Philip *Independent Non-Executive*
Lord Plumb *Independent Non-Executive*
Roberts, Dr Derek *Independent Non-Executive*

GLAXO HOLDINGS

Share record

Return on shareholders' equity	%	25.77
5-year price high	p	930.0
5-year price low	p	335.8
Dividend yield	%	5.34
5-year high	%	5.64
5-year low	%	2.01
Price/earnings ratio		13.6
5-year high		32.1
5-year low		12.9

Share price performance (in pence)

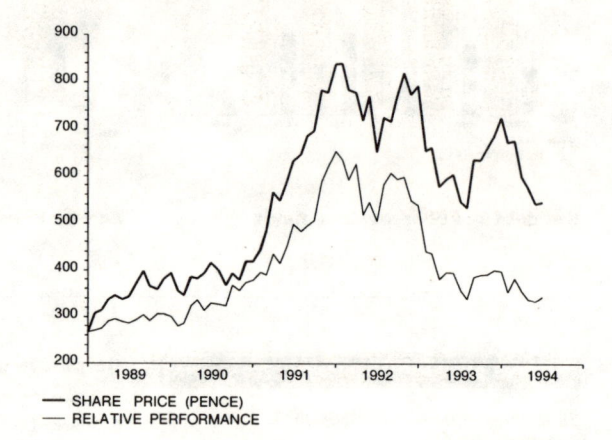

— SHARE PRICE (PENCE)
— RELATIVE PERFORMANCE

Financial record

		30/6/89	30/6/90	30/6/91	30/6/92	30/6/93
Total sales	£	2,570M	2,854M	3,397M	4,096M	4,930M
Pre-tax profit	£'000	978,000	1,144M	1,271M	1,410M	1,655M
Published retentions	£'000	428,000	464,000	461,000	521,000	540,000
Earnings per share	p	22.15	26.70	30.01	33.75	39.21
Dividend per share	p	8.75	11.00	14.00	17.00	22.00
Operating cash flow	£'000	135,000	-20,000	-5,000	73,000	403,000
Net assets per share	p	84.75	98.58	120.43	132.05	168.96
Net debt/(cash)	£	-1,120M	-1,152M	-1,118M	-1,246M	-1,688M
Shareholders' funds	£	2,292M	2,733M	3,208M	3,572M	4,546M
Return on capital	%	45.18	43.28	41.05	38.83	37.68
Profit margin	%	37.04	39.35	37.33	34.38	33.51
Sales per employee	£	89.52	91.10	95.31	110.45	123.18
Interest cover		32.65	24.40	-6.63	-11.32	-12.08
Dividend cover		2.53	2.43	2.14	1.99	1.78
Sales increase	%	24.82	11.05	19.03	20.58	20.36
Earnings growth	%	13.89	20.55	12.37	12.49	16.18
Investment x depreciation		3.91	5.04	3.90	3.05	2.33
Investment as % assets		32.38	37.60	28.30	24.90	17.71
Number of employees		28,710	31,327	35,640	37,083	40,024

DRUG COMPANIES

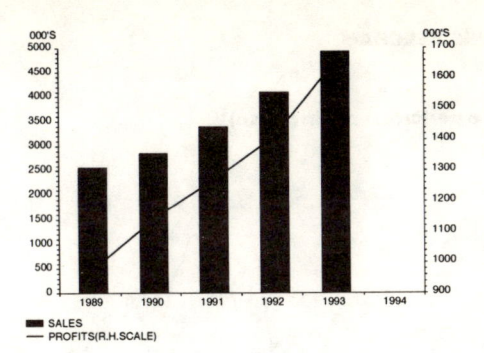

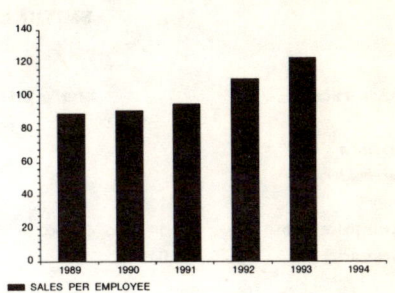

Sales and profits

Sales per employee

GLAXO HOLDINGS plc

Lansdowne House, Berkeley Square,
London W1X 6BQ
Tel: 0171 493 4060
Chairman Sir Paul Girolami (to November 1994)
Chief executive Dr Richard Sykes
Main brands Beconase, Becotide, Betnovate, Cutivate, Dermovate, Flixonase, Flixotide, Fortum, Imigran, Lacipil, Serevent, Ventolin, Zantac, Zinnat, Zofran
Size £4.9 billion sales, £17 billion stock market value, 40,000 employees
5-year growth sales 92%, earnings per share 77%, employment 39%
Solvency debt n/a, interest cover n/a
Political donations £60,000 Conservative Party, £12,000 Centre for Policy Studies
Charitable donations £7 million

Major developments
1899 company formed as London base for New Zealand trading company
1906 Glaxo infant powdered food launched
1969 Ventolin launched
1972 became public
1975 Beconase launched
1981 Zantac launched
1978 set up US subsidiary
1990 launched Zofran, Flixonase, Serevent
1991 launched Imigran

Corporate governance
Separate Chairman and Chief Executive Y
Number of Directors 16
Number of Non-Executive Directors 8
(6 Independent Directors)
Insulated Directors CE

Board Committees
Audit: Y   Remuneration: Y

Remuneration

Year end	30.06.91	30.06.92	30.06.93
Total board £M	6.65	7.17	9.27
% change		6	31
Highest paid £M	1.07	1.19	1.44
% change		11	22

Board
Sykes, Dr Richard B *Chief Executive*
Girolami, Sir Paul *Executive Chairman*
Humer, Dr Franz *Executive Director*
Konishi, Hiroshi *Executive Director*
Lance, Sean *Executive Director*
Maidment, Neil *Executive Director*
Strachan, Jeremy A W *Executive Director*
Coombe, John *Finance Director*
Armstrong, Mrs Anne A L *Ind. Non-Executive*
Cuckney, Sir John *Independent Non-Executive*
Ferguson, James L *Independent Non-Executive*
Lord Howe of Aberavon *Independent Non-Executive*
Lord Kingsdown *Independent Non-Executive*
Derx, Donald *Non-Executive*
Sanders, Dr Charles A *Non-Executive*
Southwood, Prof. Sir R *Independent Non-Executive*

SMITHKLINE BEECHAM

Share record

Return on shareholders' equity % 75.31
5-year price high p 554.5
5-year price low p 231.0

Dividend yield % 3.41
5-year high % 3.84
5-year low % 1.95

Price/earnings ratio 13.3
5-year high 23.5
5-year low 12.4

Share price performance (in pence)

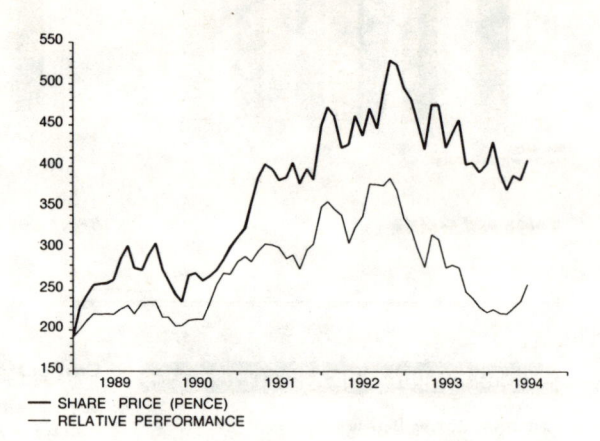

— SHARE PRICE (PENCE)
— RELATIVE PERFORMANCE

Financial record

		31/12/89	31/12/90	31/12/91	31/12/92	31/12/93
Total sales	£	4,897M	4,764M	4,685M	5,219M	6,164M
Pre-tax profit	£'000	723,700	861,000	1,002M	1,115M	1,169M
Published retentions	£'000	49,800	631,000	400,000	461,000	487,000
Earnings per share	p	17.33	19.79	23.91	26.82	28.41
Dividend per share	p	2.60	7.00	7.70	8.60	10.90
Operating cash flow	£'000	511,500	159,000	303,000	369,000	361,000
Net assets per share	p	41.03	51.73	61.11	77.38	112.15
Net debt/(cash)	£'000	1,750M	676,000	502,000	392,000	-38,000
Shareholders' funds	£'000	686,400	1,271M	1,652M	2,110M	2,343M
Return on capital	%		85.86	77.60	67.61	49.46
Profit margin	%	14.62	18.01	21.30	21.27	18.90
Sales per employee	£	77.98	83.14	86.76	97.19	116.96
Interest cover		8.02	8.80	17.92	36.81	78.67
Dividend cover		6.67	2.83	3.10	3.12	2.61
Sales increase	%		-2.72	-1.66	11.40	18.11
Earnings growth	%		14.19	20.83	12.18	5.94
Investment x depreciation		1.45	1.55	1.64	1.62	1.90
Investment as % assets		13.36	16.33	15.73	14.90	19.87
Number of employees		62,800	57,300	54,000	53,700	52,700

DRUG COMPANIES

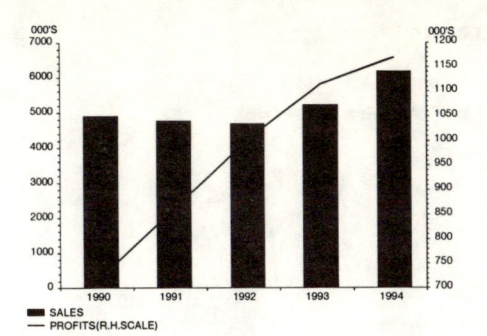

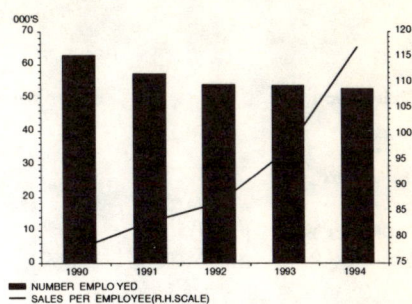

Sales and profits

Sales and employment

SMITHKLINE BEECHAM plc

New Horizons Court, Brentford,
Middlesex TW8 9EP
Tel: 0181 975 2000
Chairman Sir Peter Walters
Chief executive Jan Leschly
Main brands Amoxil, Aquafresh, Augmentin, Bactroban, Dyazide, Eminase, Engerix B, Havrix, Horlicks, Kredex, Kytril, Lucozade, Macleans, Relafen, Ribena, Seroxat, Tagamet, Timentin, Tums, Zentel
Size £6.2 billion sales, £10.0 billion stock market value, 52,700 employees
5-year growth sales 26%, earnings per share 64%, employment -16%
Solvency debt n/a, interest cover 79 times
Political donations £5,000 Centre for Policy Studies
Charitable donations £8 million

Major developments
1989 merger of Beecham Group plc and Smithkline Beckman Corporation
1990 Yardley and Lenthéric sold to management; sold Marmite, Ambrosia, Bovril
1993 agreed Over The Counter joint venture with Marion Merrell Dow; sold hair care brands Bristows, Brylcreem, Silvikrin, Vosene
1994 acquired Diversified Pharmaceutical Services for $2.3 billion

Corporate governance
Separate Chairman and Chief Executive Y
Number of Directors 15
Number of Non-Executive Directors 10
(9 Independent Directors)
Insulated Directors None

Board Committees
Audit: Y Remuneration: Y

Remuneration

Year end	31.12.91	31.12.92	31.12.93
Total board £M	7.77	8.06	9.26
% change	-1	4	15
Highest paid £M	1.73	2.09	1.90
% change	4	21	-9

Board
Leschly, Jan *Chief Executive*
Garnier, Dr Jean-Pierre *Executive Director*
Groome, Harry *Executive Director*
Poste, Dr George *Executive Director*
Collum, Hugh R *Finance Director*
Allaire, Paul A *Independent Non-Executive*
Clark, Sir Robert *Independent Non-Executive*
Grant, William *Independent Non-Executive*
Hogg, Sir Christopher *Independent Non-Executive*
McHenry, Donald *Independent Non-Executive*
White, James *Independent Non-Executive*
Yamada, Tadataka *Independent Non-Executive*
Young, John A *Independent Non-Executive*
Buxton, Andrew R F *Non-executive*
Walters, Sir Peter *Non-Executive Chairman*

50   DRUG COMPANIES

WELLCOME

Share record

Return on shareholders' equity	%	24.65
5-year price high	p	1173.0
5-year price low	p	367.0
Dividend yield	%	4.28
5-year high	%	5.29
5-year low	%	0.69
Price/earnings ratio		12.5
5-year high		40.5
5-year low		10.1

Share price performance (in pence)

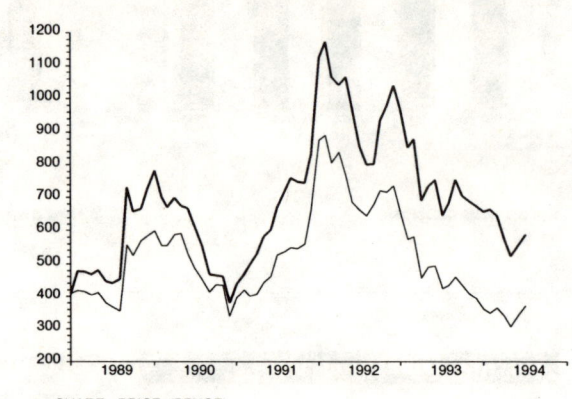

— SHARE PRICE (PENCE)
— RELATIVE PERFORMANCE

Financial record

		31/8/89	31/8/90	31/8/91	31/8/92	31/8/93
Total sales	£	1,408M	1,469M	1,606M	1,762M	2,041M
Pre-tax profit	£'000	282,800	319,300	400,100	507,870	651,200
Published retentions	£'000	138,800	123,700	164,800	146,300	267,800
Earnings per share	p	19.67	23.24	28.94	36.29	46.54
Dividend per share	p	5.05	6.50	10.00	13.00	17.30
Operating cash flow	£'000	116,300	33,000	116,500	160,700	141,800
Net assets per share	p	126.51	129.06	158.10	169.07	216.95
Net debt/(cash)	£'000	-30,400	-17,400	-198M	-410M	-567M
Shareholders' funds	£'000	821,200	867,800	1,101M	1,177M	1,615M
Return on capital	%	31.21	32.25	34.70	37.91	40.56
Profit margin	%	20.05	21.66	24.84	28.77	31.89
Sales per employee	£	69.24	77.91	85.85	99.51	116.14
Interest cover		81.46	-49.44	16.96	21.78	27.40
Dividend cover		3.89	3.58	2.89	2.80	2.69
Sales increase	%	12.63	4.30	9.35	9.69	15.82
Earnings growth	%	28.98	18.16	24.54	25.40	28.22
Investment x depreciation		1.87	3.00	2.82	2.05	1.94
Investment as % assets		17.25	25.59	22.13	17.44	15.76
Number of employees		20,340	18,853	18,711	17,706	17,571

DRUG COMPANIES

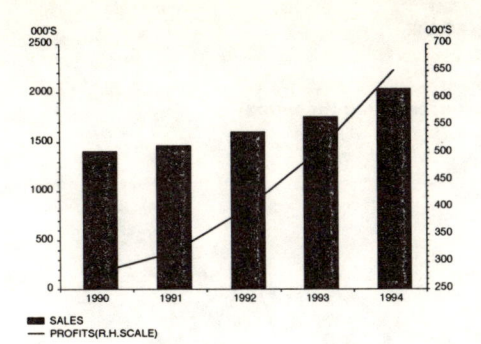

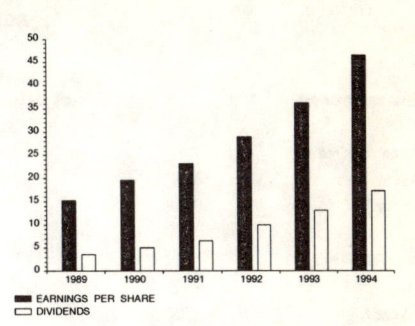

Sales and profits

Earnings and dividends

WELLCOME plc

Unicorn House, P O Box 129, 160 Euston Road, London NW1 2BP
Tel: 0171 387 4477
Chairman and chief executive John Robb
Substantial shareholdings Wellcome Trust 40%
Main brands Actifed, Calpol, Cortisporin, Exosurf, Imuran, Lamictal, Lanoxin, Mepron, Neosporin, Retrovir/AZT, Septrin, Sudafed, Tracrium, Wellferon, Zovirax, Zyloric
Size £2.0 billion sales, £5.5 billion stock market value, 17,600 employees
5-year growth sales 45%, earnings per share 137%, employment -14%
Solvency debt n/a, interest cover 27 times
Political donations 0
Charitable donations £993,900

Major developments
1880 established as Burroughs, Wellcome & Co
1936 Wellcome Trust established on death of Sir Henry Wellcome
1965 bought Calmic
1984 set up Coopers Animal Health joint venture with ICI
1986 became public when Trust sold 25% of shares
1987 Retrovir approved for the treatment of Aids
1989 sold Coopers Animal Health
1991 sold vaccines business, Calmic hygiene business
1992 sold environmental health; Wellcome Trust reduced shareholding to 40%
1993 entered joint venture with Warner Lambert

Corporate governance
Separate Chairman and Chief Executive N
Number of Directors 11
Number of Non-Executive Directors 5
(5 Independent Directors)
Insulated Directors CE

Board Committees
Audit: Y   Remuneration: Y

Remuneration

Year end	31.08.91	29.08.92	31.08.93
Total board £M	2.62	3.62	2.52
% change	-8	38	-30
Highest paid £	386,000	590,000	548,000
% change	14	53	-7

Board
Robb, John Weddell *Chairman & Chief Executive*
Barry, Dr David W *Executive Director*
Cipau, Dr Gabriel *Executive Director*
Cochrane, James M T *Executive Director*
Merrifield, Keith J *Executive Director*
Tracy, Philip R *Executive Director*
Butler, Sir Michael *Independent Non-Executive*
Hearne, Graham J *Independent Non-Executive*
Lever, Jeremy F *Independent Non-Executive*
Thompson, Clive M *Independent Non-Executive*
Tennant, Sir Anthony *Non-Executive Deputy Chairman*

52 DRUG COMPANIES

ZENECA

Share record

Dividend yield	%	27.44
5-year high	%	867.0
5-year low	%	595.0
Price/earnings ratio		4.55
5-year high		5.78
5-year low		3.96
Return on shareholders' equity	%	15.2
5-year price high	p	19.3
5-year price low	p	13.2

Share price performance (in pence)

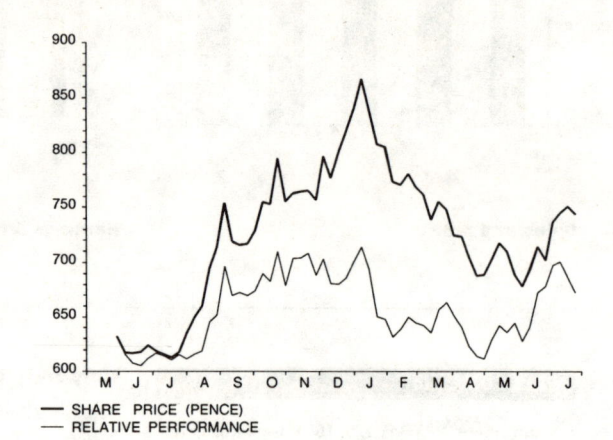

— SHARE PRICE (PENCE)
— RELATIVE PERFORMANCE

Financial record

		31/12/90	31/12/91	31/12/92	31/12/93
Total sales	£'000	3,810	3,929	3,979	4,440M
Pre-tax profit	£'000	354	531	102	627,000
Published retentions	£'000	222	345	80	110,000
Earnings per share	p				49.88
Dividend per share	p				27.50
Operating cash flow	£'000	138	64	-52	164,000
Net assets per share	p				303.53
Net debt/(cash)	£'000	n/a	1,652	1,867	197,000
Shareholders' funds	£'000	1,906	2,044	2,135	1,605M
Return on capital	%				
Profit margin	%	9.29	13.51	2.56	14.08
Sales per employee	£	105.25	111.62	117.37	137.46
Interest cover		3.06	4.13	1.63	6.90
Dividend cover					1.81
Sales increase	%	n/a	3.12	1.27	n/a
Earnings growth	%				
Investment x depreciation		1.79	1.32	1.67	1.82
Investment as % assets		21.62	15.18	17.19	18.59
Number of employees		36,200	35,200	33,900	32,300

DRUG COMPANIES

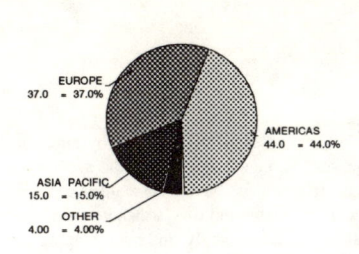

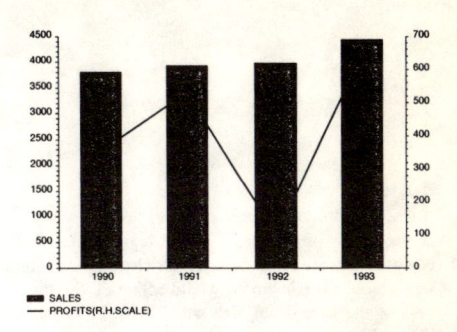

Sales by region

Sales and profits

ZENECA plc

15 Stanhope Gate, London W14 6LN
Tel: 0171 304 5000
Chairman Sir Denys Henderson
Chief executive David Barnes
Main brands Ambush, Biopol, Casodex, Diprivan, Eradicane, Fusilade, Gramoxone, Karate, Nolvadex, Reglone, Tenormin, Quorn, Zestril, Zoladex
Size £4.4 billion sales, £7.1 billion stock market value, 32,300 employees
5-year growth n/a
Solvency debt = 12% shareholders' funds, interest cover 7 times
Political donations 0
Charitable donations £1.7 million

Major developments
1993 floated from ICI

Corporate governance

Separate Chairman and Chief Executive Y
Number of Directors 11
Number of Non-Executive Directors 5
(5 Independent Directors)
Insulated Directors None

Board Committees
Audit: Y   Remuneration: Y

Remuneration
(*Comparative figures not available*)
Year end   31.12.93

Total board £M   1.9
% change

Highest paid £   373,000
% change

Board
Barnes, David *Chief Executive*
Henderson, Sir Denys *Executive Chairman*
Doyle, Peter *Executive Director*
Mayo, John Charles *Executive Director*
Pink, Alan Harvey *Executive Director*
Rogers, Anthony *Executive Director*
Lord Chilver *Independent Non-Executive*
Greenbury, Sir Richard *Independent Non-Executive*
Lewis, Gillian Margaret *Independent Non-Executive*
Morse, Sir Jeremy *Independent Non-Executive*
Wyman, Thomas Hunt *Independent Non-Executive*

ELECTRICITY COMPANIES

Outlook

It was billed in advance – as the huge state sell-offs of the 1980s often were – as the biggest and most complex privatisation ever. Electricity privatisation was a bold experiment. It would roll back the frontiers of the state in an area which most other industrialised countries considered strategically too important to be left to the vagaries of the market. It would be the Thatcher government's flagship privatisation, crowning a decade of achievement in time for the 1992 election. It was an immensely political sell-off. It would be 'power to the people', the admen said. And many believed it.

Since the first shares were traded in December 1990, privatisation of the electricity companies has steadily become more and more controversial. An industry trying to revel in the freedom of the private sector soon found itself a target for frequent attack. Fat profits, fat dividends and fat pay packets for directors overseeing massive job-cutting programmes all provoked repeated objections, made worse because the country's 22 million electricity users were seeing electricity prices continue to rise. Big industry in particular found it was paying so much more for its power, in the midst of recession, that firms like ICI, British Steel and Blue Circle began to campaign for a new deal that would allow them to compete and keep their electricity costs aligned with Continental rivals. There were calls for major changes. Complaints were made that the 12 regional electricity companies (RECs) remained regional monopolies, while the two generators, National Power and PowerGen, were a powerful duopoly allegedly rigging the newly created electricity spot market (the 'pool' by which electricity is sold to the distributors) to push up prices and bolster their already swollen margins. The House of Commons Energy Select Committee, in one of its last reports before being dissolved in April 1992, castigated the sell-off, stating that privatisation had not delivered what the government had promised it would: competition.

The three-stage sell-off – starting with the 12 RECs, moving to the sale of the two generators and then culminating in the sale of the two, vertically integrated, Scottish companies (Scottish Power and Scottish Hydro-Electric) – crystallised rumbling discontent with the notion of privatisation.

Ministers argued that it was early days: the 12 RECs would be working in a competitive market designed to evolve in predetermined stages over eight years. From 1998 all consumers would be free to shop for power almost as they shopped for bread or petrol or any other staple provided by suppliers in competition with each other. Then the market would apply controls on the power companies and replace the attentions of the industry watchdog, the director general of electricity supply, and price capping.

Meanwhile the government publicly kept an open mind on the structure of the generating industry. Having broken up the old Central Electricity Generating Board (CEGB) into to two parts (National Power and PowerGen) and then torn the nuclear industry out of National Power after the City made it clear it could not stomach the huge costs and risks involved in a privatised industry for atomic energy, Ministers repeatedly hinted that the option of a Monopolies Commission inquiry into the generators by 1995 was possible. But the government hung on to a 40 per cent holding in the generators, worth £4 billion in 1994, which was likely to be sold in February 1995. Ministers knew that any real threat of a Monopolies Commission probe would do nothing to enhance the proceeds from that sale.

Perhaps a fourth Conservative victory in April 1992 should have ushered in a more peaceful period for the sector. But then crisis struck its main supplier – British Coal – and the industry was plunged into a period of new and even more intense scrutiny. Once again the powerful duopoly of the two generators was blamed at a time when their decision to diversify fuel supplies – accounting for some 70 per cent of their costs – meant they would more than halve their supplies of British coal in favour of imported coal, gas and the polluting bitumen-based fuel from Venezuela called Orimulsion.

The RECs were also in the firing line. All but one of the 12 (MANWEB) had used the freedom acquired by privatisation to invest in new gas-fired power stations from which they would also buy power, in an attempt to break their captive link with the old CEGB and the generators born out of it.

With the government seeing gas as the quickest route to introducing competition, regulatory rules were put in place that meant the RECs could contract for this form of power and pass on the costs of it to their own captive customers, even though it was sometimes more expensive than power from old coal-fired stations.

To detractors, power privatisation was a botched affair that produced a market rigged towards gas and nuclear power which, after being pulled from the sell-off, was set up with a subsidy worth over £1.2 billion in 1993, funded through a 10 per cent charge on all electricity bills. But after five months of crisis the government decided to press ahead with a delayed programme of closures in the coal industry. The most significant aspect of Michael Heseltine's energy White Paper in March 1993 was that it maintained the *status quo*. The electricity industry remains almost totally unscathed by his proposals.

The City had shown signs of real worry that the White Paper might place curbs on the power companies – either by slowing the process of market liberalisation, or restraining gas projects, or by calling for tighter regulatory curbs on the generators. Following its publication, the City issued a sigh of relief which blew the shares of the companies to new highs.

Since the publication of the White Paper, the RECs have faced two regulatory hurdles: the first was a review of their supply businesses, which they cleared without mishap; and the second a review of distribution, the local monopolistic wires business which contributes up to 75 per cent of profits. With criticism mounting that the regulator, Professor Stephen Littlechild, had failed to deliver adequate price reductions in distribution charges to customers, he was expected to impose a one-off price cut of up to 15 per cent, as well as a tough new price cap of RPI -3 or -4 per cent. In fact the one-off cut was 14% but the price increase cap was set at just 2 per cent below inflation each year.

In the first four years after privatisation the RECs, under a generous price control, were allowed to raise their distribution charges by 1 per cent above the RPI, so the crack-down is relative. And since distribution charges account for only 25 per cent of an average bill, the new regime is unlikely to represent a great windfall for the consumer. Against that background, most companies have sought to reassure shareholders that they will be able to continue to boost dividends, whatever the outcome of the review.

In 1994 the RECs' franchise market that is subject to price controls shrank so that any customer using more than 100 kilowatts of power a year became free to shop around. Previously only those big users consuming more than 1 megawatt could do so. In 1998 the market will be open to competition at all levels, right down to the smallest of domestic users.

The aim of most RECs is to become powerful regional energy companies, with some already showing a preference for supply and others happy to stick with the safer business of distribution. Many have taken advantage of liberalisation in the gas market to become gas suppliers. In 1993 Eastern Electricity, the largest REC, even went as far as buying the output of an entire off shore gas field. Those RECs that led the rush to build gas-fired stations and managed to lay their hands on long-term gas supplies (most have contracts spanning 15 years) are likely to win out.

With the companies all looking increasingly eager to continue the cost-cutting drive that has underpinned growing profits, further restructuring of the industry is assured during the 1990s, with cuts of up to 3 per cent a year. These are all basically very similar businesses, so the potential for decreasing overheads through joint ventures and even eventually full-blown mergers is obvious. There have been only tentative moves in this direction so far. Southern and Eastern led the way by combining their retailing chains, and were later joined by Midlands Electricity. South Wales (which had to live for the first two years in the private sector with Welsh Water holding a near 15 per cent stake and calling for amalgamation) is moving closer to neighbouring SWEB; Yorkshire and East Midlands are also in the throes of a joint venture in retailing.

Once the regulatory hurdles are out of the way in 1994, further ties could be formed. Industry leaders do not see why there should always be 12 RECs – why not six or eight? The question is how will takeover occur: through friendly merger, hostile bid? Or will one REC come to the rescue of another, subject to hostile attentions from a foreign bidder or from a company outside the sector which recognises that these companies are fairly safe, recession-resistant producers of steady profits, who could soon be amassing a cash mountain of £2–3 billion between them?

The taste for diversification has, so far, been fairly limited. In fact, the one REC which has diversified most radically, East Midlands, is now in the hands of a management team spending enormous amounts of money in order to return the company to its core business.

For the generators the outlook is less certain but scarcely less robust. They face emerging competition and since early 1994 have been under instructions from the regulator to use their best endeavours to sell 6,000 megawatts of power station plant between them in order to foster competition. This, together with a two-year price cap on electricity pool prices, was the prerequisite for avoiding a reference from the Monopolies Commission. Neither the government (with its sights set on the sale of its remaining 40 per cent stake in the companies) nor the rest of the industry (fearful it would get dragged into a review) wanted that.

The two groups are considering trade sales of power plant, overseas asset swaps or demergers as a way of meeting the plant sale directive, but with only two years in which to complete deals, they look likely to use most of the available time. Meanwhile, they are losing market share: National Power has slipped from above 40 per cent to well below it, while PowerGen, once over 30 per cent, is now down to 25 per cent and expects to slip further to 22 per cent, believing it would soon be overtaken by Nuclear Electric as Britain's second-biggest power producer. Yet already it is talking confidently about returning to the mid-20 per cent level by 1997, anticipating that many of the planned independent gas stations will not eventually go ahead.

But continuing heavy job cuts and power station closures are in order, either way. Already the two have cut their combined staff from 23,000 at privatisation to around 10,000 in March 1993, and further cuts are inevitable.

The second certainty is that the generators will be

forced to look overseas for growth. National Power wants to generate £1 billion of turnover from overseas operations by the turn of the century, and PowerGen will be looking similarly to derive up to a quarter of its sales from foreign markets. Some City observers expect the generators to derive up to 12 per cent of their combined pre-tax profits from foreign projects by 1998. Europe is a prime target in the short term; the fast-expanding markets in Asia and the Pacific are the long-term goal. In the short term there is strong pressure to invest in the UK on new gas-fired power stations and to clean up coal-fired stations. But spending here is expected to peak in the mid-1990s, freeing cash for overseas expansion.

The picture is far less rosy for the only part of the electricity industry which remains in state control – nuclear power – whose future is currently being reviewed, and Ministers will decide whether to lift a four-year moratorium on the building of new atomic power stations. It is highly unlikely that further Treasury funds will be made available for new stations. So it will be up to Nuclear Electric, serving England and Wales, and Scottish Nuclear, producing nearly 50 per cent of the power north of the border, to persuade the same City financiers that called for nuclear power to be pulled from privatisation to provide the cash for new stations. Nuclear Electric wants to build a £3.6 billion Sizewell C – a twin-reactor version of the huge B station which will begin operating in 1994. Scottish Nuclear is evaluating foreign designs.

The terms of reference for the review – which the government had promised, but then failed, to bring forward to 1993 – are to see if privatisation of nuclear power is a possibility and, if so, when; to see if privately financed nuclear power stations can be built; to examine security of supply; and to consider how best to manage the industry's vast burden of decommissioning liabilities, currently running at between £22 billion and £26 billion. A separate inquiry is being conducted by the Department of Environment into the management of nuclear waste – an area where there remain considerable uncertainties.

The nuclear industry is relieved that the government appears to have accepted its case that it can produce power competitively, although critics continue to be highly sceptical and the industry is still reluctant to spell out its costings publicly.

Another issue which appears to be getting scant attention in the review is the £16 billion of reprocessing contracts between the two nuclear generators and British Nuclear Fuels, in spite of the fact that talks on reassigning risk cover have been deadlocked since the government withdrew its offer to underwrite cost escalations. The seriousness of the matter was underlined when British Nuclear Fuels produced much-delayed accounts in early 1994, which carried an auditors' warning because of the uncertainty over the contracts.

Privatisation is once again back on the government's agenda. A further phase of the power sell-off was completed in the summer of 1993 with the sale of the last part of the Northern Ireland industry. (A precursor to that sale was a massive hike in electricity prices.) The government is taking the first steps to private nuclear power by preparing part of the Atomic Energy Authority for sale. But the costs will be very great. With Nuclear Electric's liabilities outweighing its assets, it is technically bankrupt. It is urging the government to take on the £10 billion of liabilities it inherited from the CEGB and let it get on with running a smaller privatised business with a new family of reactors.

Meanwhile the industry is set fair, thanks to a five-year contract to buy coal from British Coal at a 17 per cent price reduction for the generators and about a 12 per cent reduction for the RECs. Most of the 12 RECs have announced price freezes or cuts for 1993, courtesy of the new deal. The effect of cuts in 1993 was at best to offset the consequences of VAT being imposed at 8 per cent on domestic fuel bills for the first time in April 1994. But with VAT to be imposed at the full rate of 17.5 per cent from April 1995, customers can look forward to rising electricity bills once again, even after the distribution review.

Shareholders may cheer. But consumers and those anxious for an energy policy based on more than just privatisation will have reason to remain highly critical.

Shares

The dominant influence on shares of the electricity companies, as with the water industry and to a lesser extent British Telecom and British Gas, is the industry regulator, currently Professor Stephen Littlechild, director general of the electricity regulation agency, Offer. Recessions may come and go, but what matters more than anything else is the pricing formula and any threat of an inquiry by the Monopolies Commission, which might upset the whole regime. Or rather, it is not what the regulator *actually* does, so much as what investors imagine the regulator is *thinking* of doing. The impact of regulation is particularly important since shares in utilities tend to be held for their dividend yield, rather than for prospects of capital gains as a result of earnings growth. If regulation works, the prospects of above-average earnings growth should be remote (at least until the utilities have built up significant non-regulated business), so that for the time being dividends will remain a more significant aspect of the return on investment than for most shareholdings. The electricity companies' share prices are particularly susceptible to the changing face of politics, dipping much more than the rest of the market in March 1992, for instance, when it looked as though a Labour government was going to be elected, which might be expected to be less generous to privatised companies than a Conservative administration. They bounced back up again following the Conservative victory.

Within the general picture there have been some significant divergences. The fortunes of the distribution companies (the RECs) have differed from those of the generators, while the Scottish companies, which combine generation and distribution, have had a different experience again. In fact the Scottish companies have fared worst. They have been seen as more stable, but with lower growth prospects in earnings. Dividend prospects are also worse because the Scottish companies began public life with lower dividend cover and therefore less scope for growth. The pure generators, on the other hand (National Power and PowerGen), were seen as having much greater potential for dividend growth. In the first place, they had much higher levels of dividend cover, so greater potential for increasing dividends even without growth in earnings. Secondly, the scope for cost-cutting was greater, especially after the lower coal price from the new five-year agreement beginning in 1993, so the generators were expected to produce higher earnings growth than the Scottish companies. From the middle of 1993 Powergen shares began to perform better than those of National Power, due to greater optimism over its diversification prospects. When Northern Ireland Electricity entered the scene in 1993, its shares began to rise steadily into the middle of 1994.

The shares of most of the RECs traded very similarly in the early months of privatisation, although those of Eastern and East Midlands did fall further than those of the others initially. But gradually investors began to discern differences between the management skills and strategies of each company, and the impact of regulation on one company compared to another. By the middle of 1993 MANWEB was gaining supporters, while South Wales and Yorkshire were losing popularity. In the first half of 1994 shares in Northern began to soar, reflecting investors' approval of its less conservative, more aggressive, approach. Perceived differences between the companies remained relatively insignificant, however, and quite volatile.

Corporate conscience

The electricity companies appear to have a reasonably unified approach to issues of policy, and on the whole they take the kind of responsible, enlightened approach to social and community affairs which would be expected from the utilities. Uniformity is not complete, however. For example, East Midlands, London, Midlands, Northern and South Wales all support Opportunity 2000; while Southern does not have formal equal opportunities policies. On environmental matters there is the odd divergence: for instance, South Wales does not have adequate, publicly stated, policies. Southern Electric stands out by having three advertising complaints upheld against it by the ASA, while London and NORWEB have registered one each.

Otherwise there is little to choose between these companies when it comes to ethical issues. Eastern Electricity and Scottish Power seem rather more committed than the others with regard to the environment – both were quick to hold independent audits.

All of the distributors are involved in nuclear power because they take electricity from Nuclear Electric, and all use ozone-depleting chemicals in fridges sold by their retail businesses. Only PowerGen is clear on both these fronts, while National Power does not use ozone-destroying chemicals (although, as the major generator, it is a key contributor of greenhouse gases, as is PowerGen). The generators are also subject to water pollution constraints, which they have failed to meet: National Power exceeded its discharge limits 4 times in 1990/91, and PowerGen did so once; National Power was fined £15,000 for allowing excess chlorine to be discharged into the River Trent; and Scottish Hydro-Electric also had one conviction.

As with the water companies, EIRIS measures how well these companies treat their customers, and there is a wide variation between companies. Scottish Hydro-Electric comes off worst, with one of the highest levels of disconnections (8.8 per 10,000 domestic customers) and a high level of complaints (8.3 per 10,000). Northern and Yorkshire also have high disconnection rates, while Eastern and NORWEB have a high complaints rate. London made a dramatic improvement in 1992/3, transforming the worst record among the electricity companies into one of the best.

Corporate governance

Executive pay rises have been at the centre of criticism of corporate governance standards in the electricity industry, with a doubling of salaries for almost all the regional chairmen during the post-privatisation period. The implementation of generous share-option schemes has also been condemned. It is difficult to separate worries about the rate of increase in executive remuneration from complaints that excessive profits are being made by the industry, as boardroom pay rates are said, largely, to reflect the profit performance of the companies. The largesse to senior executives sits particularly uncomfortably with the heavy and steady loss of jobs in the industry. Yet disclosure of bonus schemes and the workings of remuneration committees is generally poor, and some companies, such as Yorkshire, Southern and MANWEB, did not have remuneration committees until 1993. Several of these companies have followed the trend to distributing summarised accounts to many shareholders, and not including details of directors' pay in these glossy documents.

South Wales is an honourable exception, however, and stands out by including details of directors' pay in the directors' report rather than burying them in the notes to the accounts. National Power also sets a high standard for explanation of directors' remuneration, disclosing that the remuneration committee excludes from comparisons those companies constituting the top quartile of pay, and focuses on the median of remaining companies considered to be of a similar nature. Many of these companies still insulate the chairman from re-election by shareholders, however.

ELECTRICITY COMPANIES

NATIONAL POWER

Share record

Return on shareholders'
equity	%	18.05
5-year price high	p	509.0
5-year price low	p	175.0
Dividend yield	%	3.58
5-year high	%	6.28
5-year low	%	2.71
Price/earnings		
ratio		13.0
5-year high		16.0
5-year low		7.2

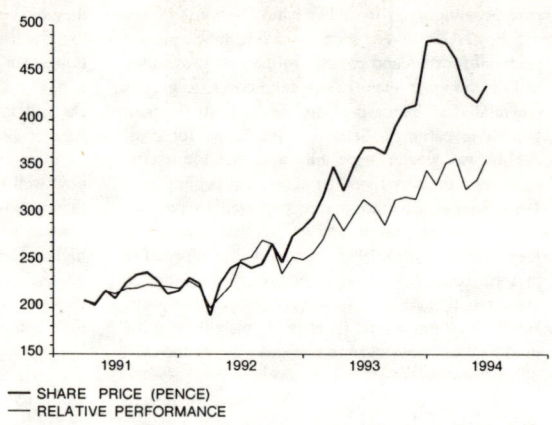

Share price performance (in pence)

— SHARE PRICE (PENCE)
— RELATIVE PERFORMANCE

Financial record

		31/3/91	31/3/92	31/3/93	31/3/94
Total sales	£	4,378M	4,701M	4,348M	3,641M
Pre-tax profit	£'000	479,000	514,000	602,000	632,000
Published retentions	£'000	136,000	249,000	285,000	362,000
Earnings per share	p	23.53	28.63	34.66	36.94
Dividend per share	p	8.25	9.10	10.60	12.50
Operating cash flow	£'000	542,000	17,000	-62,000	73,000
Net assets per share	p	211.42	246.63	265.03	316.84
Net debt/(cash)	£'000	182,000	226,000	309,000	353,000
Shareholders' funds	£	1,778M	2,027M	2,314M	2,643M
Return on capital	%		19.71	20.54	19.36
Profit margin	%	10.94	10.93	13.85	17.33
Sales per employee	£	278.62	354.07	437.69	523.51
Interest cover		-8.21	25.00	13.80	8.95
Dividend cover		2.85	3.15	3.27	2.96
Sales increase	%		7.38	-7.51	-16.26
Earnings growth	%		21.66	21.06	6.59
Investment x depreciation		2.63	2.60	2.55	1.90
Investment as % assets		16.61	19.96	19.14	13.61
Number of employees		15,713	13,277	9,934	6,955

ELECTRICITY COMPANIES

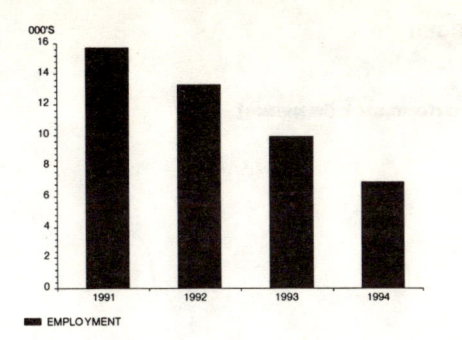

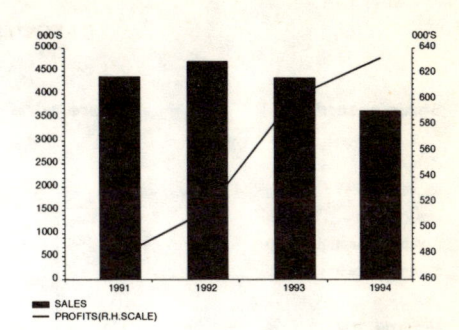

Employment

Sales and profits

NATIONAL POWER plc

Windmill Hill Business Park, Whitehill Way,
Swindon, Wiltshire SN5 6PB
Tel: 01793 877777
Chairman Sir Trevor Holdsworth
Chief executive John Baker
Substantial shareholdings H M Government 39%
Main subsidiaries British Electricity International, Deeside Power Development, English Village Nurseries, First Windfarm Holdings, National Wind Power (50%), Windelectric (35%)
Size £3.6 billion sales, £5.5 billion stock market value, 7,000 employees
Solvency debt = 13% shareholders' funds, interest cover 9 times
Political donations 0
Charitable donations £680,000

Major developments
1991 privatised

Corporate governance
Separate Chairman and Chief Executive Y
Number of Directors 13
Number of Non-Executive Directors 8
(7 Independent Directors)
Insulated Directors Ch, CE

Board Committees
Audit: Y   Remuneration: Y

Remuneration

Year end	31.03.91	31.03.92	31.03.93
Total board £M	1.22	2.04	1.94
% change		67	-5
Highest paid £	147,194	383,935	393,803
% change		161	3

Board
Baker, John   *Chief Executive*
Camsey, Granville   *Executive Director*
Jackson, Rod   *Executive Director*
Webster, Colin   *Executive Director*
Birkenhead, Brian   *Finance Director*
Banham, Sir John   *Independent Non-Executive*
Ferguson, Anne   *Independent Non-Executive*
Gill, Sir Anthony   *Independent Non-Executive*
Morton, Sir Alastair   *Independent Non-Executive*
Palmer, T Joseph   *Independent Non-Executive*
Walker, Sir David   *Independent Non-Executive*
Blackman, Gil   *Non-executive*
Holdsworth, Sir Trevor   *Non-Executive Chairman*

POWERGEN

Share record

Return on shareholders' equity — % — 18.61
5-year price high — p — 581.0
5-year price low — p — 175.0

Dividend yield — % — 3.20
5-year high — % — 6.34
5-year low — % — 2.39

Price/earnings ratio — 11.7
5-year high — 14.8
5-year low — 7.0

Share price performance (in pence)

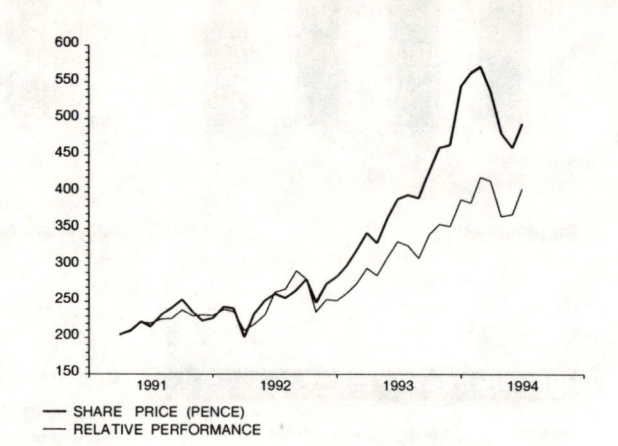

— SHARE PRICE (PENCE)
— RELATIVE PERFORMANCE

Financial record

		31/3/91	31/3/92	31/3/93	31/3/94
Total sales	£	2,651M	3,009M	3,188M	2,932M
Pre-tax profit	£'000	327,500	365,000	444,000	489,000
Published retentions	£'000	100,700	170,000	203,000	246,000
Earnings per share	p	26.52	31.74	40.41	54.44
Dividend per share	p	8.32	9.25	10.50	12.65
Operating cash flow	£'000	415,800	5,000	14,000	-224M
Net assets per share	p	210.24	239.61	275.61	337.61
Net debt/(cash)	£'000	-55,200	-9,000	12,000	288,000
Shareholders' funds	£	1,295M	1,465M	1,670M	1,919M
Return on capital	%		22.02	23.54	21.67
Profit margin	%	12.38	12.10	13.83	16.41
Sales per employee	£	299.91	387.21	557.83	613.13
Interest cover		-4.49	-10.03	56.13	21.30
Dividend cover		3.19	3.43	3.85	3.59
Sales increase	%		13.50	5.95	-8.03
Earnings growth	%		19.68	27.35	12.44
Investment x depreciation		2.10	3.74	2.78	6.35
Investment as % assets		11.28	20.46	16.37	28.31
Number of employees		8,840	7,771	5,715	4,782

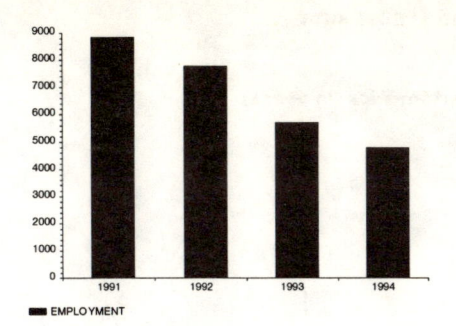

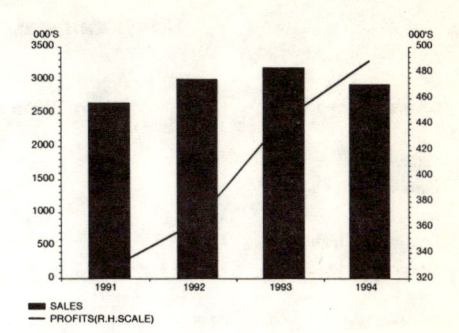

Employment

Sales and profits

POWERGEN plc

53 New Broad Street, London EC2M 1JJ
Tel: 0171 826 2826
Chairman Sir Colin Southgate
Chief executive Edmund Wallis
Substantial shareholdings H M Government 40%
Size £2.9 billion sales, £3.9 billion stock market value, 4,800 employees
Solvency debt = 15% shareholders' funds, interest cover 21 times
Political donations 0
Charitable donations £335,000

Major developments
1991 privatised
1992 bought Rumbelows' Scottish chain of shops from Thorn-EMI

Corporate governance

Separate Chairman and Chief Executive Y
Number of Directors 11
Number of Non-Executive Directors 5
(5 Independent Directors)
Insulated Directors Ch, CE

Board Committees
Audit: Y   Remuneration: Y

Remuneration

Year end	31.03.91	31.03.92	31.03.93
Total board £M	1.27	1.46	1.51
% change		14	4
Highest paid £	204,282	226,043	255,602
% change		11	13

Board
Wallis, Edmund *Chief Executive*
Dance, David *Executive Director*
Jump, Roger *Executive Director*
Reidy, Michael *Executive Director*
Roberts, Dr Alf *Executive Director*
Rennocks, John *Finance Director*
Crawford, Prof Sir F *Independent Non-Executive*
Habgood, A J *Independent Non-Executive*
Hoffman, M R *Independent Non-Executive*
Myners, Paul *Independent Non-Executive*
Southgate, Sir Colin G *Non-Executive Chairman*

NORTHERN IRELAND ELECTRICITY

Share record

Return on shareholders' equity   %   21.38
5-year price high   p   415.5
5-year price low   p   220.0

Dividend yield   %   4.20
5-year high   %   5.69
5-year low   %   3.01

Price/earnings ratio   10.0
5-year high   15.2
5-year low   8.1

Share price performance (in pence)

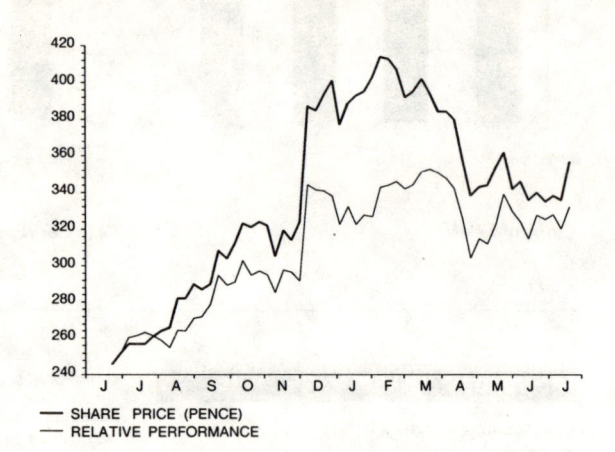

— SHARE PRICE (PENCE)
— RELATIVE PERFORMANCE

Financial record

		31/3/94
Total sales	£'000	481,900
Pre-tax profit	£'000	83,100
Published retentions	£'000	41,600
Earnings per share	p	40.22
Dividend per share	p	18.80
Operating cash flow	£'000	45,300
Net assets per share	£'000	262.39
Net debt/(cash)	£'000	-60,800
Shareholders' funds	£'000	313,000
Return on capital	%	
Profit margin	%	17.24
Sales per employee	£	136.28
Interest cover		-68.25
Dividend cover		2.14
Sales increase	%	
Earnings growth	%	
Investment x depreciation		1.81
Investment as % assets		8.64
Number of employees		3,536

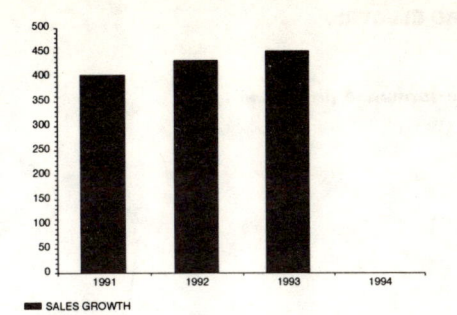

Sales growth

Employment

NORTHERN IRELAND ELECTRICITY plc

120 Malone Rd, Belfast BT9 5HT
Tel: 01232 661100
Chairman Sir Desmond Lorimer
Chief executive Dr Patrick Haren
Size £482 million sales, £560 million stock market valuation, 3,536 employees
5-year growth n/a
Solvency debt n/a, interest cover n/a

Major developments
1993 privatised

Corporate governance
Separate Chairman and Chief Executive Y
Number of Directors 8
Number of Non-Executive Directors 4
(4 Independent Directors)

Board Committees
Audit: Y   Remuneration: Y

Insulated Directors

no remuneration figures yet available

Board
Haren, Dr Patrick H *Chief Executive*
McClay, Walter *Executive Director*
McCracken, Harold *Executive Director*
Woodworth, Philip G *Finance Director*
Barnett, Robert *Independent Non-Executive*
Jefferies, David G *Independent Non-Executive*
McAleese, Mary Patricia *Ind. Non-Executive*
Lorimer, Sir T Desmond *Non-Executive Chairman*

SCOTTISH HYDRO-ELECTRIC

Share record

Return on shareholders' equity	%	16.48
5-year price high	p	477.0
5-year price low	p	218.0
Dividend yield	%	4.43
5-year high	%	5.96
5-year low	%	3.08
Price/earnings ratio		12.6
5-year high		17.4
5-year low		11.3

Share price performance (in pence)

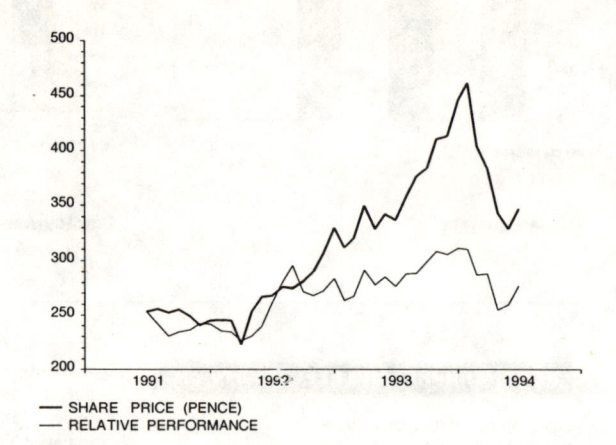

— SHARE PRICE (PENCE)
— RELATIVE PERFORMANCE

Financial record

		31/3/92	31/3/93	31/3/94
Total sales	£'000	667,400	717,800	792,400
Pre-tax profit	£'000	122,700	158,900	164,200
Published retentions	£'000	58,000	62,200	73,200
Earnings per share	p	25.29	30.86	31.73
Dividend per share	p	10.16	11.38	3.16
Operating cash flow	£'000	68,300	67,200	33,800
Net assets per share	p	239.12	222.98	259.24
Net debt/(cash)	£'000	167,200	114,000	81,500
Shareholders' funds	£'000	609,500	666,400	738,400
Return on capital	%		20.74	19.27
Profit margin	%	18.38	22.14	20.75
Sales per employee	£	191.78	205.44	223.09
Interest cover		4.86	9.84	12.73
Dividend cover		2.49	2.71	10.04
Sales increase	%		7.55	10.39
Earnings growth	%		21.98	2.85
Investment x depreciation		2.32	1.68	1.98
Investment as % assets		9.38	7.29	8.84
Number of employees		3,480	3,494	3,552

ELECTRICITY COMPANIES

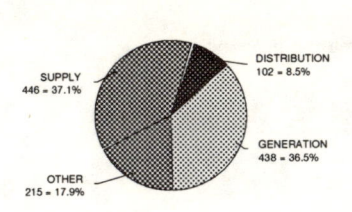

Sales analysis

- SUPPLY 446 = 37.1%
- DISTRIBUTION 102 = 8.5%
- GENERATION 438 = 36.5%
- OTHER 215 = 17.9%

Employment

SCOTTISH HYDRO-ELECTRIC plc

10 Dukeld Road, Perth PH1 5WA
Tel: 01738 455040
Chairman Lord Wilson
Chief executive Roger Young
Main subsidiaries Keadby Power (50%)
Size £792 million sales, £1.4 billion stock market value, 3,600 employees
Solvency debt = 11% shareholders' funds, interest cover 13 times
Political donations 0
Charitable donations £70,183

Major developments
1989 formed as North of Scotland Electricity
1991 privatised as Scottish Hydro-Electric
1992 bought Keadby in joint venture with NORWEB

Corporate governance

Separate Chairman and Chief Executive Y
Number of Directors 9
Number of Non-Executive Directors 5
(5 Independent Directors)
Insulated Directors None

Board Committees
Audit: Y Remuneration: Y

Remuneration

Year end	31.03.91	31.03.92	31.03.93
Total board £M	0.50	0.87	0.99
% change		72	14
Highest paid £	99,000	227,000	235,000
% change		129	4

Board
Young, Roger *Chief Executive*
Read, Arnold *Executive Director*
Young, Alan *Executive Director*
Gray, John *Finance Director*
Everett, Peter *Independent Non-Executive*
Grant, Ian *Independent Non-Executive*
Grant, Peter *Independent Non-Executive*
Walker, Michael *Independent Non-Executive*
Lord Wilson *Non-Executive Chairman*

SCOTTISH POWER

Share record

Return on shareholders' equity	%	26.09
5-year price high	p	486.0
5-year price low	p	216.0
Dividend yield	%	4.23
5-year high	%	5.68
5-year low	%	2.97
Price/earnings ratio		12.7
5-year high		17.3
5-year low		11.6

Share price performance (in pence)

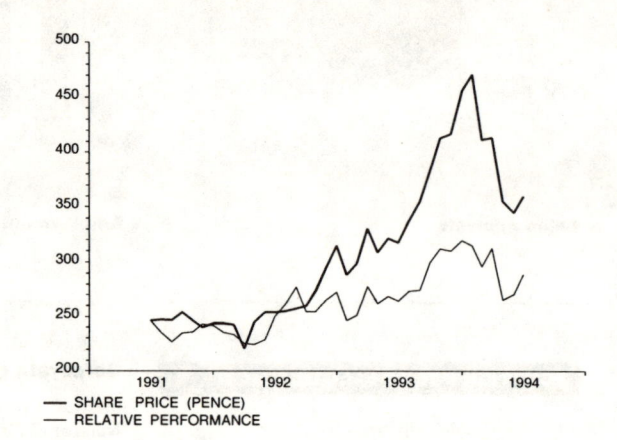

Financial record

		31/3/92	31/3/93
Total sales	£	1,385M	1,486M
Pre-tax profit	£'000	259,900	320,800
Published retentions	£'000	122,800	128,600
Earnings per share	p	25.19	29.85
Dividend per share	p	10.13	11.15
Operating cash flow	£'000	160,500	51,000
Net assets per share	p	143.10	139.29
Net debt/(cash)	£'000	123,900	97,600
Shareholders' funds	£'000	792,600	936,000
Return on capital	%		30.33
Profit margin	%	18.77	21.59
Sales per employee	£	145.82	170.32
Interest cover		13.23	36.26
Dividend cover		2.49	2.68
Sales increase	%		7.32
Earnings growth	%		18.47
Investment x depreciation		2.66	2.41
Investment as % assets		9.86	10.02
Number of employees		9,495	8,724

ELECTRICITY COMPANIES

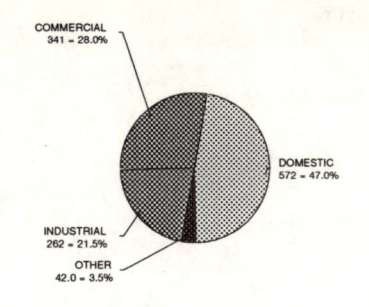

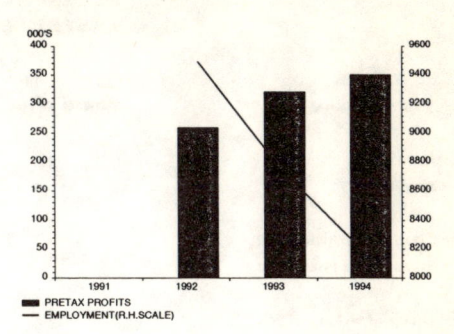

Sales analysis

Profit analysis

SCOTTISH POWER plc

1 Atlantic Quay, Glasgow G2 8SP
Tel: 0141 248 8200
Chairman Murray Stuart
Chief executive Dr Ian Preston
Main subsidiaries Caledonian Gas (75%)
Size £1.5 billion sales, £3.0 billion stock market value, 8,700 employees
Solvency debt = 10% shareholders' funds, interest cover 36 times
Political donations 0
Charitable donations £157,218

Major developments
1991 privatised

Corporate governance

Separate Chairman and Chief Executive Y
Number of Directors 10
Number of Non-Executive Directors 5
(5 Independent Directors)
Insulated Directors Ch, CE

Board Committees
Audit: Y Remuneration: Y

Remuneration

Year end	31.03.91	31.03.92	31.03.93
Total board £M	0.55	0.91	1.05
% change		64	15
Highest paid £	104,246	203,192	247,408
% change		95	22

Board
Preston, Dr Ian *Chief Executive*
Kinski, Michael *Executive Director*
Smith, Michael *Executive Director*
Whyte, Duncan *Executive Director*
Russell, Ian *Finance Director*
Black, Colin H *Independent Non-Executive*
Garrick, Ronald *Independent Non-Executive*
Kuenssberg, Nick C D *Independent Non-Executive*
Scott, James *Independent Non-Executive*
Stuart, Murray *Non-Executive Chairman*

68 ELECTRICITY COMPANIES

EASTERN ELECTRICITY

Share record

Return on shareholders' equity	%	15.90
5-year price high	p	722.0
5-year price low	p	240.0
Dividend yield	%	4.68
5-year high	%	8.03
5-year low	%	3.51
Price/earnings ratio		10.2
5-year high		15.1
5-year low		8.6

Share price performance (in pence)

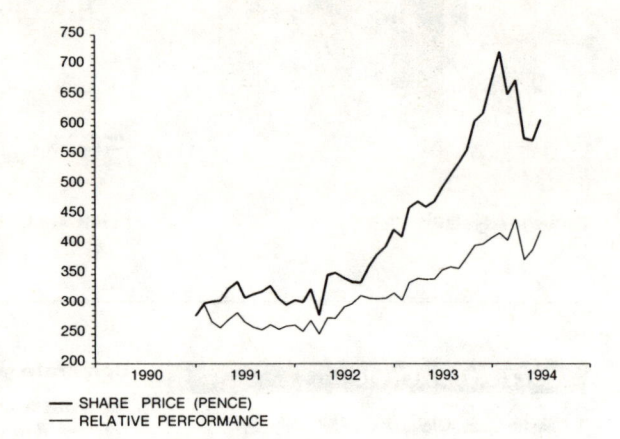

— SHARE PRICE (PENCE)
— RELATIVE PERFORMANCE

Financial record

		31/3/91	31/3/92	31/3/93	31/3/94
Total sales	£	1,720M	1,878M	1,916M	1,846M
Pre-tax profit	£'000	130,600	143,100	183,400	241,900
Published retentions	£'000	61,500	59,200	83,400	63,700
Earnings per share	p	29.75	37.68	50.04	67.01
Dividend per share	p	14.45	16.70	19.20	23.00
Operating cash flow	£'000	-93,200	33,700	125,700	264,300
Net assets per share	p	339.38	355.24	364.37	335.58
Net debt/(cash)	£'000	267,000	233,300	143,200	-28,700
Shareholders' funds	£'000	701,400	760,600	847,400	870,400
Return on capital	%		19.12	21.71	28.32
Profit margin	%	7.59	7.62	9.95	13.09
Sales per employee	£	171.99	190.15	227.66	263.64
Interest cover		8.97	4.71	8.12	15.45
Dividend cover		2.06	2.26	2.61	2.91
Sales increase	%		9.19	2.01	-3.63
Earnings growth	%		26.65	32.81	33.93
Investment x depreciation		1.97	1.74	1.14	1.48
Investment as % assets		12.76	10.03	7.69	9.88
Number of employees		10,001	9,877	8,415	7,003

ELECTRICITY COMPANIES 69

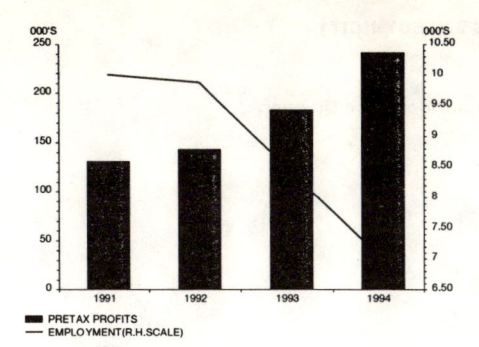

Profits and employment

Sales per employee

EASTERN ELECTRICITY plc

Wherstead Park, Wherstead, Ipswich,
Suffolk IP9 2AQ
Tel: 01473 688688
Chairman James Smith
Chief executive John Devaney
Size £1.8 billion sales, £1.6 billion stock market value, 7,000 employees
Solvency debt n/a, interest cover 15 times
Political donations 0
Charitable donations £125,916

Major developments
1990 privatised
1992 joint retail venture with Southern and Midlands Electricity

Corporate governance

Separate Chairman and Chief Executive Y
Number of Directors 11
Number of Non-Executive Directors 4
(4 Independent Directors)
Insulated Directors Ch, MD

Board Committees
Audit: Y   Remuneration: Y

Remuneration

Year end	31.03.91	31.03.92	31.03.93
Total board £M	0.59	1.10	1.31
% change		87	20
Highest paid £	114,621	242,818	237,658
% change		112	-2

Board
Smith, J C *Executive Chairman*
Devaney, J F *Chief Executive*
Connock, S L *Executive Director*
Mee, D C *Executive Director*
Swinden, Dr D J *Executive Director*
Watson, W G *Executive Director*
Anstee, Eric *Finance Director*
Coutts, I D *Independent Non-Executive*
Duncan, J N *Independent Non-Executive*
Lord Marlesford *Independent Non-Executive*
Wilkins, Sir Graham *Independent Non-Executive*

EAST MIDLANDS ELECTRICITY

Share record

Return on shareholders' equity	%	21.15
5-year price high	p	715.0
5-year price low	p	240.0
Dividend yield	%	4.69
5-year high	%	8.34
5-year low	%	3.60
Price/earnings ratio		9.5
5-year high		36.4
5-year low		7.2

Share price performance (in pence)

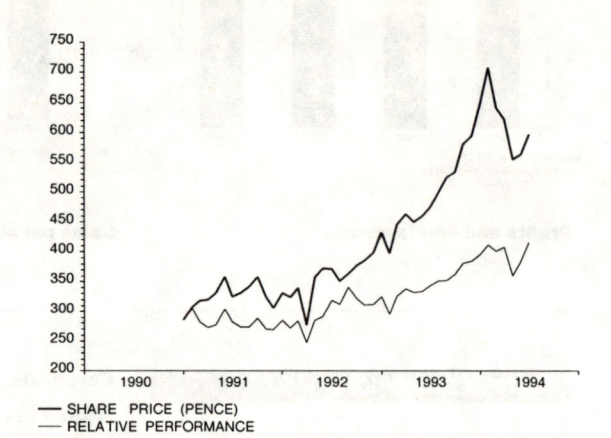

— SHARE PRICE (PENCE)
— RELATIVE PERFORMANCE

Financial record

		31/3/91	31/3/92	31/3/93	31/3/94
Total sales	£	1,327M	1,544M	1,570M	1,445M
Pre-tax profit	£'000	106,500	150,300	169,100	180,700
Published retentions	£'000	58,100	72,000	73,800	-22,000
Earnings per share	p	35.63	50.20	59.74	68.16
Dividend per share	p	15.04	17.10	19.50	22.70
Operating cash flow	£'000	-94,400	21,300	43,400	159,700
Net assets per share	p	292.81	362.91	379.73	389.39
Net debt/(cash)	£'000	156,000	180,100	141,400	2,000
Shareholders' funds	£'000	523,600	565,700	637,500	649,300
Return on capital	%		26.22	25.39	25.29
Profit margin	%	8.03	9.77	10.85	12.66
Sales per employee	£	179.72	187.29	180.79	182.41
Interest cover		5.86	7.85	8.80	11.64
Dividend cover		2.37	2.94	3.06	3.00
Sales increase	%		16.36	1.70	-7.99
Earnings growth	%		40.90	19.01	14.09
Investment x depreciation		3.83	3.10	2.88	2.70
Investment as % assets		18.93	17.03	16.42	16.01
Number of employees		7,382	8,243	8,684	7,919

ELECTRICITY COMPANIES

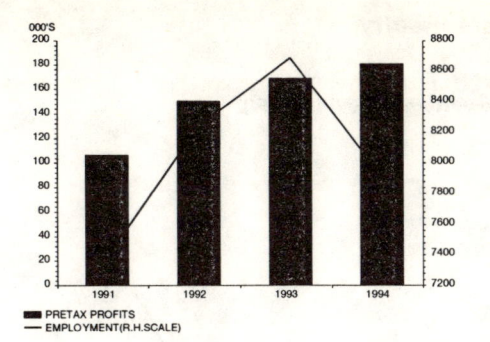

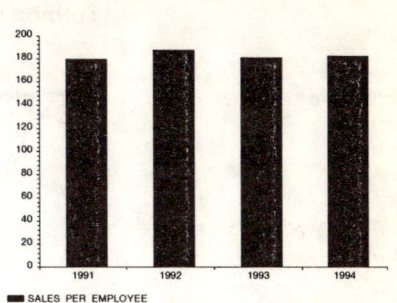

Profits and employment

Sales per employee

EAST MIDLANDS ELECTRICITY plc

Coppice Road, Arnold, Nottingham, NG5 7HX
Tel: 0115 926 9711
Chairman Nigel Rudd
Chief executive Norman Askew
Main subsidiaries Ambassador Security, W A Boulting, Derek B Haigh, Furse Specialist Contracting
Size £1.4 billion sales, £1.3 billion stock market value, 7,900 employees
Solvency debt = 0.5% shareholders' funds, interest cover 12 times
Political donations 0
Charitable donations £514,000

Major developments
1990 privatised
1991 bought 5 contracting companies from Thomas Robinson Group
1992 merged retail operation with Yorkshire Electricity

Corporate governance
Separate Chairman and Chief Executive Y
Number of Directors 8
Number of Non-Executive Directors 4
(4 Independent Directors)
Insulated Directors Ch, MD

Board Committees
Audit: Y   Remuneration: Y

Remuneration

Year end	31.03.91	31.03.92	31.03.93
Total board £M	0.60	1.06	1.18
% change		76	12
Highest paid £	114,476	230,969	225,743
% change		102	-2

Board
Askew, Norman *Chief Executive*
Keohane, James *Executive Director*
Stanyard, Keith *Executive Director*
Davies, Robert *Finance Director*
Corah, Nicholas *Independent Non-Executive*
Gunn, Robert *Independent Non-Executive*
Schroeder, Alan *Independent Non-Executive*
Rudd, A Nigel R *Non-Executive Chairman*

ELECTRICITY COMPANIES

LONDON ELECTRICITY

Share record

Return on shareholders' equity	%	20.25
5-year price high	p	727.0
5-year price low	p	240.0
Dividend yield	%	5.07
5-year high	%	8.28
5-year low	%	3.66
Price/earnings ratio		10.1
5-year high		12.9
5-year low		6.7

Share price performance (in pence)

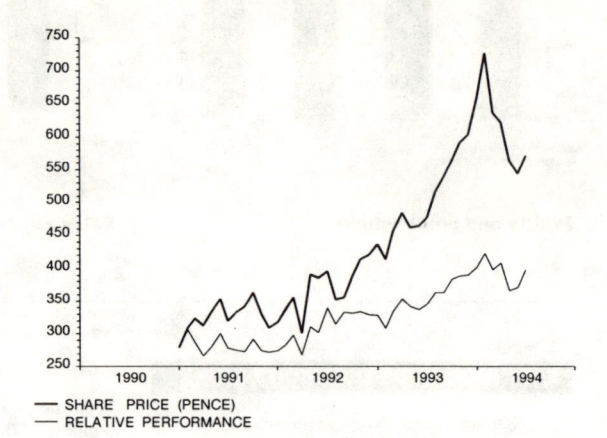

— SHARE PRICE (PENCE)
— RELATIVE PERFORMANCE

Financial record

		31/3/91	31/3/92	31/3/93	31/3/94
Total sales	£	1,224M	1,347M	1,376M	1,308M
Pre-tax profit	£'000	141,800	142,500	165,600	186,700
Published retentions	£'000	72,400	66,900	65,500	92,700
Earnings per share	p	45.77	47.00	58.71	65.08
Dividend per share	p	14.90	16.80	19.50	22.50
Operating cash flow	£'000	-92,000	31,600	102,900	157,400
Net assets per share	p	288.03	319.49	333.78	430.68
Net debt/(cash)	£'000	141,900	96,400	89,400	-64,100
Shareholders' funds	£'000	535,600	600,600	621,900	716,700
Return on capital	%		23.92	24.81	24.56
Profit margin	%	11.58	10.58	21.13	14.25
Sales per employee	£	182.93	204.70	218.50	236.51
Interest cover		-4.78	12.26	35.44	33.67
Dividend cover		3.07	2.80	3.01	2.89
Sales increase	%		10.06	1.51	-4.31
Earnings growth	%		2.68	24.91	10.86
Investment x depreciation		2.71	2.48	2.49	2.23
Investment as % assets		15.21	13.85	12.74	11.43
Number of employees		6,691	6,581	6,258	5,532

ELECTRICITY COMPANIES

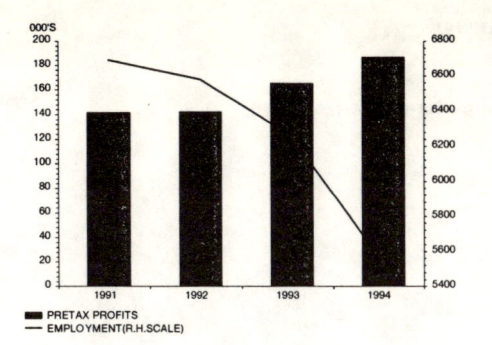

Profits and employment

Sales per employee

LONDON ELECTRICITY plc

Templar House, 81–87 High Holborn,
London WC1 6NU
Tel: 0171 242 9050
Chairman Sir Bob Reid
Chief executive Dr Roger Urwin
Main subsidiaries Barking Power (13.5%), Berkeley Environmental Systems, Combined Power Systems (14%), London Power Co
Size £1.3 billion sales, £1.2 billion stock market value, 5,500 employees
Solvency debt n/a, interest cover 34 times
Political donations 0
Charitable donations £111,466

Major developments
1990 privatised
1991 bought Berkeley Environmental Systems
1992 joint venture in combined heat and power with Northern and Norweb; stake in Barking Power power station
1993 sold retailing operation to management

Corporate governance

Separate Chairman and Chief Executive Y
Number of Directors 10
Number of Non-Executive Directors 5
(5 Independent Directors)
Insulated Directors Ch, MD

Board Committees
Audit: Y   Remuneration: Y

Remuneration

Year end	31.03.91	31.03.92	31.03.93
Total board £M	0.70	0.70	0.67
% change			-4
Highest paid £	142,879	177,114	187,843
% change		24	6

Board
Urwin, Roger *Chief Executive*
Beaumont, Ian *Executive Director*
Brown, Mike *Executive Director*
Kersey, Mike *Executive Director*
Towers, Alan *Finance Director*
Owen, Gordon M W *Independent Non-Executive*
Prendergast, Anthony *Independent Non-Executive*
Priestley, Leslie *Independent Non-Executive*
Robinson, Helen *Independent Non-Executive*
Reid, Sir Bob *Non-Executive Chairman*

MANWEB

Share record

Return on shareholders' equity	%	14.63
5-year price high	p	848.0
5-year price low	p	240.0
Dividend yield	%	4.47
5-year high	%	8.89
5-year low	%	3.23
Price/earnings ratio		9.6
5-year high		12.3
5-year low		6.8

Share price performance (in pence)

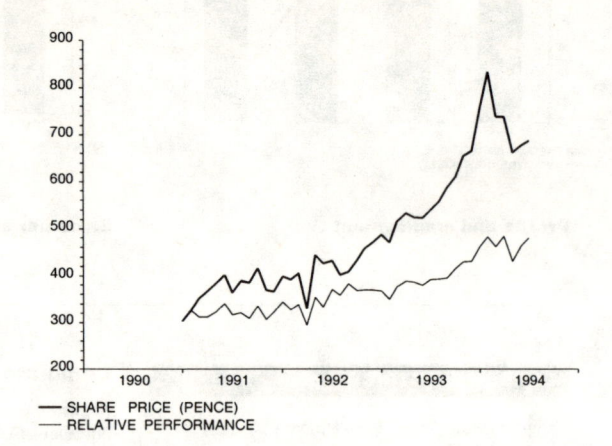

— SHARE PRICE (PENCE)
— RELATIVE PERFORMANCE

Financial record

		31/3/91	31/3/92	31/3/93	31/3/94
Total sales	£'000	829,000	834,600	919,900	929,600
Pre-tax profit	£'000	69,000	103,700	116,800	129,800
Published retentions	£'000	26,000	48,100	57,400	70,200
Earnings per share	p	42.94	66.32	73.99	86.28
Dividend per share	p	16.00	18.25	21.00	24.35
Operating cash flow	£'000	-47,000	48,800	31,100	51,600
Net assets per share	p	456.44	500.42	554.04	623.32
Net debt/(cash)	£'000	106,000	56,400	26,900	-25,300
Shareholders' funds	£'000	463,000	522,000	588,400	668,100
Return on capital	%		20.17	19.96	19.59
Profit margin	%	8.32	12.43	12.69	13.87
Sales per employee	£	151.19	180.53	202.93	201.91
Interest cover		6.27	13.92	35.63	16.14
Dividend cover		2.68	3.63	3.52	3.54
Sales increase	%		0.68	10.22	1.05
Earnings growth	%		54.44	11.56	16.61
Investment x depreciation		2.52	1.87	2.41	3.02
Investment as % assets		14.03	9.66	12.24	14.81
Number of employees		5,483	4,623	4,533	4,604

ELECTRICITY COMPANIES 75

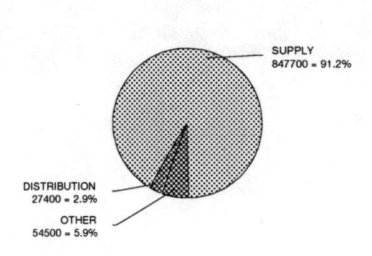

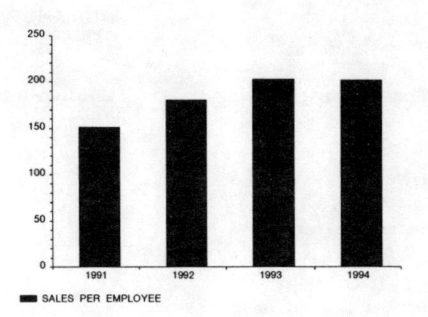

Sales analysis

SUPPLY 847700 = 91.2%
DISTRIBUTION 27400 = 2.9%
OTHER 54500 = 5.9%

Sales per employee

SALES PER EMPLOYEE (1991, 1992, 1993, 1994)

MANWEB plc

Sealand Road, Chester CH1 4LR
Tel: 01244 377111
Chairman Bryan Weston
Chief executive John Roberts
Size £993 million sales, £798 million stock market value, 4,600 employees
Solvency debt n/a, interest cover 16 times
Political donations 0
Charitable donations £76,158

Major developments
1990 privatised

Corporate governance

Separate Chairman and Chief Executive Y
Number of Directors 11
Number of Non-Executive Directors 4
(4 Independent Directors)
Insulated Directors Ch, MD

Board Committees
Audit: Y   Remuneration: Y

Remuneration

Year end	31.03.91	31.03.92	31.03.93
Total board £M	0.71	0.93	1.04
% change		31	11
Highest paid £	156,000	214,000	208,000
% change		37	-3

Board
Roberts, John E *Chief Executive*
Weston, Bryan H *Executive Chairman*
Hopkins, Peter D *Executive Director*
Kirkham, Howard *Executive Director*
Leonard, Colin W *Executive Director*
Vernon-Smith, David *Executive Director*
Astall, John *Finance Director*
Carnwath, Alison *Independent Non-Executive*
Goodall, Ralph W *Independent Non-Executive*
Morris, G Eryl *Independent Non-Executive*
Nightingale, Glen *Independent Non-Executive*

MIDLANDS ELECTRICITY

Share record

Return on shareholders'
equity	%	22.01
5-year price high	p	764.0
5-year price low	p	240.0
Dividend yield	%	4.72
5-year high	%	8.36
5-year low	%	3.48
Price/earnings		
ratio		9.9
5-year high		11.9
5-year low		6.9

Share price performance (in pence)

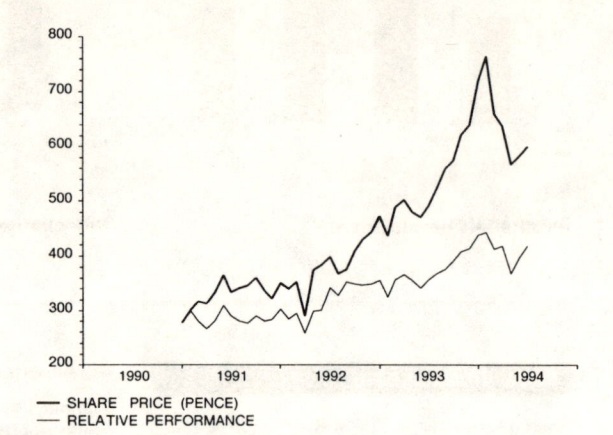

── SHARE PRICE (PENCE)
── RELATIVE PERFORMANCE

Financial record

		31/3/91	31/3/92	31/3/93	31/3/94
Total sales	£	1,329M	1,454M	1,537M	1,416M
Pre-tax profit	£'000	109,700	142,100	204,600	220,800
Published retentions	£'000	54,700	66,600	75,000	88,200
Earnings per share	p	35.71	47.60	73.71	76.51
Dividend per share	p	15.04	17.25	20.00	23.20
Operating cash flow	£'000	-34,400	85,700	78,100	205,600
Net assets per share	p	297.01	329.76	333.89	377.43
Net debt/(cash)	£'000	130,300	44,600	6,000	-167M
Shareholders' funds	£'000	531,500	598,100	671,900	756,400
Return on capital	%		23.51	30.86	29.76
Profit margin	%	8.25	9.77	13.35	15.58
Sales per employee	£	171.96	190.25	208.53	228.05
Interest cover		15.68	16.57	119.69	-50.84
Dividend cover		2.37	2.76	3.69	3.30
Sales increase	%		9.40	5.69	-7.90
Earnings growth	%		33.28	54.85	3.80
Investment x depreciation		2.35	2.30	1.97	2.19
Investment as % assets		15.21	13.80	12.78	13.23
Number of employees		7,729	7,643	7,370	6,207

ELECTRICITY COMPANIES

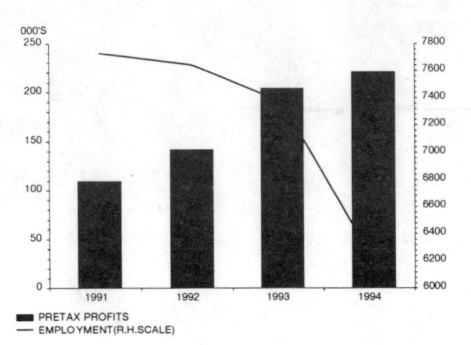

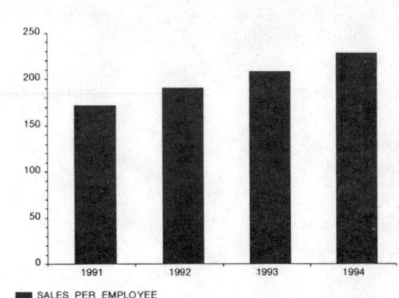

Profits and employment

Sales per employee

MIDLANDS ELECTRICITY plc

Mucklow Hill, Halesowen, West Midlands B62 8BP
Tel: 0121 423 2345
Chairman Bryan Townsend
Chief executive Mike Hughes
Main subsidiaries Central Power, Midlands Gas, Mass Energy, Teesside Power (19%)
Size £1.4 billion sales, £1.3 billion stock market value, 6,200 employees
Solvency debt n/a, interest cover n/a
Political donations 0
Charitable donations £126,579

Major developments
1990 privatised
1992 joined Eastern/Southern retail joint venture
1993 Teesside power station opened; retail business sold

Corporate governance

Separate Chairman and Chief Executive Y
Number of Directors 9
Number of Non-Executive Directors 4
(4 Independent Directors)
Insulated Directors Ch, MD

Board Committees
Audit: Y Remuneration: Y

Remuneration

Year end	31.03.91	31.03.92	31.03.93
Total board £M	0.80	1.00	1.00
% change		25	0
Highest paid £	181,790	221,399	229,524
% change		22	4

Board
Hughes, Michael *Chief Executive*
Townsend, Bryan *Executive Chairman*
Degg, Gary *Executive Director*
Murray, Roger *Executive Director*
Chapman, Peter *Finance Director*
Davies, Gareth *Independent Non-Executive*
Graves, Francis *Independent Non-Executive*
Morgan, Dr Janet P *Independent Non-Executive*
Neill, John *Independent Non-Executive*

NORTHERN ELECTRIC

Share record

Return on shareholders' equity	%	19.90
5-year price high	p	789.0
5-year price low	p	240.0
Dividend yield	%	4.61
5-year high	%	9.03
5-year low	%	3.57
Price/earnings ratio		8.9
5-year high		11.9
5-year low		6.0

Share price performance (in pence)

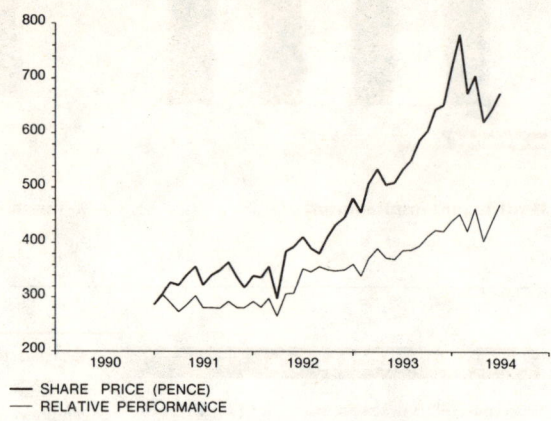

— SHARE PRICE (PENCE)
— RELATIVE PERFORMANCE

Financial record

		31/3/91	31/3/92	31/3/93	31/3/94
Total sales	£'000	776,400	813,700	882,700	1,031M
Pre-tax profit	£'000	89,200	98,200	116,300	135,600
Published retentions	£'000	45,500	50,500	58,900	67,600
Earnings per share	p	40.46	58.66	73.77	80.29
Dividend per share	p	16.25	18.55	21.45	24.85
Operating cash flow	£'000	-39,300	30,400	54,800	75,300
Net assets per share	£'000	328.29	362.41	420.95	486.10
Net debt/(cash)	£'000	86,900	59,200	38,900	-25,400
Shareholders' funds	£'000	315,200	365,700	424,700	494,000
Return on capital	%		25.51	26.01	25.59
Profit margin	%	11.49	12.07	13.18	13.16
Sales per employee	£	140.45	151.70	182.91	218.60
Interest cover		-14.42	10.26	19.53	33.78
Dividend cover		2.49	3.16	3.44	3.23
Sales increase	%		4.80	8.48	16.74
Earnings growth	%		44.98	25.76	8.83
Investment x depreciation		2.59	2.29	2.39	2.34
Investment as % assets		15.87	13.27	14.33	14.16
Number of employees		5,528	5,364	4,826	4,714

ELECTRICITY COMPANIES

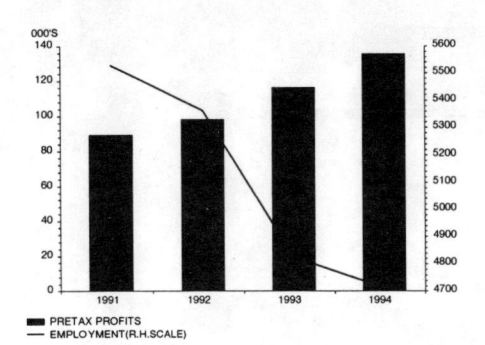

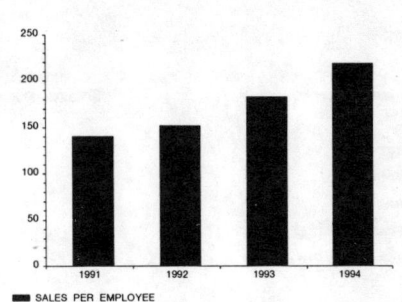

Profits and employment

Sales per employee

NORTHERN ELECTRIC plc

Carliol House, Market Street,
Newcastle upon Tyne NE1 6NE
Tel: 0191 221 2000
Chairman David Morris
Chief executive Tony Hadfield
Size £1.0 billion sales, £817 million stock market value, 4,700 employees
Solvency debt n/a, interest cover 34 times
Political donations 0
Charitable donations £700,000

Major developments
1990 privatised

Corporate governance

Separate Chairman and Chief Executive Y
Number of Directors 8
Number of Non-Executive Directors 3
(3 Independent Directors)
Insulated Directors Ch, MD

Board Committees
Audit: Y   Remuneration: Y

Remuneration

Year end	31.03.91	31.03.92	31.03.93
Total board £M	0.51	0.63	0.78
% change		24	23
Highest paid £	141,511	166,000	191,000
% change		17	15

Board
Hadfield, Tony *Chief Executive*
Morris, David *Executive Chairman*
Dixon, Ron *Executive Director*
Hook, Bill *Executive Director*
Groves, Alan *Finance Director*
Errington, Stuart *Independent Non-Executive*
McCutcheon, Ian *Independent Non-Executive*
Nicholson, Paul *Independent Non-Executive*

NORWEB

Share record

Return on shareholders' equity	%	20.80
5-year price high	p	800.0
5-year price low	p	240.0
Dividend yield	%	4.49
5-year high	%	8.68
5-year low	%	3.25
Price/earnings ratio		9.3
5-year high		14.2
5-year low		6.4

Share price performance (in pence)

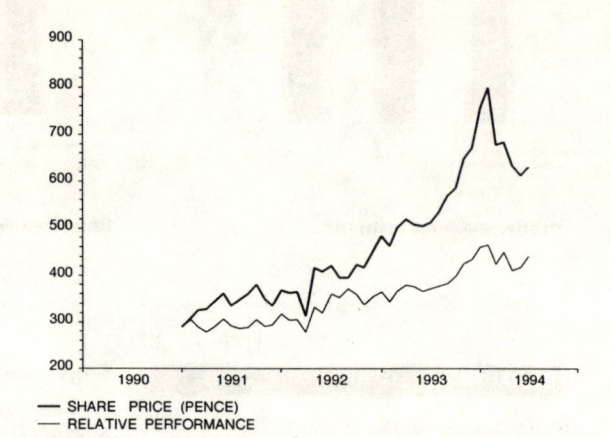

— SHARE PRICE (PENCE)
— RELATIVE PERFORMANCE

Financial record

		31/3/91	31/3/92	31/3/93
Total sales	£	1,240M	1,318M	1,414M
Pre-tax profit	£'000	80,300	137,900	157,100
Published retentions	£'000	16,500	57,500	76,900
Earnings per share	p	26.69	51.00	64.55
Dividend per share	p	15.63	17.70	20.00
Operating cash flow	£'000	23,800	36,500	55,400
Net assets per share	p	342.00	394.11	432.66
Net debt/(cash)	£'000	134,800	103,900	57,500
Shareholders' funds	£'000	419,100	471,000	540,800
Return on capital	%		24.78	24.76
Profit margin	%	6.47	10.47	11.14
Sales per employee	£	151.20	166.48	177.20
Interest cover		5.50	8.46	12.24
Dividend cover		1.71	2.88	3.23
Sales increase	%		6.26	7.25
Earnings growth	%		91.11	26.58
Investment x depreciation		1.92	1.88	2.37
Investment as % assets		13.35	13.98	16.97
Number of employees		8,203	7,917	7,977

ELECTRICITY COMPANIES

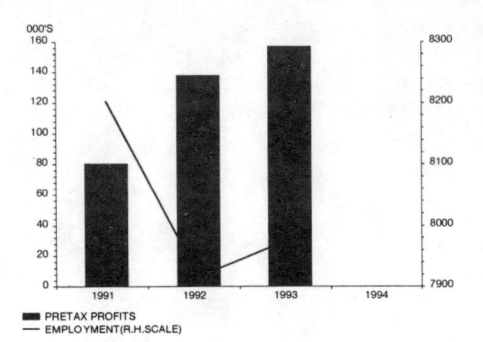

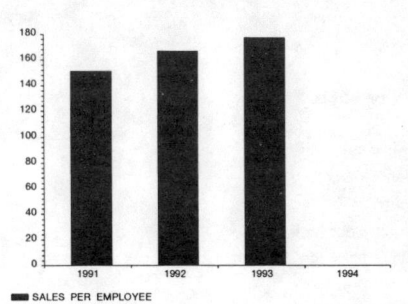

Profits and employment

Sales per employee

NORWEB plc

Talbot Road, Manchester M16 0HQ
Tel: 0161 873 8000
Chairman and chief executive Kenneth Harvey
Main subsidiaries Combined Heat and Power Co (50%), Norgen, NORWEB Gas (75%)
Size £1.4 billion sales, £1.1 billion stock market value, 8,000 employees
Solvency debt = 11% shareholders' funds, interest cover 12 times
Political donations 0
Charitable donations £104,780

Major developments
1990 privatised
1992 bought Atlantis retail superstores from Thorn-EMI; bought Keadby Power in joint venture with Scottish Hydro-Electric; bought Northern Gas in joint venture with Utilicorp

Corporate governance

Separate Chairman and Chief Executive N
Number of Directors 11
Number of Non-Executive Directors 4
(4 Independent Directors)
Insulated Directors Ch

Board Committees
Audit: Y   Remuneration: Y

Remuneration

Year end	31.03.91	31.03.92	31.03.93
Total board £M	0.53	0.85	0.88
% change		60	4
Highest paid £	105,135	184,643	208,287
% change		76	13

Board
Harvey, Ken *Chairman & Chief Executive*
Croft, Margaret *Executive Director*
Faulkner, Malcolm *Executive Director*
McTague, Peter *Executive Director*
Rothwell, Peter *Executive Director*
Simmons, Alec *Executive Director*
Wilson, Brian *Finance Director*
Booth, A Thomas *Independent Non-Executive*
Cockshaw, Sir Alan *Independent Non-Executive*
Green-Armytage, John M *Ind. Non-Executive*
Salsbury, Peter *Independent Non-Executive*

SEEBOARD

Share record

Return on shareholders' equity	%	17.00
5-year price high	p	429.0
5-year price low	p	120.0
Dividend yield	%	4.51
5-year high	%	8.20
5-year low	%	3.04
Price/earnings ratio		9.0
5-year high		13.5
5-year low		6.0

Share price performance (in pence)

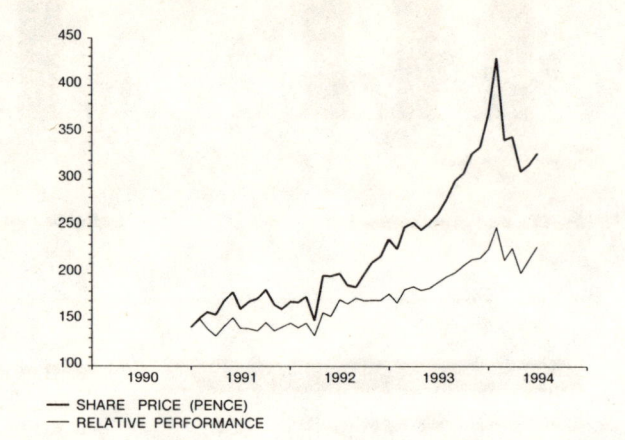

— SHARE PRICE (PENCE)
— RELATIVE PERFORMANCE

Financial record

		31/3/91	31/3/92	31/3/93
Total sales	£	1,048M	1,157M	1,226M
Pre-tax profit	£'000	81,400	98,400	112,700
Published retentions	£'000	36,700	46,200	53,800
Earnings per share	p	17.22	26.77	31.00
Dividend per share	p	7.38	8.63	10.00
Operating cash flow	£'000	-40,400	21,600	1,100
Net assets per share	p	183.83	202.77	222.92
Net debt/(cash)	£'000	89,800	50,100	32,300
Shareholders' funds	£'000	380,100	422,400	476,200
Return on capital	%		22.13	22.86
Profit margin	%	7.77	8.50	9.19
Sales per employee	£	165.22	184.91	202.98
Interest cover		23.97	10.56	17.49
Dividend cover		2.33	3.10	3.10
Sales increase	%		10.45	5.95
Earnings growth	%		55.45	15.82
Investment x depreciation		2.04	2.81	2.86
Investment as % assets		13.37	21.01	19.65
Number of employees		6,340	6,257	6,039

ELECTRICITY COMPANIES 83

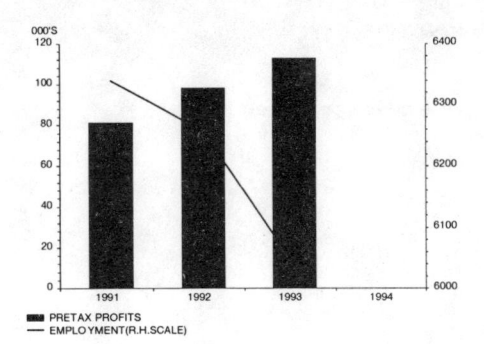

Profits and employment

Sales per employee

SEEBOARD plc

Grand Avenue, Hove, East Sussex BN3 2LS
Tel: 01273 724522
Chairman Sir Keith Stuart
Chief executive Jim Ellis
Size £1.2 billion sales, £829 million stock market value, 6,000 employees
Solvency debt = 7% shareholders' funds, interest cover 17 times
Political donations 0
Charitable donations £134,797

Major developments
1990 privatised
1992 joint venture with Medway Power Ltd

Corporate governance

Separate Chairman and Chief Executive Y
Number of Directors 11
Number of Non-Executive Directors 6
(6 Independent Directors)
Insulated Directors Ch, MD

Board Committees
Audit: Y   Remuneration: Y

Remuneration

Year end	31.03.91	31.03.92	31.03.93
Total board £M	0.72	0.95	1.00
% change		31	6
Highest paid £	116,750	184,151	156,000
% change		58	-15

Board
Ellis, Jim   *Chief Executive*
Gutteridge, Stephen   *Executive Director*
Jones, Len   *Executive Director*
Weight, Jon   *Executive Director*
Quin, John   *Finance Director*
Aldred, Ralph   *Independent Non-Executive*
Cox, Roy   *Independent Non-Executive*
Dean, Peter   *Independent Non-Executive*
McLeod, Sir Ian   *Independent Non-Executive*
Walmsley, John A   *Independent Non-Executive*
Stuart, Sir Keith   *Non-Executive Chairman*

SOUTHERN ELECTRIC

Share record

Return on shareholders' equity	%	22.86
5-year price high	p	743.5
5-year price low	p	240.0
Dividend yield	%	4.70
5-year high	%	8.03
5-year low	%	3.48
Price/earnings ratio		11.0
5-year high		15.5
5-year low		6.8

Share price performance (in pence)

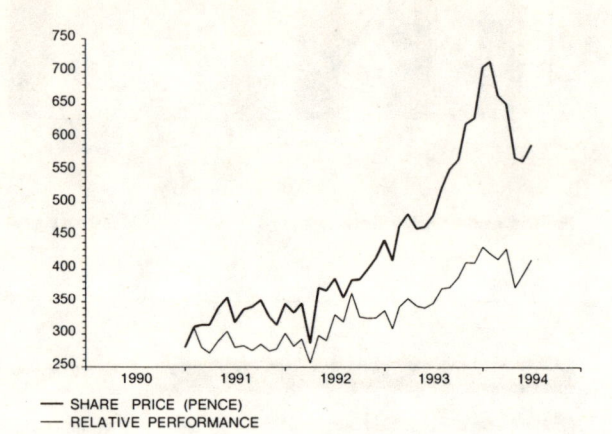

— SHARE PRICE (PENCE)
— RELATIVE PERFORMANCE

Financial record

		31/3/91	31/3/92	31/3/93	31/3/94
Total sales	£	1,546M	1,751M	1,797M	1,780M
Pre-tax profit	£'000	153,300	174,800	197,500	247,000
Published retentions	£'000	74,600	84,000	94,300	111,700
Earnings per share	p	36.20	50.95	58.86	71.37
Dividend per share	p	14.45	16.66	19.60	22.70
Operating cash flow	£'000	-107M	37,900	94,800	183,300
Net assets per share	p	282.50	302.03	327.42	380.16
Net debt/(cash)	£'000	196,200	157,700	125,400	-45,800
Shareholders' funds	£'000	544,400	628,100	693,500	815,000
Return on capital	%		25.53	27.75	27.61
Profit margin	%	9.92	9.99	11.42	13.94
Sales per employee	£	184.88	209.90	235.08	240.86
Interest cover		-26.06	8.04	9.29	23.13
Dividend cover		2.51	3.06	3.00	3.14
Sales increase	%		13.23	2.62	-0.91
Earnings growth	%		40.74	15.54	21.26
Investment x depreciation		2.99	2.55	2.71	3.38
Investment as % assets		19.07	16.88	17.20	18.79
Number of employees		8,362	8,340	7,642	7,391

ELECTRICITY COMPANIES

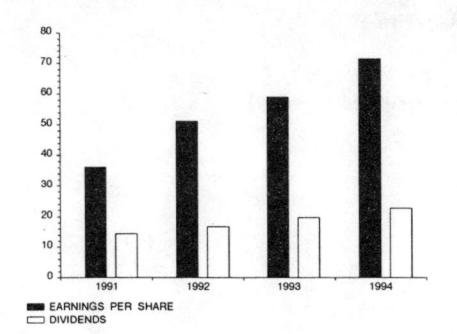

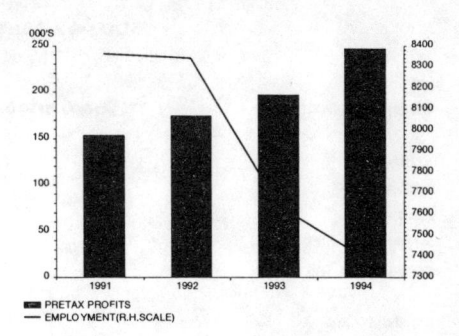

Earnings and dividends

Profits and employment

SOUTHERN ELECTRIC plc

Southern Electric House, Westacott Way,
Littlewick Green, Maidenhead, Berkshire SL6 3BQ
Tel: 01628 822166
Chairman Geoffrey Wilson
Chief executive Henry Casley
Size £1.8 billion sales, £1.6 billion stock market value, 7,400 employees
Solvency debt n/a, interest cover 23 times
Political donations 0
Charitable donations £79,000

Major developments
1990 privatised
1992 bought Thermal Transfer Holdings; bought 70% Rightmain Ltd; joint retail venture with Eastern and Midlands Electricity; set up Southern Electric Contracting; joint venture with Phillips Petroleum

Corporate governance
Separate Chairman and Chief Executive Y
Number of Directors 8
Number of Non-Executive Directors 4
(4 Independent Directors)
Insulated Directors Ch, CE

Board Committees
Audit: Y   Remuneration: Y

Remuneration

Year end	31.03.91	31.03.92	31.03.93
Total board £M	0.86	0.96	1.07
% change		12	11
Highest paid £	197,057	256,690	277,000
% change		30	8

Board
Casley, Henry R *Chief Executive*
Forbes, James A *Executive Director*
Hart, James *Executive Director*
Deane, John W *Finance Director*
Coates, Kenneth H *Independent Non-Executive*
Stoughton-Harris, Anthony *Ind. Non-Executive*
Timpson, Nicholas G L *Independent Non-Executive*
Wilson, Geoffrey H *Non-Executive Chairman*

SOUTH WALES ELECTRICITY

Share record

Return on shareholders'
equity	%	18.20
5-year price high	p	818.0
5-year price low	p	240.0
Dividend yield	%	4.95
5-year high	%	8.87
5-year low	%	3.55
Price/earnings		
ratio		9.0
5-year high		12.6
5-year low		6.9

Share price performance (in pence)

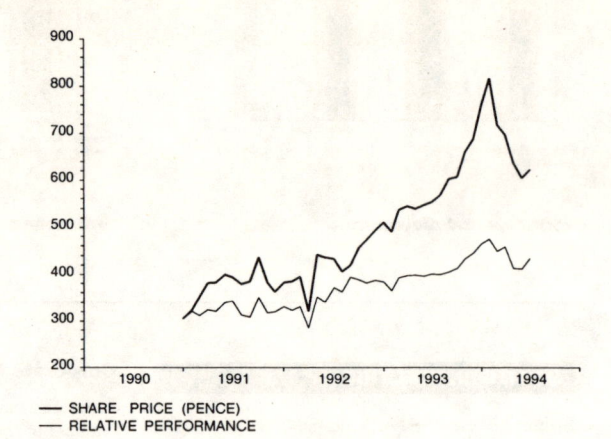

— SHARE PRICE (PENCE)
— RELATIVE PERFORMANCE

Financial record

		31/3/91	31/3/92	31/3/93
Total sales	£'000	567,200	590,200	586,000
Pre-tax profit	£'000	58,400	84,000	87,000
Published retentions	£'000	25,300	31,300	38,300
Earnings per share	p	40.20	61.55	59.99
Dividend per share	p	16.90	19.40	22.30
Operating cash flow	£'000	-19,000	38,300	24,300
Net assets per share	p	304.51	327.60	354.02
Net debt/(cash)	£'000	48,300	10,000	-9,800
Shareholders' funds	£'000	270,000	305,000	337,800
Return on capital	%		27.37	26.13
Profit margin	%	10.30	14.23	14.85
Sales per employee	£	150.57	162.50	185.09
Interest cover		17.42	35.36	-85.56
Dividend cover		2.38	3.17	2.69
Sales increase	%		4.06	-0.71
Earnings growth	%		53.11	-2.54
Investment x depreciation		2.53	3.46	2.84
Investment as % assets		19.05	25.58	21.56
Number of employees		3,767	3,632	3,166

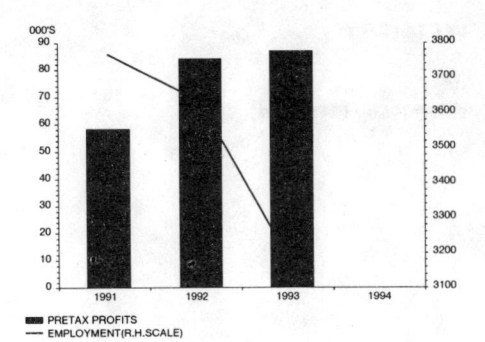

Profits and employment

Sales per employee

SOUTH WALES ELECTRICITY plc

Newport Road, St Mellons, Cardiff CF3 9XW
Tel: 01222 792111
Chairman J Wynford Evans
Chief executive Andrew Walker
Main subsidiaries BEI Lighting, Celtic Contracting
Size £586 million sales, £648 million stock market value, 3,200 employees
Solvency debt n/a, interest cover n/a
Political donations 0
Charitable donations £39,900

Major developments
1990 privatised
1991 launched Celtic Contracting
1992 joined Teesside power station joint venture; formed retail joint venture with South Western Electricity
1993 bought Phoenix Electrical Company Ltd; cable TV/telephone joint venture; formed SWALEC Gas

Corporate governance

Separate Chairman and Chief Executive Y
Number of Directors 10
Number of Non-Executive Directors 5
(5 Independent Directors)
Insulated Directors Ch, MD

Board Committees
Audit: Y   Remuneration: Y

Remuneration

Year end	31.03.91	31.03.92	31.03.93
Total board £M	0.66	0.87	0.88
% change		32	1
Highest paid £	120,687	192,709	199,670
% change		60	4

Board
Walker, Andrew   *Chief Executive*
Evans, J Wynford   *Executive Chairman*
Gibbard, David   *Executive Director*
Mackay, Mike   *Executive Director*
Myring, David   *Finance Director*
Kendall, David   *Independent Non-Executive*
Morgan, Peter   *Independent Non-Executive*
Phillips, Sir Peter   *Independent Non-Executive*
Pollard, Vivien   *Independent Non-Executive*
Prosser, David   *Independent Non-Executive*

SOUTH WESTERN ELECTRICITY

Share record

Return on shareholders' equity	%	17.06
5-year price high	p	740.0
5-year price low	p	240.0
Dividend yield	%	4.97
5-year high	%	8.44
5-year low	%	3.56
Price/earnings ratio		9.3
5-year high		12.5
5-year low		6.7

Share price performance (in pence)

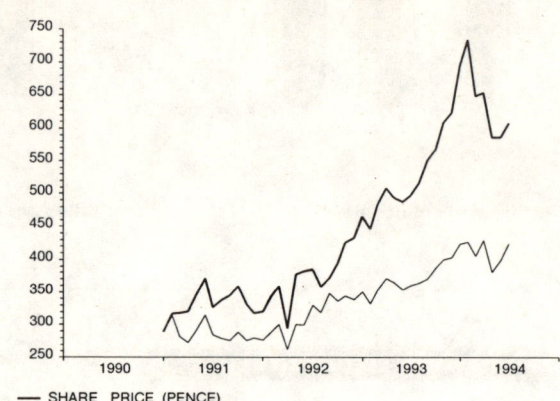

— SHARE PRICE (PENCE)
— RELATIVE PERFORMANCE

Financial record

		31/3/91	31/3/92	31/3/93
Total sales	£'000	779,400	847,100	892,000
Pre-tax profit	£'000	66,200	89,500	104,900
Published retentions	£'000	34,600	41,100	53,200
Earnings per share	p	41.62	55.88	66.21
Dividend per share	p	15.20	17.40	20.00
Operating cash flow	£'000	-22,900	21,000	31,400
Net assets per share	p	382.85	418.52	465.56
Net debt/(cash)	£'000	140,000	115,500	101,700
Shareholders' funds	£'000	384,200	425,300	478,800
Return on capital	%		21.34	21.78
Profit margin	%	8.49	10.57	11.75
Sales per employee	£	137.31	152.55	160.17
Interest cover		5.45	6.39	8.79
Dividend cover		2.74	3.21	3.31
Sales increase	%		8.69	5.30
Earnings growth	%		34.27	18.47
Investment x depreciation		3.26	2.75	2.41
Investment as % assets		17.96	15.12	13.47
Number of employees		5,676	5,553	5,569

ELECTRICITY COMPANIES 89

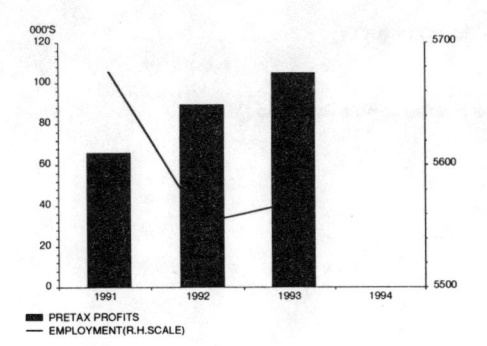

Profits and employment

Sales per employee

SOUTH WESTERN ELECTRICITY plc

800 Park Avenue, Aztec West, Almondsbury,
Bristol BS12 4SE
Tel: 01454 201101
Chairman Maurice Warren
Chief executive John Seed
Size £892 million sales, £711 million stock market value, 5,600 employees
Solvency debt = 21% shareholders' funds, interest cover 9 times
Political donations 0
Charitable donations £81,000

Major developments
1990 privatised
1992 merged retail business with South Wales Electricity

Corporate governance
Separate Chairman and Chief Executive Y
Number of Directors 8
Number of Non-Executive Directors 4
(4 Independent Directors)
Insulated Directors Ch, MD

Board Committees
Audit: Y Remuneration: Y

Remuneration

Year end	31.03.91	31.03.92	31.03.93
Total board £M	0.91	1.18	0.94
% change		30	-20
Highest paid £	163,929	217,617	238,175
% change		33	9

Board
Seed, John Jnr *Chief Executive*
Bonner, John A G *Executive Director*
Carson, Malcolm J *Executive Director*
Sellers, John E *Finance Director*
Fisher, C M *Independent Non-Executive*
Gough, John *Independent Non-Executive*
Hichens, Anthony *Independent Non-Executive*
Warren, Maurice E *Non-Executive Chairman*

YORKSHIRE ELECTRICITY

Share record

Return on shareholders'
equity	%	18.50
5-year price high	p	725.0
5-year price low	p	240.0

Dividend yield	%	5.05
5-year high	%	8.58
5-year low	%	3.68

Price/earnings
ratio		8.2
5-year high		11.7
5-year low		6.9

Share price performance (in pence)

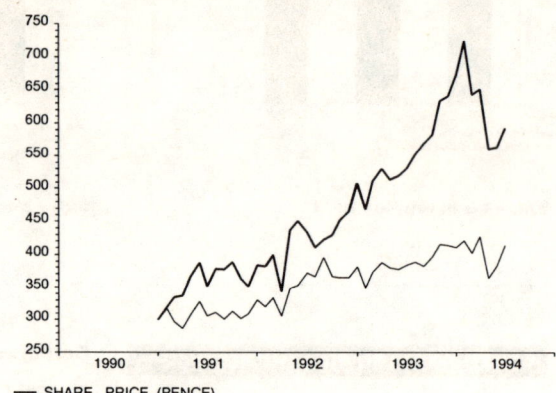

— SHARE PRICE (PENCE)
— RELATIVE PERFORMANCE

Financial record

		31/3/91	31/3/92	31/3/93
Total sales	£	1,243M	1,343M	1,325M
Pre-tax profit	£'000	139,000	145,900	164,000
Published retentions	£'000	67,000	63,400	69,000
Earnings per share	p	41.39	48.82	57.41
Dividend per share	p	15.44	17.76	20.42
Operating cash flow	£'000	18,900	30,300	46,400
Net assets per share	p	312.84	315.10	368.74
Net debt/(cash)	£'000	113,300	86,100	-33,400
Shareholders' funds	£'000	511,600	571,600	636,100
Return on capital	%		25.71	26.41
Profit margin	%	11.19	10.87	12.39
Sales per employee	£	174.36	188.97	193.43
Interest cover		35.11	11.27	21.94
Dividend cover		2.68	2.75	2.81
Sales increase	%		8.06	-1.31
Earnings growth	%		17.95	17.60
Investment x depreciation		2.07	2.51	3.17
Investment as % assets		12.54	14.86	16.66
Number of employees		7,126	7,105	6,850

ELECTRICITY COMPANIES

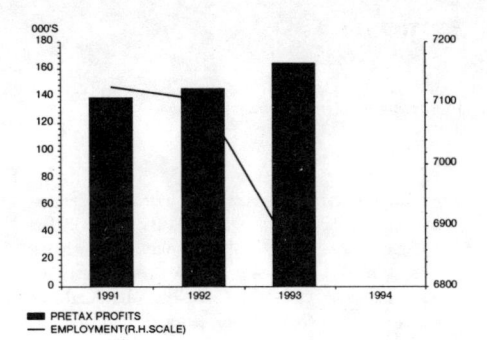

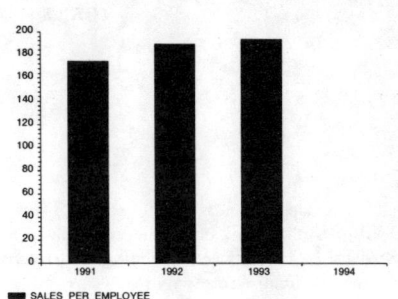

Sales analysis

Profit analysis

YORKSHIRE ELECTRICITY GROUP plc

Wetherby Road, Scarcroft, Leeds LS14 3HS
Tel: 0113 289 2123
Chairman John Tysoe
Chief executive Malcolm Chatwin
Size £1.3 billion sales, £1.2 billion stock market value, 6,850 employees
Solvency debt n/a, interest cover 22 times
Political donations 0
Charitable donations £115,000

Major developments
1990 privatised
1991 bought Cyril Exelby Ltd
1992 merged retail chain with East Midlands Electricity

Corporate governance

Separate Chairman and Chief Executive Y
Number of Directors 9
Number of Non-Executive Directors 5
(4 Independent Directors)
Insulated Directors Ch, MD

Board Committees
Audit: Y   Remuneration: Y

Remuneration

Year end	31.03.91	31.03.92	31.03.93
Total board £M	0.74	1.00	1.10
% change		36	10
Highest paid £	183,571	204,088	196,806
% change		11	-4

Board
Chatwin, Malcolm *Chief Executive*
Hall, Graham J *Executive Director*
Morgan, Bryan P *Executive Director*
Coleman, A W J *Finance Director*
Clark, D B *Independent Non-Executive*
Hardman, John N *Independent Non-Executive*
Lady Eccles *Independent Non-Executive*
Rigg, James A *Independent Non-Executive*
Tysoe, John S *Non-Executive Chairman*

INSURANCE COMPANIES

Outlook

Insurers are supposed to be careful souls, so it is a shock to find that many of their recent troubles are attributable to imprudence. Having spent the early 1990s reeling from overcapacity (too many insurers chasing too few customers), as well as being hit by huge claims from natural as well as man-made disasters such as mortgage indemnity, the industry has now reached a period of calm. Drastic action to increase premiums and to get rid of business which was doomed to incur losses created the backdrop for a healthy period of profits growth from 1993 onwards. But despite pledges that premium-rate cutting was a thing of the past, there is already evidence that some classes of business are offering discounts. And when price cutting starts, it is only a matter of time before the losses roll in.

Worrying signs that a profits slide is imminent – after the surpluses for 1994 and 1995 have fed through – include the fact that profits in many types of business are at a 20-year high and capacity in the market has increased following several capital-raising issues and as a result of the strong equity markets. At the same time, the capital-raising issues have helped to reduce concern over the industry's solvency ratio (that is, shareholders' funds as a percentage of premium income), which had been partially addressed by the business reorganisation of some companies such as Royal Insurance.

Meanwhile European insurance companies, less damaged by the downturn in the industry during the early 1990s, are aggressively seeking market share. Hence any deterioration in the total cost of claims could have a rapid impact on UK insurers. These factors are being compounded by the trend towards direct selling following the success of Direct Line, which is now being aped by the big composite companies. And while the insurers say that business demand remains unaffected by controversy over the mis-selling of endowment and private-pension policies, the industry's credibility remains fragile.

Domestic mortgage-indemnity insurance remains a huge burden to insurers. Building societies insist that house buyers must obtain this type of insurance if their mortgage loan exceeds 75 per cent of the property's value, so that the building society is protected if it loses money after repossessing the house if the owner defaults on the mortgage. The hit on the insurer in each case is not great – on average about £15,000 – but the recent accumulation of repossessions has turned this type of policy into a massive loss-maker. Although the rate at which people fell behind with their mortgages started to slow in 1992, the after-effects of the mortgage-indemnity débâcle have cast a shadow over the industry that will last well beyond the end of 1994, despite the improving housing market. Moreover, policies for professional indemnity and employers' liability show all the potential for another disaster, particularly if the rate of claims continues to increase and if the trend to take legal action intensifies.

Commercial Union (CU) raised £100 million from a preference-share issue in May 1992 in order to boost its flagging solvency margin, although this did not solve all its problems, and it opted for a massive £428 million rights issue in February 1993. Luckily for CU, it managed to present the call for cash at the same time as announcing an upsurge in its fortunes of over £100 million, thereby quashing speculation that it desperately needed the money from shareholders. CU is indeed not too badly off as far as mortgage indemnity goes, having made a conscious decision to reduce its exposure in the 1980s after a series of disasters in the US, and thus living up to its reputation as an ultra-conservative company. It is also helped by the fact that it does not cover many building society block policies. But the company is fearful that the numbers of claims for subsidence will rise fast when the housing market picks up and people panic about selling their crumbling homes. In the early 1990s CU was also busy targeting private motor business which is being discarded by other insurers. The idea is to take advantage of rising rates, although it is a strategy that could backfire badly. This should enable CU to shed unprofitable business as the market turns down again – an event which is expected to leave this company less badly dented than some of its rivals. Even so, the group's efforts to avoid the traps facing the rest of the pack failed to dampen its enthusiasm for 'direct' insurance operations, which began to take off in 1994. The company's business in life assurance continues to thrive and overall CU remains strong.

General Accident was badly hit by unexpectedly high losses in 1992 due to the ravages of Hurricane Andrew; it had to pay out £38 million, £7 million more than anticipated. Although this was just one misfortune, it does point to one of the company's weaknesses: it is the UK insurer that is most exposed to the American market, where underwriting conditions remain less than comfortable and where state regulators cap profits on some types of business, notably motor insurance. None the less, General Accident has been making the most of premium increases in Britain. This, coupled with its recent £140 million fund raising, has made solvency less of a worry for the company. Its motor insurance business is undergoing a radical change as it moves towards being 50 per cent direct sales.

Guardian The company, which shortened its name from 'Guardian Royal Exchange' to 'Guardian', has a healthy-looking book of business, helped by a large exposure to the buoyant UK market, which should keep profits high in 1994 and '95. Guardian's underwriting reputation has improved (although the market is looking for longer-term proof of success here), and an upturn in the German market should offset to some extent the effects of an inevitable downturn in the UK. Concerns do still exist, however, over the adequacy of the company's reserves, particularly regarding its large number of policies covering employers' liability.

Legal & General was hit extremely badly by mortgage-indemnity claims and its UK investment business has also struggled. A restructuring of the investment business in the UK and US has helped this side of things. The company is regarded as one of the weaker of the UK life assurance companies and is likely to remain so for some time to come, despite having mounted a spirited sales drive.

Prudential is continuing to scale down its non-life assurance business: it disposed of its UK commercial operations and its ill-fated estate agencies in order to concentrate on its huge, and profitable, core operation. Only the Mercantile and General Reinsurance business remains in the non-life sector, but Prudential has made it clear that this will be sold at the right price. Under chief executive Mick Newmarch, the company has taken an aggressive stance on financial services regulation, a position which commands some respect as the group is the largest life insurer and investor in Britain. Prudential looks set to enjoy reasonable, if not exceptional, growth in life assurance premiums for the foreseeable future.

Royal Insurance While the group has shown some success in the development of its direct writing operation – the Insurance Service – and has managed to shed some of the doubts over the strength of its balance sheet, worries remain about Royal Insurance's prospects. The company has incurred sizeable mortgage-indemnity losses and is exposed to subsidence claims. Reserves have been increased, although analysts think further strengthening may be necessary on the liability account. The US arm, which was a profits black hole for years, has shown some improvement but looks unlikely to become an attractive business during the 1990s.

Sun Alliance raised £155 million in 1993 through a convertible-bond issue, giving a fillip to a pressured balance sheet, although this is not nearly as strong, relative to that of other insurance companies, as it was a few years ago. The company has taken hard knocks from the poor state of the UK's housing market. Losses on mortgage indemnity have been enormous and there is little sign of a let-up. In other parts of the world, such as the US and Germany, and in other classes of business, such as buildings insurance, Sun Alliance is looking reasonably strong, but this is overshadowed by its losses at home in the mortgage-indemnity business and by concerns about the extent of losses (believed to be as much as £200 million) which might come from its reinsurance contract with Nationwide Anglia, although the group does insist it has sufficient provisions in place.

Eagle Star is a peculiar insurer in that it enjoys a strong safety net provided by its parent group, BAT (see also under BAT), which, at the end of 1992, pumped in £450 million to revive its ailing solvency margin. Eagle Star's investment business was combined with that of sister company Allied Dunbar during 1993, when there was considerable speculation that a Continental insurer or a UK building society would be added to the BAT portfolio. Profits improved substantially during 1993, thanks to some pruning of unattractive business, although mortgage indemnity remains a difficult area for the company.

Shares

The insurance industry generally experiences cycles of boom and bust, and the share prices of the quoted composite insurers (covering genuine insurance against fire, theft and other disasters as well as savings and investment) tend to reflect this cycle. As the industry nears the bottom of the cycle, investors deem it time to buy the shares again, ready for the upturn. And as the cycle nears its peak, it is time to sell, before profits and prospects begin to fall.

This cyclical pattern is interrupted occasionally by specific events, especially major disasters. And there were many of those in the period reviewed here. If it wasn't hurricanes in North America, it was hurricanes in south-east England, or floods, or heavy snowfalls, or excessively dry summers. Whatever the weather, the insurance companies seemed to be in trouble.

In the great stock market boom of 1986–7, the insurers generally lost out because the emphasis was on expansionist retailers, takeover bidders, and other creatures of the boom. This was also a time of overcapacity, leading to low premium levels and low profits. That began to change in 1987, with the sector advancing during the final stages of the surge in the stock market, followed by a period of relative stability.

As recession began to bite in 1989–90, investors started to favour the insurance companies as safe havens at a time when consumer demand was weak, thereby affecting many capital goods and retail sectors. Insurance was not seen as being greatly affected by recession – after all, people still need motor insurance even if they are not changing their cars, and householders still need home insurance even if they are not moving house. During this period there was also an increase in premium rates, encouraging investors to view the industry with confidence.

In the event, such confidence was misplaced, as the subsequent plunge in the sector shares illustrates. Recession did indeed affect insurers: a rise in arson, a greater tendency to claim for small sums, and a tendency to claim more, plus an increase in burglary and especially car crime. But the biggest recessionary impact was on mortgage-indemnity business, as the rate of house repossessions soared. As the scale of the losses suffered by the industry – and the rights issues necessary to repair the balance sheets – began to dawn during 1991, so the fall in the share price gathered pace. By 1993 prices had recovered somewhat, but were nowhere near their level of two years previously, having only just about clawed their way back to the level they had occupied before the 1987 recovery.

Investors who picked their companies well nevertheless stood to gain. There was a huge diversity in the performance of the different insurance companies during the period. General Accident and Royal Insurance clearly fared much worse than their rivals; indeed, thanks to its calamitous experiences in various fields, the value of shares in Royal Insurance halved relative to the sector.

Commercial Union, on the other hand, went from strength to strength. This was partly due to its lowly standing at the beginning of the period, following several dismal episodes in the US, and partly due to its low exposure to the worst disaster areas of mortgage indemnity. During the late 1980s CU also came to be regarded by investors as one of the best-managed of the industry leaders (although the competition was not fierce).

Sun Alliance used to wear that mantle, but the faltering share price from the end of 1991 illustrates that its reputation had slipped a little. While the company remained strong, it was heavily involved in the mortgage-indemnity bloodbath.

The mighty Prudential benefited from the relative stability of its savings business, but its shares made a sudden surge towards the end of the period, having languished during the late 1980s. The explanation has something to do with the arrival at the top of the company of Mick Newmarch, a no-nonsense executive who soon began to clear out unwanted businesses. While the departure from ventures such as estate agencies incurred significant losses, the relief, and the belief that Mr Newmarch was possibly worth his huge salary increase, was reflected in the performance of the share price. Legal & General also had the advantage of a greater weight of life (i.e. savings) business, and another down-to-earth, though less celebrated, new chief executive.

Although the buoyant profits of 1993 promised to continue for at least another couple of years and the insurers all had plenty of tax losses from which to benefit, in early 1994 the shares already looked to be preparing themselves for the other side of the roller coaster.

Corporate conscience

While insurance companies are not exposed to specific matters of conscience through their mainstream business (such as Third World debt, as in the case of the banks), many issues still apply to them. All except Legal & General are represented in other countries with oppressive regimes, most notably CU, which has a life insurance subsidiary in Mexico.

There is no significant military connection, but four companies are involved with the nuclear industry. CU and General Accident share an interest in Plant Safety, a company which supplies specialist engineering services for the inspection and certification of boilers in nuclear power stations. Royal Insurance, through BE Inspection, and Sun Alliance, through National Vulcan Engineering, are similarly implicated.

For companies which have suffered mightily due to storms and other environmental upheavals, these companies do not demonstrate exceptional environmental awareness. Only Guardian and General Accident have an adequate environmental policy. The only other black marks are for advertising. Royal suffered 3 adverse judgements from the ASA in 1991 and 1992; General Accident received 2.

On the positive side, all accept their responsibilities to the community, and demonstrate this through membership of bodies such as BITC. Guardian Royal Insurance and Sun Alliance are all committed to giving more than one per cent of profits to charity. CU has an undistinguished employment record, but the others operate adequate equal opportunities policies. Guardian has a woman on the board, while Legal & General and Prudential support Opportunity 2000. Guardian, General Accident, Royal Insurance and Sun Alliance are all heavily unionised.

Corporate governance

As some of Britain's largest shareholders in other large public companies, the boards of the insurance companies might be expected to pay particular attention to their own corporate governance. But this is not so. Like the banks, they inherit a tradition of heavy non-executive representation, but not all have capitalised on this to embrace the new recommendations of the Cadbury Report. Several continue to give political donations without reference to shareholders, although Legal & General is one company which has agreed to seek investor approval for such payments in future.

Most of the insurers, even die-hards like Sun Alliance, which has always derided the need for advances in its own corporate governance, have sought to improve the level of disclosure and accountability in their annual reports. As befits these powerful investors – whose industry body, the Association of British Insurers, likes to cut such a dash with its corporate governance guidelines – the insurance companies' boardrooms do have remuneration and audit committees, although nomination committees (which select boardroom members) remain far from standard. It is arguable whether the top rates of pay among the insurers respond adequately to the traumatic peaks and troughs of the companies' earnings, but even the sternest critics would be unlikely to argue that directors should return money to their company on such a routine basis.

COMMERCIAL UNION

Share record

Return on shareholders' equity   %   12.65
5-year price high   p   709.0
5-year price low   p   387.9

Dividend yield   %   5.74
5-year high   %   7.82
5-year low   %   4.29

Price/earnings ratio   16.5
5-year high   61.5
5-year low   10.7

Share price performance (in pence)

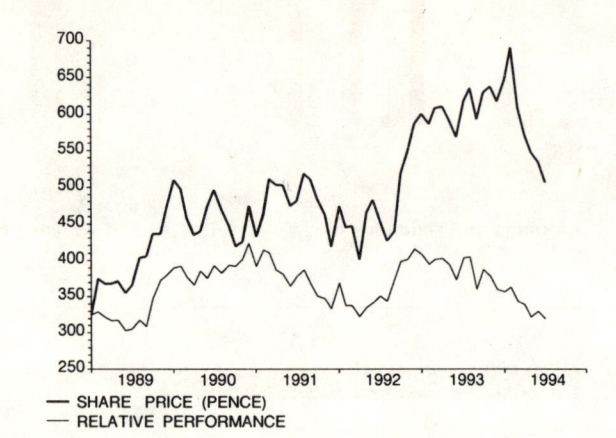

— SHARE PRICE (PENCE)
— RELATIVE PERFORMANCE

Financial record

		31/12/89	31/12/90	31/12/91	31/12/92	31/12/93
Total life premiums	£	1,024M	1,164M	1,361M	2,007M	1,899M
General premiums	£	2,454M	2,361M	2,646M	3,363M	3,919M
Insurance result	£	-245M	-345M	-463M	-431M	-277M
Pre-tax profit	£'000	150,500	1,400	-68,600	31,400	218,000
Published retentions	£'000	82,400	-76,400	-120M	122,100	168,000
Earnings per share	p	52.76	4.87	0.00	52.16	60.95
Dividend per share	p	20.80	22.25	22.87	23.55	24.85
Net assets per share	p	3,385	3,340	3,620	4,559	4,457
Shareholders' funds	£	1,708M	1,235M	1,210M	1,501M	2,529M
Borrowing ratio	%	26.0	35.0	34.0	32.0	0.13
Return on shareholders' equity	%	9.55	1.70	-1.23	14.74	12.65
Pre-tax profit margin	%	3.85	0.02	-1.93	0.23	3.52
Premiums per employee	£	166,531	163,037	183,996	237,097	254.63
Dividend cover		2.54	0.22	0.00	2.21	2.45
Premium growth	%	18.21	1.36	13.71	33.97	8.36
Earnings growth	%	9.49	-90.78	-100.00	0.00	16.83
Total insurance funds	£	12,708M	13,205M	14,825M	19,050M	21,300M
Total investments	£	4,620M	4,076M	4,364M	5,502M	7,020M
Number of employees		20,882	21,619	21,782	22,646	22,849

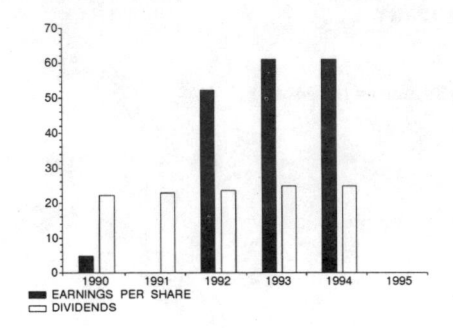

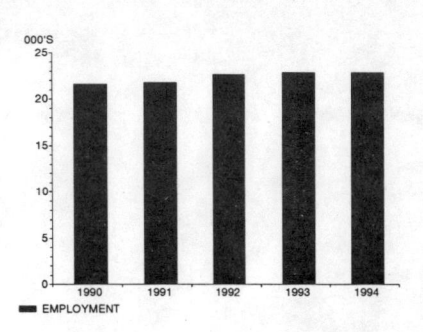

Earnings and dividends

Employment

COMMERCIAL UNION plc

St Helen's, 1 Undershaft, London EC3P 3DQ
Tel: 0171 283 7500
Chairman Nicholas Baring
Chief executive John Carter
Main subsidiaries Quilter Goodison
Size £5.8 billion premiums, £3.1 billion stock market value, 22,800 employees
5-year growth premiums n/a, earnings per share 16%, employment 9%
Solvency n/a
Political donations 0
Charitable donations £213,582

Major developments
1861 incorporated
1885 registered as a public company
1968 merger with Northern & Employers
1971 bought Employers Group Associates (US)
1990 bought unit trusts and other funds from Royal Asset Management; expanded in Italy through deal with Credito Italiano
1992 increased ownership of NCU (Australia) from 46% to 71%; expanded into Poland with a joint venture

Corporate governance
Separate Chairman and Chief Executive Y
Number of Directors 10
Number of Non-Executive Directors 7
(7 Independent Directors)
Insulated Directors None

Board Committees
Audit: Y   Remuneration: Y

Remuneration

Year end	31.12.91	31.12.92	31.12.93
Total board £M	0.80	0.94	1.10
% change	-8	18	15
Highest paid £	260,207	310,881	357,246
% change	-5	20	15

Board
Carter, J G T *Chief Executive*
Ward, P G *Executive Director*
Wyand, A B *Executive Director*
Fauroux, Roger *Independent Non-Executive*
Gillam, Patrick J *Independent Non-Executive*
Hampel, R C *Independent Non-Executive*
Heaton, F A *Independent Non-Executive*
Meij, Prof. Dr H *Independent Non-Executive*
Strachan, Ian C *Independent Non-Executive*
Baring, N H *Non-Executive Chairman*

GENERAL ACCIDENT

Share record

Return on shareholders' equity	%	10.78
5-year price high	p	752.0
5-year price low	p	356.0
Dividend yield	%	6.03
5-year high	%	7.39
5-year low	%	3.52
Price/earnings ratio		10.7
5-year high		18.4
5-year low		8.6

Share price performance (in pence)

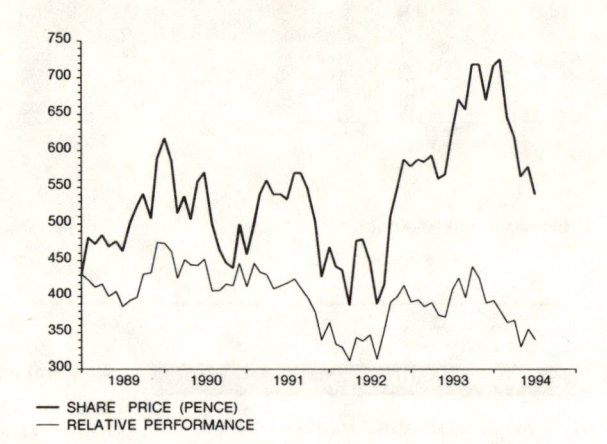

— SHARE PRICE (PENCE)
— RELATIVE PERFORMANCE

Financial record

		31/12/89	31/12/90	31/12/91	31/12/92	31/12/93
Total life premiums	£	381,300	413,500	551,900	790,400	860,100
General premiums	£	3,023M	2,966M	3,188M	3,752M	4,080M
Insurance result	£	-204M	-462M	-569M	-510M	-229M
Pre-tax profit	£'000	147,000	-121M	-171M	-29,300	294,900
Published retentions	£'000	22,100	-209M	-256M	-151M	101,000
Earnings per share	p	30.42	0.00	0.00	0.00	49.96
Dividend per share	p	25.00	26.75	26.75	26.75	27.50
Net assets per share	p	1,571	1,272	1,342	1,880	2,284
Shareholders' funds	£	2,552M	1,430M	1,373M	1,629M	2,370M
Borrowing ratio	%	27.0	37.0	28.0	38.0	0.15
Return on shareholders' equity	%	5.07	-6.60	-10.14	-2.09	10.78
Pre-tax profit margin	%	4.32	3.59	-4.58	-0.65	5.96
Premiums per employee	£	n/a	n/a	n/a	n/a	n/a
Dividend cover		1.22	0.00	0.00	0.00	1.82
Premium growth	%	23.01	-0.73	10.67	21.47	8.89
Earnings growth	%	-43.46	-100.00	0.00	0.00	0.00
Total insurance funds	£	3,723M	3,684M	4,166M	6,267M	7,702M
Total investments	£	6,702M	5,448M	5,779M	7,043M	7,681M
Number of employees		n/a	n/a	n/a	13,162	11,908

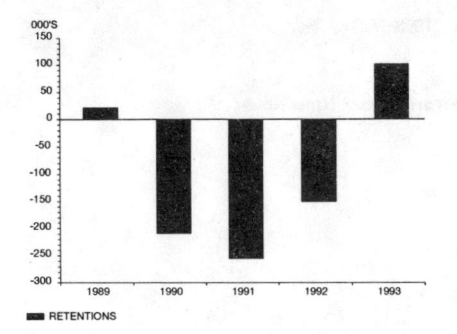

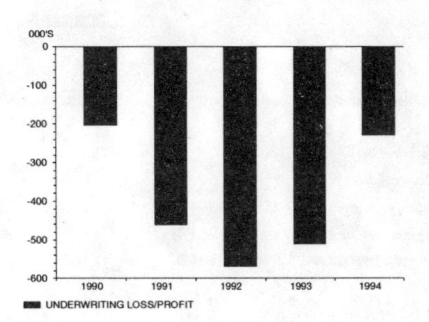

Net Retained Profit

Underwriting losses

GENERAL ACCIDENT plc

Pitheavlis, Perth, Scotland PH2 0NH
Tel: 01738 21202
Chairman The Earl of Airlie
Chief executive Nelson Robertson
Size £4.9 billion premiums, £2.6 billion stock market value, 11,900 employees
5-year growth premiums n/a, earnings per share 64%, employment n/a
Solvency n/a
Political donations 0
Charitable donations £394,142

Major developments
1885 established as General Accident Assurance Corporation
1906 became General Accident Fire and Life Assurance Corporation Ltd
1988 bought 51% NZI Corporation (New Zealand)
1989 took full control of NZI
1990 new holding company formed as General Accident plc
1991 decided to wind down NZI Bank
1993 set up SelectDirect direct sales insurance operation

Corporate governance

Separate Chairman and Chief Executive Y
Number of Directors 15
Number of Non-Executive Directors 10
(10 Independent Directors)
Insulated Directors None

Board Committees
Audit: Y   Remuneration: Y

Remuneration

Year end	31.12.91	31.12.92	31.12.93
Total board £M	1.98	1.74	2.30
% change	-5	-12	30
Highest paid £	219,442	237,822	292,881
% change	-0.2	8	23

Board
Robertson, W N *Chief Executive*
Farnam, W E *Executive Director*
Holder, B *Executive Director*
Morris, G N *Executive Director*
Scott, R A *Executive Director*
Bolton, L *Independent Non-Executive*
Botting, Mrs L *Independent Non-Executive*
Cleaver, Sir Anthony *Independent Non-Executive*
Earl of Mansfield *Independent Non-Executive*
Goodison, Sir Nicholas *Independent Non-Executive*
Lord Macfarlane *Independent Non-Executive*
Lord Nickson *Independent Non-Executive*
Middleton, Sir Peter *Independent Non-Executive*
Noel-Paton, F Ronald *Independent Non-Executive*
Earl of Airlie *Non-Executive Chairman*

INSURANCE COMPANIES

GUARDIAN ROYAL ASSURANCE

Share record

Return on shareholders'
equity	%	38.08
5-year price high	p	264.0
5-year price low	p	104.0
Dividend yield	%	5.31
5-year high	%	15.26
5-year low	%	3.52
Price/earnings ratio		2.7
5-year high		21.8
5-year low		2.4

Share price performance (in pence)

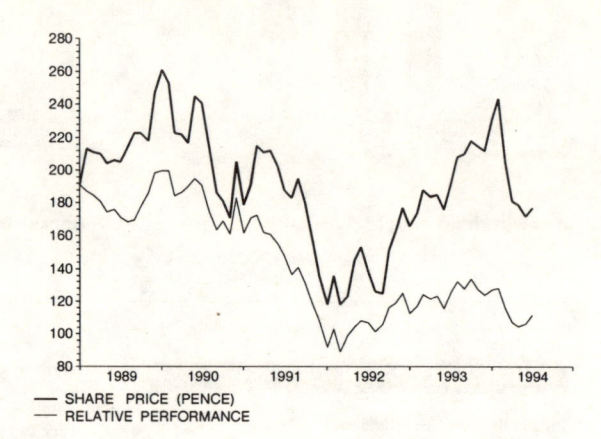

— SHARE PRICE (PENCE)
— RELATIVE PERFORMANCE

Financial record

		31/12/89	31/12/90	31/12/91	31/12/92	31/12/93
Total life premiums	£	783,600	808,700	879,000	821,000	758,000
General premiums	£	1,914M	1,992M	2,158M	2,246M	2,525M
Insurance result	£	-170M	-461M	-512M	-295M	359,000
Pre-tax profit	£'000	148,300	-157M	-210M	150,000	751,000
Published retentions	£'000	-1,300	-215M	-244M	53,000	581,000
Earnings per share	p	11.35	0.00	0.00	16.28	82.25
Dividend per share	p	11.50	11.90	7.00	7.00	7.60
Net assets per share	p	1,033	852.14	1,247	1,404	1,669
Shareholders' funds	£	1,642M	942,400	947,000	1,132M	1,681M
Borrowing ratio	%	14.0	14.0	5.0	4.0	0.12
Return on shareholders' equity	%	6.60	-18.51	-19.35	10.06	38.08
Pre-tax profit margin	%	5.50	-5.61	-6.91	4.89	22.88
Premiums per employee	£	n/a	n/a	n/a	n/a	n/a
Dividend cover		0.99	0.00	0.00	0.00	10.82
Premium growth	%	22.85	3.84	8.43	0.99	7.04
Earnings growth	%	-41.48	-100.00	0.00	0.00	405.19
Total insurance funds	£	7,235M	6,452M	9,783M	10,915M	12,607M
Total investments	£	3,641M	3,109M	9,652M	10,882M	13,414M
Number of employees		n/a	9,233	8,697	7,839	7,582

INSURANCE COMPANIES

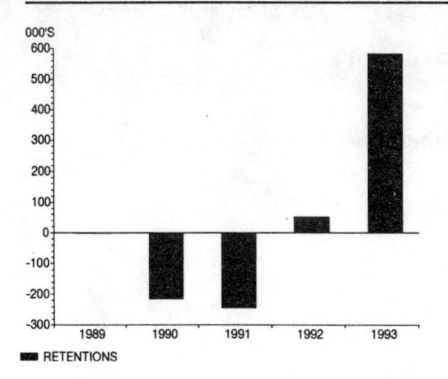

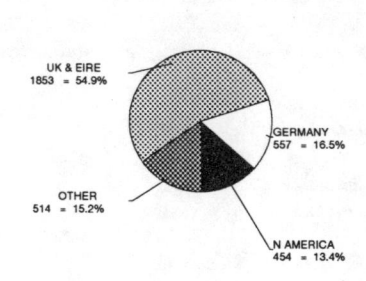

Retentions

Sales analysis

GUARDIAN ROYAL ASSURANCE plc

Royal Exchange, London EC3V 3LS
Tel: 0171 283 7101
Chairman Charles Hambro
Chief executive Sidney Hopkins
Size £3.3 billion premiums, £1.6 billion stock market value, employees 7,600
5-year growth premiums n/a, earnings per share 624%, employment n/a
Solvency n/a
Political donations £35,000 Conservative Party
Charitable donations £218,764

Major developments
1968 formed on merger of Guardian Assurance Co and Royal Exchange Assurance
1988 Minority interest in Bruton Property Holdings Ltd
1989 linked with Nationwide Anglia building society; investment in Italian insurance companies
1991 sale of Italian interests; first ever loss
1992 fined £100,000 after agents scandal

Corporate governance
Separate Chairman and Chief Executive Y
Number of Directors 14
Number of Non-Executive Directors 9
(6 Independent Directors)
Insulated Directors None

Board Committees
Audit: Y   Remuneration: Y

Remuneration

Year end	31.12.91	31.12.92	31.12.93
Total board £M	1.31	1.38	1.40
% change	-4	5	2
Highest paid £	255,776	329,322	338,179
% change		11	29	3

Board
Hopkins, Sidney A *Chief Executive*
Burton, Caroline M *Executive Director*
McDonough, James T *Executive Director*
Sinclair, John *Executive Director*
Morley, James *Finance Director*
Gordon, Donald *Independent Non-Executive*
Hayes, Sir Brian *Independent Non-Executive*
Menzies, John Maxwell *Independent Non-Executive*
Reynolds, Sir Peter *Independent Non-Executive*
Sheffield, J Julian L G *Independent Non-Executive*
Tennant, Sir Anthony J *Independent Non-Executive*
Adeane, G Edward *Non-executive*
Stoughton-Harris, Anthony *Non-executive*
Hambro, Charles E A *Non-Executive Chairman*

INSURANCE COMPANIES

LEGAL & GENERAL GROUP

Share record

Return on shareholders' equity	%	43.92
5-year price high	p	543.0
5-year price low	p	288.0
Dividend yield	%	5.70
5-year high	%	8.70
5-year low	%	4.35
Price/earnings ratio		15.2
5-year high		28.5
5-year low		14.1

Share price performance (in pence)

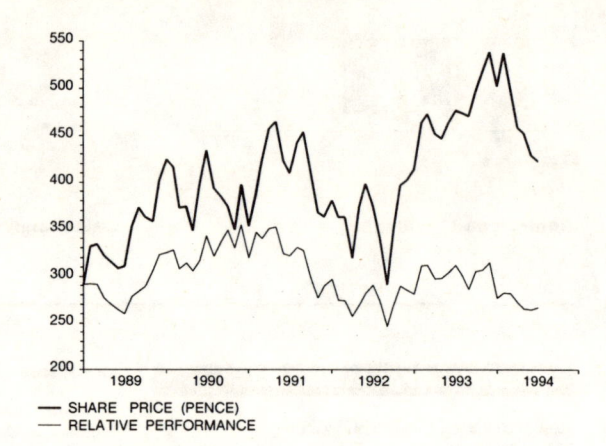

— SHARE PRICE (PENCE)
— RELATIVE PERFORMANCE

Financial record

		31/12/89	31/12/90	31/12/91	31/12/92	31/12/93
Total life premiums	£	2,314M	2,600M	2,101M	2,007M	2,358M
General premiums	£	369,200	382,500M	345,200	294,600	291,800
Insurance result	£	2,000	-88,300	-218M	-128M	27,300
Pre-tax profit	£'000	142,300	68,600	11,300	116,100	181,000
Published retentions	£'000	26,100	6,700	-58,300	-3,200	50,400
Earnings per share	p	20.76	11.77	6.60	18.65	37.14
Dividend per share	p	15.80	17.90	18.80	19.10	20.10
Net assets per share	p	3,561	3,304	3,902	4,548	6,074
Shareholders' funds	£	365,100	287,100	240,500	262,200	324,000
Borrowing ratio	%	102.0	131.0	154.0	154.0	150.0
Return on shareholders' equity	%	27.86	19.71	13.26	34.48	43.92
Pre-tax profit margin	%	5.30	2.30	0.46	5.04	6.83
Premiums per employee	£	n/a	n/a	n/a	n/a	n/a
Dividend cover		1.31	0.66	0.35	0.98	1.85
Premium growth	%	49.38	11.16	-17.97	-5.93	15.13
Earnings growth	%	2.89	-43.30	-43.89	182.37	99.15
Total insurance funds	£	16,261M	15,301M	18,348M	21,580M	29,034M
Total investments	£	16,320M	15,345M	18,315M	21,634M	29,449M
Number of employees		n/a	n/a	n/a	8,077	7,606

INSURANCE COMPANIES 103

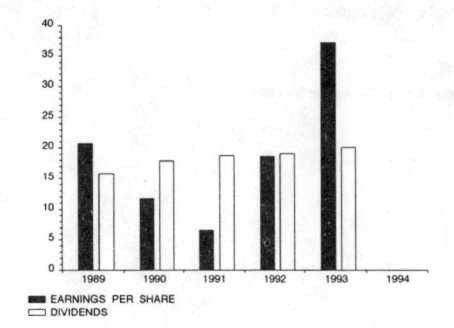

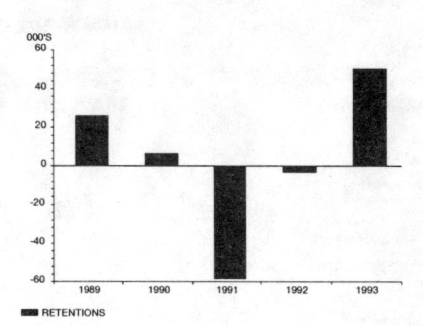

Earnings and dividends

Retentions

LEGAL & GENERAL GROUP plc

Temple Court, 11 Queen Victoria Street,
London EC4N 4TP
Tel: 0171 528 6200
Chairman Prof. Sir James Ball
Chief executive David Prosser
Size £2.6 billion premiums, £2.2 billion stock market value, employees 7,600
5-year growth premiums n/a, earnings per share 79%, employment n/a
Solvency n/a
Political donations £30,000 Conservative Party
Charitable donations £466,500

Major developments
1979 formed to acquire Legal and General Assurance Society
1983 bought minority interest in Victory Insurance Holdings
1987 acquisition of Fairmount Trust Ltd; acquisition of City & Urban Developments Ltd
1989 bought numerous estate agents; bought William Penn Life Assurance of America

Corporate governance

Separate Chairman and Chief Executive Y
Number of Directors 13
Number of Non-Executive Directors 10
(10 Independent Directors)
Insulated Directors None

Board Committees
Audit: Y   Remuneration: Y

Remuneration

Year end	31.12.91	31.12.92	31.12.93
Total board £M	1.90	1.29	1.60
% change	-20	-32	21
Highest paid £	370,010	312,473	472,889
% change	42	-16	51

Board
Prosser, David *Chief Executive*
Rough, David *Executive Director*
Hobson, Anthony *Finance Director*
Chapman, Honor *Independent Non-Executive*
Crawford, Prof. Sir F *Independent Non-Executive*
Dixon, Kenneth H M *Independent Non-Executive*
Egan, Sir John *Independent Non-Executive*
Govett, Bill *Independent Non-Executive*
Harding, Sir Christopher *Ind. Non-Executive*
Kerridge, John S *Independent Non-Executive*
Lady Howe *Independent Non-Executive*
Wheatley, Alan *Independent Non-Executive*
Ball, Prof. Sir James *Non-Executive Chairman*

INSURANCE COMPANIES

PRUDENTIAL CORPORATION

Share record

Return on shareholders' equity	%	49.87
5-year price high	p	382.0
5-year price low	p	183.5
Dividend yield	%	5.36
5-year high	%	7.28
5-year low	%	4.02
Price/earnings ratio		14.7
5-year high		45.3
5-year low		13.1

Share price performance (in pence)

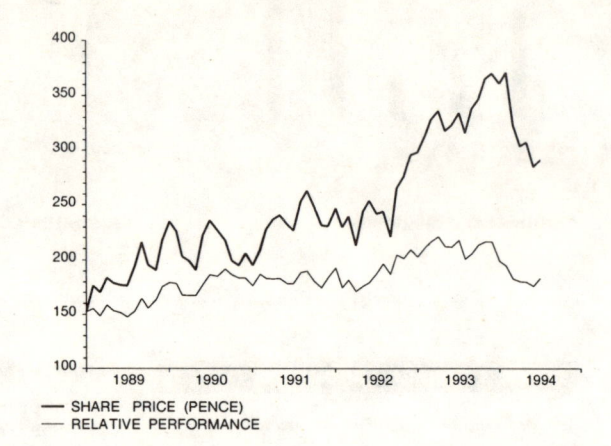

— SHARE PRICE (PENCE)
— RELATIVE PERFORMANCE

Financial record

		31/12/89	31/12/90	31/12/91	31/12/92	31/12/93
Total life premiums	£	4,721M	5,190M	6,019M	7,443M	7,699M
General premiums	£	1,037M	1,026M	1,049M	1,048M	650,000
Insurance result	£	-8,600	-185M	-149M	-121M	67,000
Pre-tax profit	£'000	385,500	243,800	267,000	406,000	589,000
Published retentions	£'000	104,900	-47,800	-119M	58,000	146,000
Earnings per share	p	15.06	7.15	7.18	14.47	31.26
Dividend per share	p	9.20	10.30	11.00	11.90	13.20
Net assets per share	p	2,010	1,850	2,225	2,726	3,361
Shareholders' funds	£	813,600	503,000	463,000	504,000	788,000
Borrowing ratio	%	101.0	156.0	171.0	141.0	87.0
Return on shareholders' equity	%	34.04	25.58	28.63	53.77	49.87
Pre-tax profit margin	%	6.69	3.92	3.78	4.78	7.05
Premiums per employee	£	n/a	n/a	n/a	n/a	n/a
Dividend cover		1.64	0.69	0.65	1.22	2.37
Premium growth	%	24.70	7.94	13.72	20.13	-1.67
Earnings growth	%	19.16	-52.50	0.41	101.44	116.07
Total insurance funds	£	35,857M	33,475M	40,528M	49,970M	61,942M
Total investments	£	37,307M	34,278M	40,538M	50,017M	62,407M
Number of employees		n/a	n/a	n/a	23,619	21,114

INSURANCE COMPANIES

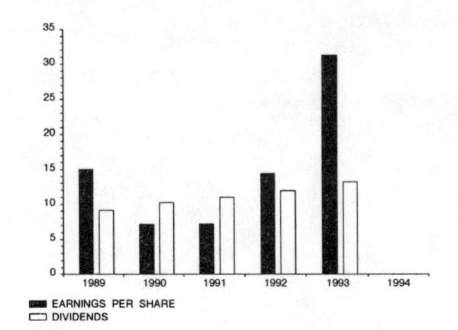

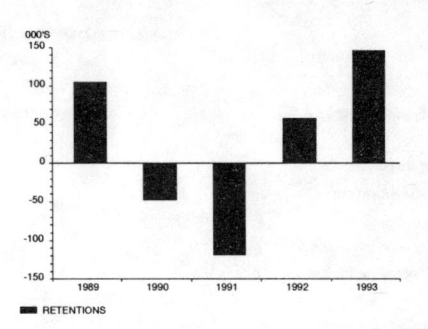

Earnings and dividends

Retentions

PRUDENTIAL CORPORATION plc

142 Holborn Bars, London EC1N 2NH
Tel: 0171 405 9222
Chairman Sir Brian Corby
Chief executive Mick Newmarch
Size £8.3 billion premiums, £5.8 billion stock market value, employees 21,100
5-year growth premiums n/a, earnings per share 108%, employment n/a
Solvency n/a
Political donations 0
Charitable donations £1 million

Major developments
1848 established
1978 became public
1985 bought part of Prudential Life of Ireland
1986 bought estate agency businesses
1988 established largest residential estate agency network
1989 bought Australian and New Zealand life assurance interests of Aetna Life
1990 began selling off estate agents
1991 concluded departure from estate agency business
1992 abandoned general insurance broking; sold commercial insurance business

Corporate governance
Separate Chairman and Chief Executive Y
Number of Directors 15
Number of Non-Executive Directors 9
(2 Independent Directors)
Insulated Directors None

Board Committees
Audit: Y   Remuneration: Y

Remuneration

Year end	31.12.91	31.12.92	31.12.93
Total board £M	2.41	3.02	3.48
% change	-18	25	15
Highest paid £	617,114	769,385	834,068
% change	14	25	8

Board
Newmarch, Mick *Chief Executive*
Bedell-Pearce, Keith *Executive Director*
Freeman, Tony *Executive Director*
Jenkins, Hugh *Executive Director*
Maxwell, John *Executive Director*
Sutcliffe, Jim *Executive Director*
Abrahams, Michael *Independent Non-Executive*
Jacomb, Sir Martin *Independent Non-Executive*
Baker, Mary Elizabeth *Non-Executive*
FitzGerald, Niall *Non-Executive*
Holdsworth, Sir Trevor *Non-Executive*
Jarratt, Sir Alex *Non-Executive*
Medhurst, Brian *Non-Executive*
Teare, Andrew Hubert *Non-Executive*
Corby, Sir Brian *Non-Executive Chairman*

106 INSURANCE COMPANIES

ROYAL INSURANCE

Share record

Return on shareholders'
equity	%	10.50
5-year price high	p	556.5
5-year price low	p	121.1
Dividend yield	%	3.80
5-year high	%	16.05
5-year low	%	0.92
Price/earnings		
ratio		15.9
5-year high		39.1
5-year low		2.8

Share price performance (in pence)

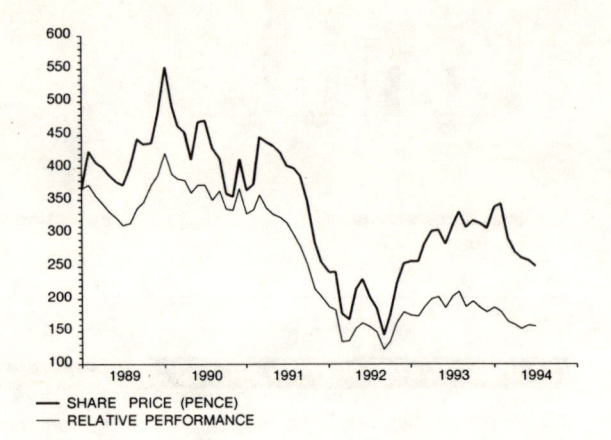

— SHARE PRICE (PENCE)
— RELATIVE PERFORMANCE

Financial record

		31/12/89	31/12/90	31/12/91	31/12/92	31/12/93
Total life premiums	£	1,068M	1,085M	1,057M	1,076M	1,432M
General premiums	£	3,582M	3,567M	3,483M	3,342M	3,607M
Insurance result	£	-400M	-726M	-887M	-588M	-371M
Pre-tax profit	£'000	126,000	-187M	-373M	-1,190M	151,000
Published retentions	£'000	-33,000	-301M	-468M	-107M	96,000
Earnings per share	p	17.39	0.00	0.00	0.00	13.46
Dividend per share	p	24.42	24.99	10.81	4.81	7.50
Net assets per share	p	3,015	2,806	3,005	1,739	1,579
Shareholders' funds	£	2,635M	1,645M	1,469M	1,462M	2,177M
Borrowing ratio	%	31.0	46.0	44.0	35.0	65.0
Return on shareholders' equity	%	3.21	-10.15	-27.14	-5.53	10.50
Pre-tax profit margin	%	1.85	-5.05	-8.96	-3.17	2.46
Premiums per employee	£	n/a	n/a	n/a	n/a	n/a
Dividend cover		0.71	0.00	0.00	0.00	1.79
Premium growth	%	20.78	0.04	-2.41	-2.69	14.06
Earnings growth	%	-40.27	-100.00	0.00	0.00	0.00
Total insurance funds	£	11,919M	11,966M	13,133M	6,899M	6,786M
Total investments	£	12,892M	12,151M	13,179M	6,655M	71,509M
Number of employees		n/a	n/a	n/a	15,890	13,495

INSURANCE COMPANIES

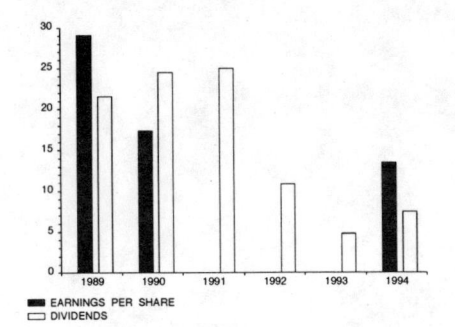

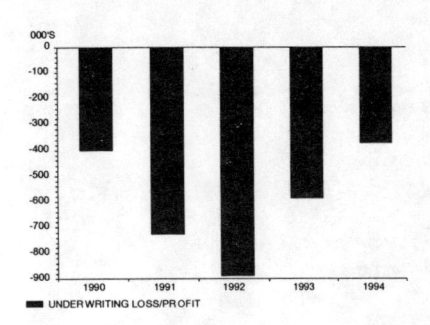

Earnings and dividends

Underwriting losses

ROYAL INSURANCE HOLDINGS plc

1 Cornhill, London EC3V 3QR
Tel: 0171 283 4300
Chairman Sir John Cuckney
Chief executive Richard Gamble
Main subsidiaries Bretton Financial Services, British Engine, Cavendish Insurance, The CareAssist Group
Size £5.0 billion premiums, £1.6 billion stock market value, employees 13,500
5-year growth premiums n/a, earnings per share -23%, employment n/a
Solvency n/a
Political donations 0
Charitable donations £460,055

Major developments
1845 formed
1919 merged with Liverpool Fire & Life Insurance
1961 merged with London and Lancashire
1985 acquired Lloyds Life
1988 bought Maccabees Life (US); acquired interests in numerous estate agencies; bought 90% of Italian insurer Lloyd Italico
1992 formed Epic alliance with Aachener and Munchener, and Fondiaria; merged Australian business with that of Sun Alliance

Corporate governance

Separate Chairman and Chief Executive Y
Number of Directors 11
Number of Non-Executive Directors 6
(6 Independent Directors)
Insulated Directors None

Board Committees
Audit: Y   Remuneration: Y

Remuneration

Year end	31.12.91	31.12.92	31.12.93
Total board £M	1.46	1.80	1.80
% change	14	25	0
Highest paid £	256,095	239,910	259,604
% change	5	-6	8

Board
Gamble, Richard A *Chief Executive*
Barker, David F *Executive Director*
Elms, Roy A *Executive Director*
Rowland, Robin W *Executive Director*
Dowdy, Michael J *Finance Director*
Alun-Jones, Sir Derek *Independent Non-Executive*
Barber, Nicholas C F *Independent Non-Executive*
Gormly, Allan G *Independent Non-Executive*
Milne, Sir John *Independent Non-Executive*
Williams, Sir Max *Independent Non-Executive*
Cuckney, Sir John *Non-Executive Chairman*

SUN ALLIANCE

Share record

Return on shareholders' equity	%	8.47
5-year price high	p	416.0
5-year price low	p	217.5
Dividend yield	%	5.80
5-year high	%	8.74
5-year low	%	4.08
Price/earnings ratio		13.5
5-year high		15.0
5-year low		8.9

Share price performance (in pence)

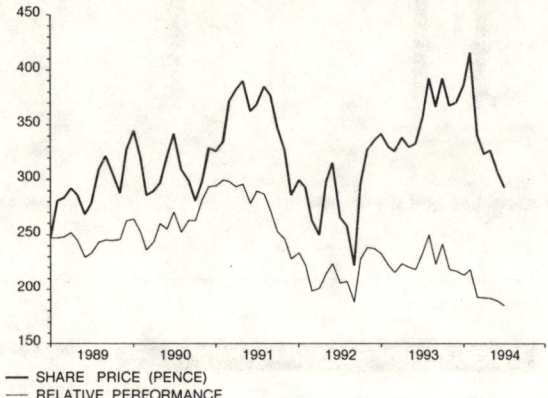

— SHARE PRICE (PENCE)
— RELATIVE PERFORMANCE

Financial record

		31/12/89	31/12/90	31/12/91	31/12/92	31/12/93
Total life premiums	£	810,600M	861,200	1,081M	1,134M	1,134M
General premiums	£	2,384M	2,453M	2,626M	3,037M	3,398M
Insurance result	£	-63,700	-551M	-834M	-243M	-243M
Pre-tax profit	£'000	318,600	-181M	-466M	-130M	221,700
Published retentions	£'000	116,400	-217M	-586M	-243M	60,600
Earnings per share	p	27.27	0.00	0.00	0.00	19.84
Dividend per share	p	12.50	14.00	14.25	14.25	14.75
Net assets per share	p	1,836	1,691	1,865	2,141	2,905
Shareholders' funds	£	2,937M	2,034M	1,684M	1,548M	2,012M
Borrowing ratio	%	6.0	15.0	21.0	24.0	20.0
Return on shareholders' equity	%	7.34	-5.22	-28.01	-8.32	8.47
Pre-tax profit margin	%	9.97	-5.46	-12.80	-2.99	4.89
Premiums per employee	£	n/a	n/a	n/a	n/a	n/a
Dividend cover		2.18	0.00	0.00	0.00	1.35
Premium growth	%	6.54	3.75	9.93	19.11	4.43
Earnings growth	%	-14.51	-100.00	0.00	0.00	0.00
Total insurance funds	£	11,418M	11,222M	12,908M	15,275M	20,857M
Total investments	£	5,750M	5,229M	5,663M	6,308M	7,194M
Number of employees		n/a	n/a	n/a	n/a	17,706

INSURANCE COMPANIES

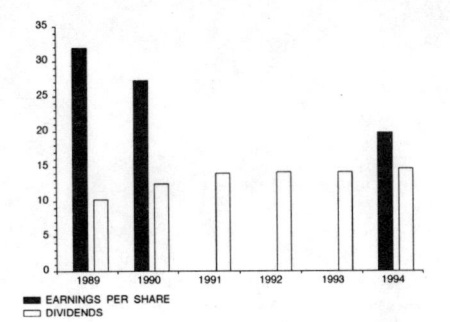

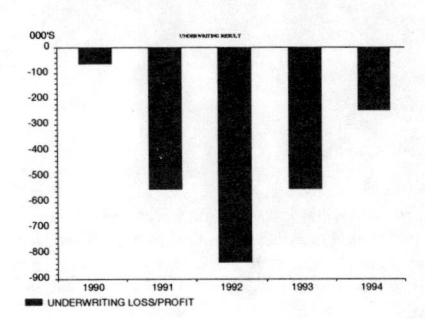

Earnings and dividends

Underwriting losses

SUN ALLIANCE plc

1 Bartholomew Lane, London EC2N 2AB
Tel: 0171 588 2345
Chairman Sir Christopher Benson
Chief executive Roger Taylor
Substantial shareholdings Chubb (US) 3%, Transatlantic Holdings (S Africa) 3%
Main subsidiaries Bradford Insurance, Legal Protection Group, London Assurance, National Vulcan, Phoenix Assurance, Swinton Holdings, Woolwich Life (49%)
Size £4.5 billion premiums, £2.6 billion stock market value, employees 17,700
5-year growth premiums n/a, earnings per share -27%, employment n/a
Solvency n/a
Political donations £50,000 Conservative Party
Charitable donations £299,000

Major developments
1959 merger of Alliance Assurance and Sun Insurance Office
1984 bought Phoenix Assurance
1988 30% stake in Swinton Insurance
1989 bought Australian and New Zealand business of AMEV Life Assurance; bought Royal Life (NZ)
1990 bought further 19% of Swinton Insurance
1991 bought Guardian Royal Exchange (NZ); bought further 26% of Swinton Insurance; first ever loss; row over loan to former chairman
1992 reduction of cross-holdings with Chubb Corporation; sold stakes in Commercial Union, London and Manchester; merger of Australian interests with those of Royal Insurance
1993 bought Hafnia's banking and insurance business (Denmark); Transatlantic took share stake

Corporate governance

Separate Chairman and Chief Executive Y
Number of Directors 13
Number of Non-Executive Directors 7
(6 Independent Directors)
Insulated Directors MD

Board Committees
Audit: Y   Remuneration: Y

Remuneration

Year end	31.12.91	31.12.92	31.12.93
Total board £M	1.76	1.70	1.72
% change	18	-4	1
Highest paid £	285,236	292,625	308,139
% change	10	3	5

Board
Taylor, Roger *Chief Executive*
Dew, M *Executive Director*
Hayes, Thomas Arthur *Executive Director*
Nelson, T S *Executive Director*
Petty, R *Executive Director*
Taylor, Peter Graham *Executive Director*
Ayling, Robert *Independent Non-Executive*
Fergusson, Sir Ewen *Independent Non-Executive*
Kemp-Welch, John *Independent Non-Executive*
Keswick, Henry *Independent Non-Executive*
Lord Kindersley *Independent Non-Executive*
de Rothschild, Leopold *Non-Executive*
Benson, Sir Christopher *Non-Executive Chairman*

SUPERMARKET GROUPS

Outlook

At the end of the Second World War there were no supermarkets in Britain. J Sainsbury opened the first one in Croydon, South London, in 1950. Now, the vast majority of grocery shopping is in supermarkets: the idea that a shopkeeper would pick the items off the shelf for the customer seems quaint, almost quirky.

Within the supermarket business, three companies have risen head and shoulders above their rivals. To say that they dominate the grocery business is misleading: the industry is too fragmented for that. But Tesco, Sainsbury and Argyll – the parent of Safeway – have shown themselves to be supremely proficient in exploiting the British shopper's liking for huge supermarkets with a vast range of goods and a large car park. In the supermarket game, big has proved itself to be beautiful. In 1992 Sainsbury overtook Marks & Spencer as Britain's most profitable retailer and pointed out that, over the previous two decades, its profits had grown by an annual compound rate of 23 per cent. Someone investing Sainsbury in 1973 saw his or her money multiply 55-fold in the following 20 years.

The last decade or so has been characterised by a steady migration of supermarkets from the high street to out-of-town and edge-of-town sites. The building of a new superstore – typically with more than 25,000 square feet of selling space – is expensive. A site alone can cost upwards of £15 million and it can cost a further £10 million to construct the building and car park, fit refrigerators and shelves and recruit the staff before the first jar of coffee is sold.

This is big money by anyone's standards, but, for the large groups, such investment has proved worthwhile: large purpose-built stores are relatively cheap to operate, they are efficient because they are purpose-built and, above all, they attract shoppers in their droves who are then content to spend upwards of £50 on a single trip to replenish their larders for the week. Take Sainsbury: in the 12 months to September 1992 it increased its number of superstores (those of 25,000 square feet or more) by 22 to 170; over the same period the number of outlets of 15,000 square feet or less actually declined. And look at the sums which Tesco has invested: in the five years to 1992 it opened 100 new outlets and 80 petrol stations, investing a total of £2.6 billion in store development. In 1992–3 the average size of new store opened was nearly 40,000 square feet. Argyll – rather different from its two main competitors in that it operates Lo-Cost and Presto supermarkets as well as Safeway – reckons to open a new Safeway once every two weeks.

Such investment has to be financed from somewhere. In 1991 Sainsbury – for the first time in the company's history – asked shareholders for money. They were asked to buy £489 million of new shares and readily agreed. In 1992 Tesco raised £572 million from its shareholders to help maintain the pace of its opening programme. And in 1993 Argyll – with its annual capital spending plans running somewhat behind its two bigger rivals at a mere £600 million – raised £150 million by issuing bonds.

These big three have, without question, been increasing their share of the total groceries market. By spending heavily on information technology that can automatically monitor what is being sold, place orders with manufacturers and even tell store managers the best way to arrange goods on their shelves so shoppers are most tempted to buy expensive, high-margin goods while looking for basic groceries, the superstore operators' profits have consistently grown.

But the apparently unstoppable march of the supermarkets has raised three key questions. First, is there not a danger of 'saturation', in which everyone in Britain is within easy reach of a superstore so that there is no scope for further growth? Second, if the superstores are gaining market share, who is losing it? And third, how seriously should the big supermarket groups take the threat posed by Britain's burgeoning discount grocery retailers? (Kwik Save is well established as a discounter, with numerous outlets, but the early 1990s have seen a dozen new entrants, selling a few hundred lines – as opposed to the 20,000 offered by a big superstore – at rock-bottom prices.)

The concern about saturation is an old one. The big groups argue, convincingly, that it will be some years before there is a superstore within 20 minutes' drive of every significant centre of population. Nevertheless, it is no coincidence that Sainsbury moved into the US in 1988, and that Tesco has just taken over a French retailer, Catteau. The idea is clearly that these geographical diversifications will provide growth in the next century when the market for superstores in Britain is mature.

The retailers who are losing out to the big, aggressive groups are easy to identify. They are often independent specialists like butchers, bakers and fishmongers. High-street supermarkets like Waitrose (part of the John Lewis Partnership) and the Co-Op have also lost market share. Asda, which in the late 1980s tried to ape the big three, has been forced to differentiate itself from the leaders by cutting prices to attract extra customers. Gateway has suffered, too, its parent having been burdened with huge debts after a highly leveraged buy-out in 1989.

And what of the impact of the discounters? Already they have had a major effect on the large supermarket groups, which have been forced to cut prices of basic items in an attempt to stem the loss of customers to new entrants like Aldi, Netto and Ed. The emergence of warehouse clubs – where customers buy in bulk at very low prices – poses a further threat. Indeed, some mainstream retailers like Asda, the Co-Op, Gateway and Argyll are experimenting with their own discount formats. All the major supermarket chains have been forced to respond by cutting prices in one way or another. The big food retailers have curtailed their opening programmes. They have accepted that they have to swallow one-off provisions to acknowledge that some of their stores are not worth as much as they thought. And the government has made it clear that planning permission for the edge-of-town retail sites, which have hitherto proved so profitable for superstore operators, will become much tougher to obtain.

Asda was the first of the large groups to recognise that it would have to adapt in order to survive. In the late 1980s the company had tried to ape the efforts of its bigger rivals' to be the smartest place to shop; it had also come up with the novel idea that people doing their Saturday shopping might also want to buy other items like fridges and televisions in a supermarket. Following a clear-out of the old management in 1992, Archie Norman, previously with Kingfisher, took over the helm and initiated a back-to-basics policy. He placed more emphasis on the core food business and on selling merchandise cheaply, in accordance with the company's tradition. There was also a £347 million rights issue to put Asda's finances back in order. As late as mid-1993, when Argyll, Sainsbury and Tesco were still trying to shrug off the threat of falling food prices and profit margins, it was Mr Norman who declared that 'the halcyon days in the industry are over'. He predicted, correctly, a continuing price war.

Greater price-consciousness among consumers finally prompted Sainsbury to launch its 'Essential for the Essentials' campaign in 1993, cutting the price of hundreds of popular lines. Yet the group's performance remained worse than observers had expected – particularly after taking into account the impact on profits of having to reduce the value of company properties.

In a similar vein, Tesco introduced brands at rock-bottom prices – so-called tertiary brands – to try to win back those customers who were deserting mainstream supermarkets for the discounters. It is also opening small, city-centre stores under the Tesco Metro name, as the scope for building new superstores becomes more limited.

Safeway held out longer than its main competitors, but finally conceded that it, too, was seeing profit margins fall. It adopted a policy which it called 'everyday low pricing' – the unoriginal catch-phrase which seems to have become the motto of every retailer in the mid-1990s.

Shares

Food retailing always had a reputation in the stock market as a safe, defensive sector. People have to buy food, whatever the economic climate. In bad times they might be more likely to buy basics rather than fancy tropical fruit and high-margin, ready-prepared meals, but the impact on supermarket profits is likely to be less than in other sectors because food is such a basic requirement. The record of the sector during the recession supports this defensive reputation, but its performance has been surprisingly volatile considering its supposedly stable business.

The 1987 crash brought investors rushing into the safety of the supermarkets, but there was a backlash as the economy appeared to be unaffected and the consumer boom took off. The onset of recession in 1990 brought with it a lengthy revival, however. The advance continued until economic recovery began in 1993, but not without interruption. Quite a marked decline occurred in the second half of 1991, partly due to false hopes of recovery and partly to fears of rights issues, and partly to perennial worries that the sector would be hit either by a Monopolies Commission inquiry or by superstore saturation, or both. Such concerns were temporarily overcome, but returned with a vengeance at the start of 1993 as the price war between supermarkets broke out. By the beginning of 1994 the worst seemed to be over, however, and the sector's rating began to recover.

Sainsbury was long seen as the most solid and most respected supermarket operator, and this was reflected in its extremely steady share price, advancing on the sector substantially in 1991 and 1992, despite already being very highly valued. But even the mighty Sainsbury could not escape the fall in the ratings for food retailers, as the full effect of price wars became apparent in 1993 and 1994.

Argyll had a similarly steady reputation. Following the excitement of its participation in the scandal-ridden Guinness bid for Distillers, it concentrated once again on supermarkets, and, with the purchase of the respected UK operation of Safeway, Argyll's shares maintained a remarkably steady path more or less in line with the sector. But then the shares also slumped in 1993/4.

Sainsbury's long-term rival Tesco has a more volatile record. Its shares did better than the sector during the late 1980s, not because it was perceived by most people to have surpassed its key rival, but because the shares began the period on a more lowly rating. During the late 1980s Tesco moved up towards Sainsbury's level, but this changed in 1991, however, when Tesco found itself suffering more than its rivals from the impact of recession. There was little consensus among investors on why Tesco's sales should be holding up less well than those of its main rivals, but it was generally believed that the company's profits were likely to be lower than had been thought, and that the shares should therefore be downgraded. Tesco remains a well-respected company, but its shares attract rather less respect than they did.

The star of the sector has undoubtedly been Wm Morrison, the Yorkshire chain which has gained more and more admirers since the late 1980s. Morrison seems to belie the notion that scale is essential; that smaller chains cannot compete with the giants because of the advantages of great size with regard to buying, distribution and technology. The company has proved that it is possible through sound management, close attention to detail and to customer markets. Morrison's shares leapt upwards as investors came to recognise that the company seemed to be one regional operator which could rapidly increase its business and its profits despite the continuing expansion of and fierce competition from the sector leaders.

While shares in Wm Morrison soared, those in Asda plunged, suggesting that the company might have been better sticking to its Yorkshire heritage rather than becoming a national chain just like the others. Asda had suffered in the mid-1980s from the fateful merger, and subsequent demerger, with MFI, and its attempt to catch up with its major rivals by acquiring a group of superstores from Gateway proved to be the final straw as far as many investors were concerned. The resulting excessive debt, at a difficult time for sales, led to dreaded rights issues and the prospect of continuing to be squeezed between the three highly regarded operators at the top, and the discount merchants at the bottom. Only when the group appointed a new chairman and chief executive, and appeared to have found a more coherent strategy, did the shares begin to pick themselves up again, and by 1993 investors were beginning to think that Asda could be due for a substantial recovery.

Worries about the discount operators were fuelled by the arrival of foreign operators in Britain. But Kwik Save has been keen to stress that it has been running a home-grown discount supermarket chain for years. It was long regarded by investors as a second-tier, if not second-rate, operation but the arrival of Hong Kong food group Dairy Farm with a substantial share stake and a new chief executive changed all that. The shares soared in 1989 on hopes that Dairy Farm might launch a full takeover bid, and consequently fell back again when those hopes were dashed. Subsequently Kwik Save entered a period of rapid and successful expansion, however, which persuaded investors that the company was worthy of attention in its own right, not just as a takeover target. Growing confidence in Kwik Save was dented slightly at the end of 1991, but investors were subsequently reassured that poor profits were just a temporary blip even though the shares slid slightly from a high point early in 1993.

Corporate conscience

Supermarketing is increasingly an international business, but British supermarket groups have not yet reached beyond Europe and the US, so they are not implicated in the issue of involvement with countries operating under repressive regimes. Nor are they exposed on military or nuclear matters. The main ethical issues that apply to supermarkets are the sale of alcohol and tobacco, tolerance of animal testing and intensive farming, and the use of ozone-depleting chemicals in refrigeration equipment. In addition, all the groups in this section have embraced Sunday trading.

Most have a reasonable record with regard to the environment, employment, and community affairs, although Wm Morrison is not the kind of company to worry about such things. All the others have strong equal opportunities and environment policies, although there are pitifully few women in senior management, and only Safeway and Tesco support Opportunity 2000. Sainsbury stands out as it has a female executive director, but scores negatively on the environment front because of tropical hardwoods sold through its Homebase DIY stores. Asda and Tesco take the lead in employment matters on account of their recognition of trade union representation.

Surprisingly, considering that supermarkets are not manufacturing companies, Asda, Argyll and Kwik Save all have water pollution records: Safeway was fined £3,000 in 1992 for allowing ammonia to be discharged into the Mersey. Less surprisingly, most have fallen foul of the ASA, with only Kwik Save and Wm Morrison escaping on this count.

Corporate governance

The supermarket sector retains significant family connections, which increases the need for better structures of corporate governance, although these are not always implemented in practice. On the whole, however, these are some of the better-run boardrooms, as well as being some of the best-run companies.

Argyll finally split the roles of chairman and chief executive in 1993 by promoting finance director Colin Smith to the position of chief executive. The company also strengthened the non-executive team in 1993 with the appointment of Ann Burdus and Neville Bain. Ms Burdus should bring considerable expertise to the remuneration committee, since she is a member of the Top Salaries Review Board. The appointment of Mr Bain as chair of the audit committee was a substantial improvement on the previous position when it was headed by the executive deputy chairman who also had overall responsibility for corporate finance. The company made very full disclosure of directors' pay in the 1994 annual report.

Asda made a full report on governance in its 1993 annual report, but there was only limited explanation of directors' pay. The ousting of the previous chairman and chief executive owed more to the power of investors than that of independent directors.

Kwik Save has a shortage of independent directors despite the heavy non-executive contingent on the board, which is due to representation by minority owner Dairy Farm. The chairman gave support to the Cadbury proposals in his 1993 report, while pointing out that some directors have contracts of up to five years. The accounts presented only outline details of directors' bonuses, and offered no explanation of the £64,000 benefits in kind.

Wm Morrison's finance director was quoted in 1992 as saying, 'Ken Morrison is the boss first, second and third.' But since Mr Morrison has worked in the business for 40 years, and owns 15 per cent of the shares, it is impossible to see how the company can argue against having a strong counterbalance in the boardroom. In a brief statement on corporate governance in the 1994 annual report, the directors said that no individual has 'unfettered powers', and while there are no plans to appoint non-executives, 'the board will review the situation from time to time'.

Sainsbury also remains a family-run company, but it is a rather larger one than Wm Morrison and has had longer to adjust to the requirements of its public status. Nevertheless, the proportion of independent directors needs to be increased, as does the level of disclosure of directors' pay, while David Sainsbury retains the top two posts.

Tesco has departed the furthest from its origins as a family business, and while it does not formally have a separate chief executive, David Malpas is managing director and Victor Benjamin is deputy chairman. Although five of the 14 directors are non-executive, the company's remuneration and audit committees are not staffed entirely by independents. Figures for performance-related pay are given, in addition to a rough guide to the basis on which bonuses are awarded.

ARGYLL GROUP

Share record

Return on shareholders' equity	%	14.23
5-year price high	p	432.0
5-year price low	p	190.3
Dividend yield	%	6.07
5-year high	%	6.25
5-year low	%	3.12
Price/earnings ratio		11.0
5-year high		20.0
5-year low		8.6

Share price performance (in pence)

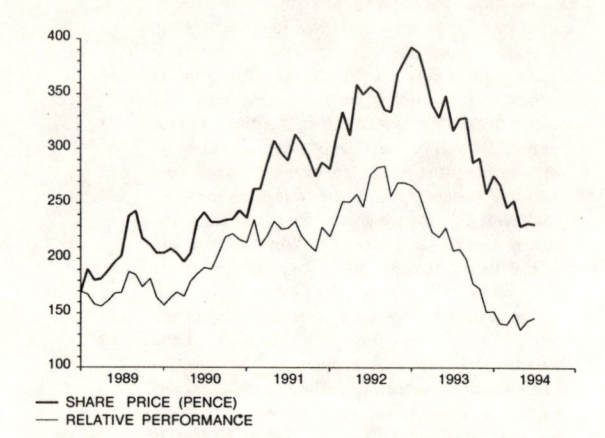

— SHARE PRICE (PENCE)
— RELATIVE PERFORMANCE

Financial record

		31/3/90	31/3/91	31/3/92	31/3/93	31/3/94
Total sales	£	3,920M	4,496M	4,729M	5,196M	5,608M
Pre-tax profit	£'000	227,500	290,800	360,500	415,200	635,200
Published retentions	£'000	94,700	126,900	232,400	180,700	124,200
Earnings per share	p	16.76	21.26	23.85	26.91	22.67
Dividend per share	p	7.07	8.49	9.75	10.90	11.50
Operating cash flow	£'000	-85,000	-162M	-27,300	-245M	-230M
Net assets per share	p	83.04	104.54	147.39	176.37	191.62
Net debt/(cash)	£'000	10,500	162,400	-204M	40,900	260,100
Shareholders' funds	£'000	683,100	815,400	1,446M	1,644M	1,776M
Return on capital	%	33.52	34.08	28.99	24.43	18.52
Profit margin	%	5.80	6.47	7.62	7.99	6.51
Sales per employee	£	60.62	68.02	72.05	78.81	81.81
Interest cover		-10.81	-97.28	-10.55	-15.12	110.67
Dividend cover		2.37	2.50	2.45	2.47	1.97
Sales increase	%	11.97	14.70	5.18	9.88	7.92
Earnings growth	%	25.42	26.81	12.21	12.84	-15.77
Investment x depreciation		5.74	5.91	5.80	6.87	3.96
Investment as % assets		26.17	24.61	22.60	24.85	20.55
Number of employees		64,660	66,099	65,635	65,937	68,546

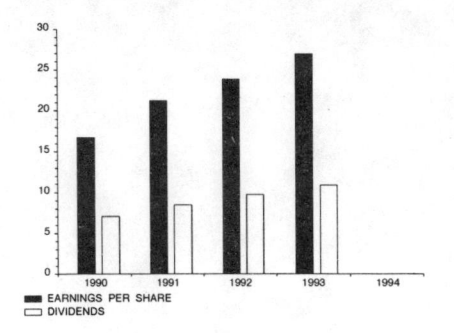

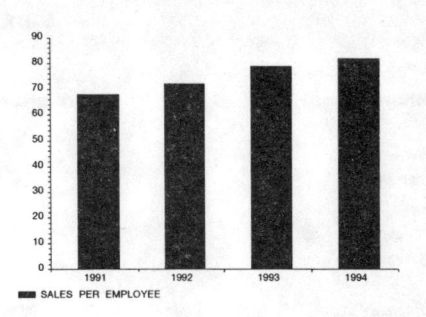

Earnings and dividends

Sales per employee

ARGYLL GROUP plc

6 Millington Road, Hayes, Middlesex UB3 4AY
Tel: 0181 848 8744
Chairman Sir Alistair Grant
Chief executive Colin Smith
Main brands and subsidiaries Lo-Cost, Presto, Safeway
Size £5.6 billion sales, £2.7 billion stock market value, 68,600 employees
5-year growth sales 43%, earnings per share 35%, employment 6%
Solvency debt = 15% shareholders' funds, interest cover 111 times
Political donations £30,000 Conservative Party
Charitable donations £568,000

Major developments
1962 Safeway began trading in the UK
1977 James Gulliver Associates formed after Gulliver left Oriel Foods
1981 Gulliver bought Oriel, including Lo-Cost
1982 Gulliver bought Allied Suppliers, including Presto
1983 merged with Amalgamated Distilled Products and changed name to Argyll
1985 bid £1.9 billion for Distillers
1986 raised Distillers bid to £2.5 billion but beaten by Guinness
1987 bought Safeway Food Stores Ltd
1988 James Gulliver left the group
1992 received £100 million compensation from Guinness over Distillers takeover

Corporate governance

Separate Chairman and Chief Executive Y
Number of Directors 11
Number of Non-Executive Directors 5
(4 Independent Directors)
Insulated Directors MD

Board Committees
Audit: Y   Remuneration: Y

Remuneration

Year end	31.03.91	31.03.92	3.04.93
Total board £M	2.30	4.33	2.72
% change		89	-37
Highest paid £	518,000	973,000	546,000
% change		88	-44

Board
Grant, Sir Alistair *Chairman*
Smith, Colin D *Chief Executive*
Kieran, Pat O *Executive Director*
Taylor, M Logan *Executive Director*
Webster, David G C *Executive Director*
Wotherspoon, Gordon *Executive Director*
Bain, Neville C *Independent Non-Executive*
Bidwell, Sir Hugh *Independent Non-Executive*
Burdus, Ann *Independent Non-Executive*
Plowden Roberts, H Martin *Ind. Non-Executive*
Leith, Prue M *Non-Executive*

ASDA GROUP

Share record

Return on shareholders'		
equity	%	6.02
5-year price high	p	173.1
5-year price low	p	21.9
Dividend yield	%	3.84
5-year high	%	12.17
5-year low	%	2.63
Price/earnings ratio		13.5
5-year high		27.0
5-year low		3.5

Share price performance (in pence)

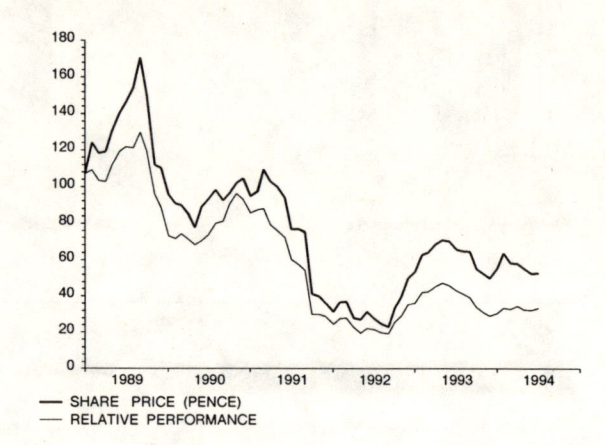

— SHARE PRICE (PENCE)
— RELATIVE PERFORMANCE

Financial record

		30/4/89	30/4/90	30/4/91	30/4/92	30/4/93
Total sales	£	2,709M	3,550M	4,468M	4,529M	4,614M
Pre-tax profit	£'000	246,800	184,700	168,300	88,200	140,800
Published retentions	£'000	111,700	152,900	62,000	-391M	113,500
Earnings per share	p	11.87	8.85	8.26	2.79	3.85
Dividend per share	p	3.92	3.92	3.92	2.00	1.60
Operating cash flow	£'000	-286M	42,500	-49,800	-90,200	181,000
Net assets per share	p	96.17	119.19	122.90	88.05	87.62
Net debt/(cash)	£'000	96,900	863,800	872,300	671,300	76,400
Shareholders' funds	£'000	941,500	1,084M	1,137M	1,108M	1,568M
Return on capital	%	19.96	16.09	15.59	10.86	11.07
Profit margin	%	8.51	5.27	3.86	1.90	3.03
Sales per employee	£	53.67	56.60	60.29	64.22	66.58
Interest cover		-5.68	7.26	2.92	1.90	3.75
Dividend cover		3.03	2.26	2.11	1.40	2.41
Sales increase	%	-0.73	31.07	25.85	1.37	1.87
Earnings growth	%	15.93	-25.44	-6.69	-66.21	38.00
Investment × depreciation		10.91	1.18	1.83	1.30	0.21
Investment as % assets		34.74	3.16	6.70	5.56	1.01
Number of employees		50,465	62,722	74,109	70,527	69,298

SUPERMARKET GROUPS

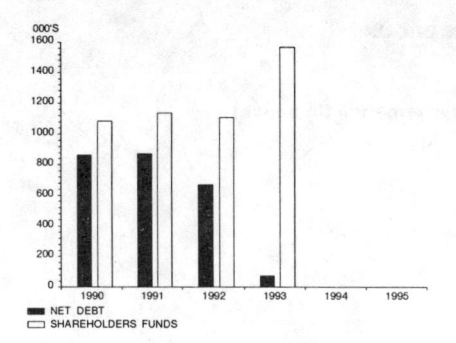

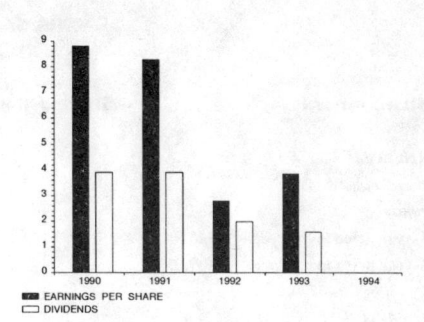

Debt and shareholders' funds

Earnings and dividends

ASDA GROUP plc

Asda House, Southbank, Great Wilson Street, Leeds LS11 5AD
Tel: 0113 243 5435
Chairman Patrick Gillam
Chief executive Archie Norman
Main subsidiaries Allied Maples, George Davies Partnership (21%), Gazeley Properties
Size £4.6 billion sales, £1.7 billion stock market value, 69,300 employees
5-year growth sales 70%, earnings per share -67%, employment 37%
Solvency debt = 5% shareholders' funds, interest cover 4 times
Political donations 0
Charitable donations £200,000

Major developments
1978 formed by merger of Associated Dairies and Allied Retailers
1985 merged with MFI Furniture Group to become Asda-MFI
1987 MFI bought out by managers
1989 bought 60 Gateway superstores
1991 management shake-up; move to Sunday trading
1993 sold Allied Maples

Corporate governance

Separate Chairman and Chief Executive Y
Number of Directors 10
Number of Non-Executive Directors 6
(6 Independent Directors)
Insulated Directors Not known

Board Committees
Audit: Y   Remuneration: Y

Remuneration

Year end	27.04.91	2.05.92	1.05.93
Total board £M	1.30	1.55	2.01
% change		19	30
Highest paid £	231,000	169,222	468,127
% change		-27	177

Board
Norman, Archie *Chief Executive*
Campbell, Tony *Executive Director*
Leighton, Allan *Executive Director*
Cox, Phil *Finance Director*
Ellen, Susan *Independent Non-Executive*
Gibson, Ian *Independent Non-Executive*
Knight, Frank *Independent Non-Executive*
Maude, Francis *Independent Non-Executive*
O'Brien, David *Independent Non-Executive*
Gillam, Patrick J *Non-Executive Chairman*

KWIK SAVE GROUP

Share record

Return on shareholders' equity	%	25.22
5-year price high	p	843.0
5-year price low	p	409.0
Dividend yield	%	4.43
5-year high	%	4.46
5-year low	%	1.99
Price/earnings ratio		9.1
5-year high		20.3
5-year low		9.1

Share price performance (in pence)

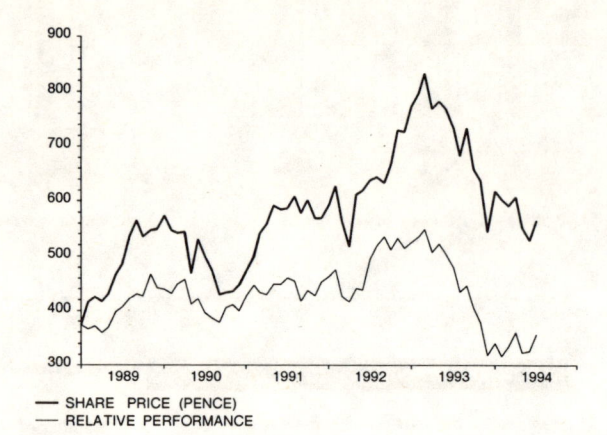

— SHARE PRICE (PENCE)
— RELATIVE PERFORMANCE

Financial record

		31/8/89	31/8/90	31/8/91	31/8/92	31/8/93
Total sales	£	1,181M	1,446M	1,785M	2,319M	2,651M
Pre-tax profit	£'000	73,157	85,137	101,961	110,475	126,200
Published retentions	£'000	32,166	36,824	45,351	49,559	57,300
Earnings per share	p	31.53	36.15	44.22	47.78	55.56
Dividend per share	p	10.50	12.10	14.70	16.00	18.30
Operating cash flow	£'000	4,300	-7,122	-12,080	-9,423	13,000
Net assets per share	p	117.05	141.12	156.51	188.42	220.99
Net debt/(cash)	£'000	-39,499	-33,057	-2,062	6,696	-2,400
Shareholders' funds	£'000	181,114	218,382	244,254	294,478	347,800
Return on capital	%	41.84	43.22	45.01	42.84	40.38
Profit margin	%	6.19	5.89	5.71	4.76	4.76
Sales per employee	£	117.45	124.19	135.08	156.23	119.44
Interest cover		-14.91	-16.59	-30.81	45.89	632.00
Dividend cover		3.00	2.99	3.01	2.99	3.04
Sales increase	%	26.81	22.36	23.45	29.95	14.33
Earnings growth	%	33.40	14.64	22.34	8.05	16.27
Investment x depreciation		4.36	3.52	4.93	3.04	2.87
Investment as % assets		22.91	21.94	29.98	21.28	19.41
Number of employees		10,059	11,640	13,211	14,843	22,196

SUPERMARKET GROUPS

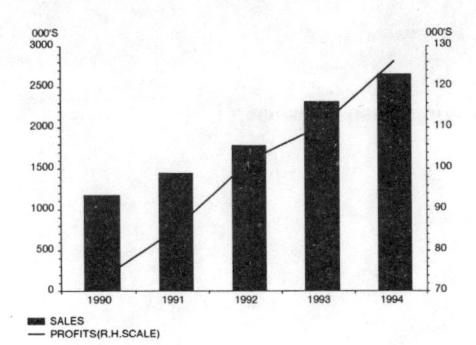

Profits and sales

Sales per employee

KWIK SAVE GROUP plc

12th Floor, Silkhouse Court, Tithebarn Street, Liverpool L2 2LE
Tel: 0151 236 7551
Chairman Sir Timothy Harford
Chief executive Graeme Bowler
Substantial shareholdings Dairy Farm 29%
Main subsidiaries Colemans, Tates
Size £2.7 billion sales, £0.8 billion stock market value, 22,200 employees
5-year growth sales 124%, earnings per share 76%, employment 121%
Solvency debt n/a, interest cover 632 times
Political donations 0
Charitable donations £81,839

Major developments

1965 first Kwik Save stored opened at Rhyl, N Wales
1970 became a public company
1981 bought Colemans
1986 bought Tates
1987 Dairy Farm bought 25% stake
1989 bought Victor Value chain
1991 bought 42 stores from Gateway; bought Liquorsave

Corporate governance

Separate Chairman and Chief Executive Y
Number of Directors 12
Number of Non-Executive Directors 8
(4 Independent Directors)
Insulated Directors All

Board Committees
Audit: Y   Remuneration: Y

Remuneration

Year end	31.08.91	29.08.92	28.08.93
Total board £M	0.91	1.01	1.40
% change	8	12	32
Highest paid £	287,000	326,000	310,000
% change	14	14	-5

Board

Bowler, Graeme *Chief Executive*
Hughes, Peter *Executive Director*
Murphy, John Conan *Executive Director*
Pretty, Derek *Finance Director*
Cook, Derek *Independent Non-Executive*
Hill, Ian Frederick Donald *Ind. Non-Executive*
Parr, Thomas Donald *Independent Non-Executive*
Howell-Price, Owen P *Non-Executive*
Keswick, Simon Lindley *Non-Executive*
Leach, Charles Guy Rodney *Non-Executive*
Seabrook, Graeme *Non-Executive*
Harford, Sir Timothy *Non-Executive Chairman*

SUPERMARKET GROUPS

Wm MORRISON SUPERMARKETS

Share record

Return on shareholders' equity

Return on shareholders' equity	%	16.0
5-year price high	p	175.0
5-year price low	p	44.5
Dividend yield	%	1.02
5-year high	%	1.25
5-year low	%	0.62
Price/earnings ratio		13.9
5-year high		27.3
5-year low		11.0

Share price performance (in pence)

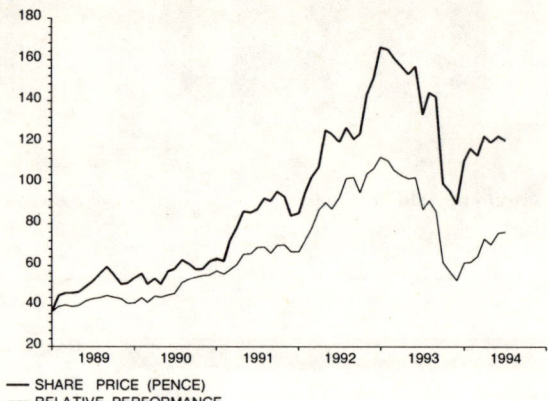

— SHARE PRICE (PENCE)
— RELATIVE PERFORMANCE

Financial record

		31/1/90	31/1/91	31/1/92	31/1/93	31/1/94
Total sales	£'000	775,681	909,599	1,118M	1,317M	1,538M
Pre-tax profit	£'000	36,647	50,077	61,683	83,838	97,959
Published retentions	£'000	19,971	28,008	35,189	48,572	53,832
Earnings per share	p	3.84	5.32	6.27	7.5	9.74
Dividend per share	p	0.43	0.51	0.67	0.8	1.00
Operating cash flow	£'000	1,841	-66,781	-32,599	-2,928	-14,653
Net assets per share	p	28.37	43.72	64.87	62.68	82.32
Net debt/(cash)	£'000	10,184	74,909	39,152	41,468	55,866
Shareholders' funds	£'000	159,262	188,358	322,750	371,940	426,034
Return on capital	%	27.09	27.02	20.84	20.43	20.98
Profit margin	%	4.71	5.49	5.52	6.37	6.37
Sales per employee	£	62.41	65.98	68.73	74.05	73.87
Interest cover		10.87	10.71	16.56	-19.40	-48.79
Dividend cover		9.03	10.50	9.41	9.37	9.74
Sales increase	%	28.50	17.26	22.91	17.78	16.84
Earnings growth	%	42.71	38.61	17.82	19.48	29.90
Investment x depreciation		7.67	6.36	5.67	4.08	4.70
Investment as % assets		27.35	22.73	22.31	18.68	19.42
Number of employees		12,429	13,787	16,265	17,782	20,827

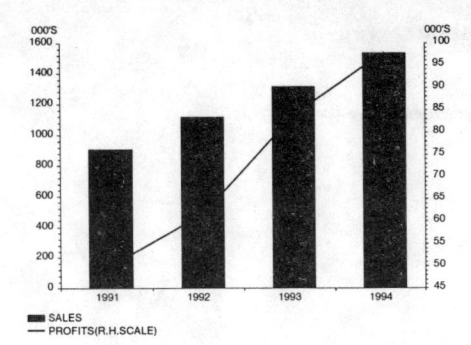

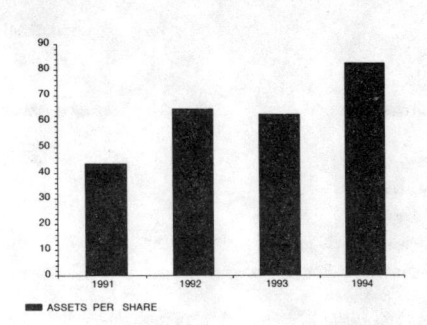

Sales and profits

Assets per share

Wm MORRISON SUPERMARKETS plc

Hilmore House, Thornton Road, Bradford BD8 9AX
Tel: 01274 494166
Chairman and managing director Kenneth Morrison
Substantial shareholders Kenneth Morrison 15%
Size £1.5 billion sales, £884 million stock market value, 20,800 employees
5-year growth sales 98%, earnings per share 153%, employment 68%
Solvency debt = 13% shareholders' funds, interest cover n/a
Political donations 0
Charitable donations £69,000

Major developments
1940 registered as a private company
1962 first supermarket opened
1967 converted into a public company

Corporate governance

Separate Chairman and Chief Executive N
Number of Directors 7
Number of Non-Executive Directors 0
(0 Independent Directors)
Insulated Directors Not known

Board Committees
Audit: N   Remuneration: N

Remuneration

Year end	31.01.92	30.01.93	30.01.94
Total board £M	0.90	1.05	1.21
% change	8	17	15
Highest paid £	210,131	284,000	300,000
% change	29	1	6

Board
Morrison, Kenneth D *Executive Chairman*
Buttle, George D *Executive Director*
Dowd, John *Executive Director*
Hutchinson, Keith *Executive Director*
Melnyk, Marie M *Executive Director*
Owen, Roger A *Executive Director*
Ackroyd, Martin *Finance Director*

J SAINSBURY

Share record

Return on shareholders' equity	%	16.88
5-year price high	p	582.0
5-year price low	p	243.2
Dividend yield	%	3.34
5-year high	%	3.72
5-year low	%	2.07
Price/earnings ratio		14.4
5-year high		21.0
5-year low		11.9

Share price performance (in pence)

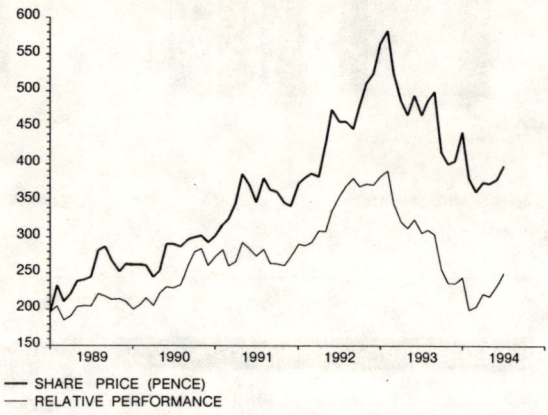

— SHARE PRICE (PENCE)
— RELATIVE PERFORMANCE

Financial record

		31/3/89	31/3/90	31/3/91	31/3/92	13/3/93
Total sales	£	5,659M	6,930M	7,813M	8,696M	9,686M
Pre-tax profit	£'000	352,300	420,700	505,700	632,200	735,200
Published retentions	£'000	175,300	221,300	240,000	284,500	325,500
Earnings per share	p	14.97	18.55	22.28	25.06	28.55
Dividend per share	p	4.99	6.03	7.27	8.75	10.00
Operating cash flow	£'000	-146M	-71,000	-183M	-136M	-65,900
Net assets per share	p	100.38	129.02	155.10	187.13	210.15
Net debt/(cash)	£'000	743,500	794,600	741,100	449,700	569,800
Shareholders' funds	£	1,168M	1,406M	1,672M	2,641M	3,029M
Return on capital	%	29.44	29.59	28.52	26.40	21.98
Profit margin	%	5.95	6.05	6.47	7.26	7.59
Sales per employee	£	64.10	69.30	71.69	77.10	80.63
Interest cover		36.44	24.54	15.20	-48.69	-201.78
Dividend cover		3.00	3.08	3.07	2.86	2.86
Sales increase	%	18.10	22.47	12.74	11.29	11.39
Earnings growth	%	17.31	23.95	20.07	12.49	13.93
Investment x depreciation		5.13	4.45	4.79	4.70	4.47
Investment as % assets		17.46	16.82	18.68	16.62	15.54
Number of employees		88,283	100,001	108,987	112,784	120,119

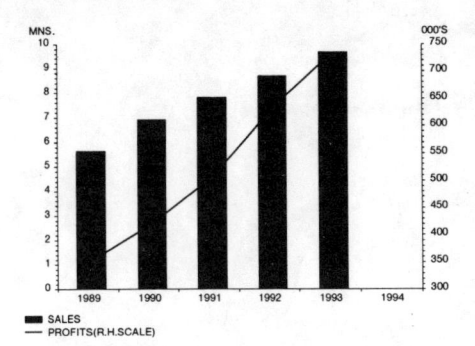

Sales and profits

Sales per employee

J SAINSBURY plc

Stamford House, Stamford Street, London SE1 9LL
Tel: 0171 921 6000
Chairman and chief executive David Sainsbury
Substantial shareholdings Sainsbury trusts 25%,
Main subsidiaries Haverhill Meat Products,
Homebase (75%), Savacentre, Shaw's Supermarkets (US)
Size £9.7 billion sales, £7.1 billion stock market value, 120,100 employees
5-year growth sales 71%, earnings per share 91%, employment 36%
Solvency debt = 18% shareholders' funds, interest cover n/a
Political donations 0
Charitable donations £1.4 million

Major developments
1869 business founded in London
1950 first supermarket opened
1969 Lord John Sainsbury became chairman
1973 became public
1975 Savacentre concept launched with BhS
1981 first Homebase opened
1986 bought stake in Shaw's Supermarkets (US)
1987 took full control of Shaw's
1989 bought outstanding 50% interest in Savacentre from Storehouse
1990 bought outstanding 50% interest in Haverhill Meat Products
1991 began Sunday trading
1992 Lord Sainsbury handed over chair to cousin David

Corporate governance
Separate Chairman and Chief Executive N
Number of Directors 18
Number of Non-Executive Directors 5
(5 Independent Directors)
Insulated Directors All execs

Board Committees
Audit: Y   Remuneration: Y

Remuneration

Year end	16.03.91	14.03.92	13.03.93
Total board £M	2.70	3.20	3.90
% change		19	22
Highest paid £	217,000	280,000	378,000
% change		29	35

Board
Sainsbury, D J *Chairman & Chief Executive*
Vyner, R T *Deputy Chairman & Managing Director*
Quarmby, D A *Joint Managing Director*
Adriano, D B *Executive Director*
Adshead, J E *Executive Director*
Clapham, David *Executive Director*
Clark, R A *Executive Director*
Cooper, R *Executive Director*
Coull, I D *Executive Director*
Harvey, C I *Executive Director*
Whitbread, R P *Executive Director*
Worrall, K C *Executive Director*
Thorne, R P *Finance Director*
Ashworth, Dr John M *Independent Non-Executive*
Barnes, J H G *Independent Non-Executive*
Heiser, Sir Terence *Independent Non-Executive*
Lady Eccles of Moulton *Independent Non-Executive*
Spooner, Sir James *Independent Non-Executive*

TESCO

Share record

Return on shareholders' equity	%	14.94
5-year price high	p	296.0
5-year price low	p	174.7
Dividend yield	%	4.16
5-year high	%	5.10
5-year low	%	2.16
Price/earnings ratio		12.9
5-year high		18.6
5-year low		8.7

Share price performance (in pence)

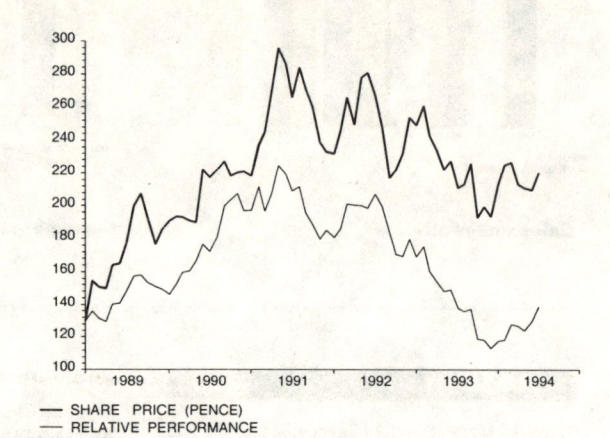

— SHARE PRICE (PENCE)
— RELATIVE PERFORMANCE

Financial record

		28/2/90	28/2/91	29/2/92	28/2/93	28/2/94
Total sales	£	5,402M	6,346M	7,097M	7,582M	8,600M
Pre-tax profit	£'000	326,600	417,100	545,000	583,200	564,800
Published retentions	£'000	186,500	205,400	273,300	278,900	146,100
Earnings per share	p	13.69	17.42	19.91	21.72	21.38
Dividend per share	p	4.17	5.25	6.30	7.10	7.75
Operating cash flow	£'000	-133M	-362M	-336M	-135M	-93,900
Net assets per share	p	103.49	154.07	162.49	178.24	190.53
Net debt/(cash)	£'000	316,600	-177M	326,800	471,100	735,700
Shareholders' funds	£	1,254M	2,160M	2,447M	2,753M	2,749M
Return on capital	%	24.55	22.43	21.21	19.37	16.99
Profit margin	%	6.05	6.57	7.68	7.69	6.57
Sales per employee	£	64.91	72.37	81.55	88.09	137.88
Interest cover		-32.33	-20.84	-7.32	-17.51	-77.44
Dividend cover		3.28	3.32	3.16	3.06	2.76
Sales increase	%	14.50	17.48	11.84	6.82	13.43
Earnings growth	%	21.16	27.27	14.30	9.08	-1.54
Investment x depreciation		5.77	7.89	6.42	4.11	3.12
Investment as % assets		22.86	27.47	20.31	13.11	15.00
Number of employees		83,224	87,691	87,033	86,066	62,374

SUPERMARKET GROUPS

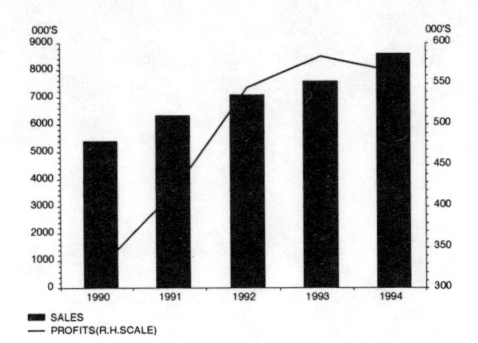

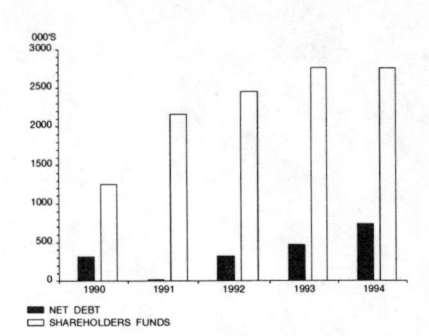

Sales and profits

Debt and shareholders' funds

TESCO plc

Tesco House, Delamare Road, Cheshunt,
Hertfordshire EN8 9SL
Tel: 01992 632222
Chairman and chief executive Sir Ian MacLaurin
Main subsidiaries Catteau (France)
Size £8.6 billion sales, £4.7 billion stock market value, 62,400 employees
5-year growth sales 59%, earnings per share 56%, employment -25%
Solvency debt = 27% shareholders' funds, interest cover n/a
Political donations 0
Charitable donations £285,000

Major developments
1932 Tesco Stores formed to acquire Jack Cohen's retailing interests
1947 became public
1977 stopped giving Greenshield stamps
1987 bought Hillards
1991 began Sunday trading
1993 bought 90% Cotteau
1994 bought Wm Low

Corporate governance

Separate Chairman and Chief Executive N
Number of Directors 15
Number of Non-Executive Directors 6
(5 Independent Directors)
Insulated Directors MD, JMD

Board Committees
Audit: Y   Remuneration: Y

Remuneration

Year end	29.02.92	27.02.93	27.02.94
Total board £M	5.51	5.31	5.05
% change	-18	-4	-5
Highest paid £M	1.00	0.97	0.79
% change	-32	-4	-18

Board
MacLaurin, Sir Ian Charter *Chairman & Chief Executive*
Malpas, David *Managing Director*
Ager, Rowley *Executive Director*
Benjamin, Victor *Executive Director*
Darnell, Michael *Executive Director*
Gildersleeve, John *Executive Director*
Leahy, Terry *Executive Director*
Wemms, Michael *Executive Director*
Reid, David *Finance Director*
Baroness O'Cathain *Independent Non-Executive*
Gardiner, John A *Independent Non-Executive*
Jones, Dr Gwyn *Independent Non-Executive*
Padovan, John *Independent Non-Executive*
Pilmott, Graham *Independent Non-Executive*
Tuffin, Dennis *Non-Executive*

WATER COMPANIES

Outlook

The privatisation of the water industry in 1989 was complex and controversial. Ten companies were sold off to the public, each at a different price and with a different formula for permitted price increases, while a further 29 statutory water companies not owned by government came under the aegis of the new Water Act. Water, essential to human life, was an emotive subject, and provoked deep debate about the morality of placing the industry wholly in the private sector, with the consequent priority of producing profits. Water companies owned large areas of natural beauty, especially around reservoirs, and there was concern about commercial development marring the countryside. Above all, the privatisation exercise was seen as a blatant manoeuvre by government to pass on the financial burden of updating Britain's antiquated water mains and sewers to others. In theory, the cost was to be borne by risk-taking investors. In practice, the customer picked up the tab.

The government, the water companies, and the financial advisers in the City worked their magic, however, and floated off the whole operation to a public eager for short-term gains and protected by the government's promise that the companies would be able to pass on the cost of upgrading the infrastructure to consumers through higher prices. But the industry continued to attract controversy. Within months French utility giants like Lyonnais des Eaux, Compagnie Générale des Eaux and Bouygues started to increase their stakes in or make takeover bids for a number of British water companies. Even before privatisation the French-owned companies had stakes in 16 of the statutory water companies. At one point it seemed that the UK consumer and the taxpayer – whose enforced munificence had delivered the companies to the market effectively free of debt – may have transformed the finances of the water companies solely for the benefit of stock market punters and French utility groups.

However, chauvinism soon raised its head, leading to the unusual sight of free-market disciple Peter Lilley, then the new Secretary of State for Trade and Industry, issuing dire threats in July 1990 about predatory French acquisitions of chunks of British industry. The Monopolies Commission concluded that Générale des Eaux's stake in Mid-Kent Water was against the public interest. The government breathed a sigh of relief, and Mr Lilley decided that the Commission's suggestion that the French should give 'effective undertakings' would not work. Instead, he ordered the regulator, Ofwat, to arrange for the French to reduce their shareholding and have no board representation. The French backed off, though some of them still have stakes in a number of British water companies.

The publication of the annual reports of the newly privatised companies created fresh controversy, revealing that many directors had awarded themselves huge pay increases. Not content with that, several companies splashed out on questionable acquisitions: why did Welsh Water, for instance, need hotels, country clubs, restaurants and Georgian lodges – and a near 15 per cent stake in South Wales Electricity?

The answer is that water companies have statutory obligations to provide water and dispose of sewage – both areas of business regulated by Ofwat. But because regulation can be expected to limit profits growth, the companies have been keen to acquire such growth by building up their non-regulated businesses as fast as possible. Water process engineering companies have been acquired, and large overseas contracts have been secured. Most of Mexico City's water and waste-water network is being upgraded by consortia, either led by or including British water companies. North West Water, whose inheritance included some of the worst areas of industrial pollution as well as beauty spots like the Lake District, successfully led a consortium which in 1994 won a contract to rebuild Malaysia's water and waste-water system – a £1.25 billion project spread over a period of at least 18 years. The Malaysian contract was won just as political relations with Malaysia broke down and North West Water parted company with its chief executive, Robert Thian. However, most water companies have realised that it is unwise to diversify into businesses not closely related to their core activities. Welsh Water, for example, has sold its electricity shares and is pulling out of hotel management.

Privatisation was done on the cheap. That was the official conclusion of Sir John Bourn, head of the National Audit Office. He condemned the government's hasty sell-off of the water industry, claiming that the £3.6 billion raised was £2.2 billion less than expected. But at least the huge infrastructure projects to improve Britain's water and waste-water operations – long delayed because of the implications of public-sector borrowing – are now under way. And the government is happy to agree to European Community legislation to improve the quality of water and British beaches, knowing that it no longer has to foot the bill. Instead, the burden has fallen on consumers, who have been faced with mounting bills. In 1993 and 1994 Ian Byatt, director general of Ofwat, frequently voiced his concern about customers' ability to pay. When in July 1994 he announced the industry's new price regime for the next 10 years, rises were limited on the whole to covering inflation and the cost of capital investment projects required by legislation. He looked to the water companies to finance any other improvements by establishing greater efficiency in their organisations.

Shares

Shares in the water sector have risen substantially compared to the market as a whole since the flotation of the water companies at the end of 1989. A feeling that these companies were subject to the most benign regulator (Ofwat), and hence would have the greatest scope for dividend increases, helped push up the share price from the summer of 1990 into the spring of 1991. The sector then suffered from political uncertainty during the rest of 1991, and until the general election in the following year, because of fears that a Labour government would either take water back into government ownership, or at least impose a fiercer regulatory regime. But the share price soared following the Conservative victory and remained at roughly the same relative position into the spring of 1993. At that point, some nervousness began to set in as investors started to focus on the impending regulatory review (in the summer of 1994). There appeared to be a conflict between the investment required by each company to meet targets for improved water quality and the maximum level of price increases preferred by the regulator – the implication being that the desire to keep prices down and the need to spend money on improving water quality would reduce the water companies' profits, and hence shareholders' dividends.

At first the performance of the shares in the 10 companies differed considerably following flotation, based largely on investors' perceptions of the level of price increases and capital investment required by each company. But these differences soon evened out, leaving little to choose between the companies. Initially the shares of Southern and Wessex fared worst, but both recovered before the beginning of 1992. Shares in Wessex went up steeply at the beginning of 1991 when the company produced the highest rise for the sector in the half-year dividend (in December 1991), and then again in February 1992 when Wessex announced a joint venture with the giant US waste company Waste Management International (WMI) to create Wessex Waste Management. This was the kind of deal which investors wanted from the utilities: a departure from the regulated activities whose profits growth was likely to be restricted in the long term, but without entailing the heavy exposure and high risk which a move into a completely new area would involve. In this case the experience of WMI, and that company's cash, helped lessen the perceived risk. After an initial rebound prior to the election, shares in Wessex continued to strengthen relative to the sector, right into 1993, but then slipped when the company asked shareholders to fund the acquisition of NFC's waste-management business, and when the US partner took a greater stake in the water company's shares.

Northumbrian's shares also began to gain new fans once it started to demonstrate some skills in diversification, but they did not gain momentum until the summer of 1992 when the company produced better-than-expected profits from its core business, thanks to one of the more generous pricing formulae, tight cost control, and some deft financial management which brought a one-off profit of £7 million from a stock market investment fund. Throughout 1993 and the early part of 1994 only Yorkshire and Welsh Water showed any significant independence from the rest of the pack. Shares in Welsh Water benefited from some of the most optimistic expectations for the dividend, while Yorkshire's shares, on the other hand, suffered a reaction to the sharp rise in the price during 1992.

As 1993 wore on, analysis of the individual companies in the sector began to be overwhelmed by the political issues, which dominated share sentiment until the new regulatory agreement was in place in the summer of 1994. From the end of 1993 the sector as a whole fell sharply, reflecting growing fears concerning the severity of the regulatory review, in addition to worries about interest rates.

Corporate conscience

Many issues of conscience do not touch most of the privatised water companies, although the diversifications of some companies do bring them into areas that are ethically sensitive. For example, Thames is involved in animal testing, through PCI Membrane Systems, which makes chemicals for effluent treatment. It also has subsidiaries in countries with oppressive regimes such as Egypt and Nigeria. Its subsidiary Stella-Meta Filters exports water purifiers for military purposes and another company, PWT Projects, supplies radioactive waste-treatment services to the nuclear industry.

Welsh Water also has a military connection through Acer, while North West is involved in the nuclear industry (through Wallace & Tiernan) as well as having interests in Brazil and Mexico. Severn Trent is involved in Mexico, and through the waste-management company Biffa it has mining interests, as does Southern. Both Northumbrian and North West Water use ozone-destroying chemicals as solvents in their manufacturing businesses.

The employment policies of the 10 companies vary widely. Wessex and Severn Trent have the strongest equal opportunities policies, while those of Anglian, Southern, Welsh and Yorkshire are above average, unlike those of the other companies. Welsh Water is the only water company to support Opportunity 2000. Both Southern and Wessex have reasonably strong trade union representation. Yorkshire is the only company to have been convicted of health and safety offences, on 2 occasions.

The business of water provision and treatment

means that environmental issues are of central concern in this industry, however. The record is mixed and, on the whole, not good. Surprisingly, North West Water does not appear to have environmental policies worth the name, while few have had independent audits. This apparently casual approach is borne out in the pollution record. Each of these companies has at least one conviction: Welsh Water had 18 from 1990 to 1993; and Severn Trent received the maximum fine (£22,000) for one of its 12 convictions during this period, when it was found guilty of causing sewage to enter the River Churnet.

Because these are regulated utilities, EIRIS is able to monitor how well (or badly) they treat their customers. In 1991/2 South West received the highest level of complaints (17.8 per 10,000 connections) and has a poor record on sewage treatment (almost a quarter of its treatment works did not comply with discharge consents in 1991/2). None of the companies has an unblemished record, however. Thames stands out as providing drinking water in 1992 with a 91 per cent probability of containing some substance which does not comply with required standards of water quality. This dwarfs Anglian's figure of 52 per cent, which is high compared with the other companies. Anglian was the only company which did not report at least one incident of below-standard water quality to the Drinking Water Inspectorate in 1991, while Welsh Water recorded 8 incidents and Severn Trent 14. Southern also had the highest disconnection rate (29.3 per 10,000 connections), while North West and Thames reported above-average water losses through leakage.

Corporate governance

In the newly privatised water industry, concern over matters of corporate governance has focused on the pay and perks of top executives which have soared despite worries about rising consumer charges. While it was largely the same executives running the companies who were in charge before privatisation, the salaries for chief executives rose by as much as 290 per cent once the industry was sold off. Generous share-option packages, agreed at the time of privatisation, started to come into operation from January 1993, giving the same executives benefits worth up to £250,000. Absolute salaries and perks are still at the lower end of the range for large companies, which suggests further 'catching up' might take place, particularly if profits continue to move ahead strongly – although in some cases the movement in salaries has been downwards from 1992.

None of these companies has an excellent record on corporate governance and disclosure, which is disappointing and a little surprising considering their recent reconstitution and the level of public interest that they arouse. All have strong non-executive representation, in most cases forming a majority of the board, and most now have the requisite committees, after some initial hesitation in introducing them. South West has gone furthest in explaining bonus payments, while Thames stands out for negative reasons, having directors insulated from re-election and being the only company to make a political contribution – although this stopped in 1993. Anglian has taken up the fashion for distributing a separate annual review to many shareholders, which provides only summary financial information and includes no details of directors' pay.

ANGLIAN WATER

Share record

Return on shareholders' equity	%	11.58
5-year price high	p	608.0
5-year price low	p	240.0
Dividend yield	%	5.89
5-year high	%	8.51
5-year low	%	4.44
Price/earnings ratio		11.1
5-year high		13.8
5-year low		5.8

Share price performance (in pence)

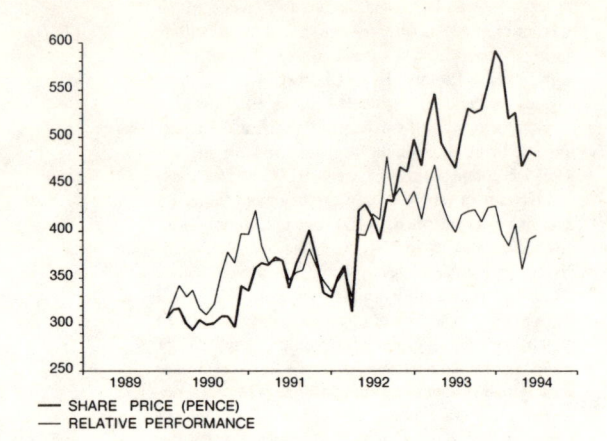

— SHARE PRICE (PENCE)
— RELATIVE PERFORMANCE

Financial record

		31/3/90	31/3/91	31/3/92	31/3/93
Total sales	£'000	401,300	460,600	523,100	583,200
Pre-tax profit	£'000	89,100	152,600	175,800	182,200
Published retentions	£'000	38,300	83,800	95,400	104,100
Earnings per share	p	43.09	45.94	53.19	55.28
Dividend per share	p	15.31	17.50	19.30	21.10
Operating cash flow	£'000	-98,700	-20,600	-103M	-49,700
Net assets per share	p	414.62	532.98	615.33	683.06
Net debt/(cash)	£'000	183,400	194,700	303,800	392,500
Shareholders' funds	£	1,134M	1,226M	1,337M	1,409M
Return on capital	%		12.79	12.60	11.85
Profit margin	%	22.20	33.13	33.61	31.28
Sales per employee	£	92.72	98.78	100.13	105.06
Interest cover		2.29	9.41	8.62	7.17
Dividend cover		2.81	2.63	2.76	2.62
Sales increase	%		14.78	13.57	11.49
Earnings growth	%		6.61	15.77	3.94
Investment x depreciation		5.72	5.67	5.81	4.58
Investment as % assets		13.10	13.81	14.94	13.03
Number of employees		4,328	4,663	5,224	5,551

Earnings and dividends

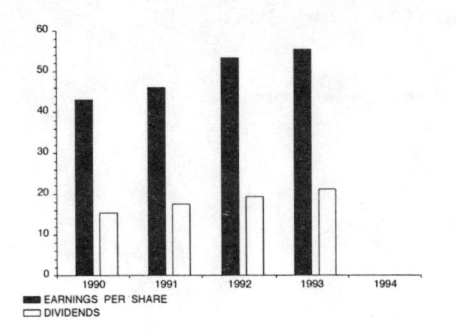

Sales per employee

ANGLIAN WATER plc

Anglian House, Ambury Road, Huntingdon, Cambs PE18 6NZ
Tel: 01480 443000
Chairman Bernard Henderson
Group managing director Alan Smith
Main subsidiaries Alphens Environmental
Size £583 million sales, £1.4 billion stock market value, 5,600 employees
Solvency debt = 28% shareholders' funds, interest cover 7 times
Political donations 0
Charitable donations £41,000

Major developments
1989 privatised
1992 bought Rosewater Engineering
1993 bought Nordic Water (Sweden)

Corporate governance
Separate Chairman and Chief Executive Y
Number of Directors 11
Number of Non-Executive Directors 7
(7 Independent Directors)
Insulated Directors None

Board Committees
Audit: Y Remuneration: Y

Remuneration

Year end	31.03.91	31.03.92	31.03.93
Total board £M	0.54	0.59	0.98
% change		9	65
Highest paid £	96,000	107,000	163,000
% change		12	52

Board
Smith, Alan *Managing Director*
Henderson, Bernard *Executive Chairman*
Green, John *Executive Director*
Mellor, Chris *Finance Director*
Cator, Francis *Independent Non-Executive*
Challen, David *Independent Non-Executive*
de Moller, June *Independent Non-Executive*
Earl of Cranbrook *Independent Non-Executive*
Gourlay, Robin *Independent Non-Executive*
Jewson, Richard W *Independent Non-Executive*
Nichols, Dinah *Independent Non-Executive*

NORTHUMBRIAN WATER GROUP

Share record

Return on shareholders' equity   %   7.92
5-year price high   p   757.0
5-year price low   p   240.0

Dividend yield   %   5.39
5-year high   %   8.91
5-year low   %   3.81

Price/earnings ratio   9.1
5-year high   13.9
5-year low   3.4

Share price performance (in pence)

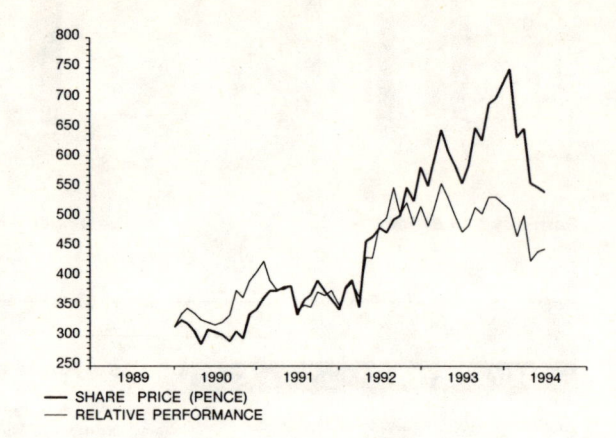

— SHARE PRICE (PENCE)
— RELATIVE PERFORMANCE

Financial record

		31/3/90	31/3/91	31/3/92	31/3/93
Total sales	£'000	150,900	167,000	203,500	252,100
Pre-tax profit	£'000	12,100	47,900	61,100	62,100
Published retentions	£'000	-2,900	30,600	43,000	52,300
Earnings per share	p	81.54	66.87	85.50	85.05
Dividend per share	p	16.00	18.60	20.50	22.50
Operating cash flow	£'000	-84,200	-39,100	-46,900	-63,000
Net assets per share	p	965.80	1,196	1,279	1,471
Net debt/(cash)	£'000	-103M	-74,700	-6,100	101,200
Shareholders' funds	£'000	622,600	671,400	706,900	749,800
Return on capital	%		7.80	10.05	9.46
Profit margin	%	8.02	29.52	30.37	24.87
Sales per employee	£	106.79	102.77	85.61	86.84
Interest cover		1.45	-2.61	-12.36	7.68
Dividend cover		5.10	3.60	4.17	3.78
Sales increase	%		10.67	21.86	23.88
Earnings growth	%		-17.99	27.86	-0.52
Investment x depreciation		5.37	5.21	4.74	4.57
Investment as % assets		10.14	13.87	10.56	11.06
Number of employees		1,413	1,625	2,377	2,903

Earnings and dividends

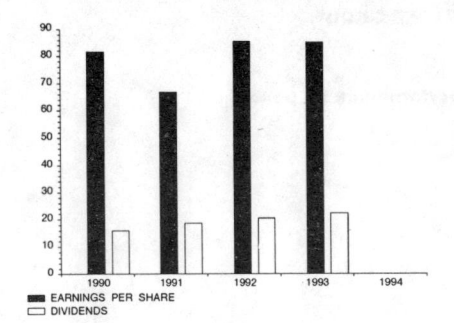

Sales per employee

NORTHUMBRIAN WATER GROUP plc

Northumbria House, Regent Centre, Gosforth, Newcastle upon Tyne NE3 3PX
Tel: 0191 284 3151
Chairman Professor Sir Edward Holliday
Chief executive David Cranston
Size £252 million sales, £381 million stock market value, 2,900 employees
Solvency debt = 14% shareholders' funds, interest cover 8 times
Political donations 0
Charitable donations £193,000

Major developments
1989 privatised
1991 bought James Duncan Holdings Ltd; bought Earth Service Ltd
1992 Detectronic Ltd acquired; entered joint venture with Thames Water which then acquired Subterra Ltd
1993 bought the European consultancy business of Simon Engineering
1994 sold pipeline cleaning business

Corporate governance
Separate Chairman and Chief Executive Y
Number of Directors 8
Number of Non-Executive Directors 5
(4 Independent Directors)
Insulated Directors Not known

Board Committees
Audit: Y   Remuneration: Y

Remuneration

Year end	31.03.91	31.03.92	31.03.93
Total board £M	0.36	0.43	0.60
% change		21	40
Highest paid £	82,000	110,000	117,000
% change		34	6

Board
Cranston, David G *Chief Executive*
Hargreaves, Jon *Executive Director*
Taylor, Michael *Finance Director*
Pescod, Prof. M B *Independent Non-Executive*
Riddell, Sir John *Independent Non-Executive*
Ward, John S *Independent Non-Executive*
Straker, Sir Michael *Non-Executive*
Holliday, Prof. Sir E *Non-Executive Chairman*

NORTH WEST WATER GROUP

Share record

Return on shareholders'
equity	%	12.16
5-year price high	p	601.0
5-year price low	p	240.0
Dividend yield	%	5.69
5-year high	%	8.72
5-year low	%	4.56
Price/earnings		
ratio		7.7
5-year high		18.9
5-year low		5.6

Share price performance (in pence)

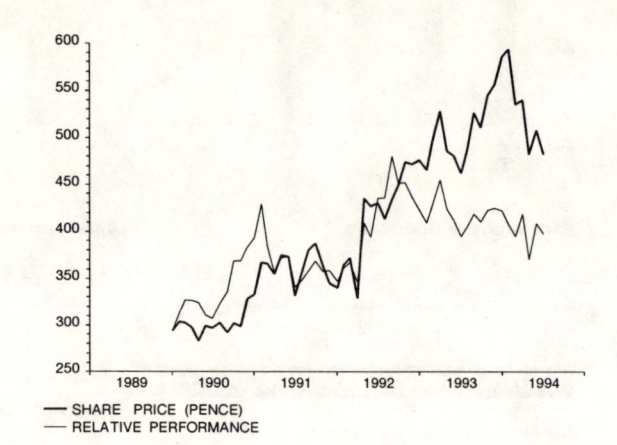

— SHARE PRICE (PENCE)
— RELATIVE PERFORMANCE

Financial record

		31/3/90	31/3/91	31/3/92	31/3/93	31/3/94
Total sales	£'000	511,400	598,500	789,100	877,900	924,200
Pre-tax profit	£'000	75,300	214,500	230,100	283,100	281,000
Published retentions	£'000	18,900	129,000	136,100	145,800	174,200
Earnings per share	p	17.68	54.27	57.90	72.24	70.41
Dividend per share	p	15.70	18.00	19.67	21.40	23.07
Operating cash flow	£'000	-74,800	-126M	-214M	-221M	-14,300
Net assets per share	p	464.72	549.53	632.00	717.95	785.89
Net debt/(cash)	£'000	-136M	-4,800	296,400	534,600	557,600
Shareholders' funds	£	1,566M	1,650M	1,702M	1,841M	2,074M
Return on capital	%		12.89	13.12	14.28	12.59
Profit margin	%	14.72	35.84	29.16	32.35	30.61
Sales per employee	£	72.03	82.10	96.22	108.91	115.34
Interest cover		1.94	-6.64	15.67	7.85	6.32
Dividend cover		1.13	3.01	2.94	3.38	3.05
Sales increase	%		17.03	31.85	11.25	5.27
Earnings growth	%		207.00	6.70	24.76	-2.53
Investment x depreciation		6.87	9.00	9.95	6.92	4.83
Investment as % assets		12.96	17.29	18.65	15.22	11.39
Number of employees		7,100	7,290	8,201	8,061	8,013

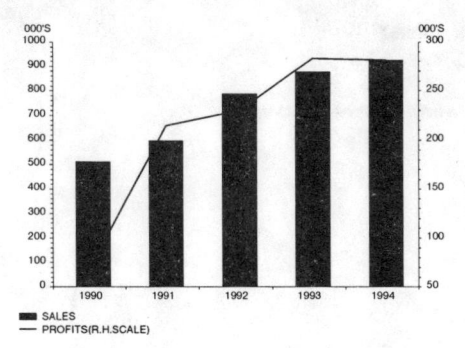

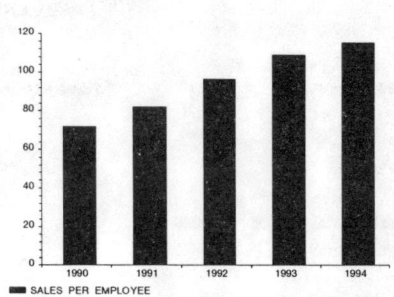

Sales and profits

Sales per employee

NORTH WEST WATER GROUP plc

Dawson House, Great Sankey,
Warrington WA5 3LW
Tel: 01925 234000
Chairman Sir Desmond Pitcher
Chief executive Brian Staples
Size £924 million sales, £1.9 billion stock market value, 8,000 employees
Solvency debt = 27% shareholders' funds, interest cover 6 times
Political donations 0
Charitable donations £60,000

Major developments
1989 privatised
1991 bought Wallace & Tiernan Group Inc and Edwards & Jones (Holdings) Ltd
1993 bought Consolidated Electric Company; won major international contracts

Corporate governance
Separate Chairman and Chief Executive Y
Number of Directors 10
Number of Non-Executive Directors 7
(7 Independent Directors)
Insulated Directors Ch, CE, MD

Board Committees
Audit: Y Remuneration: Y

Remuneration

Year end	31.03.91	31.03.92	31.03.93
Total board £M	0.60	0.90	1.25
% change		50	39
Highest paid £	144,000	189,000	255,000
% change		31	35

Board
Staples, Brian *Chief Executive*
Green, Derek *Executive Director*
Ferguson, Bob *Finance Director*
Bolton, Clare *Independent Non-Executive*
Clark, Eric *Independent Non-Executive*
Leach, Dr Rodney *Independent Non-Executive*
Middleton, Sir Peter *Independent Non-Executive*
Pendleton, Alan *Independent Non-Executive*
Sanderson, Frank *Independent Non-Executive*
Pitcher, Sir Desmond *Non-Executive Chairman*

SEVERN TRENT

Share record

Return on shareholders' equity	%	12.16
5-year price high	p	635.0
5-year price low	p	240.0
Dividend yield	%	5.65
5-year high	%	8.25
5-year low	%	4.26
Price/earnings ratio		9.3
5-year high		12.2
5-year low		4.2

Share price performance (in pence)

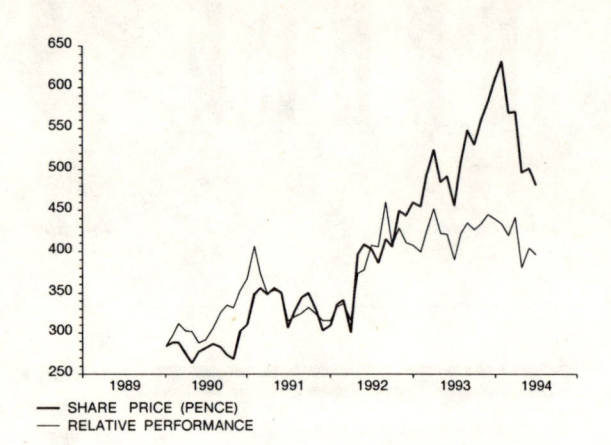

— SHARE PRICE (PENCE)
— RELATIVE PERFORMANCE

Financial record

		31/3/90	31/3/91	31/3/92	31/3/93	31/3/94
Total sales	£'000	544,100	627,000	821,700	904,600	998,000
Pre-tax profit	£'000	240,400	249,000	265,400	270,100	281,400
Published retentions	£'000	74,300	156,300	181,600	172,500	178,500
Earnings per share	p	63.02	64.44	67.98	69.43	72.28
Dividend per share	p	14.85	17.55	19.30	21.10	22.75
Operating cash flow	£'000	-8,000	-169M	-185M	-170M	-52,800
Net assets per share	p	499.86	567.37	686.80	761.76	840.29
Net debt/(cash)	£'000	-315M	-236M	169,600	422,400	575,800
Shareholders' funds	£	1,675M	1,828M	1,830M	1,980M	2,139M
Return on capital	%		14.22	15.98	12.83	12.06
Profit margin	%	44.18	39.73	32.07	29.76	28.16
Sales per employee	£	74.55	83.33	78.89	86.00	92.55
Interest cover		-3.52	-3.83	-60.21	10.31	6.82
Dividend cover		4.24	3.67	3.53	3.29	3.18
Sales increase	%		15.24	31.05	10.09	10.33
Earnings growth	%		2.25	5.49	2.14	4.10
Investment x depreciation		5.47	8.04	6.89	5.07	3.83
Investment as % assets		14.40	21.69	19.02	15.49	12.06
Number of employees		7,298	7,524	10,416	10,519	10,783

WATER COMPANIES

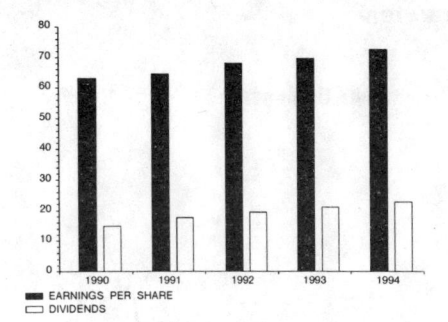

Earnings and dividends

Sales per employee

SEVERN TRENT plc

2297 Coventry Road, Birmingham B26 3PU
Tel: 0121 722 4000
Chairman John Bellak
Chief executive Roderick Paul
Main subsidiaries Acer Engineering (35%), Aztec Environmental Control, Biffa Waste Services, Capital Controls, Fusion Meters, Grafham Carbons (50%), Charles Haswell
Size £998 million sales, £1.8 billion stock market value, 10,800 employees
Solvency debt = 27% shareholders' funds, interest cover 7 times
Political donations 0
Charitable donations £158,191

Major developments
1989 privatised
1991 bought Biffa Group of companies from BET
1993 bought East Worcester Water plc

Corporate governance

Separate Chairman and Chief Executive Y
Number of Directors 10
Number of Non-Executive Directors 5
(5 Independent Directors)
Insulated Directors Ch, CE, MD

Board Committees
Audit: Y   Remuneration: Y

Remuneration

Year end	31.03.91	31.03.92	31.03.93
Total board £M	1.02	1.01	1.17
% change		-2	16
Highest paid £	158,800	148,200	195,000
% change		-7	32

Board
Paul, Roderick S *Chief Executive*
Bellak, John G *Executive Chairman*
Cocker, Victor *Executive Director*
Upstone, Michael P *Executive Director*
Costin, Alan *Finance Director*
Boissier, Roger H *Independent Non-Executive*
Ireland, Richard *Independent Non-Executive*
Simon, Andrew H *Independent Non-Executive*
Tritton, Clare *Independent Non-Executive*
Wilbraham, Sir Richard B *Ind. Non-Executive*

WATER COMPANIES

SOUTHERN WATER

Share record

Return on shareholders' equity	%	12.18
5-year price high	p	682.0
5-year price low	p	240.0
Dividend yield	%	5.83
5-year high	%	8.35
5-year low	%	4.01
Price/earnings ratio		9.6
5-year high		13.6
5-year low		5.4

Share price performance (in pence)

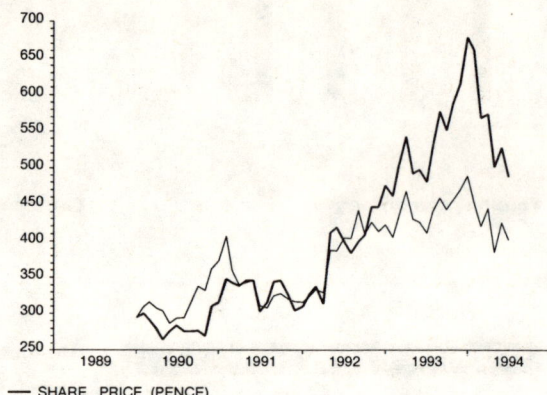

— SHARE PRICE (PENCE)
— RELATIVE PERFORMANCE

Financial record

		31/3/90	31/3/91	31/3/92	31/3/93
Total sales	£'000	225,800	251,200	290,700	319,200
Pre-tax profit	£'000	60,300	97,200	109,100	119,200
Published retentions	£'000	32,400	58,400	73,200	74,100
Earnings per share	p	46.48	53.44	60.56	66.34
Dividend per share	p	15.00	17.70	19.50	21.30
Operating cash flow	£'000	-32,500	-45,000	-10,000	11,800
Net assets per share	p	416.19	481.45	581.37	640.27
Net debt/(cash)	£'000	-25,300	-6,000	-1,700	-15,500
Shareholders' funds	£'000	677,000	741,800	815,900	898,500
Return on capital	%		13.39	14.03	13.54
Profit margin	%	26.71	38.69	n/a	37.34
Sales per employee	£	80.93	85.79	93.68	94.30
Interest cover		4.31	-13.73	-35.27	594.50
Dividend cover		3.10	3.02	3.11	3.11
Sales increase	%		11.25	15.72	9.80
Earnings growth	%		14.97	13.32	9.55
Investment x depreciation		4.90	4.51	4.79	2.88
Investment as % assets		15.53	16.06	15.82	9.93
Number of employees		2,790	2,928	3,103	3,385

WATER COMPANIES

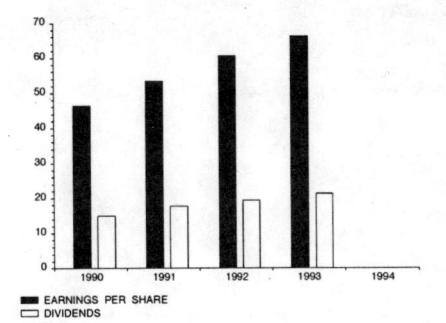

Earnings and dividends

Sales per employee

SOUTHERN WATER plc

Southern House, Yeoman Road,
Worthing BN13 3NX
Tel: 01903 264444
Chairman William Courtney
Chief executive Martyn Webster
Main subsidiaries Aquaclear, Coastal Wastewater Consultants, Ecoclear, Greenhill Enterprises, Hazeley Down, McDowells, Southern Projects, Southern Science
Size £319 million sales, £846 million stock market value, 3,400 employees
Solvency debt n/a, interest cover n/a
Political donations 0
Charitable donations £26,000

Major developments
1989 privatised
1991 bought McDowells Ltd; bought Greenhill Enterprises Ltd, Aquaclear Ltd and Monk Rawling

Corporate governance

Separate Chairman and Chief Executive Y
Number of Directors 8
Number of Non-Executive Directors 4
(2 Independent Directors)
Insulated Directors Ch, CE, MD

Board Committees
Audit: Y   Remuneration: Y

Remuneration

Year end	31.03.91	31.03.92	31.03.93
Total board £M	0.43	0.53	0.60
% change		21	14
Highest paid £	142,000	169,000	170,000
% change		19	1

Board
Webster, Martyn *Chief Executive*
Courtney, William *Executive Chairman*
Tozzi, Keith *Executive Director*
King, Raymond *Finance Director*
Girle, Philip *Independent Non-Executive*
Thomas, Vivian *Independent Non-Executive*
Midmer, Francis *Non-Executive*
Westhead, John *Non-Executive*

SOUTH WEST WATER

Share record

Return on shareholders' equity	%	10.60
5-year price high	p	664.0
5-year price low	p	240.0
Dividend yield	%	6.20
5-year high	%	9.68
5-year low	%	4.57
Price/earnings ratio		10.4
5-year high		13.2
5-year low		3.9

Share price performance (in pence)

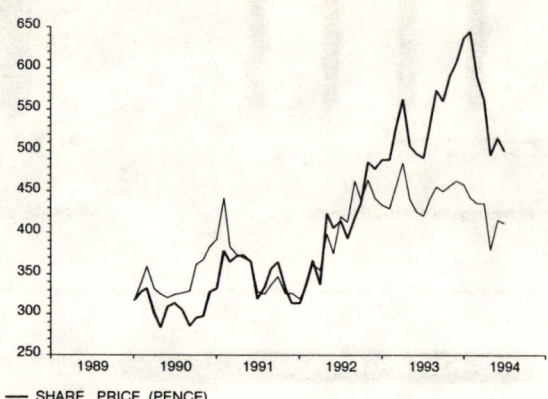

— SHARE PRICE (PENCE)
— RELATIVE PERFORMANCE

Financial record

		31/3/90	31/3/91	31/3/92	31/3/93
Total sales	£'000	121,000	143,800	166,500	194,400
Pre-tax profit	£'000	83,200	88,400	90,000	92,700
Published retentions	£'000	22,600	56,000	54,300	54,700
Earnings per share	p	62.25	65.93	66.12	67.87
Dividend per share	p	17.40	20.00	21.70	23.70
Operating cash flow	£'000	-11,300	-39,000	-67,100	-135M
Net assets per share	p	520.01	673.88	880.63	1,027
Net debt/(cash)	£	-259M	-230M	-151M	13,100
Shareholders' funds	£'000	631,900	688,100	747,200	794,000
Return on capital	%		12.83	11.37	11.14
Profit margin	%	68.76	61.54	54.11	48.71
Sales per employee	£	70.68	69.40	67.99	76.06
Interest cover		-1.16	-1.70	3.51	2.14
Dividend cover		3.58	3.30	3.05	2.86
Sales increase	%		18.84	15.79	16.76
Earnings growth	%		5.91	0.28	2.65
Investment x depreciation		8.97	11.13	10.11	15.84
Investment as % assets		18.58	23.05	19.35	23.76
Number of employees		1,712	2,072	2,449	2,556

Earnings and dividends

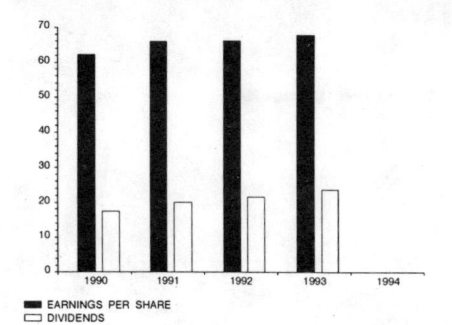

Sales per employee

SOUTH WEST WATER plc

Peninsula House, Rydon Lane, Exeter EX2 7HR
Tel: 01392 446688
Chairman and chief executive Keith Court
Main subsidiaries Copa Holdings, ELE Group, Haul-Waste, Peninsular Group, TJ (Brent)
Size £194 million sales, £645 million stock market value, 2,600 employees
Solvency debt = 1.5% shareholders' funds, interest cover 2 times
Political donations 0
Charitable donations £33,000

Major developments
1989 privatised
1991 bought Copa Holdings
1992 process technology joint venture formed with Weir Group; joint venture with Fomento de Construcciones y Contras SA to form Peninsular Waste Management
1993 Haul-Waste Ltd and ELE Group acquired

Corporate governance
Separate Chairman and Chief Executive N
Number of Directors 11
Number of Non-Executive Directors 6
(6 Independent Directors)
Insulated Directors Ch, CE, MD
Board Committees
Audit: Y   Remuneration: Y

Remuneration

Year end	31.03.91	31.03.92	31.03.93
Total board £M	0.53	0.68	0.69
% change		29	2
Highest paid £	89,000	124,000	136,000
% change		39	2

Board
Court, Keith William *Chairman & Chief Executive*
Fraser, William Hamilton *Managing Director*
Drummond, Colin Irwin John *Executive Director*
Hewett, Bruce *Executive Director*
Hill, Kenneth Leslie *Finance Director*
Chipperfield, Sir Geoffrey *Ind. Non-Executive*
Day, Simon James *Independent Non-Executive*
Fletcher, Alan *Independent Non-Executive*
Lady Holborow *Independent Non-Executive*
Yassukovich, Stanislas *Independent Non-Executive*
Leader, Timothy Charles *Non-Executive Deputy Chairman*

THAMES WATER

Share record

Return on shareholders' equity	%	13.10
5-year price high	p	602.0
5-year price low	p	240.0
Dividend yield	%	6.01
5-year high	%	8.10
5-year low	%	4.37
Price/earnings ratio		10.1
5-year high		15.2
5-year low		5.8

Share price performance (in pence)

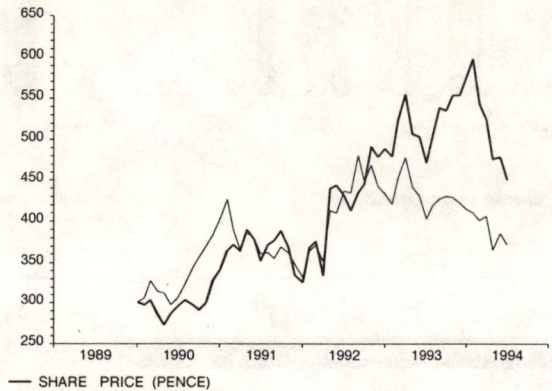

Financial record

		31/3/90	31/3/91	31/3/92	31/3/93
Total sales	£'000	611,500	835,500	899,300	1,043M
Pre-tax profit	£'000	167,900	214,000	236,300	243,200
Published retentions	£'000	108,900	126,000	137,000	147,900
Earnings per share	p	40.66	50.55	54.83	57.18
Dividend per share	p	15.11	17.50	19.20	21.00
Operating cash flow	£'000	4,500	-142M	-151M	-147M
Net assets per share	p	378.80	418.65	534.65	598.37
Net debt/(cash)	£'000	-48,700	88,600	327,500	516,000
Shareholders' funds	£	1,347M	1,483M	1,627M	1,783M
Return on capital	%		14.90	14.59	13.76
Profit margin	%	27.44	25.60	26.30	23.52
Sales per employee	£	78.50	92.68	96.20	100.73
Interest cover		-17.40	-17.25	27.54	9.37
Dividend cover		2.69	2.89	2.86	2.72
Sales increase	%		36.63	7.64	15.96
Earnings growth	%		24.33	8.48	4.28
Investment x depreciation		6.99	9.34	6.36	5.19
Investment as % assets		16.09	21.74	16.30	14.69
Number of employees		7,790	9,015	9,348	10,352

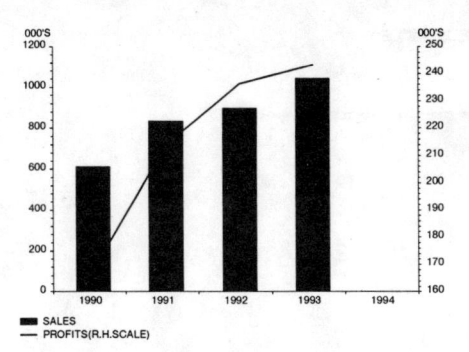

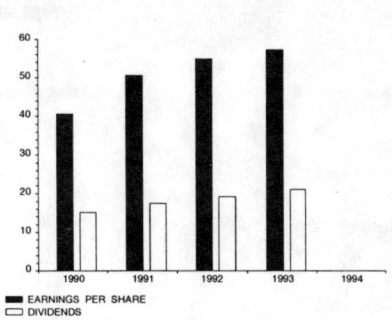

Sales and profits

Earnings and dividends

THAMES WATER plc

14 Cavendish Place, London W1M 9DJ
Tel: 0171 636 8686
Chairman Sir Robert Clarke
Chief executive Michael Hoffman
Main subsidiaries Metro Rod, Permutit, PWT
Size £1.0 billion sales, £1.9 billion stock market value, 10,400 employees
Solvency debt = 29% shareholders' funds, interest cover 9 times
Political donations 0
Charitable donations £110,000

Major developments
1989 privatised
1990 bought Metro Rod
1991 bought Morgan Collis Group
1992 joint venture with Northumbrian Water to acquire Subterra and A J Whiteside
1993 bought the water and waste treatment business of Simon Engineering

Corporate governance
Separate Chairman and Chief Executive Y
Number of Directors 9
Number of Non-Executive Directors 5
(5 Independent Directors)
Insulated Directors Ch, CE, MD

Board Committees
Audit: Y   Remuneration: Y

Remuneration

Year end	31.03.91	31.03.92	31.03.93
Total board £M	0.85	0.82	0.87
% change		-3	7
Highest paid £	209,000	254,000	274,000
% change		22	8

Board
Hoffman, Mike *Chief Executive*
Alexander, William *Executive Director*
Harper, Bill *Executive Director*
Luffrum, David *Finance Director*
Harrop, Sir Peter *Independent Non-Executive*
Leaver, Sir Christopher *Independent Non-Executive*
Thomson, John *Independent Non-Executive*
Worlidge, E John *Independent Non-Executive*
Clarke, Sir Robert C *Non-Executive Chairman*

WELSH WATER

Share record

Return on shareholders' equity	%	12.39
5-year price high	p	739.0
5-year price low	p	240.0
Dividend yield	%	5.53
5-year high	%	9.31
5-year low	%	4.08
Price/earnings ratio		8.7
5-year high		11.4
5-year low		4.1

Share price performance (in pence)

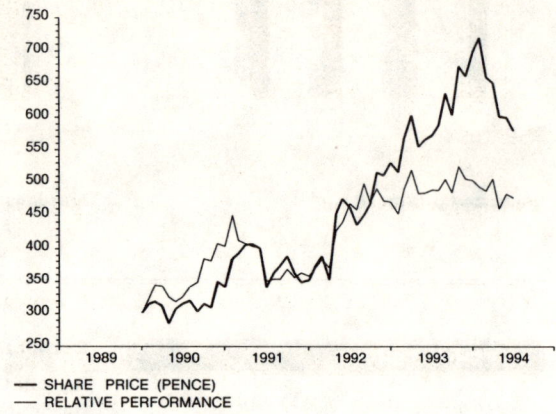

— SHARE PRICE (PENCE)
— RELATIVE PERFORMANCE

Financial record

		31/3/90	31/3/91	31/3/92	31/3/93
Total sales	£'000	255,300	293,000	341,900	382,400
Pre-tax profit	£'000	46,600	128,500	139,400	138,400
Published retentions	£'000	12,700	90,300	96,500	116,100
Earnings per share	p	66.63	82.46	89.18	90.72
Dividend per share	p	16.70	19.50	21.40	23.50
Operating cash flow	£'000	-110M	-4,400	-52,900	-38,900
Net assets per share	p	560.11	646.11	829.45	898.33
Net debt/(cash)	£'000	-177M	-166M	-86,900	-58,300
Shareholders' funds	£'000	781,800	899,300	996,800	1,073M
Return on capital	%		15.08	13.91	12.76
Profit margin	%	18.25	43.96	40.95	36.19
Sales per employee	£	68.80	70.89	72.81	76.51
Interest cover		2.93	-2.86	-6.46	-13.55
Dividend cover		3.99	4.23	4.17	3.86
Sales increase	%		14.77	16.69	11.85
Earnings growth	%		23.75	8.16	1.72
Investment x depreciation		4.77	6.40	6.09	4.88
Investment as % assets		14.20	18.67	19.14	15.89
Number of employees		3,711	4,133	4,696	4,998

Earnings and dividends

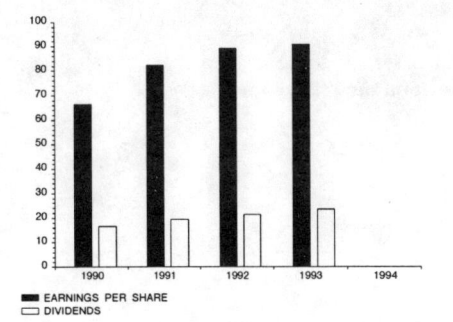

Sales per employee

WELSH WATER plc

2 Alexandra Gate, Rover Way, Cardiff CF2 2UE
Tel: 01222 500600
Chairman Iain Evans
Chief executive Graham Hawker
Main subsidiaries Acer Consultants, Brecon Insurance Company, Hamdden, Wallace Evans
Size £382 million sales, £840 million stock market value, 5,000 employees
Solvency debt n/a, interest cover n/a
Political donations 0
Charitable donations £44,000

Major developments
1989 privatised
1990 bought Wallace Evans Ltd; bought 10% South Wales Electricity on its privatisation
1991 increased stake to 15%
1992 sold the stake in South Wales Electricity
1993 bought engineering consultant Acer Group Ltd

Corporate governance

Separate Chairman and Chief Executive Y
Number of Directors 9
Number of Non-Executive Directors 5
(5 Independent Directors)
Insulated Directors Not known

Board Committees
Audit: Y   Remuneration: Y

Remuneration

Year end	31.03.91	31.03.92	31.03.93
Total board £M	0.44	0.62	0.70
% change		40	13
Highest paid £	143,000	141,000	156,000
% change		-1	11

Board
Hawker, Graham A *Chief Executive*
Charles, Brian H *Executive Director*
James, John M *Executive Director*
Twamley, Paul J *Finance Director*
Hales, Antony *Independent Non-Executive*
Hawkins, D Grant *Independent Non-Executive*
Knowles, Timothy *Independent Non-Executive*
Sellier, Robert *Independent Non-Executive*
Evans, Iain R *Non-Executive Chairman*

146 WATER COMPANIES

WESSEX WATER

Share record

Return on shareholders' equity % 9.39
5-year price high p 752.0
5-year price low p 235.3

Dividend yield % 4.97
5-year high % 8.45
5-year low % 3.69

Price/earnings ratio 13.1
5-year high 19.2
5-year low 5.0

Share price performance (in pence)

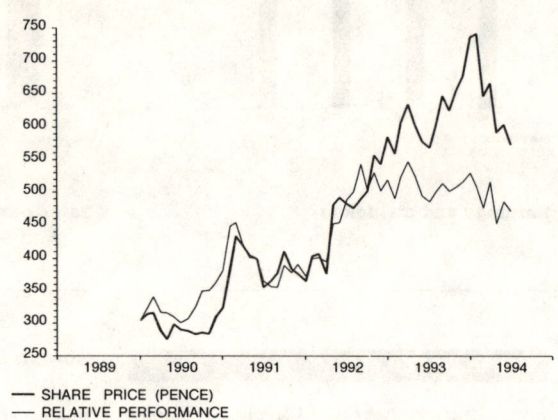

— SHARE PRICE (PENCE)
— RELATIVE PERFORMANCE

Financial record

		31/3/90	31/3/91	31/3/92	31/3/93
Total sales	£'000	147,800	166,900	190,800	205,600
Pre-tax profit	£'000	28,700	66,500	79,200	86,000
Published retentions	£'000	8,900	41,700	49,900	51,000
Earnings per share	p	50.65	56.82	58.53	57.29
Dividend per share	p	14.81	17.35	19.12	21.50
Operating cash flow	£'000	-79,400	-17,800	-35,800	-55,800
Net assets per share	p	539.93	693.45	701.12	792.32
Net debt/(cash)	£'000	-37,300	-94,400	-15,500	-54,400
Shareholders' funds	£'000	558,500	665,900	670,400	817,500
Return on capital	%		10.49	10.91	11.10
Profit margin	%	19.42	39.84	41.04	39.64
Sales per employee	£	90.18	95.10	102.09	109.89
Interest cover		2.64	-6.81	-8.19	-161.40
Dividend cover		3.42	3.27	3.06	2.66
Sales increase	%		12.92	14.32	7.76
Earnings growth	%		12.19	3.00	-2.11
Investment x depreciation		6.16	5.03	6.20	6.58
Investment as % assets		16.81	13.86	16.36	16.66
Number of employees		1,639	1,755	1,869	1,871

Earnings and dividends

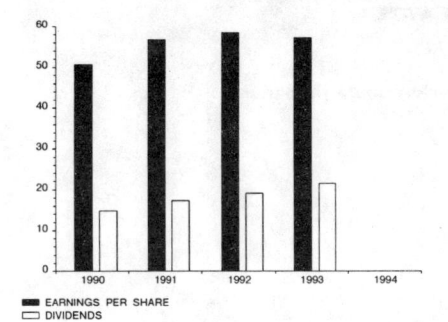

Sales per employee

WESSEX WATER plc

Wessex House, Passage Street, Bristol BS2 0QJ
Tel: 0117 929 0611
Chairman Nicholas Hood
Managing director Colin Skellett
Main subsidiaries UK Waste Management, Wessex Waste Management (50%), Wimpey Wessex Water (50%)
Size £205 million sales, £742 million stock market value, 1,900 employees
Solvency debt n/a, interest cover n/a
Political donations 0
Charitable donations £45,000

Major developments
1989 privatised
1991 joint venture with Waste Management International; bought Wimpey Waste Management
1993 joint venture bought Waste Management Ltd from NFC; formed Avon Waste Management, joint venture company with Avon County Council

Corporate governance

Separate Chairman and Chief Executive Y
Number of Directors 10
Number of Non-Executive Directors 6
(6 Independent Directors)
Insulated Directors Ch, CE, MD

Board Committees
Audit: Y   Remuneration: Y

Remuneration

Year end	31.03.91	31.03.92	31.03.93
Total board £M	0.58	0.53	0.57
% change		-8	6
Highest paid £	128,000	146,000	154,000
% change		14	6

Board
Skellett, C F *Chief Executive*
Hood, W Nicholas *Executive Chairman*
Huntingdon, R *Executive Director*
Wheatley, N A W *Finance Director*
Barbour, Dr A K *Independent Non-Executive*
Falkman, E G *Independent Non-Executive*
Heiser, Sir Terence *Independent Non-Executive*
Kent, R D *Independent Non-Executive*
McLure, D N A *Independent Non-Executive*
Thornhill, A R *Independent Non-Executive*

148 WATER COMPANIES

YORKSHIRE WATER

Share record

Return on shareholders' equity   %   10.0
5-year price high   p   626.0
5-year price low   p   240.0

Dividend yield   %   5.79
5-year high   %   8.57
5-year low   %   4.25

Price/earnings ratio   10.2
5-year high   14.0
5-year low   5.4

Share price performance (in pence)

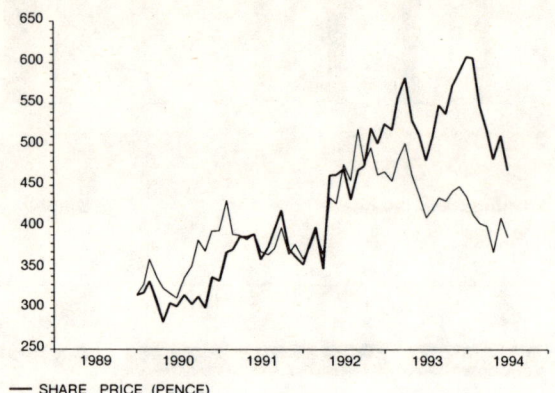

— SHARE PRICE (PENCE)
— RELATIVE PERFORMANCE

Financial record

		31/3/90	31/3/91	31/3/92	31/3/93
Total sales	£'000	354,700	388,900	441,200	481,600
Pre-tax profit	£'000	61,400	114,100	123,900	134,200
Published retentions	£'000	25,800	67,800	75,000	86,400
Earnings per share	p	48.40	52.21	57.59	62.81
Dividend per share	p	15.42	17.70	19.50	21.07
Operating cash flow	£'000	-115M	-106M	-47,500	-93,300
Net assets per share	p	527.89	609.58	754.55	841.53
Net debt/(cash)	£'000	-21,500	45,200	140,100	215,800
Shareholders' funds	£'000	965,100	1,045M	1,129M	1,234M
Return on capital	%		11.49	10.92	10.68
Profit margin	%	17.31	29.34	28.08	28.07
Sales per employee	£	77.26	81.21	90.00	101.60
Interest cover		2.67	-13.05	112.82	10.85
Dividend cover		3.14	2.95	2.95	2.98
Sales increase	%		9.64	13.45	9.16
Earnings growth	%		7.88	10.30	9.08
Investment x depreciation		4.37	5.20	5.63	5.75
Investment as % assets		15.54	18.33	17.61	16.55
Number of employees		4,591	4,789	4,902	4,740

Earnings and dividends

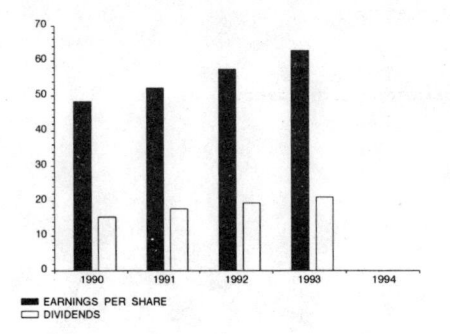

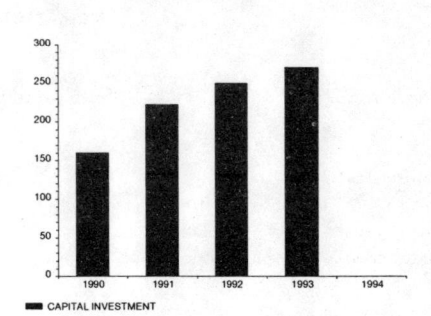

Capital investment

YORKSHIRE WATER plc

2 The Embankment, Sovereign Street,
Leeds LS1 4BG
Tel: 0113 234 3234
Chairman Sir Gordon Jones
Managing director Trevor Newton
Size £482 million sales, £1.0 billion stock market value, 4,700 employees
Solvency debt = 17% shareholders' funds, interest cover 11 times
Political donations 0
Charitable donations £79,000

Major developments
1989 privatised
1991 bought Fospur water treatment company from Burmah Castrol
1992 YW Enterprises set up joint venture with Babcock International
1993 bought Alcontrol Labs and Third Finance Leasing Co.
1994 bought Dyvell and Heinrici environmental business; joint venture in US

Corporate governance

Separate Chairman and Chief Executive Y
Number of Directors 10
Number of Non-Executive Directors 5
(5 Independent Directors)
Insulated Directors Ch, CE, MD

Board Committees
Audit: Y   Remuneration: Y

Remuneration

Year end	31.03.91	31.03.92	31.03.93
Total board £M	0.51	0.68	0.73
% change		35	7
Highest paid £	119,000	143,000	156,000
% change		20	9

Board
Jones, Sir Gordon *Executive Chairman*
Newton, Trevor *Managing Director*
Bell, John *Executive Director*
Ward, Anthony *Executive Director*
Batty, Malcolm *Finance Director*
Cramb, David *Independent Non-Executive*
Flesher, Peter *Independent Non-Executive*
Honeybourne, Dr Christopher *Ind. Non-Executive*
Jackson, Thomas *Independent Non-Executive*
Shaw, Sir Giles *Independent Non-Executive*

INDIVIDUAL COMPANIES

ARGOS plc

489–499 Avebury Boulevard, Saxon Gate West, Central Milton Keynes MK9 2NW
Tel: 01908 690333
Chairman David Donne
Chief executive Michael Smith
Size £1.1 billion sales, £1.0 billion stock market value, 12,500 employees
5-year growth n/a
Solvency debt n/a, interest cover n/a
Political donations 0
Charitable donations £82,190

Major developments
1973 concept launched
1979 bought by BAT Industries
1990 demerged from BAT
1993 abandoned Chesterman furniture venture

Outlook

Argos is a retailer which has never been afraid to be boring. While others like Next and Burton became caught up with the frenzied late-1980s fashion for expansion and diversification, Argos stuck to its knitting. The result has been to create a company with cash in the bank and more than 320 'catalogue shops'. The formula is simple: shoppers choose what they want from a brochure that is rather slimmer than the normal mail-order offering, fill in a slip of paper, pay at a till and then wait for their purchase to be retrieved from the warehouse. The formula may be simple, but it seems to be successful. And because most Argos shoppers have already chosen what they want from the catalogue before they arrive at the store, there is little need for display space and the company can often make do with what it terms 'secondary' sites. It has to worry less than most conventional retailers about attracting shoppers by using glitzy window displays and lavish shop fittings: instead, it can concentrate on the workaday issues of making sure that the right items are in stock at the right time.

The company was the brainchild of the late Richard Tompkins, the man who made a fortune from Green Shield stamps in the 1960s and 1970s. It was bought by BAT Industries in 1979 for £32 million. Then in 1990, after Sir James Goldsmith and friends had tried to take over BAT, the group's shareholders were given Argos shares so that they directly owned the retailer: it became independent.

Since then, the company has had to cope with the worst recession that the current generation of retailers has known. Argos has weathered the storm rather better than most: by offering much the same goods as that of the cheap variety store (like a 1970s Woolworths), it taps into a market which is rather less dependent on the vagaries of the economic cycle than most.

Of course it has not been able to avoid completely the effect of the downturn in retail spending. Argos is Britain's second-biggest jeweller after Ratners, is one of the country's three largest toy retailers (alongside Woolworths and Toys R Us) and a leader in selling small electrical appliances like kettles and shavers. All these areas were hit badly by the decline in retail spending, so inevitably Argos suffered. But it suffered less than most of its rivals, and clocked up record profits in 1992 by sticking to its established formula.

The key question now facing Argos is the degree to which it should rely on its tried-and-tested sales formula to generate future profits. There are still hundreds of towns without an Argos outlet where the company would like to open one. Argos is already reckoned to be among the retailing industry's leaders in making full use of computers in placing orders, controlling stocks and analysing which lines should be added and which should be dropped each time it prints a new edition of its twice-yearly catalogue. But further savings could be made, and thus profit margins protected, even if there is renewed growth in high-street sales.

The alternative approach is to use Argos's accumulated profits to start up or buy a completely different retail business in an area which might enjoy really strong growth during an upturn in the economy. So far its only attempt at serious diversification has been to set up a furniture retailing operation under the Chesterman name. Unfortunately, this venture coincided with the long, deep housing slump, and Argos was forced to close it down in March 1993.

Argos's solid but unexciting image has served it well in the early 1990s. The question is whether it can afford to maintain this image when (or perhaps if) the outlook for the high street becomes rather brighter.

Shares

The Argos flotation in 1990 produced, after an initial dip in line with falling share prices generally, an 18 per cent premium over the rest of the market and put it on a similar price/earnings ratio to the mighty Marks & Spencer. It was seen as a core holding by most institutional shareholders. For a chainstore in a

ARGOS

Share record

Return on shareholders' equity	%	22.25
5-year price high	p	388.0
5-year price low	p	192.0
Dividend yield	%	2.95
5-year high	%	4.42
5-year low	%	2.30
Price/earnings ratio		17.8
5-year high		24.4
5-year low		13.2

Share price performance (in pence)

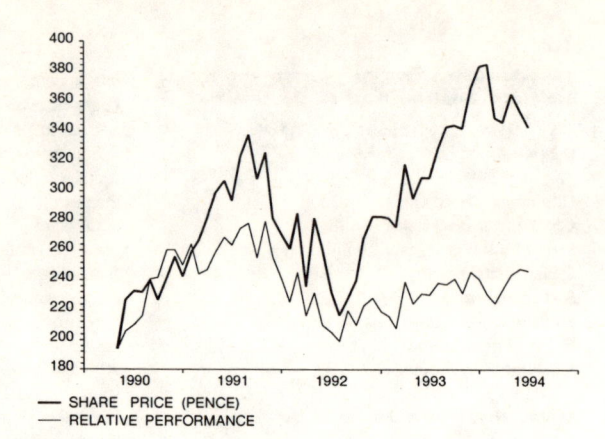

— SHARE PRICE (PENCE)
— RELATIVE PERFORMANCE

Financial record

		31/12/90	31/12/91	31/12/92	31/12/93
Total sales	£'000	905,568	926,649	1,004M	1,110M
Pre-tax profit	£'000	75,106	63,591	67,823	85,143
Published retentions	£'000	28,985	22,272	13,975	31,377
Earnings per share	p	16.22	14.05	16.55	19.10
Dividend per share	p	6.00	6.40	7.00	8.00
Operating cash flow	£'000	12,295	29,203	-54,016	44,111
Net assets per share	p	58.03	68.78	76.35	87.44
Net debt/(cash)	£	-151M	-179M	-234M	-298M
Shareholders' funds	£'000	184,011	206,337	220,461	253,780
Return on capital	%		33.92	31.76	35.22
Profit margin	%	8.29	6.86	6.76	7.67
Sales per employee	£	77.94	76.25	83.24	87.85
Interest cover		-9.93	-8.56	-6.60	-10.74
Dividend cover		2.67	2.20	2.36	2.39
Sales increase	%		2.33	8.30	10.58
Earnings growth	%		-13.37	17.80	15.39
Investment x depreciation		1.95	0.98	1.66	1.42
Investment as % assets		27.92	16.58	27.27	23.91
Number of employees		11,619	12,152	12,056	12,631

Earnings and dividends

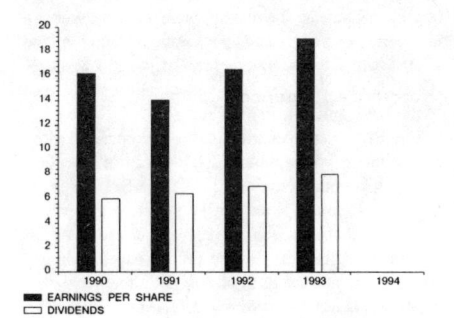

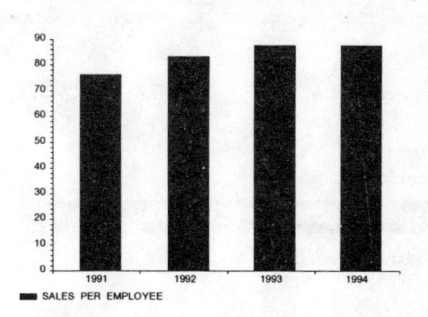

Sales per employee

deepening recession this was an impressive début and was attributed to the quality of its management.

Save for a little uncertainty ahead of its reporting seasons, the company continued to outperform most shares during 1991, but while it was seen as a growth stock, it gradually lost its premium rating against other chainstores. The fact that Argos continued to build up its cash pile and would not need a rights issue helped to keep its shares buoyant until 1992 when profits fell and the board was criticised for mishandling the launch of Chesterman – its first major initiative since flotation. The shares fell almost as far as they had risen and by August that year had underperformed the stores sector by 31 per cent.

Yet since 1993 the company's defensive virtues have remained attractive to investors, and in the medium term the shares are expected to retain a modest premium to the stores sector.

Corporate conscience

Argos had the chance, as a new company, to make a fresh start on ethical and social issues. It took the company some time to realise this, but by 1993 it had developed adequate environmental and equal opportunities policies, including support for Opportunity 2000. There was more than the obligatory reference to employee involvement in the formal directors' report (1993), but there was no discussion of environmental issues, even though the company is committed to phasing out the use of tropical hardwoods. The only other ethical matter that impinges on the group is that of animal testing on some products.

Corporate governance

Separate Chairman and Chief Executive Y
Number of Directors 9
Number of Non-Executive Directors 3
(3 Independent Directors)
Insulated Directors None

Board Committees
Audit: Y   Remuneration: Y

Remuneration

Year end	31.12.91	31.12.92	31.12.93
Total board £M	1.14	1.30	1.32
% change	8	14	1
Highest paid £	191,921	214,358	217,383
% change	-1	12	1

Board
Smith, Michael J *Chief Executive*
Beattie, W Keith C *Executive Director*
Fishbourne, Peter J *Executive Director*
Green, Trevor B *Executive Director*
O'Callaghan, J P (Sean) *Executive Director*
Stewart, Robert D *Finance Director*
Birch, Peter G *Independent Non-Executive*
Mackinlay, J Lindsay *Independent Non-Executive*
Donne, David L *Non-Executive Chairman*

The company retains some of the feel of a subsidiary, rather than of a fully fledged public company in its own right. There are only three independent directors, including chairman David Donne. Argos has followed the fashion for separating the formal report and accounts from the annual review, which is published separately together with summary financial statements. Shareholders must request the full accounts if they wish to receive them. The 1993 review included a statement on corporate governance, which described changes that have been made

154 ARJO WIGGINS APPLETON plc

in order to comply with the Cadbury Code. There is still no nominations committee, however, as this is not considered appropriate by the company.

ARJO WIGGINS APPLETON plc

Gateway House, Basing View, Basingstoke, Hampshire RG21 2EE
Tel: 01256 723000
Chairman Anthony (Cob) Stenham
Chief executive Alain Soulas
Substantial shareholder Arjomari/Saint Louis/Worms 40%
Main brands Conqueror, Courier, NCR, Idem
Main subsidiaries Arjo UK Merchants, Arjo Wiggins Appleton (Holdings), Wiggins Teape Group Ltd
Size £2.7 billion sales, £2.4 billion stock market value, 18,800 employees
5-year growth n/a
Solvency debt = 28% shareholders' funds, interest cover 5 times
Political donations 0
Charitable donations £110,000

Major developments

1919 Wiggins Teape became public
1970 Wiggins Teape bought by BAT Industries
1978 Appleton bought by BAT
1990 Wiggins Teape Appleton demerged from BAT; merged with Arjomari-Prioux; name changed from Wiggins Teape Appleton to Arjo Wiggins Appleton
1991 bought 62.5% of Buhl Group, 95.2% of Organizzazione Calegari, 40% of Usiplast
1992 boardroom split leading to departure of chief executive

Outlook

This company is the result of a merger between Wiggins Teape Appleton and Arjomari-Prioux, following the 1990 demerger of the former company from Bat Industries. But these latest developments are merely the latest in a long line of corporate rearrangements.

The separate flotation of this paper company was just the latest event in a long history of corporate reshuffling which has affected the constituent parts of BAT over the years. The Appleton end of the business belonged to the US business-machine and electronics company NCR from 1970–78. Prior to that, Appleton, as an independent business, had a long association with NCR because of the joint development by the two companies of carbonless (NCR) paper.

Wiggins Teape, the British arm of the company, was also independent once and has a long history as a stationer and paper manufacturer. The Conqueror brand was launched in 1888 and the company was first quoted on the stock exchange in 1919. BAT first began to take an interest in what had become an international paper and packaging group in the 1960s, when the conglomerate built up a sizeable shareholding. Wiggins Teape eventually became part of the BAT group in 1970.

The British and American arms had operated more or less independently, but came together in one company when both were floated off from BAT in 1990. Yet they were not alone for long. Before the end of that year, ambitious chief executive Stephen Walls had agreed a merger with the French paper company Arjomari; hence the birth of Arjo Wiggins Appleton.

Mr Walls did not have much time to build on this success, however. Following disagreements with his fellow directors, he departed in the summer of 1992 to take up the chairmanship of troubled foods group Albert Fisher. (This made a hat trick of pay-offs: he was previously made redundant when Plessey, where he was finance director, was taken over by GEC and Siemens, and he came to Plessey after losing his job with Chesebrough-Pond's when Unilever bought the US toiletries group.)

The affair was more than a boardroom tiff. It brought into question (so far as British shareholders were concerned) the nature of the new group and, especially, who was pulling the strings. Union with Arjomari had not proved to be a full merger with a discrete, independent company. Arjomari was at the centre of a typical French web of shareholdings: a food-manufacturing company called St Louis owned 43 per cent of its shares; St Louis was 38 per cent owned by a conglomerate called Pechelbronn, which in turn was largely controlled by the merchant bank Worms. Wiggins Teape had issued shares to Arjomari shareholders to satisfy the terms of the merger, and as a result, St Louis, and hence eventually Worms, ended up owning almost two-fifths of the Arjo Wiggins Appleton shares. The Worms interest is represented on the board by Nicholas Worms, senior partner of Maison Worms.

While this network of shareholdings was fine in principle, British shareholders began to wonder in whose interests the group was being run when, in September 1992, they were hit with a shock dividend cut. Without warning, and, in British eyes, without good cause, Arjo announced a drop of almost a fifth in its interim dividend, along with a fall in profits for the half-year of more than a quarter.

In such circumstances it might seem sensible to conserve cash rather than pay it out to shareholders, and this indeed is what the French owners argued. But to British investors brought up on the stiff-upper-lip tradition of holding the dividend until disaster looms, the cut seemed inexplicable. Debts were low, the company was not in serious trouble, prospects seemed better than for many other European paper companies. Suspicious Brits muttered darkly about self-serving St Louis interests, and the share price fell by 29 per cent. A plunge of more than a third in the earnings for 1993 made the dividend cut seem

ARJO WIGGINS APPLETON

Share record

Return on shareholders' equity	%	6.28
5-year price high	p	315.0
5-year price low	p	127.0
Dividend yield	%	2.81
5-year high	%	8.08
5-year low	%	2.58
Price/earnings ratio		28.4
5-year high		30.9
5-year low		7.0

Share price performance (in pence)

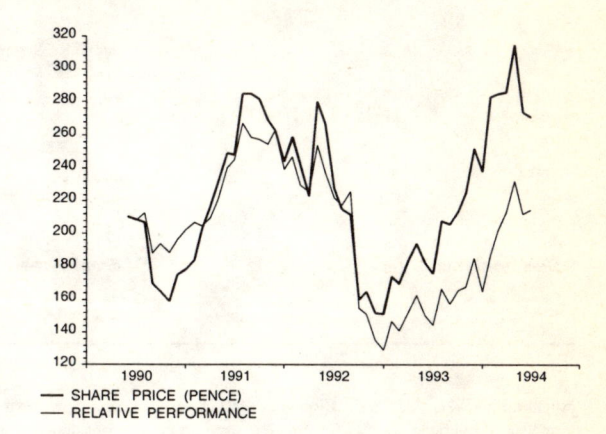

— SHARE PRICE (PENCE)
— RELATIVE PERFORMANCE

Financial record

		31/12/90	31/12/91	31/12/92	31/12/93
Total sales	£'000	1,506M	2,487M	2,623M	2,727M
Pre-tax profit	£'000	167,600	231,600	166,700	136,600
Published retentions	£'000	61,400	80,700	43,400	12,200
Earnings per share	p	22.85	17.09	12.53	9.08
Dividend per share	p	8.35	8.35	6.50	6.50
Operating cash flow	£'000	-82,900	55,700	-54,800	9,000
Net assets per share	p	265.13	161.22	182.82	188.51
Net debt/(cash)	£'000	172,700	173,000	315,800	326,600
Shareholders' funds	£	1,009M	1,075M	1,207M	1,181M
Return on capital	%		21.53	14.91	11.63
Profit margin	%	10.62	9.38	6.47	5.53
Sales per employee	£	126.88	131.49	134.94	145.28
Interest cover		15.15	18.92	6.86	5.44
Dividend cover		2.71	2.05	1.93	1.40
Sales increase	%		65.08	5.47	3.98
Earnings growth	%		-25.21	-26.69	-27.49
Investment x depreciation		1.68	1.39	1.60	1.46
Investment as % assets		11.20	13.09	14.95	14.91
Number of employees		11,873	18,911	19,436	18,771

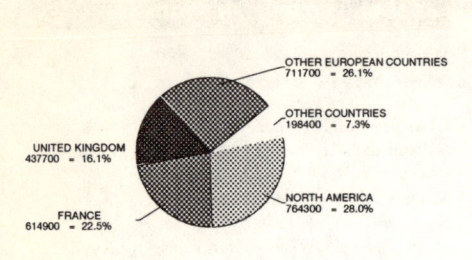

Sales analysis

Employment

prudent, however. Yet the situation was not as bad as it appeared: operating profits for the year were down by only 5 per cent, and business was improving sharply in the UK and US by the beginning of 1994.

In fact prospects do look promising, especially once the European recession is over. The French, British and US bases give the company a very broad spread, although North America dominates so far as profits are concerned. The group also has expertise in the growth areas not just of carbonless paper (stemming from the NCR connection) but of all kinds of coated products, including thermal papers. It intends to build on these strengths, by investing heavily in manufacturing and by capitalising on its unique European distribution network.

Successful examples of Franco-British co-operation are rare, whether in business or other fields. There is a chance that this company could be one of them.

Shares

When Wiggins Teape Appleton was first demerged from BAT in 1990, the market had no other company to compare it with for valuation purposes, so the shares tracked the market, although helped by an undercurrent of bid speculation. The group's attractiveness to a bidder was increased by the £126 million it was to get from selling its Portuguese pulp business. The deal with Arjomari late in 1990 snuffed out the bid premium in the shares just before the Portguese deal was blocked at the start of 1991.

The new company was seen as being a defensive stock to hold and there was the prospect of a progressive dividend policy – its dividends rising faster than inflation. 1991 started off well for shareholders as the market took the view that the group's business looked good in the long term as its trading cycle was bound to recover some time. But its results through that year proved disappointing and management talk of a slowdown in trading hit the shares. The cracks in confidence started to appear in 1992 when, having reached a new peak on the back of the Tory election victory, the shares dropped after the board parted with its chief executive.

The shares underperformed the market and shareholders were unnerved as differences in policy emerged at the group. By the autumn, shareholders were up in arms when a cut in the dividend and a poor trading outlook sent the shares crashing down by 29 per cent in one day. They reached a record low of 129p before picking up a little in the market's December rally. In 1993 City analysts warned that the group faced a higher interest bill on a rising debt, predicted more tough trading and feared that worries over the cut dividend would keep the shares pinned to the floor. Nevertheless, hopes of economic recovery encouraged the shares to continue rising until April 1994.

Corporate conscience

Paper-making is an intensive industrial process which uses substantial amounts of electricity and tends to produce unpleasant effluent. Arjo Wiggins Appleton is therefore one of many industrial companies which needs to take strenuous measures to limit its impact on the environment. In the original flotation document for Wiggins Teape Appleton the group did make a commitment to environmental care. It said that senior officers have responsibility on a group-wide basis, while environmental issues are continually reviewed with the aim of anticipating adverse impacts, a process that is aided by regular environmental audits. The company does not appear to have followed up this statement with much enthusiasm, though. The 1993 annual report contained a brief section on environment and safety, but this did not go beyond a few pieces of good publicity and included no serious reporting.

The record suggests the company takes this policy seriously. The group has no record of conviction for water pollution, and in recent years there is only one instance of its exceeding permitted limits for discharges into water – at its Stoneywood mill near Aberdeen, in 1990. The group also has a clean record on health and safety.

Ethically, Arjo is relatively untainted. Like most multinationals, it operates in countries with oppressive regimes – mostly in South America – and it does business in some of the poorest countries of the world. But Arjo has not attracted particular attention for its cavalier attitude. Back home, it attempts to demonstrate a responsible attitude through membership of BITC.

Corporate governance

Separate Chairman and Chief Executive Y
Number of Directors 11
Number of Non-Executive Directors 6
(3 Independent Directors)
Insulated Directors None

Board Committees
Audit: Y   Remuneration: Y

Remuneration

Year end	31.12.91	31.12.92	31.12.93
Total board £M	2.11	3.03	2.28
% change		78	44	-25
Highest paid £	380,955	307,166	422,345
% change		-9	-19	37

Board
Soulas, Alain *Chief Executive*
Stenham, Cob *Executive Chairman*
Beylier, Philippe *Executive Director*
Schumaker, Dale *Executive Director*
Isaac, Tony *Finance Director*
Loudon, George *Independent Non-Executive*
Powell, Sir Charles *Independent Non-Executive*
Tegner, Ian *Independent Non-Executive*
Dumon, Bernard *Non-Executive*
Galateri, Gabriele *Non-Executive*
Worms, Nicholas Clive *Non-Executive*

During the period in 1992 which saw the departure of the chief executive and an unexpected dividend cut, there was some concern that the board was unduly influenced by the French minority shareholders. The independent non-executives have since been strengthened, although they remain heavily outnumbered. At least the company retains a separate chairman, plus audit, nomination and remuneration committees, and all directors are elected periodically.

ASSOCIATED BRITISH FOODS plc

Weston Centre, 68 Knightsbridge,
London SW1X 7LR
Tel: 0171 589 6363
Chairman and Chief executive Garry Weston
Substantial shareholder Wittington Investments (Weston family) 63%
Main brands Sunblest, Allinson, Speedibake, Kingsmill, Mighty White and Vit-Be, The Baker's Oven, Silver Spoon sugar, Burton biscuits, Ryvita, Twinings
Main subsidiaries Allied Bakeries, Silbury Frozen Foods Ltd, British Sugar, R Twining & Co, Jacksons of Piccadilly.
Size £4.4 billion sales, £2.5 billion stock market value, 50,000 employees
5-year growth sales 76%, earnings per share 35%, employment -6%
Solvency debt n/a, interest cover n/a
Political donations 0
Charitable donations £300,000

Major developments
1935 became public as Allied Bakeries
1960 name changed to Associated British Foods Group
1967 Garry Weston appointed chairman
1986 the ABF Investments group (comprising the Finefare and Headway Construction groups) sold to Dee Corporation (subsequently Gateway)
1987 abandoned bid for Berisford
1991 bought British Sugar; Anglia Canners sold to Hillsdown Holdings
1994 sold most of Baker's Oven chain

Outlook
Associated British Foods (ABF) is one of the most private of public companies. The large Weston family shareholding (63 per cent) must have something to do with it, limiting the necessity to butter up other investors. The reclusive personality of chairman and chief executive Garry Weston is the other factor. Consequently the company does not go out of its way to explain its strategies and actions and to report the results of operations.

These characteristics are very clearly reflected in the group's operations. It is a careful, conservative business, sticking to the food-processing industry it knows best, and concentrating mainly on keeping costs down in order to squeeze extra efficiency out of the factories. Having seen the antics of many less careful companies during the late 1980s, this approach has a lot to commend it. But the result is an unexciting business and a pile of cash with which it ought to be possible to do something more productive than the corporate equivalent of sticking it in the building society. (See also GEC in manufacturing and GUS in retailing, similarly private and conservatively run companies.)

ASSOCIATED BRITISH FOODS

Associated British Foods

Share record

Return on shareholders' equity	%	11.23
5-year price high	p	607.0
5-year price low	p	370.0
Dividend yield	%	3.34
5-year high	%	4.59
5-year low	%	2.91
Price/earnings ratio		10.1
5-year high		13.0
5-year low		8.3

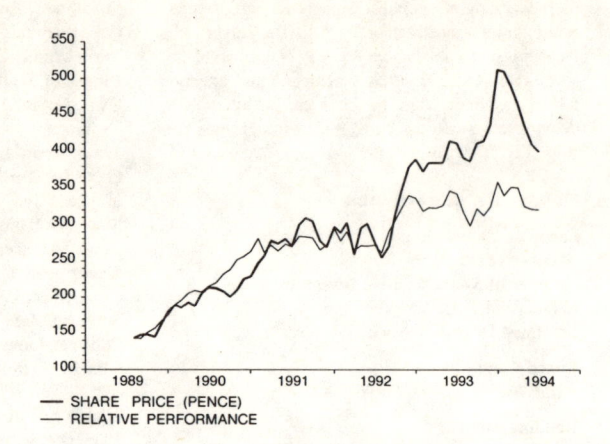

Share price performance (in pence)

— SHARE PRICE (PENCE)
— RELATIVE PERFORMANCE

Financial record

		31/3/89	31/3/90	14/9/91 76 weeks	12/9/92	18/9/93
Total sales	£	2,496M	2,775M	4,877M	3,954M	4,386M
Pre-tax profit	£'000	231,400	283,500	459,400	297,000	320,000
Published retentions	£'000	154,600	217,900	118,600	103,000	161,000
Earnings per share	p	34.61	41.86	45.93	43.64	46.76
Dividend per share	p	9.30	11.00	16.70	14.00	15.00
Operating cash flow	£'000	67,900	69,500	159,900	74,000	99,000
Net assets per share	p	393.00	446.59	416.38	429.40	468.82
Net debt/(cash)	£	-936M	-1,083M	-417M	-409M	-501M
Shareholders' funds	£	1,702M	1,925M	1,637M	1,708M	1,879M
Return on capital	%	14.29	15.48	26.26	17.82	17.56
Profit margin	%	9.27	10.22	9.42	7.51	7.30
Sales per employee	£	47.08	53.01	90.36	76.44	87.78
Interest cover		-2.98	-1.45	-2.17	-12.32	-6.20
Dividend cover		3.72	3.81	2.75	3.12	3.12
Sales increase	%	9.88	11.15	75.78	-18.93	10.93
Earnings growth	%	14.28	20.97	9.71	-4.97	7.14
Investment x depreciation		1.96	1.85	1.79	1.58	1.28
Investment as % assets		18.04	17.95	19.54	14.63	12.87
Number of employees		53.024	52,345	53,975	51,724	49,968

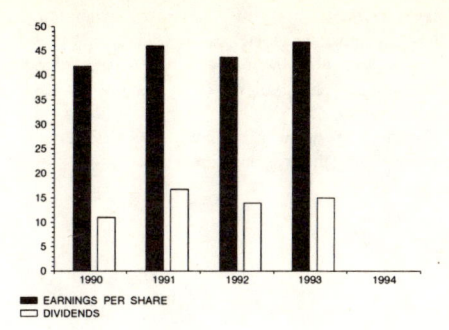

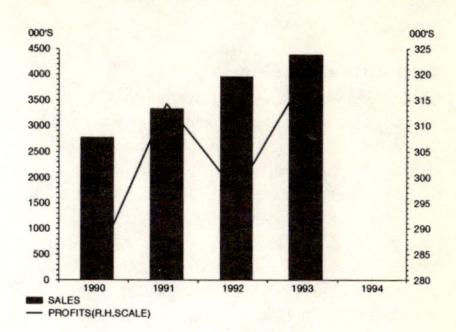

Earnings and dividends

Sales and profits

ABF's personality is clearly illustrated by its dogged pursuit of British Sugar, which it finally managed to acquire in 1990. The pursuit began back in 1987, when the sugar company was owned by commodities business S & W Berisford (now Berisford International). Berisford had acquired British Sugar in 1982 after a prolonged takeover battle. It retained the business only because the Monopolies Commission prevented Italian sugar group Feruzzi taking a controlling share stake and ruled out a merger with Tate & Lyle, which Berisford had considered when it was under attack from Hillsdown. ABF subsequently picked up the 24 per cent shareholding in Berisford which had been held by Ferruzzi, and used this as a platform for a takeover bid.

Fortunately for ABF the stock market crash of 1987 intervened, just in time for ABF to abandon its bid, which looked mightily over-priced in the wake of the crash. Mr Weston was not to be denied, however. In 1990 he returned, not with a takeover bid for the whole of Berisford, but with £880 million just for British Sugar. This time he was successful. The acquisition paid dividends in 1993 when British Sugar proved a major element in ABF's 27 per cent profits rise. Thanks to windfall gains from the devaluation of sterling, British Sugar increased profits by 17 per cent to £162 million – 59 per cent of total operating profits.

Success leaves ABF with a range of (mainly British) basic food-processing businesses, though still with a toe in retailing through the Baker's Oven shops and the remnants of a grocery chain in Ireland, left behind when Fine Fare was sold to Dee Corporation in 1986 to become part of the ill-fated Gateway operation.

The addition of sugar has lessened the importance of bread, though ABF remains Britain's biggest baker with Sunblest. While being a solid business of the kind beloved by ABF, bread has been subject to repeated price wars, the latest of which forced Mr Weston to admit in 1992 that milling and baking were not earning an adequate return on capital. Supermarket price wars, although largely funded at present by the participants rather than their wholesalers, are expected to increase pressures on ABF's core business, making price rises almost impossible to implement successfully. ABF's strong balance sheet does, however, make it more able to withstand this than some of its rivals. The balance sheet is expected to be bolstered, moreover, as the group has admitted that it is in negotiation to sell its Baker's Oven retail chain.

Apart from bread and sugar, ABF owns a number of other valuable, but probably underexploited, brands including Twinings tea, Burton biscuits and Ryvita. What these brands need is a little consumer marketing flair to increase their appeal to shoppers. They are unlikely to get it from ABF.

Shares

Apart from a flourish in 1986 when the group sold its Fine Fare supermarket chain, ABF's shares tracked the FTSE 100 index until the peak of the 1987 bull market. Then ABF attracted investors as its basic food products were relatively safe in the bear market which ensued. It was helped by the fact that it was conservatively run and averse to taking risks, as well as having a great deal of money in the bank. The safe and steady image stuck with the group until 1989 when it began to outperform a jittery stock market and shrewdly sold its shares in the Gateway supermarket chain.

The following year it finally pounced on British Sugar. This boosted the group's rating just in time for it to become a safety-first share once more as the recession bit. The share rating slipped in 1992 as a bread price war hit profits just as lower interest rates cut the income from its savings. The slide continued throughout most of 1993, but the shares then staged a brief recovery, thanks to the prospect of some improvement in bread prices.

Corporate conscience

As an old-fashioned, very private company, ABF does not appear to have adopted any of the 'trendy' ethical issues, but pays for a clean conscience through corporate donations and involvement in BITC, including membership of the Per Cent Club.

Ethically, it may cause offence by selling in its Irish supermarkets tobacco, alcohol, and toiletries tested on animals, in addition to selling food products and ingredients likely to have been tested on animals, including sugar in British Sugar. ABF has no direct links with oppressive regimes, however.

Environmentally, British Sugar has a poor record on discharges into water, having exceeded permitted levels at least once in both 1990 and 1991 at several plants. Nor does ABF appear to have made any special effort to remove chemicals which damage the ozone layer from its refrigeration units. But it has made some efforts on recycling and reclamation. The 1993 annual report included a statement on environmental policy, showing that this issue is being taken seriously. Yet the policy does not include the crucial element of audit and quantified measurement.

The group also has a black mark against it on health and safety, with a £500 fine awarded against Allied Bakeries in 1989 for breaches of the Factories Act.

Corporate governance

Separate Chairman and Chief Executive N
Number of Directors 6
Number of Non-Executive Directors 1
(0 Independent Directors)
Insulated Directors None

Board Committees
Audit: N   Remuneration: N

Remuneration

Year end	14.09.91	12.09.92	18.09.93
Total board £M	0.67	0.75	0.70
% change		12	-7
Highest paid £	236,000	165,000	188,000
% change		-30	14

Board
Weston, Garry H   *Chairman & Chief Executive*
Bailey, Harold W   *Executive Director*
Jackson, Peter J   *Executive Director*
Shaw, Trevor H M   *Executive Director*
Tidey, Donald J   *Executive Director*
Weston, W G Galen   *Non-Executive*

For such a huge company ABF acknowledges its public status only minimally. But in 1993 this most private of public companies was finally forced to begin addressing many of the governance issues raised by the Cadbury Code. Admittedly ABF still has only one non-executive director (a relative of the chairman) and admits to not meeting Cadbury guidelines on other central issues such as audit committees and executive directors' pay. But its annual report finally 'recognises the force of circumstance and current opinion' underlying the Code and is now considering falling into line. In May 1994 the family shareholdings were reorganised, but ABF remains controlled by the Weston Foundation.

BAA plc

130 Wilton Road, London SW1V 1LQ
Tel: 0171 834 9449
Chairman Dr Brian Smith
Chief executive Sir John Egan
Main subsidiaries Heathrow Airport, Gatwick Airport, Stansted Airport, Airports UK (Southampton) Ltd, Skycare Cargo Ltd, Glasgow Airport Ltd, Edinburgh Airport Ltd, Aberdeen Airport Ltd, BAA Hotels Ltd, Lynton Properties
Size £0.9 billion sales, £4.9 billion stock market value, 8,500 employees
5-year growth sales 44%, earnings per share 26%, employment -11%
Solvency debt = 49% shareholders' funds, interest cover 6 times
Political donations 0
Charitable donations £541,000

Major developments
1987 privatised
1988 bought Lynton Property and Reversionary plc
1989 bought Scottish Express Ltd
1990 acquired freehold of Southampton Eastleigh airport
1992 Prestwick Airport sold to British Aerospace

Outlook

BAA was British Airports Authority, one of the Thatcher era's smaller privatisations. For a while in the late 1980s it toyed with the notion of becoming a diversified property company, but the property slump soon put a stop to that and it returned to being mainly just BAA, which is essentially a retailer. It is experimenting with non-airport property/retail developments, but on a minor scale in 1994.

True, BAA's premises are a little different from most stores: they are not in city centres and they do have rather a lot of ancillary services. But the way BAA is moving, there will soon be little difference between somewhere such as Heathrow and one of the new, out-of-town shopping malls such as Lakeside at Thurrock or the Gateshead Metro Centre except that you need an air ticket and a passport to get to most of

BAA

Share record

Return on shareholders' equity	%	9.45
5-year price high	p	1081.0
5-year price low	p	326.0
Dividend yield	%	2.36
5-year high	%	4.95
5-year low	%	1.91
Price/earnings ratio		23.1
5-year high		25.4
5-year low		9.2

Share price performance (in pence)

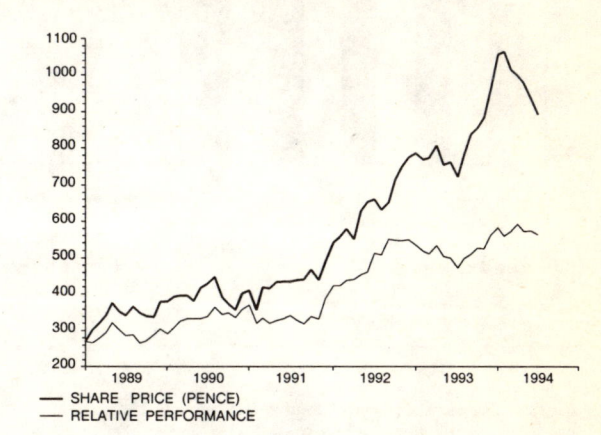

— SHARE PRICE (PENCE)
— RELATIVE PERFORMANCE

Financial record

		31/3/90	31/3/91	31/3/92	31/3/93	31/3/94
Total sales	£'000	662,000	724,600	787,900	808,300	952,800
Pre-tax profit	£'000	256,300	284,000	282,800	291,900	322,400
Published retentions	£'000	204,700	124,300	81,200	129,500	147,800
Earnings per share	p	37.22	44.97	47.76	42.25	46.92
Dividend per share	p	11.50	13.00	14.50	16.00	18.00
Operating cash flow	£'000	-52,000	-196M	-23,000	173,000	32,000
Net assets per share	p	473.74	525.89	533.57	567.55	651.90
Net debt/(cash)	£'000	557,200	868,500	926,600	737,400	725,500
Shareholders' funds	£	1,884M	1,876M	1,880M	2,047M	2,543M
Return on capital	%	12.44	11.84	12.95	13.13	12.20
Profit margin	%	38.72	39.19	35.89	36.11	n/a
Sales per employee	£	69.53	66.76	76.21	96.03	112.13
Interest cover		0.00	0.00	6.04	5.62	8.02
Dividend cover		3.24	3.46	3.29	2.64	2.61
Sales increase	%	13.84	9.46	8.74	2.59	17.89
Earnings growth	%	35.94	20.83	6.20	-11.53	11.05
Investment x depreciation		4.40	7.34	2.90	0.98	2.51
Investment as % assets		19.10	25.01	13.23	4.66	11.12
Number of employees		9,521	10,854	10,338	8,417	8,498

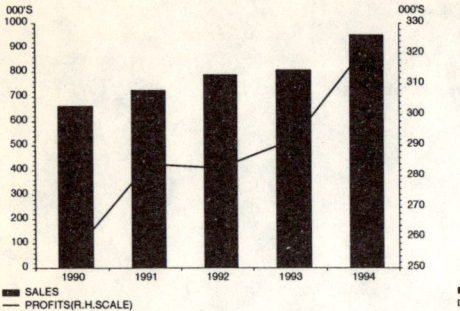

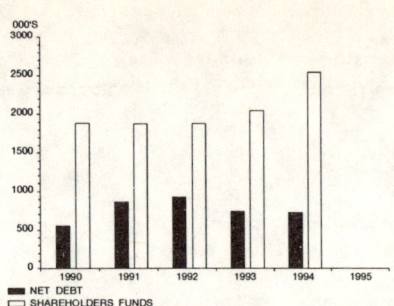

Sales and profits

Debt and shareholders' funds

the airport shops. The group's airport operations have gradually shifted from loss to (probably) a small profit in 1993, but the bulk of profits comes from other income – primarily from duty-free and other sales, plus car parking, rental of retail space, catering and other commercial activities.

Heathrow and Gatwick produce the vast bulk of BAA's profits, suggesting that if this really was just another public company, it would have sold off or closed smaller sites in Scotland. In fact Prestwick was sold in 1992, but BAA added to its provincial locations with the acquisition of Southampton during the previous year. In any case, BAA is not just another public company. It is a privatised business, with a virtual monopoly in the south east and a regulator in the form of the Civil Aviation Authority. The CAA was once thought to be somewhat ineffectual as a regulator, compared to the fierce oppressors of British Gas and Telecom. That was until 1991, when the Author-ity shocked everybody by going much further than a Monopolies Commission recommendation. The CAA came up with a pricing formula for the two years from April 1992 of RPI -8 per cent – BAA must keep increases in aircraft landing fees at least 8 per cent below the rate of inflation, so that with inflation below 8 per cent, BAA's prices must fall.

At the time a shocked Sir John Egan warned that investment plans would be jeopardised. But they have not been. BAA profits continue to rise, and plans for expansion continue to be made. BAA wants to build a fifth terminal at Heathrow, almost doubling capacity to nearly 80 million passengers a year. It is also helping to build a fast rail link from Heathrow to London's Paddington station. All this suggests that the CAA got its formula about right. If anything, the regulator erred on the lenient side. The formula relaxes swiftly to just RPI -1 by 1996. Yet BAA is a low-risk, high-growth business. Heathrow, its princi-

pal asset, is the world's leading international airport. Gatwick has been improved considerably since the mid-1980s, while Stansted is likely to continue slowly increasing its traffic figures, and hence its financial performance. Air travel seems as certain to keep rising, as does road travel, despite the blip at the start of the 1990s caused first by the Gulf War and then by recession. And BAA has shown that it can squeeze many more shops into its airports, and thus squeeze out much more profit.

There are threats, of course. The end of duty-free sales within the EC has been postponed, but not abandoned. North Atlantic traffic, which accounts for a quarter of Heathrow's business, has shown itself to be very sensitive to recession and to war or other political unrest in Europe. And the prediction of sustained increases in air travel could be proved to be entirely unfounded in 10 years' time. But in the meantime, BAA seems set to fly high.

Shares

BAA has been a great success since its privatisation in 1987. The market crash that year served to underline its appeal to shareholders seeking a bid-proof, steady profit-earner which could maintain dividend payments. The company's appeal made it a core holding for institutions and the shares' standing was little affected by a flurry of acquisitions in the late 1980s.

However, in 1989 the board overreached itself, spoiling the shares' track record, when the company moved into hotels and non-airport retailing just as the bubble in those businesses was bursting. The policy was reversed, and even property write-downs in 1991 and 1992 failed to pull the shares back. There was a slight dip in the share rating when air traffic was adversely affected by the Gulf War, but BAA is seen as a safe investment in the long term and is expected to benefit strongly from an easing in the world recession. So 1992 saw a surge in the shares and investors had digested the new pricing regime. This was sustained, and even improved on, in 1994.

Corporate conscience

BAA has made serious efforts to develop an effective environmental policy which is comprehensive and includes goals and targets that can be measured. Yet it also has a record of exceeding water discharge consents at Stansted on a number of occasions, and at Aberdeen. Intrinsically, its activity of encouraging people to undertake high-energy travel makes it one of many companies implicated in the build-up of greenhouse gas – albeit indirectly in this case because it does not own the aircraft which make the emissions. BAA has ventured into environmental reporting, but promises only in 1995 to report against specific performance targets. It has adopted an innovative stance on noise pollution, however: fining airlines which exceed night noise limits, which raised £107,000 for local charities in 1993.

By the nature of its business (catering and retailing), BAA is also implicated in the sale of alcohol and tobacco, and of cosmetics and toiletries which are likely to have been tested on animals. In addition, one recorded complaint was upheld against BAA in 1991 by the ASA and another at the start of 1994.

The company is publicly committed to equal opportunities but has yet to satisfy EIRIS that it has a sufficiently rigorous public policy on this issue.

Corporate governance

Separate Chairman and Chief Executive Y
Number of Directors 12
Number of Non-Executive Directors 5
(4 Independent Directors)
Insulated Directors None

Board Committees
Audit: Y   Remuneration: Y

Remuneration

Year end	31.03.92	31.03.93	31.03.94
Total board £M	1.65	1.88	2.33
% change	-3	14	24
Highest paid £	311,000	398,000	533,000
% change	-6	28	34

Board
Egan, Sir John   *Chief Executive*
Edington, Gordon   *Executive Director*
Everitt, Richard   *Executive Director*
Gibson, J M Barry   *Executive Director*
Hodgkinson, Mike   *Executive Director*
Maine, Michael   *Executive Director*
Ellis, Nigel   *Finance Director*
Middleton, P J   *Independent Non-Executive*
Urquhart, Lawrence M   *Independent Non-Executive*
Lord Wright   *Non-Executive*
Smith, Dr N Brian   *Non-Executive Chairman*
Maxmin, Dr Tim   *Independent Non-Executive*

Disclosure to shareholders has improved in recent years. In the boardroom the balance between executives and non-executives is healthy and, in addition to remuneration and audit committees, there is a top-level safety committee. The company prominently reveals details of executives' salaries. The annual report includes a clear and comprehensive section entitled 'How we run the company'. Generous service contracts exist for top executives, as does a bonus scheme entitling executives to as much as 40 per cent of salary subject to earnings growth, but also taking account of their improvements to customer service and productivity.

BAT INDUSTRIES plc

P O Box 345, Windsor House, 50 Victoria Street, London SW1H 0NL
Tel: 0171 222 7979
Chairman Sir Patrick Sheehy
Deputy chairman and chief executive Martin Broughton
Main brands Kent, Lucky Strike, State Express 555, Barclay, Kool, Capri
Main subsidiaries British American Tobacco Co Ltd, Henri Wintermans' Sigarenfabrieken BV (Netherlands), The Allied Dunbar Group, Eagle Star Insurance, Farmers Group (US), W D & H O Wills (Australia), Souza Cruz (Brazil), Threadneedle Asset Management
Size £17.9 billion sales, £13.4 billion stock market value, 190,000 employees
5-year growth sales 34%, earnings per share 8%, employment 22%
Solvency debt = 49% shareholders' funds, interest cover 9 times
Political donations £5,000 Centre for Policy Studies
Charitable donations £7.7 million

Major developments
1902 British American Tobacco formed to acquire overseas business of American Tobacco and Imperial Tobacco
1912 became quoted on UK stock market
1914 acquired Souza Cruz in Brazil
1932 acquired HBZ in Germany
1966 bought Henri Wintermans
1976 name changed from British American Tobacco to BAT Industries; bought Saks Fifth Avenue
1979 bought Argos
1982 bought Marshall Field's
1984 bought Eagle Star Insurance
1985 bought Allied Dunbar
1988 bought Farmers Group
1989 fought off Hoylake Investments; demerged its UK stores and paper divisions, sold US stores
1990 Argos floated; Wiggins Teape Appleton

BAT INDUSTRIES

Share record

Return on shareholders' equity	%	22.77
5-year price high	p	565.0
5-year price low	p	261.0
Dividend yield	%	5.76
5-year high	%	7.94
5-year low	%	3.02
Price/earnings ratio		15.6
5-year high		31.1
5-year low		7.0

Share price performance (in pence)

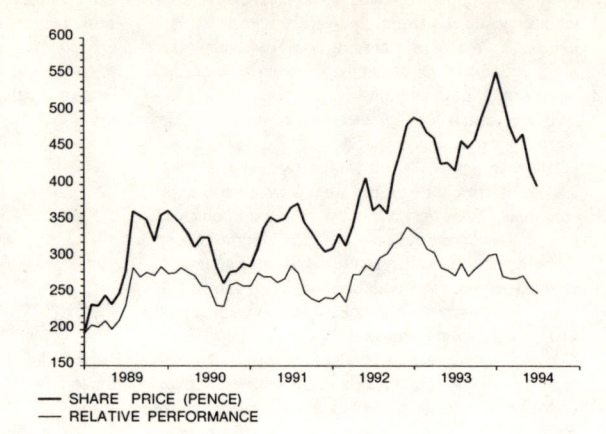

— SHARE PRICE (PENCE)
— RELATIVE PERFORMANCE

Financial record

		31/12/89	31/12/90	31/12/91	31/12/92	31/12/93
Total sales	£	13,311M	15,027M	13,817M	16,006M	17,879M
Pre-tax profit	£'000	2,027M	957,000	1,102M	1,586M	1,778M
Published retentions	£'000	751,000	521,000	71,000	344,000	525,000
Earnings per share	p	32.63	11.72	15.72	25.91	35.40
Dividend per share	p	13.15	15.55	16.80	18.60	20.10
Operating cash flow	£'000	259,000	-538M	-236M	420,000	744,000
Net assets per share	p	233.27	728.89	828.18	977.57	1,132
Net debt/(cash)	£	1,895M	1,513M	1,563M	2,201M	2,055M
Shareholders' funds	£	4,683M	2,874M	2,989M	3,855M	4,679M
Return on capital	%	31.90	8.90	6.05	6.86	6.43
Profit margin	%	8.16	5.40	6.90	8.99	8.92
Sales per employee	£	85.57	135.59	130.53	80.84	93.95
Interest cover		7.48	2.76	4.70	9.36	8.72
Dividend cover		2.48	0.75	0.94	1.39	1.76
Sales increase	%	17.19	12.89	-8.05	15.84	11.70
Earnings growth	%	20.74	-64.08	34.12	64.85	36.61
Investment x depreciation		1.18	1.27	1.73	1.44	1.56
Investment as % assets		12.19	16.78	20.38	17.01	19.61
Number of employees		155,563	110,823	105,855	197,989	190,308

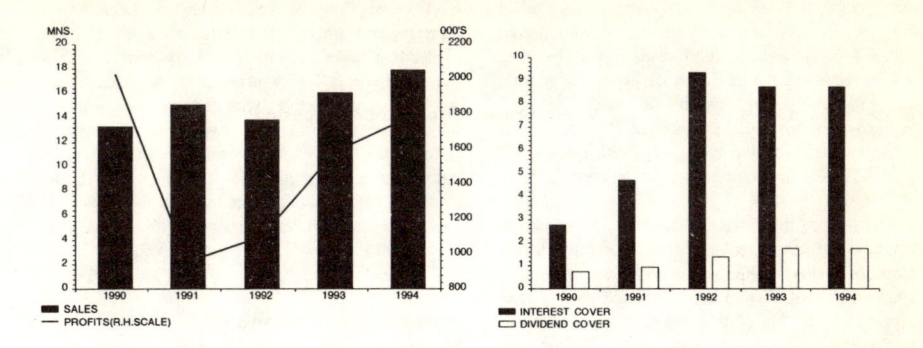

Sales and profits

Interest and dividend cover

floated; VG Instruments sold
1991 bought Pecs Tobacco Factory in Hungary
1994 combined fund management businesses in Threadneedle Asset Management; bought American Tobacco for £1 billion.

Outlook
Like most of the world's tobacco companies, BAT has faced an uphill struggle finding something sensible to do with the huge cash flows generated by its cigarettes. This kind of mature business, which needs relatively little investment because it is not expanding, throws off cash in trainloads. Some tobacco companies, such as Philip Morris in the US, have tied up with beer, but that is no more a growth business than cigarettes. R J Reynolds (another US tobacco com-pany) tried food manufacturing when it merged with Nabisco, but that particular initiative ended in the huge buy-out which has seen the dismemberment of the latter.

BAT has strong US connections. Indeed the 'American' in its original title, British American Tobacco, was rather more important than the 'British', since BAT and Imperial Tobacco (now part of Hanson) once had a cosy agreement which carved up the world, leaving the UK to Imperial. BAT owns Players and Benson & Hedges, but not in the UK, although a brand swap with American brands gave the company the right to sell Lucky Strike and Pall Mall in France, for instance. BAT's main brands are Lucky Strike, Kent and Barclay, not best known to British smokers. Despite its US exposure, however, BAT has not tried beer or food manufacturing, although it has tried most things.

Lately it has been forced to abandon most of its diversifications. Ace financier Sir James Goldsmith (and a handful of his financial friends) shook BAT to its foundations, and showed the world that sheer size was no protection, when he launched a £13 billion takeover bid for the group in 1988. He argued that the days of conglomerates were over, that BAT shareholders gained nothing from their joint ownership of cigarettes, insurance, retailing and paper. Sir James and his friends coined the term 'unbundling' for their plan to tear the group apart.

BAT was not impressed, but its major shareholders were, and they made it plain to the group that the price of their loyalty in the face of the bid was for it to do at least some of the unbundling itself. Stores such as Saks Fifth Avenue and Marshall Fields in the US and Horten in Germany were eventually sold. In the UK Argos was floated off as a separately quoted company, as was Wiggins Teape Appleton (see Arjo). BAT is left with just tobacco and financial services.

Sadly for BAT and its shareholders, any benefit from the clear-out has been obscured by the disasters in its insurance companies. Farmers, the huge US acquisition which marked the end of the expansionary years, seems to have fared well enough. But in the UK the recession has hit Eagle Star probably harder than other insurance companies. The company was snapped up by BAT in 1984 to rescue it from the advances of German insurance giant Allianz, and, with BAT's financial clout behind it, was eager to grab business. It was particularly aggressive in the mortgage-indemnity market, under the common misapprehension that house prices only go up, not down. Recession brought the realisation that this was not so, and with the rising tide of repossessions the building societies called on their insurers to pay up on the indemnity policies. Eagle Star lost over £200 million on this business in 1991, and not much less in 1992. It did manage to claw back some ground in 1993 and, despite possible loss of market share, attempted to stick to good-quality business. Recession did not help its financial products compa-

BAT INDUSTRIES plc

ny, Allied Dunbar. Despite (like many other insurance companies) having to make provisions against the mis-selling of private pensions, market leader Allied Dunbar (whose fund management business was merged with that of Eagle Star) is set for growth, although BAT complains that its insurance companies are having to pay a princely £30 million a year to compensate for the collapse of other insurance ventures and to comply with the cost of City regulation.

Meanwhile the tobacco business trundles on, although the impact of price wars in the US and recession in major European markets was evident in 1993 when profits from tobacco fell. This is widely supposed to be a declining business, as the habit of smoking meets with increasing disapprobation. But while the proportion of smokers in developed Western countries continues to fall, the cigarette companies are compensated by growth in consumption in the developing world, plus access to new markets in Eastern Europe, China and Japan.

BAT is probably the most international of the major tobacco companies, having a monopoly in some developing countries, although facing state monopolies in others. Yet its record does not suggest that this has helped to produce better-than-average performance. The group remains a puzzle. There seems little reason to put tobacco and insurance together, and despite BAT's intention to give more profits to shareholders (in the form of dividends), it may not be long before BAT is looking for something else on which to spend its excess cash. Despite denials that the French Groupe Victoire was its target, in 1994 BAT was clearly planning a sizeable European acquisition. With tobacco profits showing the strain of the US price war, BAT took little time in suggesting that its profits growth, courtesy of the upturn in insurance earnings, was a vindication of the group's diversification.

Shares

The two key events of the 1980s for BAT were the acquisition of Eagle Star in 1984, which lost the group so much money, and the abortive takeover bid from Hoylake, the vehicle for Sir James Goldsmith, in 1988–9, which for a time jerked the group's share price out of its rut. The failure of the bid left the shares to fall relative to the rest of the market, although it also jolted the board into hiving off the Argos and Wiggins Teape businesses.

BAT's chief attraction to shareholders has continued to be the dividend income which flows mostly from tobacco sales. But the fluctuating fortunes of the Eagle Star insurance business have periodically hurt the group's rating compared with tobacco rivals like Rothmans which have been nothing like as ambitious in their diversification programmes. In 1991 Eagle Star's exposure to mortgage-protection schemes weakened BAT's status as a recession-resistant stock.

In 1992 the group kept faith with investors by paying a dividend that was not covered by earnings. This determined stance on dividend policy, the strength of BAT's cash flow, its renewed grip on Eagle Star's finances and its resumed status as a tax-efficient investment raised its rating over the course of that year. But since 1993 worries about America's anti-smoking stance, coupled with persistent rumours of a major Continental takeover, have undermined confidence in BAT shares, exacerbating the market's difficulty in rating a company that combines tobacco and insurance. Shares have lagged behind the FTSE 100 index and seem unlikely to sparkle without some dramatic push for growth by the group.

Corporate conscience

As a tobacco company, BAT does not stand much chance so far as many people's ethics are concerned. In addition to the health implications of smoking, however, tobacco companies like BAT are tainted because their product is tested on animals. (BAT contracts out this activity.) As a major transnational company, it also operates in many countries where human-rights violations have been recorded, from Angola to Zimbabwe, taking in South Korea and Thailand on the way. BAT has a sizeable operation in South Africa, which may now be a positive indicator for some investors, especially as the group does recognise trade unions in that country.

In general, and disregarding South Africa, the group's employment and social policies and practices compare well with those of its peers. It has a formal equal opportunities policy which is actively implemented, and makes substantial efforts concerning employee involvement. BAT has also supported Fullemploy. This responsible approach is reflected, too, in community involvement, where the company makes substantial donations to charities and to the community as a whole, and has a payroll-giving scheme. (Some of the charitable donations, it must be said, go to the tobacco industry's Health Promotion Research trust.) BAT is a member of BITC and the Per Cent Club, while Allied Dunbar, the personal savings subsidiary, has a reputation for substantial charitable activity and is a separate member of the Per Cent Club. Allied Dunbar also supports Opportunity 2000.

BAT has an effective environmental policy which includes regular monitoring and review of its industrial practices, and has used independent environmental auditors. The group has also taken steps to minimise the use of wood for tobacco curing by its suppliers.

There is no record of advertising complaints having been upheld against members of the group.

Corporate governance

Separate Chairman and Chief Executive Y
Number of Directors 11
Number of Non-Executive Directors 5
(4 Independent Directors)
Insulated Directors None

BET plc

Board Committees
Audit: Y   Remuneration: Y

Remuneration

Year end	31.12.91	31.12.92	31.12.93
Total board £M	4.57	6.33	5.5
% change	-44	39	-13
Highest paid £	638,416	980,679	777,091
% change	22	54	-21

Board
Broughton, Martin Faulkner *Chief Executive*
Bramley, Barry David *Executive Director*
Denlea, Leo Edward *Executive Director*
Greener, Dr George *Executive Director*
Herter, Ulrich George Volk *Executive Director*
Allvey, David Philip *Finance Director*
Earl Cairns *Independent Non-Executive*
Lord Armstrong of Ilminster *Independent Non-Executive*
Rankin, Sir Alick *Independent Non-Executive*
Yeutter, Clayton *Independent Non-Executive*
Sheehy, Sir Patrick *Non-Executive Chairman*

One-third of the company's directors is non-executive. Details of the performance element of executive remuneration are included in the notes to the accounts but, like so many other companies, BAT disappointingly uses abbreviated accounts in addition to a more detailed set of financial statements to avoid much useful disclosure to a majority of shareholders. A company of the stature of BAT, whose Eagle Star subsidiary is a big shareholder on behalf of its insurance policyholders, could have been expected to outline its corporate governance philosophy to a wider number of shareholders. BAT has been given credit for nimble boardroom action to attempt to ensure a smooth handover when chairman Sir Patrick Sheehy eventually retires. This has involved the creation of a separate chief executive in Martin Broughton, but also a delay in Mr Sheehy's retirement date. And the separation of roles does little to introduce external influences, since Mr Broughton is a long-serving BAT man.

BET plc

Stratton House, Piccadilly, London W1X 6AS
Tel: 0171 629 8886
Chairman Sir Christopher Harding
Chief executive L John Clark
Main brands and subsidiaries Initial UK Ltd, Laundrycraft, Shorrock Ltd, United Transport
Size £2.2 billion sales, £990 million stock market value, 101,000 employees
5-year growth sales 3%, earnings per share -88%, employment -23%

Solvency debt n/a, interest cover 5 times
Political donations £12,500 Conservative Party
Charitable donations £145,900

Major developments
1896 The British Electric Traction Co formed
1934 first link with Advance Services
1955 BET became majority shareholder of Advance
1968 merger of Rediffusion TV with ABC to form Thames TV
1984 bought Anglian Windows; sold Rediffusion TV rental to Granada; took full control of Advance cable; TV interests sold to Robert Maxwell
1985 name changed to BET; bought Initial; failed bid for SGB
1986 bought HAT Group, Shorrock
1988 bought ADT's European commercial cleaning business, Pritchard Security, sold Argus Press
1989 bought Savam (France); sold United Transport Holdings (Australia); sold HAT Merchanting Ltd to Bowater Industries; bought Hestair
1990 sold Anglian Windows
1991 sold Biffa waste management business; sold Thames TV stake to Thorn-EMI; boardroom shake-up brings in new chief executive
1992 sold Initial USA; management buyout of Boulton & Paul

Outlook
Recession is merciless in testing corporate strategies to destruction. It cruelly exposed the attempts of BET to become a diversified service conglomerate, and left former chairman Sir Timothy Bevan and chief executive Nicholas Wills to carry the can.

In 1990, at the beginning of the recession, Mr Wills made the unfortunate and misguided claim that BET was recession-proof. A year later it was clear that he was wrong not only about that prediction, but also about his entire strategy of building a service group with interests stretching from scaffolding through distribution to the Initial laundry service. At first it seemed that the chief executive would escape the tumbrils, for he took over as chairman. But his survival was brief and his successor, John Clark, was soon left with a clear run to implement his recovery programme.

At least Mr Wills had a strategy. For years BET's problem was that it meandered rather aimlessly around the corporate jungle, not seeming to know what it wanted to do, or how to do it. Nationalisation was the problem. The initials BET used to represent British Electric Traction. The company ran trams, and generated the electricity to make them run. From electricity it moved to gas; then all three activities were nationalised, thereby depriving the company of its core businesses.

Like many other companies it found great difficulty knowing how to spend the compensation money. The result was that BET entered the 1980s with an incoherent collection of unrelated businesses, including publishing, tele-vision (the Rediffusion heritage

BET

Share record

Return on shareholders' equity	%	8.74
5-year price high	p	313.5
5-year price low	p	81.0
Dividend yield	%	3.80
5-year high	%	17.85
5-year low	%	1.74
Price/earnings ratio		8.9
5-year high		65.0
5-year low		3.6

Share price performance (in pence)

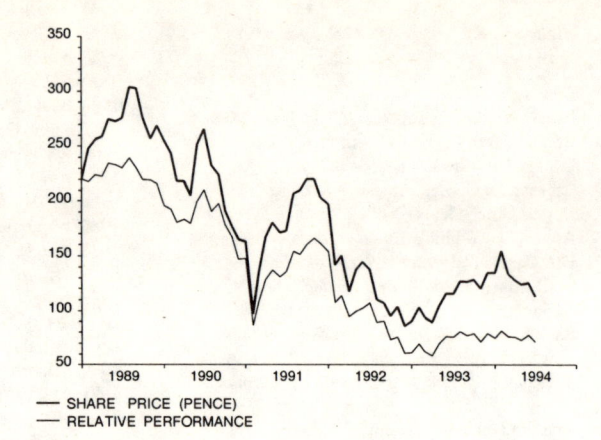

— SHARE PRICE (PENCE)
— RELATIVE PERFORMANCE

Financial record

		31/3/89	31/3/90	31/3/91	31/3/92	31/3/93
Total sales	£	2,106M	2,586M	2,636M	2,345M	2,176M
Pre-tax profit	£'000	270,700	322,300	217,000	109,300	62,400
Published retentions	£'000	148,400	115,800	51,900	-531M	-65,100
Earnings per share	p	24.67	27.26	17.84	11.16	2.77
Dividend per share	p	11.16	12.62	12.86	6.31	3.25
Operating cash flow	£'000	83,400	-45,700	22,400	175,000	128,400
Net assets per share	p	117.82	143.45	139.78	98.16	68.35
Net debt/(cash)	£'000	98,000	434,200	425,000	107,100	-93,200
Shareholders' funds	£'000	888,700	1,272M	1,258M	401,200	808,900
Return on capital	%	38.32	40.57	29.62	17.86	14.07
Profit margin	%	12.36	12.14	7.99	4.55	2.50
Sales per employee	£	15.95	18.86	21.24	22.54	21.46
Interest cover		12.86	8.27	3.62	3.74	5.46
Dividend cover		2.21	2.16	1.39	1.77	0.85
Sales increase	%	4.52	22.78	1.93	-11.04	-7.19
Earnings growth	%	15.98	10.51	-34.55	-37.43	-75.16
Investment x depreciation		1.42	1.49	0.97	0.19	0.25
Investment as % assets		27.13	24.93	19.00	4.69	6.69
Number of employees		132,025	137,101	124,118	104,019	101,408

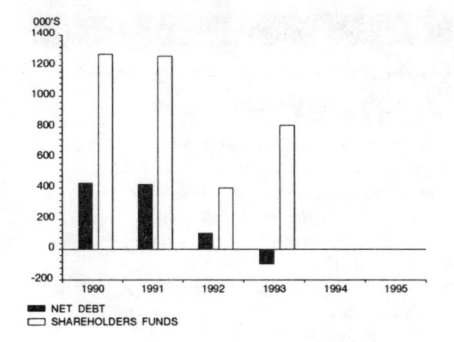

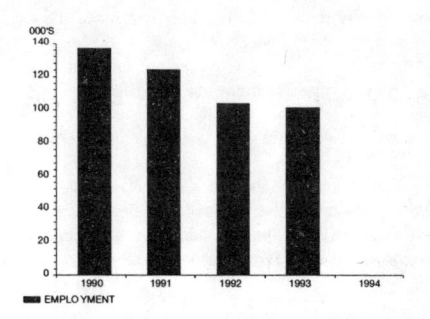

Debt and shareholders' funds

Employment

which left it with a stake in Thames Television), distribution and building services. Under Mr Wills there followed a hectic spree of selling off those businesses that were not wanted and using the money to try and create a more coherent group built around the concept of industrial services. A bid for scaffolding company SGB failed, but BET continued to invest in scaffolding, as well as in plant hire (especially cranes). Apart from SGB, most acquisitions did not reach the headlines, but when at one stage the group was making three purchases a week, it certainly kept the lawyers and bankers busy, not to mention Mr Wills and his colleagues.

By 1991 realisation dawned that these activities were by no means unaffected by recession and the spree came to a shuddering halt, but not before the group had spent far too much to win a tussle for the employment agency group Hestair. This, together with the other purchases, resulted in a debt mountain which threatened to bury the company. When the new chief executive, John Clark, took over from Nicholas Wills, he found that financial and management controls were almost non-existent due to the previous preoccupation with acquisitions, and the philosophy of decentralisation which left individual businesses to go their own ways. This was quickly changed: Mr Clark installed managers and instituted proper financial controls, making cash flow a top priority. A series of disposals helped restore the cash position, including window company Boulton & Paul and Initial USA, but the sales went much more slowly that had originally been intended.

Despite all this, BET remains a group lacking coherence and without attractive prospects as far as investors are concerned. It is left with a collection of low-margin businesses which offer little potential for growth. By 1993 the hunt had begun for acquisitions which might produce a better growth and margin profile. So the circle begins again.

Shares

BET spent the 1980s building up a portfolio of business, but as far as investors were concerned the whole never seemed to exceed the sum of the parts and the rating went nowhere relative to other shares, except during the market crash of 1987 when the group was briefly seen as a safe haven.

In 1991 the group's persistent underperformance was punished when pressure from major institutional shareholders brought in changes on the board and in group policy. After a severe collapse the rating improved against the market in general as cost-cutting made the dividend look more secure and hope rested on the new chief executive. The next blow fell in mid-1992 when the shares were sapped by fears that accounting changes would slash profits. Such fears were justified and the dividend was halved, but shareholders were then hit by a rights issue. Their disillusionment with BET was illustrated by the fact that less than half the rights shares were bought. And there was no let-up in the misery for shareholders: yet another dividend cut late in the year triggered a 20 per cent fall in the share price in one day. With the shares languishing at a low price relative to the market, analysts were still worried about dividend cover for 1993 and were doubtful about the group's long-term prospects.

Corporate conscience

BET is a member of BITC and the Per Cent Club, but that seems to be as far as its conscience extends. It does not broadcast an equal opportunities policy, nor does it operate a full public environmental policy. Its record in these two areas, while not bad, is not entirely clean. On the employee front, the Four Seasons Roofing Group was convicted in 1989, 1990 and 1991 for breaches of health and safety regulations, as was Hireplant in 1990. And on the environmental front, United Transport exceeded discharge consents at Felixtowe in 1990/91. BET is also tainted environmentally in two other respects. As a distribution company, its lorry fleet is clearly a contributor of carbon dioxide and other greenhouse gases to the atmosphere. And its cleaning activities are likely to use chemical solvents which are damaging to the ozone layer.

On other issues, BET has some minor involvement in questionable regimes such as those of Brunei and Tanzania; it is a supplier of security systems and cleaning services to the Ministry of Defence and the US Air Force; and Shorrock also supplies security systems for Sizewell B nuclear power station.

Corporate governance

Separate Chairman and Chief Executive Y
Number of Directors 9
Number of Non-Executive Directors 5
(5 Independent Directors)
Insulated Directors Not known
Board Committees
Audit: Y   Remuneration: Y

Remuneration

Year end	31.03.92	31.03.93	31.03.94
Total board £M	3.32	2.79	2.22
% change	14	-16	-20
Highest paid £	483,977	545,000	161,000
% change	68.5	13	40

Board

Clark, L John *Chief Executive*
Allan, John *Executive Director*
Payne, Keith *Executive Director*
Mackenzie, Robert *Finance Director*
Chataway, Christopher *Independent Non-Executive*
Duncan, George *Independent Non-Executive*
Lord Mark Fitzalan Howard *Ind. Non-Executive*
Lord Tebbit *Ind. Non-Executive*
Harding, Sir Christopher *Non-Executive Chairman*

Changes following the 1991 shake-up have rectified the inadequate non-executive contingent in the boardroom, but a little late, considering the group's poor financial and strategic record. A strong band of non-executives now makes up more than half the directors and they run the audit and remuneration committees. The company makes a point that it believes in the separation of the roles of chairman and chief executive. Details of performance-related bonuses have also improved. On the plus side, however, BET is just about the only FTSE 100 company which regularly, every three years, seeks a shareholder vote on political donations.

BICC plc

Devonshire House, Mayfair Place, London W1X 5FH
Tel: 0171 629 6622
Chairman and chief executive Sir Robin Biggam
Main subsidiaries Balfour Beatty, BICC Cables
Size £3.6 billion sales, £1.4 billion stock market value, 39,000 employees
5-year growth sales 4%, earnings per share -67%, employment -15%
Solvency debt = 51% shareholders' funds, interest cover 3.8 times
Political donations 0
Charitable donations £200,000

Major developments

1945 formed as British Insulated Callenders Cables
1969 bought Balfour Beatty
1975 name changed to BICC
1986 bought Haden group's building services operations and North American businesses
1987 bought Clarke Homes
1989 bought GEGC
1992 bought Reynolds and German cable group KWO

Outlook

If BICC were just the cable company suggested by its former name (British Insulated Calendar's Cables), it would have had to struggle for survival during the recession, since cable is used in construction projects involving the kind of major capital expenditure that tends not to get approval when times are hard. But, to make matters worse, the group had itself diversified into property and construction, and, furthermore, it was involved in three of the most difficult developments of the era: the Channel tunnel, the redevelopment of London's Spitalfields area, and the much-delayed extension of the Jubilee Underground line.

That the company emerged from the recession in reasonable financial health must be some kind of tribute to a respected management team, to the strength of its core businesses, and to relatively conservative financing – not so conservative as to forswear off-balance-sheet finance, or to avoid paying a dividend that was not covered by earnings, but cautious enough to ensure that there was sufficient cash flow to pay the dividend, and sufficient cash to keep interest payments reasonably low.

Indeed, BICC's cash record is rather better than its profit record, but it has the potential for marked improvement. The fall in profit and earnings during 1991 was due partly to substantial write-offs as the property slump hit the value of assets, as BICC took its share of the Transmanche Link consortium losses on the Channel tunnel. These provisions emphasise how unwise it was for BICC to diversify into property in the first place, although of course it was not the

BICC

Share record

Return on shareholders' equity	%	16.22
5-year price high	p	538.6
5-year price low	p	207.0
Dividend yield	%	5.94
5-year high	%	12.40
5-year low	%	3.85
Price/earnings ratio		27.9
5-year high		31.7
5-year low		6.2

Share price performance (in pence)

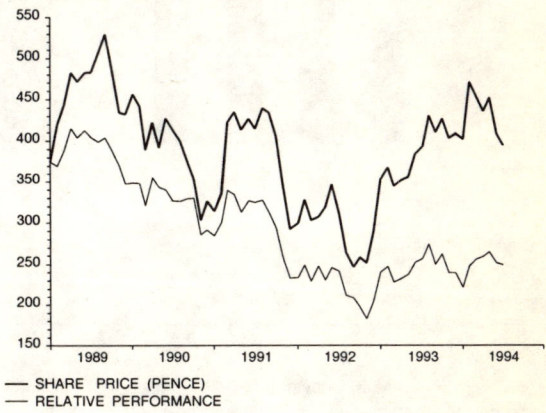

— SHARE PRICE (PENCE)
— RELATIVE PERFORMANCE

Financial record

		31/12/89	31/12/90	31/12/91	31/12/92	31/12/93
Total sales	£	3,462M	3,555M	3,452M	3,388M	3,614M
Pre-tax profit	£'000	200,600	182,500	123,000	120,000	107,000
Published retentions	£'000	67,300	40,300	-51,000	-51,000	-15,000
Earnings per share	p	44.27	38.10	24.44	19.89	14.52
Dividend per share	p	18.34	18.58	18.58	19.25	19.25
Operating cash flow	£'000	24,800	40,900	n/a	52,000	146,000
Net assets per share	p	285.10	317.20	323.97	352.58	284.93
Net debt/(cash)	£'000	88,100	142,200	179,000	218,000	245,000
Shareholders' funds	£'000	384,500	368,600	374,000	685,000	477,000
Return on capital	%	36.02	28.21	19.42	18.75	16.44
Profit margin	%	5.17	4.51	2.69	3.04	2.57
Sales per employee	£	75.20	80.11	82.44	84.45	92.31
Interest cover		7.06	6.53	5.04	4.68	3.82
Dividend cover		2.41	2.05	1.32	1.03	0.75
Sales increase	%	27.65	2.70	-2.90	-1.85	6.67
Earnings growth	%	20.05	-13.94	-35.87	-18.60	-26.99
Investment x depreciation		1.25	1.34	n/a	0.64	-0.16
Investment as % assets		18.33	23.08	n/a	8.78	-2.20
Number of employees		46,035	44,379	41,874	40,118	39,151

BICC plc

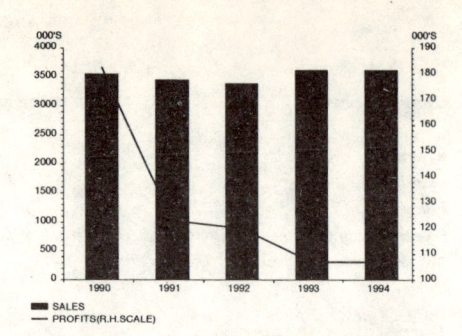

Employment

Sales and profits

only company which thought the 1980s property boom would continue for ever, and that it should partake of the spoils even though property was not one of its main businesses or key strengths, or even part of its strategy.

In 1986, with ex-Post Office boss Sir William Barlow as chairman and Robin Biggam (now Sir) as chief executive (after Sir William's retirement, Mr Biggam combined the two posts – particularly unfortunate in the light of subsequent strategic mistakes, which might have been avoided with better scrutiny), corporate strategy aimed to emphasise strengths in cable-making and contracting by improving margins through reducing costs, and by adding acquisitions which would contribute to their market positions and create global businesses. In those respects, as the following points indicate, BICC has been remarkably successful. That success was spoilt, however, by adventures in property, and there is an underlying feeling that if demerger specialists were looking for candidates, they might find it easy to demonstrate that civil engineering (even in the power industry) and cables gained little from being part of the same group.

Balfour Beatty The hammering inflicted on the construction industry in the late 1980s and early 1990s hardly seemed to touch Balfour Beatty. The reason is that the company does little commercial construction work (offices and shops, for instance). Instead it specialises in major civil engineering projects – tunnels and bridges, roads and railways. Its strength in the power generation sector was the (dubious) rationale for its takeover by BICC in the first place. Balfour Beatty has an excellent reputation, and hopes to use this to expand its interests abroad in order to lessen its dependence on the UK market. Indeed, it already has a presence in the US, and has a history of involvement in Asia, including, unfortunately, building the Pergau Dam in Malaysia, which caused a huge political storm in spring 1994.

Cables BICC entered the 1980s like many British companies, with an historic attachment to Commonwealth territories at the expense of Europe and North America. But by the early 1990s it had become one of the world's top three cable companies, with substantial interests in North America and on the Continent following a series of acquisitions, and with much more efficient operations. Greater manufacturing efficiencies have resulted in wider margins even though selling prices have steadily declined.

Life in the 1990s is likely to remain tough, however, although the growth of telecommunications bodes well for increased demand in that sector, and power cables (a slightly larger BICC business at the start of the 1990s) should benefit from the regeneration of Eastern Europe. BICC also believes there is plenty of scope for investment in the US, where the industry is still highly fragmented. More acquisitions are intended in the US.

Shares

BICC is a stock perpetually tipped for recovery, but whose recovery never seems to arrive. By 1987 BICC's profits had clawed their way back to the level of 1981, but the shares, relative to the rest of the market, had not and they have continued to languish. The company has enjoyed strong cash flow and paid good dividends, so the shares have been wanted for their yield. What has been missing is that feeling which fund managers like to have that at some point the shares will outperform the market.

In 1987, when most shares were booming, the group produced good results but its shares did no more than track the index until the crash, when they crashed too. It was not until 1989 that they enjoyed an upward burst. Between October 1988 and the following August they doubled in value as the group seemed poised to benefit from years of restructuring, but, like a man at the top a of a hill, they trudged on down again as recession began to take its toll. By mid-1990 the group was asking shareholders for £177 million through a rights issue, and as the group's involvement in property and the Channel tunnel looked less and less attractive, the shares continued to underperform. By 1992 BICC was once more asking for cash from its shareholders, and profits were again struggling to reach the levels of 1981. However, with the refinancing came a possible end to the group's property troubles, so the shares climbed 30 per cent into the beginning of 1993. The surge did not continue, however, as recovery proved to be slow.

Corporate conscience

Military involvement and connections with the nuclear industry are the main ethical issues for BICC. Apart from its obvious involvement through participation in Devonport Management, the naval dockyard, various parts of the group are also military suppliers. Supplies range from telephone and other cables, perimeter fence systems, military aircraft shelters, facilities management at Catterick and RAF Bonnington, to the construction of military airfields by Balfour Beatty. The latter also makes BICC a military exporter. In addition, Balfour Beatty is a supplier to the nuclear industry, including construction work for British Nuclear Fuels and the Torness nuclear power station, generator equipment and cabling at Sizewell. WasteChem is involved in decommissioning nuclear facilities and handling radioactive waste, while Haden Young has supplied heating and ventilation for a number of nuclear plants. Balfour Beatty also supplied a transmission line linking a nuclear power station in China to Hong Kong.

While the group is a member of BITC and a supporter of Opportunity 2000, it does not publicly operate an equal opportunities policy, although it has made a commitment to equal opportunities in its annual report. BICC has a number of convictions for health and safety violations, including an £800 fine under the Control of Asbestos at Work Regulations. A comprehensive environmental policy was developed during 1993, and includes specific rules and a commitment to regular monitoring. Individual units are expected to have their own detailed policies, and report annually to the board. Various parts of the group use ozone-depleting chemicals (for example, CFC-11 and CFC-12 in Protocoat protective aerosol spray) and the housing operations use tropical hardwoods such as sapele and mahogany. The group's record on water pollution is not good. In the three years to March 1993 there were a number of occasions on which consent levels were exceeded; Balfour Beatty has been convicted 5 times in the last five years for water pollution, including a fine of £2,300 for allowing oil to enter a tributary of the River Wansbeck in Northumbria; and in 1992 Stent Foundations was fined £10,000 for polluting the Medway in Kent.

Corporate governance

Separate Chairman and Chief Executive N
Number of Directors 10
Number of Non-Executive Directors 5
(5 Independent Directors)
Insulated Directors None

Board Committees
Audit: Y   Remuneration: Y

Remuneration

Year end	31.12.91	31.12.92	31.12.93
Total board £M	1.54	1.37	1.42
% change	10	-11	4
Highest paid £	279,139	300,000	314,332
% change	22	8	5

Board
Biggam, Sir Robin A   *Chairman & Chief Executive*
Clark, Eric   *Executive Director*
Mason, Peter   *Executive Director*
Zinkin, Peter   *Executive Director*
Henderson, Ronald   *Finance Director*
Bonfield, P L   *Independent Non-Executive*
Davidson, Sir Robert   *Independent Non-Executive*
Lord Howe of Aberavon   *Independent Non-Executive*
Reeves, Christopher   *Independent Non-Executive*
Viscount Weir   *Non-Executive Deputy Chairman*

The group insists that it complies with the main proposals of the Cadbury Code, and in a specific corporate governance section in the 1991 and 1992 annual reports, deputy chairman Viscount Weir explained the board structure and workings. Yet Sir Robin Biggam remains executive chairman, and there is no separate chief executive or managing director. The answer to this conundrum lies in the role of Viscount Weir and the fact that the operating units (BICC Cables and Balfour Beatty) have separate chief executives, which BICC considers adequate. The make-up of the board gives equal weighting to executive and (truly independent) non-executives.

BLUE CIRCLE INDUSTRIES plc

84 Eccleston Square, London SW1 1PX
Tel: 0171 828 3456,
Chairman Sir Peter Walters
Group managing director Keith Orrell-Jones
Main brands and subsidiaries Potterton, Myson, New World, Armitage Shanks
Size £1.7 billion sales, £2.3 billion stock market value, 21,000 employees
5-year growth sales 31%, earnings per share -55%, employment -1%

BLUE CIRCLE INDUSTRIES plc

BLUE CIRCLE INDUSTRIES

Share record

Return on shareholders' equity	%	11.41
5-year price high	p	387.0
5-year price low	p	124.0
Dividend yield	%	4.42
5-year high	%	12.10
5-year low	%	3.63
Price/earnings ratio		24.7
5-year high		71.9
5-year low		6.7

Share price performance (in pence)

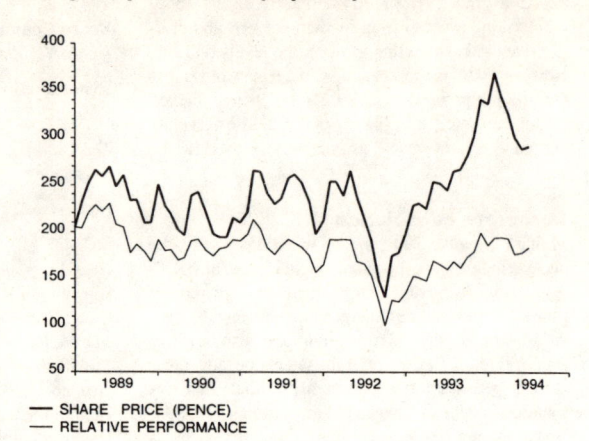

— SHARE PRICE (PENCE)
— RELATIVE PERFORMANCE

Financial record

		31/12/89	31/12/90	31/12/91	31/12/92	31/12/93
Total sales	£	1,283M	1,215M	1,114M	1,370M	1,679M
Pre-tax profit	£'000	231,900	195,800	134,100	106,700	165,900
Published retentions	£'000	120,000	53,000	-12,200	-50,400	22,100
Earnings per share	p	28.60	22.07	11.96	4.70	12.86
Dividend per share	p	10.65	10.89	10.89	11.25	11.25
Operating cash flow	£'000	100,000	-14,700	-1,100	-61,700	35,200
Net assets per share	p	284.99	259.12	250.31	267.51	215.23
Net debt/(cash)	£'000	266,500	352,100	396,300	404,500	360,300
Shareholders' funds	£'000	857,300	833,900	811,800	964,900	982,100
Return on capital	%	19.28	17.15	13.42	11.01	14.42
Profit margin	%	14.88	13.01	8.27	4.99	7.48
Sales per employee	£	61.65	61.06	61.02	61.75	81.38
Interest cover		57.18	144.64	5.04	3.65	4.83
Dividend cover		2.69	2.03	1.10	0.42	1.14
Sales increase	%	14.08	-5.35	-8.31	23.01	22.53
Earnings growth	%	5.37	-22.85	-45.82	-60.72	173.90
Investment x depreciation		1.02	1.06	0.53	0.84	0.70
Investment as % assets		7.51	9.37	4.56	7.59	6.57
Number of employees		20,818	19,893	18,253	22,188	20,629

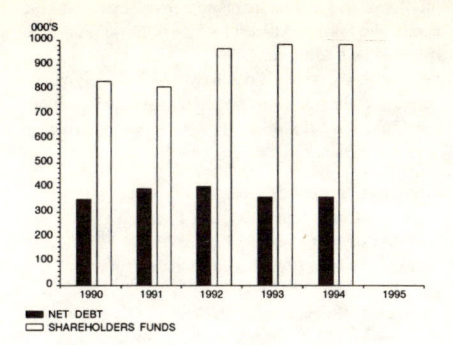

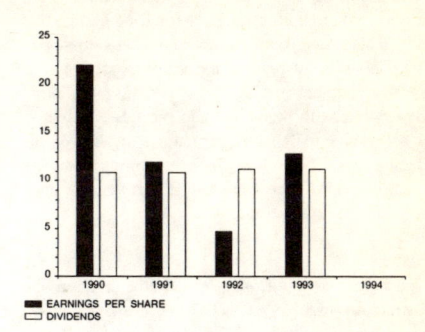

Debt and shareholders' funds

Earnings and dividends

Solvency debt = 37% shareholders' funds, interest cover 5 times
Political donations 0
Charitable donations £535,197

Major developments
1900 formed as The Associated Portland Cement Manufacturers
1920s Blue Circle brand name adopted
1978 became Blue Circle Industries
1988 bought Birmid Qualcast
1990 bought Myson Group; sold five foundry businesses of Birmid Qualcast; bought Ceramica Dolomite, Italy
1991 bought Thermopanel AB, Sweden
1992 42% of Blue Circle (South Africa); sold Atco Qualcast sold; bought Celsius heating group

Outlook
Blue Circle *is* cement – the biggest cement producer in the UK. But it is also Armitage Shanks, the name which stares up from so many toilet and bathroom fittings. And it is Potterton, Myson and New World boilers and cookers. Until the end of 1992 it was also Qualcast mowers ('a lot less bovver than a hover'), but that business was the subject of a £17 million management buy-out.

The group is still best known for its cement, however, and as with so many British companies, it could be argued that it should not have attempted to diversify, but should have concentrated instead on what it knows best. There is certainly a view in the City that any departures from that specialism during the 1980s have been neither well directed nor well executed, an opinion that is supported by the sizeable slump in profits during the recent recession.

Blue Circle might well respond, on the other hand, that it would have been in a much worse position without the contribution of the non-cement activities, and, more significantly, that under new chairman Sir Peter Walters (late of BP) it had adopted a rather more aggressive strategy. The very least that can be said for the group is that it did not allow itself to become more than marginally seduced by the 1980s lure of building and property development. It did not entirely resist the temptation, but its involvement (and therefore the associated write-downs or provisions) was minimal.

Blue Circle has built up substantial cement operations in Chile and Malaysia, but has been too timid in moving away from its UK cement base with its expensive acquisitions. Armitage Shanks was acquired in 1980, but there was little apparent impact on either it or Blue Circle of the two companies having merged. The next move outside cement did not come until 1988, when Birmid Qualcast was acquired (at the second attempt – the first having narrowly failed, after a recount, to breach the required 50.1 per cent barrier which gives a bidder control). Again, there seemed little impact on the two companies, and Qualcast lawnmowers, which were presumably surplus to requirements from the start, did not depart the group for four years. The acquisition of Myson in 1990, on the other hand, did seem to create something more than the sum of the parts, but that sum is no less subject to the UK building cycle than the rest of the UK business since Myson is inescapably wedded to the housing market.

Latterly, Blue Circle seems to have grasped that it should have been concentrating on building a pan-European business, not an Anglo-American one. Earlier in the 1980s the group's cement business expanded into the US, where it promptly became bogged down in the Atlanta cement price wars. Later in the decade, and in the early 1990s, the focus finally shifted back to Europe, with acquisitions such as Ceramica Dolomite in Italy, Thermopanel in Sweden and Celsius in France helping to transform Potterton

Myson into a European, not just a British, business.

The group has also built up a waste-management business, although unfortunately for Blue Circle, this rarely made news until it incurred heavy losses in 1993. This did not prevent the group reporting substantially higher profits, however, as economic recovery began to boost its main businesses. Recovery will revive the cement companies' cash flow, so reducing the debt levels which mounted up during the early 1990s. Then Blue Circle can venture once again into the takeover market.

Shares

As a company still largely dependent upon the construction industry, Blue Circle's share performance is generally driven by the economy. It was curious, then, that following the stock market crash of 1987 the group's shares rose strongly – on speculation that it was a bid target, which was confirmed by an abortive dawn raid just before Christmas. Hopes of a takeover kept the shares strong through 1988, even though Blue Circle itself bid for Birmid Qualcast. They stayed strong through to the middle of 1989, when the property boom was clearly beginning to wane. Shareholders liked the way the group raised cash from the sales of overseas businesses, but the shares weakened when it bought Myson.

From that time on the shares were remarkably steady until the group really fell out of favour in June 1992 when it popped in a rights issue. By the end of 1992, growing confidence in the City that Blue Circle was coming out of the recession saw its shares recover and outperform the all-share index by more than 10 per cent. Some of this recovery was reversed in the first half of 1994, however.

Corporate conscience

Making cement is by its nature an unpleasant business, inevitably having an environmental impact, from the quarrying of the original material to the high-energy manufacture of the cement itself, and its subsequent distribution. Blue Circle has a comprehensive environmental policy, however, and has had a recent, independent environmental audit. Its environmental policy was published in the report and accounts for 1991, and in 1992 Blue Circle moved on to publish a separate environmental report. By 1993 this report included specific measures in relation to energy and water consumption and waste management, detailing several fines in the US, in addition to one prosecution in the UK during that year.

Potterton Myson and the parent company have previously both been convicted recently under health and safety regulations, aberrations that mar an otherwise solid commitment to the social responsibilities of big business. The group was a founder member of the Foundation for Business Responsibilities, is a member of BITC and the Per Cent Club. It operates a payroll-giving scheme, places employees on secondment to charities and makes substantial donations to community, environmental and other causes.

Blue Circle also takes equal opportunities reasonably seriously, including the provision of paid paternity leave and arrangements to help women combine career and family. At least half its employees are represented by trade unions.

Finally, the group does have some operations in countries which have infringed human rights, including Chile and Sri Lanka, but it is no longer involved in South Africa.

Corporate governance

Separate Chairman and Chief Executive Y
Number of Directors 12
Number of Non-Executive Directors 6
(6 Independent Directors)
Insulated Directors MD

Board Committees
Audit: Y   Remuneration: Y

Remuneration

Year end	31.12.91	31.12.92	31.12.93
Total board £M	1.39	1.91	2.50
% change	-37	37	30
Highest paid £	234,558	234,166	345,961
% change	8	-0.2	74

Board
Orrell-Jones, Keith *Chief Executive*
Jackson, Tony J *Executive Director*
Lovett, David *Executive Director*
McKenzie, Ian S V *Executive Director*
Young, Charles G *Executive Director*
Loudon, James R H *Finance Director*
Hubbard, R David C *Independent Non-Executive*
Hunter, John F B *Independent Non-Executive*
Lord Moore *Independent Non-Executive*
Wilson, Geoffrey H *Independent Non-Executive*
Wyatt, C Terrel *Independent Non-Executive*
Walters, Sir Peter *Non-Executive Chairman*

The board is divided evenly between executives and non-execs, and follows the prescriptions of the Cadbury Code, although the annual report gives no details of how these are put into practice. Reasonably full information regarding directors' pay is provided, even if it does not explain the large increase in pay in 1993.

THE BOC GROUP plc

Chertsey Road, Windlesham, Surrey GU20 6HJ
Tel: 01276 477222
Chairman Richard Giordano
Chief executive Alexander Dyer
Main brands Boco, Cryocell, Enlon Plus, Forane, Kryoclean, Kwik Film
Size £3.1 billion sales, £3.5 billion stock market value, 38,400 employees

THE BOC GROUP

Share record

Return on shareholders' equity	%	13.7
5-year price high	p	773.0
5-year price low	p	440.0
Dividend yield	%	4.01
5-year high	%	6.02
5-year low	%	3.87
Price/earnings ratio		17.5
5-year high		25.3
5-year low		9.2

Share price performance (in pence)

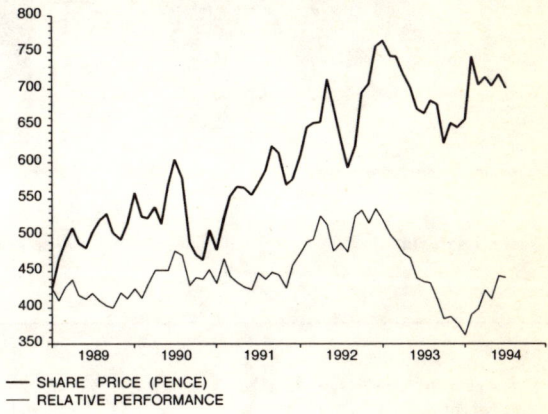

— SHARE PRICE (PENCE)
— RELATIVE PERFORMANCE

Financial record

		30/9/89	30/9/90	30/9/91	30/9/92	30/9/93
Total sales	£	2,309M	2,644M	2,719M	2,731M	3,068M
Pre-tax profit	£'000	330,500	354,300	335,100	341,900	337,600
Published retentions	£'000	149,200	153,200	97,500	-12,700	93,800
Earnings per share	p	47.56	50.62	44.12	45.0	41.68
Dividend per share	p	16.60	19.00	20.40	22.00	23.20
Operating cash flow	£'000	-1,100	86,200	-56,000	1,300	-7,200
Net assets per share	p	390.43	378.55	453.41	494.77	533.14
Net debt/(cash)	£'000	695,900	657,300	768,900	718,800	965,200
Shareholders' funds	£	1,151M	1,181M	1,286M	1,388M	1,489M
Return on capital	%	24.51	25.68	22.27	19.22	17.76
Profit margin	%	13.24	12.66	11.72	70.57	10.14
Sales per employee	£	59.39	66.83	67.81	5.92	79.81
Interest cover		5.94	6.05	5.24	2.10	5.01
Dividend cover		3.00	2.73	2.16		1.80
Sales increase	%	8.95	14.50	2.82	0.47	12.31
Earnings growth	%	8.87	6.43	-12.84	2.01	-7.38
Investment × depreciation		1.90	1.55	1.64	1.52	1.42
Investment as % assets		20.51	16.88	16.79	15.16	14.04
Number of employees		38,879	39,560	40,088	38,702	38,434

THE BOC GROUP plc

Sales analysis

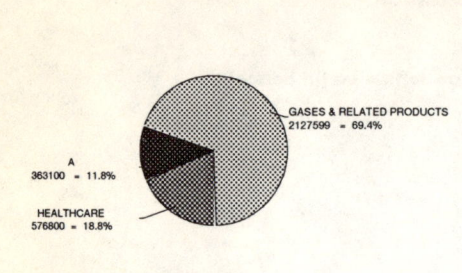

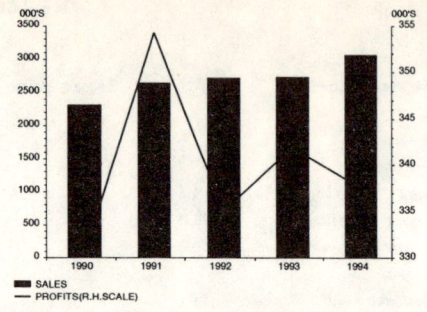

A = VACUUM TECHNOLOGY & DISTRIBUTION
- GASES & RELATED PRODUCTS 2127599 = 69.4%
- A 363100 = 11.8%
- HEALTHCARE 576800 = 18.8%

Sales and profits

5-year growth sales 33%, earnings per share -12%, employment -1%
Solvency debt = 65% shareholders' funds, interest cover 5 times
Political donations 0
Charitable donations £490,000

Major developments
1886 formed as Brin's Oxygen Co Ltd
1906 became British Oxygen Co
1975 changed to BOC
1978 bought Airco
1983 bought Glasrock
1988 bought Selox, Baxter Health Care Corp
1989 bought Albion Instruments and Ramam Technology Inc
1991 bought Delta Biotechnology
1992 sold Glasrock
1993 expiry of Forane
1994 re-appointment of Giordano as chairman

Outlook

BOC is probably best known for making Richard Giordano one of the first £1 million-a-year company bosses, and for its involvement in various investigations by the Monopolies Commission concerning gas supplies to the health service. In most people's minds the group is firmly associated with industrial processes, and its most public image must be that of the truck carrying gas cylinders.

Sir Richard, as he has been since acquiring an honorary knighthood (honorary because he is American), retired at the start of 1992, handing over to the aptly named Patrick Rich, a Frenchman who, despite his name, had to get by on just over half a million pounds in his first spell at the top from January to September 1992. By spring of 1994 Giordano was back in the chair, however. At the end of 1993 the board took the commendable view that the roles of chair and chief executive should be split, and while Mr Rich wrote in the annual report that he was happy to take the chairmanship only, two months later he announced he was stepping down – for health reasons. The other images are also misconceived. Gas cylinders are a minor part of the business, while customers in heavy industry are only one source of profits. Most of the oxygen and argon that BOC produces does indeed go into metal-working and steel-making, but the food industry is a major user of nitrogen for chilling and freezing, while this gas is also required by the electronics industry.

In the mid-1980s BOC was keen to stress its healthcare connections, but enthusiasm for expanding this aspect of the business has waned somewhat, as evidenced partly by the sale of the US company Glasrock in 1992. This company was bought in 1983 and turned into a nationwide supplier of oxygen systems for people with breathing difficulties to use at home. It never met profit expectations, however, partly because the patients' poor health record meant that many did not survive for long despite the benefits of Glasrock's product, making it rather more difficult than usual to get paid.

BOC has also stepped back a little from its involvement in pharmaceuticals, in view of the growing problems with drug pricing and competition from generic drugs, which hit group profits in 1994 after the expiry of patent protection on the anaesthetic Forane. Healthcare continues to be an important part of the business, however, providing about 15% of the group's operating profits. There was an abortive attempt in 1990 to float off this business, but the motivation was similar to that which may have initiated ICI's split. It was due not to disdain for healthcare, but to an expectation that a separate health company would be more highly valued by stock markets in the UK and US, and its higher valuation would make it easier to use the separate company's shares to make acquisitions.

BOC exhibits the usual schizophrenia about diversifying from its gas core. Mr Giordano's first task when he first took over in 1979 was to clear out some of the mistaken acquisitions of the 1960s and 1970s, including fish farming and other food interests. It was a curious role for somebody who had just been on the receiving end of that acquisition process, as boss of US gas company Airco (taken over by BOC). BOC's other priorities during the 1980s were to invest in the core activities to improve productivity, and to expand its businesses worldwide. Productivity improvements have certainly been made, as many redundant workers can testify. Airco and BOC have been welded together, and the group has established a strong business in Asia. The challenge for the 1990s is to establish a strong European business in gases to match those in the US and Asia.

Healthcare remains both a disappointment and a challenge. This side of the business was reorganised as part of Giordano's final act as chief executive, creating separate divisions for Medical Systems (mainly anaesthetics); Medical Devices (for instance, catheters); Specialty Products (used in suction and oxygen therapy); and Pharmaceutical Products (again mostly related to anaesthetics). It remains to be seen whether BOC will retain all these divisions. It could be argued that the group should concentrate on the one division where it is particularly strong: anaesthetics.

Shares

BOC shares failed to boom in the stock market rally of 1986–7, but repaid their followers by not falling very far when the market crashed, and went on to show their defensive qualities by handsomely outperforming the rest of the market until well into 1988. The company pleased investors with its policy of announcing at the start of each year what its dividend was going to be at the end, and while the shares never caught fire, nor was their performance too disappointing.

The group's staid image improved in 1990 when it announced plans to hive off its US healthcare business, and its recession-proof reputation again helped the shares to outperform the market. The demerger failed to mat- erialise, however, and as well as a deepening recession, a change in accounting policy at the end of 1991 caused some doubts. Yet 1992 saw the shares rise relative to the rest of the market as, despite the recession, BOC continued to generate a strong enough cash flow to sustain its dividend yield. Analysts concluded that even if shares in other companies promised better short-term prospects, BOC was still a good long-term bet for investors. A profound fall began at the end of 1992 as the group's specific problems with Forane and with reorganisation costs added to general worries about the healthcare industry. The return of Richard Giordano boosted spirits again and the share price sustained a rally through the first half of 1994.

Corporate conscience

Like most multinationals, BOC operates in countries which have infringed human rights. But there are also more specific issues: some of its pharmaceutical products, and even special pest-control gases, are tested on animals; its record in South Africa is questionable; and certain of its products are used for military purposes as well as the nuclear industry, and have negative implications for the environment.

Environmental issues are probably the most substantial area of concern. BOC distributes a number of products which incorporate CFCs, mainly as refrigerants, in addition to Halon products such as Freon 13B1, for use in fire extinguishers, and carbon tetrachloride for the electronics industry. The Edwards High Vaccum subsidiary supplies pumps to the nuclear industry, while Special Gases sells methane for use as a coolant in nuclear-reactor cores. In its operations, the group has also infringed consent levels for water discharges on a few occasions at its Brinsworth plant. While the group is not notoriously careless in its attitude to the environment, nor does it appear to take the issue as seriously as many large companies. The annual report includes only a brief, formal policy statement on the matter, although the group has established the BOC Foundation for the Environment and Community.

The company's military involvement is small, but perhaps the least expected ethical issue. BOC supplies gases and gas cylinders for military use, such as for missile propellants; Edwards High Vaccum sells pumps and similar products to the military; and the group has developed copper processes for military circuitry.

Regardless of all this, the group is a member of BITC and the Per Cent Club.

Corporate governance

Separate Chairman and Chief Executive Y
Number of Directors 14
Number of Non-Executive Directors 8
(7 Independent Directors)
Insulated Directors None

Board Committees
Audit: Y   Remuneration: Y

Remuneration

Year end	30.09.91	30.09.92	30.09.93
Total board £M	6.92	4.76	5.53
% change	49	-31	16
Highest paid £	1,047,771	696,417	786,393
% change	2	-34	13

Board
Dyer, Alexander P *Chief Executive*
Chatterji, Dr Debajyoti *Executive Director*
Clubb, Ian *Finance Director*
Chow, C K *Executive Director*
Rosenkranz, Danny *Executive Director*
Stoll, Dr Roger *Executive Director*
John, David *Independent Non-Executive*

THE BODY SHOP INTERNATIONAL plc

Tedman, Dr Craig *Independent Non-Executive*
MacDonald, J Howard *Independent Non-Executive*
Malpas, Robert *Independent Non-Executive*
Nevin, Crocker *Independent Non-Executive*
Taverne, Dick *Independent Non-Executive*
Tugendhat, Sir Christopher *Ind. Non-Executive*
Giordano, Richard V *Non-Executive Chairman*

The board has a majority of non-executives, and the group's annual report gives encouragingly detailed biographies of its board members, plus a full account of the aims of its board committees. As befits a company which traditionally remunerates its executives highly, there is better-than-average disclosure of remuneration and share-incentive packages which explained for example that the increase in the highest-paid director's salary was due to sterling devaluation because the salary was paid in dollars. The group is also among those companies which, before being forced to reveal this by statute, listed as a separate item the non-audit fees earned by its auditors.

THE BODY SHOP INTERNATIONAL plc

Watersmead, Littlehampton, Sussex BN17 6LS
Tel: 01903 731500
Chairman T Gordon Roddick
Managing director Anita Roddick
Main subsidiary Soapworks Ltd
Size £195 million sales, £454 million stock market value, 2,456 employees
5-year growth sales 131%, earnings per share 97%, employment 94%
Solvency debt = 12% shareholders' funds, interest cover 20 times
Political donations 0
Charitable donations £881,068

Major developments
1976 company formed
1977 first franchise awarded
1984 became public
1988 Mostly Men range launched; Soapworks soap factory opened in Easterhouse, Glasgow
1991 helped launch *The Big Issue* magazine to help the homeless

Outlook

In 1984, when Body Shop was floated on the stock market, 'the City was positively orgasmic about the whole niche-market concept,' admits the company's founder, Anita Roddick. It was a good start. And the company was able to cash in not only on the 1980s consumer boom that benefited virtually every retailer in the land, but also on the growing environmental awareness which persuaded shoppers to use their spending power to make a statement about their concern for the planet.

The growth in sales was phenomenal. In a single year, 1987, Body Shop's turnover rose by more than 60 per cent. By marketing improbable concoctions like cocoa-butter hand and body lotion and all manner of cosmetics made from natural products, Body Shop prospered and grew. By mid-1992 the company had more than 800 shops in 41 countries.

The City, as ever, was pretty indifferent to the manner in which the company made its money: institutional investors are a cold and calculating lot with little interest in the ethics of the companies in which they invest. They were quite happy to back Body Shop as long as its success continued: by February 1992 an investor who had put money into the company when it made its stock-market début had multiplied his or her money 76-fold.

But even Body Shop, using its highly publicised commitment to good causes and concern for the environment in order to attract concerned shoppers, could not remain immune from the effects of recession. And in 1992 the cracks began to show. The company was forced to admit that the sales through its British shops were below expectations. In the lead-up to Christmas its underlying level of sales – the volume of sales going through each existing outlet, not including new shops – was lower than it had been a year earlier. Profits fell by 15 per cent.

Having expanded aggressively overseas, Body Shop in 1993 had fewer than a quarter of its outlets in the UK. Nevertheless, Britain is still important for the company. And just like other niche retailers, Body Shop has had to cope with increasing competition from its far larger retailing rivals who tried to snap up its market. Marks & Spencer spotted how much money Sock Shop was making in the mid-1980s, and, as a result, started selling much snazzier socks and tights: Sock Shop went under. Tie Rack successfully exploited the market for more interesting ties for men, but eventually excited the interest of bigger clothing retailers who in turn spruced up their ranges. And Body Shop has had to face the same challenge: just as it was complaining that it had had a poor Christmas in 1992, Boots was boasting how well its own range of 'natural' cosmetics was doing.

Unlike the late Sock Shop, Body Shop did not borrow huge amounts of money to open new stores: its expansion was achieved by franchising the format to individuals who wanted to try their hand at retailing. So Body Shop has not been so heavily exposed to dips in retail spending: it has shared the burden with its franchisees. What is more, it still has huge untapped markets overseas. Although Body Shop is near to saturating the market in Britain, it has hardly scratched the surface in Japan and Asia, for example; there are also plenty of gaps to be filled in Europe.

But the company has had to accept that the days when its sales would increase by more than 60 per cent in a year are over. It has been forced, belatedly, to turn its attention to dreary details like the control of stocks and working capital. All in the name of the environment, of course.

THE BODY SHOP INTERNATIONAL

Share record

Return on shareholders' equity	%	19.25
5-year price high	p	370.0
5-year price low	p	130.0
Dividend yield	%	1.04
5-year high	%	1.52
5-year low	%	0.25
Price/earnings ratio		24.3
5-year high		81.5
5-year low		16.2

Share price performance (in pence)

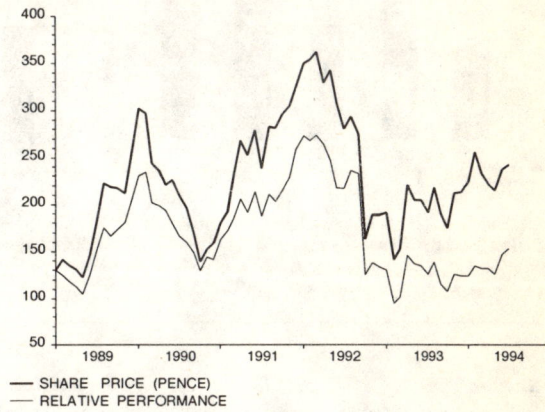

— SHARE PRICE (PENCE)
— RELATIVE PERFORMANCE

Financial record

		31/1/90	28/2/91	29/2/92	28/2/93	28/2/94
Total sales	£'000	84,480	115,599	147,441	168.272	195,400
Pre-tax profit	£'000	14,508	20,037	25,203	21,544	28,900
Published retentions	£'000	6,977	9,842	13,400	7.37	15,600
Earnings per share	p	5.00	6.70	8.79	1.70	9.90
Dividend per share	p	0.91	1.22	1.60	10,623	2.00
Operating cash flow	£'000	-17,081	-18,900		12,433	16,300
Net assets per share	p	19.32	38.93	42.73	62.19	68.68
Net debt/(cash)	£'000	25,540	16,291	31,766	27,278	12,000
Shareholders' funds	£'000	25,992	65,149	74,178	82,209	96,900
Return on capital	%	59.07	43.69	37.94	25.53	25.59
Profit margin	%	17.17	17.33	17.09	12.80	14.79
Sales per employee	£	66.78	62.69	76.55	79.22	79.56
Interest cover		7.13	11.28	10.43	8.85	20.27
Dividend cover		5.48	5.49	5.49	4.34	4.95
Sales increase	%	15.71	36.84	27.55	14.13	16.12
Earnings growth	%	39.44	33.98	31.12	-16.10	34.30
Investment x depreciation		9.69	5.16	3.62	2.06	1.57
Investment as % assets		59.68	41.52	30.23	20.59	18.56
Number of employees		1,265	1,844	1,926	2,124	2,456

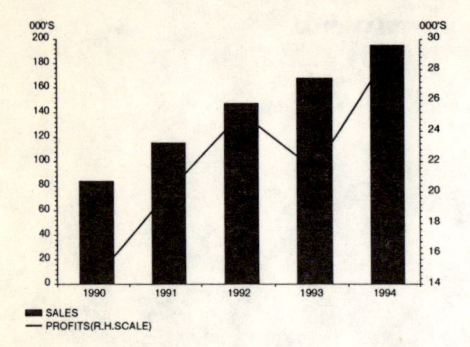

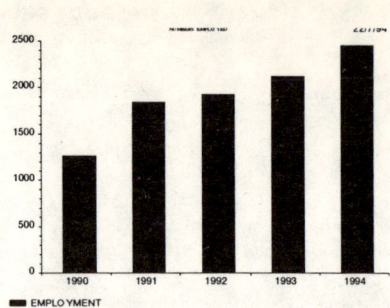

Sales and profits

Employment

Shares

Body Shop was one of the classic flotation successes of the 1980s. As the most original of the 'niche' retailers, its shares easily outperformed the rest of the market for most of the time, and came into their own after the market crash of 1987 when the difference between its prospects and those of other retailers became clear to investors. Its shares dipped at the end of 1988 as reports came through of poor Christmas trading elsewhere in the high street. But Body Shop proved itself to be the exception, and throughout 1989 and 1990 the company's rating soared.

The shares began to flag, however, as major retailing chains began to muscle their way into the Body Shop's niche. They continued to fall after a poorly received share issue in mid-1990, but profits kept increasing and shares once again outperformed the market the following year.

The process stopped in 1992, however, when the market realised that Body Shop was not growing fast enough to justify its high rating, and the shares went into free fall that September when the group issued a profit warning. The shares stabilised, then fell again at the beginning of 1993 after the company reported poor Christmas sales. Signs that the business was starting to recover helped the shares to climb again from late 1993 into spring 1994.

Corporate conscience

Body Shop is *the* company with a conscience. Founders Anita and Gordon Roddick explicitly embrace a philosophy of caring about the products and processes the company is involved in, as well as employment and other social issues. That has not prevented Body Shop being involved in controversy, however, but the company defends it record vigorously.

The Roddicks' informal approach to business also means that formal policies on issues such as equal opportunities do not exist. Nevertheless, apart from Anita Roddick, the board also includes another female executive director and provides excellent childcare arrangements, including 10 days' paternity leave.

Social and environmental issues are clearly crucial to this company. Staff are expected to spend several (paid) hours a month on community work, and the company is a heavy donor to charities. It has an environmental department charged with maintaining high standards, carries out an annual audit, operates schemes for recycling and minimising packaging, and asks that suppliers adhere to certain environmental criteria, including the avoidance of animal testing. In addition to its environmental aims, the group's purchasing policy is regarded as a means of supporting development in Third World Countries, notably through a Trade Not Aid project. In addition, suppliers are required to ensure a certain standard of conditions of employment for its workers.

Corporate governance

Separate Chairman and Chief Executive N
Number of Directors 6
Number of Non-Executive Directors 0
Insulated Directors None

Board Committees
Audit: N   Remuneration: N

Remuneration

Year end	28.02.92	28.02.93	28.02.94
Total board £M	0.89	1.04	0.98
% change	8	18	-6
Highest paid £	196,000	205,000	210,000
% change	7	5	2

Board
Roddick, Anita L *Managing Director*
Roddick, T Gordon *Executive Chairman*
Forster, Jilly C *Executive Director*
Helyer, Eric G *Executive Director*
Rose, Stuart A *Executive Director*
Ross, Michael *Executive Director*

Britain's most consciously 'ethical' public company does not take such a vigorous stance on corporate governance as it does on other business issues. But in his 1993 annual statement, chairman Gordon Roddick acknowledged the Cadbury Report, saying that the company agreed with its spirit and the Code of Conduct, and that Body Shop had been looking for non-executive directors 'who will make a real contribution to the future of Body Shop'. A year later the situation had not been changed, although consultants had been recruited to search for appropriate people to fill the role. Non-executives are particularly necessary because the notional separation between Gordon and Anita remains insufficient to qualify as separate chairman/chief executive.

THE BOOTS COMPANY plc

Nottingham NG2 3AA
Tel: 0115 950 6111
Chairman Sir Michael Angus
Chief executive Sir James Blyth
Main Subsidiaries Crookes Healthcare Ltd, Farley Health Products Ltd
Size £4.2 billion sales, £5.6 billion stock market value, 80,100 employees
5-year growth sales 23%, earnings per share 38%, employment 2%
Solvency debt n/a, interest cover 37 times
Political donations 0
Charitable donations £1.4 million

Major developments
1888 formed Boots Pure Drug Co
1933 1000th shop opened
1968 bought Timothy Whites chemist chain
1969 launch of Ibuprofen painkiller
1971 name changed to Boots Company; bought Crookes Laboratories
1986 bought Farley Health products
1987 Sir James Blyth appointed as chief executive; first Childrens World opened
1989 bought Underwoods; bought Ward White Group; bought Miller and Santhouse
1990 joint venture DIY stores formed with W H Smith Do It All
1993 dropped development of Manoplax heart drug
1994 sold Farley

Outlook
As a brand name, Boots is one of the best: it conveys an aura of cleanliness, reliability and familiarity. As a retailer, Boots the Chemist is widely respected: it is one of the safest areas of retailing; even when times are tough, after all, people continue to buy basics like aspirin and shampoo. But as an overall business, the Boots company is regarded with a little more reservation. There is much more to it than chemist shops, and it is those other bits which have proved troublesome over recent years.

Until 1989 the shape of the company was relatively simple. In essence, it had two parts: the chemist shops and a pharmaceuticals operation. The pharmaceuticals side was not a big player in the corporate world – nothing to compare with a Glaxo or a Merck – but it made decent money from over-the-counter potions like Nurofen and Optrex. And Boots invested great hope in a new heart drug, Manoplax. But in 1993 development of the drug was halted, and in 1994 the group admitted that it was considering disposing of the pharmaceuticals business.

The other part of the empire, the retailing business, was – after the abandonment of some earlier misguided efforts to broaden the chemist shops' range of merchandise – beautifully simple. Boots had made one or two small diversifications: it had built up a tiny chain under the name of Childrens World and had a string of opticians. But above all, Boots concentrated on what it was good at: running chemist shops – more than a thousand of them. It proved itself to be a leader in exploiting new technology to the full – not only to ensure that shops remained properly stocked, but also to allow Boots to charge different prices in different outlets in order to maximise its profits according to the social mix of a particular area.

Then in 1989, following the arrival of Sir James Blyth as chief executive, Boots decided to make its big move. There is only so much growth that can be achieved from chemist shops, so the company bid for, and won control of, Ward White, a group which had in the 1980s, along with so many other companies, sold its history and acquired new businesses. Ward White became the owner of bicycle and car parts chain Halfords, the DIY business Payless and the Fads wallpaper and paint shops. Boots paid £900 million for the group.

Within a year it emerged that the price had been too high. The full extent of the downturn in the markets served by Halfords and Payless became clear. Boots had bought Ward White to give its own business some fizz, whereas in fact Ward White was denting the profitability of a group whose solid and efficient high-street business, chemist shops, was coping far better with the recession than were its retailing rivals.

With Payless, Boots felt that it was contending with much the same problem that W H Smith faced with its DIY offshoot, Do It All: neither operation was big and powerful enough to compete strongly with the two giants of the sector, B&Q and Texas. So

THE BOOTS COMPANY

Share record

Return on shareholders' equity	%	21.76
5-year price high	p	605.0
5-year price low	p	249.0
Dividend yield	%	3.42
5-year high	%	5.54
5-year low	%	2.83
Price/earnings ratio		16.4
5-year high		22.5
5-year low		11.1

Share price performance (in pence)

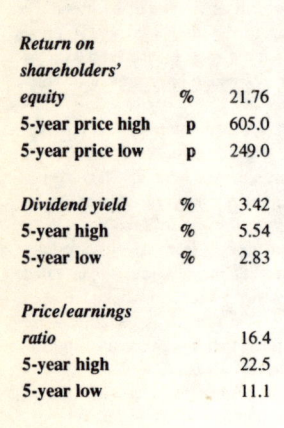

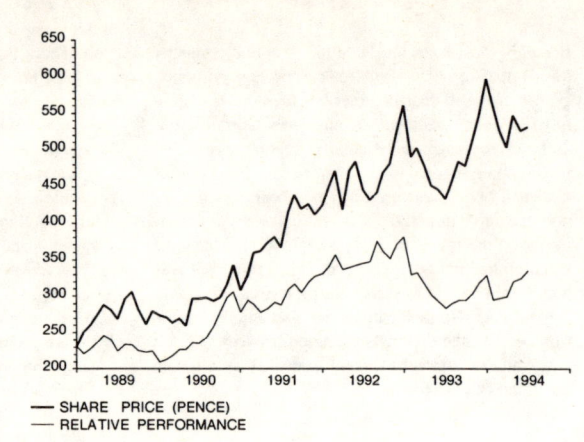

— SHARE PRICE (PENCE)
— RELATIVE PERFORMANCE

Financial record

		31/3/90	31/3/91	31/3/92	31/3/93	31/3/94
Total sales	£	3,381M	3,565M	3,656M	3,954M	4,167M
Pre-tax profit	£'000	358,200	358,500	374,200	405,200	484,400
Published retentions	£'000	136,100	149,800	120,800	26.97	131,900
Earnings per share	p	25.56	24.89	26.09	13.40	35.29
Dividend per share	p	11.00	11.60	12.40	140,100	15.00
Operating cash flow	£'000	152,300	110,900	94,700	62,100	291,100
Net assets per share	p	148.44	151.67	161.95	177.93	182.55
Net debt/(cash)	£'000	475,500	393,500	239,600	184,000	-69,000
Shareholders' funds	£	1,131M	1,272M	1,432M	1,479M	1,609M
	%					
Return on capital	%	26.83	29.40	28.08	26.07	28.20
Profit margin	£	10.55	9.82	10.25	10.77	12.85
Sales per employee		42.99	42.57	45.22	49.58	52.02
Interest cover		11.82	7.22	9.67	26.64	37.02
Dividend cover		2.32	2.15	2.10	2.01	2.35
	%					
Sales increase	%	25.03	5.44	2.54	8.15	5.40
Earnings growth		19.75	-2.62	4.82	3.40	30.85
Investment x depreciation		1.70	1.65	1.67	1.53	1.49
Investment as % assets		8.14	8.95	9.28	10.62	12.89
Number of employees		78,648	83,745	80,847	79,738	80,099

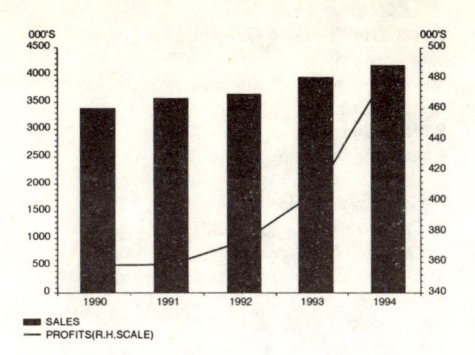

Sales and profits

Sales per employee

Payless and Do It All were rolled into a single business, jointly owned by Boots and W H Smith. It is likely that W H Smith will eventually pull out of DIY altogether: Do It All might be floated as a business in its own right, sold to someone more committed to the sector, or Boots could take full control of the company.

In the meantime, Boots has to try to deal with the legacy of its unfortunately timed takeover of Ward White – praying for a recovery in the DIY market, closing those Do It All outlets that have lost money, and persevering with Halfords. Indeed, Halfords was showing signs of recovery in 1994.

And all the while, the old Boots the Chemist ploughs on – tried, tested and profitable. Boots must hope that, once the recession is over, Halfords and Do It All will give the group the zest which the chemists' chain cannot. It is a shame they had to have the downside first.

Shares

Boots's shares underperformed the market for most of the shopping-mad 1980s and the group almost prided itself on its dull but dependable stock market image. The shares were bought for the yield rather than the market ride and their safe qualities helped when the market crash of 1987 made them preferable to others in the stores sector.

The shares began to outperform the market in 1989 as nicely honed retail skills increased cash levels and with speculation that the group might be a bid target. Then the board amazed everyone that year by bidding for Ward White, its first contested takeover in a generation. The market did not predict how detrimental this purchase would prove to be for the group, so the shares resumed an upward trend which accelerated sharply in mid-1990 when the group put its DIY interests into a joint venture with W H Smith. Early in 1991 Boots was the first to admit that its sales had been weak over the Christmas season and the group's rating sagged.

The autumn of 1991 saw the shares begin a sustained, if unspectacular, appreciation against the rest of the market which continued until 1993. This was based on the strength of the group's drugs business and the perception that its hard work on the retail operations was paying off. Yet another poor Christmas and worries about DIY and music sales pulled the rating down in early 1993. Despite the Manoplax débâcle, the shares then rallied strongly in the latter part of 1993.

Corporate conscience

Boots has a long paternalist tradition which is largely maintained by the present management. But commitment in principle to the best ethical behaviour is not always matched in practice. For example, in the employment field it does not negotiate with the shop workers' union USDAW (although the union does represent staff in grievance procedures), but in other respects the group operates progressive employment policies. There is a profit-sharing scheme and an active equal opportunities policy, including measurement of progress. Boots supports Opportunity 2000. It is also an active member of BITC and makes substantial charitable donations. Despite all this, the group was fined £400 for a breach of the Factories Act in 1990.

Boots is also open to attack on Third World issues: not just because of small operations in oppressive regimes such as the Philippines and Pakistan, but also because of the questionable marketing of drugs. In the UK the group had a total of three complaints upheld against it (including Do It All) by the ASA in 1992 and 1993.

Boots has a comprehensive environmental policy and is phasing out CFCs in some aerosols; Do It All sells some products which use tropical hardwoods,

BOWATER plc

but only from managed areas of woodland. Boots also sells some drugs and toiletries which have been tested on animals, although its own brands are not, and it has supported research into alternatives to animal testing.

Corporate governance

Separate Chairman and Chief Executive Y
Number of Directors 11
Number of Non-Executive Directors 5
(5 Independent Directors)
Insulated Directors All execs

Board Committees
Audit: Y Remuneration: Y

Remuneration

Year end	31.03.91	31.03.92	31.03.93
Total board £M	2.25	3.47	3.70
% change		54	6
Highest paid £	343,000	571,000	620,000
% change		67	9

Board
Blyth, Sir James *Chief Executive*
Hawksworth, Alan H *Executive Director*
Hourston, Gordon M *Executive Director*
Ruddell, Michael F *Executive Director*
Solway, Gordon R *Executive Director*
Thompson, David A R *Finance Director*
Davis, Peter J *Independent Non-Executive*
Prosser, Ian M G *Independent Non-Executive*
Reynolds, Sir Peter *Independent Non-Executive*
Wilson, Robert P *Independent Non-Executive*
Angus, Sir Michael *Non-Executive Chairman*

Sir James Blyth is the kind of powerful chief executive who needs a weighty counterbalance on the board. Boots does reasonably well on this score, with a separate chairman and the independent directors making up almost 50 per cent of the board and including some heavyweights from the top of other large groups, such as Peter Davis, late of Reed Elsevier, and Ian Prosser of Bass. The company has a tradition of corporate responsibility, which includes a board committee for 'social responsibility' as well as audit and remuneration. Some details of directors' bonus schemes are provided in the annual accounts.

BOWATER plc

Bowater House, Knightsbridge, London SW1X 7NN
Tel: 0171 584 7070
Chairman Michael Woodhouse
Chief executive David Lyon
Main subsidiaries Cope Allman, DRG, McCorquodale, Speciality Coatings International, Tower Packaging

Size £2.1 billion sales, £2.2 billion stock market value, 26,400 employees
5-year growth sales 64%, earnings per share 10%, employment 51%
Solvency debt = 16% shareholders' funds, interest cover 17 times
Political donations 0
Charitable donations £129,000

Major developments
1923 formed as Bowater's Mills
1947 changed to Bowater Paper Corporation
1973 planned takeover of Hanson Trust blocked by Monopolies Commission
1981 closed last UK paper mill
1984 demerger of US and UK businesses
1987 new management installed
1989 bought Norton Opax; bought Viking Packaging Group; sold Evode Group stake; De La Rue stake
1990 became Bowater plc; sold Crossley Builders Merchants
1992 bought DRG Packaging and Cope Allman Packaging
1993 bought Tower Packaging and Speciality Coatings International

Outlook

Demerger is usually seen as a late-1980s fashion: after the takeover boom came the urge to take apart. Courtaulds, BAT and ICI are the names which spring to mind, but Bowater was breaking this ground back in 1984. Curiously the process changed it from a fairly focused paper company into a conglomerate – the very target that demergers are supposed to aim at. More curious still, in the process of building up following the demerger Bowater acquired the rump of two other conglomerates – Cope Allman and DRG – and DRG itself had become available as the result of a break-up bid.

Bowater was a British newsprint company. In the 1930s it moved into Canada, an important source of raw material (namely wood pulp) for companies making newsprint, and subsequently into southern USA. For a while it was the world's biggest newsprint company. The recession of the early 1980s claimed the British end of the newsprint business, however, as high energy costs and the impact of soaring sterling turned profits into losses. Bowater stopped making newsprint in the UK in 1981 when it closed its Ellesmere Port mill.

From then on, tensions grew between the two sides of the Atlantic, between the US newsprint company and the UK business, which was now concentrating on more specialised paper products, including a joint venture in tissues with US company Scott Paper, and moving into new areas such as building products. Both sides of the business needed investment, but had become very different kinds of company (a scenario very similar to the one experienced by Courtaulds), and the scale of investment needed in the US was becoming too much for the UK company to cope with. The answer was to split in two.

BOWATER

Share record

Return on shareholders' equity	%	23.93
5-year price high	p	521.0
5-year price low	p	175.8
Dividend yield	%	3.51
5-year high	%	6.76
5-year low	%	2.87
Price/earnings ratio		17.3
5-year high		24.9
5-year low		8.5

Share price performance (in pence)

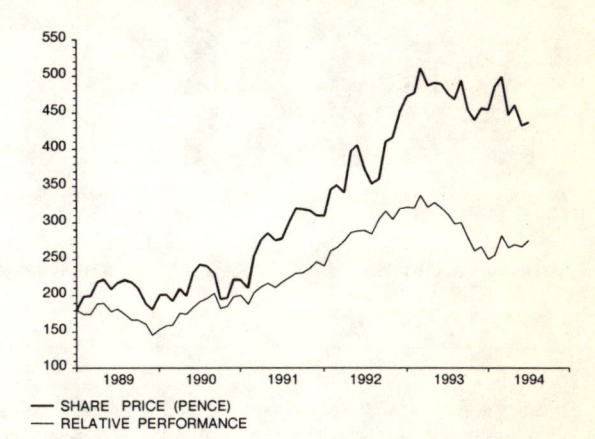

— SHARE PRICE (PENCE)
— RELATIVE PERFORMANCE

Financial record

		31/12/89	31/12/90	31/12/91	31/12/92	31/12/93
Total sales	£	1,288M	1,274M	1,206M	1,510M	2,112M
Pre-tax profit	£'000	100,400	113,100	112,700	147,800	201,600
Published retentions	£'000	105,500	66,500	26,600	50,900	72,500
Earnings per share	p	23.33	21.66	23.18	24.18	25.78
Dividend per share	p	8.17	9.64	10.72	11.20	12.55
Operating cash flow	£'000	11,500	47,800	31,900	47,100	61,600
Net assets per share	p	262.54	267.12	240.52	209.21	214.50
Net debt/(cash)	£'000	375,700	99,600	113,200	276,100	261,700
Shareholders' funds	£'000	263,800	427,200	447,400	1,298M	1,667M
Return on capital	%	21.81	22.21	21.19	28.74	29.27
Profit margin	%	6.69	7.94	9.10	9.42	9.40
Sales per employee	£	73.61	64.68	64.15	68.33	80.00
Interest cover		10.70	18.93	-24.20	-17.82	16.57
Dividend cover		2.85	2.25	2.16	2.16	2.05
Sales increase	%	-7.08	-1.09	-5.34	25.20	39.87
Earnings growth	%	19.47	-7.18	7.01	4.33	6.62
Investment x depreciation		1.41	1.90	1.52	1.25	1.26
Investment as % assets		9.58	17.01	13.81	11.61	12.89
Number of employees		17,500	19,700	18,800	22,100	26,400

BOWATER plc

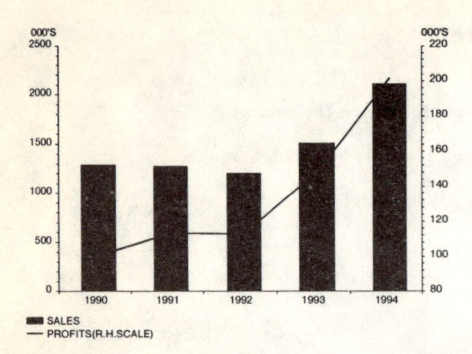

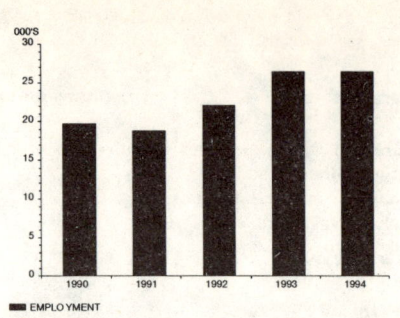

Sales and profits

Employment

Since then, Bowater Industries, as the UK company became, has set about turning itself into a separate, more manageable entity. It has not been an easy process, though. The sale of its remaining paper interests, including the joint venture with Scott Paper (but excluding the Australian division), left the company with the familiar problem of having money and not knowing quite what to do with it. The result was an unfocused hotch-potch of different industries which briefly attracted the interest of Hanson as a potential break-up opportunity. The arrival in 1987 from BTR of new chairman Norman Ireland changed all this. Under Mr Ireland, Bowater has gained a sense of direction – the initial impetus being towards becoming a conglomerate much in the style of the hugely successful BTR.

Like all conglomerates these days, Bowater would prefer not to be thought of as a conglomerate, since the model is currently out of favour. It claims to be 'first and foremost a print and packaging group', and to be fair, acquisitions from 1989 onwards have pushed Bowater increasingly in that direction, while also broadening its international spread of businesses, notably in the US. The Australian tissue-paper and timber operations are a survival from the Scott Paper joint venture. There is still a windows business, but the bulk of the building products industry has been sold, as have the freight operations. The acquisition of Norton Opax, Cope Allman and DRG have significantly increased the group's concentration on print and packaging activities.

As in the best BTR tradition, the company is also seeking to become well ensconced in niches where profit margins are unlikely to be severely depressed – in cosmetics and pharmaceuticals packaging, for example. Bowater finally seems to have found a role that is international in scale and has plenty of potential for growth. In 1993 it bought Speciality Coatings International, Tower – which makes medical packaging – and acquired a controlling stake in Mitek, a manufacturer of connecting plates used in the building trade.

Shares

Bowater started the 1980s with a wide and umpromising range of activities, but increasingly concentrated on its print and packaging businesses and emerged in 1987 under new mangement as an attractive investment. It built up a wide City following and, having switched back on to the takeover trail in 1989 with the bid for Norton Opax, it was able to ask its investors for cash to finance expansion in 1990 without hurting its rating.

It has proved to be one of the safest havens from recession. From 1990 on, its performance relative to the market as a whole improved steadily while other, formerly more glamorous, shares shrank along with the major world economies. In 1992 the management asked its shareholders for more money in order to fund the acquisition of Cope Allman and DRG. The money was granted without demur, and the shares continued their seemingly inexorable rise. But fears about fierce competition in Bowater's markets pushed the shares downwards throughout 1993.

Corporate conscience

Bowater has a proper environmental policy, and for the first time devoted space to the subject in its 1993 annual report. The chief executive's special report did not include quantified measures, however. In 1992 the subsidiary NFI Electronics was (like most such companies) still using CFC-113 as a solvent in the manufacture of electronic control panels, and the group has given no commitment to phasing it out. Bowater does, how-ever, have a clean record on discharges to water.

Three subsidiaries have been successfully prosecuted under the Factories Act in recent years: the

Standard Check Book Company, Bowater Containers Scotland, and Bowater PKL. Zenith Windows has had complaints upheld by the ASA. In the small South African operations the group has also been found to pay low wages to some black African employees.

Corporate governance

Separate Chairman and Chief Executive Y
Number of Directors 10
Number of Non-Executive Directors 5
(5 Independent Directors)
Insulated Directors None

Board Committees
Audit: N   Remuneration: Y

Remuneration

Year end	31.12.91	31.12.92	31.12.93
Total board £M	1.59	1.91	2.56
% change	22	20	34
Highest paid £	381,000	444,000	522,000
% change	56	17	18

Board
Lyon, David *Chief Executive*
Priestly, Eric *Executive Director*
Tutt, Leo *Executive Director*
Wallis, Stuart *Executive Director*
Hartnall, Michael *Finance Director*
Crawford, Prof. Sir F *Independent Non-Executive*
Lord Sheppard *Independent Non-Executive*
Mackrell, Keith A V *Independent Non-Executive*
Warren, John *Independent Non-Executive*
Woodhouse, Michael *Non-Executive Chairman*

In his last annual report before he retired, chairman Norman Ireland made a robust statement on corporate governance, describing it as an issue for all directors, not just non-executives. Hence the audit committee consisted of all directors. In 1994 this changed: the company now complied with the requirements of the Cadbury Committee, as explained in the directors' report for 1993, wittily entitled 'The Small Print'. The annual report gives details of the overseas directors' pay and directors' bonuses, and includes pension contributions.

BPB INDUSTRIES plc

Langley Park House, Uxbridge Road,
Slough SL3 6DU
01753 573273
Chairman Alan Turner
Chief executive Jean-Pierre Cuny
Main subsidiaries Artex, British Gypsum, C Davidson & Sons, Gyproc Insulation, Purfleet Board, Radcliffe Paper and Board

Size £1.2 billion sales, £1.7 billion stock market value, 11,300 employees
5-year growth sales 11%, earnings per share -25%, employment -9%
Solvency debt = 21% of shareholders' funds, interest cover 7 times
Political donations £10,000
Charitable donations £33,000

Major developments

1917 British Plasterboard opened first UK plant
1968 became sole UK manufacturer of plasterboard
1976 monopolies inquiry, and pricing undertakings given to Office of Fair Trading
1987 moved into Germany with purchase of Rigip's interests for £69 million
1988 fined by European Commission for monopolistic practices
1990 monopolies inquiry; bought 65% Inveryeso, Spain, for £97 million; bought plaster business of Poliet, France, for £128 million
1991 rights issue raised £125 million

Outlook

It is curious that the building materials industry has seen so many near-monopolies: Pilkington in glass, Redland in roof tiles, RMC in readymix, and BPB in plasterboard. And it is interesting that such UK monopolies have crumbled in the face of competition from the continent, which has also spurred on companies like BPB to retaliate with vigour and great success.

Plasterboard is a relatively modern invention, but probably not as modern as it usually seems. Only in the 1970s did use of the product really take off, after decades of struggling against conventional plastering techniques since BPB's forerunner opened its first UK factory during the first world war. So tough was the struggle that competitors such as ICI gave up the fight in the 1960s, leaving BPB with a clear run. For 20 years it had an almost perfect monopoly, with competition only from imports, which managed to take barely 5 per cent of the UK market.

In an unusual example of markets following economic theory, however, competitors were attracted by the great rewards which stemmed from this position and by a surge in use of the product during the 1970s and 1980. One competitor would have been bad enough, but in 1987 not only did Redland enter in a joint venture with Australian company CSR, but also the German company Knauf decided that the UK market was too much to resist, possibly stung by BPB's invasion of Germany when it bought Rigip's interests.

The result was predictable. A price war ensued which saw plasterboard prices fall by more than a quarter, aided by the recession which hit demand just as the new capacity was coming on stream. BPB has emerged victorious, however, if wounded. Redland's partner changed from CSR to the French group Lafarge Coppée {acute accent on first e} but Redland quickly saw its mistake and sold out to Lafarge.

BPB INDUSTRIES plc

BPB INDUSTRIES

Share record

Return on shareholder's equity	%	12.53
5-year price high	p	360.0
5-year price low	p	121.0
Dividend yield	%	3.07
5-year high	%	12.40
5-year low	%	2.64
Price/earnings ratio		21.1
5-year high		36.5
5-year low		6.4

Share price performance (in pence)

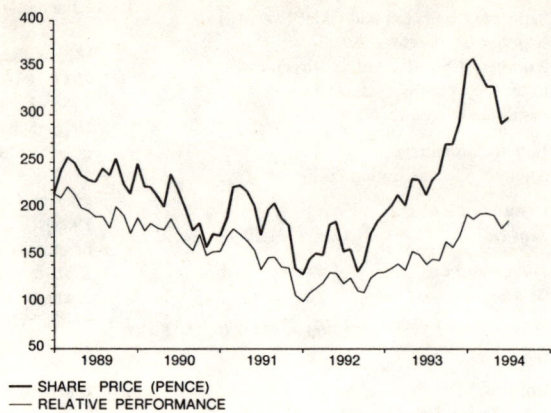

— SHARE PRICE (PENCE)
— RELATIVE PERFORMANCE

Financial record

		31/3/90	31/3/91	31/3/92	31/3/93	31/3/94
Total sales	£	1,033M	1,001M	1,021M	1,125M	1,151M
Pre-tax profit	£'000	135,400	70,000	45,400	65,800	121,700
Published retentions	£'000	44,400	17,500	-27,000	3,000	34,500
Earnings per share	p	22.84	11.11	6.31	9.15	17.17
Dividend per share	p	10.95	10.95	11.25	7.50	8.10
Operating cash flow	£'000	-117M	-98,800	2,000	44,400	99,200
Net assets per share	p	161.07	228.94	194.94	203.88	181.79
Net debt/(cash)	£'000	99,400	306,700	203,000	242,400	138,200
Shareholders' funds	£'000	593,400	531,600	629,600	649,000	653,600
Return on capital	%	22.35	13.11	8.71	10.48	15.34
Profit margin	%	11.63	6.01	3.96	5.54	9.99
Sales per employee	£	83.11	70.98	81.15	92.54	101.91
Interest cover		66.83	3.22	2.41	3.04	7.28
Dividend cover		2.09	1.02	0.56	1.22	2.12
Sales increase	%	7.54	-3.16	2.05	10.14	2.34
Earnings growth	%	-28.26	-51.35	-43.25	45.16	87.57
Investment x depreciation		3.40	1.95	1.17	0.54	0.53
Investment as % assets		28.57	15.25	8.88	4.40	4.82
Number of employees		12,432	14,096	12,581	12,152	11,292

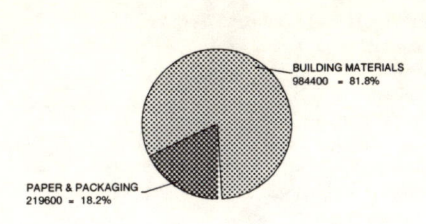

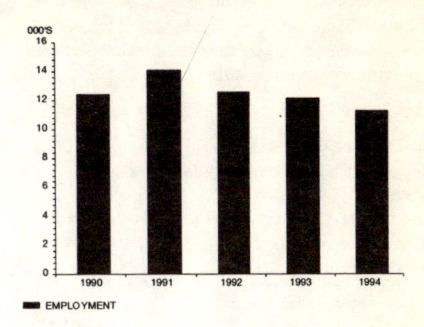

Sales analysis

BUILDING MATERIALS
984400 = 81.8%

PAPER & PACKAGING
219600 = 18.2%

Employment

BPB's market share in the UK slumped from 96 per cent to 'only' 65 per cent and its profits slumped in 1991 to barely a fifth of what they had been in 1988. By 1992, however, the worst seemed to be over. Prices began rising again, and in the meantime BPB had been spurred on by the competitive threat sufficiently to reduce costs by 30 per cent.

BPB had also been spurred on to continue its strategy of European expansion. Acquisitions in Germany, France and Spain have seen overseas profits overtake the contribution from Britain, even including the paper and packaging interests in the UK total. The group has become a leading supplier throughout Europe, estimated to have more than half the market, joining RMC as a major British company at the top of the German building materials industry. That position was strengthened in 1994 with the announcement of a new plasterboard plant in Berlin.

Plasterboard is made from a combination of gypsum and liner board which is manufactured from waste paper. The board-making process throws off other paper products, leaving BPB with a substantial business, mostly in the UK, producing board for cartons and other packaging. Thanks to Britain's tardiness in meeting European Union recycling targets, the business has suffered from a cost disadvantage since waste paper is subsidised in several European countries as a means of encouraging recycling, whereas British paper users have to pay for supplies.

Nevertheless the division has continued to make profits, and the cost position should improve once the UK recycling scheme has been implemented. The main plasterboard business can also expect to see improved conditions as Europe's building industry recovers from recession. For some observers, the main problem is avoiding the attention of competition authorities - something which has been a long-standing problem for BPB over the years.

Shares

Redland's announcement that it was to enter the plasterboard market knocked a tenth off the stock market value of BPB in just a few days in 1987, and the shares continued on a downward trend against the market for the next four years. As recession in Britain and then the rest of Europe added to problems of overcapacity by cutting demand there seemed little point in buying the shares, especially as the dividend came under pressure in 1991. A rights issue in June 1991 did not help, and killed a tentative recovery in the shares' standing. But investors finally reckoned that enough was enough by the end of 1991, when it seemed that there were prospects of economic recovery in the UK at least, and when it became clear that the worst of the price war in the industry was over. Sentiment was knocked back again in November 1992 when the dividend was belatedly cut, but this disappointment was soon countered by continuing news of price increases and improvements in the group's financial performance. This good news even allowed investors to treat the sudden departure of chief executive John Maxwell with equanimity in September 1993. Just two months later the shares rose by 4 per cent when the group announced a 60 per cent rise in half-year profits.

Corporate conscience

Gypsum is mined or quarried, thus BPB meets familiar environmental concerns on this issue, especially as it has not demonstrated an adequate public environment policy. Indeed, in its 1993 annual report the company said such issues were best addressed by individual subsidiaries rather than group-wide policies. Nevertheless its environmental record is not bad. It has no recent record of pollution convictions, and few cases of exceeding discharge consent levels to water. There have been health and safety convictions, however, and the ASA upheld a complaint

192 BRITISH AEROSPACE plc

against Albertay Paper Sacks on decency grounds in 1993. Otherwise, the group has some military connections. These issues are not balanced by any positive involvements, in community, equal opportunities or environmental commitments.

Corporate governance
Separate Chairman and Chief Executive Y
Number of Directors 12
Number of Non-Executive Directors 6
(6 Independent Directors)
Insulated Directors none

Board committees
Audit: Y   Remuneration committee : Y

Remuneration

Year end	31.03.92	31.03.93	31.03.94
Total board £M	1.34	1.58	1.73
% change		18	9
Highest paid £	304,000	305,000	322,000
% change		0.3	6

Board
Turner, Alan *Chairman*
Cuny, Jean-Pierre *Chief Executive*
Bushell, Chris *Executive Director*
Herring, Peter *Executive Director*
Sydney-Smith, Peter *Finance Director*
Beckett, Michael *Independent Non-Executive*
Carey, Sir Peter *Independent Non-Executive*
Clark, Martin *Independent Non-Executive*
Connolly, Eugene *Independent Non-Executive*
Dowdall, Michael *Independent Non-Executive*
Fredjohn, Den *Independent Non-Executive*

Board membership meets Cadbury criteria for numbers of non-executives, and the requisite committees exist, although chairman Alan Turner sits on them. These structures did not prevent the group making a mess of the succession to Mr Turner, however, when it appointed John Maxwell. He lasted less than a year before the non-executives fulfilled one of their purposes and told him it was time to go. Unfortunately, while Jean-Pierre Cuny has been designated as the next occupant of the chief executive post, in the meantime Mr Turner has resumed both of the top two roles. The note in the accounts on directors' pay shows bonuses separately, explains them as being based on 'specific and challenging targets', and gives general details of what those targets are. In 1994 it also pointed out that the chairman's salary had been the same since April 1991, and this £40,000 bonus was the first he had received for four years.

BRITISH AEROSPACE plc
Warwick House, PO Box 87, Farnborough, Hants GU14 6YU
Tel: 01252 373232
Chairman Bob Bauman
Chief executive Dick Evans
Main subsidiaries Arlington Securities, Royal Ordnance
Size £10.8 billion sales, £1.9 billion stock market value, 96,800 employees
5-year growth sales 18%, earnings per share -70%, employment -24%
Solvency debt = 5% shareholders' funds, interest cover 1 time
Political donations 0
Charitable donations £1.3 million

Major developments
1977 brought into state ownership
1981 government sold 50% to public
1985 government sold the remaining half
1987 bought Royal Ordnance
1988 bought Rover Group; bought Arlington Securities
1991 rights issue and departure of Professor Roland Smith
1993 attempted joint venture with Taiwan Aerospace
1994 departure of chairman John Cahill; sale of Rover to BMW

Outlook
British Aerospace (BAe) is one of many companies for which it would have been better if the 1980s had not existed. The group spent the decade appearing to consolidate on its shotgun marriage and diversify from dependence on defence, yet it entered the 1990s in more disarray than at the outset, and apparently having done few of the things which it was supposed to be concentrating on all those years, such as cutting costs and instituting effective business controls.

The group came together in 1978, as a result of the nationalisation of British Aircraft Corporation (BAC), Hawker Siddeley and Scottish Aviation. The antecedents of these companies include all the famous names in British aviation: Avro, De Havilland, Sopwith, Bristol Aeroplane and Vickers. But the intention to create a powerful, unified aircraft and missile company was never realised, apparently because BAe management never got to grips with rationalising production. The various components of the new group seem to have been allowed too much freedom to carry on much as before, operating from too many sites and duplicating too many activities.

The true state of affairs was obscured during the run-up to privatisation, which began in 1981, and during the 1980s the cushion of defence work plus the buoyant civil aircraft industry helped to convey a picture of reasonable progress. The picture remained

BRITISH AEROSPACE

Share record

Return on shareholders' equity	%	3.50
5-year price high	p	729.4
5-year price low	p	113.0
Dividend yield	%	2.10
5-year high	%	19.0
5-year low	%	1.39
Price/earnings ratio		30.5
5-year high		68.5
5-year low		4.6

Share price performance (in pence)

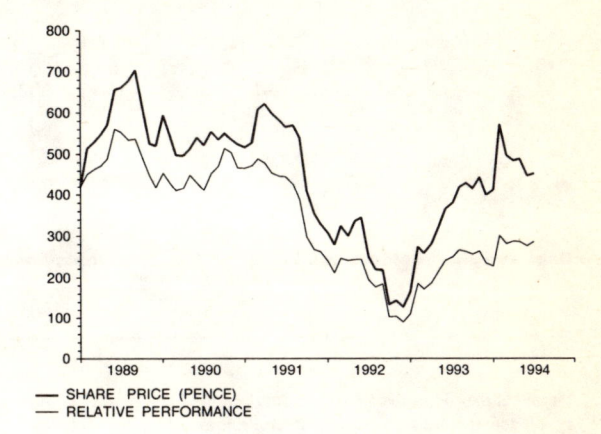

— SHARE PRICE (PENCE)
— RELATIVE PERFORMANCE

Financial record

		31/12/89	31/12/90	31/12/91	31/12/92	31/12/93
Total sales	£	9,085M	10,540M	10,562M	9,977M	10,760M
Pre-tax profit	£'000	265,000	372,000	125,000	-201M	74,000
Published retentions	£'000	166,000	174,000	-206M	-935M	-266M
Earnings per share	p	55.35	90.33	39.53	10.86	16.15
Dividend per share	p	22.34	24.61	24.86	7.00	8.30
Operating cash flow	£'000	587,000	-147M	-329M	-388M	-297M
Net assets per share	p	1,719	1,755	1,669	1,211	1,105
Net debt/(cash)	£'000	-1,142M	-711M	-323M	91,000	79,000
Shareholders' funds	£	2,380M	2,534M	2,697M	1,780M	1,510M
Return on capital	%	10.24	12.07	7.64	1.18	8.14
Profit margin	%	2.72	3.50	1.21	-2.07	0.61
Sales per employee	£	71.25	82.41	85.73	91.95	111.16
Interest cover		5.49	3.09	1.21	-1.38	1.40
Dividend cover		2.48	3.67	1.59	1.55	1.95
Sales increase	%	61.11	16.02	0.21	-5.54	7.85
Earnings growth	%	-9.27	63.21	-56.24	-72.52	48.66
Investment x depreciation		2.58	1.17	1.13	1.11	1.14
Investment as % assets		22.59	11.37	10.80	11.60	12.94
Number of employees		127,500	127,900	123,200	108,500	96,800

194 BRITISH AEROSPACE plc

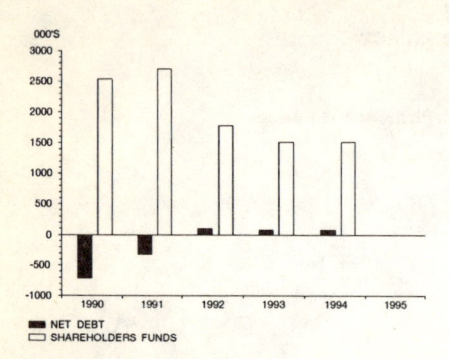

Debt and shareholders' funds

Employment

blurred at the end of the 1980s as a result of the flurry of activity initiated by chairman Professor Sir Roland Smith. Apart from machinations over the (eventually highly successful) European Airbus consortium, BAe took first Royal Ordnance and then, even more outrageously, the Rover group off the government's hands. Controversy, especially over payments for Rover, clouded the question of why BAe should buy these companies in the first place. And the same applied to its purchase of property company Arlington and construction operation Ballast Needham.

The only possible answer lay in the fact that BAe needed to diversify away from defence, which was becoming an increasingly difficult sector as the Ministry of Defence attempted to turn the screw on suppliers. But maybe the answer had more to do with politics than business. (BAe, as one of the largest suppliers to the Ministry of Defence, operates in a highly political environment. Any political favours it can do for the government of the day are likely to be excellent investments.) The 1990s showed, however, that BAe would have done better getting its aircraft business into shape rather than dabbling in other activities. Recession caused a downturn in both the car and property industries, but it was not until the middle of 1992 (and after the departure of Professor Smith) that the true extent of the problems in the aircraft business became apparent.

1991 had been difficult enough, with pre-tax profits slumping and extraordinary write-offs eradicating what was left of them. That year, and Professor Smith's reputation, was further marred for BAe by a bungled rights issue. But that was nothing compared to the shock in September 1992 when new chairman John Cahill had to announce a half-year loss of £129 million, which did not allow for a provision of £1 billion (before tax) for sorting out the regional jet business – including the closure of the famous Hatfield site. In the event BAe recorded a loss for the year of £1.2 billion.

More encouraging news emerged at the start of 1993: BAe assumed it had concluded a joint venture on regional jets with Taiwan Aerospace; and there was at last to be some progress on the long-awaited second stage of the Al Yamamah military project for Saudi Arabia. Cars and even property could also both be expected eventually to bounce back strongly with an economic upturn. But it was a false dawn. The Taiwan deal was never finalised and further huge provisions left BAe with another net loss and another big cash outflow in 1993. The controversial sale of Rover to BMW did go through, helping the cash position, but plenty of problems remain: Airbus must be counted a success, but the huge overhang of orders from the civil aircraft boom of the late 1980s compared to current airline demand casts a shadow over its prospects; the whole defence industry is threatened by the end of cold war; and there are still question marks over what is left of BAe's civil aircraft programme. It will be a long time before the group's credibility is fully restored even with the departure of John Cahill and his replacement.

Shares

British Aerospace has long been perceived as a volatile stock, though its recent performance has fluctuated particularly wildly. Traditionally the group's shares have moved erratically in response to orders for aeroplanes, but in 1987 the board implemented

its plan to smooth the ride by acquiring allied businesses. The first acquisition, Royal Ordnance, came as the stock market peaked and had not been assimilated before the market crash in October.

After the crash the group's shares began to rise relative to the market, due to optimism over orders, and the purchase of the Rover group in 1988 speeded the process up. All seemed well until BAe bought the Arlington property group at the top of the market the following year. The shares promptly headed downwards and remained at best volatile in 1990 as the recession hit, despite claims from some analysts at the time that profits and the dividend were safe, and the view of one that it was one of the most recession-proof shares on the stock market. After a brief recovery at the time of the Gulf War, uncertainty continued until echoes of boardroom rows reached the market in 1991 and, assisted by a profit warning, the shares plummeted.

The failure that year of the rights issue intended to save the group made matters worse, and even talk of a break-up bid or rescue by GEC failed to halt the slide in BAe's shares. Cost-cutting and internal reorganisation failed to dispel the City's doubts about the shares although they did gain some ground as a result of hopes that an economic recovery would float the group off the rocks.

In 1993, with the clinching of the second part of the Saudi Tornado deal and with continuing speculation that a GEC joint venture of some sort in military operations would provide the group with a safety net, the picture began to brighten and analysts started to describe BAe as a prime recovery stock. Optimism became limited however as it became clear that the Rover sale would not transform BAe prospects and after a sharp rise at the start of 1994 the shares moved sideways relative to the market.

Corporate conscience

It is the military involvement which dominates this company's 'conscience' record. Apart from building military aircraft such as the Tornado and Harrier, and making weapons, the group is also heavily implicated in exports to countries with suspect regimes, notably Indonesia.

But, while the company can hardly avoid these aspects, because they are its business, it appears to make little effort on other issues of conscience. BAe is a member of BITC and the Per Cent Club, and has a good record of charitable donations. But it does not broadcast an equal opportunities policy it has a lengthy list of health and safety convictions, and a poor environmental record. The ASA even upheld two complaints against its mobile communication associate Hutchinson Telecom at the end of 1993. Health and safety convictions include a £25,000 fine in 1988, one of the largest recorded in this book. They also reveal some fascinating laws, such as the Horizontal Milling Machines Regulations 1928, and under which Royal Ordnance was fined.

In addition, the group's environmental record is blotted by one conviction for water pollution, leading to a £2,000 fine in 1991 for breaching consent levels on 2 occasions at Royal Ordnance. BAe also uses some CFCs in solvent cleaners, but has pledged to phase out all ozone-depleting chemicals by the end of 1995.

Corporate governance

Separate Chairman and Chief Executive Y
Number of Directors 12
Number of Non-Executive Directors 7
(6 Independent Directors)
Insulated Directors None

Board Committees
Audit: Y   Remuneration: Y

Remuneration

Year end	31.12.91	31.12.92	31.12.93
Total board £M	2.50	2.67	3.01
% change	-8	7	13
Highest paid £	338,110	439,318	724,855
% change		-18	30	65

Board
Evans, R H *Chief Executive*
Gillibrand, S *Executive Director*
Turner, Mike *Executive Director*
Weston, John *Executive Director*
Lapthorne, Richard D *Finance Director*
Biggam, Sir Robin *Independent Non-Executive*
Brown, K C *Independent Non-Executive*
Hampel, R C *Independent Non-Executive*
Lord Heskett *Independent Non-Executive*
Kirk, R L *Independent Non-Executive*
Lord Hollick *Independent Non-Executive*
Bauman, Bob *Non-Executive Chairman*

Succession has caused problems at the company, but the lack of non-executive representation in the boardroom has belatedly been addressed by the appointment of several powerful figures so that independents now outnumber executive directors. These directors were instrumental in negotiating Mr Cahill's departure, but could not get away with compensation of less than £3.1 million given the length of Mr Cahill's contract remaining. Remuneration disclosure is adequate although there was no attempt to justify Mr Cahill's huge pay-off.

BRITISH AIRWAYS plc

P O Box 10, Speedbird House, Heathrow Airport,
London TW6 2JA
Tel: 0181 759 5511
Chairman Sir Colin Marshall
Group managing director Robert Ayling
Size £6.3 billion sales, £4.2 billion stock market value, 49,600 employees
5-year growth sales 30%, earnings per share -4%, employment -5%
Solvency debt = 148% shareholders' funds, interest cover 3 times
Political donations 0
Charitable donations £479,000

BRITISH AIRWAYS plc

BRITISH AIRWAYS

Share record

Return on shareholders' equity	%	17.83
5-year price high	p	495.0
5-year price low	p	119.3
Dividend yield	%	3.08
5-year high	%	9.48
5-year low	%	2.71
Price/earnings ratio		19.0
5-year high		31.4
5-year low		3.4

Share price performance (in pence)

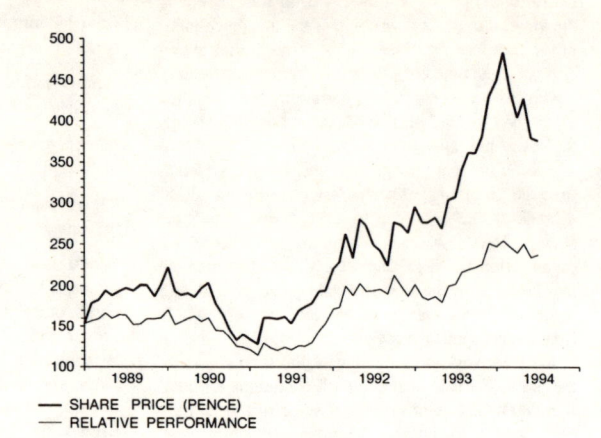

— SHARE PRICE (PENCE)
— RELATIVE PERFORMANCE

Financial record

		31/3/90	31/3/91	31/3/92	31/3/93	31/3/94
Total sales	£	4,838M	4,937M	5,224M	5,566M	6,303M
Pre-tax profit	£'000	365,000	221,000	302,000	196,000	342,000
Published retentions	£'000	182,000	31,000	321,000	99,000	180,000
Earnings per share	p	35.25	20.46	34.74	24.53	33.80
Dividend per share	p	8.48	8.48	9.76	10.16	11.10
Operating cash flow	£'000	306,000	-707M	123,000	-52,000	211,000
Net assets per share	p	271.46	357.31	468.95	583.74	592.95
Net debt/(cash)	£'000	754,000	1,545M	1,492M	2,773M	2,695M
Shareholders' funds	£'000	912,000	958,000	1,284M	1,214M	1,827M
Return on capital	%	23.82	13.45	14.32	9.61	11.00
Profit margin	%	7.90	4.35	5.78	3.83	5.60
Sales per employee	£	92.94	90.71	103.63	113.68	127.00
Interest cover		7.87	7.42	4.45	3.07	3.37
Dividend cover		4.16	2.38	3.56	2.41	3.05
Sales increase	%	13.65	2.05	5.81	6.55	13.24
Earnings growth	%	42.46	-41.95	69.77	-29.39	37.82
Investment x depreciation		0.90	3.10	0.99	1.52	0.74
Investment as % assets		10.67	26.87	8.38	11.21	5.94
Number of employees		52,054	54,427	50,409	48,960	49,628

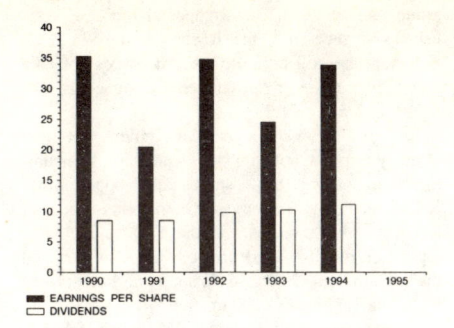

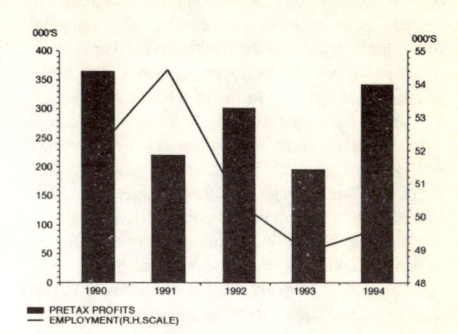

Earnings and dividends

Profits and employment

Major developments
1987 privatised bought British Caledonian
1989 abandoned attempt to invest in United Airlines
1991 The World's Biggest Offer marketing campaign; sale of engine overhaul business to GE
1992 KLM merger talks failed; bought 49% of Delta Air Regionalflugverkehr (renamed Deutsche BA), 50% TAT; bought Dan Air
1993 bought 25% of USAir, 25% of Qantas
1994 suspended further investment in USAir; launched new flights to Paris only

Outlook
The airline business is all about filling seats – and preferably the most expensive seats that deliver the highest yields per passenger. In the depths of the recession this proved to be a tough task even for market leader British Airways. With signs that the gloom was lifting, BA's own performance began to perk up. It was helped particularly by a marked recovery in premium traffic (Club and first class seats) coupled with a rigorous cost-cutting regime.

BA ploughed £100 million into a programme of improvements to its Club World business class, First Class and its flagship Concorde, over an 18-month period spanning 1993. The improvements enabled passengers to take their pick from plush arrivals lounges as well as departure lounges, and further improvements were planned for the end of 1994 when Club World was to be completely relaunched.

A general recovery in passenger numbers helped boost premium traffic by 14 per cent in the first three months of 1994 alone, compared with a 4 per cent fall in the same quarter of the previous year. Total passenger numbers rose by nearly 9 per cent in that period. But the industry still had too many seats available – BA itself was filling only 90 per cent of available seats – and over-capacity helps to hold down prices, as BA knows only too well. In 1994 it launched a new `World Offers' programme _ a constant round of cut-price tickets to fill leisure seats.

But although the recovery in premium traffic undoubtedly helped BA's financial recovery, the details were overshadowed by a big black cloud: its tricky relationship with loss-making partner USAir.

Since the late 1980s BA's major preoccupation has been its lengthy `global shopping list', as it went round the world on a much publicised spree, picking up foreign partners. It spent nearly £700 million on these new allliances, financing the deals partly through a £442 million rights issue.

But all has not been rosy at USAir, where BA's partnership with the sixth biggest US carrier had been planned to be the centrepiece in its global strategy. With USAir, there was not only a ticket code-sharing agreement, designed to give passengers a wider choice of destinations by allowing BA to sell tickets to USAir destinations, but also sizeable investment planned over several stages – Government approval permitting. In March 1994, BA issued its first warning of trouble with its partner by saying it would not make any further equity investment until it was reassured of the viability of the business. But the real thunderbolt came with the results in May, when BA admitted it might be forced to write off the £275 million invested so far in USAir unless the restructuring programme was in place by the autumn.

In contrast to the problems with its transatlantic partner, the alliances with other partners seem to be moving ahead well, with Qantas in profit and benefits emerging from its links with TAT and Deutsche BA, its French and German partners.

But the inherent problems with USAir have undoubtedly raised questions about whether BA's management has been over-zealous in its globalisation policy, suffering from the same over-ambition which damaged so many companies in the late 1980s.

Also, tucked away in the 1993 annual report was a

198   BRITISH AIRWAYS plc

provision of £22 million for litigation – a discreet reference to the possible outcome of legal action by Richard Branson's Virgin Atlantic, which successfully humiliated BA in the libel courts in 1993.

These little sideshows apart, however, BA seems as well placed as any airline in what seems likely to remain a difficult industry. BA's determined management has successfully pushed through a rigorous and continuing cost-cutting programme, slashing £580 million off annual costs over the last three years. This has been achieved through better working practices, better deals struck with suppliers, more efficient use of aircraft and trimming back its management team.

If any airline can survive, it is undoubtedly BA, so long as its marriage with USAir does not go horribly wrong.

Shares

Privatised in the boom market of 1987, BA's shares held up well against the rest of the market. During the dramatic crash of that year they briefly fell to below their offer price but pulled out of their dive before most other companies. The group's shares continued to do well relative to the market, and were also popular on account of their dividend yield. They weakened in 1988, when BA bought British Caledonian, but recovered quickly.

In 1991 the Gulf War severely disrupted air traffic, and the group's shares again fell to below their flotation price. Profits recovered next year, along with air traffic, and BA's shares soared to new heights relative to the market. As recession gripped the UK, business kept growing, with successive cuts in interest rates and timely sales of aircraft helping to feed profits.

The next big hurdle for the group appeared to be finding a major airline partner, preferably in the US. Although deals like the Dan-Air acquisition in 1992 kept investor interest alive, there was increasing concern over the group's cash flow and the shares peaked that year. The Virgin episode in 1993 did not affect BA's trading position but did put a question mark over the board and its policy-making, which adversely affected the shares, as did the continuing struggle to find a North American partner – at an acceptable price. The USAir deal was welcomed and the share rating rose to a peak at the start of 1994. It fell back only slightly, despite subsequent worries about the US investment.

Corporate conscience

Revelations in 1992 concerning the campaign against Virgin stand in contrast to the high degree of social responsibility that BA has otherwise demonstrated. And there have been some interesting developments on issues of conscience, especially on the environmental front. At the end of 1989 BA began to take this matter seriously, giving responsibility to a senior manager and taking the important first step of an environmental audit (at Heathrow). The result of the audit was also published, and some of the criticisms were acted on. This approach has been developed with typical professionalism throughout the company. Audits have been extended throughout the group and an annual environmental report is published – so successfully that it won an award in 1992. But there are still criticisms that BA does not take issues like noise pollution seriously enough, nor report such matters fully.

BA's record on employment is similarly excellent in many respects, but with significant gaps. It is committed to training, has a strong equal opportunities policy, including clear targets. On the other hand, BA has a record of disputes with trade unions and has a reputation for high-handedness. It has also infringed the Health and Safety at Work Act, being fined £3,000 in 1989 and £1,500 in 1990.

On mainstream ethical issues BA is implicated as it sells drink (and pours it down the throats of Business and First Class passengers) and tobacco, and toiletries tested on animals. It also has a military connection, with a contract from the Ministry of Defence worth between £25 million and £50 million a year. And finally, BA's aggressive marketing has brought its several adverse judgements by the ASA (five in 1992).

Corporate governance

Separate Chairman and Chief Executive Y
Number of Directors 10
Number of Non-Executive Directors 6
(4 Independent Directors)
Insulated Directors All

Board Committees
Audit: Y   Remuneration: Y

Remuneration

Year end	31.03.92	31.03.93	31.03.94
Total board £M	2.44	2.38	1.83
% change	43	-3	-23
Highest paid £	669,350	540,916	665,379
% change	64	-19	23

Board

Marshall, Sir Colin *Chairman*
Ayling, Robert *Managing Director*
Stevens, Derek *Finance Director*
Davies, Michael *Independent Non-Executive*
Kennedy, Sir Francis *Independent Non-Executive*
Lord White of Hull *Independent Non-Executive*
Price, Charles H, II *Independent Non-Executive*
Angus, Sir Michael Richard *Non-Executive*
Barnes, Capt. Colin *Non-Executive*
Mackay, Charles *Independent Non-Executive*
O'Cathain, Baroness *Independent Non-Executive*

Attention to, and disclosure of, governance matters improved considerably in 1993/4. The 1994 report and accounts included a separate corporate governance statement, which explained the workings of board committees, including an 'Air Safety Review Committee'. The report also detailed directors' membership of the board committees, and listed senior executives as well. Details of directors' pay remain sketchy, however, with bonuses explained only as being 'driven by corporate goals'.

BRITISH GAS plc

Rivermill House, 152 Grosvenor Road, London SW1V 3JL
Tel: 0171 821 1444
Chairman Richard V Giordano
Chief executive Cedric Brown
Size £10.4 billion sales, £12.2 billion stock market value, 79,300 employees
5-year growth sales 30%, earnings per share 32%, employment -1%
Solvency debt = 55% shareholders' funds, interest cover 5 times
Political donations 0
Charitable donations £2 million

Major developments
1986 privatised
1987 bought Consumers Gas, Canada
1988 bought Acre Oil; bought Bow Valley Industries; bought Tenneco's oil & gas division
1991 signed agreement to develop Miskar gas field, Tunisia
1992 formed Transco to build pipelines; formed Premier Energy Suppliers to market gas
1993 announced sale of Consumers Gas; findings of Monopolies Commission inquiry published
1994 restructuring of gas business into 5 units; announced sale of Bow Valley Energy

Outlook
It did not take long for the government to realise that the privatisation of British Gas in 1986 was seriously flawed. But it took ministers nearly seven years to admit it. Then the company was plunged into a reorganisation as radical as anything a privatised utility has had to endure. As a result, its future, the outlook for its shareholders, its 18 million domestic customers and its workforce, is highly uncertain.

The underlying problem is due to the very structure of gas privatisation. The company was simply transformed from being a public sector monopoly to being a powerful private sector one. This was partly the result of the lobbying skills of then chairman Sir Denis Rooke, who made the case for the company being kept intact. Lord Marshall later tried to do the same with the power industry but by then the government had learned its lesson. The government too must take much of the blame. In the heyday of privatisation the emphasis was on large and flashy sell-offs which could spill billions into Treasury coffers. Competition and the consumer were afterthoughts and it was left to the government-appointed regulator, Ofgas, to deliver what the government had failed to think deeply enough about.

Unfortunately for British Gas, it was landed with a regulator who, in the shape of Sir James McKinnon, took his responsibilities very seriously. In the absence of clear guidelines setting out the powers of the regulator, this left him too much room to use his discretion, according to some critics, and he became engaged in an increasingly bitter public battle with his charge. For the consumer this was good news, however. Sir James engineered a post-privatisation price cap which constrained British Gas from raising its prices by more than the RPI minus 5 percentage points. As a result, domestic gas prices have fallen by some 23 per cent since privatisation. Further regulatory squeezes were imposed on the group, too, including a directive to give up all but 40 per cent of the industrial gas market to competitors and to release gas supplies to potential rivals in order to encourage them to ease their way into the marketplace.

Despite these developments, Sir James began increasingly to concern himself with the company's monopolistic hold on the market. With Robert Evans taking over from Sir Denis on his retirement, the new chairman's inability to deal effectively with civil servants meant that the war of words intensified and culminated in an almost total breakdown in relations between Ofgas and the company. Ofgas was determined to push for a separation of British Gas's transportation system – the pipelines which move gas around the country – and its supply business, which sells gas to the consumer. With that in mind, Sir James pressed for a Monopolies Commission investigation into the gas pipeline business in 1992. But the company, showing a deftness that had been previously been lacking, outmanoeuvred him and pursuaded Trade and Industry Secretary Michael Heseltine to refer the entire gas industry for scrutiny by the Monopolies Commision.

A year-long investigation followed. In August 1993 the Monopolies Commission recommended that the company be split in two and that its transportation arm be hived off either through a flotation or a trade sale. It recommended that the domestic market be opened to full competition, but only slowly and probably not before the year 2002. Notably it warned that in the short term consumers were likely to have to pay a higher price for gas; investing for the longer term assumed the benefits of a competitive market.

It was one of the most exhaustive Monopoly inquiries ever mounted. But in December Michael Heseltine announced that he was preparing to ignore its recommendations almost entirely. Never before had the recommendations of the Monopoly Commission been so comprehensively binned. Instead, Mr Heseltine revealed his determination to keep British Gas in one piece, having listened to the company's argument that to split it would undermine its efforts to become one of Britain's biggest and most successful international companies. And he proposed to take

BRITISH GAS

Share record

Return on shareholders' equity	%	19.37
5-year price high	p	360.0
5-year price low	p	185.0
Dividend yield	%	6.38
5-year high	%	7.89
5-year low	%	4.93
Price/earnings ratio		12.0
5-year high		21.8
5-year low		9.0

Share price performance (in pence)

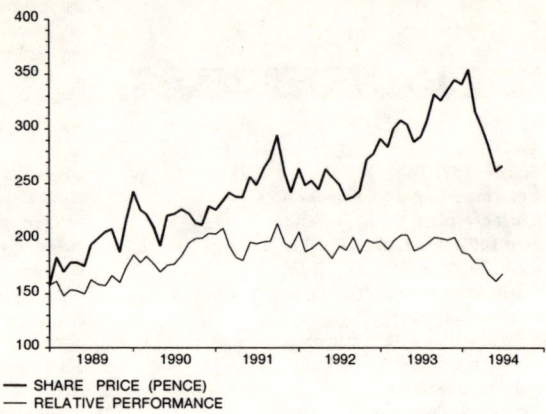

— SHARE PRICE (PENCE)
— RELATIVE PERFORMANCE

Financial record

		31/3/90	31/3/91	31/12/91 39 weeks	31/12/92	31/12/93
Total sales	£	7,983M	9,491M	6,794M	10,254M	10,386M
Pre-tax profit	£'000	1,267M	1,783M	590,000	1,277M	1,367M
Published retentions	£'000	233,000	385,000	-158M	-140M	-913M
Earnings per share	p	20.38	27.59	12.70	21.80	26.91
Dividend per share	p	10.50	12.50	13.40	14.20	14.50
Operating cash flow	£	-252M	-564M	-263M	-1,003M	-82,000
Net assets per share	£'000	206.38	263.27	267.87	292.18	310.11
Net debt/(cash)	£	1,193M	2,459M	2,462M	3,926M	3,991M
Shareholders' funds	£	7,407M	8,042M	8,026M	8,123M	7,211M
Return on capital	%	17.40	20.47	7.79	13.94	13.69
Profit margin	%	15.87	18.79	8.68	12.39	12.87
Sales per employee	£	99.19	116.02	80.36	122.04	130.88
Interest cover		13.30	11.19	4.19	5.08	4.75
Dividend cover		1.94	2.21	0.95	1.54	1.86
Sales increase	%	6.07	18.89	-28.42	50.93	1.29
Earnings growth	%	-4.11	35.43	-53.97	71.64	23.43
Investment x depreciation		1.56	2.23	2.40	2.19	1.53
Investment as % assets		7.38	10.63	10.44	17.54	12.71
Number of employees		80,481	81,805	84,540	84,023	79,358

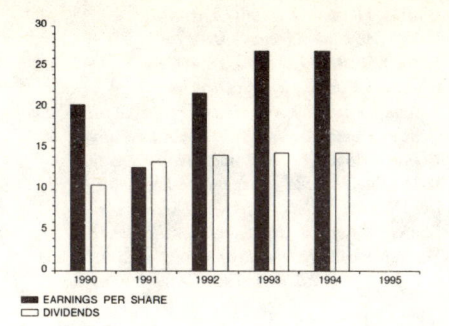

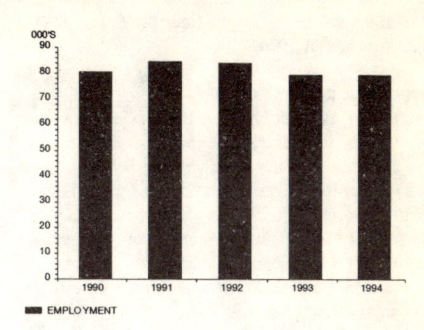

Earnings and dividends

Employment

the high-risk course of rushing through measures to increase competition in the domestic market in the two years between 1996 and 1998. In conjunction with the new Gas regulator, Clare Spottiswoode – an entirely different, though no less independent, official from Sir James – Mr Heseltine promised to deliver a joint consultation document on the competitive market. But as the document failed to materialise over the next few months, it became clear that the government was hesitating as it realised that the introduction of competition would mean the eradication of cross-subsidies that allowed British Gas to offer a universal tariff. Result: the distinct possibility of higher gas bills for those least able to afford it.

For a government still struggling against the backlash from the controversy about imposing VAT on fuel, promises from would-be competitors to British Gas – that they could cut bills for everyone and would not 'cherry pick' the most lucrative customers – would not suffice. The consultation document was only finally published after the May local council elections were over. Ministers proposed to open up the market for 18.5 million customers by 5 per cent chinks each year in 1996 and 1997, before moving to full competition the year after. It was a tight schedule, particularly as new legislation needed to be put through in the Parliamentary session starting in Autumn 1994. And there were fears that the government might miss that deadline and defer the controversial move a little longer.

The sop for British Gas – about to witness a major erosion of its domestic market – was that the McKinnon RPI-5 formula had been relaxed to RPI-4. But the company was subsequently given a tough new price cap regulating its pipelines business – at the old RPI-5 level. In the face of this, it warned that it was likely to freeze dividends in 1994 and would be hard pushed to increase earnings on its UK gas business in 1995 and 1996. Critics suggested that British Gas was overreacting, but the City took the company at its word.

The escape from regulation, as with all the privatised utilities, is to build up its international presence, a strategy British Gas has been adopting with considerable aplomb. Some earlier adventures in foreign parts have not been so successful, though. For instance, expansion into Canada with the purchase of Consumers Gas was wound up in 1994 as British Gas decided it would be better served by going for higher-risk, higher-return investments. Excursions into eastern Europe, Argentina and the former Soviet Union are now being added, together with pioneering developments in places like Vietnam.

As regards the core domestic business, the steady pressure to reduce costs in the early post-privatisation days has been stepped up. In 1994 the company was in the midst of a programme to axe 25,000 jobs over three to five years. Observers accept that the company may have to do more if it is to meet the regulatory pressures of a tough price cap on its £17 billion network of pipelines.

Shares

From the time of the company's début on the stock market in 1986, the sheer size of British Gas ensured that it was a core holding for investing institutions, as well as being snapped up by the famous army of 'Sids'. For much of its life as a public company, it has been a stable investment, moving broadly in line with the market. The lowest point occurred early in 1989, largely as a consequence of the mild winter, which hit gas consumption. But this was followed by a swift rise relative to the market as thoughts of the advancing recession focused investors' minds on the fundamentally stable nature of the business. Subsequently, the main influence has been the regulatory threat, the share price dipping to reflect a number of temporary 'frights' from 1991 to 1993. The shares finally began to dive steeply as the seriousness of the threat to break up British Gas became apparent at the end of 1993, and the rating continued to fall throughout the first half of 1994.

Corporate conscience

Of all the privatised companies, British Gas has probably retained its culture as a nationalised industry more than most. On the negative side, British Gas is still a white, male preserve, although the group is sufficiently aware of this to take the unusual step of publishing the figures in its annual report. At the end of 1993 only 13 per cent of managers were women, and less than 3 per cent of the workforce were from ethnic minorities.

On the positive side, the pre-privatisation culture of the company is reflected in the way it takes its social responsibilities seriously. As part of an employment policy that maintains the tradition of patient trade union negotiations, it has put equal opportunities into practice, offering – unusually – career breaks for men as well as women, and responsibility at director level. British Gas also supports Opportunity 2000. It is a member of BITC and the Per Cent Club, has an extensive educational programme and is one of the largest corporate donors to charitable and community causes. It has a comprehensive environmental policy and was scheduled to complete an environmental audit in the autumn of 1994.

This high level of awareness of corporate responsibility has not prevented the group from breaching various laws and standards. Three advertising complaints were upheld in 1992; there have been a number of successful prosecutions in recent years under health and safety legislation, and occasionally excess discharge into water. In 1993 the group was also still using CFC-113 as a refrigerant to control the dew-point of natural gas, with no commitment to phase it out.

Unexpectedly, given its overwhelmingly domestic business, British Gas has also received criticism for its activities in the Third World. Exploration has spread to countries such as Tunisia, Gabon, Thailand, Malaysia and Ecuador.

Corporate governance

Separate Chairman and Chief Executive Y
Number of Directors 13
Number of Non-Executive Directors 8
(8 Independent Directors)
Insulated Directors Ch, CE, +1 exec

Board Committees
Audit: Y   Remuneration: Y

Remuneration

Year end	31.12.91	31.12.92	31.12.93
Total board £M	1.66	1.91	2.02
% change	0.4	15	6
Highest paid £	435,222	379,484	386.246
% change		18	-13	2

Board
Brown, Cedric *Chief Executive*
Blacker, Norman *Executive Director*
Dalton, Howard *Executive Director*
Herbert, Russell *Executive Director*
Rogerson, Philip *Finance Director*
Baroness Platt of Writtle *Independent Non-Executive*
Benson, David H *Independent Non-Executive*
Boissier, Roger H *Independent Non-Executive*
Kalms, Stanley *Independent Non-Executive*
Lord Walker *Independent Non-Executive*
Mackvell, Keith *Independent Non-Executive*
Perry, Michael *Independent Non-Executive*
Giordano, Richard V *Non-Executive Chairman*

After clinging to a joint chairman and chief executive, the company finally bowed to pressure in 1992 to split the two roles. By 1994 more than half the boardroom was non-executive, and the annual report provided ample biographical details. British Gas now divulges more information to shareholders, but the existence of an audit committe is barely mentioned in the annual report, and only the figures for executive remuneration are provided in the summary statement for shareholders. In 1994 the group also removed the exemption from re-election, which had applied to three directors, including the chairman. It stated, moreover, that from 1995 pay details for each individual director would be reported.

BRITISH PETROLEUM CO plc

Britannic House, 1 Finsbury Circus,
London EC2M 7BA
Tel: 0171 496 4000
Chairman Lord Ashburton
Chief executive David Simon
Size £47.7 billion sales, £22.0 billion stock market value, 72,600 employees
5-year growth sales 27%, earnings per share -55%, employment -39%
Solvency debt = 84% shareholders' funds, interest cover 4 times.
Political donations 0
Charitable donations £21 million

Major developments
1909 formed as Anglo-Persian Oil Co
1914 government took control
1935 name changed to Anglo-Iranian Oil Co
1954 name changed to British Petroleum
1977–87 government sold its shareholding
1987 bought Standard Oil
1988 bought Britoil
1989 sold mineral assets to RTZ; bought back its shares from Kuwait Investment Office
1992 Bob Horton ousted as chairman and chief executive

BRITISH PETROLEUM

Share record

Return on shareholders' equity	%	9.16
5-year price high	p	411.5
5-year price low	p	184.0
Dividend yield	%	2.75
5-year high	%	11.23
5-year low	%	2.63
Price/earnings ratio		22.3
5-year high		31.1
5-year low		8.7

Share price performance (in pence)

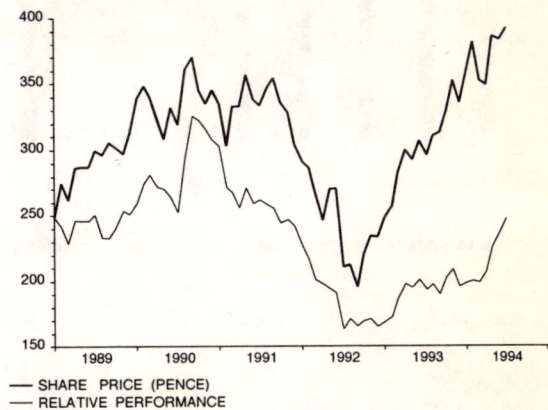

— SHARE PRICE (PENCE)
— RELATIVE PERFORMANCE

Financial record

		31/12/89	31/12/90	31/12/91	31/12/92	31/12/93
Total sales	£	37,394M	41,711M	41,267M	43,314M	47,655M
Pre-tax profit	£	2,533M	2,768M	1,203M	1,107M	1,542M
Published retentions	£'000	1,339M	827,000	-490M	-1,027M	157,000
Earnings per share	p	30.87	30.36	7.70	8.83	13.85
Dividend per share	p	14.90	16.05	16.80	10.50	8.40
Operating cash flow	£'000	563,000	937,000	-357M	-431M	n/a
Net assets per share	p	390.32	380.26	405.45	427.49	411.89
Net debt/(cash)	£	7,870M	6,299M	7,437M	9,909M	8,170M
Shareholders' funds	£	10,785M	11,001M	10,654M	9,979M	9,748M
Return on capital	%	15.75	16.49	9.14	7.92	9.75
Profit margin	%	6.07	6.16	2.51	1.93	2.78
Sales per employee	£	312.01	353.33	358.06	409.59	656.40
Interest cover		8.67	7.43	3.80	3.21	3.91
Dividend cover		2.07	1.89	0.46	0.84	1.65
Sales increase	%	12.97	11.54	-1.06	4.96	10.02
Earnings growth	%	63.43	-1.66	-74.65	14.69	56.99
Investment x depreciation		0.94	1.01	1.25	0.93	n/a
Investment as % assets		9.87	11.38	13.56	10.70	n/a
Number of employees		119,850	118,050	115,250	105,750	72,600

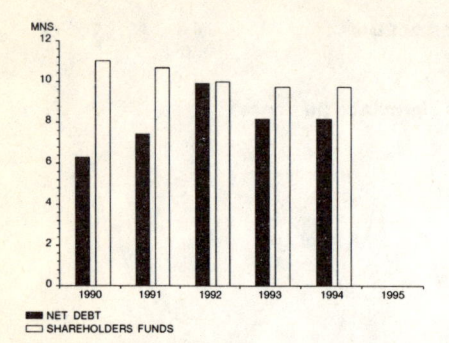

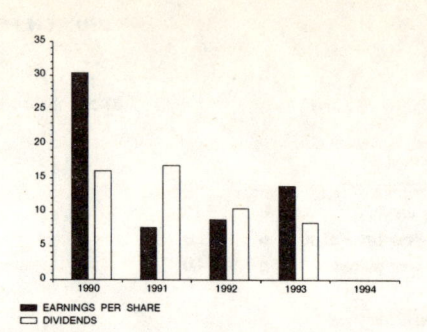

Debt and shareholders' funds

Earnings and dividends

Outlook

If BP were still nationalised, it would be held out as an example of Whitehall incompetence, an indisputable argument for the government staying out of commercial operations. Yet this is supposedly one of the private sector's biggest and best companies, with some of the toughest and most professional managers in Britain, in one of the most capitalistic sectors. So what went wrong?

Ironically, part of the answer is privatisation – specifically the sale in 1987 of more than two billion shares in the company, continuing a process which the last Labour government had started in 1977. The sale unfortunately coincided with the stock market crash; as a result it failed to attract the private investors it needed and, instead, caught the attention of the Kuwait Investment Office (KIO) who picked up a 22 per cent stake in the company, to the great embarrassment of BP and the British government. The KIO insisted that this was just another investment, but the thought of a Middle Eastern government (indirectly) controlling such an important stake in Britain's premier oil company was too much. After much toing and froing and a Monopolies Commission inquiry, BP ended up buying back 12 per cent of the shares, hence worsening its already looming indebtedness and triggering what amounts to a long-term crisis at the company.

In 1992 that crisis claimed the head of chairman and chief executive Bob Horton; cost an additional 16,000 jobs as the group slashed costs everywhere; led to the dividend being cut for the first time since the Second World War, along with cuts in capital spending; and accelerated the sale of its non-oil businesses. It was a miserable year, except perhaps for David Simon, the man who lost out when Bob Horton was originally appointed, but had the last laugh when he took over as chief executive following Mr Horton's departure.

The KIO fiasco was not the only cause of this crisis. Indeed, the £2.4 billion spent buying back the KIO shares was almost insignificant by comparison with its greatest extravagance – £5 billion to take complete control of Standard Oil in the US in 1987. On top of these two items, BP paid £2.2 billion to buy the privatised Britoil in 1988. This was all in the heady days before the recession, when people still believed the Lawson boom would continue for ever and, more importantly for BP, that the oil prices would remain high. The decline of Opec's power in the 1980s brought oil prices sliding down, which, combined with a decreasing demand for oil as a result of the recession, made matters worse for the industry. Moreover, profits have tumbled in oil-refining, where capacity has remained too high for current needs, although the exploration side of the business has maintained returns (on a current cost basis, which excludes the swings on stock prices which distort traditional accounting, based on historical costs). BP faces the mid-1990s struggling under a mountain of debt, just like all the other expansionist businesses which charged full speed into the recession. The company responded quickly as the scale of the financial crisis became apparent, but despite the early sale of coal and mineral interests, and despite further disposals, BP's debts hit £8.5 billion in 1992, costing over £700 million in interest charges in 1991 and not much less in 1992.

This calamity was the result of over-optimism in the mid-1980s, especially regarding the buoyancy of the oil price, and self-aggrandisement which encouraged the company to believe it could challenge Shell and Exxon for leadership in the industry. The price of those mistakes has been heavy, but BP still has a future.

1993 was a year of financial progress with costs greatly reduced and almost £2 billion removed from the debt burden (now standing at £8.2 billion). This should put the group in a better position than some oil companies to withstand lower oil prices, particularly if BP manages, as forecast, to lop another $1 billion off costs by 1996 as well as decrease its debt by roughly $1 billion a year. The company's discovery and development costs are said to be running at about $3.40 a barrel – just about as low as the industry boasts – which should augur well if oil prices pick up. Although they group is still stuck in its uninspiring chemicals business and is far from out of the woods in its main activities, despite its resolve to cut costs, BP's financial and operating fortunes look to be on the up despite a 20-year low oil price in spring 1994.

Shares

BP's value to investors has lain not in a strong share price, but in the high yield of its shares compared with the rest of the market. After the effect of the flotation flop of 1987 had worn off, the group's shares rose relative to the market as growing economies increased the demand for oil. But over the 1980s as a whole, Shell, its arch-rival, raised its dividend progressively and narrowed the yield gap between the two companies. This put pressure on BP whose shares over that decade had underperformed Shell's by some 25 per cent. As a result – and despite recognising the usual fluctuation in share values caused by oil prices, currency values, exploration finds and the like – shareholders began to ask themselves as 1990 approached, 'Why stick with BP?'

In March that year the board announced plans for major restructuring and reorganisation, aimed at making the group the most successful oil company of the 1990s and beyond. BP's share price relative to the rest of the market began to rise, slumped, and then soared as Iraq invaded Kuwait and sent oil prices skywards. Windfall profits from stock appreciation masked a fall in the underlying profit position, and the City worried about BP's dividend cover. As recession set in the shares' performance relative to the rest of the market began a slide that only stabilised in mid-1992.

The group was saddled with high debts as a result of buying back the Kuwaiti holding and of investing in new field developments, but the board protected the share price by ruling out a rights issue and sought to generate enough cash to meet debt payments until money came in from its new ventures. In May 1992 the group recorded its first-ever quarterly loss and in June a boardroom *coup* was the prelude to a dividend cut. The shares fell to levels last seen in 1986.

Shares have recovered remarkably since the dark days of 1992, and market attention now focuses on the timing and size of a dividend increase versus greater debt reduction or increased capital spending – something which only too recently would have been considered an impossibly luxurious choice for the oil giant.

Corporate conscience

As an international oil company, environmental issues are clearly the most significant for BP. While the company cannot get away from the fact that its main business is selling fossil fuel to burn, it is involved in renewable energy projects, does sponsor conservation programmes, and has long had a wide-ranging environmental policy. This includes independent audits, plus monitoring and review of performance. The 1993 annual report included a section on environmental investment, reporting capital expenditure of £250 million in this area, down on £350 million for the previous year. But there was no asttempt to report on other areas of environmental performance. The group has been criticised, however, for employing much lower standards outside the developed countries of the West, especially in some exploration projects – for instance, in Papua New Guinea and Indonesia. Likewise, the group's international spread takes it to many countries with oppressive regimes, including Algeria, Chile, Turkey and Vietnam. Back home, there are some examples of BP exceeding its discharge limits to water, and it was convicted of water pollution in 1992, being fined £1,500 for allowing the discharge of sodium lauryl ether sulphate into the River Irk.

BP's operations also transgress other ethical issues: various oil and chemical products are commonly tested on animals; BP Nutrition (up for sale at the start of 1993) is involved in intensive farming; the group is a substantial supplier to the Ministry of Defence; dangerous pesticides such as Amitrole are used in some BP Oil products; and of course BP's petrol stations sell cigarettes.

On the social front, the group makes an effort to be a good employer, not assisted by the massive redundancies over the past few years. It has an active community programme, including placing employees on secondment and making hefty charitable contributions, and has one of the more advanced equal opportunities policies. There is paid paternity leave as well as childcare facilities. In addition, BP Oil is a member of Opportunity 2000. For an oil company BP's health and safety record is also good: it had only one conviction in recent years, bringing a fine of £2,000 at the beginning of 1989. In South Africa all its black employees are paid above reasonable minimum levels.

Corporate governance

Separate Chairman and Chief Executive Y
Number of Directors 16
Number of Non-Executive Directors 9
(9 Independent Directors)
Insulated Directors None

Board Committees
Audit: Y   Remuneration: Y

Remuneration

Year end	31.12.91	31.12.92	31.12.93
Total board £M	3.70	3.62	4.30
% change	18	-2	19
Highest paid £	797,000	534,507	615,000
% change	-20	-33	15

BRITISH STEEL plc

Board
Simon, David A G *Chief Executive*
Browne, E J P *Executive Director*
Chase, Rodney *Executive Director*
Norton, H E *Executive Director*
Sanderson, Bryan *Executive Director*
Seal, K R *Executive Director*
Ahearne, Steve *Finance Director*
Glover, Sir James *Independent Non-Executive*
Hahn, Dr Carl H *Independent Non-Executive*
Horn, Dr Karen *Independent Non-Executive*
Knight, Charles F *Independent Non-Executive*
Miles, Michael *Independent Non-Executive*
Nicholson, Sir Robin *Independent Non-Executive*
Sheehy, Sir Patrick *Independent Non-Executive*
Wright, Sir Patrick *Independent Non-Executive*
Lord Ashburton *Non-Executive Chairman*

The *coup* in 1992 which toppled Robert Horton, former chairman and chief executive, is indicative of the strength of the company's non-executive contingent, which outnumbers the executive directors. In addition to remuneration and audit committees, there are also a non-executive health and safety audit committee and an external affairs committee. Under the new regime the roles of chairman and chief executive have been separated. Although the performance-related elements of executive pay are shown in the annual report, BP does not indicate how these are calculated The company's new share-option scheme for senior managers met with a storm of protest at the 1994 AGM and may well be revised.

BRITISH STEEL plc

9 Albert Embankment, London SE1 7SN
Tel: 0171 735 7654
Chairman and Chief executive Brian Moffat
Deputy chairman Sir Nicholas Goodison
Main subsidiaries ASW (20%), Coated Metals, Cold Drawn Tubes Ltd, UES Holdings (50%)
Size £4.2 billion sales, £3.1 billion stock market value, 41,300 employees
5-year growth sales -18.3%, earnings per share -91%, employment -24%
Solvency debt n/a, interest cover 6 times
Political donations 0
Charitable donations £363,000

Major developments
1967 formed by Iron & Steel Act
1988 privatised
1989 bought C Walker
1990 bought Kloeckner Werke AG's Mannstaedt division; bought Canadian Steel Manufacturing Inc; closed hot strip mill at Ravenscraig; closed Clydesdale tube works
1991 closed one of Ravenscraig's two blast furnaces
1992 Ravenscraig closed completely
1994 fined £28 million by European Commission for price-fixing; launched court action against European Union state aid package

Outlook

Steel is an industry crying out for planning – state planning, or preferably supra-state planning. British Steel is a company that has been cast uncomfortably adrift from the ship of state, yet competes with companies which have not been. In the 1980s it proved itself extremely efficient, not just at staying afloat, but also at making some progress despite the stormy waters. But from the late 1980s the environment for steel became so unfriendly that it overwhelmed any progress the company tried to make. The consequences were closures and job losses on a massive scale.

Free marketeers could argue, of course, that the industry would never have got into this mess if it were not for state planning; planning which, in the late 1960s, saw the need in the UK for 40 million tonnes of steel (compared with production in 1992 of just over 16 million tonnes); planning which spent a decade at European Community level dealing with what the EC described as a 'manifest crisis' of over-capacity, yet began the 1990s with a European industry able to produce 30 million tonnes more than customers wanted. The free-market argument would be that, without state support, that excess capacity would have gone out of business.

Whichever system is to blame, British Steel is stuck, rather like British Coal, having spent billions of pounds on investment and redundancy, only to find that the market for its more efficient production is continually shrinking. At the start of the 1980s, before the vain three-month strike to try and prevent huge job cuts, British Steel employed approaching 200,000 people. By the beginning of 1994 the numbers employed had shrunk to nearly 40,000. Yet the volumes of steel produced were very similar to those of a decade ago, illustrating the huge strides which have been made in improving productivity.

Much of this was achieved before privatisation in 1988, proving that nationalised industries can produce effectively if given the chance by governments. Since privatisation, however, the recession gathering across Europe, but particularly in the UK, has undermined the company's best efforts, justifying the warnings from those who said that British Steel was being privatised at the top of the market. This is an industry with high fixed costs, so the combination of falling volumes and prices soon eroded the profits which had built up to a peak of almost £1 billion in 1989–90. In the first half of 1992 the company plunged into loss and was forced to abandon the interim dividend although a small sum was paid at the end of the year. Substantial cash flows turned negative despite the slashed dividend and reduced capital spending. A cash balance of £651 million in March 1990 turned into net debt just two years later.

BRITISH STEEL

Share record

Return on shareholders' equity	%	1.62
5-year price high	p	159.0
5-year price low	p	46.5
Dividend yield	%	1.59
5-year high	%	18.67
5-year low	%	0.96
Price/earnings ratio		61.8
5-year high		62.6
5-year low		4.1

Share price performance (in pence)

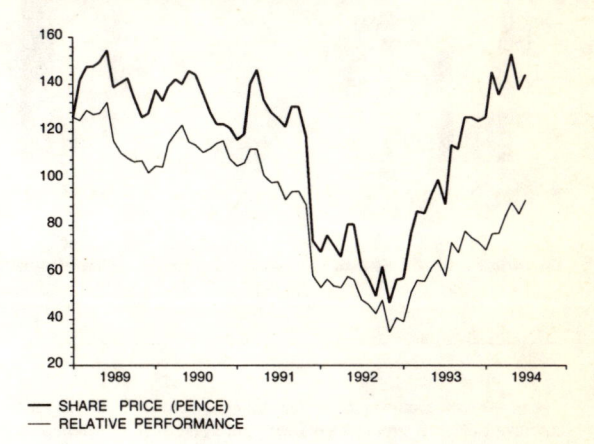

— SHARE PRICE (PENCE)
— RELATIVE PERFORMANCE

Financial record

		31/3/89	31/3/90	31/3/91	31/3/92	31/3/93
Total sales	£	4,906M	5,113M	5,041M	4,598M	4,303M
Pre-tax profit	£'000	726,000	878,000	469,000	106,000	-105M
Published retentions	£'000	461,000	399,000	18,000	-124M	-150M
Earnings per share	p	32.05	32.25	16.60	4.77	0.00
Dividend per share	p	7.50	8.25	8.75	4.50	1.00
Operating cash flow	£'000	573,000	390,000	169,000	-302M	-52,000
Net assets per share	p	202.50	226.49	244.73	246.20	230.60
Net debt/(cash)	£'000	-372M	-651M	-342M	11,000	82,000
Shareholders' funds	£	3,910M	4,293M	4,050M	3,911M	3,834M
Return on capital	%		20.75	10.44	3.08	-1.07
Profit margin	%	14.08	15.69	7.97	2.17	-2.39
Sales per employee	£	88.88	93.99	89.06	89.11	94.36
Interest cover		-15.83	-7.61	-3.77	-2.91	-5.82
Dividend cover		4.27	3.91	1.90	1.06	0.00
Sales increase	%		4.22	-1.41	-8.79	-6.42
Earnings growth	%		0.62	-48.54	-71.24	-100.00
Investment x depreciation		1.62	2.17	1.97	1.00	0.86
Investment as % assets		14.99	18.57	16.08	8.72	7.77
Number of employees		55,200	54,400	56,600	51,600	45,600

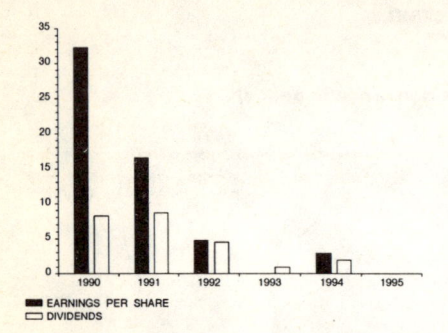

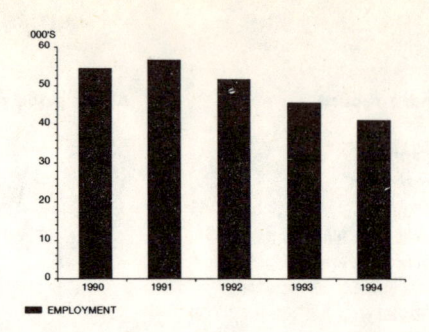

Earnings and dividends

Employment

There was some recovery in 1993, enabling the group to move back into profit as volumes rose again and prices also began their recessionary losses.

Excess capacity remains, however, and as long as it remains, it will keep prices below what could otherwise be achieved. But since every EC country wants to retain its steel-making, it has proved impossible to negotiate closures, while state support keeps otherwise untenable plants open. And meanwhile, cheaper imports from Eastern Europe make matters even worse, while trade disputes with the US threaten a further source of sales. Economic recovery will help to set the graphs swinging upwards again, but will not solve the problem that governments and the EC have been grappling with for years. In a desperate bid to force some progress on reducing output throughout Europe, British Steel announced in spring 1994 that it was taking European Commission to court. That was as much a political as a legal measure, but its chances of success must be thin.

Shares

Since flotation in 1988 British Steel has given its shareholders a poor ride. Within the main downward trend there have been variations in line with the rise and fall of selling prices for steel, while fluctuations in the exchange rate, especially relative to the Deutschmark, have cut across this pattern.

The main attraction of the shares in their early days was their dividend and yield, and even when prices were down, the dividend was held. The shares were at their strongest relative to the market as a whole in 1989 and again in early 1990 when profits were good. But doubts over the safety of the dividend crept in as the recession cut into demand, and the shares fell sharply in 1991 when the board confirmed City fears by issuing a warning on future dividend levels.

There was worse to come from their flotation price of 125p the shares dropped to just 52p when the dividend cut came in 1992. They recovered strongly since the end of 1992, as a return to profits, the prospects of economic recovery, and an increase in the dividend payment combined to improve the attraction.

Corporate conscience

On many issues British Steel's conscience is clean. However, the company does operate in what might be considered oppressive regimes (e.g. Turkey), is involved with the military, in mining, nuclear power and uses ozone-depleting chemicals (the latter in solvent cleaners). Its involvement in the nuclear industry consists of manufacture of flasks for spent fuel, special steels for advanced gas-cooled reactors, and stainless steel tubes for Sellafield's reprocessing works. And the military connection includes making armour, steel, alloy and titanium for Tornado aircraft, gas cylinders for firing torpedos, and ferrous metals for the navy. Producing armour plate is even an export activity.

The most substantial matters of corporate conscience for British Steel, though, are employment and the environment. Group employment has fallen 160,000 since the start of the 1980s, which clearly makes this a crucial issue. British Steel naturally argues that it had no choice but to advance productivity in this way, in order to be competitive with other manufacturers, especially given the increasingly international and competitive market. And through its 'enterprise arm', British Steel Industry, it has sought to soften the impact of unemployment on the neighbourhoods affected by plant closures (such as Shotton and Corby) by helping set up new businesses. Nevertheless the company was widely criticised over the closure of Ravenscraig in Scotland, after years of half-promises to keep it open, and with trade unions alleging that British Steel had not invested sufficiently while taking advantage of a co-operative workforce.

Other employment issues include health and safety where there have been several convictions.

British Steel also had 5 convictions for pollution in 1991 and 1992, the largest fine being £10,000 in February 1992 for contravening discharge consents in Northumbria. As might be expected, given this record, there have also been many cases of subsidiaries exceeding consents, but which did not lead to prosecutions. These breaches cast some doubt on the group's public commitment to taking the environment seriously, as does its decision to transfer some of its transport from rail to road.

Corporate governance

Separate Chairman and Chief Executive N
Number of Directors 12
Number of Non-Executive Directors 6
(6 Independent Directors)
Insulated Directors None

Board Committees
Audit: Y   Remuneration: Y

Remuneration

Year end	31.03.92	31.03.93	31.03.94
Total board £M	1.58	1.87	2.09
% change		-5	18	12
Highest paid £	331,361	321,630	496,190
% change		15	-3	54

Board
Moffat, Brian *Chairman & Chief Executive*
Bodington, Dr Jeff *Executive Director*
Homer, Harold *Executive Director*
McDowall, John *Executive Director*
Pedder, Tony *Executive Director*
Hampton, Philip *Finance Director*
Goodison, Sir Nicholas *Independent Non-Executive*
Bond, John *Independent Non-Executive*
Sanderson, Bryan *Independent Non-Executive*
Turner, Richard *Independent Non-Executive*
Runciman, Peter *Independent Non-Executive*
Shaw, Sir Giles *Independent Non-Executive*

British Steel has avoided the rows over top pay rises and lack of accountability which have rocked other privatised companies, despite its troubled and highly political public life. The group has always had sufficient numbers of non-executives, and they are sufficiently independent as well, but their 'weight' in the sense of business experience and seniority was not great before some new appointments in 1993. Despite new appointments there is no plan to reverse the backward step of combining the roles of chairman and chief executive which originally arose because of the early departure of former chairman Sir Alastair Frame. The membership of audit, remuneration and environment committees is published and there is very full disclosure of directors' pay, although not the reason for the bonus payments which resulted in the huge pay rise for Brian Moffet in 1993/4.

BRITISH TELECOMMUNICATIONS plc

81 Newgate Street, London EC1A 7AJ
Tel: 0171 356 5000
Chairman Sir Iain Vallance
Group managing director Michael Hepher
Size £13.7 billion sales, £24.7 billion stock market value, 156,000 employees
5-year growth sales 11%, earnings per share 33%, employment -37%
Solvency debt = 9% shareholders' funds, interest cover 13 times
Political donations 0
Charitable donations £2 million

Major developments
1984 privatised
1987 further government holding sold off
1989 bought 20% of McCaw Cellular Communications Inc
1991 another tranche of Government shares sold
1992 sold International Aeradio Sharelink sold 51% Mitel stake sold
1993 Telecom Security sold final tranche of BT shares sold; agreed to buy 20 per cent of MCI for £2.8 billion

Outlook

Government ministers regard British Telecommunications (BT) as one of the great successes of the privatisation programme. Hived off from the Post Office and launched into a liberalised domestic telecommunications market in 1984, it notched up huge profit increases as it shed labour and invested heavily in new equipment. The cost of telephone calls fell. Privatisation of the company was deemed by the government to provide a shining example of how its European partners should break up their public telephone monopolies.

The financial record shows dramatic progress from the £1.1 billion profit earned in its final year as a nationalised industry to £2 billion in 1992, even after £1 billion of redundancy costs, as does the share price. The government sold 50.2 per cent of BT in 1984 at 130p a share, valuing the company at less than £8 billion. The next 26 per cent was sold in November 1991 at between 335p and 350p a share. The remaining 22 per cent was sold in 1993 with the stock market value at around £25 billion. Since privatisation the workforce has been slashed from 241,000 (including 10,000 part-time employees) to 172,000 by the end of 1992, mainly through voluntary redundancy programmes. A further 30,000 jobs were to go in 1993–4.

BRITISH TELECOMMUNICATIONS

Share record

Return on shareholders' equity	%	17.3
5-year price high	p	486.5
5-year price low	p	245.0
Dividend yield	%	5.31
5-year high	%	6.75
5-year low	%	4.09
Price/earnings ratio		10.6
5-year high		20.1
5-year low		8.9

Share price performance (in pence)

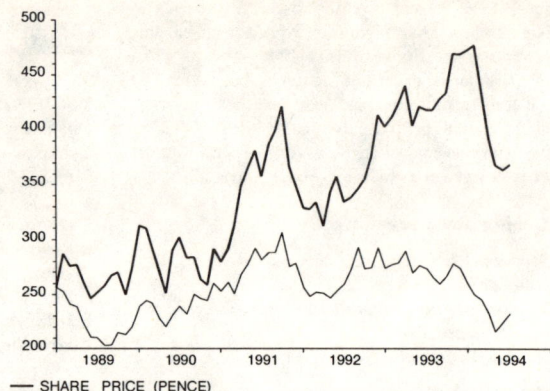

— SHARE PRICE (PENCE)
— RELATIVE PERFORMANCE

Financial record

		31/3/90	31/3/91	31/3/92	31/3/93	31/3/94
Total sales	£	12,315M	13,154M	13,337M	13,242M	13,675M
Pre-tax profit	£	2,643M	3,025M	3,094M	3,194M	3,290M
Published retentions	£'000	789,000	1,262M	1,156M	253,000	728,000
Earnings per share	p	27.91	32.17	33.24	39.17	37.04
Dividend per share	p	11.80	13.30	14.40	15.60	16.70
Operating cash flow	£'000	3,000	768,000	1,133M	851,000	1,118M
Net assets per share	p	235.79	256.88	266.10	273.15	275.29
Net debt/(cash)	£	4,473M	3,641M	2,505M	1,762M	1,226M
Shareholders' funds	£	9,224M	10,572M	11,754M	12,218M	13,026
Return on capital	%	23.66	24.15	22.77	22.26	21.68
Profit margin	%	21.51	23.04	23.15	24.02	23.93
Sales per employee	£	49.67	55.41	60.90	72.32	87.66
Interest cover		6.24	7.05	7.94	10.14	13.22
Dividend cover		2.37	2.39	2.31	2.51	2.22
Sales increase	%	11.24	6.81	1.39	-0.71	3.27
Earnings growth	%	10.10	15.26	3.32	17.85	-5.45
Investment x depreciation		1.69	1.34	1.20	0.97	0.92
Investment as % assets		20.47	16.72	15.65	13.07	12.79
Number of employees		247,912	237,400	219,000	183,100	156,000

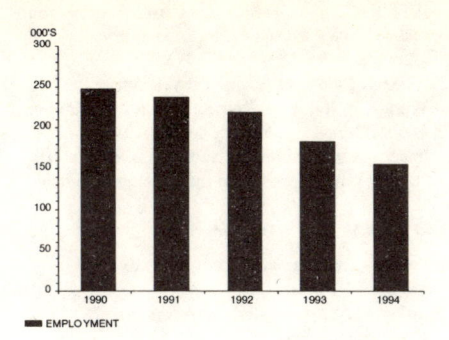

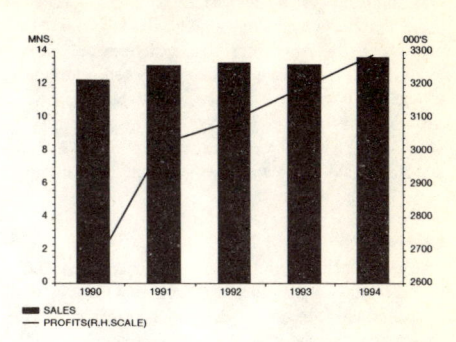

Employment

Sales and profits

Despite eight years of competition from Mercury Communications, BT still has about 90 per cent of the UK telecommunications market. It has exploited to the full the benefits of an established network, a gigantic customer base, and substantial research and development facilities. Its real opponent at the moment is not Mercury, or the cable companies offering telephony as an extra, but Oftel, the watchdog of the telecommunications industry. In the crucial early years Oftel was blessed with a tough director general, Sir Bryan Carsberg, who was more than able to stand up to the might of BT and its youthful chairman, Iain Vallance. (Indeed, so successful was Sir Bryan that he eventually became director general of the Office of Fair Trading.) The business background of the present director general, Don Cruikshank, makes him a worthy and equally tough opponent.

In spite of tough price restraints instituted by Oftel, BT achieved spectacular rises in profits to accompany improved productivity. It was accused of making excessive profits while adding thousands to the dole queues, but the criticism became more muted as the cost of restructuring ate into the group's financial performance. And there were other costs besides the purely financial ones: the huge and rapid reduction in the workforce has left morale low, so much so that the group has embarked on a project to monitor morale among all its employees for several years to come.

BT has a stated goal of becoming a global telecommunications company. But it has suffered several setbacks along the road. It had hoped to set up a global partnership with other international telecommunications companies in order to handle the networking operations of multinational organisations. The partners failed to materialise, however, and BT was forced to go it alone with Syncordia, launched in 1991 and based in Atlanta. But in September 1993 BT agreed to buy 20 per cent of MCI, America's third largest long-distance carrier, for £2.8 billion and merge their multinational service operations into a single entity, 75 per cent owned by BT. Regulatory approval of the deal was expected by the end of 1994.

BT's hopes of establishing itself as a major player in the American cellular-phone business through its 20 per cent holding in McCaw Cellular Communications came to an end in 1992 when it announced it was selling its McCaw shares to US giant AT&T, albeit at a £250 million profit. It still has a big stake in the UK cellular-phone market through its 60 per cent stake in Cellnet, which vies with Vodafone for the dominant position in Britain's growing mobile-phone industry.

BT has, however, sold off businesses which it sees as no longer part of its core operations. Competition broke BT's monopoly on the supply of telecommunications equipment to homes and business, and BT finally pulled out of that manufacturing market when it sold its 51 per cent holding in the Canadian company Mitel in 1992. Other firms to go were Internationa Aeradio, a provider of airport and telecommunications services; Sharelink, a telephone-based share-dealing operation; and Telecom Security, a security alarms business.

National and international telephones still provide BT with its core business, with commercial accounts being far more profitable than domestic ones (though BT claims Mercury has been 'cream-skimming' its profitable commercial subscribers). It is one of the two companies (the other being Mercury) licensed for international business, an area it hopes will expand as and when other countries liberalise their telecommunications markets. Data transmission is also a growth area. But BT provides many other services, ranging from private leased lines and networks to video-conferencing facilities and videophones.

BRITISH TELECOMMUNICATIONS plc

BT faces increased competition on many fronts as new companies, some with sizeable financial backing, enter the telecommunications market over the next few years. It will not give up its market share easily. Since privatisation, the entrenched attitude of the civil service which pervaded the company has increasingly been replaced by a more market-sensitive approach. The company is leaner and fitter, and will fight at all levels to ensure that there are no easy pickings for newcomers.

Shares

Investors doubled their money on the first day that BT traded on the stock market in 1984 after a flotation at 130p a share. Since then the company has offered shareholders a good income through the dividend and a robust share price. The shares outperformed the rest of the market most strongly in 1985, but while they were overtaken by more speculative shares in the run up to the market crash of 1987, they proved a safe haven. The emergence of Mercury as a rival in the mid-1980s made little difference to BT's rating.

The second tranche of shares was floated at 335p in 1991 without the same built-in instant profit as the first. The market regulator, Oftel, took a tougher stance on profits and over 1992, while the shares gained ground against the rest of the market, the old glamour rating was not repeated. However, cost-cutting offset lower profits and the shares showed a strong defensive quality during the recession.

The government announced its intention to sell off the third tranche of shares in late 1992, but the price did not fall. Analysts predicted a successful flotation and argued that the group's strong potential cash flow made its likely return on investment attractive at a time of low interest rates. They were not disappointed.

Corporate conscience

Though much hated, often quite unfairly because of its size and near-monopoly status, BT is at the forefront on most ethical issues. It has an extensive community involvement programme, is a member of BITC and the Per Cent Club, and a major charitable donor as well as placing many employees on secondment to charities. A similarly enthusiastic approach also applies to equal opportunities. BT has a sound policy, including monitoring, and offers reasonable childcare provision as well as paid paternity leave. The com-pany is still heavily male-dominated: only 16 per cent of all managerial grades were occupied by women in 1992, but BT supports Opportunity 2000 and is pursuing greater equality with some vigour and imagination.

The same applies to the environment, which BT takes very seriously. Having adopted a comprehensive policy, including an independent audit, it has also developed regular reporting, so successfully that BT was joint winner with British Airways of an environmental reporting award in 1992. It still uses CFC-13 as a cleaner, but is committed to phasing it out by 1996.

This shining record has not prevented BT falling foul of the law or similar monitoring agencies on occasions. The ASA upheld three complaints against the company in 1991 and 1992; BT was fined £10,000 in 1988 for breaching the Health and Safety at Work Act; and it was convicted of water pollution in 1990. BT is also caught by one other issue of conscience: it earns substantial sums from the Ministry of Defence for work on military communications.

Corporate governance

Separate Chairman and Chief Executive Y
Number of Directors 13
Number of Non-Executive Directors 6
(4 Independent Directors)
Insulated Directors Not known

Board Committees
Audit: Y   Remuneration: Y

Remuneration

Year end	31.03.92	31.03.93	31.03.94
Total board £M	3.00	3.65	3.67
% change	16	22	0.4
Highest paid £	539,065	616,000	757,000
% change	0.5	14	23

Board
Vallance, Sir Iain D T *Executive Chairman*
Hepher, Michael L *Managing Director*
Argent, Malcolm *Executive Director*
Brett, Michael *Executive Director*
Booth, Anthony J *Executive Director*
Rudge, Dr Alan W *Executive Director*
Brace, Robert D *Finance Director*
Bosonnet, Paul G *Independent Non-Executive*
Lord Tebbit *Independent Non-Executive*
Mulcahy, Sir Geoffrey J *Independent Non-Executive*
Newbold, Mrs Yve M *Independent Non-Executive*
Brett, Michael *Non-Executive*
Scholey, Sir David *Non-Executive*

Unusually, BT provides its non-executives with service contracts. Disappointingly, though, the overall quality of disclosure to shareholders is below average for those who receive only the annual review, which contains summary financial statements, along with a warning that 'it does not contain sufficient information to allow for a full understanding of the group'. The review gives brief details of the non-executive directors and the way they work, and there is further explanation in the full report and accounts. While there is improved disclosure of board payments in the 1993 report, no detail is given of the criteria for performance pay. The boardroom does contain some eminent non-executives such as Sir Geoff Mulcahy of Kingfisher, Sir David Scholey of Warburg Group and ex-Cabinet Minister Norman Tebbit, representing the great and the good.

BTR plc

Silverton House, Vincent Square, London SW1P 2PL
Tel: 0171 834 3848
Chairman Norman Ireland
Chief executive Alan Jackson
Main subsidiaries Brook Crompton Motors, Brush Traction, Chloride Industrial Batteries, DCE Group, Dunlop, Dunlopillo, Dunlop Slazenger, Hawker Siddeley Group, Mirrlees Blackstone, Nordstrom, Oldham Batteries, Permali, Pilkington's Tiles, Rest Assured, Rexnord, Rockware, Serck, Schlegel Corporation, Stewart Warner, Tilcon, Westinghouse Brake and Signal, Worcester Controls
Size £9.8 billion sales, £13.5 billion stock market value, 130,000 employees
5-year growth sales 39%, earnings per share 1%, employment 19%
Solvency debt = 95% shareholders' funds, interest cover 8 times
Political donations 0
Charitable donations £678,408

Major developments
1898 formed as Leyland & Birmingham Rubber Co
1969 Owen Green became managing director
1972 changed to BTR
1983 bought Thomas Tilling for £637m
1985 bought Dunlop for £549m; bought Mylex, Australia
1986 failed bid for Pilkington
1989 sold National Tyre Service
1990 failed bid for Norton
1991 bought Rockware Group; bought Hawker Siddeley
1992 sold ACI glass and Soda ash
1993 bought Rexnord for £547m; sold Newey & Eyre
1994 sold Hawker Siddeley Canada stake; flotation of Graham builders merchants

Outlook

At one time BTR was seen as just another acquisitive conglomerate. By the beginning of the 1990s, however, it had become one of Britain's most respected companies. Whereas in the early 1980s it was lumped with Hanson, BTR emerged free from the taint of asset-stripping and from the mistakes which damaged the reputations of Lords Hanson and White. During the 1980s it became clear that Hanson's strengths were in asset-trading, while BTR excelled at running companies – running them better than pretty well anyone else.

The 1990s present BTR with plenty of challenges, however. Not least among these is coping with the departure of Sir Owen Green, the chairman who retired in 1993 and was the chief architect of the group. He became managing director of what was then Birmingham Tyre and Rubber Company in 1969 and in 20 years of leadership he transformed a sleepy Midlands business into a global industrial group.

The secret of BTR's success is simple, yet rather negative in business terms: it avoids risks. This policy does not, of course, account solely for the group's dramatic growth; the other aspect of its success lies in the fact that it does what it does extremely well. But every major company aims for such operational effectiveness, whereas the avoidance of risk is more specific to BTR. It takes a number of forms. First, the group only takes on businesses that employ relatively low technology – so avoiding technological obsolescence or the unpleasant surprises that can come from the unknown – and, ideally, that produce low-value but crucial industrial products so that customers are prepared to pay decent prices. Second, it avoids competitive risk: its businesses must be in well-protected areas, with minimal direct competition. Sir Owen has summed up this approach as seeking 'niche positions in major markets, or major positions in niche markets'. The third aspect of risk avoidance concerns market risk. Sir Owen preaches the gospel of caution in anticipating market growth: factories make most profit when they are running at full capacity. BTR is therefore very suspicious of factory managers who ask for capital expenditure to expand production. A company that is desperate for business to fill production lines can easily be forced to accept orders at less profitable prices. The busy factory, on the other hand, can turn away such business, concentrating instead on higher-margin work.

As a result of this approach, BTR has proudly calculated that the £554 million growth in profits in the second half of the 1980s owed nothing whatsoever to higher volumes, but came instead from higher margins and acquisitions. This highly conservative policy was summed up long ago in 1983, in BTR's offer document for Thomas Tilling – the acquisition which first shot the group into the headlines, and which few thought could possibly come off because Tilling was such an established, even establishment, company and much larger than BTR. In its letter to Tilling shareholders BTR explained its philosophy thus:

BTR's success is based on certain fundamental principles:

The objective is continuing growth – growth directly reflected in increased earnings and dividends.

Growth is influenced by contiguity – the presence of a common feature, whether in technology, in process, in market, in geography or in any combination thereof.

The management style is specific and simple, based on responsibility at the centre but decentralisation of authority and decision-making to operational units whose results are regularly and carefully monitored.

The key indicator of BTR's success is the group's pre-tax return on sales.

It is an accountant's approach to business, pragmatic but unexciting; the lack of interest in volume growth

BTR

Share record

Return on shareholders' equity	%	33.64
5-year price high	p	407.0
5-year price low	p	164.7
Dividend yield	%	4.05
5-year high	%	7.31
5-year low	%	3.31
Price/earnings ratio		17.5
5-year high		20.0
5-year low		7.6

Share price performance (in pence)

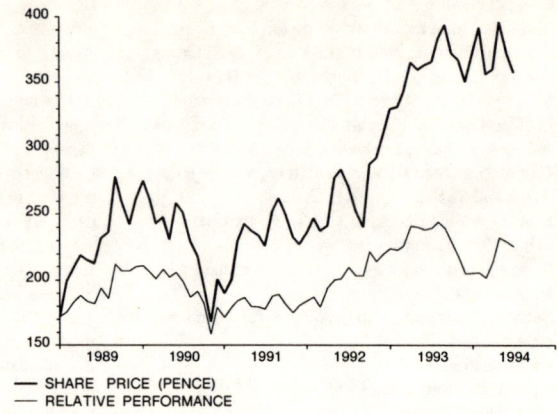

— SHARE PRICE (PENCE)
— RELATIVE PERFORMANCE

Financial record

		31/12/89	31/12/90	31/12/91	31/12/92	31/12/93
Total sales	£	7,025M	6,742M	6,742M	8,841M	9,772M
Pre-tax profit	£'000	1,080M	966,000	883,000	1,080M	1,208M
Published retentions	£'000	399,000	262,000	246,000	320,000	386,000
Earnings per share	p	21.33	18.58	16.95	20.22	21.58
Dividend per share	p	8.85	9.35	9.82	10.80	12.25
Operating cash flow	£'000	151,000	371,000	162,000	122,000	198,000
Net assets per share	p	113.99	112.81	128.25	143.02	131.97
Net debt/(cash)	£'000	1,035M	902,000	2,106M	2,053M	1,999M
Shareholders' funds	£	1,597M	1,601M	1,428M	1,840M	2,102M
Return on capital	%	43.78	35.54	30.24	31.41	30.95
Profit margin	%	14.76	13.82	12.59	11.84	12.13
Sales per employee	£	64.15	63.85	64.24	65.42	75.28
Interest cover		7.42	7.79	7.76	6.65	7.96
Dividend cover		2.41	2.02	1.73	1.86	1.76
Sales increase	%	28.36	-4.03	0.00	31.13	10.53
Earnings growth	%	26.56	-12.87	-8.80	19.32	6.71
Investment x depreciation		1.89	1.67	1.30	1.21	1.29
Investment as % assets		16.27	15.75	9.89	9.44	10.91
Number of employees		109,501	105,594	104,950	135,133	129,814

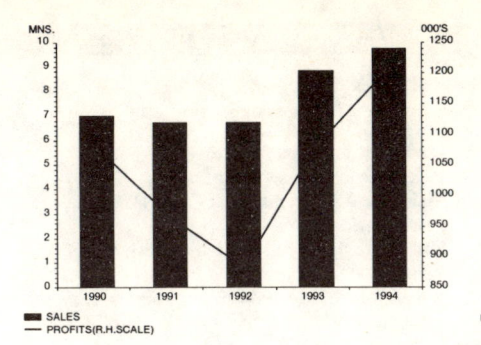

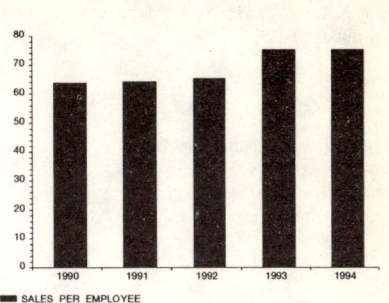

Sales and profits

Sales per employee

may offer little hope for increased employment in manufacturing, but it has certainly delivered growth in earnings and dividends, and a few of the more extravagant companies that ran out of control in the late 1980s would have done well to ponder this cautious strategy.

The question now is whether caution is enough to further BTR's success in the 1990s. And like Hanson, BTR faces the problem of being too big to achieve its customary rate of growth merely by making acquisitions. The additions of Rockware, Hawker Siddeley and Rexnord will help profits, and the sale of non-manufacturing businesses may also help. But it is unlikely that the group will easily escape from the relatively pedestrian performance it has recently exhibited.

Shares

As predators go BTR is a blue chip. Its market rating grew dramatically as a result of successive acquisitions in the 1980s, brought to a halt when it failed to acquire Pilkington in 1986. When the market crashed in 1987, BTR recovered quite quickly and it was soon strongly outperforming. This lasted until 1990 when the US and Australian dollar affected profits, coinciding with decreased demand in its basic businesses. At that time there was also a shortage of acquisitions. Its bid for the US Norton group, the biggest attempted since Pilkington, failed that year and, while the group made a profit on the foray, the share rating began to slip as the City questioned whether the group could maintain its growth as the recession deepened.

The acquisition of Rockware and a new policy of being readier to sell off companies failed to quell doubts, although the rating did begin a slow recovery from the end of 1990. When the group succeeded in its bid for Hawker, this propelled the shares to new heights. The second half of 1993 saw the shares slip back but this was reversed from the start of 1994.

Corporate conscience

BTR became notorious in the 1980s for a long-running dispute in South Africa, during which trade unions insisted that the British company had consistently denied their rights, while BTR maintained that it had operated entirely fairly. It is involved in many strategic sectors in South Africa, including chemicals and transport. The group employs over 6,000 people there, almost two-thirds of them black Africans. Pay levels are on the whole above required minima, but a few examples have been reported of pay below the supplemented living level.

As a huge, diverse conglomerate, BTR is inevitably exposed to more ethical issues than many companies. Military and environmental matters are the most significant ethical issues. BTR is not a huge supplier to the military, but has in recent years received contracts worth between £25 million and £50 million a year. Its military involvement was greatly increased by the acquisition of Hawker Siddeley, but other subsidiairies are also involved. Dunlop, for example, supplies wheel and braking systems and tyres for Harrier jets; Brush supplies motors to the Canadian navy; Oldham batteries are used in tanks; Crompton Lighting produces night-vision lamps for the British navy. Various parts of the group are also involved in exporting military equipment.

In addition, BTR companies are suppliers to the nuclear industry: Mirrlees Blackstone diesel generators are used at Sizewell B, for example. Other environmentally questionable products include the use of ozone-depleting chemicals in making base boards and other products for the electronics industry, air-conditioning systems and adhesives.

216   BURMAH CASTROL plc

BTR sites have also been guilty of exceeding water discharge consents on many occasions.

On the plus side, BTR does it bit for the community through BITC.

Corporate governance

Separate Chairman and Chief Executive Y
Number of Directors 9
Number of Non-Executive Directors 5
(0 Independent Directors)
Insulated Directors MD

Board Committees
Audit: Y   Remuneration: Y

Remuneration

Year end	31.12.91	31.12.92	31.12.93
Total board £M	2.78	2.55	3.64
% change	21	-8	43
Highest paid £	254,086	272,590	285,253
% change	19	7	5

Board
Jackson, A R *Chief Executive*
Fairclough, R F *Executive Director*
Pearson, Graeme *Executive Director*
Sharp, E E *Executive Director*
Smith, J D M *Executive Director*
O'Donovan, K A *Finance Director*
Laughland, Hugh W *Non-Executive*
Yardley, G J *Non-Executive*
Ireland, Norman C *Non-Executive Chairman*

Recently retired chairman Sir Owen Green made no secret of his opposition to independent directors, so it is no surprise that BTR does not have any – its five non-executive directors all have connections which disqualify them on this score: for example, Norman Ireland and John Cahill, who retired at the 1994 annual meeting, have both been long-serving associates of Sir Owen. His opposition can be justified by BTR's record of boardroom sanity as well as financial performance, but that does not justify limited disclosure and lack of board structures on matters such as boardroom pay. Under new chairman Norman Ireland, BTR came closer to Cadbury. In 1994 an Audit committee was set up, but consisting of the entire board. And there were still no independent directors on the board. BTR does not have bonus schemes for directors, which at least saves any fuss about non-disclosure of payment rates. BTR did disclose in 1993 that the highest paid overseas director received more than £500,000.

BURMAH CASTROL plc

Burmah Castrol House, Pipers Way,
Swindon SN3 1RE
Tel: 01793 511521
Chairman Lawrence Urquhart
Chief executive Jonathan Fry
Main brands and subsidiaries Castrol, Foseco, Fosroc, Sericol
Size £2.8 billion sales, £1.7 billion stock market value, 22,000 employees
5-year growth sales 34%, earnings per share 1%, employment 94%
Solvency debt = 59% shareholders' funds, interest cover 5 times.
Political donations 0
Charitable donations £228,000

Major developments
1886 Burmah Oil formed
1899 C C Wakefield (Castrol) formed
1905 Burmah backed Concessions Syndicate to explore in Middle East
1909 Burmah backed Anglo-Persian Oil (later BP) Castrol brand launched
1914 sold majority stake in Anglo-Persian Oil to British government
1942 refineries, oil wells destroyed in Burmese invasion
1960 C C Wakefield changed name to Castrol
1963 Burmese government seized Burmah assets; joint takeover by BP and Shell fought off
1966 Burmah bought Castrol
1968 bought Rawlplug
1970 bought Halfords
1972 bought Quinton Hazell and Veedol
1974 bought Signal Oil and Gas; propped up by Bank of England
1975 sold remaining stake in BP to Bank of England
1976 majority of North Sea Oil interests sold to the government
1980 sold Assam Oil Co and 50% of Oil India to Indian government
1983 buys Sericol Group
1984 sold Halfords
1985 sold Rawlplug
1990 bought Foseco

Outlook
Burmah Castrol has had a rather accident-prone history. By rights it should be one of the world's largest oil companies but instead it is trying to sell off its last interests in exploration in Pakistan. In 1909 it helped to set up the Anglo-Persian Oil Company, forerunner of British Petro-leum (BP), after having discovered the first oil in the Middle East. By 1909 it had been drilling for oil in Burma (where the company takes its name from, using the original Victorian spelling) for 20 years. Unfortunately its focus remained mainly in Burma and the Indian sub-continent – where some

BURMAH CASTROL

Share record

Return on shareholder's equity	%	16.33
5-year price high	p	881.0
5-year price low	p	438.0
Dividend yield	%	4.08
5-year high	%	6.70
5-year low	%	3.63
Price/earnings ratio		15.3
5-year high		20.2
5-year low		7.5

Share price performance (in pence)

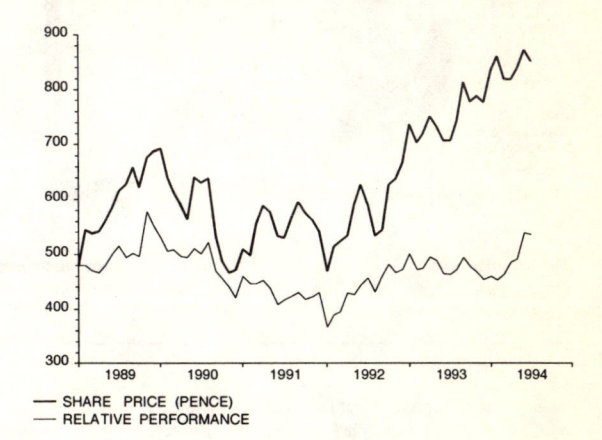

— SHARE PRICE (PENCE)
— RELATIVE PERFORMANCE

Financial record

		31/12/89	31/12/90	31/12/91	31/12/92	31/12/93
Total sales	£	2,054M	2,264M	2,956M	2,387M	2,758M
Pre-tax profit	£'000	148,000	158,200	158,800	167,900	183,600
Published retentions	£'000	74,100	132,800	200	38,100	49,000
Earnings per share	p	48.36	47.93	40.26	39.13	48.86
Dividend per share	p	21.50	23.00	24.00	25.25	27.50
Operating cash flow	£'000	-38,200	183,000	-161M	15,900	73,600
Net assets per share	p	429.32	487.37	563.19	678.91	624.59
Net debt/(cash)	£'000	145,300	138,200	355,200	370,300	349,800
Shareholders' funds	£'000	585,900	551,900	496,200	547,700	592,400
Return on capital	%	25.60	22.59	22.25	19.27	19.29
Profit margin	%	6.50	5.98	4.71	6.07	5.93
Sales per employee	£	180.32	152.07	122.00	106.31	125.14
Interest cover		7.91	8.33	4.01	4.47	5.30
Dividend cover		2.25	2.08	1.68	1.55	1.78
Sales increase	%	11.27	10.26	30.55	-19.26	15.55
Earnings growth	%	11.32	-0.89	-15.99	-2.83	24.88
Investment x depreciation		2.83	0.96	0.97	1.00	0.91
Investment as % assets		18.89	6.46	9.29	9.35	9.75
Number of employees		11,388	14,889	24,230	22,450	22,038

BURMAH CASTROL plc

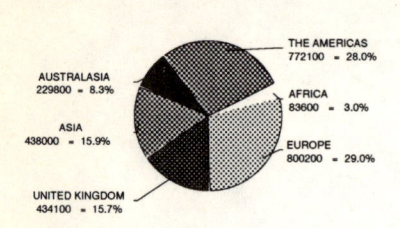

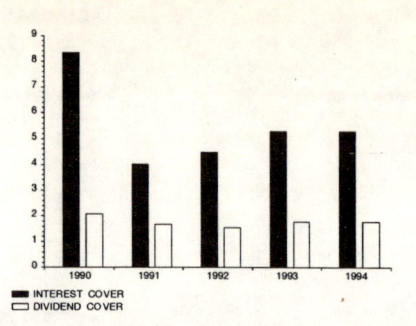

Sales analysis

- THE AMERICAS 772100 = 28.0%
- AUSTRALASIA 229800 = 8.3%
- AFRICA 83600 = 3.0%
- ASIA 438000 = 15.9%
- EUROPE 800200 = 29.0%
- UNITED KINGDOM 434100 = 15.7%

Interest and dividend cover

of its most important operations were destroyed by war – rather than the Middle East, and its 90 per cent holding in what was to become BP was diluted.

More recently, in 1966, Burmah was in on the first (though non-commercial) oil discovery in the North Sea. But in the early 1970s the group, which had acquired Castrol in 1966, moved heavily into oil-tanker operation, and paid $420 million to buy US oil company Signal Oil and Gas – just in time for the first Arab-Israeli war. The group was made bankrupt, and was saved only by the Bank of England. The price of being baled out by the Bank of England was the loss of much of its oil and gas interests and a huge cost of extricating itself from the tanker business. It matched Rolls-Royce as one of the more spectacular non-property crashes of the 1970s.

But Burmah began paying dividends again in 1979 and since then it has striven to become a more coherent company, making plans that are more in keeping with its reduced standing in the world. It has certainly not kicked the habit of corporate deals, though. There were failed bids for Croda Chemicals and Calor at either end of the 1980s, and an aborted approach from Gerald Ronson's Heron group in between. Successes included the sale of most of the remaining drilling interests (in Burmah's centenary year) and the consumer businesses of Rawlplug, Halfords and Quinton Hazell, plus the purchase of consumer chemicals business Foseco in 1990.

For all this activity, Castrol remains the group's main profit-earner, generating more than half the operating profit. Despite the fact that Burmah has traditionally been associated with exploration alone, Castrol is a highly successful marketing operation. It does no refining, but buys lubricant from the other major oil companies. While Castrol blends the various components of the final product, its real skill is in protecting and developing the superb global brand. The lubricant is mostly sold in Europe, but almost half the profits come from sales elsewhere, with a solid foothold in high-growth Asia.

Despite the Foseco acquisition, Castrol still dwarfs the other operations. Burmah's petrol station business, though spread around Europe, is small by the standards of the group and the industry as a whole. As with Castrol, the fuel is bought from Burmah's competitors, but in petrol the group has no discernible brand-name or other advantage, especially in the face of the onslaught on the market from the superstore operators.

Chemicals is a more substantial business, since being boosted by Foseco. The interests are in specialities rather than bulk manufacture which is so vulnerable to declines in volume, but the business suffered in the early 1990s because of the fading fortunes of its main customers – steel and construction. The main problem is that the group still seems intent on building up the smaller divisions by acquisition, and Burmah's record of paying too much for acquisitions is no better than most companies'. If only it could find another Anglo-Persian oil company.

Shares

Burmah Castrol began to appeal to investors in the mid-1980s when it was seen as a takeover target. The shares rose. By 1986 its strong financial performance was underpinning this strength. The rating was little affected by fluctuations in the oil price, although the group was a major consumer.

By 1990 the City felt that Burmah needed to find new markets for its lubricants and was further disconcerted by rising oil prices. The group's bid for Foseco thus came at an awkward time and the shares fell 9 per cent in one day, despite a rising market. Burmah's victory brought with it tax and debt problems, but the shares recovered some ground in 1991 relative to the market as a whole until it was revealed that the Foseco deal had reduced earnings per share by 18 per cent. The following year the company was re-rated as it became clear that despite the recession, and thanks to the weakness of sterling (beneficial to exports), earnings were strong once again and the group could maintain its growth rate without another large acquisition. The 1992 growth was more or less sustained, and built on with a surge in the shares' standing in spring of 1994 as the possibility of recovery in the chemicals business was appreciated as well as the strength of Castrol.

Corporate conscience

Burmah's main issue of conscience is pesticides, especially Fosroc makes Protim, a timber treatment which has been implicated in health and safety incidents (when used by others), and which contains pentachlorophenol and other active ingredients which have been questioned as potential health hazards in certain circumstances, and which have been banned in some countries.

In the past Burmah has not appeared to be especially concerned about health and safety, environmental or other ethical issues. This now seems to be changing. The 1992 annual report referred to what is accurately described as 'corporate citizenship' changed in the following year to 'Corporate Responsibility'. It reported on charitable donations, health and safety and the environment, including the news that the group had begun an environmental review which would lead to the implementation of a new policy. The policy does not include full environmental reporting, however. The record is not bad: Burmah has only one recent health and safety conviction, and that was against Foseco before its acquisition, when it was fined £300 for an offence under the rather esoteric, but obviously important, Dangerous Substances (Conveyance by Road in Road Tankers and Tank Containers) Regulations 1981.

The group's record on discharges to water is also relatively good. There are only a couple of recent examples of exceeding consent limits, all at the Burmah Castrol site at Ellesmere Port. Otherwise, on the environmental front, Burmah companies use CFCs in a number of aerosols and are not yet committed to phasing them out.

Like most international companies, Burmah also trades in countries with oppressive regimes such as Pakistan and the Phillipines. And in South Africa it has paid some of its black workforce a rate that is below a reasonable standard of living. Burmah has some military involvement, selling lubricants, chemicals and sealants to the Ministry of Defence. Castrol's Special Products division also supplies the nuclear power industry.

Corporate governance

Separate Chairman and Chief Executive Y
Number of Directors 10
Number of Non-Executive Directors 5
(4 Independent Directors)
Insulated Directors None

Board Committees
Audit: Y   Remuneration: Y

Remuneration

Year end	31.12.91	31.12.92	31.12.93
Total board £M	1.33	1.45	1.94
% change	11	9	34
Highest paid £	385,000	418,000	472,000
% change	39	9	13

Board
Fry, Jonathan *Chief Executive*
Ellicock, John H *Executive Director*
Owen, Dr Gerald *Executive Director*
Stevenson, Tim *Executive Director*
Hardy, Brian *Finance Director*
Dobbie, Iain G *Independent Non-Executive*
Jansen, P *Independent Non-Executive*
Mellor, Hugh Salusbury *Independent Non-Executive*
Magnusson, Bernt *Independent Non-Executive*
Urquhart, Lawrence M. *Non-Executive Chairman*

Burmah Castrol takes corporate governance seriously enough to describe its non-executives as 'independent' directors. But the annual report gives details of their backgrounds and connections, and a reasonable explanation of how board committees work. This also explains the basis of the executive incentive plan, and the total amount of the bonuses paid is shown in the relevant accounts note.

BURTON GROUP plc

214 Oxford Street, London W1N 9DF
Tel: 0171 636 8040
Chairman Sir John Hoskyns
Chief executive John Hoerner
Main brands and subsidiaries Burton Menswear, Debenhams, Dorothy Perkins, Evans, IS, Principles, Principles for Men, Top Shop, Top Man
Size £1.9 billion sales, £0.8 billion stock market value, 36,600 employees
5-year growth sales 4%, earnings per share -89%, employment -1%
Solvency debt = 23% shareholders' funds, interest cover 2 times
Political donations 0
Charitable donations £212,851

Major developments
1929 formed as Montague Burton, the Tailor of Taste
1969 changed to Burton Group
1981 Ralph Halpern took over as chairman and chief executive
1985 bought Debenhams

BURTON GROUP

Share record

Return on shareholders' equity	%	2.80
5-year price high	p	222.9
5-year price low	p	29.4
Dividend yield	%	4.24
5-year high	%	22.38
5-year low	%	2.88
Price/earnings ratio		25.2
5-year high		155.3
5-year low		2.2

Share price performance (in pence)

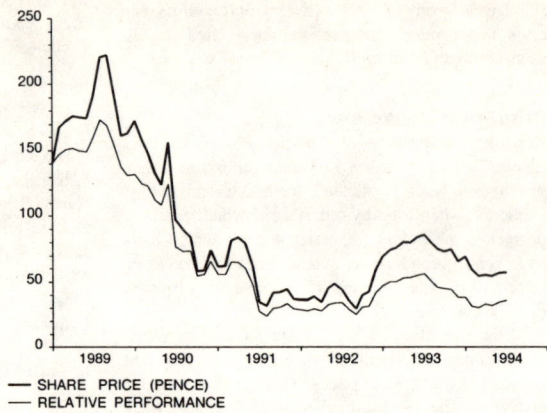

— SHARE PRICE (PENCE)
— RELATIVE PERFORMANCE

Financial record

		31/8/89	31/8/90	31/8/91	31/8/92	31/8/93
Total sales	£	1,819M	1,801M	1,661M	1,765M	1,893M
Pre-tax profit	£'000	220,600	139,400	13,400	12,700	37,800
Published retentions	£'000	98,500	-21,200	-188M	-13,000	-14,100
Earnings per share	p	20.78	14.09	0.79	0.99	2.21
Dividend per share	p	7.65	4.99	2.61	1.93	2.00
Operating cash flow	£'000	-40,500	-8,500	71,300	-121M	25,600
Net assets per share	p	151.60	142.75	136.44	82.12	85.88
Net debt/(cash)	£'000	319,400	339,000	301,500	375,900	193,700
Shareholders' funds	£'000	737,900	737,500	714,100	701,100	853,100
Return on capital	%	26.59	19.81	5.29	4.37	7.16
Profit margin	%	9.46	5.65	0.81	0.72	2.00
Sales per employee	£	49.05	47.34	47.00	49.07	51.78
Interest cover		8.11	3.68	1.53	1.45	2.09
Dividend cover		2.72	2.82	0.30	0.51	1.11
Sales increase	%	14.36	-0.95	-7.78	6.23	7.28
Earnings growth	%	0.25	-32.18	-94.37	25.18	122.48
Investment x depreciation		2.20	1.63	0.93	-0.13	0.32
Investment as % assets		15.84	12.64	6.79	-1.12	2.87
Number of employees		37,077	38,054	35,344	35,964	36,562

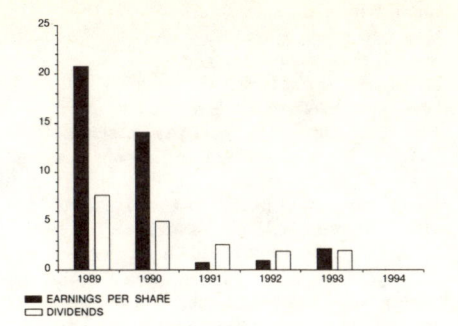

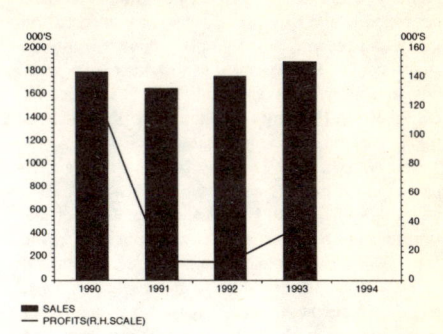

Earnings and dividends

Sales and profits

1990 Sir Ralph Halpern left; sold Burton Group Financial Services; sold Debenhams Investment Services
1991 sold Harvey Nichols
1993 sold Champion Sport

Outlook

The story of Burton over the last decade is like a caricature of British retailing. Run by Sir Ralph Halpern, who in 1986 became Britain's highest-paid executive, with a £1 million pay packet, the company prospered on the back of the 1980s consumer-spending boom.. In 1985 it bid for, and won control of, Debenhams, in which it invested heavily in order to make the large stores far grander and glitzier than before. Then, exasperated at the rises in rents it was facing for its shops, Burton moved into the business of developing whole shopping centres. It also expanded Debenhams's financial services operations, fatefully.

Come the recession, the cracks began to show. Burton was one of the first of the 1980s retailing success stories to reveal its fragility. Halpern was asked to resign in November 1990. Under Laurence Cooklin, the process of trying to rebuild Burton began. In 1991 the company announced that it would close 100 stores; as a consequence, 1,600 jobs were to go. And the company conceded that it would have to set aside £139 million to cover the cost of pulling out of its disastrous venture into the property business. To shore up its finances, shareholders were persuaded to part with £161 million, money that was needed to prevent Burton breaking the conditions attached to its bank loans.

Mr Cooklin did not last; he left in February 1992 (with a £773,000 pay-off to soften the blow) and was replaced by John Hoerner, who had been brought in under Halpern to sort out Debenhams. On the day that Hoerner took over, the company was worth less than £430 million; in 1986, when Burton was riding high, the stock market had valued it at more than £1,800 million. Since Hoerner's accession to the chief executive's job, two major themes have dominated the story of Burton. First, there has been a great deal of staff-cutting: almost 1,000 posts at the company's head office went early in 1993. And Burton announced that a further 1,000 full-time jobs in its shops would be converted into 3,000 part-time posts – part of an ongoing programme of cutting the number of full-time employees and replacing them with part-timers. Second, the formats of the individual chains have been tidied up, aiming to give shoppers a better idea of what each is trying to do and what sort of customers it is trying to attract.

Without doubt, the fortunes of Debenhams improved when Hoerner was running it. Since taking over the group as a whole, he tried to introduce simple, pragmatic changes to increase sales. This strategy worked, initially at least, and sales through the 'multiples' – the non-Debenhams outlets – rose strongly in 1992. The City's view of Burton improved, and at the beginning of 1993 the company was again able to ask its shareholders for money through a rights issue: this raised £163 million to be used over the following three years. But the group's margins were being squeezed once again in the latter half of 1993, and in 1994 came the poignant news that Burton – originally launched as the 'Tailor of Taste' – would stop selling its own suits. Those departments selling suits would be run instead by clothing manufacturer William Baird.

Shares

Burton's rise during the 1980s from less than 22p a share in 1981 to 275.3p a share in 1987 was mirrored by its fall back to 30p in 1992. By the market crash in 1987 the shares were already beginning to lose their premium rating. Share options for top directors – thought by many shareholders to be excessively generous – heightened worries over the group's off-balance-sheet financing of its financial services and property operations. In 1990 the group's decline steepened as the City realised just how exposed the group had become to the property market. Burton's announcement that it wanted to withdraw from property and financial services made little difference, nor did Sir Ralph Halpern's departure. The 1991 distress rights issue did nothing to halt the slide.

In 1992, with the economy showing no signs of recovery, the group's cost-cutting was not regarded as enough in itself to boost the shares as its chainstores needed revitalising. But by the end of 1992 the City could see signs that Burton was turning around as a result of Hoerner's management of the company, and the shares began to lift again, so that a futher rights issue in early 1993 was well received. The company's timing of the issue was clever: mounting pressure on margins and worries about new trading formats sent the shares tumbling in late 1993 and early 1994.

Corporate conscience

This company has a patchy record on ethical issues. It appears to have little truck with formal approaches to these issues, although a refusal to take part in surveys does not help to make its position clear.

The one area where Burton is active is in community involvement. It is a member of BITC and the Per Cent Club and a major donor to charity. It has been involved in a number of special projects to counter unemployment in inner-city areas, and has mounted special campaigns in conjunction with Comic Relief. Debenhams has also been a significant supporter of Great Ormond Street children's hospital.

The group has stated that it is concerned with environmental issues, but does not have a comprehensive environmental policy. Nor does it appear to operate an equal opportunities policy. Its approach to employment has been criticised for replacing full-time workers with part-timers, who do not participate in some of the conditions for employment such as pension schemes. But John Hoerner has at least removed the many archaic divisions between staff on different levels, including higher pay for men than women in some activities.

Corporate governance

Separate Chairman and Chief Executive Y
Number of Directors 8
Number of Non-Executive Directors 4
(4 Independent Directors)
Insulated Directors None

Board Committees
Audit: Y   Remuneration: Y

Remuneration

Year end	31.08.91	31.08.92	28.08.93
Total board £M	2.52	2.34	2.53
% change	-19	-7	8
Highest paid £	640,000	392,000	624,000
% change	-22	-39	59

Board

Hoerner, John *Chief Executive*
Green, Terry A *Executive Director*
McNamee, Martin *Executive Director*
North, Richard *Finance Director*
Brown, John *Independent Non-Executive*
Jarvis, Peter J *Independent Non-Executive*
Marland, Caroline *Independent Non-Executive*
Hoskyns, Sir John *Non-Executive Chairman*

The effectiveness of the company's non-executives, led by chairman Sir John Hoskyns since late 1990, has been amply demonstrated in the removal in recent years of failing chief executives Sir Ralph Halpern and Laurance Cooklin (although both departed with generous pay-offs and other executives enjoy three-year service contracts). Half the boardroom is non-executive and these run the audit and remuneration committees. Cancellation of the company's former generous performance-related incentive pay scheme for executives will have come as a relief to shareholders, and this has been followed by a cleaning-up of the entire executive perks system.

CABLE AND WIRELESS plc

Mercury House, Theobalds Road,
London WC1X 8RX
Tel: 0171 315 4000
Chairman Lord Young of Graffham
Chief executive James Ross
Main subsidiaries Hong Kong Telecommunications (57.7%), Mercury Communications Ltd (80%), Mercury One-2-One (50%)
Size £4.7 billion sales, £9.3 billion stock market value, 41,300 employees
5-year growth sales 103%, earnings per share 46%, employment 10%
Solvency debt = 10% shareholders' funds, interest cover 63 times
Political donations 0
Charitable donations £826,000

Major developments
1872 Eastern Telegraph Company (ETC) formed
1929 ETC merged with Marconi to form Imperial and International Communications
1934 name changed to Cable & Wireless
1947 nationalised
1981 privatised
1982 Mercury won licence to compete against BT
1984 Mercury became wholly owned subsidiary; bought controlling stake in Hong Kong Telephone
1986 became first British company on the Tokyo stock exchange
1988 bought Telephone Rentals

CABLE & WIRELESS

Share record

Return on shareholders' equity	%	14.20
5-year price high	p	538.0
5-year price low	p	198.5
Dividend yield	%	2.36
5-year high	%	3.58
5-year low	%	1.74
Price/earnings ratio		23.9
5-year high		33.1
5-year low		16.0

Share price performance (in pence)

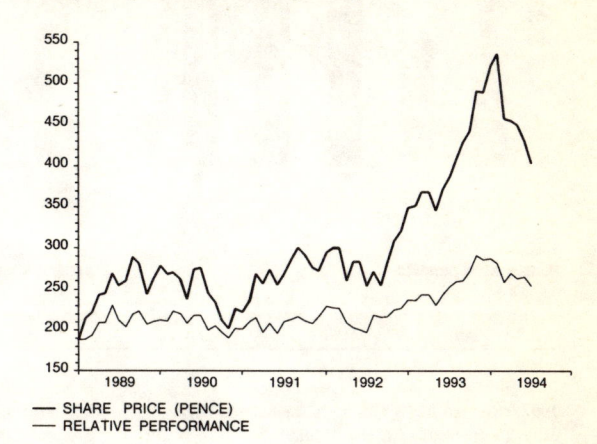

— SHARE PRICE (PENCE)
— RELATIVE PERFORMANCE

Financial record

		31/3/90	31/3/91	31/3/92	31/12/93	31/3/94
Total sales	£	2,316M	2,593M	3,176M	3,826M	4,699M
Pre-tax profit	£'000	528,800	607,600	711,800	846,800	1,068M
Published retentions	£'000	707,800	178,200	180,800	352,900	22.22
Earnings per share	p	15.26	14.69	17.79	19.95	8.25
Dividend per share	p	5.00	5.90	6.63	7.42	333,800
Operating cash flow	£'000	-56,700	-307M	-121M	-121M	169,800
Net assets per share	p	159.16	159.36	177.85	235.77	264.14
Net debt/(cash)	£'000	-192M	323,000	610,100	369,500	352,400
Shareholders' funds	£	2,209M	2,236M	2,363M	3,018M	3,275M
Return on capital	%	22.03	19.53	21.31	21.07	21.46
Profit margin	%	22.39	22.80	21.71	21.88	23.02
Sales per employee	£	61.65	65.95	81.96	96.04	113.65
Interest cover		11.93	-39.31	23.01	21.00	62.71
Dividend cover		3.11	2.55	2.69	2.69	2.69
Sales increase	%	50.99	11.94	22.50	20.45	22.83
Earnings growth	%	22.32	-3.74	21.09	12.13	11.38
Investment x depreciation		3.37	3.25	2.68	2.16	1.96
Investment as % assets		24.72	25.24	22.77	20.06	19.95
Number of employees		37,574	39,316	38,754	39,837	41,348

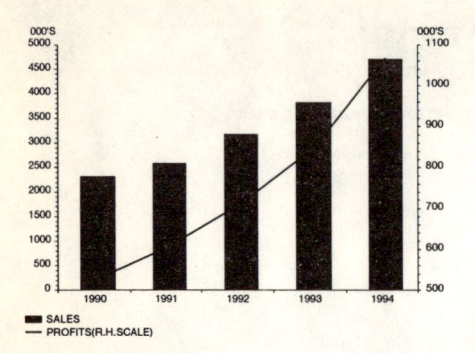

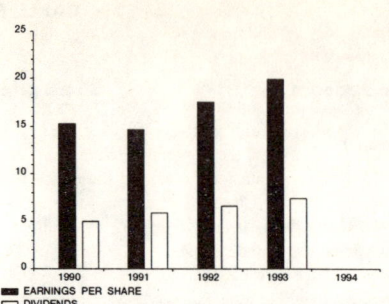

Sales and profits

Earnings and dividends

1992 swapped 20% of Mercury for stake in UK cable TV interests of BCE of Canada
1993 launched Mercury One-2-One in joint venture with US West

Outlook

Cable & Wireless (C&W) is one of the world's oldest and largest international telecommunications groups, with a corporate history stretching back some 125 years. But it was virtually unknown in Britain until it helped launch Mercury Communications as the first direct rival to British Telecom in 1982. Mercury was the government's not-so-secret weapon for breaking BT's telecom monopoly. The cards were stacked in its favour with the new industry regulator, Oftel, policing negotiations between the two operators on crucial matters like interconnection costs.

Oftel's brief was to ensure that BT did not strangle Mercury – and other new telecom operators like Vodafone – at birth. But despite being fully owned by C&W since 1984 and launching its all-digital network in 1986, Mercury has only managed to capture about 10 per cent of the UK telecom market. It has, however, successfully lured away some of BT's most profitable customers, particularly big business and City institutions. BT recognised the need to fight back, and a special team was set up to win back customers.

C&W reduced its Mercury stake to 80 per cent in November 1992 by selling a 20 per cent holding to Canada's largest company, BCE, for £480 million. BCE, which owns Bell Canada, is expected to give Mercury some R&D muscle through its ownership of Bell Northern Research, Canada's biggest R&D organisation, and through its 58 per cent stake in Northern Telecom, a leading supplier of digital telecom equipment. C&W agreed to invest £30 million in BCE's cable television operations in Britain.

One of Mercury's more unexpected achievements was to give a new lease of life to UK's near-moribund cable television industry through a series of deals which enabled the cable companies to offer telephony as well as television. Most of the cable companies which offer a telephone service have opted for links with Mercury rather than BT.

By early 1993 investment in Mercury had topped £2.5 billion. Mercury's network covered 90 per cent of the population and carried more than 14 million calls a day. In September 1993 C&W and US West, one of the big American regional telephone groups, launched Mercury One-2-One, their jointly owned UK mobile-phone service. Its network was limited initially to the London area, but it achieved a marketing *coup* by offering free off-peak local calls to domestic subscribers.

C&W's history goes back to the first successful trans-Atlantic cable laid in 1866 by the Brunel-designed steamship the *Great Eastern*. Behind the venture was Manchester textile merchant Sir John Pender, who in 1872 welded together the companies which laid the submarine cable from Cornwall in England to Bombay in India. The new company, the Eastern Telegraph Company (ETC), extended its network to China, Australia, and took over businesses with cable links with Africa, the Caribbean and South America.

During the 30 years after Sir John's death in 1896, the company began to lose out to a new invention, wireless, which was faster, cheaper and used less power than cable networks. Communications were a politically sensitive subject, and government intervention led to the 1929 merger of ETC and the Marconi Company to form a single entity, renamed Cable & Wireless in 1934. After a crucial role during the Second World War, C&W was nationalised in 1947. Telephone links replaced telegraph. The break-up of the British Empire led to the loss of some overseas networks, and the formation of joint ventures to run others. The wheel came full circle when Mrs Thatcher's government decided to privatise C&W in 1981, though cautiously retained a 'golden share'.

The biggest legacy from C&W's colonial days is its control of Hong Kong's highly profitable national and international telecommunications business. But this looks a little less attractive as 1997 draws nearer and Britain prepares to hand the colony back to mainland China. However, the company's chairman, former Secretary of State for Trade and Industry Lord Young, is committed to enterprise and opportunity, and likes to think positively: 'There are only a billion and a half people with adequate telecommunications, another billion with poor services, and more than three billion people in the world who can only dream today of a telephone.' And he is in no doubt about who can make those dreams come true.

Shares

Cable & Wireless was one of the brightest successes of the privatisation programme, being offered for sale at 50p a share in 1981 and topping 600p a share by 1989. Over that decade the group produced a 20 per cent growth rate per year in its earnings. It patiently developed its markets in the Far East and used cash to build up its Mercury phone company. The earnings growth rate slowed in 1990 and the group lost some ground relative to the rest of the market as currency factors reduced earnings per share and the launch of Mercury's challenge to British Telecom left investors in two minds about the shares. There was a surge of interest at the end of 1991 on speculation that Mercury was to be floated off or form a global alliance with the US group AT&T.

By May 1992 the dust had cleared, although nothing had been achieved, and the shares plunged steeply when the board announced plans for restructuring, including the mobile-phone business. A sustained improvement in the company's rating began soon afterwards and was reinforced when it sold a stake in Mercury in the US.

Corporate conscience

Telecommunications is a relatively 'clean' business. The group is a member of BITC and the Per Cent Club and supports the arts through ABSA, although, for its size, its generosity is unexceptional. Otherwise it does not wear any concern on its corporate sleeve. And while the nature of its business does not involve the group in many ethical issues, it is tainted in some respects, through involvement with the military and with oppressive regimes. For example, Cable & Wireless has an associate company in the Philippines, which employs several hundred people, and in Bahrain. The group also provides telecommunications services to the military, and Mercury is part of the consortium carrying out a Defence Fixed Telecommunications study.

There have been only limited brushes with the law. The ASA upheld one complaint against Mercury in 1991 and another in 1993, for an offence under the Health and Safety at Work Act.

Corporate governance

Separate Chairman and Chief Executive Y
Number of Directors 13
Number of Non-Executive Directors 5
(5 Independent Directors)
Insulated Directors Ch, DCh, MD

Board Committees
Audit: Y   Remuneration: Y

Remuneration

Year end	31.03.92	30.03.93	30.03.94
Total board £M	5.41	6.02	4.29
% change	10	11	-28
Total highest paid £M	0.49	1.03	0.95
% change	15	111	-8

Board

Ross, James H *Chief Executive*
Lord Young of Graffham *Executive Chairman*
Harris, Michael *Executive Director*
Solomon, Jonathan H M *Executive Director*
Olsen, Rodney J *Finance Director*
Bischoff, Winfried F W *Independent Non-Executive*
Carey, Sir Peter *Independent Non-Executive*
Morgan, Dr Janet P *Independent Non-Executive*
Robins, Sir Ralph *Independent Non-Executive*
Smith, Dr N Brian *Independent Non-Executive*

A brief paragraph on corporate governance in the directors' report for 1993–4 states that the group complies with the Cadbury Code, which is confirmed by the company's auditors. The annual report includes full biographies of the directors, though it does not explain how the board works, and the pay report gives a brief explanation of directors' bonus schemes.

CADBURY SCHWEPPES plc

25 Berkeley Square, London W1X 6HT
Tel: 0171 409 1313
Chairman Dominic Cadbury
Chief executive David Wellings
Main brands A&W Brands, Bassett's, Bouquet D'Or, Crunchie, Fry's Turkish Delight, Fry's Chocolate Cream, Gini, Kia-Ora, Schweppes, Sharps, Sunkist, Trebor, Time Out, Twirl
Main subsidiaries Trebor Bassett Ltd, Chocolat Poulain SA (France), Coca-Cola & Schweppes Beverages Ltd (51%), Sodastream Ltd, Canada Dry
Size £3.7 billion sales, £3.8 billion stock market value, 39,000 employees
5-year growth sales n/a, earnings per share n/a, employment 12%

CADBURY SCHWEPPES

Share record

Return on shareholders' equity	%	29.69
5-year price high	p	540.0
5-year price low	p	295.5
Dividend yield	%	4.05
5-year high	%	4.84
5-year low	%	2.66
Price/earnings ratio		14.3
5-year high		20.7
5-year low		11.6

Share price performance (in pence)

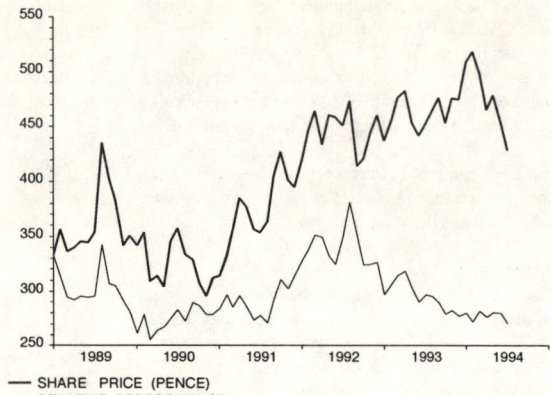

— SHARE PRICE (PENCE)
— RELATIVE PERFORMANCE

Financial record

		31/12/89	31/12/90	31/12/91	31/12/92	31/12/93
Total sales	£	2,843M	3,146M	3,232M	3,372M	3,725M
Pre-tax profit	£'000	251,000	279,600	316,900	347,200	424,800
Published retentions	£'000	101,100	95,800	106,200	97,600	120,400
Earnings per share	p	24.39	24.81	26.59	26.70	30.27
Dividend per share	p	10.54	11.33	12.31	13.00	14.40
Operating cash flow	£'000	-41,500	79,300	76,300	100,400	184,400
Net assets per share	p	131.76	154.38	186.36	186.87	184.12
Net debt/(cash)	£'000	421,700	362,600	330,900	375,600	354,800
Shareholders' funds	£'000	595,300	772,800	886,100	1,093M	1,372M
Return on capital	%	37.39	37.86	34.29	31.99	35.26
Profit margin	%	8.73	8.80	9.47	9.88	11.04
Sales per employee	£	81.28	88.24	91.38	92.19	95.35
Interest cover		8.63	5.73	6.36	7.52	10.38
Dividend cover		2.31	2.19	2.16	2.06	2.10
Sales increase	%	19.38	10.65	2.74	4.33	10.45
Earnings growth	%	8.04	1.71	7.19	0.43	13.37
Investment x depreciation		2.28	1.86	1.86	1.36	1.21
Investment as % assets		22.92	18.90	18.91	13.69	14.23
Number of employees		34,982	35,653	35,372	36,579	39,066

CADBURY SCHWEPPES plc

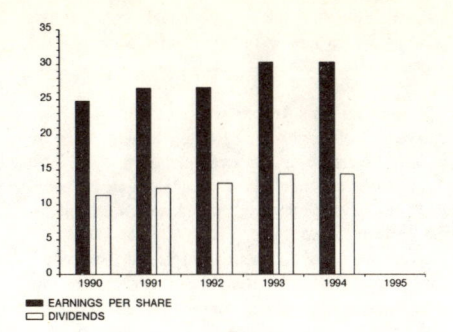

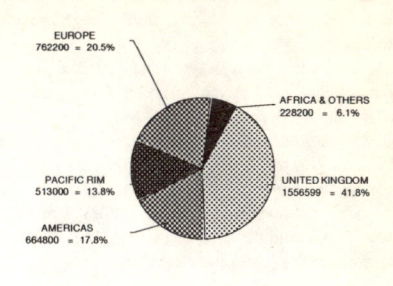

Earnings and dividends

Sales analysis

Solvency debt = 34% shareholders' funds, interest cover 8 times
Political donations 0
Charitable donations £650,000

Major developments
1969 merger to create Cadbury Schweppes
1986 management buy-out of Jeyes; management buy-out of Premier Brands
1987 creation of Coca-Cola & Schweppes Beverages
1988 withdrawal from US chocolate market; bought Chocolat Poulain; bought Lion confectionary
1989 bought Bassett Foods; bought Trebor group; bought Crush International
1992 bought Victory V and Hacks brands; bought Aquas Minerales, Mexico
1993 bought A&W Brands
1994 bought Bouquet D'Or

Outlook
Until about 10 years ago, Cadbury was as traditional a British family business as you could find. Now it has moved forwards, changing itself into a tightly run, well-directed branded goods operation. Curiously, the transformation has been wrought by a Cadbury – Dominic Cadbury – when he became chief executive in 1983, and proved to be a shrewd and effective boss. He took over from Sir Graham Day as chairman in 1993.

Under previous Cadburys the company had behaved like a traditionally run British company, with the additional motivation of Quaker good intentions. It had gobbled up competitors, so that by the time Rowntree was taken over by Nestlé in 1988, it was the only sizeable British-owned confectionery company. It had interests in the old Commonwealth and had wasted years in the US failing to become a force to be reckoned among confectioners there. It had diversified into other businesses: jam, mixer drinks and disinfectant in a multi-product grocery business.

All this changed in a series of dramatic moves during the 1980s, following a strategy that was to become very fashionable: concentrating on substantial, core strengths. Those strengths were identified as chocolate and fizzy drinks – the two product areas brought together by the merger of Cadbury and Schweppes in 1969. The rest went: the US part of the business was ceded to arch-rival Hershey a brave and poignant move after years of fierce competition; Typhoo tea, Kenco coffee, Hartleys and Chivers jam and even Cadbury's Smash were sold off as Premier Brands (subsequently acquired by Hillsdown); Jeyes chemicals and cleaning products were also sold off as a management buy-out and became a separate quoted company.

Despite having achieved all this, Cadbury looked at one time as though it would not live to reap the benefit. But in 1987 the slightly unexpected predator General Cinema (a US company which was interested because of its involvement in bottling) eventually lost interest, leaving Cadbury Schweppes to concentrate on building up the businesses it retained. A distribution agreement with Pepsi was swapped for one with Coke. Cadbury was convinced there would be a difference between the companies, and this does seem to have been reflected in the good performance of the joint-venture UK company Coca-Cola & Schweppes Beverages. The group has also done several deals to redress the historical imbalance towards the US and the old Commonwealth. In 1993 it lifted its holding in Dr Pepper of the US to 25 per cent and took over the root-beer company A&W Brands – a deal which required a rights issue to raise £324 million from Cadbury's shareholders. Other acquisitions have included mineral water in Mexico and Germany, chocolate in France and Spain. And back home the group has added Trebor mints,

CADBURY SCHWEPPES plc

Bassett liquorice all-sorts and Victory V lozenges to its portfolio, while increasing its marketing investment to ensure that it is not outgunned by Mars and Rowntree.

The result has been a five-year financial record which reflects little impact from recession (though some from the new accounting standard). There is still little discernible benefit from having Schweppes and Cadbury in the same group, so it would be difficult to argue against an ICI-style demerger. But while the group continues to to be so profitable and to maintain its standing in the market-place, there is little cause to upset the chocolate cart.

Shares

Cadbury's heavy investment and restructuring programme of the 1980s did not reap benefits for the company until the bull market of 1986–7. As 1987 opened, the group was seen as being vulnerable to a bid, but no takeover took place and the shares dipped relative to the rest of the market, which was galloping away towards its crash that October. When the market fell, Cadbury was among those relatively robust companies which gained ground, helped by stakebuilding on the part of the American General Cinema soft drinks group. There followed a complete re-rating of the shares in 1988, topped up with more bid speculation after Nestlé's takeover of Rowntree focused attention on the sector as a whole and on the worth of Cadbury in particular. This took the shares to an all-time high relative to the market.

The absence of a bid saw the rating ease back down again throughout 1989, apart from a wild surge in the price when Coca-Cola was said to have its eye on the group. Over the next year Cadbury's defensive qualities were appreciated as the recession set in, and the share price did not fall after General Cinema sold its holding in the company. The group's rating then rose further as margins and sales improved despite the recession, and borrowings eased.

The market's expectation that the recession would end in 1993 caused less defensive shares to rise strongly and Cadbury lost ground by comparison. The management's success in coping with mounting competition encouraged a revival in the shares in early 1994.

Corporate conscience

Cadbury retains some of the Quaker morality of its founders, but this has not prevented the group from triggering a number of ethical alarm bells. It operates in a number of countries with questionable regimes, including Ghana and Nigeria. And it has paid black African employees in South Africa below even the minimum recommended earnings level. It is also implicated in animal testing.

In the UK the group is generally considered to be a good employer, and includes a special section on environmental and community issues in the annual report. Women account for a fifth of managers, and the group does monitor female employees and those from ethnic minorities, as well as offering reasonably advanced childcare benefits. In addition, there are adequate environmental and equal opportunities policies. The group has been convicted once in recent years under health and safety laws, being fined £4,000 in 1990.

Trebor Bassett's Kreemy works in Maidstone has a bad record of discharges to water, having exceeded consent levels on several occasions in 1990/91. But the rest of the group had a completely clean record that year, having improved considerably on its previous performance.

Community involvement is probably the group's strongest point, as befits the inheritors of the Bournville village. The group is a member of BITC and the Per Cent Club, with Trebor also being a member of the latter. Cadbury is a major donor to charity, places employees on secondment and makes gifts in kind to community ventures.

Corporate governance

Separate Chairman and Chief Executive Y
Number of Directors 12
Number of Non-Executive Directors 5
(5 Independent Directors)
Insulated Directors CE

Board Committees
Audit: Y   Remuneration: Y

Remuneration

Year end	31.12.91	31.12.92	31.12.93
Total board £M	4.61	3.35	4.72
% change	23	-27	41
Highest paid £	54,000	429,000	852,000
% change	13	23	99

Board

Wellings, David G *Chief Executive*
Cadbury, Dominic *Executive Chairman*
Stradwick, R C *Executive Director*
Sunderland, John *Executive Director*
Swan, F J *Executive Director*
Williams, D R *Executive Director*
Jinks, D *Finance Director*
Davison, Ian F Hay *Independent Non-Executive*
Hutchison, Thomas O *Independent Non-Executive*
Vinton, Mrs A M *Independent Non-Executive*
Waddell, Gordon H *Independent Non-Executive*
Whitehead, Sir John *Independent Non-Executive*

As the company whose former chairman gave his name to the Cadbury Code, it could hardly fail to make an effort to comply with that committee's recommendations. It publishes full details of the functioning and aims of its non-executive boardroom committees, in keeping with a generally very informative annual report. The chief executive is still insulated from re-election, however. The enormous pay increase in 1993 for the highest-paid director was due to a long-term bonus scheme, and the group gave a reasonable explanation for this in the annual report.

CARADON plc

Caradon House, 24 Queens Road, Weybridge, Surrey KT13 9UX
Tel: 01932 850850
Chairman Antony Hichens
Chief executive Peter Jansen
Main brands Celuform plastic timber replacement systems, Duraflex and Caradon window and door systems, Everest windows and double glazing, Ideal boilers, Mira showers, MK electrical products, Stelrad and Henrad radiators, Terrain plastic pipes, Twyfords and Doulton bathroom products
Size £961 million sales, £2.0 billion stock market value, 12,900 employees
5-year growth sales 133%, earnings per share -25%, employment 69%
Solvency debt = 8% shareholders' funds, interest cover n/a
Political donations 0
Charitable donations £53,816

Major developments

1988 formed to acquire non-packaging businesses of MB Group after merger of Metal Box with Carnaud of France
1989 bought ABS Holdings Corp; bought Caradon plc
1990 name changed to MB-Caradon
1993 bought Pillar for £809 million from RTZ; name changed to Caradon

Outlook

The genesis of this company is more complex than most. It constitutes the packaging 'remnants' of Metal Box combined with the building material activities of Reed International and the industrial interests of RTZ.

Metal Box was one of the many long-established, comfortable British companies which dozed through the post-war years not quite realising that the Empire was over. When it awoke, it found itself in the 1980s, facing a fierce recession. Years of cut-backs and closures followed as the group scaled back its operations to a profitable core, and then it suddenly embarked on a brave and ingenious strategy which opened a new era as a building products rather than a packaging company.

The transformation occurred in a flurry of activity in 1988 and 1989. First the group changed its name from Metal Box to MB (not the most imaginative part of this imaginative exercise) and renamed the packaging activities Metalbox. Next it merged Metalbox with the French packaging group Carnaud, creating a powerful European packaging operation, Carnaud Metalbox (CMB), which, though still partly owned by MB, remained a public company in its own right. Having semi-divested its packaging activities, MB then had to find something else to do. Its first acquistion was the US cheque-printing business, ABS. Then, more significantly, it merged with Caradon, the Twyfords and Mira bathroom equipment company which had been a management buy-out from Reed International in 1985 and had been floated on the stock market two years later. In fact this deal looked remarkably like a reverse takeover of MB, since the top management at Caradon soon assumed control of the enlarged group. But the move into building products was not as strange as it looks, since this was not an entirely new area. MB already owned Stelrad radiators (acquired in 1973 as an extension of its metal-bashing past) and Doulton bathroom products, as well as similar businesses on the Continent

All this seems somewhat tortuous in retrospect, but it was based on the now-familiar fashion for building pan-European businesses with dominant market positions. CMB became Europe's largest packaging group, and while the combination could have been achieved either by MB acquiring Carnaud or vice versa, neither was a practical option. Unfortunately it took MB-Caradon a further five years before the process was completed. Only in the spring of 1993 did the group manage to sell its stake in CMB. But when the sale was finally achieved – at a far higher price than had anticipated originally, because of the success of new management at CMB – it raised over £450 million for MB-Caradon. That sum, together with at least as much again in available borrowings, gave the group a £1 billion war chest with which to continue the process of creating an international building products group. In the event, £809 million was spent on purchasing the Pillar company from RTZ. Pillar had represented RTZ's attempt to diversify from mining – it included the electrical and electronics company MK Electric in addition to a window and door business – in the US as well as the UK. The Pillar acquisition broadened Caradon's geographical and product base, creating an international building materials group. The next task for Caradon was to show that the new group could be run as effectively as it had been put together.

Shares

In its old form Metal Box managed to keep pace with the market average through 1987, the year that the Caradon company's stock flotation was oversubscribed 39 times. While Caradon carried on rising in market esteem, Metal Box perked up only when John Elliott's Elders group revealed its holding in 1988. The period of outperformance by Metal Box ended the next year when it became clear that Elliott was not going to bid. The rating failed to lift in 1989 despite the complex tie-up with the French Carnaud group or the bid for Caradon.

Given the group's burden of debt, the City saw no reason to re-rate the shares until after its fears about exposure to the building industry proved groundless at the end of 1990. With confidence in the new management increasing, the shares outperformed the market by 23 per cent in 1991. A rights issue – to raise cash to cut debt – was well received. The rating

CARADON

Share record

Return on shareholders' equity	%	24.18
5-year price high	p	447.5
5-year price low	p	119.3
Dividend yield	%	3.36
5-year high	%	8.10
5-year low	%	2.44
Price/earnings ratio		22.8
5-year high		30.5
5-year low		6.6

Share price performance (in pence)

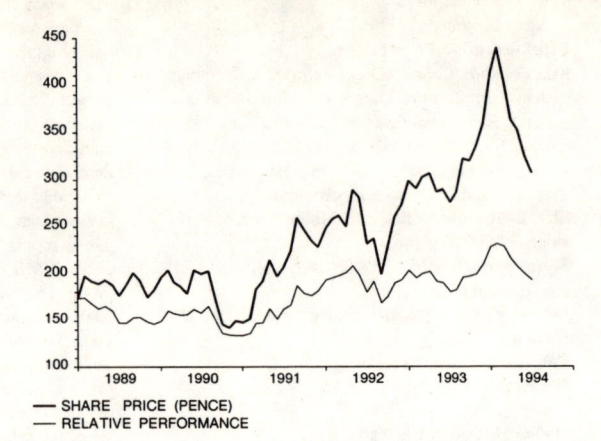

— SHARE PRICE (PENCE)
— RELATIVE PERFORMANCE

Financial record

		31/12/89 39 weeks	31/12/90	31/12/91	31/12/92	31/12/93
Total sales	£'000	309,300	695,500	679,200	664,400	960,700
Pre-tax profit	£'000	80,900	102,900	105,500	125,700	132,000
Published retentions	£'000	37,500	33,200	23,100	32,300	108,400
Earnings per share	p	19.34	14.92	14.35	12.79	14.53
Dividend per share	p	5.99	7.98	8.08	8.29	8.91
Operating cash flow	£'000	-9,400	n/a	13,600	17,200	51,600
Net assets per share	p	149.62	144.59	147.33	136.68	140.73
Net debt/(cash)	£'000	224,400	204,700	42,900	46,600	39,800
Shareholders' funds	£'000	322,100	388,500	572,000	525,100	481,900
Return on capital	%	19.20	26.42	22.10	21.38	20.53
Profit margin	%	15.81	10.22	10.85	13.25	13.17
Sales per employee	£	40.68	55.62	60.69	64.57	74.57
Interest cover		-2.11	4.59	4.65	18.20	-13.67
Dividend cover		3.23	1.87	1.78	1.54	1.63
Sales increase	%	-77.72	124.86	-2.34	-2.18	44.60
Earnings growth	%	-3.11	-22.87	-3.84	-10.82	13.57
Investment x depreciation		0.00	n/a	1.07	1.70	0.95
Investment as % assets		0.00	n/a	13.62	19.79	7.63
Number of employees		7,603	12,505	11,192	10,290	12,884

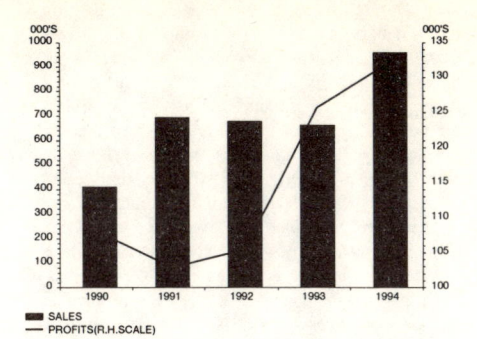

Sales and profits

Sales per employee

improved into 1992 but then it dipped as the market waited to see if the group had anything other than cost efficiency to offer.

The answer came in 1993 when the board revealed its plan to sell off its stake in CMB, which would leave the group cash rich in an environment where that cash could pick up some cheap assets. The Pillar deal, completed in August 1993, proved the value of this strategy, and signalled a surge in the share price that lasted until the beginning of 1994. But a feeling that the rise had been exaggerated, combined with disappointment over the slow recovery in the housing market, caused the share price to retreat during the first half of 1994, almost as far as it had risen.

Corporate conscience

The acquisition of Pillar has increased Caradon's exposure to issues of conscience. For example, tropical hardwoods are used in Duraflex double-glazing units and Indal doors. The Caradon group has also now become subject to advertising complaints, and uses ozone-depleting chemicals. The annual report includes a brief statement of environmental policy, but gives the impression that the board has been far too preoccupied in other ways to be overly concerned about such matters.

Corporate governance

Separate Chairman and Chief Executive Y
Number of Directors 9
Number of Non-Executive Directors 5
(3 Independent Directors)
Insulated Directors MD, JMD, CE

Board Committees
Audit: Y   Remuneration: Y

Remuneration

Year end	31.12.91	31.12.92	31.12.93
Total board £M	1.27	1.73	2.33
% change	-14	37	35
Highest paid £	223,227	330,037	537,766
% change	-13	48	63

Board

Jansen, Peter *Chief Executive*
Cohen, Daniel *Executive Director*
Hewett, Peter *Executive Director*
Walker, Tim *Executive Director*
Minton, Kenneth J *Independent Non-Executive*
Robinson, Gerry *Independent Non-Executive*
Thompson, Clive M *Independent Non-Executive*
Parker, Sir Eric *Non-Executive*
Hichens, Antony P *Non-Executive Chairman*

The board of Caradon includes a chairman's committee which encompasses all non-executives and is reponsible for appointments, remuneration and audit matters. The governance statement in the 1992 annual report also explained the constitution of the pension trustees, though unfortunately this revealed the fact that the trustee company was run by senior managers with no employee representation. The standard of disclosure in the 1993 annual report was generally good, with improved disclosure of directors' pay and bonus schemes. Details revealed, for instance, that one director waived a pay rise of £30,000 and a bonus of £25,800. The highest-paid director, on the other hand, received a performance-related bonus of almost £246,000, although the basis for this huge sum was not divulged to shareholders.

CARLTON COMMUNICATIONS plc

15 St George Street, London W1R 9DE
Tel: 0171 499 8050
Chairman Michael Green
Managing director to be appointed
Main brands and subsidiaries Abekas, Central TV, Complete Post, Harry, Henry, Hal ImMix, Moving Picture Company, Pickwick, Paintbox, Picturebox, Post Perfect, Quantel, Solid State Logic, Technicolor, Video Time, Zenith (51%)
Size £1.0 billion sales, £2.0 billion stock market value, 7,300 employees
5-year growth sales 94%, earnings per share -18%, employment 63%
Solvency debt n/a, interest cover n/a
Political donations 0
Charitable donations £915,000

Major developments
1939 formed as Fleet Street Letter
1983 changed to Carlton Communications; bought Moving Picture Company
1985 bought Abekas; bid for Thames TV blocked by broadcasting authority
1986 sold Fleet Street Letter
1987 bought 20% Central TV from Ladbroke
1988 bought Modern Video Productions Inc; bought Cambridge Computer Graphics; bought Technicolor Holdings
1989 bought UEI
1990 sold Cosworth to Vickers
1991 awarded the new Channel 3 London weekday TV licence
1992 bought Pickwick Group
1993 bought rest of Central TV

Outlook
In 1985 the Independent Broadcasting Authority (IBA) ruled out a planned takeover of Thames Television by Carlton. It is one of the business (and television) world's wonderful ironies that the IBA no longer exists, that Carlton is now probably the most powerful of the independent television (ITV) companies, and that it cemented its pivotal role in ITV with the agreed £760 million takeover of Central Television. The IBA originally claimed that Carlton had a very limited track record in anything and none in the television business. It took just nine years to make that assertion appear ludicrous.

Carlton had joined the stock market only in 1983, through a reverse takeover of the Fleet Street Newsletter, a tiny publishing operation which served its purpose as a shell company and was subsequently sold off. Armed with his new share-issuing powers, Michael Green wasted no time pursuing that 1980s hobby of buying up companies. The first was the Moving Picture Company, which temporarily brought Mike Luckwell into Carlton as well as giving it full control over International Video Corporation and entry to the market for video production equipment. During the mid to late 1980s Carlton built on this video business with acquisitions of Abekas, Complete Post and Modern Video Productions – all in the US – and UEI in the UK. This gave the group a strong portfolio of products and services for use in the burgeoning digital television and video production industry. UEI's Quantel is the market leader in television graphics, originally with the Paintbox and subsequently Harry, Flash Harry, Henry and Domino. Abekas specialises in digital video special effects. Complete Post is a post-production business which services both television and advertising companies.

All this cost Carlton approaching $150 million for the US companies, plus £520 million for the UK acquisitions, mostly financed by plentiful issues of shares. But that was not enough to keep Mr Green busy. He also snapped up 20 per cent of Central Television, the Midlands ITV operator, and shortly before the UEI acquisition, in September 1988, Carlton paid $780 million for Technicolor, the film- and video-processing laboratory whose name is famous as the founder of the colour film industry but whose main business now is churning out copies of films and videos. Central finally gave Michael Green the entry into the television world, while Technicolor was a solid business which shared with Rank most of the market for film and video reproduction.

The acquisitions of Technicolor and UEI in less than a year almost put Carlton into the category of expansionist businesses that went a bid too far, but the company managed to escape not only intact but eventually much strengthened, thanks to its ITV franchise victories. As profits fell in 1990, investors worried about the quality of the previous profits' spurt (i.e. how much was due to takeover accounting), the strength of top management, and the prospects for the group. But Carlton did not make the mistake of those other companies by becoming hugely debt-laden. In any case, worries were soon soothed by greater financial disclosure, the appointment of a managing director to separate that role from Michael Green's job as chairman, and a tough non-executive director in Sir Derek Birkin, of RTZ. In addition, a profits recovery in 1992 must also have helped to calm nerves frayed by too many corporate disasters in 1991 and 1992.

Success in the ITV franchise bids also set Carlton back on the expansionist road, although the extent of that success brought Mr Green up against the television establishment once again, because of the extent of his interests in the new ITV network. As well as taking over the London weekday franchise from Thames, Carlton still owned a fifth of Central – which it now controls 100 per cent – through which it also gained a 20 per cent stake in the southern area with the acquisition of Meridian. That stake became even more valuable following the acquisition by Meridian of Anglia Television in 1993, although a squabble with Meridian's major shareholder, MAI, ensured a less than happy transition.

Carlton was also a 20 per cent shareholder in the breakfast television victor GMTV, and soon launched

CARLTON COMMUNICATIONS

Share record

Return on shareholders' equity	%	34.89
5-year price high	p	1029.0
5-year price low	p	301.0
Dividend yield	%	2.75
5-year high	%	6.23
5-year low	%	1.14
Price/earnings ratio		21.3
5-year high		27.8
5-year low		6.3

Share price performance (in pence)

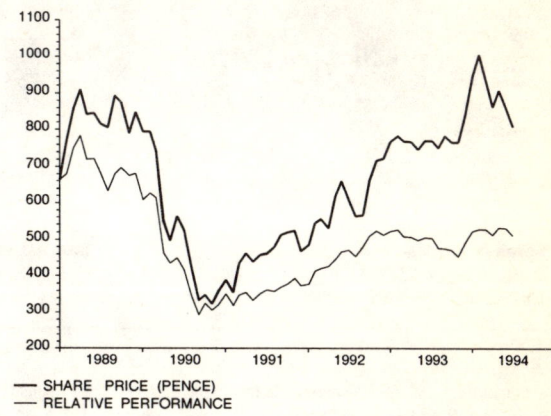

— SHARE PRICE (PENCE)
— RELATIVE PERFORMANCE

Financial record

		30/9/89	30/9/90	30/9/91	30/9/92	30/9/93
Total sales	£'000	518,249	697,619	537,967	635,215	1,005M
Pre-tax profit	£'000	112,323	129,293	88,509	102,320	128,954
Published retentions	£'000	59,106	158,957	18,334	29,243	46,091
Earnings per share	p	51.38	43.36	29.65	32.96	42.04
Dividend per share	p	9.37	14.05	15.50	17.00	18.70
Operating cash flow	£'000	-8,768	88,780	n/a	13,152	-20,914
Net assets per share	p	228.12	233.75	n/a	273.39	292.10
Net debt/(cash)	£'000	64,310	-130M	-193M	-147M	-78,283
Shareholders' funds	£'000	248,162	355,195	390,794	383,292	424,733
Return on capital	%	54.09	37.20	n/a	n/a	16.90
Profit margin	%	20.52	17.84	15.94	15.05	12.20
Sales per employee	£	116.12	121.11	109.05	101.36	138.53
Interest cover		16.15	-52.61	-3.78	-8.13	-28.43
Dividend cover		5.48	3.09	1.91	1.94	2.25
Sales increase	%	197.35	34.61	-22.89	18.08	58.17
Earnings growth	%	38.26	-15.60	-31.61	11.15	27.56
Investment x depreciation		1.23	0.82	0.69	1.28	1.80
Investment as % assets		13.22	14.07	12.86	20.42	31.98
Number of employees		4,463	5,760	4,933	6,267	7,253

CARLTON COMMUNICATIONS plc

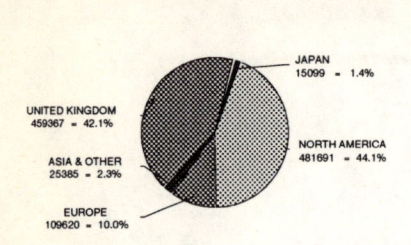

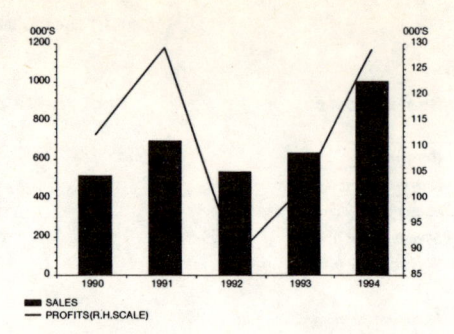

Sales analysis

UNITED KINGDOM 459367 = 42.1%
ASIA & OTHER 25385 = 2.3%
EUROPE 109620 = 10.0%
JAPAN 15099 = 1.4%
NORTH AMERICA 481691 = 44.1%

Sales and profits

■ SALES
— PROFITS(R.H.SCALE)

a consortium bid for the news station ITN, jointly with Central and London Weekend Television plus the news agency and electronic information company Reuters.

Although Michael Green quickly emerged as one of the three most powerful figures in ITV, following the relaxation of the takeover rules in late 1993, it is still not clear that he has won a licence to print money. ITV is still in turmoil, with cost savings nowhere near as evident as some have suggested and a rationalisation of the network's sales houses scheduled for 1995. Rupert Murdoch's Sky satellite station, in addition to other cable channels, is growing in strength. And, having failed to award a Channel 5 licence in 1993, the Independent Television Commission appears set to do just that – very much against Green's desires – in 1994. The outlook for video remains uncertain, both in terms of demand and technology. The acquisition of Central may, therefore, simply have added another declining business to the Carlton stable rather than offering an alternative to an inexorable downward spiral.

Shares

During the 1980s a string of acquisitions made Carlton's profits and rating grow, especially its purchases of Technicolor in 1988 and UEI in 1989. Apart from speculation about their future performance, the shares had a good yield and the group achieved high compound growth between 1986 and 1990: 36 per cent in earnings per share and 33 per cent in its dividend, thanks to its strong cash flow.

In early 1990 confidence in the stock collapsed, with more than £1 billion wiped off its market value. No concrete reason emerged for the downturn, just a feeling that the company could not maintain the fast pace of growth or that competition was growing for its video-copying operation. It later emerged that profits had fallen, debt had risen, and that the market

had sensed something was up. The fizz created by TV takeover wars in late 1993 did wonders for Carlton's share price recuperation, however. Despite paying more than £750 million for Central, Carlton's shares had by early 1994 regained some of their former glamour.

Corporate conscience

Carlton's conscience is fairly clear as far as most ethical issues are concerned, though its record is not entirely without stain. Quantel and Abacus supply equipment to the military, and the group also owns a business called Yewlands Engineering, which makes heat exchangers for the Tornado bomber. In addition, Yewlands makes fabrications for the nuclear industry, as does Quantel. The group uses some ozone-depleting chemicals as solvents for cleaning printed circuit boards, but is committed to phasing them out by the end of 1995. Its employment practices do not stand out, but the group is a member of BITC and the Per Cent Club, while Carlton Television supports Opportunity 2000.

Corporate governance

Separate Chairman and Chief Executive Y
Number of Directors 10
Number of Non-Executive Directors 5
(3 Independent Directors)
Insulated Directors All execs

Board Committees
Audit: Y   Remuneration: Y

Remuneration

Year end	30.09.91	30.09.92	30.09.93
Total board £M	1.31	2.32	2.31
% change	24	77	-0.4
Total highest paid	287,807	530,020	631,705
% change	13	84	19

COATS VIYELLA plc

Board
Green, Michael P *Executive Chairman*
de Moller, June *Managing Director*
Epley, Tom *Executive Director*
Walmsley, Nigel N *Executive Director*
Cragg, Bernard A *Finance Director*
Birkin, Sir Derek *Independent Non-Executive*
Lipworth, Sir Sydney *Independent Non-Executive*
Wray, Nigel W *Independent Non-Executive*
Green, David B *Non-Executive*
Lord Sharp of Grimsdyke *Non-Executive*

The company was forced to shake up its cosy boardroom when investors blamed some of its troubles during the early 1990s on poor governance. Starting with the appointment of a separate chief executive (who moved on in 1993) and then the promotion of June de Moller to managing director, Michael Green moved some way to accommodate City worries, although few doubt that he is still the most powerful influence in the group. The company now has five non-executive directors, not all of whom are independent, but as a result Carlton is much more clearly in the mainstream.

COATS VIYELLA plc

28 Saville Row, London W1X 2DD
Tel: 0171 734 5321
Chairman Sir David Alliance
Chief executive Neville Bain
Main brands Coats, Dorma, Jaeger, Louis Phillipe, Patons, Peter England, Rocola, Van Heusen, Trutex, Wilton Royal, Viyella
Main subsidiaries Vantona Viyella Ltd, Coats Patons plc, British Van Heusen Co Ltd, Jaeger Holdings Ltd, Lantor, Youghal Carpets
Size £2.4 billion sales, £1.5 billion stock market value, 78,100 employees
5-year growth sales 28%, earnings per share -6%, employment 23%
Solvency debt = 33% shareholders' funds, interest cover 4 times
Political donations 0
Charitable donations £175,000

Major developments
1909 formed as Spirella Company of Great Britain
1974 taken over by David Alliance
1982 bought Carrington Viyella
1983 became Vantona Viyella on takeover of Vantona
1986 merged with Coats Paton, name changed to Coats Viyella
1989 sold Nottingham Group
1991 bought Tootal Group

Outlook

The British textile industry has been in decline for so long that it sometimes seems surprising that there are any textile companies left at all. Coats Viyella incorporates most of the major companies which existed 20 years ago – Tootal, Vantona, Coats Patons and Carrington Viyella. It is the product of a one-man Industrial Reorganisation Corporation for the industry – Sir David (anglicised during the 1980s from the Iranian 'Davoud') Alliance. Only Courtaulds and Dawson escaped his net.

His is not exactly a storybook rags-to-riches tale, except in the literal sense that he began in the cloth trade and is now not short of a bob or two. But it is a noteworthy story all the same. Sir David originally came to Britain as a representative of his father's business, but gradually built up his own companies. His first move into the public arena came in 1974 when he put his various interests together and made a successful bid for the corset company Spirella. This proved a useful foundation, which was soon built on with the purchase of household textiles company Vantona. But Sir David really shot to attention a few years later when he came to the rescue of ICI, extricating the chemical giant from its part-owned and debt-ridden yarn and fabric business, Carrington Viyella. In the 1980s a series of opportunistic acquisitions created the current group – Nottingham Manufacturing, Scottish thread company Coats Patons, and finally Tootal, which was itself an agglomeration of English Sewing thread, Calico Printers cloth, and Tootal Broadhurst Lee clothing (which, incidentally, gave the editor of this book his first pay packets).

Sir David seemed to be better at deal-making than running his group, however. But in 1990 he made what may have been his best acquisition, when he attracted Neville Bain from Cadbury Schweppes to become chief executive. Mr Bain had spent his working life in the confectionery business and knew nothing about textiles. Yet this was probably his greatest strength, since those who have been steeped in the industry seem to have been incapable of saving it. He is certainly seen as having brought to Coats Viyella some of the professionalism and strategic thinking which has blessed Cadbury in recent years.

Coats Viyella now has a very strong base on which to build, having become the world's number one thread-maker following the takeover of Tootal. Through Coats Paton it has acquired a global distribution network for industrial and domestic sewing thread, including significant interests in South America (which is a rarity for a British company, and offers substantial long-term potential even if Brazil's economy jeopardises success in the short term). Tootal's industrial thread business spans the globe as well, including the unusual factor of being a major player in the US, as well as in Asia.

Since thread is the group's main business, accounting for almost half its profits, it is tempting to think that Coats Viyella would be better off if it dealt in that commodity alone. Clothing, yarn and fabrics face the perennial problems of competition from

COATS VIYELLA

Share record

Return on shareholders' equity	%	10.00
5-year price high	p	284.0
5-year price low	p	91.0
Dividend yield	%	4.59
5-year high	%	13.19
5-year low	%	3.30
Price/earnings ratio		14.9
5-year high		27.9
5-year low		5.7

Share price performance (in pence)

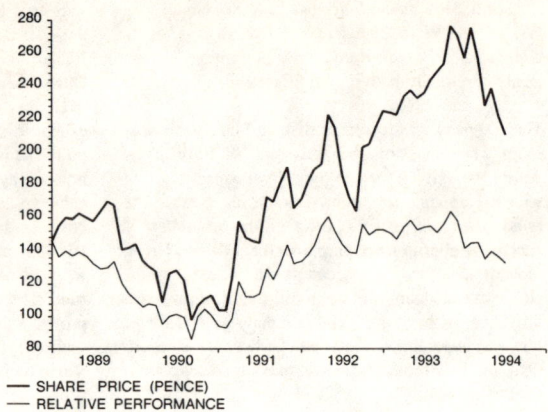

— SHARE PRICE (PENCE)
— RELATIVE PERFORMANCE

Financial record

		31/12/89	31/12/90	31/12/91	31/12/92	31/12/93
Total sales	£	1,904M	1,828M	1,948M	2,110M	2,444M
Pre-tax profit	£'000	136,400	117,500	120,000	114,200	145,100
Published retentions	£'000	32,400	4,100	26,900	16,700	36,800
Earnings per share	p	14.39	11.36	10.94	10.51	13.54
Dividend per share	p	9.00	7.00	7.00	7.25	8.00
Operating cash flow	£'000	-28,500	111,000	-4,200	21,700	71,600
Net assets per share	p	239.68	221.89	217.55	221.33	216.01
Net debt/(cash)	£'000	136,700	82,000	261,100	403,000	263,900
Shareholders' funds	£'000	751,600	705,700	644,700	707,000	791,300
Return on capital	%	16.24	12.60	13.77	14.34	16.15
Profit margin	%	7.00	6.10	5.88	5.26	5.88
Sales per employee	£	29.93	31.32	31.90	33.89	31.29
Interest cover		5.04	5.79	4.91	3.12	4.23
Dividend cover		1.60	1.62	1.56	1.45	1.69
Sales increase	%	2.64	-4.00	6.57	8.33	15.83
Earnings growth	%	-7.41	-21.02	-3.70	-3.98	28.88
Investment x depreciation		0.84	0.67	0.48	0.61	0.61
Investment as % assets		7.93	7.46	4.97	6.10	6.58
Number of employees		63,598	58,353	61,055	62,248	78,097

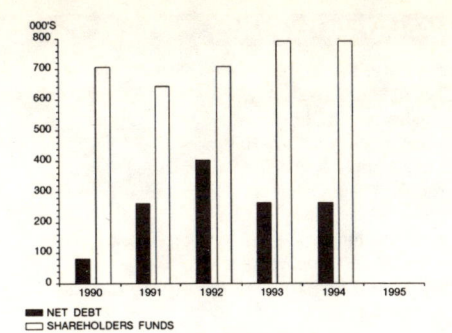

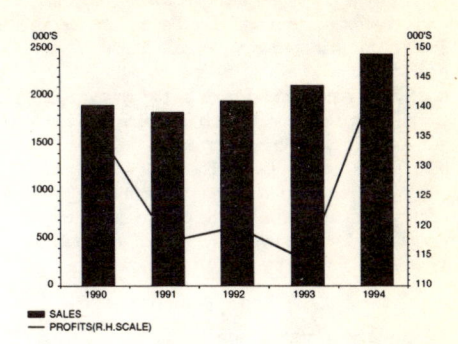

Debt and shareholders' funds

Sales and profits

cheap imports, although Tootal's pre-acquisition efforts to combine the best of both cheap imports and domestic finishing could help the group in the long term. What is now called Homewares suffered from the housing recession, but includes solid brands in Dorma, Osman, Stiebel and Youghal carpets, and could prove more profitable in better economic times. At the retail end, Jaeger and Viyella never seem to have lived up to their potential, but the addition of some specific retailing skills in the shape of Fiona Harrison from Clairol could change that. And finally there is Engineering, a curiosity which should not be there, but which is (financially) one of the best divisions in the group.

Sir David made a habit of collecting those companies that remained of the UK textile industry. It is now down to Mr Bain to build them up.

Shares

Its ambitious acquisition policy propelled what was then called Vantona Viyella to stock market stardom in the 1980s. The shares soared from 32p in 1980 to 420p in 1987 as each deal increased cost savings, and the benefits of investment were enhanced by a cyclical recovery in the textile sector. Enthusiasm waned briefly in 1986 as the group bid successfully for Coats, but revived in 1987 as post-bid profits started to come in.

Shares in the renamed group failed to gain much ground after the market crash, and in late 1988 investors' confidence was shattered when the board gave a profit warning. The bad news coincided with an industry-wide downturn in the textile cycle, so while there were periodic rallies in the share price, Coats Viyella consistently underperformed the market until 1990. That year profits were half what they had been in 1987, and the group was seen as having missed its chance to link with Tootal at the first attempt in 1989 and not to have rationalised its businesses fast enough.

Strengthened by a re-rating of the shares and a reinforced management, the group finally clinched the acquisition of Tootal in 1991. As other companies in other sectors entered the recession, Coats Viyella was perceived as having already slimmed itself down and this helped to boost its shares. Despite a slide in the share price in early 1994, the benefits of a weak pound helped performance, although the company's almost universally pessimistic outlook dampened resilience.

Corporate conscience

Textile companies are not generally renowned for their progressive attitudes, perhaps because of long traditions, perhaps because times have been so tough for them for so long that they have felt too constrained by commercial pressures. In that context, Coats Viyella's record is not too bad. It is a member of BITC and the Per Cent Club, and it has taken environmental issues seriously (a comprehensive policy and no recent record of exceeding discharges to water). The 1993 annual report included a substantial section on the environment. This described the group's environmental policy but was mostly concerned with reporting performance, including the news that 44 operating units had breached legislation of one form or another, though none were prosecuted. While the statement is 'audited', it does not attempt to provide any comprehensive quantitative reporting. Coats Viyella also has a reasonably good employment record, though lacks great commitment to equal opportunities. But some Coats subsidiaries have made chemicals or specialist fabrics which have involved animal testing, and there are a couple of recent convictions under health and safety laws.

The group's main exposure to issues of conscience

238 COURTAULDS plc

concerns human rights and military involvement. Coats Viyella is a hugely international company, particularly strongly represented in South America. In South Africa it employs several hundred black Africans, some of whom have been paid below a reasonable level. Various parts of the group supply the military: Compton Sons & Webb is a famous manufacturer of uniforms; Carrington Novare makes protection suits for use in chemical warfare; and the group produces threads and other materials for military purposes. It has in the past made contributions to the Conservative Party, but did not do so in 1993.

Corporate governance

Separate Chairman and Chief Executive Y
Number of Directors 9
Number of Non-Executive Directors 3
(2 Independent Directors)
Insulated Directors None

Board Committees
Audit: Y   Remuneration: Y

Remuneration

Year end	31.12.90	31.12.91	31.12.92
Total board £M	1.54	2.06	1.54
% change		34	-25
Highest paid £	209,000	499,000	481,000
% change		139	-4

Board
Bain, Neville C *Chief Executive*
Alliance, Sir David *Executive Chairman*
Flower, Martin C *Executive Director*
Macdiarmid, Alistair H *Executive Director*
White, Peter M *Executive Director*
Walls, J Russel F *Finance Director*
Djanogly, Harry A S *Independent Non-Executive*
Thomson, William C *Independent Non-Executive*
Blank, Maurice Victor *Non-Executive*

In recent times the group has shaken off its image as communications-shy. Having formerly been loath to provide shareholders with anything more than the basics, Coats Viyella then won top prize in early 1994 in the Stock Exchange and Chartered Accountants award for published accounts. The annual report for 1993 showed the company to be a convert to the Cadbury principles of corporate governance. It also included an environmental report and the early adoption of the Accounting Standards Board's changes on financial statements.

COURTAULDS plc
50 George Street, London W1A 2BB
Tel: 0171 612 1000
Chairman Sir Christopher Hogg
Chief executive Sipko Huismans
Main brands Amtico flooring, Clarifoil film, International Paint, Cellophane, Courtelle and Tencel fibres, P-Plus packaging film
Size £2.1 billion sales, £2.0 billion stock market value, 21,600 employees
5-year growth sales -20%, earnings per share 23%, employment -66%
Solvency debt = 41% shareholders' funds, interest cover 11 times.
Political donations 0
Charitable donations £219,714

Major developments
1913 formed as Courtaulds
1961 fought off takeover bid from ICI
1968 acquired International Paint
1988 first production of Tencel Fibre
1989 Samuel Courtauld sold
1990 textiles business demerged as Courtaulds Textiles
1991 expansion of coatings business

Outlook
In 1830 Samuel Courtauld founded the textile empire which still bears his surname, building a fortune by making silk crêpe at a mill in Essex. But the company of that name, now a rather small producer of polyester for trousers and blouses, was sold by the group in 1989 and the entire surviving textiles side of the business was hived off as a separate public company (Courtaulds Textiles) when the subsequent group split in two in 1990 in a similar fashion to the ICI demerger. The Courtaulds which remains, and which is the subject of this chapter, is a chemical company.

The ICI connection is apt. The chemical group failed to acquire Courtaulds in a bitter takeover battle back in the 1960s, which resulted not only in Courtaulds's continuing independence, but also in the rise to the top of Lord Kearton as chairman. He created a vertically integrated textile group covering everything from fibre production through cloth manufacture to retailing just as he tried to do later for the rest of industry as head of the Labour government's Industrial Reorganisation Corporation (IRC). This strategy worked for Courtaulds no better than it did for the rest of the country. Demerger was the culmination of attempts by Sir Christopher Hogg, Kearton's eventual successor at Courtaulds (and one of his lieutenants at the IRC), to undo the integrated group.

Sir Christopher's justification for demerger always seemed a little feeble – that the board was unable to deal adequately with decisions about the very different businesses of textiles and chemical products such

COURTAULDS plc

COURTAULDS

Share record

Return on shareholders' equity	%	27.64
5-year price high	p	605.0
5-year price low	p	269.0
Dividend yield	%	3.63
5-year high	%	5.75
5-year low	%	2.70
Price/earnings ratio		35.0
5-year high		36.2
5-year low		9.3

Share price performance (in pence)

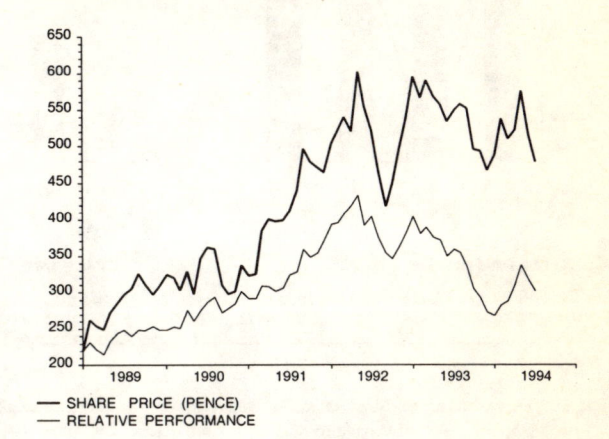

— SHARE PRICE (PENCE)
— RELATIVE PERFORMANCE

Financial record

		31/3/89	31/3/90	31/3/91	31/3/92	31/3/93
Total sales	£	2,610M	2,627M	1,912M	1,943M	2,074M
Pre-tax profit	£'000	197,100	201,700	186,300	201,400	191,000
Published retentions	£'000	205,600	44,200	27,900	90,100	94,300
Earnings per share	p	29.66	34.28	36.26	38.16	36.65
Dividend per share	p	10.89	11.10	12.00	13.00	14.00
Operating cash flow	£'000	84,600	214,600	46,200	-4,800	64,800
Net assets per share	p	225.21	168.85	186.84	201.33	209.86
Net debt/(cash)	£'000	15,700	206,900	236,000	232,600	222,000
Shareholders' funds	£'000	754,900	445,500	435,900	500,900	541,800
Return on capital	%	23.64	29.03	30.82	31.73	29.95
Profit margin	%	6.98	7.36	9.55	10.21	9.13
Sales per employee	£	41.29	55.30	78.99	84.10	96.03
Interest cover		16.30	25.16	38.24	25.49	11.07
Dividend cover		2.72	3.09	3.02	2.94	2.62
Sales increase	%	7.78	0.65	-27.22	1.62	6.77
Earnings growth	%	-12.21	15.55	5.79	5.25	-3.98
Investment x depreciation		1.73	1.25	1.64	1.89	1.44
Investment as % assets		22.25	17.87	18.21	19.68	15.91
Number of employees		63,200	47,500	24,200	23,100	21,600

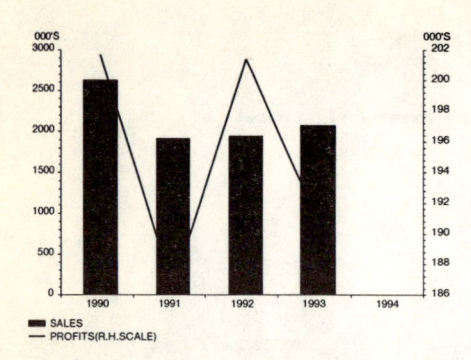

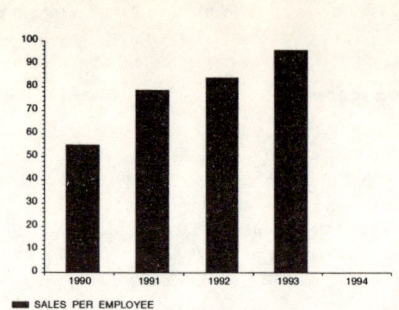

Sales and profits

Sales per employee

as films and coatings. Most board-level directors of major public companies have to deal with similarly diverse businesses: at Bass, the difference between brewing beer and franchising hotels; at BAT, cigarettes and insurance; at BOC, industrial gases and operating-theatre drugs; at Northern Foods, doorstep milk deliveries and recipe dishes for Marks & Spencer.

Nevertheless the demerger went ahead, to wide acclaim, and appears to have done neither party any harm. It has left Courtaulds as a specialised chemical company, still with a strong base in the wood pulp which shot it to fame at the beginning of the century as the inventor of the first artificial fibre (viscose). The Fibres and Chemicals division is the largest profit-maker in the group, with acetate-based products made from wood-derived cellulose as its core including Cellophane, Courtelle teabags, non-woven medical products and cigarette filters. Coatings and Sealants division has been built up over years mainly by acquisition as a specialist paint business. The Polymer Products division, which is the smallest, includes rigid packaging, such as packs produced for the toiletries and drug industries. A textile connection remains here, with the Amtico carpet-tile business.

In many of these areas Courtaulds comes up against the international chemical giants. But it has striven hard through the 1980s to move away from direct competition with them in bulk chemicals or to negotiate deals such as the Hoechst joint venture in acrylics to build a more substantial market position. Mostly, however, Courtaulds operates in specialist niches where it can command leading positions and which rely much more on advanced technology, service and quality rather than volume, and are therefore both more profitable to it and less attractive to the larger players. Tencel is a good example, being based on lengthy research and designed for use in high-class fashion rather than for mass production at the bottom end of the market. There have been enough new 'wonder' fibres over the years to remain cautious for the time being, but with Tencel Courtaulds seems set fair to carry on the tradition of innovation in textiles, even if it is no longer supposed to be a textile company.

Shares

The profound restructuring enabled Courtaulds to increase its market rating through the 1980s and the group was regarded as a model recovery stock. Its rating peaked in the 1987 bull market, but it was a victim of the October crash. The shares underperformed the market by 25 per cent over 1988, which was poor even by comparison with the sector. Interest in the shares was only aroused with the revelation in mid-1988 that Australian magnate Kerry Packer had a stake in the group. This concentrated minds on Courtaulds's potential, but when Mr Packer's flirtation with the group ended and he sold his shareholding, the market became disillusioned.

The components for the group's recovery were in place, however, and in 1989, after further tinkering with the mix of businesses, the board came up with its plan to hive off the textile business and press on with speciality chemicals. This triggered a re-rating which continued into 1992 and was fully justified as cost-cutting fuelled sustained growth in earnings.

The rating of the chemical business achieved greater heights than the combined business had enjoyed in the boom years, but Courtaulds could not keep up the pace as the effects of recession caught up with it. The weakness of the pound in 1993 encouraged investors for a time but the underlying trend in the group's trading was downward until the beginning of 1994.

Corporate conscience

For a chemical company, Courtaulds has a reasonable record. True, it makes pesticides and uses some

CFCs in aerosols and as refrigerants, some products involve animal testing, and the group is implicated in the military and nuclear industries. Courtaulds even has a tobacco connection, because it produces acetate tow for cigarette filters. But it has a strong environmental policy which is reflected in a complete absence of water pollution offences. It was fined £2,000 at the start of 1991 for an offence under the Highly Flammable Liquids and Liquified Petroleum Gases Regulations, but that is the only conviction since 1989.

Like most companies in this book, Courtaulds has some small operations in countries with oppressive regimes, notably Mexico, where it makes paints. And as with some other companies, the most surprising ethical issue that concerns it is military involvement. Courtaulds Aerospace makes various military components, including missile fins and camouflage products, while a couple of other subsidiaries are also involved in the military market. Aerospace exports some products for military use, such as body armour, helmets and protective fabric. In addition, this company supplies sealants for radiation shielding in the nuclear industry, while an American subsidiary supplies carbon tubes for nuclear research.

Corporate governance

Separate Chairman and Chief Executive Y
Number of Directors 11
Number of Non-Executive Directors 4
(3 Independent Directors)
Insulated Directors None

Board Committees
Audit: Y   Remuneration: Y

Remuneration

Year end	31.03.92	31.03.93	31.03.94
Total board £M	1.51	1.21	1.31
% change		6	-20	10
Highest paid £	303,788	284,150	355,353
% change		5	-7	25

Board
Huismans, Sipko *Chief Executive*
Campbell, Gordon A *Executive Director*
Giachardi, David J *Executive Director*
Morris, G Eryl *Executive Director*
Pragnell, Michal P *Executive Director*
Petersen, Neville *Executive Director*
Evans, Howard *Finance Director*
Grubman, Wallace K *Independent Non-Executive*
Hearne, Graham J *Independent Non-Executive*
Lees, Sir David *Independent Non-Executive*
Hogg, Sir Christopher *Non-Executive Chairman*

The good balance between executives and non-executives has been tilted the wrong way by the retirement of Sir Geoffrey Allen and the appointment of two new executive directors. But Courtaulds gives the impression of taking governance seriously. The company has separated the positions of chairman and chief executive, and Sir Christopher Hogg made reference in the 1992 annual report to the increased assurance which shareholders should derive from improved corporate governance. In his 1993 statement Sir Christopher explained the introduction of a new bonus scheme, which he said would help to counter short-termism. Details of bonus payments were spelled out in the accounts.

DE LA RUE plc

6 Agar Street, London WC2N 4DE
Tel: 0171 836 8383
Chairman Lord Limerick
Chief executive Jeremy Marshall
Main subsidiaries Inter Innovation, Fortronic
Size £593 million sales, £1.9 billion stock market value, 7,700 employees
5-year growth sales -70%, earnings per share 124%, employment -31%
Solvency debt n/a, interest cover n/a
Political donations 0
Charitable donations £104,000

Major developments
1898 Thomas De La Rue and Co formed
1981 bought Printrak
1987 bought Fortronic
1988 bought Ebway Industries Inc
1989 sold Crosfield Electronics; Norton Opax takeover bid defeated; new management installed; sold Printrak
1991 name changed to De La Rue plc
1992 bought Inter Innovation

Outlook
After 20 years of blundering, it is surprising that De La Rue is still around, and it is also difficult to be sure that the company has learned from its mistakes as it embarks on yet another acquisition spree. The main reassurance (on this score, at least) comes from the presence of ex-Hanson man Jeremy Marshall as chief executive.

De La Rue's strength is, and always has been, printing banknotes. It has been doing that since the 1830s and has a huge share of the available market in those countries around the world which allow foreign suppliers in (but not in the UK, where the Bank of England retains control of printing money). A natural adjunct to this business was the printing of bonds, cheques, passports and similar documents. Inevitably, given the impatience of business people, all this eventually began to seem rather boring (though highly profitable). So in the 1970s De La Rue set off to acquire more exciting businesses.

Formica and Potterton Boilers might not seem

DE LA RUE

Share record

Return on shareholders' equity	%	27.53
5-year price high	p	1021.0
5-year price low	p	1929.9
Dividend yield	%	2.58
5-year high	%	8.53
5-year low	%	2.34
Price/earnings ratio		23.7
5-year high		35.7
5-year low		11.5

Share price performance (in pence)

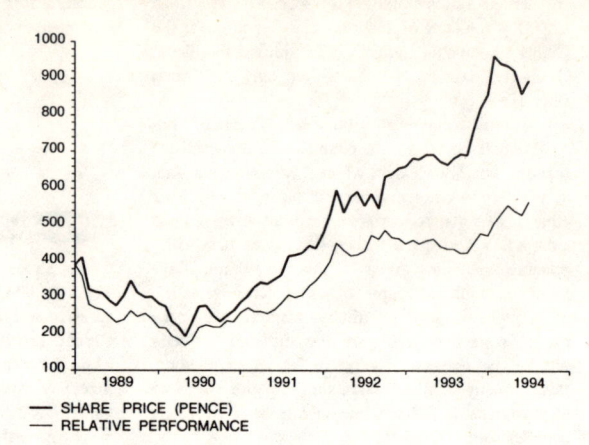

Financial record

		31/3/90	31/3/91	31/3/92	31/3/93	31/3/94
Total sales	£'000	349,463	369,627	415,400	559,500	592,700
Pre-tax profit	£'000	50,274	67,245	76,700	102,900	123,700
Published retentions	£'000	-56,212	26,440	25,800	41,700	57,300
Earnings per share	p	19.97	29.83	31.29	37.44	44.73
Dividend per share	p	12.35	12.82	15.00	17.00	20.00
Operating cash flow	£'000	173,186	10	55,500	69,500	66,400
Net assets per share	p	154.27	150.38	180.30	180.86	211.90
Net debt/(cash)	£'000	-39,485	-16,030	-112M	-171M	-268M
Shareholders' funds	£'000	145,902	158,649	346,000	271,600	321,900
Return on capital	%	25.16	35.61	33.16	34.55	34.30
Profit margin	%	11.73	15.39	16.71	16.26	18.24
Sales per employee	£	31.09	42.32	49.34	65.07	76.55
Interest cover		-11.39	27.52	-16.79	-6.84	-8.16
Dividend cover		1.62	2.33	2.09	2.20	2.24
Sales increase	%	-33.88	5.77	12.38	34.69	5.93
Earnings growth	%	847.49	49.34	4.91	19.65	19.49
Investment x depreciation		0.52	0.89	1.11	1.20	1.47
Investment as % assets		12.45	11.48	14.22	17.22	20.69
Number of employees		11,240	8,734	8,419	8,599	7,743

DE LA RUE plc

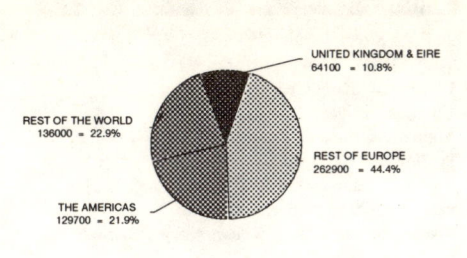

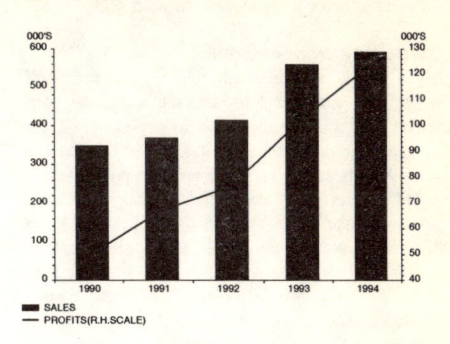

Sales analysis

- UNITED KINGDOM & EIRE 64100 = 10.8%
- REST OF EUROPE 262900 = 44.4%
- THE AMERICAS 129700 = 21.9%
- REST OF THE WORLD 136000 = 22.9%

Sales and profits

■ SALES
— PROFITS(R.H.SCALE)

terribly exciting now, but if you have been printing banknotes for almost 150 years, it might be a different matter. The group never made a terribly successful conglomerate, however, and these businesses were sold off in the early 1970s, only to be followed by more acquisitions, this time in apparently more logical areas. In the late 1980s De La Rue's core business acitivities could be neatly arranged in a triangle, with printing, security and technology at the points, thus encompassing security printing, printing technology and electronic security. This formula worked well enough until 1989, when it became apparent that technology formed one interest too many as the Crosfield subsidiary hit the electronic rocks. Early in 1989 the resignation of managing director Brian Malpass was accompanied by a profit warning. During that year matters went from bad to worse as more difficulties emerged in the electronics businesses, and finally a takeover bid was made by Norton Opax. This fellow struggler was merely trying to escape the unwelcome attentions of Bowater, however, which it failed to do.

With Norton Opax consumed by Bowater, De La Rue thereby gained an extra life, and under the leadership of Mr Marshall the group seemed to be using it to good effect. Crosfield has been sold and the money used to reduce debts but also to embark on a new round of acquisitions. This time, though, the pace seems to have been slower and the underlying logic a little clearer. Indeed, the only acquisition in Mr Marshall's first four years at the helm was the Swedish company Inter Innovation, a competitor in the markets for cash-handling and dispensing systems, which also brought to the group a bank security business.

This acquisition was generally well regarded by the City, which welcomed Jeremy Marshall's professionalism and gladly paid up £160 million in a rights issue, even though Inter Innovation cost only £95 million. De La Rue promised that the spare cash would be used to make further acquisitions. With £200 million still in the group's pocket, pressure is mounting for deals to be made. But buying privately owned businesses, in which De La Rue is interested, can take time. And everyone will be keen for the company to avoid the hasty mistakes of its past.

Shares

De La Rue's core businesses have made it a safe haven in time of recession or market panic, and its participation in the Camelot consortium bidding for the national lottery has added some glamour. During the latter part of the 1980s the company struggled with acquisitions but the shares outperformed the market strongly during the 1987 crash, while bid speculation boosted them the following year. Worries over the group's trading caused the shares to fall sharply in late 1988 and matters came to a head in 1989 when the board issued a profit warning and the managing director resigned. It became clear that the acquisitions had gone wrong, trading was bad and debt was rising. Only renewed bid interest aided the share price. Then in July the board's sale of Crosfield and an abortive bid from Norton Opax cleared the way for new management.

The cash generated by the sale of Crosfield was used to reorganise the group and while the shares reached their low point relative to the market in 1990, the recovery was already under way. The distribution of Robert Maxwell's stake among City institutions was followed by strong results in 1991 and the group was even able to make a rights issue. With recession affecting other shares, the group's defensive qualities came into their own and, by mid-1992, the stock had gained 140 per cent against the rest of the market.

During the New Year market rally of 1993 other shares were bought for recovery and the group's rela-

DIXONS GROUP plc

tive market value dropped. However, De La Rue was still seen as being a sound investment in itself.

Corporate conscience
De La Rue is an exceedingly 'clean' company as far as ethics, social and enironmental issues are concerned. It is not the most community-minded company, having avoided the attentions of BITC. But it is relatively open, has an environmental policy which includes clear goals and measurable objectives, as well as regular monitoring, though not audit. De La Rue also operates an equal opportunities policy, though not one which requires monitoring. The subsidiary Fortronic currently uses CFCs or other ozone-damaging chemicals for cleaning printed circuit boards, but the group has a commitment to phasing out such chemicals by the end of 1995. Otherwise, the only blot on its copybook is a minor interest in Nigeria and Sri Lanka.

Corporate governance

Separate Chairman and Chief Executive Y
Number of Directors 11
Number of Non-Executive Directors 6
(5 Independent Directors)
Insulated Directors None

Board Committees
Audit: Y   Remuneration: Y

Remuneration

Year end	31.03.91	31.03.92	31.03.93
Total board £M	0.68	1.22	1.22
% change		80	0
Highest paid £	327,000	272,000	256,000
% change		-17	-6

Board
Marshall, Jeremy J S *Chief Executive*
Gardner, Robert *Executive Director*
Pugh, Michael J *Executive Director*
White, John *Executive Director*
Cullen, Les G *Finance Director*
Birkenhead, S Brian *Independent Non-Executive*
Cazalet, Sir Peter *Independent Non-Executive*
Gough, Brandon *Independent Non-Executive*
Robb, John *Independent Non-Executive*
Wright, Sir Patrick *Non-Executive*
Earl of Limerick *Non-Executive Chairman*

De La Rue strengthened its non-executive team substantially in 1993, further improving its previously wayward approach to corporate governance. It has also made an attempt to be more open on the issue of directors' pay.

DIXONS GROUP plc

29 Farm Street, London W1X 7RD
Tel: 0171 499 3494
Chairman Stanley Kalms
Chief executive John Clare
Main subsidiaries Mastercare, Currys Group, PC World
Size £2.0 billion sales, £727 million stock market value, 14,500 employees
5-year growth sales 13%, earnings per share -58%, employment -2%
Solvency debt n/a, interest cover n/a
Political donations £25,000 Conservative Party
Charitable donations £567,000

Major developments
1937 formed as Dixons Studios Ltd
1962 became Dixons Photographic
1982 became Dixons Group
1984 bought Currys
1986 failed bid for Woolworths (now Kingfisher)
1987 bought Silo
1989 sold film processing division; Kingfisher bid launched
1990 Monopolies Commission rules out the Kingfisher bid
1993 sold Silo; bought PC World

Outlook
At the zenith of its fortunes, Dixons had much to be proud of. Run by Stanley Kalms, who had joined his father's portrait-photography business just after the war and realised that selling cameras was far more lucrative than taking pictures, the company had grown Topsy-like as Britons developed an appetite for cheap electrical and photographic equipment.

In 1984 Dixons bought Currys. By 1986 the company was able to boast that its sales per square foot were the highest of any retailing group in Britain. Dixons felt so confident of its own abilities that it even launched a £1.8 billion bid for Woolworths (later to be renamed Kingfisher) which owned rival Comet but also embraced B&Q as well as the eponymous variety stores with 700 outlets on high streets throughout the UK. The bid failed by a whisker. But Dixons was full of its own success: it had done so well with its own stores (which, in retrospect, was not such an achievement at the peak of the 1980s spending boom) that it felt it had to expand. In 1987, therefore, the group paid £210 million for Silo, an electrical retailer in the US.

With the benefit of hindsight, it is now clear that the Silo purchase was a disaster. Dixons was buying at exactly the wrong point in the business cycle. In the early years under Dixons's tutelage, Silo made modest amounts of money. But as competition intensified and US consumers went into hiding, Silo slid into the red, losing £22 million in the financial year to May 1993. Four months later Silo was finally sold

DIXONS GROUP

Share record

Return on shareholders' equity	%	30.41
5-year price high	p	292.0
5-year price low	p	103.0
Dividend yield	%	4.35
5-year high	%	6.49
5-year low	%	2.65
Price/earnings ratio		18.9
5-year high		61.7
5-year low		9.5

Share price performance (in pence)

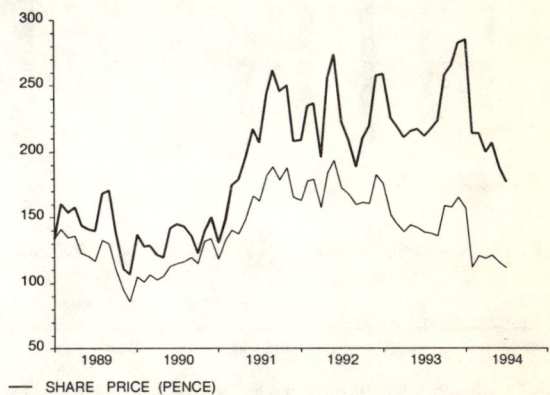

— SHARE PRICE (PENCE)
— RELATIVE PERFORMANCE

Financial record

		30/4/89	30/4/90	30/4/91	30/4/92	30/4/93
Total sales	£	1,755M	1,771M	1,695M	1,863M	1,986M
Pre-tax profit	£'000	78,400	80,100	82,200	70,300	76,700
Published retentions	£'000	26,200	17,100	26,300	2,300	-49,900
Earnings per share	p	11.65	12.12	12.59	9.05	4.92
Dividend per share	p	4.73	5.60	5.80	6.00	6.20
Operating cash flow	£'000	2,100	47,400	34,000	-45,700	53,500
Net assets per share	p	148.25	153.01	158.28	157.66	176.18
Net debt/(cash)	£'000	-21,100	-51,900	-69,400	-36,900	-74,300
Shareholders' funds	£'000	286,400	304,400	325,800	332,900	589,100
Return on capital	%	21.08	17.75	17.40	15.32	15.20
Profit margin	%	4.39	4.43	4.77	3.67	3.86
Sales per employee	£	94.99	114.58	119.16	128.94	136.74
Interest cover		15.81	-42.61	-5.80	-6.43	-6.59
Dividend cover		2.46	2.16	2.17	1.51	0.79
Sales increase	%	4.48	0.92	-4.29	9.89	6.61
Earnings growth	%	-27.53	4.04	3.91	-28.18	-45.66
Investment x depreciation		0.73	0.94	1.22	0.70	1.22
Investment as % assets		10.54	14.35	19.11	13.13	24.08
Number of employees		18,474	15,456	14,225	14,446	12,523

DIXONS GROUP plc

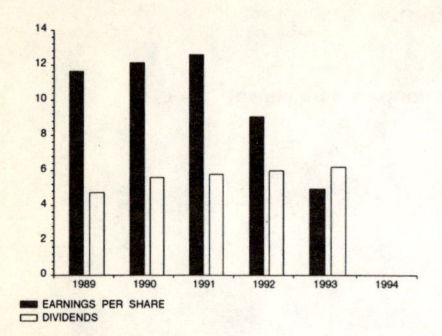

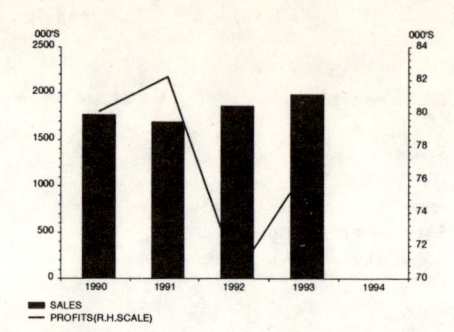

Earnings and dividends

Sales and profits

– for a meagre $50 million. Dixons had to make huge provisions to cover the loss on the sale – hence the group's overall loss of nearly £200 million for the first half of its 1992/93 financial year.

The last few years have not been easy on Dixons's home territory, either. At Christmas 1993 the company was hit by a collapse in the price of computer games, but nevertheless showed its faith in computer retailing with the acquisition of PC World. Like others in retailing, Dixons made the mistake of being seduced into thinking that because it was paying exorbitant prices to rent stores when sales were booming, it should also enter the property market. The move was ill timed, and in 1992 the company decided to pull out at a cost of £17 million. While Dixons suffered, Kingfisher (the renamed Woolworths which had proved itself to be a model of reliability) saw its chance and pounced, launching a £480 million bid for the company at the end of 1989.

The takeover assault was frustrated, however. The Monopolies Commission decided that combining an electrical retailer of the size of Dixons with Kingfisher's Comet would create a group with too strong a grip on the market. But the tussle brought to light some interesting aspects of Dixons's business. Most notably, it emerged that although the core business of selling electrical goods might be going through hard times, the company had built up a useful surplus from selling extended warranties to customers: electrical goods these days are generally pretty reliable, so there are handsome profits to be made from selling insurance cover that lasts for three or five years.

Now Dixons is trying to increase the profitability of its UK operation by closing high-street Currys outlets and opening new superstores with plenty of space for car parking away from established shopping areas. The company has already passed a minor milestone: although it has more than three times as many high-street Currys outlets as it does superstores, the square footage of the newer format has overtaken that of the conventional shops. These big outlets are relatively cheap to build and run. Moreover, shoppers seem to like them. Stanley Kalms says resignedly that he does not think that 'white goods' like fridges and cookers will continue to be sold in the high street for much longer. He has seen the future and the future is retail parks.

Shares

The 1980s consumer boom made Dixons one of the decade's glamour stocks – until 1986 when its fortunes were at their highest with the bid for Woolworths. Underlying the group's high profits the City detected an unsustainable trend, so while the shares themselves held up strongly, and did not peak until 1987, their value relative to the rest of the market began to fall in 1986. Profits started to shrink and the shares did not stop falling until late 1989 when Kingfisher bid for Dixons, thereby raising the latter's market rating once again.

Previously Dixons's shares had lost two-thirds of their value, and Kingfisher launched an assault on Dixons's management, accounting and retailing. The bid was blocked but had a galvanising effect on Dixons's management, which promised customers a new deal, with the emphasis on service and quality. Investors, on the other hand, got the old deal plus a recession.

From 1990 to 1992 the shares were bought several times ahead of a predicted recovery in consumer confidence which repeatedly failed to arrive. While the share rating recovered some of the lost ground despite a poor trading performance, investors' confidence was further dented early in 1993. The group's long-running difficulties with its Silo operation in the US resurfaced just as margins were being squeezed by the increasing cost of products caused by the weak pound. News of poor trading around Christmas 1993 again felled the share price. By January 1994 Dixons's shares had underperformed the sector by 30 per cent over the previous 12 months.

Corporate conscience

Like many self-made men, Stanley Kalms believes in the responsibilities of success. He has a long record at Dixons of charitable and community involvement. This now extends to funding a chair in business ethics at London Business School, and Dixons is naturally an active member of BITC and of the Per Cent Club. Mr Kalms is also a great believer in training, and the company has won awards for its retail and service training programmes (not that it is always possible to notice the effect in a business which traditionally suffers very high rates of staff turnover). The group has an effective equal opportunities policy, including monitoring of performance, and supports Opportunity 2000.

On the negative side, Currys sells fridges using ozone-depleting chemicals. Otherwise, the only area of ethical interest is advertising. Seven complaints were upheld by the ASA during 1991 and 1992.

Corporate governance

Separate Chairman and Chief Executive N
Number of Directors 7
Number of Non-Executive Directors 3
(3 Independent Directors)
Insulated Directors None

Board Committees
Audit: Y   Remuneration: Y

Remuneration

Year end	27.04.91	2.05.92	30.04.93
Total board £M	1.90	1.64	1.41
% change		-11	-13
Highest paid £	566,132	563,109	562,675
% change		-0.5	

Board
Kalms, Stanley *Chairman*
Clare, John *Chief Executive*
Shrager, Robert *Executive Director*
Souhami, Mark *Executive Director*
Curry, John *Independent Non-Executive*
Hornby, Sir Derek *Independent Non-Executive*
Lewis, Henry *Independent Non-Executive*

The promotion of John Clare to group managing director at the beginning of 1992 reduced the responsibilities of Dixons's chairman, Stanley Kalms, who subsequently also relinquished the role of chief executive. This separation is particularly important in what remains partly a family business with the founder in the chair. Dixons was one of the first companies to include a corporate governance statement in its annual report, however, before the final Cadbury Report was published. This revealed that the audit committee meets quarterly, and its chairmanship rotates between the non-executives. There are two remuneration committees, a non-executive one that considers executive pay, and an executive one which considers non-executive pay. In 1993 this report was accompanied by a formal statement from the auditors.

ENTERPRISE OIL plc

Grand Buildings, Trafalgar Square,
London WC2N 5EJ
Tel: 0171 925 4000
Chairman and chief executive Graham Hearne
Size £546 million sales, £2.1 billion stock market value, 657 employees
5-year growth sales 62%, earnings per share -65%, employment 76%
Solvency debt = 48% shareholders' funds, interest cover 3 times
Political donations 0
Charitable donations £188,401

Major developments
1983 formed to take over offshore oil interests of British Gas
1984 privatised
1987 merged with ICI Petroleum
1989 bought Texas Eastern
1990 ICI sold its stake
1991 bought Occidental UK jointly with Elf-Aquitaine
1994 bid for Lasmo failed

Outlook

When the government was privatising British Gas, it lost the battle to break up the national monopoly into a series of regional monopolies, but it did manage to extricate the exploration business from the still-nationalised gas company. (Both of these moves have since been reversed: the regulator, Ofgas, has gradually weakened British Gas's market position, while the company has gone back into the exploration business.) The exploration arm of British Gas became Enterprise Oil when this was privatised in 1984, and by 1989 the company had become the biggest pure oil-exploration business in the world – 'pure' in the sense that it sticks to exploration and production (E&P), instead of also getting involved in the downstream businesses of refining and marketing.

Since its birth, however, oil experts have been waiting for Enterprise Oil to be taken over. And while the company is large by E&P standards, total net assets of around £2 billion represents so much petty cash to one of the oil majors. From its inception the company has also been in the uncomfortable position of having at least one major shareholder sitting on a large chunk of its shares. A quarter of the

ENTERPRISE OIL plc

ENTERPRISE OIL

Share record

Return on shareholders' equity	%	8.06
5-year price high	p	693.0
5-year price low	p	298.0
Dividend yield	%	4.68
5-year high	%	7.05
5-year low	%	2.22
Price/earnings ratio		44.3
5-year high		55.9
5-year low		11.9

Share price performance (in pence)

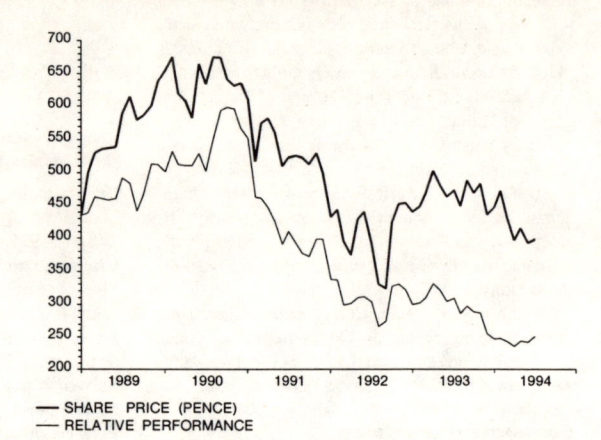

— SHARE PRICE (PENCE)
— RELATIVE PERFORMANCE

Financial record

		31/12/89	31/12/90	31/12/91	31/12/92	31/12/93
Total sales	£'000	337,100	497,100	487,600	538,100	546,100
Pre-tax profit	£'000	129,000	191,700	150,000	108,200	111,900
Published retentions	£'000	56,400	88,100	38,600	6,000	1,100
Earnings per share	p	27.35	31.17	25.12	11.91	9.63
Dividend per share	p	13.00	15.00	15.75	16.00	16.00
Operating cash flow	£'000	-186M	-125M	-117M	-154M	6,400
Net assets per share	p	392.14	377.88	437.37	520.58	493.49
Net debt/(cash)	£'000	-122M	-28,200	331,900	407,300	459,300
Shareholders' funds	£'000	548,600	636,300	679,400	901,800	951,300
Return on capital	%	12.61	13.55	10.60	7.75	6.74
Profit margin	%	38.27	38.56	30.15	21.50	20.11
Sales per employee	£	901.34	969.01	720.24	821.53	831.20
Interest cover		-1.08	-1.88	-2.36	2.04	2.71
Dividend cover		2.10	2.08	1.60	0.74	0.60
Sales increase	%	75.48	47.46	-1.91	10.36	1.49
Earnings growth	%	61.19	13.94	-19.40	-52.58	-19.16
Investment x depreciation		6.20	3.06	2.48	2.35	1.07
Investment as % assets		46.33	27.30	22.03	21.29	10.33
Number of employees		374	513	677	655	657

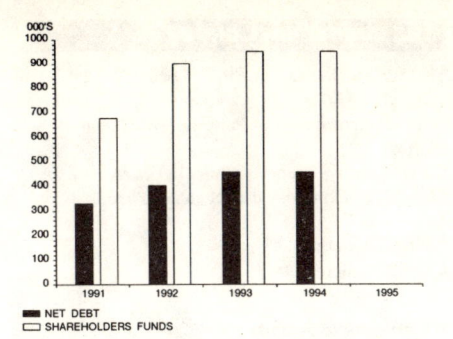

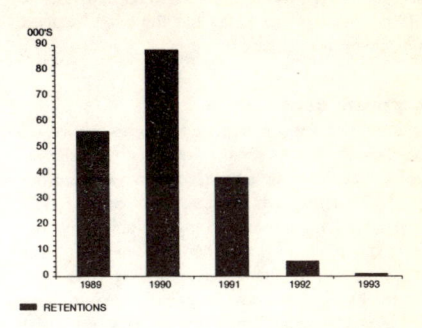

Debt and shareholders' funds

Retentions

shares were held first by mining group RTZ, then Lasmo, the other major UK exploration company. In 1988 they were sold to French oil group Elf-Aquitaine (Elf), and by that time chemical giant ICI had also become a big shareholder, acquiring shares in exchange for its own oil and gas interests, which were sold in one of the group's many divestments.

ICI eventually sold out in 1990, but instead of passing on its 25 per cent stake to another potential predator, or to Elf, as had been feared, ICI placed the shares with financial institutions. The threat from the Elf stake was also dissipated: Enterprise Oil and Elf jointly acquired Occidental UK, creating Elf Enterprise Petroleum and effectively neutralising any takeover threat from Elf since the French company paid for its Occidental stake in bonds which were exchangeable into Enterprise Oil shares. This was the sort of deal which has led Enterprise Oil to be respected as much for its deal-making as for its drilling. It was followed in 1989 by another *coup* – the acquisition of Texas Eastern, which gave Enterprise Oil a significant presence in oil and gas exploration beyond the UK, mostly in Norway but also in Indonesia. The group has also been effective at its real business of finding oil and gas, notably in the North Sea Nelson field but also in foreign locations. As a result, it has built up reserves dramatically, with the promise of strong cash flows once the new fields begin producing in the mid-1990s. In the meantime the group has sustained its cash position by selling some assets in the North Sea, and through a share offer in the US.

Inevitably, the fortunes of oil companies depend upon the international price of crude oil and the dollar exchange rate, whose vagaries are well known to Enterprise Oil. The company was launched on to the stock market just as the oil price slumped when the Saudis fell out with the rest of the Opec cartel. As a result, it was not one of the most successful privatisations. Almost a decade later, in 1993, the oil price did nothing to help Enterprise Oil. And by the beginning of 1994 it became clear that the company – through no fault of its own – might begin to struggle to cover its dividend.

In May 1994 the group bid £1.4 billion for Lasmo, arguing that the reserves of its target, enfeebled by the disastrous takeover of Ultramar, could better be developed by the financially robust Enterprise Oil. In particular, the Lasmo acquisition, it was argued, would help Enterprise Oil to cover a threatened fall in output from its existing fields around the end of the decade. The bid was not well received by investors, however, and Enterprise Oil won only 36 per cent of the shares.

Shares

Enterprise Oil has long been part of most fund managers' portfolios, thanks to the management's expansion of the group through effective deals and successful exploration. Apart from a huge spike in its share price in 1988, when Lasmo's stake in the group was sold to Elf-Aquitaine, the shares showed a steady appreciation in value against the rest of the market from 1986 to 1990. Enthusiasm for the shares peaked that year when ICI's stake was dispersed around the City just in time for investors to benefit from the Gulf crisis.

The windfall profits made that year further assisted the City's interest in the shares, but the share price weakened as recession began to hit the world's major economies. Lower oil prices and rising costs depressed the shares until the UK's exit from the ERM in 1992 left the group free to benefit from the pound's fall.

The shares outperformed the market as a whole by 25 per cent once interest in the shares was resumed in late 1992, but by 1993 the market was waiting for the benefits of development in two new fields to be reflected in earnings and cash flow. Lower debt and rising cash in 1994 were expected to boost dividends in 1995, although the failed bid for Lasmo caused some nervousness among investors.

Corporate conscience

For an oil company, Enterprise Oil raises few issues of conscience, except for the obvious environmental problem that the group's existence centres on a product which causes such environmental damage. The group naturally seems fairly sanguine about this, but to the point of ignoring all other issues as well. It has not satisfied EIRIS that it operates a rigorous environmental policy. Nor does it appear to take employment and community involvement very seriously. The annual report makes minimal reference to these issues.

Corporate governance

Separate Chairman and Chief Executive N
Number of Directors 13
Number of Non-Executive Directors 6
(5 Independent Directors)
Insulated Directors CE

Board Committees
Audit: Y   Remuneration: Y

Remuneration
Year end	31.12.91	31.12.92	31.12.93
Total board £M	1.86	2.01	2.10
% change	-4	8	4
Highest paid £	368,000	397,000	395,000
% change	-15	8	-0.5

Board
Hearne, Graham J   *Chairman & Chief Executive*
Pink, M J   *Chief Operating Officer*
Harris, E J   *Executive Director*
Paterson, I S   *Executive Director*
Watt, J F   *Executive Director*
West, J D   *Executive Director*
Shilston, A B   *Finance Director*
Bates, M R   *Independent Non-Executive*
Gardiner, John A   *Independent Non-Executive*
Quartano, Ralph N   *Independent Non-Executive*
Ramsay, G M   *Independent Non-Executive*
Shaw, Sir Brian   *Independent Non-Executive*
Bell, W E   *Non-Executive*

Enterprise Oil is another organisation which, against the trend, has moved to combine the roles of chairman and chief executive, but the board does contain some non-executives of substance. In addition, Mr Hearne came under pressure to relinquish one of his roles following the Lasmo bid. A reasonable outline is given in the annual report of the long-term bonus scheme for senior employees, including directors, and, hearteningly, it is based on comparison with a group of other oil and gas companies. Directors appear to be on 12-months' notice periods.

THE EUROTUNNEL GROUP plc

The Adelphi, John Adam Street, London WC2N 6JT
Tel: 0171 747 6747
Joint Chairmen Patrick Ponsolle, Sir Alastair Morton
Chief executive Georges-Christian Chazot
Size £2.5 billion stock market value; other financial data n/a
Political donations 0
Charitable donations 0

Major developments

1986 concession awarded to Eurotunnel until 2042; construction contract agreed with Transmanche Link (TML)
1986 two share issue raised £252 million from partners and private investors
1987 £5 billion loan finance agreed shares issued to public raising; £770m, completing initial financing; tunnelling began
1990 additional loan and share capital raised £2.7 billion
1991 first rail tunnel breakthrough
1993 TML handed tunnel over to Eurotunnel. Concession extended to 2052
1994 State opening by the Queen and President Mitterand. Launch of freight and passenger services.

Outlook

Eurotunnel is in the unusual, indeed unenviable, position of building the Channel tunnel with a huge pot of borrowed money which will all be spent before the project earns a penny (or, indeed, a centime) of income. In addition to the pressures of tackling such a vast construction project, the company has faced unusual difficulties stemming from the practicalities of linking the public infrastructure of two countries with a private sector enterprise funded by 200 banks and shareholders worldwide.

The role of the Anglo-French company initially was to commission the construction work from the 10-strong team of contractors Transmanche Link (TML). It also had the task of commissioning and testing the trains and the tunnel – which proved much more problematic than anticipated. And finally, once the Tunnel opened, it was down to Eurotunnel to operate and maintain it – and eventually pocket the revenue.

But a series of much-publicised wranglings between Eurotunnel and TML over the costs of the project meant that the crucial opening date was repeatedly delayed. The company's shaping of its finances took an unusual twist because of the way that unforeseen delays wrought havoc with its original cash projections. At the time of the project's inception, Eurotunnel costed the scheme at £2.5 billion, a figure which it forecast would rise to nearly £4 billion by the intended opening date in 1993, when

THE EUROTUNNEL GROUP

Share record

Return on shareholders' equity	%	-1.11
5-year price high	p	842.3
5-year price low	p	260.0
Dividend yield	%	0.00
5-year high	%	n/a
5-year low	%	n/a
Price/earnings ratio		59.0
5-year high		125.6
5-year low		37.8

Share price performance (in pence)

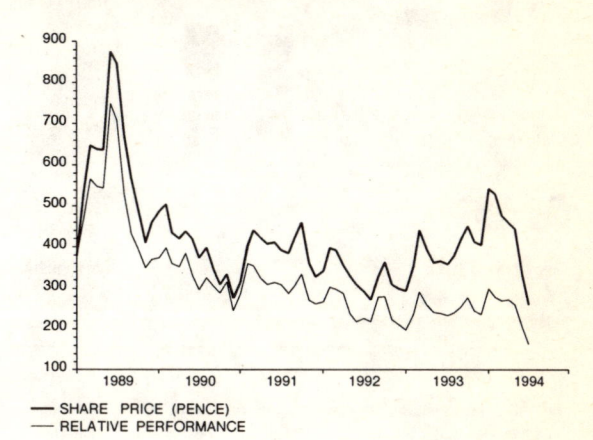

— SHARE PRICE (PENCE)
— RELATIVE PERFORMANCE

Financial record

		31/12/89	31/12/90	31/12/91	31/12/92	31/12/93
Total sales	£'000	0	0	0	0	0
Pre-tax profit	£'000	26,647	-9,814	-2,390	28,638	-15,174
Published retentions	£'000	1,147	242	-109	-1,562	-1,892
Earnings per share	p	6.18	0.00	0.00	4.64	0.00
Dividend per share	p	0.00	0.00	0.00	0.00	0.00
Operating cash flow	£	-945M	-1,377M	n/a	-1,901M	-1,678M
Net assets per share	p	397.73	639.20	820.35	1,076	1,377
Net debt/(cash)	£'000	895,666	1,663M	3,189M	5,361M	6,906M
Shareholders' funds	£'000	997,416	1,587M	1,556M	1,241M	1,367M
Return on capital	%	7.67	6.83	7.72	10.11	8.07
Profit margin	%	0.00	0.00	0.00	0.00	0.00
Sales per employee	£	0.00	0.00	0.00	0.00	0.00
Interest cover		0.87	0.94	0.94	1.04	0.97
Dividend cover		0.00	0.00	0.00	0.00	0.00
Sales increase	%	0.00	0.00	0.00	0.00	0.00
Earnings growth	%	0.00	-100.00	0.00	0.00	-100.00
Investment × depreciation		18.98	16.38	11.28	21.50	17.96
Investment as % assets		51.70	45.31	21.05	18.34	9.98
Number of employees		418	485	594	878	1,491

252 THE EUROTUNNEL GROUP plc

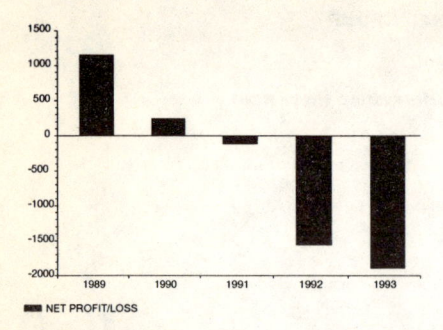

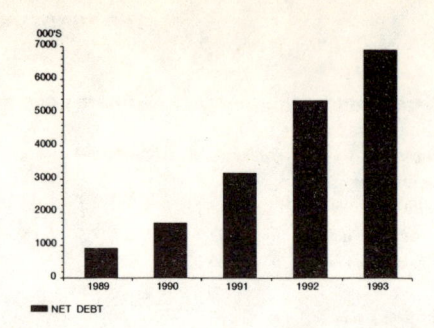

Profit and loss

Net debt

inflation and financing costs were taken into account. In fact, the final bill looks set to run to almost £11 billion, more than double the original forecast. Less than a month after the official inauguration of the tunnel by the Queen and President Mitterrand in May 1994, shareholders were asked to dig deep into their pockets to raise another £816 million in the fifth cash call in the company's history, which was a key plank in a £1.5 billion rescue package designed to stave off bankruptcy.

Eurotunnel's long-suffering banks agreed to put up a further £693 million as part of the plan. The 220-strong consortium have already injected more than £7 billion into the project. Eurotunnel claims the £1.5 billion further projected cash requirements mostly represented interest costs on the increased debt not covered by cash flow until the expected breakeven of the project in 1998. But analysts have been concerned at the way the tunnel's costs had spiralled out of control as one problem after another delayed progress, wreaking havoc with its original revenue projections. The rescue deal left it with a 'funding margin' of £470 million designed to act as a financial cushion for the project to cover the various unknown quantities. But the delays in the launch of full revenue-earning services were a major obstacle, and analysts were not convinced that Eurotunnel would be able to meet its ambitious expectations of big market shares in cross-Channel traffic.

There are opportunities for raking some money in, however. In March 1993 a legal ruling was made in Eurotunnel's favour, allocating to TML the responsibility for itemising the outstanding claims between the two parties for the cost of the fixed equipment in the tunnel.

In addition, Eurotunnel is taking legal action against both the British and French governments to claim compensation for the delayed start of scheduled passenger train services, and for the lateness and inadequacy of the railway infrastructure on the British side of the tunnel.

As far as Eurotunnel, its shareholders and its competitors are concerned, there are now two key dates on the horizon: the date when revenues from the tunnel first cover operating costs, and the date when all the bank loans are finally paid off. The banks themselves appear to have no choice but to continue to back the project. The short-term prospects for shareholders (of which Eurotunnel has 630,000) are not very good, with no chance of any dividend payments being made before the end of the century. After 2005 prospects are due to improve, but it is only from 2010 onwards that dividend payments are expected to be of sufficient size to reward the forbearance of the original, long-suffering equity investors. It is worth noting that, with the English selling out in some numbers to the French, the latter seem to have been the more patient investors. They outnumber the English by five to one.

Shares

Eurotunnel is a unique investment since the shares have a wholly speculative value with no dividend payment expected until the next century. Normal share valuation is impossible, although the market ride so far has been extraordinary. Floated at 350p in the aftermath of the crash in 1987, the shares soared to £10 over 1988–9. They then fell by £7 in six months as the series of conflicts started between the group and contractors TML. At one point a rumour that co-chairman Alastair Morton was resigning wiped £200 million off the company's market value in one day.

The share price rose and fell with the level of optimism or pessimism over project cost and completion dates. The peak in 1991 coincided with the tunnel breakthrough, but the series of disappointments which followed drove down the price once again. Approaching completion helped sustain the shares during 1993, but they collapsed to new lows in 1994 as the opening date was deferred.

Corporate conscience

As the commissioner of the Channel tunnel, Eurotunnel clearly has overall responsibility for its construction. But because the company is not actually responsible directly for the building work, which is carried out by the constituent companies of Transmanche Link, Eurotunnel has virtually no ethical impact. It is a member of BITC and the Per Cent Club, and that is about all that can be said for, or against, it.

Corporate governance

Separate Chairman and Chief Executive Y
Number of Directors 16
Number of Non-Executive Directors 13
(13 Independent Directors)
Insulated Directors Not known

Board Committees
Audit: Y   Remuneration: Y

Remuneration
Year end	31.12.91	31.12.92	31.12.93
Total board £M	0.74	0.84	0.91
% change	-33	13	8
Highest paid £	266,000	275,112	306,974
% change		-6	3	12

Board
Morton, Sir Alastair } *Joint Chairmen*
Ponsolle, Patrick
Chazot, Georges-Christian *Chief Executive*
Bertrand, Alain *Executive Director*
Corbett, Graham *Finance Director*
Bénard, André *Independent Non-Executive*
Child, Denis Marsden *Independent Non-Executive*
de Wouters, Baron *Independent Non-Executive*
Foulds, Jon *Independent Non-Executive*
Lafayette, Philippe *Independent Non-Executive*
Lion, Robert *Independent Non-Executive*
Malpas, Robert *Independent Non-Executive*
Meerhaut, John *Independent Non-Executive*
Thiolon, Bernard *Independent Non-Executive*
Tugendhat, Lord *Independent Non-Executive*
Wahl, Jacques-Henri *Independent Non-Executive*

For a company whose main activity is negotiation with builders, the role and personality of the chief executive is particularly important, emphasising the need of a strong board to act as a counterbalance to this. Indeed, Eurotunnel has no shortage of independent directors, although many fall into the 'good and great' category rather then the 'powerful and prescient'. The board has separate audit, remuneration and safety committees and the 1993 annual report explains how they work.

FORTE plc

166 High Holborn, London WC1V 6TT
Tel: 0171 836 7744
Chairman and chief executive Rocco Forte
Main brands and subsidiaries Little Chef, Happy Eater, Welcome Break, Harvester restaurants, Lillywhites, Puritan Maid
Size £2.1 billion sales, £2.0 billion stock market value, 50,000 employees
5-year growth sales -12%, earnings per share -61%, employment -46%
Solvency debt = 52% shareholders' funds, interest cover 2 times
Political donations £80,000 Conservative Party
Charitable donations £369,502

Major developments

1970 merger of Forte and Trust Houses to create Trust Houses Forte
1971 fought off bid from Allied Breweries
1981 began battle for control of Savoy group
1983 Rocco Forte became chief executive
1986 bought Happy Eater, Welcome Break motorway services and Pier House Inns
1987 bought Kentucky Fried Chicken chain in the UK
1988 bought Kennedy Brookes hotel and restaurant chain
1989 truce called with Savoy
1990 bought Crest Hotels from Bass
1991 name changed to Forte
1993 sold Gardner Merchant; Lord Forte retired; abandoned sales of Harvester pubs and restaurants; bought Relais motorway services, France; sold interest in Kentucky Fried Chicken
1994 flotation of airport services business

Outlook

Lord Forte (as he now is) founded the company of which he is now president as a milk bar in London's Regent Street, after learning the trade in his father's Brighton café. He was one of a clutch of post-war entrepreneurs who made it big through good luck, good management and good deals – Charles Clore at Sears and Maxwell Joseph of Grand Metropolitan were in a similar mould. But despite being one of Britain's largest companies, with the vast majority of the shares held by outsiders, Forte still retains much of the feel of a family business. The fact that Lord Forte only relinquished the chairmanship in 1992 has something to do with it, as does his long vendetta to gain control of the Savoy hotel group. What is more, he handed over the chairmanship to his son, Rocco, a position which Rocco combined with the role of chief executive. In addition, the board also includes Rocco's sister, Olga Pollizzi, who is responsible for building and design.

Keeping top jobs in the family would be of less consequence if Rocco's period as chief executive had been gloriously successful. But the figures show that

FORTE

Share record

Return on shareholders' equity	%	2.52
5-year price high	p	357.0
5-year price low	p	119.0
Dividend yield	%	4.23
5-year high	%	11.10
5-year low	%	3.14
Price/earnings ratio		25.2
5-year high		68.2
5-year low		15.1

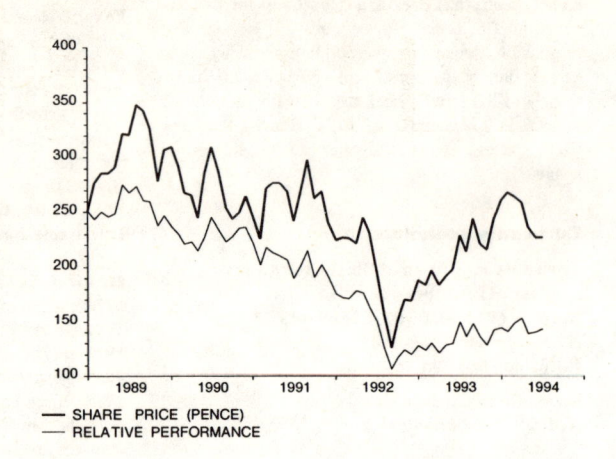

Share price performance (in pence)

— SHARE PRICE (PENCE)
— RELATIVE PERFORMANCE

Financial record

		31/1/90 65 weeks	31/1/91	31/1/92	31/1/93	31/1/94
Total sales	££'000	2,983M	2,641M	2,662M	2,721M	2,106M
Pre-tax profit	£'000	224,000	179,000	72,000	71,000	87,000
Published retentions	p	141,000	70,000	-33,000	54,000	22,000
Earnings per share	p	16.12	16.54	5.59	1.96	6.30
Dividend per share		9.66	9.91	9.91	7.50	7.50
	£'000					
Operating cash flow		-74,000	191,000	-189M	-130M	38,000
	p					
Net assets per share	£'000	438.45	478.06	498.48	432.97	402.26
Net debt/(cash)	£	939,000	1,008M	1,160M	1,178M	1,199M
Shareholders' funds		2,712M	2,961M	2,916M	2,637M	2,316M
	%					
Return on capital	%	10.44	7.76	4.76	5.50	5.90
Profit margin	£	7.04	6.51	2.63	2.65	4.13
Sales per employee		32.11	28.68	29.74	33.59	42.12
Interest cover		2.96	2.79	1.65	1.56	1.83
Dividend cover		1.67	1.67	0.56	0.26	0.84
	%					
Sales increase	%	45.94	-11.46	0.80	2.22	-22.60
Earnings growth		-3.59	2.57	-66.22	-64.91	221.40
Investment x depreciation		2.19	-0.42	2.20	1.73	1.14
Investment as % assets		4.86	-0.85	4.67	4.23	3.31
Number of employees		92,900	92,100	89,500	81,000	50,000

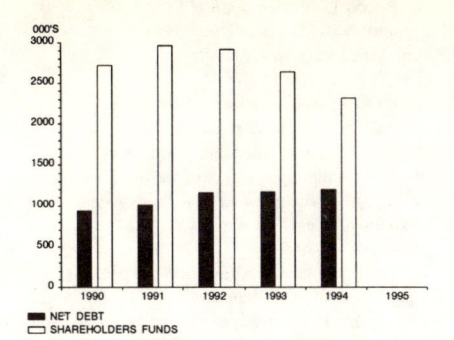

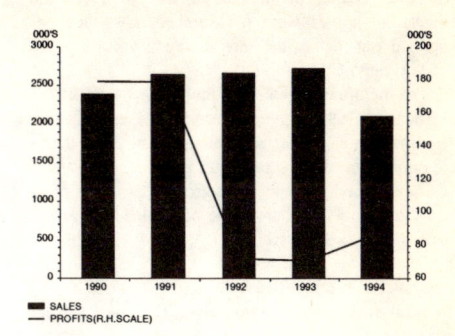

Debt and shareholders' funds

Sales and profits

this was not the case. Indeed the many disposals in 1993 and 1994 were as close as makes no difference to being forced sales to raise cash.

The hotel business is notoriously subject to the vagaries of tourism and international business travel. The number of Americans venturing over the Atlantic is particularly important for hotels in Britain, yet the numbers have been particularly erratic in recent years because of international incidents: Chernobyl, the US attack on Libya and the Gulf War all kept Americans at home. On top of these troubles, UK hoteliers have had to cope with the more general impact of recession, just like any other business. There is no doubt that the late 1980s and early 1990s were difficult times, but Forte did not handle the situation as well as it could.

Like many other businesses, it built up debts to unsustainable levels. The hotel industry being an adjunct of property investment, high debt levels were not considered worrying until it was too late and trading profits crashed in 1991–2. Soaring interest costs further dented profits and this, together with negative cash flow, meant that there was clearly a need to cut the dividend, which had already been stretching resources for the previous two years. But this opportunity to conserve cash was not taken, to the general dismay of the City which for once seemed more interested in the longer-term direction of the group than the short-term return on shares. Furthermore, the hope that 1991–2 was an errant year due to the impact of the Gulf War was not borne out when profits for the first half of the following year proved to be no better than during the war.

Confidence in the company was not improved by the decision to sell Gardner Merchant, the contract catering company that was the best-performing division. This business may have been less glamorous than running hotels, or even than consumer catering through outlets such as Kentucky Fried Chicken, Happy Eater and Little Chef and the Welcome Break motorway service stations. Nevertheless, it was consistently profitable, showed steady growth, used little capital and produced good cash flows. Given the volatility of hotels and restaurants, these seemed like valuable qualities, but the subsidiary's financial value was apparently more important to Forte and it was eventually sold in 1992, though only at the second attempt and at a lower price than talked about the first time round.

In its subsequent efforts to build faith in its potential, Forte reorganised the hotel businesses into four coherent brands in 1992. Further moves on to the Continent also helped build City confidence that the group knew where it was going, although the cash position had not improved. In addition, the appointment of two heavyweight non-executive directors in 1992 went some way to diminish worries about family whim ruining what could be a great company. But in 1994 concerns remained about Forte's ability to develop and pursue a strategy that would make the most of its widespread assets.

Shares

Forte's shares appreciated steadily against the market as a whole through the market boom in 1987 until 1989. The dividend cover was increased and a succession of deals kept investors interested. There was even the occasional mystery stakebuilder to add spice to a share holding.

Bid speculation, and the share price, climaxed in 1989. There was a probe by the Stock Exchange into share movements, but no bid, and from 1989 until 1992 the shares underperformed the market by 55 per cent. At first the shares lost ground (relatively) because other companies in its sector looked to have more growth potential. But then it was appreciated that the group's debts were high at a time of high interest rates, and profits began collapsing dramatically as the recession grew. In 1991-2 the group made a smaller profit than it had in 1983 and investors' nerves were not soothed when analysts pointed out that in the intervening years the group had invested £2.7 billion.

The picture changed when the UK left the ERM in September 1992. Lower interest rates and cheaper sterling that would attract tourists enabled the shares to outperform the market by 22 per cent. The sale of Gardner Merchant helped the group clear some of its debt, but while the share rating continued to improve, the advance was muted.

Corporate conscience

Forte is one of those groups which professes concern about many ethical issues, but whose supposed concern often does not seem to be borne out in practice, perhaps because it is not carried through into rigorous policies. For example, the group is a member of BITC and has made clear a belief in community involvement, in practice it is a relatively small donor to charity especially by comparison with its hefty donation to the Conservative Party. In association with the Conservative Foundation, Forte launched the imaginative Community Chest scheme in 1984, under which small sums are granted to local organisations for environmental improvements. But the group does not have an adequate public environmental policy. Similarly, on the employment front, Forte is a great believer in training, but has had a strained relationship with trade unions, and appears to pay scant attention formally to equal opportunities, although a substantial proportion of managers are women. (Olga Polizzi is an executive director, but since she is a member of the Forte family that scarcely counts as an example of an equal opportunities policy in action.)

Forte is involved with alcohol and tobacco, is a small-scale supplier to the military, and uses CFCs as refrigerants, with no stated phase-out target for these. Forte hotels suffered one adverse judgement by the ASA in 1992; Puritan Maid was fined £2,500 in 1989 for an offence under the Health and Safety at Work Act; and the group has a surprisingly long list of convictions for water pollution.

Corporate governance

Separate Chairman and Chief Executive N
Number of Directors 10
Number of Non-Executive Directors 4
(3 Independent Directors)
Insulated Directors None

Board Committees
Audit: N   Remuneration: Y

Remuneration

Year end	31.01.92	31.01.93	31.01.94
Total board £M	3.89	2.58	1.89
% change	53	-34	-27
Highest paid £	249,721	344,631	319,898
% change	2	38	-7

Board
Forte, Rocco *Chairman & Chief Executive*
Chiandetti, G B *Executive Director*
Hearn, Alan J *Executive Director*
Polizzi, Olga *Executive Director*
Proctor, George F L *Executive Director*
Hamill, Keith *Finance Director*
Girolami, Sir Paul *Independent Non-Executive*
Tennant, Sir Anthony J *Independent Non-Executive*
Wheatley, Alan *Independent Non-Executive*
Hardie, Sir Charles *Non-Executive*

Criticism of the advanced age and possible lack of independence of some the company's non-executives, coupled with unease about the father-and-son double act at the top of the company, prompted boardroom changes which have addressed some of the areas of concern although at 84, with 24 years' service on the board, Sir Charles Hardie can hardly be thought of as 'independent'. In the process, however, a new cause for disquiet has arisen: Rocco Forte has decided to combine the roles of chairman and chief executive, flying in the face of current thinking and accepted practice elsewhere. Salary disclosure is miserly.

GENERAL ELECTRIC COMPANY plc

1 Stanhope Gate, London W1A 1EH
Tel: 0171 493 8484
Chairman Lord Prior
Managing director Lord Weinstock
Main brands and subsidiaries AEI Cables, Avery, Creda, A B Dick, Express Lifts, GEC Alsthom (50%), GPT (60%), General Domestic Appliances (50%), Gilbarco, Hotpoint, Marconi, Picker International, Plessey Semiconductors, Redring, Yarrow Shipbuilders, Xpelair
Size £5.6 billion sales, £7.6 billion stock market value, 93,200 employees
5-year growth sales -5%, earnings per share 4%, employment -36%
Solvency debt n/a, interest cover n/a
Political Donations 0
Charitable Donations £947,000

Major developments
1900 formed as General Electric Co
1963 Weinstock became managing director
1967 merged with AEI
1968 merged with English Electric
1979 bought A B Dick, Averys
1981 bought Picker International
1985 bought Yarrow Shipbuilders
1986 bid for Plessey blocked by Monopolies Commission
1987 bought Creda, Gilbarco, Lear Astronics

GENERAL ELECTRIC COMPANY

Share record

Return on shareholders' equity	%	17.78
5-year price high	p	366.0
5-year price low	p	167.0
Dividend yield	%	4.77
5-year high	%	7.39
5-year low	%	3.52
Price/earnings ratio		14.4
5-year high		18.4
5-year low		8.6

Share price performance (in pence)

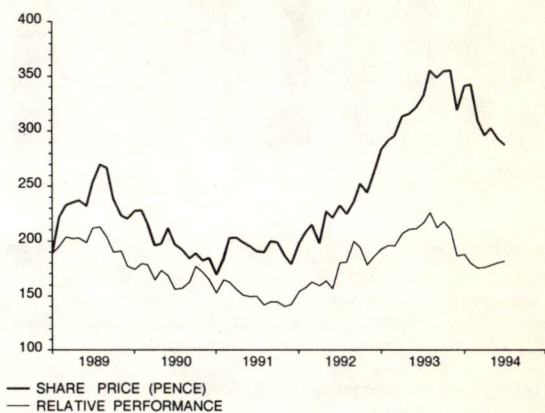

— SHARE PRICE (PENCE)
— RELATIVE PERFORMANCE

Financial record

		31/3/89	31/3/90	31/3/91	31/3/92	31/3/93
Total sales	£	5,878M	5,254M	6,043M	5,774M	5,612M
Pre-tax profit	£'000	796,700	872,100	817,600	829,000	863,000
Published retentions	£'000	314,100	433,400	251,700	279,000	258,000
Earnings per share	p	19.22	20.13	18.69	18.64	19.93
Dividend per share	p	7.80	9.25	9.25	9.60	10.30
Operating cash flow	£'000	-139M	-2,700	343,900	375,000	390,000
Net assets per share	p	135.11	126.71	121.92	130.16	144.01
Net debt/(cash)	£	-1,035M	-195M	-378M	-801M	-1,216M
Shareholders' funds	£	2,987M	2,328M	2,484M	2,712M	3,101M
Return on capital	%	23.33	25.85	26.06	25.59	24.53
Profit margin	%	12.07	12.66	10.09	10.37	10.92
Sales per employee	£	40.53	48.90	50.98	54.99	60.20
Interest cover		-6.17	-5.50	-105.34	-33.50	-17.33
Dividend cover		2.46	2.18	2.02	1.94	1.94
Sales increase	%	5.86	-10.62	15.01	-4.45	-2.81
Earnings growth	%	13.68	4.72	-7.14	-0.26	6.93
Investment x depreciation		1.20	0.99	0.85	0.82	0.77
Investment as % assets		28.79	19.20	22.05	21.30	18.90
Number of employees		145,029	107,435	118,529	104,995	93,288

GENERAL ELECTRIC COMPANY plc

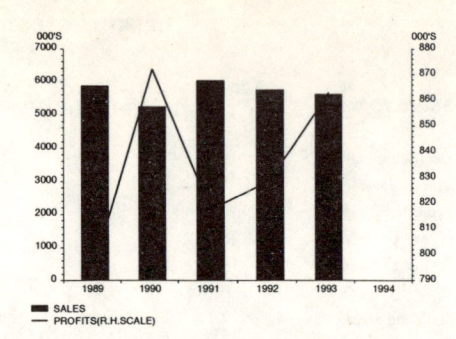

Employment

Sales and profits

1988 merged telecoms interests with Plessey to form GPT
1989 joint ventures formed with Alsthom in power systems and GE of the US in domestic appliances; takeover of Plessey jointly with Siemens approved by Monpolies Commission
1993 abandoned talks to buy Thorn-EMI defence interests; fruitless talks on merger with British Aerospace
1994 bought Ferranti defence businesses; shareholders asked to approve Lord Weinstock staying until 1996

Outlook

Lord Weinstock has been managing director of GEC since 1963 – a length of tenure challenged among leaders of large UK companies only by Barrie Stephens at Siebe and Tiny Rowland at Lonrho. Judgements still vary widely with regard to Weinstock's management of GEC over the years. The group is said by critics to have coasted along on the back of lucrative defence contracts, which enabled it to ignore or avoid serious strategic issues. GEC certainly did relatively little during the 1970s and 1980s so far as corporate moves are concerned. This was partly due to Lord Weinstock's legendary tightness with his shareholders' money, and partly due to the fact that some deals he wished to do were blocked by rulings of the Monopolies Commission or by the nationalistic interests of other governments. It is also true that some of his business transactions did not prove successful in the long run. Medical equipment (Picker) has continued to be a problem, for example. And Lord Weinstock himself has admitted he should never have got out of television production, while not moving into consumer electronics was perhaps a missed opportunity.

During the 1980s boom, corporate inactivity (and the resulting cash mountain) led GEC to be seen as a very sleepy company, reluctant to move ahead. In the recession-hit 1990s, however, that seemed less like a criticism than it used to, and, in any case, Lord Weinstock has a number of big deals under his belt. The basis for the modern GEC, in which a UK electrical-appliance maker was transformed into a diverse industrial conglomerate, was established during the late-1960s burst of activity which brought AEI and English Electric into the group. No equally significant moves were made until the late 1980s, but in the interim GEC acquired international interests and moved into lighter engineering with the purchases of office equipment company A B Dick, weighing and measuring machine specialists Avery, and petrol-pump maker Gilbarco.

In the late 1980s the group achieved its long-held ambition to acquire Plessey (jointly with Siemens) and Ferranti's defence-systems business, and set up substantial European joint ventures in power engineering (with Alsthom) and domestic electrical equipment (with General Electric of the US). This spate of joint ventures was very much in keeping with the times, but was perhaps a second best to the preferred option of European takeovers, which had proved impossible. It can also be seen as attempting to copy on a European level the rationalisation which the 1960s deals achieved in the UK – cutting costs, building market positions, combining research skills and budgets. The result of all the deals has produced a group with major strengths in the UK defence industry (albeit less advantageous in the era of the peace dividend), shares in companies with significant positions in 'white goods' and power engineering, and subsidiaries in many other areas of electrical equipment which would count as sizeable players if they were independent companies. On the other hand, GEC has some low-technology businesses which it would prefer to dispose of, such as Express lifts and Walsall Conduits.

These are relatively minor issues, however, compared to the questions of whether GEC could or should seek to acquire some or all of British Aerospace and, most difficult of all: who will succeed Lord Weinstock, how will the transition be managed, and is there any justification in the suspected plan for his son, Simon, to take over? The answers to these questions seemed as far away as ever in the summer of 1994. GEC reported little profits progress and a further increase in the cash pile, while Lord Weinstock announced that he wanted to stay on for at least another two years.

Shares

GEC missed out on the mid-1980s boom in earnings, and while its dividend was covered five times and its shares were part of every City portfolio, its relative share rating fell steadily. But the shares held up well during the market rout of October 1987, owing to the magnetic attraction of its £1.7 billion cash pile, although the rating bottomed the next year when the market got its nerve back.

The dividend was steadily increased, however, and the joint venture with Siemens to bid for Plessey in 1989 caught the City's imagination. For a brief time the shares handsomely outperformed the market but the dynamic image faded within a year, and despite further joint ventures and dividend hikes, the rating sagged. Apart from a brief flurry during the Gulf War in 1991, the relative rating dropped and hit the floor in 1991. The company's shares had nearly halved in value in eight years (relative to the market).

The big shock that year was that for the first time within memory the dividend had not been raised. Amid the City inquest investors recalled that GEC's ability to generate cash was supposed to make the dividend secure. However, analysts began to calculate what the group was worth and concluded that the fall in rating had been steeper than necessary.

The group's reputation was rapidly restored when the dividend was increased and the recession made returns elsewhere seem more precarious. Indeed, as a result of the failure of the UK economy to recover in 1992, the company's shares rose 41 per cent relative to a 15 per cent increase in the market as a whole. GEC's shares continued to gain ground in the 1993 bull market, thanks to steady earnings, good cash flow and a full order book, but then suffered at the end of the year after Lord Prior warned that profits would be static.

Corporate conscience

The group is second only to British Aerospace as a military supplier and exporter, and is also heavily involved in the nuclear industry, so that these are the main ethical matters of concern regarding GEC. Yarrow Shipbuilders makes frigates; Marconi provides torpedos; military communications and missiles; GEC Ferranti is a supplier to Tornado aircraft; while other subsidiaries also make components for the Tornado as well as armoured vehicles and missile systems. Military exports include night-vision devices, fire control systems, communications systems and power units. Customers have included the Saudi Air Force, Malaysia, Finland, Australia, Oman, Spain, Canada, the Netherlands and Germany.

GEC companies are also members of the British Nuclear Forum. GEC Alsthom has supplied power plant to Sellafield and the Daya Bay nuclear power station in China; NNC has done development work on Dounreay; and other parts of the group are involved in making nuclear containers, radioactive waste treatment systems, and nuclear dosimeters.

The group is also implicated to some extent in other issues of conscience. It has some operations in countries with questionable regimes (mainly India). Regarding employment, environmental and community issues, however, GEC performs rather better than might be expected. It is no longer a member of BITC but does make community donations and operates a payroll-giving scheme. It has made substantial efforts on equal opportunities, especially compared to some engineering companies whose pratices leave a lot to be desired. There is a female executive director and formal monitoring of the numbers of women and ethnic minorities employed. While GEC does not go in for group-wide approaches to most things, some units do have crèche facilities. The health and safety record is also fairly good.

There have been no convictions for water pollution, but there are some examples of discharge consents being exceeded. GEC came rather late to environmental issues, but has now begun to take them more seriously, and has made a commitment to phasing out use of CFCs by 1996. It has also done work for dam projects in Third World countries such as Brazil – projects that have serious environmental implications.

Corporate governance

Separate Chairman and Chief Executive Y
Number of Directors 17
Number of Non-Executive Directors 7
(7 Independent Directors)
Insulated Directors None

Board Committees
Audit: Y   Remuneration: Y

Remuneration

Year end	31.03.91	31.03.92	31.03.93
Total board £M	3.40	3.79	3.24
% change		11	3
Highest paid £	469,000	472,000	514,000
% change		1	9

Board
Lord Weinstock *Chief Executive*
Bates, M R *Executive Director*
Dixson, Dr M C S *Executive Director*
Lester, M *Executive Director*
Leppitt, A J *Executive Director*
MacBean, Dr I G *Executive Director*
Morrison, Sara *Executive Director*

Reynolds, R G *Executive Director*
Weinstock, Simon *Executive Director*
Newlands, D B *Finance Director*
Artus, Ronald E *Independent Non-Executive*
de Ferranti, S Z *Independent Non-Executive*
Giraud, A L Y *Independent Non-Executive*
Harding, Sir Christopher *Independent Non-Executive*
Lord Rees-Mogg *Independent Non-Executive*
Scholey, Sir David *Independent Non-Executive*
Lord Prior *Non-Executive Chairman*

The company's boardroom is comparatively large, with a broad non-executive contingent. Despite references to the Cadbury Code by chairman Lord Prior in his 1992 annual statement, there was subsequently no explanation of how board committees work. But the company is one of the very few in the top rank to have appointed a woman as an executive director. There is no disclosure of the basis on which pay increases are awarded, nor any elements of performance bonus.

GKN plc

P O Box 55, Ipsley, Church Lane, Redditch, Worcs B98 0TL
Tel: 01527 517715
Chairman and chief executive Sir David Lees
Main subsidiaries Sankey Vending, GKN Chep (70%), Cleanaway (50%), Westland
Size £2 billion sales, £2.1 billion stock market value, 27,500 employees
5-year growth sales -4%, earnings per share -61%, employment -25%
Solvency debt = 2% shareholders' funds, interest cover 5 times
Political donations £25,000 Conservative Party
Charitable donations £174,534

Major developments
1900 formed as Guest, Keen and Co
1902 merged to become Guest, Keen and Nettlefolds
1972 bought Firth Cleveland
1974 launch of Chep pallet joint venture in UK
1984 agreed bid for AE blocked by Monopolies Commission
1986 became GKN plc; remaining steel interests put into United Engineering Steels joint venture with British Steel
1988 bought stake in Westland Group
1994 acquired rest of Westland

Outlook
Steel used to be GKN's life-blood, but now it is getting thinner by the year. As Guest, Keen and Nettlefolds (until 1986, when the name was abbreviated to GKN), the company lost its direct interests in steel through nationalisation in the 1960s, but it was still 'one of the world's major engineering groups and the largest user of steel in the UK,' as the company modestly put it in the early 1970s. Little did it know then that this was not a very promising position to be in as the UK manufacturing sector prepared to meet the onslaught of inflation and recession.

Steel still features in the group's businesses, but to nothing like the same extent. Once a great user of steel, the car-parts business now focuses more on transmission products. GKN initially moved into services through its scaffolding interests and the Sankey vending machine business – both subsidiaries originally acquired because they used steel. GKN is also still a UK manufacturer, but it is by no means as great as it was. And the fact that it now relies less upon steel and upon the UK explains why the recession of the 1990s was not as disastrous for GKN as that of the early 1980s. In 1980 the group made a small loss of £1 million, which sounds minimal until one compares it with the profit in 1979 of £126 million. This last figure casts a dismal light on the 1993 profits performance of £128 million, even without adjusting for inflation.

Nevertheless, GKN is widely regarded as having done a good job during the 1980s. It cleared out some unpromising businesses; it reduced its reliance on the UK manufacturing sector by building up a service division; and it further reduced its reliance on the UK by expanding operations abroad. None of this made GKN immune from recession, but it made it better able to cope, aided by careful cash management, a cautious approach born of the disasters of the early 1980s (though not careful enough to avoid paying an uncovered dividend 1991), and a solid, profitable product like the constant velocity joint, used in vehicle axles. The group might have entered the 1990s in even better shape but for its one strategic mistake – the move into the defence business with a stake in Westland helicopters and tank manufacturing. Undeterred by the difficulties of military sales, however, GKN acquired the rest of Westland after a hostile bid in 1994.

Like other car-component suppliers, GKN is benefiting from the influx of Japanese manufacturers setting up in Britain. But the company has not been sitting around waiting: it has long been a European manufacturer of car parts, with sales from the Continent surpassing those from the UK in 1989. And the growth of Japanese manufacturers in the US has also helped spread the number of customers and offset the decline of business from Ford. Major new orders in the US have led to a substantial expansion of GKN's manufacturing capacity there, with a $50 million investment being announced towards the end of 1992. True to an international instinct which has guided GKN for decades, the group has also established a foothold in south-east Asia, with a joint venture in Malaysia.

Given the success of the traditional engineering side of the group, it is difficult now to see the sense of putting so much money and effort into building up

GKN

Share record

Return on shareholdes' equity	%	8.88
5-year price high	p	624.0
5-year price low	p	268.3
Dividend yield	%	4.13
5-year high	%	9.94
5-year low	%	4.11
Price/earnings ratio		27.3
5-year high		27.5
5-year low		5.5

Share price performance (in pence)

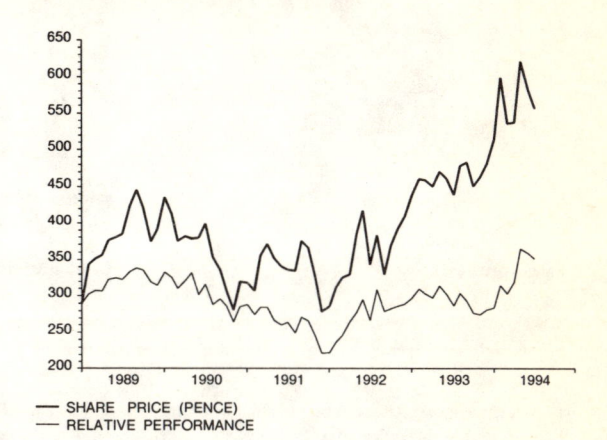

— SHARE PRICE (PENCE)
— RELATIVE PERFORMANCE

Financial record

		31/12/89	31/12/90	31/12/91	31/12/92	31/12/93
Total sales	£	2,115M	2,040M	1,925M	1,994M	2,2022M
Pre-tax profit	£'000	220,900	179,300	110,100	140,100	128,400
Published retentions	£'000	72,500	-6,500	-14,900	-2,300	-13,100
Earnings per share	p	52.13	31.77	14.38	20.80	20.41
Dividend per share	p	19.51	20.00	20.00	20.00	20.00
Operating cash flow	£'000	-7,700	62,600	78,000	49,200	158,500
Net assets per share	p	474.64	428.19	431.71	429.34	388.73
Net debt/(cash)	£'000	301,700	220,000	178,900	156,900	10,100
Shareholders' funds	£'000	665,100	680,100	662,500	654,700	655,700
Return on capital	%	26.09	20.93	13.58	15.46	14.81
Profit margin	%	7.77	5.95	4.24	5.81	5.03
Sales per employee	£	57.56	60.18	61.37	67.59	73.57
Interest cover		5.89	4.45	3.82	6.06	5.14
Dividend cover		2.67	1.59	0.72	1.04	1.02
Sales increase	%	6.41	-3.52	-5.63	3.54	1.44
Earnings growth	%	20.93	-39.05	-54.73	44.60	-1.87
Investment x depreciation		1.68	1.35	0.63	0.79	0.92
Investment as % assets		19.32	15.86	7.38	9.01	10.82
Number of employees		36,737	33,904	31,372	29,495	27,487

262   GKN plc

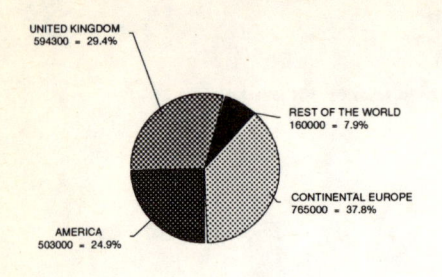

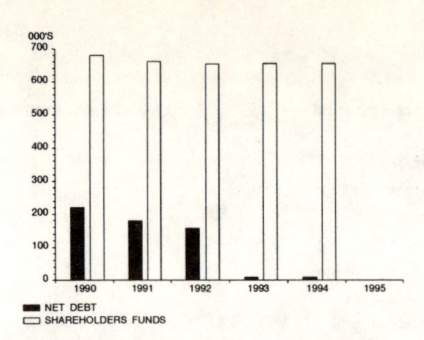

Sales analysis

UNITED KINGDOM 594300 = 29.4%
REST OF THE WORLD 160000 = 7.9%
CONTINENTAL EUROPE 765000 = 37.8%
AMERICA 503000 = 24.9%

Debt and shareholders' funds

000'S, 1990–1995
■ NET DEBT
□ SHAREHOLDERS FUNDS

---

a service operation. At one time the strategy seemed a good idea – in order to offset the anticipated decline in manufacturing and to lessen dependence on the car industry. But the performance of services in recession was disappointing, the influence of the slump in the building industry being an important factor, along with the service division's greater reliance on the UK. The latter is being addressed, notably by expansion of the Chep pallet-hire business into the US – an enormous project which carries great uncertainties but could deliver huge returns, if it works. With GKN's reputation to support it, it should succeed, but the group knows from its past that reputations count for nothing in the face of vicious economic circumstances.

Shares

Like the UK motor industry, GKN's shares have seen better times – the early 1970s, to be precise. While the actual price of shares has soared since then, their value compared with the whole stock market has shrivelled. Since 1965 the company's shares have underperformed the market by some 80 per cent, although there have been periods when it clawed back some of the lost ground. The last such phase came in 1985 as the group sold off some of its traditional steel businesses and concentrated on services and car components.

There followed a spell of renewed underperformance, enlivened by bids and steady expansion. The group even rejoined the FTSE 100 index in 1989, although its presence in the élite has been erratic since then. The shares fell despite record profits and rising dividend in 1990 and 1991 reflecting the management's pessimism about the dismal outlook for industry through the deepest part of the recession. But the group conserved its cash and held its dividend, as a result of which the shares were re-rated in 1992. The UK's exit from the ERM enabled the group to benefit from the weak pound, so that by 1993 the shares were wanted again in anticipation of an economic recovery. The Westland victory brought even more supporters.

Corporate conscience

GKN's main products are used in the production of cars; the company also makes armoured vehicles and Westland helicopters. Its service operations include Cleanaway, a waste-management company. All this exposes the group to several important areas of concern, notably greenhouse gases and other environmentally unfriendly by-products, and warfare. As well as the obvious military connections, the associated company United Engineering Steels makes components for Tornado aircraft, while Chesterfield Cylinders supplies high-pressure gas cylinders for torpedo firing and other military uses. (These two companies are also suppliers to the nuclear industry.) Even GKN Axles manufactures axles for military vehicles. Some of GKN's products are for export as well as the domestic market: for instance, Simba personnel carriers are sold to the Phillipines.

While these activities will be distasteful to some people, in carrying them out GKN is a reasonably conscientious company. It is a member of BITC and the Per Cent Club, is highly unionised and has a good employment record and reputation, including equal opportunities training of recruiters, and monitoring of the numbers of female personnel. It has full environmental policy including independent environmental audit and has sponsored conservation projects. It is committed to phasing out CFCs (currently used as cleaning agents) by 1996.

GKN's record reflects this mixed, perhaps subdued, approach. There have been several health and safety convictions and one for water pollution in

1991. Also, Cleanaway (despite its name) broke consent levels several times in 1992/3 at its Pitsea treatment plant.

GKN has some operations in countries which threaten human rights, such as India and Mexico.

Corporate governance

Separate Chairman and Chief Executive N
Number of Directors 11
Number of Non-Executive Directors 5
(5 Independent Directors)
Insulated Directors Ch, CE

Board Committees
Audit: Y   Remuneration: Y

Remuneration

Year end	31.12.91	31.12.92	31.12.93
Total board £M	1.63	1.94	1.76
% change	6	19	-9
Highest paid £	271,000	289,000	332,347
% change	13	7	15

Board
Lees, Sir David *Chairman & Chief Executive*
Beresford, Marcus *Executive Director*
Bonner, Trevor C *Executive Director*
Daly, Alec *Executive Director*
Insch, Brian D *Executive Director*
Turner, David *Finance Director*
Cazalet, Sir Peter *Non-Executive Deputy Chairman*
Davies, Howard J *Independent Non-Executive*
Nicholson, Sir Bryan *Independent Non-Executive*
Seipp, Dr Walter *Independent Non-Executive*
Parker, Dr John *Independent Non-Executive*

Sir David Lees continues to combine the roles of chairman and chief executive, and argued in his report on 1992 that this was compatible with the Cadbury recommendations because the group has sufficient, and sufficiently strong, independent directors, headed by a recognised senior member. The annual report indicates that this role is carried out by deputy chairman Sir Peter Cazalet. The annual report also details the workings of board committees, and gives some details of directors' bonus payments.

GRANADA GROUP plc

36 Golden Square, London W1R 4AH
Tel: 0171 734 8080
Chairman Alex Bernstein
Chief Executive Gerry Robinson
Main brands and subsidiaries LWT, Sutcliffe Catering, Spring Grove Services
Size £1.6 billion sales, £3.1 billion stock market value, 28,400 employees

5-year growth sales -1%, earnings per share -14%, employment 1%
Solvency debt = 86% shareholders' funds, interest cover 7 times
Political donations 0
Charitable donations £0.3 million

Major developments

1934 formed as Granada Theatres
1957 became Granada Group, after winning north west ITV franchise
1984 bought Rediffusion TV rental from BET
1985 bought SMS, CFM computer services
1986 bought Laskys
1988 bought Electronic Rentals, DPCE computer services
1989 sold Laskys to Kingfisher
1991 boardroom shake-up; bingo clubs sold; sold Canadian TV rental business; retained north west ITV licence
1993 bought Sutcliffe Services
1994 bought LWT

Outlook

Granada has tried hard over many years to be something other than a television company. It is more than just a television franchise, but its other main business is television rental. These two activities contribute the bulk of profits, just as they did 20 years ago, yet they remain vulnerable, so the need for diversification has not diminished, even if the company's history suggests that the prospects for success are not great.

There are parallels with its leisure sector rival Rank, with the important difference that Granada did not stumble upon a lucrative sideline such as Xerox. (The similarities were so great that Rank attempted a takeover in the mid-1980s, which was prevented only by the intervention of the Independent Broadcasting Authority.) The group began as a theatre company in 1934, and subsequently moved into cinemas and related areas of the leisure industry. Like Rank, Granada has or used to have a foothold in bingo halls, motorway service areas, ten-pin bowling and nightclubs. But while Rank's energies were concentrated mainly on the film industry, Granada moved into independent television (ITV) at its inception, and has held the franchise in north-west England ever since.

For many years this was a very profitable business, but the new franchise arrangements which commenced in 1992, and the advent of satellite and cable television, have diminished its attractions. At the same time the prospects for the television rental operation appear to be declining. Renting televisions and video recorders made sense when the equipment was erratic and the capital outlay was substantial. But that is no longer the case, and while the rapid technological developments in the field – plus the recession – might have been expected to give renting a boost, the market continues to shrink, as it has done since the early 1980s.

GRANADA

Share record

Return on shareholders' equity	%	23.19
5-year price high	p	596.0
5-year price low	p	129.4
Dividend yield	%	2.12
5-year high	%	12.24
5-year low	%	1.84
Price/earnings ratio		19.3
5-year high		29.6
5-year low		3.9

Share price performance (in pence)

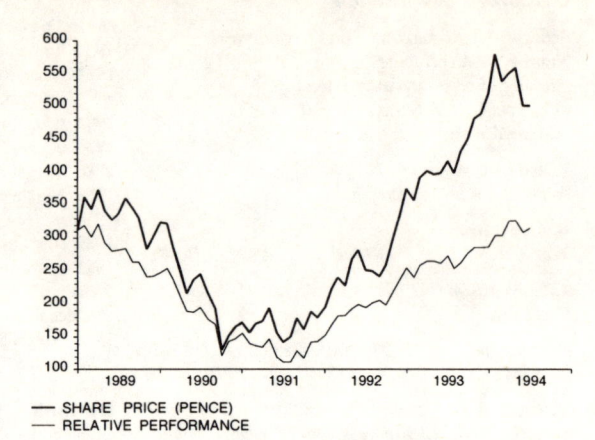

— SHARE PRICE (PENCE)
— RELATIVE PERFORMANCE

Financial record

		30/9/89	30/9/90	30/9/91	30/9/92	30/9/93
Total sales	£	1,631M	1,391M	1,391M	1,328M	1,615M
Pre-tax profit	£'000	164,100	121,400	73,300	130,000	182,800
Published retentions	£'000	71,300	17,300	-29,100	34,400	73,500
Earnings per share	p	31.05	22.26	11.85	18.76	26.32
Dividend per share	p	11.88	11.88	7.00	7.70	8.75
Operating cash flow	£'000	39,600	-50,900	122,200	41,200	130,100
Net assets per share	p	246.32	317.81	254.82	214.38	220.47
Net debt/(cash)	£'000	326,100	435,900	262,100	218,500	402,200
Shareholders' funds	£'000	510,700	508,700	527,600	561,500	464,300
Return on capital	%	27.18	20.04	16.48	20.32	24.22
Profit margin	%	10.00	8.74	5.29	9.77	11.29
Sales per employee	£	58.71	55.06	61.64	72.25	57.63
Interest cover		5.56	3.74	2.42	4.98	7.31
Dividend cover		2.61	1.87	1.69	2.44	3.01
Sales increase	%	11.70	-14.74	0.01	-4.48	21.58
Earnings growth	%	23.01	-28.33	-46.75	58.24	40.31
Investment x depreciation		0.96	1.63	0.25	1.02	0.93
Investment as % assets		14.77	22.39	4.37	17.06	15.05
Number of employees		27,782	25,257	22,562	18,385	28,025

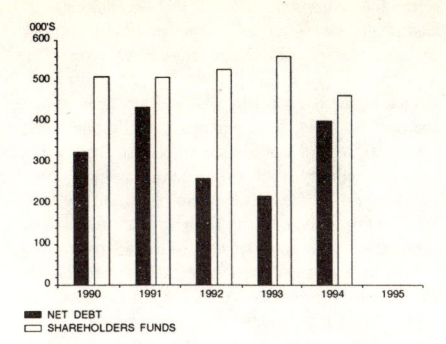

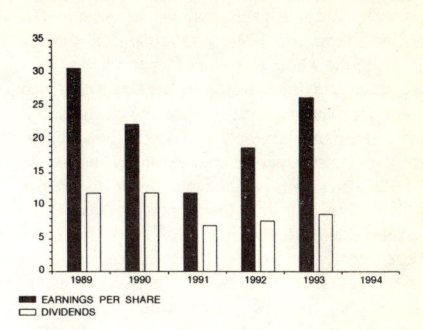

Debt and shareholders' funds

Earnings and dividends

The unexciting prospects for these two core businesses explain the need to diversify. Like most companies, however, Granada has found it extremely difficult to move into new, unrelated areas. And, indeed, following the easing of restrictions on ITV ownership, Granada invested more heavily in one of its existing businesses with the £765 million acquisition of London Weekend Television – the first hostile takeover battle in UK television, an industry which, despite its glamorous image, is under pressure regarding its long-term revenue. Few would bet against Granada taking a tilt at Yorkshire Tyne Tees if the takeover rules are relaxed still further. The LWT deal and the price brinkmanship demonstrated by Granada did, however, encourage the City to believe that the group keeps its money under tight control, although the company still has to demonstrate that rationalisation between Granada and LWT will go ahead as indicated.

Television rental was intended to be a 'cash cow' – a mature business providing money for expansion elsewhere – and to that end it was built up by a series of acquisitions to give it control of the market. That cash was not needed for, and growth would not come from, the television franchise, but other leisure interests could fulfil that role. In addition, the group was deemed to be too dependent on UK consumer spending, so it needed to diversify both internationally and into industrial markets. The answer, it seemed, was to extend the rental operation abroad, and to use the group's service skills to build a computer service operation. Both proved expensive mistakes, although Granada has persisted with computer services. Almost £170 million was spent acquiring computer service companies, notably DPCE, but in the five years from 1985 to 1990 the accumulated operating profits (before interest) did not quite reach £50 million, and in 1991 there was a £12 million loss. The division is now back in profit, thanks to aggressive cost-cutting, but it remains doubtful whether it will ever repay the investment. Overseas developments fared no better, while the leisure operations appear to be too fragmented and the main activity – motorway services – is exposed to deregulation.

Mr Lewis was succeeded in 1991 by another outsider, Gerry Robinson, though the latter has a background in service industry. Mr Robinson impressed the City with his initial success in driving down costs, and simultaneously depressed fans of Granada's history of high-quality programme-making with his cost-cutting drive, which also drove out long-standing television mogul David Plowright. Fears that an eye on the bottom line might damage programming quality not only at Granada but also, now, at LWT were aired copiously during the bid battle.

Like Pearson, Granada retains an investment in BSkyB as a hangover from its launch investment in the ill-fated BSB. This promises to be a worthwhile profit provider in the longer term, to the benefit of Granada as its terrestrial TV stations start to lose advertising share to 'new media' such as cable, Channel 5 and Sky. Granada is, however, thought to 'be willing' to sell its Sky stake for the right price.

Granada has restored order to its house, and a certain amount of credibility to its reputation in the City, but it seems little further down the road to escaping its television heritage than it was 15 years ago, while risking damage to that heritage in the meantime.

Shares

Granada's rating suffered in the late 1980s as it became clear that the board's attempt to switch its strong cash flow into areas of supposed faster growth was failing. The group fell out of the FTSE 100 index in 1989. Growing disquiet among investors came to a head that year when the group sold Lasky's for £9 million, having paid £30 million for it.

The fall in the shares accelerated the following

year: analysts threw doubt on the management's judgement as profits fell and debt rose, and there were even doubts that the group would retain its ITV franchise. Between 1989 and 1991 the shares underperformed the whole market by 50 per cent and there was talk of a major rights issue; large investors were pressing for changes on the board. When the deeply discounted rights issue came in 1991, it was bigger than the market expected and was in addition to the sale of the bingo business. Despite Mr Lewis's departure, the shares hit their lowest point relative to the market in the middle of 1991.

The franchise was retained and the steady re-rating that followed was helped by sales of assets, so that by mid-1992 the shares had outperformed the market by nearly 80 per cent. Shares benefited from optimism following retention of the franchise and by the media hype which became a market hallmark of late 1993 as takeover regulations were relaxed. Even issuing shares to pay for LWT did not fully dampen investors' ardour.

Corporate conscience
Granada offends on the ethical issue of the sale of tobacco and drinks because of its entertainment interests, and the computer services subsidiary has some military contracts. Otherwise, this is a relatively 'clean' company. It has joined the Per Cent Club and operates an adequate equal opportunities but not environmental policy. It has suffered one adverse judgement (against its motorway service stations) from the ASA in recent years, as has the new subsidiary LWT.

Corporate governance
Separate Chairman and Chief Executive Y
Number of Directors 10
Number of Non-Executive Directors 4
(4 Independent Directors)
Insulated Directors MD

Board Committees
Audit: Y   Remuneration: Y

Remuneration
Year end	30.09.91	30.09.92	30.09.93
Total board £M	1.16	1.65	1.51
% change	-9	43	9
Highest paid £	235,000	346,000	407,000
% change	0	47	18

Board
Robinson, Gerry *Chief Executive*
Bernstein, Alex *Executive Chairman*
Allen, Charles *Executive Director*
Parrott, Graham *Executive Director*
Wallace, Graham *Executive Director*
Staunton, Henry *Finance Director*
Ashworth, Dr John *Independent Non-Executive*
Clements, Alan W *Independent Non-Executive*
Martin, Ian A *Independent Non-Executive*
Orr, Michael *Independent Non-Executive*

Granada had a separate chairman and chief executive before the boardroom shake-up in 1991, demonstrating that this measure is not always proof against poor performance and falling out among directors. The roles are sill separate, but, given that the chairman is a scion of the founding family, and has been on the board since 1964, it is perhaps more important to have a majority of independent directors. They do not form a majority, but their numbers have been strengthened by the appointment of Ian Martin and Michael Orr, although both of these share Grand Met connections with new chief executive Gerry Robinson. In his chairman's report, Alex Bernstein claims that the group complies with the main Cadbury recommendations, providing some information on the audit, remuneration and nomination committees, although little on directors' pay.

THE GREAT UNIVERSAL STORES plc

Universal House, Devonshire Street, Manchester
M60 6EL
Tel: 0161 273 8282
Chairman Lord Wolfson of Marylebone
Deputy chairman Richard Pugh
Substantial shareholdings Wolfson Foundation 9% ordinary shares
Main brands and subsidiaries All Counties Insurance Company, Burberrys, Family Album, Family Hampers, General Guarantee Corporation, Kays, Marshall Ward, Scotch House, White Arrow Express
Size £2.8 billion sales, £5.6 billion stock market value, 29,600 employees
5-year growth sales 7%, earnings per share 25%, employment -8%
Solvency debt n/a, interest cover n/a
Political donations 0
Charitable donations £42,000

Major developments
1917 formed as Universal Stores
1931 became public as Great Universal Stores
1986 sold Thoms, Times Furnishing and Home Charm to Harris Queensway
1987 bought Superior Acceptance Corporation Ltd of Canada
1988 bought Pantharella plc and Andy Hampers Ltd
1991 founder Sir Isaac Wolfson died
1993 share reorganisation

Outlook
Few companies as large and as successful as Great Universal Stores (GUS) are as withdrawn, as conservative, or – to be frank – as dull. Associated British Foods (ABF) is the only close contender. Like ABF,

THE GREAT UNIVERSAL STORES

Share record

Return on shareholders' equity	%	9.44
5-year price high	p	654.0
5-year price low	p	178.9
Dividend yield	%	2.83
5-year high	%	3.57
5-year low	%	1.36
Price/earnings ratio		16.7
5-year high		20.3
5-year low		6.8

Share price performance (in pence)

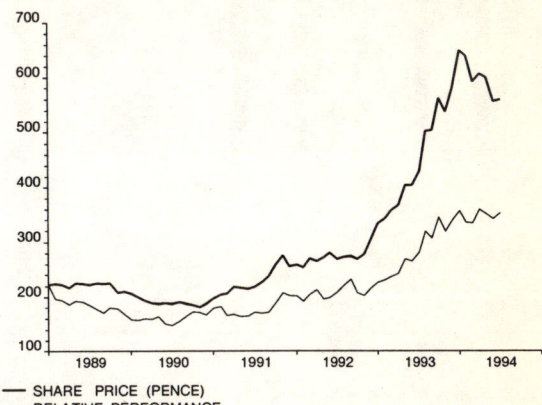

— SHARE PRICE (PENCE)
— RELATIVE PERFORMANCE

Financial record

		31/3/89	31/3/90	31/3/91	31/3/92	31/3/93
Total sales	£	2,626M	2,693M	2,523M	2,597M	2,810M
Pre-tax profit	£'000	392,000	411,400	419,200	441,500	471,400
Published retentions	£'000	219,500	197,400	206,900	210,400	208,000
Earnings per share	p	14.05	14.87	15.44	16.39	17.55
Dividend per share	p	4.37	4.79	5.21	5.56	6.11
Operating cash flow	£'000	33,500	104,900	253,000	309,200	245,300
Net assets per share	p	163.90	174.37	176.76	189.37	203.41
Net debt/(cash)	£	-449M	-587M	-845M	-1,155M	-1,420M
Shareholders' funds	£	2,669M	2,828M	2,846M	3,048M	3,298M
Return on capital	%	14.28	13.79	13.70	13.84	13.68
Profit margin	%	14.93	15.28	16.62	16.95	16.72
Sales per employee	£	81.66	87.76	100.80	107.74	94.85
Interest cover		-7.31	-4.16	-2.59	-2.43	-2.64
Dividend cover		3.21	3.10	2.96	2.96	2.87
Sales increase	%	4.54	2.55	-6.31	2.94	8.21
Earnings growth	%	3.59	5.81	3.83	6.14	7.08
Investment x depreciation		1.53	1.65	0.73	0.51	0.66
Investment as % assets		4.60	5.84	3.40	2.49	3.29
Number of employees		32,156	30,686	25,028	24,106	29,631

THE GREAT UNIVERSAL STORES plc

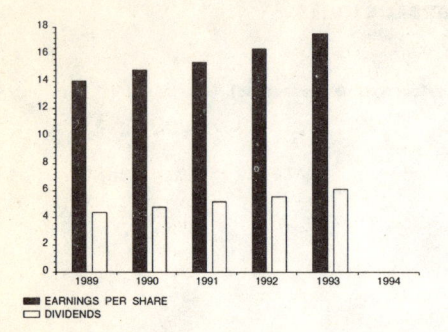

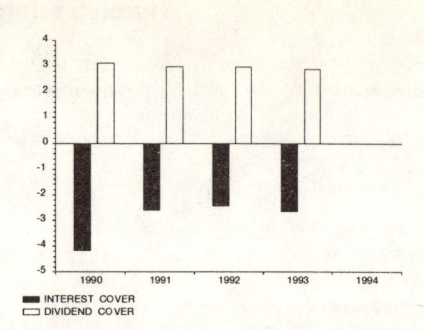

Earnings and dividends

Interest and dividend cover

GUS prefers to keep itself to itself, and to keep its profits to itself as well: thanks partly to a parsimonious dividend policy, GUS has built up a huge cash pile.

Exciting possibilities lurk in the shadows of GUS, waiting to break out. Burberry is a superb international brand, the rump of a retail operation which used to include Times Furnishing, the Paige fashion chain and Home Charm DIY outlets. Retail operations remain in North America and South Africa. The group's credit, banking and information division is a powerful financial force, and could perhaps make the banks quake if its flexed its muscles to the full. And GUS owns the freeholds of more than £700 million worth of properties. The history of the retail businesses is a good argument for GUS treading carefully in that sector, however. Times Furnishing and Home Charm were sold to Sir Phil Harris when Harris Queensway was still flourishing. (Sir Phil remains on the board, the only non-executive at the start of 1993, but the fate of his chain highlights the danger of adventurism.)

The profits arising from property rentals, banking and financial services are generally higher than those generated by the real business of the group – mail order. This is perhaps just as well, since the mail-order industry has seemed to be in steady decline for years, but the decline is slow and has not prevented GUS scoring a remarkable record of increasing profits every year since the Second World War.

The mail-order industry does have problems, though. The business was built on the basis of clubs, run by the companies' agents, who collected contributions from friends, family and work colleagues every week, and sold from the catalogue. In effect, mail order was an easy way of saving, or alternatively an easy form of credit. That system now belongs to another age, a 1950s era of tight money and even tighter credit. Even with the return of austerity in 1990s Britain, it seems remarkably out of date. Moreover, the agency system has disintegrated, with few agents now selling beyond their immediate family. So mail order has become 'home shopping', but the result is that agents have become expensive to run, taking account of both the price of catalogues and agents' commissions, as well as the cost of recruiting and training agents. GUS has a record better than most of using its agents efficiently, but it faces the apparently inexorable decline of the market just the same as every other player. And even though it remains clear market leader (ahead of privately owned Littlewoods), it lost substantial market share during the 1980s and faces new competition from Continental invaders.

All is not lost, however. Even in gentle decline and despite the recession which has ravaged so many of its competitors, the GUS profits juggernaut has continued to drive forward, even though, in a period of low interest rates, the group has derived less of the important income from its cash than in previous times. Continental operations have had a far tougher time than in the UK, although currency factors have helped earnings. And expansion is still underway in Asia and the Pacific region. Although GUS is a company that is far from setting the world alight, there continues to be a sense that the group will keep quietly up with the pack and may well achieve more than its glitzier rivals.

Shares

GUS's reputation for being one of the safest stocks available was founded on the security of the dividend and strength of the yield. While the retail-mad stock market of the 1980s chased other shares higher in the boom, leaving GUS's rating to sag, the company smartly outperformed the market in relative terms during the crash of October 1987. Its defensive qualities seemed to impress even its own board, which said it wanted to buy in the company's shares in 1988. But after this stimulus wore off there was a period of relative underperformance which lasted until the recession began to affect most shares in 1990. GUS's defensive qualities then came into their own once more, attaining a particularly high peak in the price during the Gulf crisis.

In 1991 the shares rose following the death of the group's founder, Sir Isaac Wolfson, but few expected the rise to last. It appeared, however, that the shares were being re-rated as the City came to appreciate a solid earnings performance, enhanced by the effect of high interest rates on its cash pile. The shares outperformed both the stores sector and the market as a whole through into 1992. The rating slowed relative to the bull market which followed the UK's exit from the ERM, but the group again surprised pundits with the strength of its cash generation.

The company's shares soared relative to the FTSE index in 1992-3, helped by the fashionable enfranchisement of the non-voting 'A' stock which removed the protection that had been afforded by leaving all the votes in the hands of ordinary shareholders – that is the founding Wolfson family for the most part. Analysts see GUS looking for ways of returning money to shareholders, which should continue to buoy up the market price, in the absence of much greater than expected capital spending or a major acquisition.

Corporate conscience

GUS is notoriously shy. It has always appeared to see no reason why outsiders (which seems to include shareholders) should want to know anything about the company that is not absolutely required by law, nor why it should be interested in anything which is not directly related to making profits. This has begun to change in recent years, however. But GUS still makes tiny charitable donations, has no equal opportunities or environmental policies and appears to care little about these or other issues of conscience. In South Africa, where it employs about 1,500 black African workers, it pays a few below even a minimum wage level.

The group uses some tropical hardwoods in furniture, and the mail-order catalogues have been subject to several adverse judgements from the ASA 7 times in the latest two years.

Corporate Governance

Separate Chairman and Chief Executive N
Number of Directors 11
Number of Non-Executive Directors 5
(4 Independent Directors)
Insulated Directors None

Board Committees
Audit: N   Remuneration: N

Remuneration

Year end	31.03.91	31.03.92	31.03.93
Total board £M	0.90	1.00	1.20
% change		11	20
Highest paid £	306,500	341,600	374,600
% change		12	10

Board

Lord Wolfson of Marylebone *Chairman & Chief Executive*
Barnes, Eric M *Executive Director*
Barnett, Victor J *Executive Director*
Harris, Paul M *Executive Director*
Peacock, Stanley T *Executive Director*
Pugh, Richard H C *Executive Director*
Harris, Sir Philip *Independent Non-Executive*
Blank, Victor *Independent Non-Executive*
Charkham, Jonathan *Independent Non-Executive*
Roberts, Derek *Independent Non-Executive*
Lord Wolfson of Sunningdale *Non-Executive*

GUS is one of those very private public companies which has bowed to the Cadbury Code and thrown a little light on its boardroom operations. It has appointed a raft of, largely independent, non-executive directors, even if the annual report for 1993 still gives little detail of what they actually do. Enfranchisement of the non-voting 'A' shares had added to the sense of corporate daylight. The company still shows remarkable restraint both regarding the amounts paid to its executives and the justification for those payments.

HANSON plc

1 Grosvenor Place, London SW1X 7JH
Tel: 0171 235 3455
Chairman Lord Hanson
Chief executive Derek Bonham
Main brands Castella, Panama, Henry Wintermans cigars; Embassy, John Player, Lambert & Butler, Regal cigarettes; Golden Virginia, St Bruno tobacco; Seven Seas health products; Rollalong cabins; Smith Meters; United Chair seating; Andersen Hickey office equipment
Main subsidiaries ARC, Butterley Brick, Cavenham Forest Industries (US), Gold Fields Mining Corporation, Imperial Tobacco, Jacuzzi (USA), Kaiser Cement (US), Lindustries, London Brick, Peabody (US), SCM Chemicals, Smith Corona (48%)
Size £9.8 billion sales, £13.0 billion stock market value, 71,000 employees
5-year growth sales 39%, earnings per share -29%, employment -20%
Solvency debt = 85% shareholders' funds, interest cover n/a

HANSON

Share record

Return on shareholders' equity	%	17.26
5-year price high	p	299.5
5-year price low	p	179.3
Dividend yield	%	5.64
5-year high	%	7.91
5-year low	%	4.15
Price/earnings ratio		19.5
5-year high		29.5
5-year low		10.2

Share price performance (in pence)

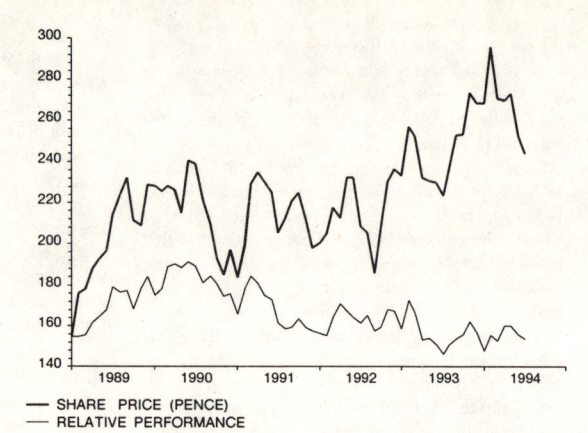

— SHARE PRICE (PENCE)
— RELATIVE PERFORMANCE

Financial record

		30/9/89	30/9/90	30/9/91	30/9/92	30/9/93
Total sales	£	6,998M	7,153M	7,691M	8,798M	9,760M
Pre-tax profit	£'000	1,064M	1,285M	1,149M	1,114M	992,000
Published retentions	£'000	764,000	501,000	577,000	824,000	183,000
Earnings per share	p	20.55	20.32	17.89	18.84	14.62
Dividend per share	p	8.50	10.40	11.00	5.50	11.40
Operating cash flow	£'000	1,051M	507,000	511,000	207,000	67,000
Net assets per share	p	192.45	219.87	246.36	294.07	351.93
Net debt/(cash)	£'000	806,000	-564M	-356M	768,000	3,348M
Shareholders' funds	£	1,086M	2,834M	3,325M	4,224M	3,953M
Return on capital	%	21.60	21.27	16.91	14.55	10.22
Profit margin	%	15.00	17.36	14.68	12.46	9.97
Sales per employee	£	78.63	89.41	109.87	117.31	137.46
Interest cover		-4.77	-5.51	-4.94	-22.37	-68.14
Dividend cover		2.43	1.95	1.64	3.43	1.28
Sales increase	%	-5.38	2.21	7.52	14.39	10.93
Earnings growth	%	18.27	-1.15	-11.97	5.35	-22.40
Investment x depreciation		1.28	1.03	0.07	0.87	0.80
Investment as % assets		6.59	3.68	0.24	2.39	1.93
Number of employees		89,000	80,000	70,000	75,000	71,000

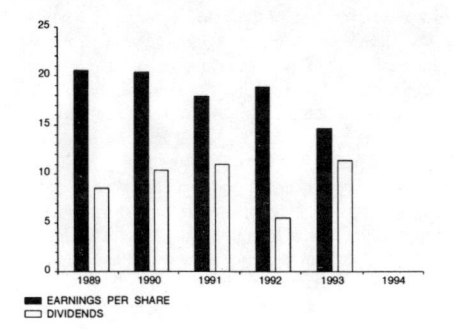

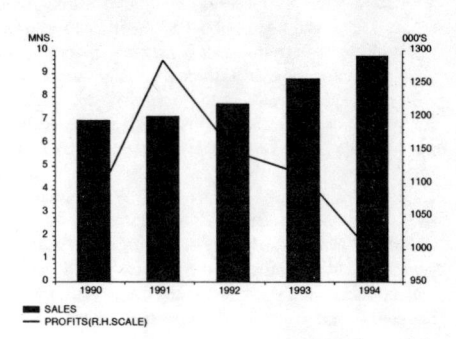

Earnings per share

Sales and profits

Political donations £115,000 Conservative Party and Centre for Policy Studies
Charitable donations £721,000

Major developments
1964 became public; bought Tillotson motor business
1969 name changed to Hanson Trust
1970 sold motor business
1975 bought Carisbrook (US)
1976 bought Hygrade (US)
1981 bought McDonough (US)
1982 bought British Ever Ready (Berec)
1982 sold Ever Ready European operations; bought United Drapery Stores
1983/4 sold Richard Shops, John Collier, Allders UDS units
1984 bought London Brick
1986 bought Imperial Group
1986 sold Imperial's hotels and pubs, Golden Wonder, Courage brewing and Ross Young's
1987 name changed to Hanson plc; bought Kidde (US)
1989 bought Consolidated Gold Fields
1990 bought Peabody Holdings; bought Cavenham Forest Industries
1991 bought Beazer plc; bought 2.8% stake in ICI
1992 sold ICI stake; sold Ever Ready; offer for Ranks Hovis McDougall beaten by Tomkins
1993 won legal battle for ownership of Costain's Australian coal mining; bought Quantum Chemicals
1994 sold office products company; floated Beazer; opened Hong Kong office

Outlook
The case of Hanson is the supreme example of the overweening role of financial markets in the Anglo-American economies. During the 1980s the group earned a reputation as one of Britain's 'best' companies, yet there was little pretence among Hanson's supporters that it produced any benefits for the British and American economies. Few would claim that Hanson has ever been particularly good at running businesses; some allege that it is actually bad at that basic function. The group's US supremo, Lord White, has even boasted that he never goes near the operating companies which he has bought.

To believers in the notion that businesses should struggle to benefit society as well as their shareholders, there is therefore some grim satisfaction in the sight of financial markets falling out of love with Hanson, as has happened in the 1990s.

During the 1980s the group established an unrivalled reputation for asset-trading: buying groups cheap and selling their component companies dear. In the UK the Imperial group provides the best, or worst, example. Imperial Tobacco had lost its way, like many tobacco companies, in trying to find something sensible to do with its tobacco cash flows. It had made one too many bad acquistions during the 1970s (the Howard Johnson hotel chain in the US), but in the early 1980s had begun to deal with the resulting problems. Too late: Hanson pounced, and despite an attempt to set up a business (as opposed to financial) deal with United Biscuits, Imperial went under the Hanson hammer.

Hanson paid about £2.5 billion for it, a huge sum even by its standards. At the time (1986) the group's sales were about £4 billion and shareholders' funds were a mere £1.6 billion. But in a very short while Hanson had recouped almost all (lent £200m), of this vast outlay in such deals as the sale of Golden Wonder to Dalgety, Courage breweries to Elders, and Ross Young's to United Biscuits. As a result, Hanson won the large and stable profits and cash flows of Imperial Tobacco for next to nothing.

The purchase of Imperial was noteworthy, but it was not unique. Hanson pulled off an even deal with chemicals group SCM, actually making a profit on the deal as well as receiving continuing earnings, before interest and tax, of about $200 million a year. Earlier in the 1980s the group had begun its love affair with the stock market through similar takeovers such as the Ever Ready battery company Berec and the retail group UDS. And these high-profile deals were merely larger versions of what the group had been doing since the mid-1960s.

Lord Hanson and his partner, Lord White, clearly have great skill in deal-making. But there is an underlying factor which prevents many in the business world from emulating them. Most people running businesses are interested in the business they are running. In many cases they have been in the business, or at least the industry, all their working lives; sometimes there are family or other emotional connections. That is a huge disadvantage when it comes to doing deals: it leads such people to pay too much for companies which they want to own too badly. One of the secrets of Hanson's success is that it cares not a jot what companies it owns: the companies are merely cash machines, vehicles for producing earnings per share.

This detachment is also crucial in squeezing as much as possible out of owned businesses before they are sold. Those who love the businesses they own will lavish 'too much' investment on them, will be reluctant to cut back research and development spending when times are hard, and will be slow to close loss-makers in the hope that they will recover. Hanson has therefore come in for much criticism for failing to invest sufficiently, for having short-term time horizons, for using tax havens to reduce its tax bill, and for leaving the companies it sells in a worse state than when they were bought.

This is a little unfair on Hanson. The culprit is surely the financial market structure and operation which not only allows but encourages such an approach. Accounting in the 1980s must also share some of the blame, especially for allowing acquisitive groups such as Hanson to bypass the profit and loss account with reorganisation costs, to hide the profits from asset-trading in its basic profit figures, and to inflate the value of acquired assets.

These weaknesses make it virtually impossible to draw absolute conclusions about the group's internal financial performance during the 1980s, though it is clear that dealing profits were responsible for a substantial part of profits growth over that period. At the end of the decade and in the early 1990s Hanson also earned huge sums by exploiting differential interest rates between the US and UK. Large deposits in high-interest Britain were offset by borrowings in low-interest (and depreciating) dollars, leaving this activity as one of the largest profit earners in 1989–91.

All this was fine so long as the financial markets were happy to turn a blind eye to it. But at the end of the 1980s analysts and investment managers began to worry about underlying profits growth, about the prospects for further large takeovers and large interest profits, and about what would happen to Hanson when its ageing leaders finally departed. The result was a downgrading of the group's share price, which only served to exacerbate the problem. A relatively low share price makes share-based acquisitions expensive, prohibitively so for any large deal. Yet despite the group's huge resources, it was not in a position to make large debt-based acquisitions either. Hanson's permitted borrowing limit soared to almost £20 billion after changes to its articles of association, but in practice investors would probably not be happy with debts as high this. Based on the traditional gearing ratio of debt to equity or net assets, some estimates suggest a practical borrowing limit of little more than £2 billion, smaller than the Imperial Tobacco bid, even without adjusting for inflation, and likely to have relatively little impact on a group of Hanson's current size.

Hemmed in by the difficulty of making a large deal pay, but with the need to make a deal to offset falling profits from spare cash, Hanson appears to have made some uncharacteristically poor decisions. Beginning with the purchase of Consolidated Gold Fields in 1989, the group has built up major resources interests – the kind of capital-intensive, commodity business which it avoided in the past. Through a series of deals and asset swaps following the ConsGold acquisition, Hanson has ended up owning Peabody, the largest US coal miner (the company was half-owned by Newmont Mining, which was half-owned by ConsGold), and Cavenham Forest Industries, a large US timber company. Then Hanson bought Beazer, a UK building company which had become one of North America's top two aggregates companies after an over-ambitious acquisition of Koppers. The asking price for Beazer was ostensibly less than £300 million in cash, but with the addition of Beazer's debt the price was almost £2 billion, and if the provisions Hanson subsequently set up are included as well, Beazer could cost a total of £3.6 billion. On the same basis, Hanson's foray into resources has cost a total of almost £11 billion, bringing almost a third of the group's profits from these companies, albeit a poor return on the capital invested. The Beazer housing businesses were floated off separately on either side of the Atlantic in 1994, but Hanson had by then moved further into commodity businesses with the purchase of Quantum Chemicals, a deal made possible largely because of Hanson's ability to cut Quantum's interest bill by reorganising its debts.

If these moves began to prompt questions about Hanson's strategy and whether the 'dynamic duo' of peers had begun to lose their touch, such doubts were hardened by the extraordinary ICI episode. In the spring of 1991 Hanson bought a stake of just under 3 per cent in the chemical giant. Lord Hanson professed his aversion to a takeover bid but suggested he might be able to help ICI in its struggle against recessionary forces. It was generally assumed that a full bid would follow brief and abortive talks with ICI's chairman, but the howls of protest from virtually all sides at the thought of one of Britain's premier industrial groups being broken up for a quick profit appeared to take Lord Hanson by surprise and persuade him that a bid would either not be allowed, or could not succeed. Eventually Hanson was forced to withdraw with its tail between its legs, adding to growing scepticism about its normally unerring touch.

A further demonstration of the group's fallibility came the following year, when Hanson was beaten to the purchase of food group RHM by Tomkins, one of the new breed of conglomerates. The defeat of the master, Hanson, by a former student, Greg Hutchings, strengthened the image of an ageing group with declining powers which had lost its way as well as many of its former friends. It is dangerous to write off such a successful company, and its eminent leaders. But it is difficult to see how Hanson can escape from the vicious circle of a low share rating caused by doubts about performance and prospects, which itself hampers future performance and especially takeover prospects. And the prospect of Hanson falling victim to one of the newer takeover merchants becomes ever less preposterous.

Shares

At its best, Hanson has been the investors' friend, with strong earnings and dividend growth, augmented by the ability to outperform the market suddenly on the strength of a deal or acquisition. The shares easily outperformed the market in the 1980s, but fared no better than the rest during the 1987 crash. Yet they soon returned to favour and by 1990 were at their accustomed premium relative to the market as a whole.

It was expected that the group's basic businesses would underpin earnings and also allow the group to pick up weaker companies during the recession. The expected acquisitions spree did not happen, however, and investors' restlessness surfaced in speculation about the management succession and in a slide in the share price. Their lordships' announcement in 1991 that they would continue in office rallied the shares despite a warning that recession was having an effect on the group. The tilt at ICI that year first raised expectations, which were subsequently deflated when the ICI shares were sold; this raised questions about the group's real quality. The Beazer bid did not catch the market's imagination and the shares did not perk up until the group sold its ICI stake in 1992. The cut in profit that year sent them back down again until the weakness of the pound after the UK's exit from the ERM stirred interest in the group's dollar earnings at the end of that year. By 1993 the shares gained strength as the market waited for the US economy to lift off, taking Hanson's profits with it. But once again the gain was short-lived and the shares resumed the general downward drift which had begun in 1990.

Corporate conscience

Hanson does not have group-wide policies on many issues, notably equal opportunities. It does have an environmental policy, however, although this does not encompass independent audit.

There is certainly a need for effort on this issue. Hanson group companies are heavily involved in areas with important environmental consequences (such as brick-making, quarrying, mining and the production of titanium dioxide) and have an appalling record on water pollution. ARC was convicted for water pollution 7 times in 1990 and 1991, its largest fine being £4,500 for polluting a stream with quarry solids on several occasions in 1990. Butterley Brick was also fined (£1,500) in 1991 for clay pollution. The record of exceeding effluent consent levels matches that conviction rate. Nine separate sites broke consent levels in the year to March 1991, ARC's Old Gasworks Site living up to its name and being found on 10 occasions to have exceeded consent levels for suspended solids. That subsidiary's Whatley quarry in Somerset was almost as bad, with 9 separate examples, plus one of pollution by fats, oil and grease. SCM chemicals exceeded chromium levels twice at Stallingborough, with one example each of excess sulphuric acid and excess chemical oxygen demand. The group had 5 convictions under health and safety laws during the three years to March 1992, including a £10,000 fine for London Brick in 1989.

In South Africa, Hanson subsidiaries pay a few black workers below reasonable wage levels, but of course the major ethical issue with this group is tobacco, since Imperial Tobacco is one of the UK's leading cigarette-makers. The group is also involved to some extent in the military and nuclear industries: refuelling hoses, special cranes, and valves for use in military rafts, boats and protective suits; and some building projects on nuclear sites.

Corporate governance

Separate Chairman and Chief Executive Y
Number of Directors 19
Number of Non-Executive Directors 6
(5 Independent Directors)
Insulated Directors All execs

Board Committees
Audit: Y   Remuneration: Y

Remuneration

Year end	30.09.91	30.09.92	30.09.93
Total board £M	8.00	8.00	9.10
% change	14	0	12
Highest paid £M	1.38	1.35	1.36
% change	-5	-2	1

Board

Bonham, Derek C *Chief Executive*
Lord Hanson *Executive Chairman*
Alexander, Anthony G.L. *Executive Director*
Clarke, David H *Executive Director*
Collins, Christopher D *Executive Director*
Cotton, Anthony R *Executive Director*
Dransfield, Graham *Executive Director*

Hanson, Robert *Executive Director*
Harper, Peter J *Executive Director*
Hellings, Brian A *Executive Director*
Raos, John G *Executive Director*
Taylor, Martin Gibbeson *Executive Director*
Landuyt, William M *Finance Director*
Baker, Rt. Hon. Kenneth *Independent Non-Executive*
Hardy, Sir David W *Independent Non-Executive*
Keswick, Simon L *Independent Non-Executive*
Price, Charles H, II *Independent Non-Executive*
Scott-Barrett, Jonathon *Independent Non-Executive*
Harding, Sir Christopher *Non-Executive*

Shareholders could be forgiven some puzzlement over exactly who is on the Hanson board and how it works. The annual report lists numerous associate directors, as well as two vice-chairmen in addition to the chairman and chief executive, none of whom is Lord White, Lord Hanson's long-serving partner. He appears only in the accompanying list for Hansen Industries, which is actually not a company but merely a branch of a UK subsidiary. Hanson appears to be one of the companies conforming with the letter rather than the spirit of recommendations in the Cadbury Code, which Lord Hanson lambasted in his 1992 annual report as being 'long on accountability and short on encouraging efficiency and enterprise'. In addition to doubts about the independence and 'weight' of Hanson's non-executives and the appointment of his son to the board, the committees, contrary to recommendation, are not entirely non-executive: the audit committee now consists entirely of non-executives, while the compensation committee includes the chief executive and three non-executives. All directors are insulated from re-election. There is no attempt to explain the huge pay levels at the company.

IMPERIAL CHEMICAL INDUSTRIES plc

9 Millbank, London SW1P 3JF
Tel: 0171 834 4444.
Chairman Sir Denys Henderson
Chief executive Ronnie Hampel
Major brands Dulux paints, Melinar PET plastic, Perspex acrylic sheet, Melinex polyester film
Main subsidiaries Tioxide Group, European Vinyl Corporation (50%)
Size £10.6 billion sales, £5.9 billion stock market value, 87,100 employees
5-year growth sales -19%, earnings per share -39%, employment -35%
Solvency debt = 12% shareholders' funds, interest cover 2 times
Political donations 0
Charitable donations £3.5 million

Major developments

1926 formed with merger of 4 large chemical companies
1961 failed takeover bid for Courtaulds
1962 sold first tranche of Imperial Metals Industries
1978 final disposal of IMI
1982 sold polyethylene business; sold Carrington Viyella
1985 bought Beatrice chemical operations
1986 set up EVC joint venture for PVC with Enimont; bought Glidden American paint
1987 bought Stauffer Chemicals; merged oil interests with Enterprise Oil
1990 sold Savlon and Cepton consumer pharmaceuticals business; bought out partner to take full control of Tioxide Group; launched 'reshaping' programme to slim the group
1991 Hanson bought 2.8% stake; sold stake in Ellis & Everard; pulled out of fertiliser and soda ash businesses
1992 announced plan to swap nylon interests in Europe for Du Pont's acrylics; Hanson sold 2.8% stake
1993 demerged drug, speciality chemicals and agrochemical operations as Zeneca

Outlook

ICI is dead. Long live ICI. On 28 May 1993 the shareholders of Britain's leading chemical group voted to accept the directors' proposal to split the group in two. The new ICI consists of the mainly chemical parts of the group, tending to be capital-intensive and based on chemical engineering. The other part of the old ICI, based more on biological science than engineering, and research-intensive, is now a separate public company called Zeneca (see under drugs sector).

A harsh view of the new ICI depicts it as the unwanted, unpromising 'rump', cut off from the more vibrant, more profitable body and now left to wither in a hostile environment. That may not be entirely fair. The new ICI does include the basic chemical businesses which produce commodity products, are therefore subject to wild swings throughout the economic cycle, and have been the cause of most of ICI's *angst* in the last 20 years. The future for such businesses throughout Europe looks bleak in the face of competition from new producers in emerging countries such as Korea. ICI's current chief executive, Ronnie Hampel, has promised to increase pressure on costs and to limit reinvestment in the company's petrochemical businesses. But the new ICI does not just comprise basic chemical products, and even in this field the hope is that for some products ICI can establish itself as one of the few global leaders.

Apart from industrial chemicals, the new ICI includes paint, explosives and a Materials division which manufactures acrylic sheet such as Perspex, plastic film and polyurethane products. Since the trauma of the early 1980s recession (which included a dividend cut in 1980 that shocked the UK financial

IMPERIAL CHEMICAL INDUSTRIES

Share record

Return on shareholders' equity	%	7.50
5-year price high	p	853.0
5-year price low	p	397.5
Dividend yield	%	4.27
5-year high	%	9.08
5-year low	%	4.03
Price/earnings ratio		26.6
5-year high		34.4
5-year low		6.4

Share price performance (in pence)

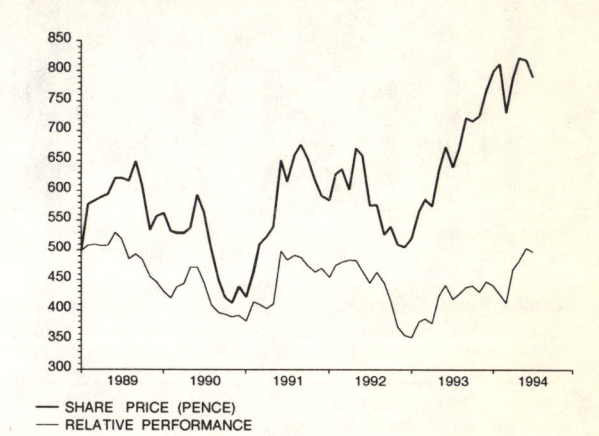

— SHARE PRICE (PENCE)
— RELATIVE PERFORMANCE

Financial record

		31/12/89	31/12/90	31/12/91	31/12/92	31/12/93
Total sales	£	13,171M	12,906M	12,488M	12,061M	10,632M
Pre-tax profit	£'000	1,468M	957,000	809,000	565,000	527,000
Published retentions	£'000	676,000	281,000	151,000	-963M	-424M
Earnings per share	p	62.19	41.92	35.25	24.49	38.66
Dividend per share	p	27.06	27.06	27.06	27.06	27.50
Operating cash flow	£'000	-732M	461,000	243,000	-598M	-36,000
Net assets per share	p	546.23	514.46	523.88	524.87	935.60
Net debt/(cash)	£	2,156M	1,728M	1,592M	2,301M	496,000
Shareholders' funds	£	5,108M	4,734M	4,844M	4,335M	4,022M
Return on capital	%	25.15	16.50	14.94	11.23	11.75
Profit margin	%	9.45	6.37	6.51	4.30	4.51
Sales per employee	£	98.44	97.70	97.11	102.65	122.07
Interest cover		6.26	4.63	4.27	3.24	1.97
Dividend cover		2.30	1.55	1.30	0.91	1.41
Sales increase	%	12.58	-2.01	-3.24	-3.42	-11.85
Earnings growth	%	-0.54	-32.59	-15.92	-30.51	57.85
Investment x depreciation		1.79	1.60	1.29	1.39	1.00
Investment as % assets		19.81	17.00	13.85	14.48	12.05
Number of employees		133,800	132,100	128,600	117,500	87,100

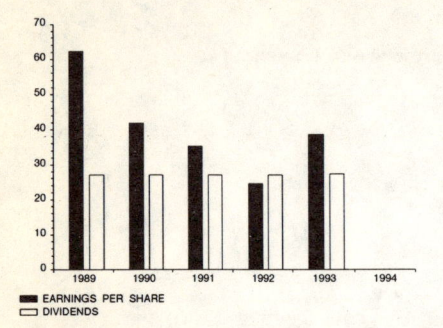

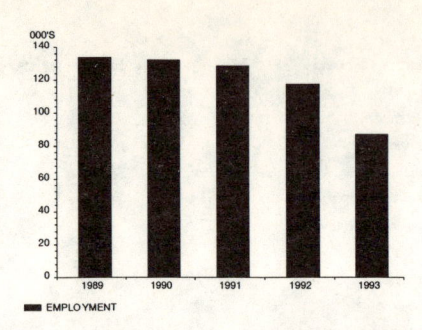

Earnings and dividends

Employment

world), ICI has been striving to gain a foremost position worldwide for those businesses that it could. Major plants have been constructed in Taiwan and elsewhere in the Pacific region to ensure a substantial presence in this fast-growing market. The acquisition of Glidden paints in the US pushed ICI's Dulux business to the top of the world paint league. A number of asset swaps have helped to build up the acrylics business, notably in 1993 when Du Pont was given ICI's nylon and polyester fibres business in exchange for the American group's acrylics operations in the United States. Similarly, ICI took full control of what had previously been the Tioxide joint venture.

This process left ICI with a number of operations where it had a leading global position and good cost competitiveness. These businesses include paints, explosives (the legacy of Nobel Industries – the force behind the foundation of ICI in 1926), titanium dioxide, acrylics and polyester film, and polyester products such as PET (for plastic drinks bottles). Within the industrial chemicals operation there is also hope for CFC replacements, although there is no certainty that ICI's controversial Klea product will turn out to be a long-term replacement for the ozone-destroying CFCs.

While these businesses all stand at least a chance of surviving and possibly prospering because of their scale and market position, it seems possible that the European base will continue to shrink at the expense of expansion in Asia. But there is a collection of other businesses which would seem to have little future in the new ICI. Foremost among these are probably the chlorine-based activities, much hated by environmental campaigners, and with a serious question mark over their future because of the environmental impact of chlorine and chlorine products, and the high electricity cost (in Britain) of the manufacturing process. This unpromising group of businesses also includes many basic intermediate chemicals and the half share in PVC with Italian group Enimont. It seems likely that the future for these operations is either gradual contraction and eventual closure, or sale to or exchange with businesses from another chemical group.

This can be seen as the continuation of a trend which goes back to the 1960s. In a series of substantial corporate moves since then, ICI has withdrawn from textiles (Carrington Viyella), metals (IMI) and oil. On the other hand, the split into two companies is a reversal of another trend which gathered pace during the 1980s: to concentrate increasingly on 'added value' businesses such as drugs, agrochemicals (hence the acquisition of Stauffer) and the developing markets of biotechnology. Disposals have continued. In 1994 the company sold its Indian fertiliser business, pulled out of European polypropylene manufacture, withdrew from small operations in the US and Argentina, and indicated that other operations were earmarked for sale later in the year.

Shares

ICI's attempts through the 1980s and 1990s to move away from trade in bulk products and towards those with added value brought little benefit to the shares, although the company's status as a core holding for major investors was never questioned. ICI's peak performance relative to the market as a whole came in 1987 after a strong phase of acquisitions. A long period of underperformance then set in while the whole industry tried to adjust to the end of a boom in petrochemicals.

The group's strategic review in 1990 came at the end of that decline, although it had no impact on the shares, which were depressed by fears that analysts' profit forecasts for that year were too high. The recession affected the bulk side of the business and masked any benefit from reorganisation. The shares were then jerked from their rut in the summer of 1991 by Hanson's share swoop. This focused a strong light on the group's problems and proposed solutions, and for a time the shares outperformed the market. When Hanson placed the stake the next year without bidding, the rating dropped again, helped along by a profit warning.

Shares started to climb back again when the demerger plan was announced, and a rise at the start of 1993 reflected excitement over the potential of the demerger. The climb was sustained, well into 1994.

Corporate conscience

ICI is one of the country's great, paternalistic employers. That leaves the group with a good employment record, including one of the oldest profit-sharing schemes. But environmental critics have fiercely attacked ICI as the country's leading producer of CFCs, and a major polluter.

On the negative side, the group not only uses live animals for testing, but insists that it must continue to do so, although it has reduced the number used, and contributes to research on alternative methods. As a multinational, ICI has operations in many countries with oppressive regimes, including a significant presence in Indonesia, Sri Lanka, Brazil, Argentina and Tanzania. It has some military connections, mainly through the explosives businesses, and makes some supplies to nuclear installations. In South Africa, a handful of its black employees have been paid below a reasonable level.

The group's employment and community record offsets these minus points. It is a member of BITC and gives large donations to charity as well placing staff on secondment to charitable organisations. It has a good record of employee and trade union relations, despite frequent and sizeable job losses in recent years. ICI has a strong equal opportunities policy, including support for Opportunity 2000. While the industry is traditionally male-dominated, more than a third of graduate recruits are women, and about an eighth of managers. The group has also taken steps to increase recruitment from ethnic minorities. It has suffered 6 convictions under health and safety laws in 1988–91, including 2 heavy fines. Nobel Explosives was fined £100,000 in 1988 and £250,000 the following year.

The environment remains the crucial issue for ICI, however. The main controversy has been over its polluting products: specifically CFCs, but also wastes from the titanium dioxide process. The group suffered a prolonged campaign against a Tioxide site in Canada, which eventually resulted in prosecution in 1993, and there was outrage when ICI responded by moving its operation to a new joint-venture company in the US. On CFCs, ICI has developed alternatives and has brought forward planned phase-out of CFCs but the replacement product has been criticised by Greenpeace, which argues for a completely different approach.

So far as ICI's record on pollution is concerned, the group is criticised as one of the country's largest polluters, but since it is also one of the largest manufacturers, that has little meaning – just as ICI's satisfaction in seeing emission figures decline recently is meaningless at a time when output is declining. But like most of the chemical industry, ICI is now entirely serious about improving its environmental performance. It has developed thorough environmental policies with clear targets at site and group level (a 50 per cent reduction in waste between 1990 and 1995) and an annual group report supplemented by site reports to local communities. ICI has also committed itself to achieving global environmental standards equivalent to the highest standards (for that process) anywhere in its worldwide operations. Back in the UK, the record on water pollution is better than it was, though there is still some way to go. The record clearly shows room for improvement, but ICI is also quite clearly working to improve it.

Corporate governance

Separate Chairman and Chief Executive Y
Number of Directors 9
Number of Non-Executive Directors 4
(4 Independent Directors)
Insulated Directors None

Board Committees
Audit: Y   Remuneration: Y

Remuneration

Year end	31.12.91	31.12.92	31.12.93
Total board £M	3.02	2.83	2.55
% change	13	-6	-10
Highest paid £	499,000	528,000	494,000
% change	11.6	6	-6

Board
Hampel, R C *Chief Executive*
Henderson, Sir Denys *Executive Chairman*
Margetts, R J *Executive Director*
Miller Smith, Charles *Executive Director*
Spall, A G *Finance Director*
Short, Colin M *Executive Director*
Hurn, Roger *Independent Non-Executive*
Pilkington, Sir Antony R *Ind. Non-Executive*
Schneider-Lenné, Miss E *Ind. Non-Executive*

A report on the company's standards of corporate governance is given by the senior non-executive in the first annual report since the demerger. This provides the terms of reference for boardroom committees. Although detail on executive earnings and the basis for bonuses has improved, the company could go further on this issue.

INCHCAPE plc

23 King Street, London SW1Y 6QY
Tel: 0171 321 0110
Chairman Sir David Plastow
Chief executive Charles Mackay
Main subsidiaries Bain Clarkson, Mann Egerton, Toyota (GB)
Size £5.9 billion sales, £2.4 billion stock market value, 38,200 employees
5-year growth sales 99%, earnings per share 13%, employment -18%
Solvency debt = 8% shareholders' funds, interest cover 8 times
Political donations £28,000 Conservative Party
Charitable donations £604,000

Major developments
1958 formed as IGD Ltd
1981 changed to Inchcape plc
1991 bought insurance broking business of Rutland Trust plc; sold off tea interests
1992 bought Spinneys group of companies; bought Tozer Kemsley & Milbourn
1993 sold Far East timber interests; took share stake in Gestetner

Outlook

There are many similarities between most large companies: their origins, histories, products or markets usually have something in common. Inchcape is unique, however. Almost half of its sales, and rather more of its profits, come from east and south-east Asia – the region most British companies are desperately scrambling to get into. On the other hand, more than half its sales and profits come from car distribution and sales – a business most companies would be glad to have nothing to do with. The conundrum is explained by Inchcape's background, established by a clerk (later to become Lord Inchcape) in India in the early 19th century, and developed into a sort of market trader to the Empire, with the emphasis on south and east Asia.

The first Earl floated the Assam Tea Company (which subsequently became part of the group) on the London stock market more than 150 years ago, but Inchcape itself only became public in the 1950s. The third Earl (who died in early spring, 1994) then proceeded to buy similar family businesses, creating a messy web of trading interests stretching around the globe, but still centred on Asia, and containing the kernels of today's rather more focused activities. The whole operation almost foundered in the early 1980s, however, when it appeared that lack of control and clear direction had allowed Inchcape to drift into trouble and possible takeover, especially with the departure of the third Earl to look after the other family business, P&O. But Inchcape escaped, and has subsequently tidied up its rambling interests. Peripheral and low-growth activities have been sold, including the tea interests on which it was founded, and timber. Activities with better prospects have been built up, notably by the £376 million acquisition of car distributor Tozer Kemsley Millbourn (TKM) in 1992.

The result is a group for which cars are extremely important, but which also has many other interests – interests that have been acquired over decades of trading in different businesses, and which have only now been assembled into a slightly more coherent whole. Motor distribution is by far the largest activity, while marketing and distribution makes a clear second. But then the order of activities becomes less clear: the collection of service businesses together represents only about a seventh of profits, and in truth there seems little in common between insurance broking and inspection and testing.

Immediate prospects are promising, however, partly because of continued economic growth in south-east Asia – Inchcape has a foothold in China where it recently won a contract to sell Jaguars – and partly because of Inchcape's link in the UK with Toyota. The Japanese company has followed Nissan in setting up a UK plant and is likely to obtain a growing share of the British market. Hence Inchcape's Mann Egerton subsidiary, through which Toyota cars are distributed, can expect to sell more and more cars.

The fly in the ointment is that Inchcape will own less and less of the Toyota distributorship. Under the agreement between the two companies, Toyota will gradually build up its share to 51 per cent in by 1998. This explains the acquisition of TKM, but illustrates the hazards of distributing other people's products in markets which they want to enter. And the same lesson applies to much of the distribution business in Asia. The trend in international consumer goods clearly indicates that manufacturers should control more of their distribution of their own goods – witness the drinks companies.

The group came a long way in the 1980s, and has come even further from its Indian origins. It also achieved an important transition when Sir George Turnbull, the architect of the transformed group, had to retire earlier than planned in 1991. The handover to Charles Mackay as chief executive, and ex-Vickers boss Sir David Plastow as chairman, seems to have gone smoothly. Inchcape looked to be adding a new dimension with the 15 per cent acquisition of office equipment group Gestetner in 1993. Yet, although the share purchase was regarded as a bargain, doubts about Gestetner's prospects made some analysts worried aabout just where this investment would lead. Inchcape may be unique among large British companies, but it shares one characteristic with many: it is still not entirely clear where it is heading, or how it will get there.

Shares

Few companies can boast a record like Inchcape's. It has consistently outperformed the all-share index since the mid-1980s, thanks to the strong cash flow, impeded somewhat in recent years, which has kept

INCHCAPE

Share record

Return on shareholders' equity	%	19.87
5-year price high	p	632.0
5-year price low	p	176.5
Dividend yield	%	4.13
5-year high	%	8.06
5-year low	%	2.72
Price/earnings ratio		16.4
5-year high		26.2
5-year low		7.3

Share price performance (in pence)

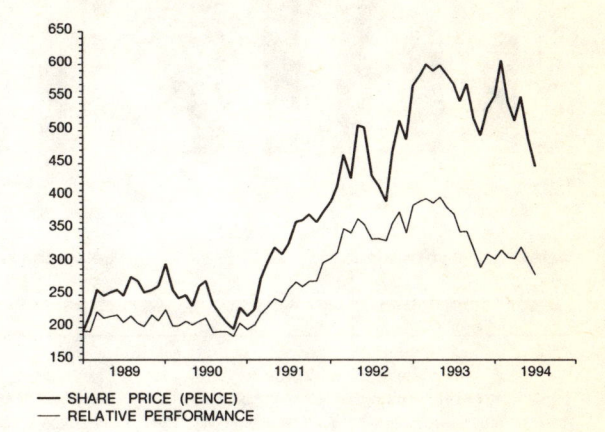

— SHARE PRICE (PENCE)
— RELATIVE PERFORMANCE

Financial record

		31/12/89	31/12/90	31/12/91	31/12/92	31/12/93
Total sales	£	2,950M	3,291M	3,636M	5,037M	5,877M
Pre-tax profit	£'000	161,100	159,100	180,300	249,000	252,400
Published retentions	£'000	54,700	53,900	75,600	78,100	99,500
Earnings per share	p	24.17	20.62	24.87	27.69	27.36
Dividend per share	p	10.38	11.14	11.80	13.75	14.80
Operating cash flow	£'000	-7,700	76,100	51,600	100,200	79,800
Net assets per share	p	125.41	148.41	158.96	172.84	213..55
Net debt/(cash)	£'000	103,500	32,300	6,200	141,800	110,600
Shareholders' funds	£'000	499,000	620,000	715,800	1,231M	1,412M
Return on capital	%	43.61	38.73	37.83	39.81	32.24
Profit margin	%	4.42	3.97	4.19	3.92	3.39
Sales per employee	£	62.99	66.19	98.70	130.58	153.89
Interest cover		9.37	7.69	22.99	16.66	8.01
Dividend cover		2.33	1.85	2.11	2.01	1.85
Sales increase	%	20.33	11.58	10.46	38.53	16.68
Earnings growth	%	6.09	-14.69	20.58	11.36	-1.19
Investment x depreciation		-0.20	1.54	1.91	1.22	0.67
Investment as % assets		-2.11	14.78	21.84	10.47	6.91
Number of employees		46,831	49,724	36,837	38,573	38,189

INCHCAPE plc

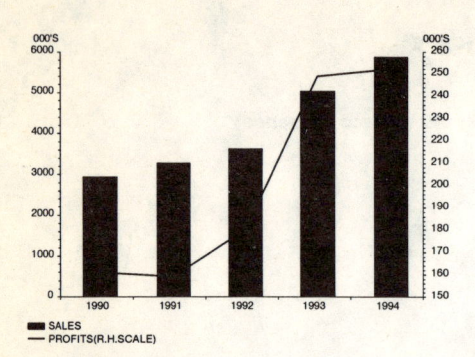

Sales and profits

Sales per employee

dividend payments rolling in. To a great extent the shares benefit from a weak pound as around half the group's profits are derived from dollar-linked currencies. From 1986 the new management's policies sent the group roaring along until 1988. Then a slowdown in world economies flattened out the growth curve, and the group's strength, its independence from the UK economy, was not apparent until 1991.

In that year the group announced a restructuring which commanded the attention of investors. It went on to achieve a 9 per cent growth in earnings at a time when earnings for industrial companies generally fell by 15 per cent. Inchcape also asked shareholders for £379 million through a rights issue to buy TKM in a deal which actually pleased investors because of its good prospects. Inchcape earned itself a re-rating which enabled the shares to trade at a premium of some 20 per cent to the market as a whole.

The following year the change of chief executive did not curb the rise in the shares, while the UK's exit from the ERM sent the pound spiralling down but also boosted the group's profits. Analysts continued to support the stock into 1994, citing its strong balance sheet and the benefit of exposure to overseas markets. Yet Inchcape remains out of sympathy with its stock market classification as a vehicle distributor.

Corporate conscience

As one of Britain's most international groups, Inchcape operates in one of the longest lists of countries with poor human rights records, with significant interests in Ethiopia, Thailand and Bahrain. In total, Inchcape has subsidiaries or associates in 85 overseas countries.

The group also registers on several other issues of conscience. As a major importer and distributor of cars, it is implicated in the production of greenhouse gases. It has an involvement in alcohol, as an importer and distributor of wines and spirits in Australia and south-east Asia, and as a distributor of Heineken in the Middle East and Australia. And there is a military involvement, through Wadham Stringer, which makes special-purpose commercial vehicles. In addition, Inchcape has fallen foul of the ASA, and some of its products involve animal testing. All this is barely offset by positive aspects: there do not appear to be full environmental and equal opportunities policies.

Corporate governance

Separate Chairman and Chief Executive Y
Number of Directors 13
Number of Non-Executive Directors 5
(5 Independent Directors)
Insulated Directors None

Board Committees
Audit: Y   Remuneration: Y

Remuneration

Year end	31.12.91	31.12.92	31.12.93
Total board £M	3.51	3.63	3.03
% change	30	3	-16
Highest paid £	450,000	418,000	424,000
% change	55	-7	1

Board
Mackay, Charles D *Chief Executive*
Plastow, Sir David *Executive Chairman*
Arnold, Simon *Executive Director*
Cummins, Andrew *Executive Director*
Cushing, Peter *Executive Director*
John, David *Executive Director*
Whittaker, Derek *Executive Director*
O'Donoghue, Rod *Finance Director*
Alexander, A J *Independent Non-Executive*
Baring, Peter *Independent Non-Executive*

Baxendell, Sir Peter *Independent Non-Executive*
Lord Armstrong of Ilminster *Ind. Non-Executive*
Hintz, Jürgen *Independent Non-Executive*

The successful management of the enforced early retirement of chief executive Sir George Turnbull and the simultaneous change of chairman suggests that Inchcape's board works well. Its constitution is better than many, although the independent directors are outnumbered by the executives. The intention to slim down the number of executives on the board, following the retirement of Reg Heath and Alan Marsh, was announced in November 1993. There are audit, remuneration and nomination committees consisting almost exclusively of non-executives. In addition, there is a chairman's committee, which comprises the chairman and the non-executives and meets before each board meeting, with the prime responsibility of 'reviewing the performance of the executive directors and senior management', according to a full explanation in his review of 1992 by chairman Sir David Plastow. Sir David also reported that he had asked Peter Baring to act as the senior independent director 'to take responsibility for monitoring my own performance, and if necessary arranging my replacement'. He adds that this goes beyond the recommendations of the Cadbury Report, which he praises highly.

KINGFISHER plc

119 Marylebone Road, London NW1 5PX
Tel: 0171 724 7749
Chairman Sir Geoffrey Mulcahy
Chief executive Alan Smith
Main subsidiaries B&Q, Darty, Comet Group, Superdrug Stores, Woolworths, Chartwell Land.
Size £4.5 billion sales, £3.5 billion stock market value, 72,000 employees
5-year growth sales 54%, earnings per share 1%, employment 13%
Solvency debt = 27% shareholders' funds, interest cover 41 times
Political donations £25,000 Conservative Party
Charitable donations £940,863

Major developments

1982 formed to buy F W Woolworths and B&Q
1984 bought Comet Group
1986 Dixons bid fought off
1987 bought Superdrug
1988 changed to Kingfisher; bought Tip Top Drug stores and Share Drug stores
1989 bought Laskys stores; bought Medicare bid for Dixons blocked by Monopolies Commission
1993 joint stationery venture with Staples; bought French group Darty

Outlook

Kingfisher is a company for which the word caution could have been invented. It is run by a group of determinedly grey people. As a non-food retailer, it is one of a tiny group of companies which managed to get through the recession without seeing their profits fall. It is also arguable whether Kingfisher is a retailer at all: rather it is a holding company which happens to own retailing businesses – Woolworths, B&Q, Comet and Superdrug in the UK, plus the French electrical retailer Darty, bought in 1993. Indeed the group could be said to be the BTR of retailing.

The group was born in 1982 when John Beckett and a small team spearheaded a buy-out of Woolworths from its US parent. The first Woolworths store had opened in Liverpool more than 70 years before and thrived on its 'nothing more than 6d' formula until the Second World War. It lumbered through the 1960s and 70s and arrived in the 1980s looking rather sorry for itself, owning more than 1,000 outlets in not very good shape. Mulcahy and team set about slimming down the operation by selling shops and cutting drastically the number of product areas which Woolworths tried to cover: the shops remained 'variety stores', but the 'variety' was rather less than it had been.

The approach worked. But the new management was also lucky: it had taken control just at the time when Britain was about to embark upon an extraordinary bout of consumer spending. Moreover, with Woolworths the group had inherited a small chain of do-it-yourself outlets called B&Q just as the market for DIY goods was taking off, helped especially by the rising level of home ownership during the 1980s as the Conservative government gave council tenants the right to buy their properties. By the end of that decade, B&Q was making larger profits than Woolworths, and 30 new outlets – 'sheds' in the parlance of DIY retailing – were being opened each year. By 1993 the group had around 300 B&Q stores. In the meantime, it had also picked up Superdrug and the electrical retailer Comet. In 1989, reflecting the broadening of its activities beyond the Woolworths chain, the company changed its name to Kingfisher.

There was excitement along the way: in 1986 Dixons bid for the company but was rebuffed; and in 1989 Kingfisher bid for Dixons, only to be told by the Monopolies Commission that bringing Dixons (and its offshoot Currys) under the same umbrella as Comet would put too great a share of the electrical retail market in the hands of a single company. Only in 1993 did Kingfisher make its next significant moves, first entering a joint venture in the UK with US stationery retailer Staples, then striking a deal to buy France's leading electrical retailer, Darty. For some years Kingfisher had indicated its interest in buying a business overseas: it had looked at operations in the US as well as on the Continent. The Darty takeover effectively locked the French company's management into Kingfisher by giving it shares in the UK group as part payment for its business.

KINGFISHER

Share record

Return on shareholders' equity	%	20.61
5-year price high	p	778.0
5-year price low	p	260.7
Dividend yield	%	3.49
5-year high	%	5.68
5-year low	%	2.23
Price/earnings ratio		16.0
5-year high		25.0
5-year low		8.0

Share price performance (in pence)

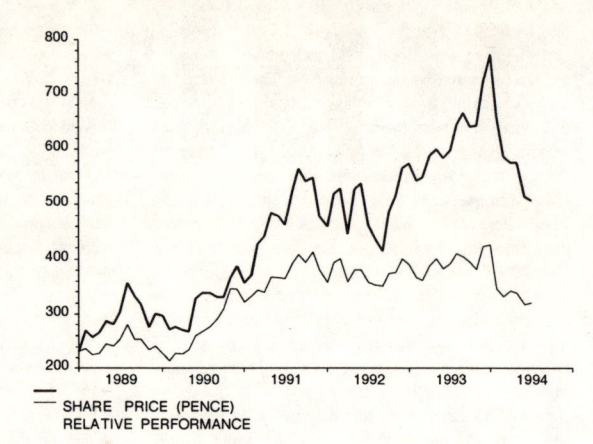

— SHARE PRICE (PENCE)
  RELATIVE PERFORMANCE

Financial record

		31/1/90	31/1/91	31/1/92	31/1/93	31/1/94
Total sales	£	2,910M	3,117M	3,389M	3,548M	4,479M
Pre-tax profit	£'000	209,800	215,300	222,300	208,000	310,600
Published retentions	£'000	175,000	129,100	102,800	72,800	130,900
Earnings per share	p	31.75	31.99	31.02	28.71	35.86
Dividend per share	p	11.19	11.87	12.64	13.33	14.90
Operating cash flow	£'000	108,300	74,900	51,800	-17,600	96,100
Net assets per share	p	278.63	288.82	268.27	252.04	250.80
Net debt/(cash)	£'000	251,100	231,500	97,300	17,900	290,700
Shareholders' funds	£'000	961,800	974,600	1,082M	1,158M	1,091M
Return on capital	%	21.00	20.28	19.98	18.99	26.13
Profit margin	%	7.21	6.89	6.51	5.80	6.83
Sales per employee	£	49.49	50.69	54.71	56.50	62.18
Interest cover		6.59	7.50	19.69	295.00	41.25
Dividend cover		2.84	2.70	2.45	2.15	2.41
Sales increase	%	9.38	7.12	8.72	4.69	26.25
Earnings growth	%	10.79	0.77	-3.05	-7.46	24.93
Investment x depreciation		0.31	0.64	0.70	1.97	1.56
Investment as % assets		1.37	3.53	4.99	14.07	10.17
Number of employees		58,796	61,497	61,941	62,799	72,036

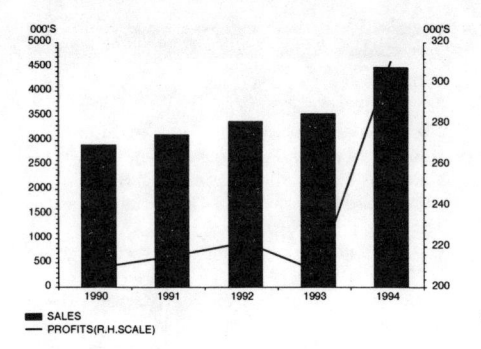

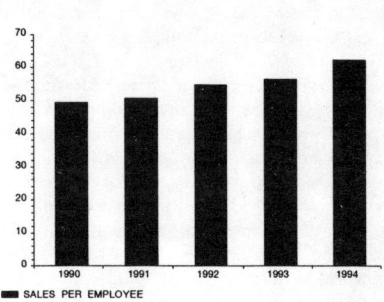

Sales and profits

Sales per employee

More importantly, the acquisition gave Kingfisher the bridgehead it sought to set up business across Europe: already Kingfisher has indicated that it is interested in transplanting the Darty formula into Germany and Spain.

From 1991 B&Q, which had been the driving force behind Kingfisher's growth in profits (the DIY business's operating surplus more than doubled in the final four years of the 1980s), felt the squeeze of recession. Fewer people were moving house; less was being spent on home improvement. But as the recession took hold, so Kingfisher saw the value of having a spread of businesses: Woolworths and Superdrug, whose performance seemed perhaps a little pedestrian during the years of booming consumer spending, proved remarkably resilient during the slump – in 1992 the profits of both rose.

The company's chairman, Sir Geoff Mulcahy, makes much of the idea that retailers in the 1990s will have to cut margins in order to generate extra sales. But in 1994 it became clear that this approach was faltering: profits from three of the four main British chains fell; only B&Q's rose. The overall corporate strategy may be sound, but there are doubts about Kingfisher's ability to attend to the humdrum details of retailing.

Shares

Kingfisher's rating against the rest of the market has never been higher than when Dixons bid for it in 1986 and in recent years has not been lower than when it turned the tables in 1989. Both events focused City minds on the group's value.

In 1986 what was then Woolworths was caught by Dixons in an apparently incoherent phase after a period of acquisition and change. After recovering from its disappointment at the group's escape, the market gave the shares a fairly high rating that lasted until 1987. Midway through that year the shares slid against the market average, only to outperform most others during the crash itself as the company's defensive qualities were established. Once the panic was over, the share rating slid again until the group's relaunch as Kingfisher in 1989, which coincided with promising results. After the bid for Dixons, the rating took off. Even though the bid was blocked, the shares kept rising as the onset of recession brought the group's defensive qualities back into demand.

The shares were weakened in 1992 by concern about the discount war in the DIY sector, although by 1993 such worries had receded. In 1994, however, the share price plunged due to anxiety about the underlying performance of Kingfisher's UK retail chains.

Corporate conscience

Kingfisher has some excellent policies on issues of conscience, although it has suffered adverse advertising judgements and is exposed on the issue of human rights through its involvement in Ghana, India, Kenya, Nigeria and Pakistan. However, the group is a supporter of Opportunity 2000 and has strong equal opportunities policies. Almost a fifth of senior managers are women and in 1990 the group decided to set specific targets for female representation: by 1996 to have women forming 20 per cent of management, and to increase the number at senior management level by half.

Kingfisher is also a strong supporter of community and charitable causes, including some unfashionable ones such as Aids charities, as well as the likes of a Crime Concern project (called Crucial Crew) aimed at young children. It is a member of BITC, as is the B&Q subsidiary, but has not joined the Per Cent Club. The group does, however, give substantial sums as well as placing staff on secondment and making gifts in kind.

On environmental matters, some parts of the group

284 LADBROKE GROUP plc

are further ahead than others. For example, B&Q applies environmental criteria to its purchasing, which led it to stop buying peat from Fisons and to insist that tropical hardwoods must come from what are considered sustainable sources by 1996. Other subsidiaries have not been as enthusiastic on this score, but the group has developed a strong environment policy which includes an independent audit as well as regular monitoring and review. And Superdrug has attempted to match Body Shop by insisting on cosmetics and toiletries which have not been tested on animals. Superdrug also supports FRAME (Fund for the Replacement of Animals in Medical Experiments).

Corporate governance

Separate Chairman and Chief Executive Y
Number of Directors 12
Number of Non-Executive Directors 7
(4 Independent Directors)
Insulated Directors None

Board Committees
Audit: Y   Remuneration: Y

Remuneration

Year end	1.02.92	31.01.93	29.01.94
Total board £M	1.75	1.77	3.27
% change	-32	1	85
Highest paid £M	0.72	0.77	1.05
% change	-4	7	36

Board
Smith, Alan *Chief Executive*
Mulcahy, Sir Geoffrey J *Executive Chairman*
Breene, Tim *Executive Director*
Whittaker, Nigel *Executive Director*
Kerr-Muir, James *Finance Director*
Hollingbery, Michael *Independent Non-Executive*
Lady Howe *Independent Non-Executive*
Mobbs, Sir Nigel *Independent Non-Executive*
Thiolon, Bernard *Independent Non-Executive*
Bullock, John *Non-Executive*
Goldstein, Ronald *Non-Executive*
Hardy, Peter B *Non-Executive*

For a company which prides itself on progressive management, Kingfisher's communication with shareholders through the annual report has been scanty. The 1993 annual report made amends, though, reporting the existence of committees for audit, remuneration, nomination and social responsibility, as well as the operation of executive and management committees. Although a non-executive majority exists in the boardroom, three of the six have question marks over their 'independence'. The persistence of Kingfisher in combining the roles of chairman and chief executive finally came to an end in April 1993. Three-year service contracts exist for executives, but the annual report now provides very full details on executive remuneration.

LADBROKE GROUP plc

Chancel House, Neasden Lane, London NW10 2XE
Tel: 0181 459 8031
Chairman John Jackson
Managing director Peter George
Main subsidiaries Hilton International Hotels, Gable House Estates, Vernons Organisation, Texas Homecare
Size £4.3 billion sales, £2 billion stock market value, 55,100 employees
5-year growth sales 24%, earnings per share -82%, employment 8%
Solvency debt = 59% shareholders' funds, interest cover 1 time
Political donations 0
Charitable donations £338,000

Major developments
1967 became public as Ladbroke Group
1979 lost casino licences
1986 bought Home Charm Group (Texas Homecare); sold bingo and amusement centres to Rank
1988 sold Home and Law Magazines; bought Hilton hotels
1989 bought Thomson T-line including Vernons Pools
1993 Cyril Stein announces resignation

Outlook

Ladbroke was once a bookie to the gentry. That was in the days when it was illegal to take bets except at racecourses; and when off-course betting was legalised in the early 1960s, chairman Cyril Stein concluded that Ladbroke should not demean itself by getting involved. Much has changed since then, however: Ladbroke has now been the largest chain of betting shops for many years, and has long since abandoned its attachment to the gentry, in favour of more mundane (and probably more profitable) businesses such as DIY.

In 1994 the start of a new era was signalled for Ladbroke, primarily with the retirement of former chairman and leading light Cyril Stein, whose departure arter 37 years made way for a fundamental rethink of the group's businesses – it was now seeking a way back into casinos after a 15-year absence – as well as a cut in the dividend and a shake-up of the boardroom. Apparently aware of how out of step he would be with the new management under chairman John Jackson and chief executive Peter George, Mr Stein bowed out with a one-off £200,000 payment and a £160,000-a-year consultancy deal designed to cash in on his, particularly property-market, expertise.

When the dividend was cut in early 1994, it put an end to the group's much vaunted record of increasing payments to shareholders in every year since it joined the stock market in 1967. The company's progress has been far from smooth and uneventful since then.

LADBROKE GROUP

Share record

Return on shareholders' equity	%	5.19
5-year price high	p	333.5
5-year price low	p	130.0
Dividend yield	%	4.21
5-year high	%	11.44
5-year low	%	3.24
Price/earnings ratio		27.8
5-year high		32.5
5-year low		8.3

Share price performance (in pence)

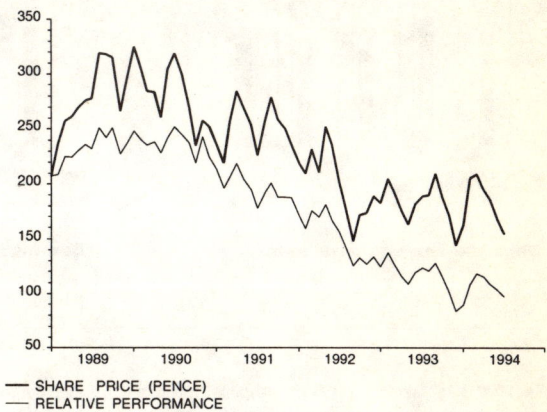

— SHARE PRICE (PENCE)
— RELATIVE PERFORMANCE

Financial record

		31/12/89	31/12/90	31/12/91	31/12/92	31/12/93
Total sales	£	3,448M	3,564M	3,560M	3,934M	4,269M
Pre-tax profit	£'000	302,200	305,600	210,500	158,900	96,900
Published retentions	£'000	128,200	124,000	43,700	-120M	-42,600
Earnings per share	p	22.78	25.90	15.55	7.82	4.08
Dividend per share	p	9.35	10.14	11.15	11.15	6.00
Operating cash flow	£'000	-99,900	-39,200	-58,400	4,300	64,200
Net assets per share	p	358.15	368.01	364.92	287.16	226.34
Net debt/(cash)	£	1,413M	1,566M	1,203M	1,341M	1,270M
Shareholders' funds	£	2,434M	2,493M	2,853M	2,513M	2,164M
Return on capital	%	13.46	11.65	9.64	8.78	8.42
Profit margin	%	8.61	8.38	5.73	3.95	2.28
Sales per employee	£	67.59	68.49	66.63	74.37	77.49
Interest cover		6.00	5.24	2.51	1.75	1.18
Dividend cover		2.43	2.55	1.39	0.72	0.68
Sales increase	%	27.10	3.36	-0.12	10.50	8.52
Earnings growth	%	23.75	13.71	-39.98	-49.70	-47.83
Investment x depreciation		2.63	3.12	0.85	0.88	1.44
Investment as % assets		7.73	8.50	2.37	2.70	5.57
Number of employees		51,015	52,039	53,429	52,894	55,089

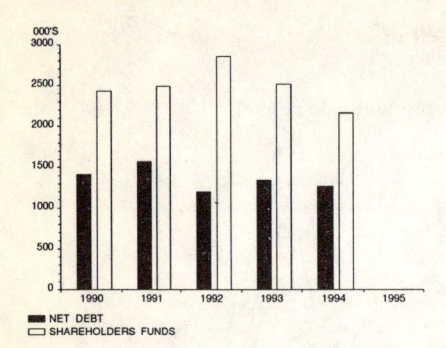

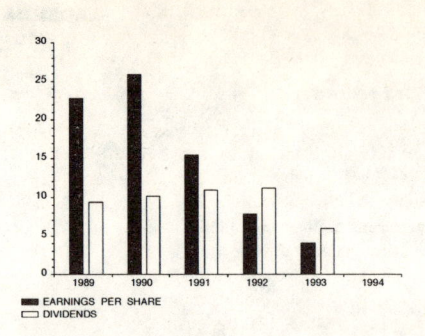

Debt and shareholders' funds

Earnings and dividends

In 1979 Ladbroke's heart was virtually ripped out when the gaming authorities declined to renew its London casino licences. At the time this form of betting accounted for half the group's profits, so it was left with a huge hole to fill. It took Ladbroke a long time to recover from this set-back, but from the mid-1980s onwards the group was reshaped in a rapid series of corporate deals which put it in a more promising position. Out went bingo, holiday camps, investment in the television network (through a stake in Central) and in the television industry (through ownership of electrical retailer Lasky's, subsequently sold by Granada to Kingfisher, which promptly closed down most of the shops to boost its own Comet chain).

Having apparently attempted to model the group on Rank, Forte and Granada, and having been thwarted in a mooted takeover of Granada, Mr Stein seemed to settle on the hotel industry as the core of the new Ladbroke – ironically, as it proved, just as another possible model, Grand Metropolitan, decided to get out of this business. The expansion of its hotel interests fitted with the group's affection for property (as with the old Grand Met), which is still reflected in a large property portfolio that, unfortunately for the company, resulted in losses and heavy write-downs in the early 1990s.

Having built up UK hotel interests, Ladbroke made a quantum leap in this business in 1988 when it paid £645 million to acquire ownership of the Hilton hotel chain outside North America. Converting its existing hotels (where suitable) to the Hilton brand, and adding new properties or management contracts, expanded the Hilton operation to 160 sites and 53,000 beds by the end of 1992. This comprised a wide geographical spread: 16 per cent of beds in 40 UK hotels; slightly more beds, though fewer hotels, in the rest of Europe; and the largest number of beds in just 19 hotels in Asia. Tighter management, including moving the operation's headquarters from New York to the rather less cosmopolitan Watford, boosted profits significantly in the first couple of years of ownership. Then came the Gulf War and recession, leading to lower occupancy levels and hence lower profits. Nevertheless, the Hilton chain remains a valuable asset, occupying a strong position in the hotel industry.

Ladbroke had a similar experience with its other major mid-1980s purchase, Texas Homecare. The DIY chain was bought in 1986, in time to gain from the great do-it-yourself boom associated with the ballooning housing market. Having reaped that benefit, and taken part in the huge expansion of the DIY outlets, however, Ladbroke then found itself embroiled not only in recession but also in the worst housing market for decades. With DIY purchases very closely associated with the housing market, Texas's profits stuttered. (The reported figures show a very slight fall, but this was made to look better by a change in accounting policy, and analysts have always felt a little uncertain about Ladbroke's accounting analysis.)

In the early 1990s the company remained second to Kingfisher's B&Q in a still-promising market, seeking to benefit by concentrating on the 'softer' end of the market (furnishing and decoration) while its rivals clustered around the hardware and building segment. Nevertheless, Ladbroke was widely thought to have decided in 1990 to sell Texas, and did not achieve it only because of the failure of potential buyers to offer a high enough price.

Although Ladbroke remains something of an enigma, reflecting the dominance for so long of Mr Stein, light is at last beginning to enter. Change is already bringing benefits, and analysts forecast strong profit gains in the next few years. Excitement for investors could come if the group pursues plans to relaunch its casino business.

Shares

Ladbroke has long been seen as a stock to hold for its yield, although group expansion meant the shares themselves had a good run, compared to the rest of the market, throughout the 1980s. The group announced a rights issue early in 1987, but 98 per cent was left with the underwriters. This spoilt the company's rating but meant it had less far to fall when the market crashed. By 1988 Ladbroke's rating was again on the rise, thanks partly to a strong performance by the hotels division, while deals like the purchase of the Vernon's pools business and Hilton saw the rating peak in 1989.

After that year the rise in interest rates to 15 per cent began to sap the group's investment in property and hotels. By mid-1990 the group had £1.5 billion of net debt and the recession was taking its toll on business; the rating slid downwards as a result. In the following year, despite a set-back attributed to the effects of the Gulf War, recession and the weak property division, the board tried another rights issue. Despite the high yield of the shares, the rating fell further in 1992 on account of worries about exposure to property, and there were doubts about the dividend.

Ladbroke persisted with big dividend payments even though its rating was low. And when at last the time came for the shareholder payout to be cut, shares lost considerable ground. Hopes now rest on the fact that lower interest rates should be good for the hotels business and may stimulate the housing market to the benefit of Texas.

Corporate conscience

Ladbroke's heritage is gambling, which exposes the group on that ethical issue. Through Hilton hotels and at race tracks it also sells alcohol and tobacco, which rings another couple of ethical bells.

Otherwise the record is mostly neutral. The group does not stand out, positively or negatively, on social or employment issues. There does not appear to be a policy on equal opportunities, although Texas has adopted some innovative employment policies and supports Opportunity 2000. Ladbroke is a member of the Per Cent Club, but curiously not of BITC. The group has no stated environmental policy. It has thus made no commitment to phasing out CFCs, or worrying about the tropical hardwoods used in Texas Homecare furniture. Hilton's network means that it operates in countries such as Israel and Venezuela. Finally, the ASA has upheld complaints against Texas and Vernon's pools.

Corporate governance

Separate Chairman and Chief Executive Y
Number of Directors 11
Number of Non-Executive Directors 5
(5 Independent Directors)
Insulated Directors None

Board Committees
Audit: Y   Remuneration: Y

Remuneration

Year end	31.12.91	31.12.92	31.12.93
Total board £M	1.93	2.00	2.17
% change		-10	4	8
Highest paid £	584,000	586,000	583,000
% change		-4	0.3	-0.5

Board

George, Peter M *Chief Executive*
Jackson, John *Executive Chairman*
Anderson, John *Executive Director*
Andrews, Christopher H *Executive Director*
Hirst, Michael B *Executive Director*
O'Mahony, Jeremiah *Finance Director*
Collum, Hugh *Independent Non-Executive*
Earl of Gowrie *Independent Non-Executive*
Janner, Greville *Independent Non-Executive*
Patten, Louise *Independent Non-Executive*
Williams, Derek *Independent Non-Executive*

Ladbroke has always given the impression of wanting to be a private company. But in the post-Stein era greater openness in the boardroom is expected to be a welcome change. Already, in succession to Mr Stein, the two top jobs have been separated and the overall balance of boardroom power has improved. The company held its first ever press conference in early 1994 and announced that Hugh Collum, chief financial officer of SmithKline Beecham, and Derek Williams of Cadbury Schweppes are to swell non-executive numbers on the board during 1994. *Glasnost* seems finally to have arrived at Ladbroke.

LAND SECURITIES plc

5 Strand, London WC2N 5AF
Tel: 0171 413 9000
Chairman and chief executive Peter Hunt
Main subsidiaries Ravenseft Properties, The City of London Real Property Company
Size £5.0 billion assets, £3.4 billion stock market value, 537 employees
5-year growth assets 3%, earnings per share 40%, employment 14%
Solvency borrowing ratio 25%, interest cover 3 times
Political donations 0
Charitable donations £108,000

Major developments

1944 company founded
1955 became public
1968 acquired City Centre Properties
1969 acquired City of London Real Property
1971 acquired Westminster Trust

LAND SECURITIES

Share record

Return on shareholders' equity	%	5.01
5-year price high	p	800.0
5-year price low	p	353.0
Dividend yield	%	4.44
5-year high	%	8.22
5-year low	%	3.13
Price/earnings ratio		20.0
5-year high		29.4
5-year low		11.3

Share price performance (in pence)

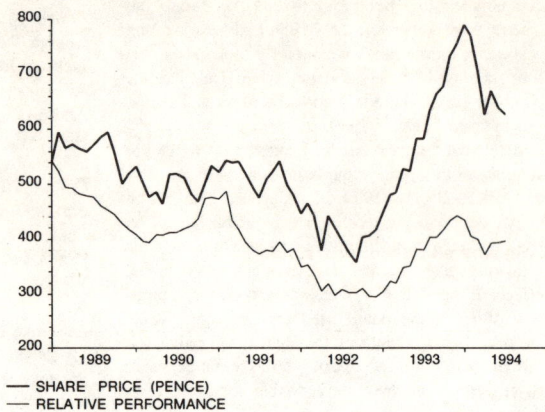

— SHARE PRICE (PENCE)
— RELATIVE PERFORMANCE

Financial record

		31/3/90	31/3/91	31/3/92	31/3/93	31/3/94
Total revenue	£'000	296,300	359,700	406,700	436,900	448,900
Pre-tax profit	£'000	175,100	215,200	227,500	234,800	234,800
Published retentions	£'000	38,500	55,900	54,800	54,700	58,400
Earnings per share	p	24.29	29.69	31.99	33.44	33.93
Dividend per share	p	17.00	19.75	21.75	22.85	24.00
Fully diluted assets per share	£	9.30	6.68	5.63	4.94	6.81
Net debt/(cash)	£	1,013M	1,100M	1,209M	1,281M	1,332M
Shareholders' funds	%	4,432M	3,371M	2,800M	2,544M	3,453M
Rent as % assets		16.19	32.97	43.76	9.95	8.28
Return on capital	%	8.85	9.95	8.28	9.18	8.52
Return on shareholders' capital	%	2.78	4.49	5.84	6.72	5.01
Trading profit margin	%	81.81	81.29	81.49	82.12	82.07
Interest cover		2.58	2.82	2.73	2.63	2.59
Dividend cover		1.43	1.50	1.47	1.46	1.41
Income growth	%	19.00	21.40	13.07	7.43	2.75
Earnings growth	%	16.39	22.21	7.76	4.54	1.48
Changes in assets	%	7.67	-16.09	-8.61	-4.70	22.78
Number of employees		473	476	492	547	537

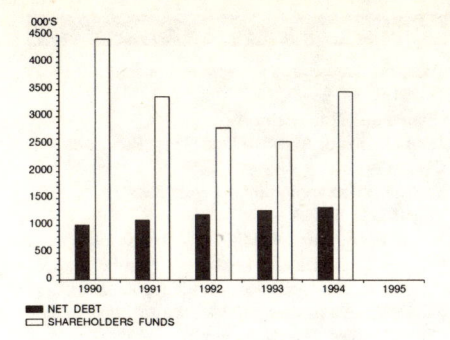

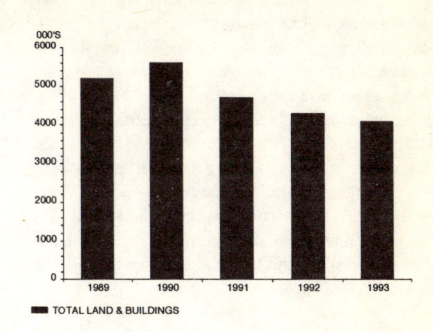

Debt and shareholders' funds

Total asset value

Outlook

Land Securities is the UK's largest property company by far and as such remained relatively oblivious to the property crash of the late 1980s, during which period its loyal fans never seriously considered desertion.

On the downside, however, a sizeable proportion of the group's massive portfolio is in the West End of London, much of it around Victoria, including a large number of leases which are due to expire in the latter part of this decade. Even though demand is now increasing for these parts of London, Land Securities may still find it necessary to redevelop some of its oldest properties if it is to attract sufficient numbers of tenants willing to pay good rents. The company spent £600 million on properties in the early 1990s.

On the other hand, Land Securities owns shopping centres as well as offices and is therefore well diversified. Historically it has always introduced a few highly remunerative redeveloped properties on to the market each year. It prides itself on receiving more money in rent than it does in running costs, and it is lowly geared.

At £237 million, group results for the financial year to the end of March 1994 showed an increase in pre-tax profits of 3.5 per cent. The figures were accompanied by an upbeat statement which stressed that the assets of the company had risen sharply over the previous year – by £934 million to over £5 billion. What is more, the company noted that although rental values in most sectors continued to fall during the year, the pace of decline had slowed and the downturn appeared to be coming to an end. In particular, Land Securities was confident about the strengthening and stability of demand, especially for top London locations. But the group was well aware that the potential for increasing rents and revenue would remain limited until the economic recovery was really in full swing. Only then would businesses have the confidence, and the cash, to demand more space.

In the meantime, Land Securities is undoubtedly in a good position. More than 80 per cent of its total rental income is secured on leases expiring beyond the year 2000 – leases without break clauses and with upward-only rent reviews. Building on this, the group was one of the few property companies to have gently resurrected its development programme by the beginning of 1994. The reconstruction of Eland House, a 250,000 square-foot development in Victoria, pre-let to the Department of the Environment, is the most significant manifestation of this change of attitude. But the group is also believed to be looking for other sites – in and out of London, possibly with retail potential.

In addition, Land Securities began addressing the other area of its activities which tends to come under fire. Critics have argued that the company needs to step up its property acquisition programme and that it may have been left behind during 1993 by other key market players starting to buy once more. In spring 1994 Land Securities bought a small trading estate in Heston, and announced that it was keen on making industrial purchases, close to both the M4 and Heathrow. So look out for more spending.

Shares

Land Securities is reputedly the safest of the property companies, not merely because it is the largest, but because of its strong finances and the prime location of its properties. That makes it popular when the market is in recession but slow to benefit when there is a boom.

Even Land Securities, large as it is, was not immune to the property crash, though, and at the end of 1991 its share price dipped almost as dramatically as that of its rivals. Then the shares recovered sharply throughout 1992 and the first half of 1993, dropping slightly in the second part of that year. Early in 1994 they were on the rise again, and City analysts were very positive about short-term prospects. They pointed out that the company was one of the few to have the financial strength to start a development programme again, and they were reassured by the long-running leases in its portfolio. Yet the critics believed that the rise in the group's fortunes owed more to the uplift in the property sector generally, and little to anything magical which the company itself had done. Moreover, there was still very little sign of market rents increasing significantly, indicating that Land Securities' profits might stay flat throughout the mid-1990s.

Corporate conscience

Property companies register on few of the issues addressed by EIRIS, and Land Securities is no exception. The only negative mark is in connection with ozone-depleting chemicals, since the company is not committed to avoiding them in properties with which it is involved. On the positive front, it has developed adequate equal opportunities and environmental policies.

Corporate governance

Separate Chairman and Chief Executive N
Number of Directors 8
Number of Non-Executive Directors 3
(2 Independent Directors)
Insulated Directors MD

Board Committees
Audit: Y   Remuneration: Y

Remuneration

Year end	31.03.92	31.03.93	31.03.94
Total board £M	1.57	1.65	1.42
% change	1	5	-14
Highest paid £	259,000	258,000	265,000
% change	4	-0.4	3

Board
Hunt, Peter J *Chairman & Chief Executive*
Griffiths, Michael R *Executive Director*
Henderson, Ian J *Executive Director*
Redshaw, Keith *Executive Director*
Murray, James I K *Finance Director*
Connick, H Ivor *Independent Non-Executive*
Hull, John *Independent Non-Executive*
Hardy, Peter B *Non-Executive*

In the 1994 annual report the company refers to the fact that Peter Hunt is both chairman and chief executive. It says the presence of three non-executives counts as a 'strong independent element'. Their independence has certainly been strengthened by the addition in 1992 of Peter Hardy, formerly with Warburg. His brief tenure balances that of John Hull, who has been on the board since 1976.

LONRHO plc

Cheapside House, 138 Cheapside, London EC2 6BL
Tel: 0171 606 9898
Chairman René Leclézio
Joint chief executives Roland (Tiny) Rowland and Dieter Bock
Substantial shareholdings Dieter Bock 24.7%, Tiny Rowland 6.3%
Main brands and subsidiaries Ashanti Goldfields (45%), Jack Barclay, Dovercourt, Dutton-Forshaw, Greenaways, Harrison & Sons, Metropole Hotels (67%), Eastern Platinum (73%), Western Platinum (73%), Princess Hotels, Sunley Turriff
Size £2.0 billion sales, £1.0 million stock market value, 130,000 employees
5-year growth sales n/a, earnings per share n/a, employment n/a
Solvency debt interest cover n/a
Political donations 0
Charitable donations £39,030

Major developments

1909 formed as London and Rhodesian Mining and Land Company
1961 Tiny Rowland joined the board
1963 changed to Lonrho
1968 bought Ashanti Goldfields
1973 Rowland became sole MD
1975 bought Volkswagen GB
1976 bought Brentford Nylons
1979 acquired SUITS, Princess Hotels, Dutton-Forshaw
1981 bought *Observer* newspaper; bid for House of Fraser (Harrods)
1982 bought casinos
1987 sold casinos to Brent Walker
1988 bought 50% of Krupp Handel GmbH
1989 sold Whyte & Mackay Distillers
1990 bought 10% of ASKO German retailer
1992 sold 50% stake in Kühne & Nagel; sold Scottish & Universal Newspapers, George Outram & Co
1993 sold Volkswagen–Audi (UK); sold the *Observer*; sold stake in Krupp Lonrho
1994 announced plans to float African interests; board changes led to departure of Rowland supporters

Outlook

It is remarkable how little Lonrho changed between 1992 and 1993 and how much has changed since then. Despite much activity on many continents, it is still predominantly a mining and trading group with its feet planted firmly in Africa. Interests range from oil in the United States to printing in Britain, but over three-quarters of its profits came from Africa in 1993 and two-thirds were earned from mining, motor and

LONRHO

Share record

Return on shareholders' equity	%	1.51
5-year price high	p	292.7
5-year price low	p	59.0
Dividend yield	%	3.82
5-year high	%	26.46
5-year low	%	2.92
Price/earnings ratio		n/a
5-year high		n/a
5-year low		n/a

Share price performance (in pence)

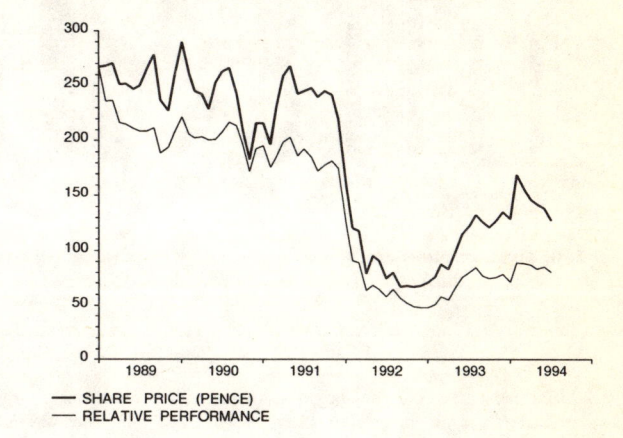

— SHARE PRICE (PENCE)
— RELATIVE PERFORMANCE

Financial record

		30/9/89	30/9/90	30/9/91	30/9/92	30/9/93
Total sales	£	3,609M	3,146M	2,998M	2,923M	1,990M
Pre-tax profit	£'000	227,900	270,000	174,000	78,000	76,000
Published retentions	£'000	142,500	49,000	-10,000	59,000	81,000
Earnings per share	p	19.34	22.24	5.26	0.00	1.35
Dividend per share	p	14.55	16.00	13.00	4.00	4.00
Operating cash flow	£'000	-296M	-123M	-173M	-35,000	-144M
Net assets per share	p	360.19	385.72	364.95	350.98	241.19
Net debt/(cash)	£'000	795,600	817,000	1,032M	847,000	430,000
Shareholders' funds	£	1,460M	1,485M	1,454M	1,080M	1,060M
Return on capital	%	16.05	16.91	13.05	8.74	8.25
Profit margin	%	5.32	6.61	4.07	1.20	1.71
Sales per employee	£	35.17	28.93	26.51	21.30	15.30
Interest cover		3.72	3.25	2.04	1.33	1.47
Dividend cover		1.33	1.39	0.40	0.00	0.34
Sales increase	%	10.49	-12.82	-4.70	-2.50	-31.92
Earnings growth	%	2.17	14.97	-76.35	-100.00	0.00
Investment x depreciation		4.43	7.02	3.39	2.39	1.02
Investment as % assets		13.17	18.78	9.76	7.24	3.89
Number of employees		102,601	108,759	113,094	137,214	130,044

292 LONRHO plc

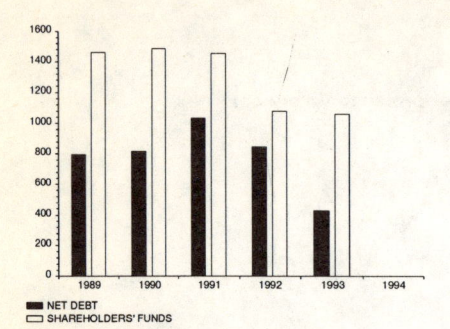

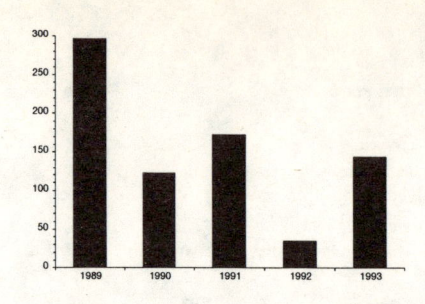

Debt and shareholders' funds

Operating cash outflow

general trading. The company began in African mining (in 1909), while the chief executive, Tiny Rowland, started his business career in Africa, which is where the man and the company came together, in 1961.

Tiny Rowland and Lonrho have been intimately intertwined ever since. Mr Rowland has been a managing director since 1961, and the sole managing director for more than 20 years after a famous coup which ousted his opponents. Now he once again shares the leadership with the German investor Dieter Bock who bought a substantial chunk of Mr Rowland's shares in 1992. Rowland was originally recruited to invigorate the sleepy company, and his negotiating skills and African contacts are widely credited with building Lonrho into a group with a £5 billion turnover. But he has also been a liability: the boardroom *coup* in 1973 prompted the famous phrase from prime minister Ted Heath about the unacceptable face of capitalism; his disregard for the niceties of City life alienated investors and so threatened the very survival of the company in the early 1990s. His 10-year feud with the Al Fayed brothers over ownership of the Harrods group, House of Fraser, also bedevilled Lonrho throughout the 1980s. The company's ownership of the ailing *Observer* newspaper until 1993 owed more to Mr Rowland's desire to have a vehicle for his views than to any business strategy.

Apart from these idiosyncrasies, the group remains an old-fashioned conglomerate. Despite original plans to make Harrods the centrepiece of a powerful retail group, there has been little attempt at creating logical business links between Lonrho's various arms, or even between the many companies within each division. Companies have been bought primarily for opportunistic reasons – because they were cheap – or for specific trading purposes. Likewise, they have been sold, and continue to be sold, to raise cash when it was needed (as in 1991–3) or simply if the price was right.

Under Mr Bock's guidance, it seems the next step is to hive off much of the minor African interests into a separately quoted company, then to merge the mining business with another mining company in southern Africa.

Mining remains the most important division as far as profits are concerned, and has received huge amounts of capital investment since the late 1980s – one of the main reasons for the cash crisis which beset the group in the early 1990s. The Ashanti gold mine, a joint venture with the Ghanaian government which was floated on the stock exchange in 1994,, and the Western Platinum/Karee/Eastern Platinum mines in South Africa are the key sources of profit. Lonrho also operates gold mines in South Africa, Zimbabwe and Mozambique. Platinum, and its associated metal, rhodium, have received a substantial boost in the last few years because of the advent of catalytic converters in cars, which use more than a third of the world's platinum, but profits have been hit by falling prices.

General Trading, the second-largest profit contributor (after the end of the Volkswgen–Audi distributorship in the UK in 1993 reduced the size of the motor division), encompasses a huge range of companies and activities. These are mostly in Africa since the German business has been reduced by the sale of the half share in freight company Kühne and Nagle and Krupp Lonrho as part of the group's fund-raising activity and various trading activities throughout Africa.

Motor Trading spreads throughout Africa, where the group has agencies for Mercedes, Toyota, Peugeot, VW-Audi, Mitsubishi, Fiat, Massey Ferguson, Rover and General Motors. This is one of the few areas where the UK was more important, until the ending of the VW-Audi distributorship. The group also owns dealerships for these and other makes, notably Jack Barclay, the Rolls-Royce dealer.

Hotels include the Metropole group, based in London, Brighton, Birmingham and Blackpool; a collection of hotels in various parts of Africa; and the Princess chain in the US, the Bahamas, Mexico and Bermuda. Considerable spending has been invested recently in expanding and upgrading several properties, but the Princess chain is thought to be a prime candidate for disposal if Lonrho can obtain the right price. Mr Rowland pulled off one of his most controversial deals in 1992 when he attracted investment in the Metropole group from the Libyan government.

Manufacturing consists of a wide collection of mostly insubstantial activities based mainly in the UK. The most substantial sector is printing and publishing, although this has been reduced by the sale of the *Observer* and Scottish newspapers. It still includes the *Standard* in Kenya, and in this country Greenaways and Harrison & Son – printer of 90 per cent of British postage stamps. Lonrho also owns Tariff and steel and textile businesses in the UK.

Agriculture is where Mr Rowland began, when he emigrated to Rhodesia after the Second World War. Sugar is now the most important crop, but Lonrho's interests encompass tea, coffee, cotton and wheat, as well as cattle and vegetables.

This hugely varied collection of companies has increasingly seemed to add up to very little, especially in cash terms. Heavy investment in hotels and mining left Lonrho with excessive debts by the end of the 1980s, and falling metal prices crippled the cash flows which were required to service those debts. The group was forced to make a series of disposals simply to raise money, and Mr Rowland eventually had to cede some of his power to Mr Bock in exchange for a crucial investment in the group.

In the early 1990s those who had watched Mr Rowland over three decades wondered whether Mr Bock would remain once it was clear that Lonrho's survival was assured. But Mr Bock has an option to buy the rest of Mr Rowland's holdings in Lonrho in 1996, which seemed to put him in an impregnable position. The more important question was what would be left and how much it would be worth after the two men had sold enough assets to stabilise the financial situation.

Shares

The steady rating of Lonrho's shares, little affected by the stock market crash of 1987, soared in 1988 to levels not seen since the mid-1970s when Australian predator Alan Bond took a stake. The shares more than doubled, and while speculators pulled out when the affair looked like dragging on, the rating stayed high. It was helped by a scrip issue and a 250 per cent rise in dividend early the next year, although, based on the group's subsequent performance, that increase proved to have been foolhardy.

While Mr Bond's challenge collapsed, Lonrho's shares clung to part of their re-rating as the market absorbed some of the virtues revealed by the raid. The next year brought a 46 per cent rise in dividend, but by 1990 the City was speculating that debt was rising and the group was losing momentum. A revival of interest came with rumours that South African mining group Gencor was interested in a merger, but by the end of 1991 the doubters were winning and the share price fell sharply.

The board said there was no reason for the fall but the next month, January 1992, brought the first cut in the dividend for 20 years, further undermining the group's credibility. Doubts continued over whether Lonrho could maintain its reduced dividend level and the share rating slipped further, taking the company out of the FTSE 100 index. The year ended with the introduction of Mr Bock and a rights issue, neither of which helped the shares. The absence of any surprises in the February 1993 results did bring a small rise in the shares, although analysts noted that nothing fundamental had changed and Lonrho still faced huge difficulties recovering its former glory. The shares managed to recover some of their glory, however, sustaining a rise into 1994.

Corporate conscience

Lonrho's philosophy seems rooted firmly in old-fashioned capitalism: anything goes if it legally benefits shareholders, and if companies concentrate on these, others will also benefit. As a result, Lonrho does not disappoint expectations that it would not be interested in policies on equal opportunities or environmental protection. Nor does it have a distinguished record as a caring employer – or caring very much about any other issue of conscience, either.

There are no blemishes on the health and safety record, however, although Lonrho has exceeded water discharge consents. Lonrho is involved in military supplies (Dutton-Forshaw exhaust controls). Ozone-depleting chemicals are used in hotel refrigeration, while the Ashanti goldfield is in an area of former tropical forest.

Lonrho operates in many Third World countries where human rights are under threat. In South Africa the group employs more than 14,000 people in mining, metal production, construction and engineering, some of whom have been paid well below an acceptable minimum level. Mr Rowland would claim that his company has done enormous amounts for many black African countries, but contrast this with Lonrho's pay-rates in these countries of less than half the accepted minimum.

Corporate governance

Separate Chairman and Chief Executive Y
Number of Directors 13
Number of Non-Executive Directors 3
(3 Independent Directors)
Insulated Directors none

Board Committees
Audit: Y   Remuneration: Y

LUCAS INDUSTRIES plc

Remuneration

Year end	30.09.91	30.09.92	30.09.93
Total board £M	5.37	5.12	5.21
% change	1	-5	2
Highest paid £M	1.60	1.65	1.6
% change	5	3	-2

Board
Bock, D *Chief Executive*
Rowland, R W *Chief Executive*
Leclézio, M J J R *Executive Chairman*
Hewlett, J A *Executive Director*
Jonah, S E *Executive Director*
Morrell, N J *Executive Director*
Platts-Mills, J L *Executive Director*
Tarsh, P M *Executive Director*
Whitten, R E *Executive Director*
Wilkinson, Terence *Executive Director*
Harper, Peter *Independent Non-Executive*
Leahy, Sir John *Independent Non-Executive*
Walls, Stephen *Independent Non-Executive*

The Lonrho board was still in transition in 1994. The search for a chairman to replace René Leclézio continued, while other long-time associates of Mr Rowland, Paul Spicer and Robert Dunlop, were scheduled to retire during the year. Three independent non-executives were appointed in 1993, bringing a semblance of normality to the boardroom, including the creation of audit and remuneration committees. Despite this, and despite paying Mr Rowland in excess of £1.6 million, the annual report does not indicate how this was composed, nor how it was justified. On the plus side, however, service contracts for executives are restricted to one year only, and the annual report volunteers that less than 0.2 per cent of its £300 million pension fund is invested in Lonrho shares.

LUCAS INDUSTRIES plc

Brueton House, New Road, Solihull, West Midlands B91 3TX
Tel: 0121 627 6000.
Chairman Sir Anthony Gill
Chief Executive George Simpson
Size £2.4 billion sales, £1.4 billion stock market value, 48,900 employees
5-year growth sales 17%, earnings per share -87%, employment -13%
Solvency debt = 46% shareholders' funds, interest cover 2 times
Political donations £25,000 Conservative Party
Charitable donations £360,600

Major developments
1897 formed as Joseph Lucas
1975 became Lucas Industries
1988 bought Amfas Corporation and AUL Instruments; sold Francis Searchlights and Lucas clearax
1989 bought AMP Keyboard Technologies; bought Krug Power & Control UK
1992 sold Fluid Power Systems
1993 formed Lucas Electronics

Outlook

This company could hardly be a better case study of Britain's manufacturing history. Joseph Lucas founded it towards the end of the last century. It grew prodigiously from the original product area of bicycles and bicycle equipment, such as lamps, to become the dominant supplier of electrical parts to the British motor industry. The important word there is 'British', because during the recession in 1980 Lucas found itself too dependent on the unreliable British market, and, having been cosseted by it for too long, not sufficiently competitive with international rivals.

Copying the move from bicycles to cars, Lucas attempted to gain a foothold in aerospace, but with limited success. In the mid-1970s workers belonging to manufacturing trade unions attempted to save their jobs, their consciences, and perhaps the company, with a famous Alternative Plan which proposed making high-tech products for commercial/domestic use instead of engaging in the military-related work of the Aerospace division. Predictably, their plan was dismissed, but the management could not ignore the group's plight, especially when its arrogance was punctured with the shock of a £21 million loss in 1981. Swingeing cuts followed, but it was not until 1986 that Lucas gave up trying to update its traditional business and management decided on its own Alternative Plan.

It was a classic of the time: jettison the commodity style products such as lamps, windscreen wipers and starter motors; concentrate on 'value-added' areas where the group's skills and market position would help to protect margins and volumes of business – Girling brake systems and CAV fuel-injection devices were the prime examples. Next, the strategy identified the need to diversify beyond the motor industry and the British Isles, which led to aerospace activities being built up, primarily in the US, and to a fairly misguided attempt to create a third leg constituting broader interests in industrial technology.

The strategy is a familiar one, having been employed by fellow companies in the motor industry like GKN and Smiths Industries, but also by many in other fields: focus on strengths, diversify away from the weakness of Britain. Sadly, 10 years after the shock of 1981, Lucas was once more in the grip of a British recession, and in 1992 it was saved from a loss only by clever use of its pension fund surplus. Another restructuring followed; more jobs went. The company found itself suffering from having paid less

LUCAS INDUSTRIES

Share record

Return on shareholders' equity	%	3.07
5-year price high	p	234.0
5-year price low	p	78.0
Dividend yield	%	4.61
5-year high	%	11.97
5-year low	%	3.74
Price/earnings ratio		49.9
5-year high		91.5
5-year low		6.3

Share price performance (in pence)

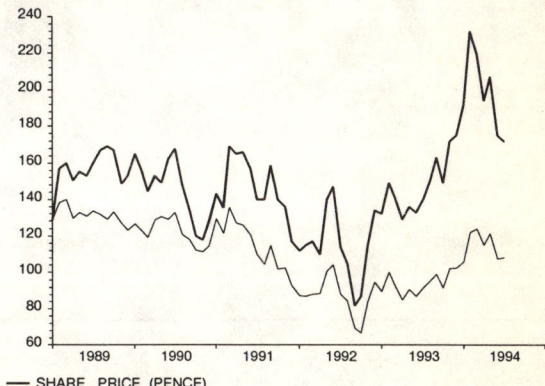

Financial record

		31/7/89	31/7/90	31/7/91	31/7/92	31/7/93
Total sales	£	2,087M	2,229M	2,365M	2,253M	2,434M
Pre-tax profit	£'000	199,400	191,100	101,800	45,000	49,400
Published retentions	£'000	95,000	91,500	1,200	-58,100	-25,100
Earnings per share	p	22.16	20.70	8.67	1.68	2.86
Dividend per share	p	6.21	7.00	7.00	7.00	7.00
Operating cash flow	£'000	56,200	33,500	-98,400	1,500	10,500
Net assets per share	p	171.24	172.28	171.52	187.99	208.34
Net debt/(cash)	£'000	116,500	175,800	327,200	328,700	337,600
Shareholders' funds	£'000	805,700	811,100	805,900	725,100	730,900
Return on capital	%	22.11	19.94	12.65	8.70	8.64
Profit margin	%	9.32	8.37	4.05	2.11	2.14
Sales per employee	£	37.29	38.83	43.05	43.85	49.81
Interest cover		24.14	12.51	4.20	2.27	2.35
Dividend cover		3.57	2.96	1.24	0.24	0.41
Sales increase	%	13.83	6.82	6.10	-4.75	8.05
Earnings growth	%	8.32	-6.59	-58.11	-80.63	70.28
Investment x depreciation		1.32	1.70	1.57	0.94	0.40
Investment as % assets		12.19	16.77	16.66	10.07	4.57
Number of employees		55,957	57,399	54,942	51,377	48,866

LUCAS INDUSTRIES plc

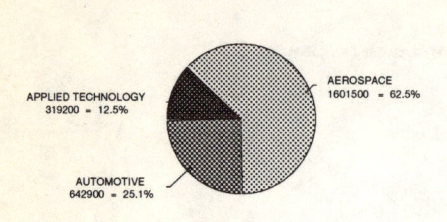

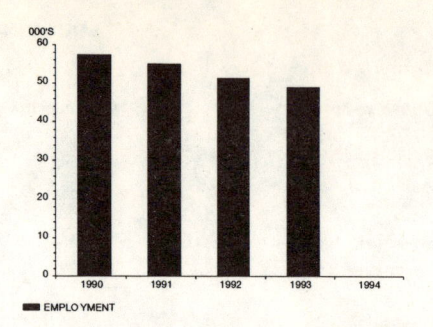

Profit analysis

APPLIED TECHNOLOGY 319200 = 12.5%
AEROSPACE 1601500 = 62.5%
AUTOMOTIVE 642900 = 25.1%

Employment

attention to its City investors than to its internal research and development.

The City's opinion of the group has not been helped by the apparent difficulty that chairman Sir Anthony Gill had in getting on with colleagues, especially finance directors, as evidenced by several swift departures from the boardroom. The importance of this has diminished as Sir Anthony's retirement – planned for late 1994 – approached, especially after the company finally found a suitable chief executive in the form of ex-Rover boss George Simpson. The City was also reassured by the announcement in April 1994 that former Midland Bank chief executive Sir Brian Pearse would take over as chairman.

Lucas has excellent technology in braking and engine systems, and should benefit from the future growth of the electronics business in cars and trucks. Aerospace is also likely to be a long-term growth industry, although the surge of deliveries stemming from orders made in the late 1980s has created too much aircraft capacity for current, depressed demand. Manufacturers have therefore been forced to cut their production levels, and output is not expected to start rising again until 1995. Lucas faces additional worries over a Pentagon inquiry into the performance of its US subsidiaries on defence contracts. The worst fears included the possibility of a a ban on the group, although Lucas has insisted this was highly unlikely. Now that the key question of succession has been resolved the danger of the group losing its independence, so that somebody else benefits from the upturn, has receded.

Shares

The heyday of the Lucas shares was in 1977, but if the trend has been downhill since, there has been the odd flurry of interest as in 1986 when the management took a holiday from pension contributions at the same time as taking an axe to jobs – and prompting bid speculation. This proved too thin a mixture to power a re-rating, however, and while the shares peaked in absolute terms, just ahead of the 1987 market crash, the relative value only rose to a respectable level again in 1988.

Once again there was talk of the City re-rating the shares, but while the group made a successful rights issue that year, the rating slipped until a turning point seemed to have been reached in 1990. Brighter prospects for the group's aerospace business triggered a rally but recession caught up with the results the next year. Perennial hopes for an upturn continued to be disappointed until late in 1992 when the City decided that Lucas had to recover at some point, and that even if it did not, the company would be taken over. Bid hopes sustained the shares into 1993 when news of the succession gave further support. But pessimism returned in 1994 on worries about the aerospace industry and fears of a Pentagon ban on Lucas products.

Corporate conscience

Lucas does not have an adequate equal opportunities policy (but does support Opportunity 2000), nor environmental policy and only limited interest in group-wide community support.

It has been convicted under Health and Safety and water pollution laws, and unusually for a manufacturing company has also fallen foul of the ASA.

Lucas has some operations in countries such as India and Brazil, which can be considered to have oppressive regimes. Most significantly, however, it is a military supplier: apart from the aerospace connection, Rists makes wiring for military use; Automotive makes power systems for tanks; and Electrical makes special military ignition sysems and windscreen washers. The group is classified as a 'major arms trader' by Campaign Against the Arms Trade, having an input to Patriot missiles and the B-2 Stealth bomber, among other means of destruction.

Corporate governance

Separate Chairman and Chief Executive Y
Number of Directors 13
Number of Non-Executive Directors 7
(7 Independent Directors)
Insulated Directors none

Board Committees
Audit: Y   Remuneration: Y

Remuneration

Year end	31.07.91	31.07.92	31.07.93
Total board £M	1.27	1.56	1.26
% change		-9	23	-19
Highest paid £	332,420	369,640	355,659
% change		2	11	-4

Board
Gill, Sir Anthony *Chairman*
Simpson, George *Chief Executive*
Dale, Robert A *Executive Director*
Mason, Bryan G *Executive Director*
Turner, Frank *Executive Director*
Grant, John A M *Finance Director*
Bossonet, Paul *Independent Non-Executive*
Edwards, Sir Sam *Independent Non-Executive*
Fairclough, Sir John *Independent Non-Executive*
Giordano, Richard *Independent Non-Executive*
Morton, Sir Alastair *Independent Non-Executive*
Pearse, Sir Brian *Independent Non-Executive*
White, James *Independent Non-Executive*

The share price suffered seriously in 1992, not only because of poor financial results, but also because the City's fragile confidence in the Lucas board was hit by the departure of finance director David Hankinson and recently appointed chief executive designate Tony Edwards. Chairman Sir Anthony Gill was accused of being unable to hang on to talented colleagues, and unable to hand over power to potential successors. Reassurance was required, and came in the form of a significant strengthening of independent directors in March 1993: in the form of Richard Giordano (former boss of BOC), Eurotunnel's Sir Alastair Morton and BT deputy chairman Paul Bosonnet. Mr Giordano was made chairman of the nominations committee, which was urgently seeking to appoint a chief executive for the company and would subsequently decide on a chairman to take over from Sir Anthony on his planned retirement in 1994. Having completed his job with the appointments of George Simpson and Sir Brian Pearse, Mr Giordano then departed for British Gas and BOC, leaving behind a much stronger board in compliance with Cadbury requirements.

MAI plc

8 Montague Close, London Bridge, London SE1 9RD
Tel: 0171 407 7624
Chairman and chief executive Lord Hollick
Main subsidiaries Anglia Television, Garban, Harlow Butler, Meridian television, NOP market research, Safeguard insurance, Wagon Finance
Size £147 million sales, £0.8 billion stock market value, 5,088 employees
5-year growth sales 67%, earnings per share 98%, employment 22%
Solvency debt = 34% shareholders' funds, interest cover n/a
Political donations 0
Charitable donations £47,000

Major developments
1973 rescue of Vavasseur; change of name to Mills and Allen
1983 set up personal financial services business
1986 bought Wagon Finance
1987 acquired London and Continental Advertising
1989 bought NOP and MIL market research; merged outdoor advertising business with Havas
1991 began to sell shares in Avenir Havas; won southern England ITV franchise as Meridian
1994 bought Anglia Television for £292 million; sold last share stake in Havas

Outlook
The initials of this company once represented 'Mills and Allen International', the billboard advertising company. Now the only connection MAI has with advertising is through its independent television (ITV) interests, Anglia and Meridian. The other side of the business is involved in the more arcane aspects of the financial system – money and securities broking (that is, acting as the intermediary between two parties which want to buy or sell funds or securities such as government bonds).

This curious combination of businesses is a consequence of the origins of the group as the fringe bank Vavasseur. Having suffered during the financial crash of 1973/4, Vavasseur was rescued by the Bank of England, under the auspices of Hambros bank and the supervision of company doctor Sir Ian Morrow. A young Hambros corporate finance executive, Clive Hollick, was brought in with Sir Ian to act as managing director. Between them they arranged a series of financial restructurings to return the company to normality. Sir Ian finally retired from the chair in 1993, although he remains on the board. The now ennobled Lord Hollick continues the quietly effective job he has done for almost 20 years, although the company's entry into the world of television means it is much less quiet than it has been.

The peerage, at the relatively early age of 45, was awarded not because of his excellent work in busi-

MAI

Share record

Return on shareholder's equity	%	30.28
5-year price high	p	321.5
5-year price low	p	87.0
Dividend yield	%	3.27
5-year high	%	7.66
5-year low	%	2.68
Price/earnings ratio		14.4
5-year high		20.4
5-year low		6.5

Share price performance (in pence)

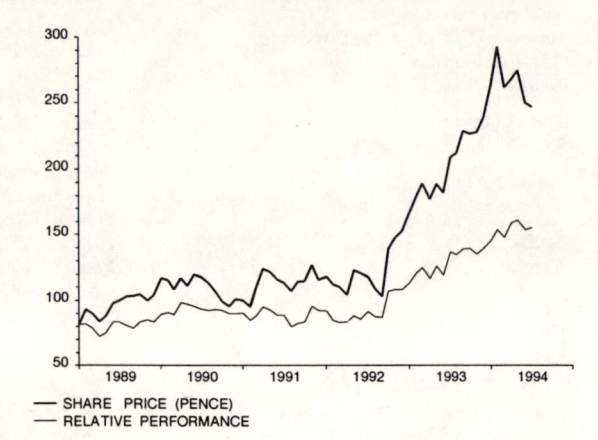

— SHARE PRICE (PENCE)
— RELATIVE PERFORMANCE

Financial record

		30/6/89	30/6/90	30/6/91	30/6/92	30/6/93
Total sales	£'000	87,901	76,400	51,400	54,200	147,000
Pre-tax profit	£'000	48,043	55,000	66,300	71,230	80,200
Published retentions	£'000	10,982	105,900	40,400	25,100	28,900
Earnings per share	p	8.00	8.63	12.61	13.77	15.85
Dividend per share	p	4.50	5.00	5.50	6.00	6.90
Operating cash flow	£'000					
Net assets per share	p	67.25	92.22	121.79	77.09	144.51
Net debt/(cash)	£'000	-22,614	5,800	97,800	110,100	123,300
Shareholders' funds	£'000	210,634	319,600	361,100	343,300	361,400
Return on capital	%	29.29	28.40	22.41	24.01	24.94
Profit margin	%					
Sales per employee	£					
Interest cover		34.67	11.46	-5.77	-5.31	-7.25
Dividend cover		1.78	1.73	2.29	2.29	2.30
Sales increase	%	14.21	-13.08	-32.72	5.45	171.22
Earnings growth	%	-1.16	7.95	46.07	9.19	15.77
Investment x depreciation						
Investment as % assets						
Number of employees		4,163	4,790	4,619	4,690	5,088

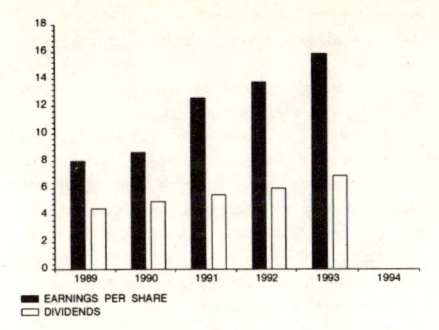

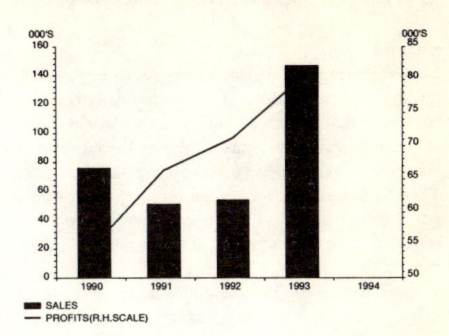

Earnings and dividends

Sales and profits

ness, but due to his involvement in Labour politics, and specifically his role in setting up the left-wing think-tank, the Institute for Public Policy Research. His support for Labour is another curious aspect of a group with such a solid City background, and something which he is sensitive about, preferring to be regarded by the business world as merely another businessman.

MAI's transition from crashed fringe bank to financial and media conglomerate was relatively slow, and not entirely steady, but picked up speed susbstantially from the late 1980s. Having restored stability and direction to the core money-broking businesses in the 1970s, the group spent the 1980s trying to build up personal financial services, on the one hand, and a broad marketing business on the other. But by the early 1990s the focus had switched to television. The advertising business was sold off, first by merging Mills and Allen with the Avenir advertising interests of French group Havas. Then the shareholding in the merged group was gradually sold. The money was invested first in Meridian, which won the ITV franchise for southern England, previously held by TVS. Then at the beginning of 1994, as part of the consolidation of ITV companies, Anglia was acquired for almost £300 million.

The prospects for ITV contractors are not as bright as such prices might suggest. Their market share, and thus their advertising base, is under sustained and successful assault from BSkyB, while the financial regime introduced with the new franchises is much less attractive than the previous system. This double-edged attack has led to the process of consolidation which has seen Granada acquire LWT and Carlton merge with Central, as well as the Meridian/Anglia marriage. The scope for economies of scale seems fairly limited for MAI, however, since Meridian was essentially a 'publisher' and commissioner of programmes. In other words, it did not have the kind of substantial production facilities of the old operators such as Anglia, and which would have offered merger benefits when combined. Yet benefits could be expected as the result of combining the advertising sales departments. This required the break-up of Meridian's joint venture with HTV, and buying out Anglia's partners – Central and Ulster – in its TSMS sales operation.

The internecine dealings in the world of television make money broking look straightforward by comparison. This much more low-profile financial operation is likely to remain the largest contributor to MAI profits for some time, even if MAI is successful in bidding for a new Channel 5 licence. It took much effort on the part of MAI to convince a sceptical City audience that this was a good business for it to be in. The general view is that the risks are high because of thin margins, high fixed costs and the volatile nature of the markets. But MAI has gradually built a leading global network of respected operators and can boast a very steady record of profits growth since the early 1980s. To some extent, the volatility of the currency and bond markets is counteracted in MAI because their cycles are likely to be out of step: currency markets are less active when bond markets are busy, and vice versa.

Nevertheless, brokers remain at the mercy of markets, and in this case also at the mercy of technological developments, such as Reuters's development of electronic trading through its Dealing 2000 product. This is unlikely to present a significant threat for several years, however, by which time MAI may have built up its media interests and further expanded the growing market research side of the business. On the other hand, the much less promising personal financial operatrions of Wagon Finance and Safeguard insurance seem more likely to be candidates for disposal. Perhaps one day MAI will be a purely media group, which would at least save Lord Hollick the

300 MARKS & SPENCER plc

annoyance of forever having to justify the unconventional mix of businesses that comprise his group.

Shares

MAI's shares only began to be fully appreciated towards the end of 1992, as investors finally became convinced that the money-broking business was more stable than many had thought, and as the move into television was seen to be proceeding satisfactorily. There had been some variation in the group's share rating before then, but it had been minor. The relative standing of the shares peaked at the end of 1987, during the final months of the stock market surge, and dropped until 1989. But these undulations were relatively minor, as MAI continued to produce financial results which belied its volatile reputation. Indeed, it is one of the few companies represented in this book whose earnings have risen in each year since 1989, a trend that has finally penetrated the scepticism of investors. Since 1992 the share rating has risen dramatically, and showed no sign of dropping in 1994, although the rise did level out following the acquisition of Anglia Television.

Corporate conscience

MAI is virtually untouched by issues of conscience. While its money-broking activities are central to the operations of many companies which do infringe many areas of ethical concern, MAI itself is not directly involved. It scores negatively only with regard to its interests in countries which might be considered to have oppressive regimes: that is, Indonesia, Malaysia, the Philippines and Saudi Arabia. On the other hand, MAI does not have a high 'positive' score, either. Anglia Television is a member of the Per Cent Club, but that is all. The group has not demonstrated a commitment to equality, the environment or other issues of social responsibility measured by EIRIS.

Corporate governance

Separate Chairman and Chief Executive Y
Number of Directors 7
Number of Non-Executive Directors 4
(3 Independent Directors)
Insulated Directors none

Board Committees
Audit: Y   Remuneration: Y

Remuneration

Year end	30.06.91	30.06.92	30.06.93
Total board £M	1.17	1.40	1.41
% change		20	1
Highest paid	348,000	426,000	491,000
% change		22	15

Board
Lord Hollick *Managing Director*
Gregson, Charles *Executive Director*
Hickson, Peter *Finance Director*
Day, Sir Graham *Independent Non-Executive*
Wheeler, Ray *Independent Non-Executive*
Morrow, Sir Ian *Non-Executive*
McKinnon, Sir James *Non-Executive Chairman*

This small board includes the requisite number of non-executives, who form the audit, remuneration and nomination committees. The 1993 annual report made the briefest mention of corporate governance and attempted no explanation of how the board works or how it complies with the Cadbury Code, suggesting limited enthusiasm for such matters. Likewise, the accounts did not go out of their way to expose details of directors' pay, although the necessary information was provided.

MARKS & SPENCER plc

Michael House, 47-67 Baker Street,
London W1A 1DN
Tel: 0171 935 4422
Chairman and chief executive Sir Richard Greenbury
Size £5.9 billion sales, £11.9 billion stock market value, 62,100 employees
5-year growth sales 18%, earnings per share 38%, employment -18%
Solvency debt = 5% shareholders' funds, interest cover n/a
Political donations £50,000 Conservative Party, £10,000 Liberal Democrats
Charitable donations £3.4 million

Major developments
1884 company began trading as Penny Bazaar
1926 became public
1975 opened first Paris store
1984 Lord Rayner became first non-family chairman
1985 launched Chargecard
1988 bought Brooks Brothers USA; bought Kings Supermarkets USA; introduced own brand Unit Trust

Outlook

Marks & Spencer (M&S) is an institution. Long before the company ventured on to the Continent by opening a store on Boulevard Haussmann in Paris in 1975, its shops were so well known that French visitors to Britain would talk excitedly about how much they were looking forward to buying some underwear in 'le Marks & Spencer'. It was a company which set the benchmark for British retailing to which others aspired.

Nothing has changed. M&S still towers above its rivals. Its professionalism is universally acknowledged. The value of its merchandise is rarely bettered. And above all, it is big: Marks & Spencer single-handedly accounts for one-quarter of the earn-

MARKS & SPENCER

Share record

Return on shareholders' equity	%	16.83
5-year price high	p	460.0
5-year price low	p	177.5
Dividend yield	%	2.70
5-year high	%	4.21
5-year low	%	2.28
Price/earnings ratio		20.9
5-year high		24.1
5-year low		13.6

Share price performance (in pence)

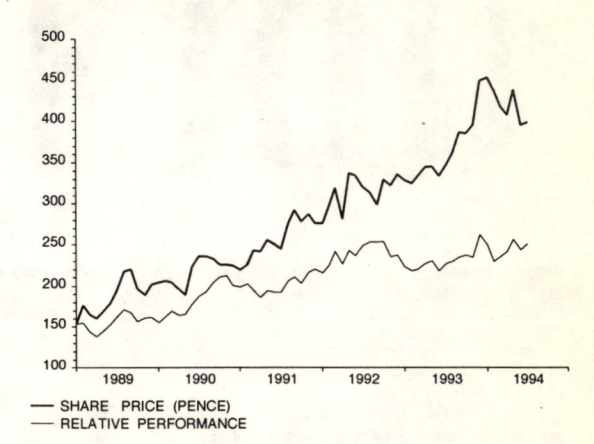

— SHARE PRICE (PENCE)
— RELATIVE PERFORMANCE

Financial record

		31/3/89	31/3/90	31/3/91	31/3/92	31/3/93
Total sales	£	5,057M	5,528M	5,775M	5,793M	5,951M
Pre-tax profit	£'000	531,000	604,200	631,500	670,400	741,100
Published retentions	£'000	193,200	216,500	215,300	178,300	271,900
Earnings per share	p	12.93	14.48	15.13	16.26	17.84
Dividend per share	p	5.60	6.40	6.70	7.10	8.10
Operating cash flow	£'000	42,000	187,800	-32,100	29,800	139,300
Net assets per share	p	92.97	101.60	109.95	113.48	124.29
Net debt/(cash)	£'000	528,000	379,800	327,000	261,300	139,500
Shareholders' funds	£	1,919M	2,175M	2,427M	2,670M	2,950M
Return on capital	%	23.97	26.13	23.33	23.06	23.71
Profit margin	%	10.50	10.93	10.94	11.57	12.45
Sales per employee	£	66.77	74.15	77.77	85.33	95.86
Interest cover		-51.06	-22.69	-52.39	-60.97	-39.70
Dividend cover		2.31	2.26	2.26	2.29	2.20
Sales increase	%	11.59	9.30	4.47	0.32	2.72
Earnings growth	%	7.08	12.00	4.48	7.50	9.69
Investment x depreciation		1.98	2.52	2.45	2.24	1.92
Investment as % assets		8.97	11.07	10.87	10.15	8.17
Number of employees		75,736	74,548	74,258	67,894	62,080

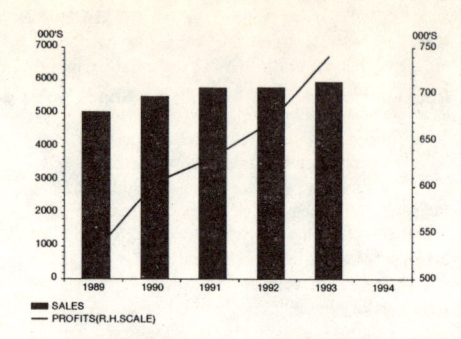

Employment

Sales and profits

ings of Britain's 34 largest quoted non-food stores groups; its shares constitute one-third of the entire stock market value of that sector. Of the £1.3 billion spent on women's underwear in Britain each year, about £500 million is spent at M&S.

Certainly, its overall business performance has not been completely without blemish. Two decades ago Marks & Spencer ventured into Canada, but the shops there either lost money or made only marginal profits. In 1988 the company bought Brooks Brothers (an old-fashioned, upmarket group of clothing stores) in the US for $750 million, but as Sir Richard Greenbury, who took over as chairman of M&S in 1991, was eventually forced to admit, the price was too high: Brooks Brothers was good, but not that good. M&S-watchers have tended to delight in the company's travails in North America, yet in a curious way this is a compliment, proving how little there is to criticise in the performance of the main British business. The Brooks Brothers deal, for example, should be kept in perspective: M&S's largest store, at Marble Arch in London's West End, takes more money in a year than does the whole of the US chain.

When retail sales were shooting upwards in the mid-1980s, there were suggestions that in M&S's core business of selling clothes it was losing its touch. Some observers suspected that it was being outclassed by newer, flashier rivals like Next and the Burton group in its various guises. But unlike these upstarts, M&S had the huge advantage of owning the freeholds on most of its outlets: it did not have to worry about meeting the enormous increase in rent which landlords were able to extract from other retailers eager to cash in on the spending boom. When growth in retail sales began to slow down, and those in leased premises were faced with continuing increases in rent, M&S was able to plough on regardless. In any case, M&S was by this time rather more than just a clothes shop. It had entered the financial services market with typical professionalism. And food sales now account for 45 per cent of sales through the company's British shops. It is expensive food, certainly. Few people would choose to (or could afford to) do all their weekly shopping at M&S, and in any case a typical store carries only 2,200 different products compared with 15,000 in a large outlet of Sainsbury or Tesco. But the company cashed in with ruthless efficiency on the British shopper's apparent liking for high-quality, high-margin, 'value-added' groceries.

Looking ahead, it is arguably the M&S food operation which faces the greatest threat from competition. The big three supermarket groups, Tesco, Sainsbury and Safeway, have expanded their superstore networks aggressively. And all make great play of being able to offer classy groceries to rival those at M&S. But no one should underestimate Marks & Spencer's resilience. As well as its professionalism and efficient systems, the company has formidable strength as a buyer and can squeeze the best possible terms from manufacturers. When times got tough, it told its suppliers that they would have to share some of the burden by accepting lower prices. (M&S also cut head-office staff.) In addition, the company is investing more than £300 million a year to expand its existing UK stores and open new ones – in Britain, Continental Europe and, in the longer term, the Far East.

Despite any worries about M&S's businesses in North America or new competition for its food sales in Britain, Marks & Spencer remains large, immensely powerful, and the envy of its rivals. It is still an institution.

Shares

While Marks & Spencer is one of the key shareholdings for any portfolio because of its size and its yield, the share rating tends to rise against the market only in times of trouble. Thus during the boom years 1986 and 1987 the rating slipped as the market found shares in other, fast-growing stores like Next more seductive, but the crash of 1987 caused the rating to leap upwards. The following year the group's virtues as a safe and reliable company were overlooked once more, but in 1989 a re-rating began again as other stars in the retailing firmament fell to earth.

As the recession worsened, the attraction of M&S increased, for it not only performed better than other companies, but showed promise, with its improved margins, of becoming more than a defensive stock. The shares rose steadily and outperformed the market by 40 per cent in 1990.

A round of job cuts the next year proved popular with shareholders (fewer jobs meaning higher profits). Even a dip in sales volumes and a weak rise in profits could not stop the rise in the share price, but this changed at the end of 1992 when the market anticipated an economic recovery which would see a surge in the price of less defensive shares. The company's rating began to slide as a result, but the shares climbed throughout 1993.

Corporate conscience

M&S has a tradition of being a paternalistic employer, a supporter of community ventures, and, on a larger scale, of the British textile industry. It was probably a little late in coming to environmental awareness, but has subsequently addressed the issue with characteristic vigour and thoroughness, although its policy does not include independent audits, nor regular monitoring. The group was famous for reducing electricity consumption, however, long before environmental issues were popular – for the very simple reason that it wished to save money.

Such parsimony does not extend to staff, however, who are generally well paid by comparison with the rest of the retail sector, and sincerely well regarded by top management. M&S started to employ part-timers long before this became a trend in retailing, but unlike many other companies, it gives permanent part-timers full pension rights. M&S has also recently made great strides on equal opportunities, although still has a pitifully low proportion of senior women, compared to the proportion they represent in the total workforce. The equal opportunities policy does include monitoring, however, and targets for ethnic recruitment. The company's childcare policy includes job-sharing and paternity leave.

M&S is tainted on account of the sale of alcohol and of meat-processing, and the group has made no commitment to phasing out CFCs in refrigeration. It also stopped selling organic produce in 1990, on the grounds that M&S customers want the pesticide-controlled but perfectly formed variety. The group has said that it wishes to replace the tropical hardwoods used to make its furniture with more ecologically sound timber.

Corporate governance

Separate Chairman and Chief Executive N
Number of Directors 22
Number of Non-Executive Directors 4
(4 Independent Directors)
Insulated Directors Ch

Board Committees
Audit: Y   Remuneration: Y

Remuneration

Year end	31.03.92	31.03.93	31.03.94
Total board £M	5.00	5.80	5.60
% change	14	16	-3
Highest paid £	634,675	721,126	688,938
% change	8	14	-4

Board
Greenbury, Sir Richard *Chairman & Chief Executive*
Aldridge, R *Executive Director*
Benfield, J R *Executive Director*
Colne, N L *Executive Director*
Hayes, Derek *Executive Director*
Littmoden, C *Executive Director*
McCracken, P G *Executive Director*
Morris, Barry *Executive Director*
Oates, J K *Executive Director*
Rowe, J T *Executive Director*
Sacher, S J *Executive Director*
Salsbury, Peter L *Executive Director*
Sieff, David *Executive Director*
Silver, C V *Executive Director*
Smith, P P D *Executive Director*
Stone, A Z *Executive Director*
Trangmar, D G *Executive Director*
Colvill, R W C *Finance Director*
Baroness Young *Independent Non-Executive*
Jacomb, Sir Martin *Independent Non-Executive*
Lanigan, D G *Independent Non-Executive*
Robins, Sir Ralph H *Independent Non-Executive*

For such a well-run company which has always valued its staff, M&S does not seem to be terribly enthusiastic about the latest trends in corporate governance, although audit and compensation committees exist. An unusually large boardroom of 22 includes just four non-executives, and the company is among those which persists in combining the roles of chairman and chief executive. The presence of a bonus scheme for directors is revealed but targets remain a close secret.

MEPC plc

12 St James's Square, London SW1Y 4LB
Tel: 0171 911 5300.
Chairman Lord Blakenham
Chief Executive James Tuckey
Substantial shareholdings Harry Hyams 5.5%
Main subsidiaries English Property Corporation, The Oldham Estate Co, Threadneedle Property Co
Size £2.9 billion assets, £1.9 billion stock market value, 1,110 employees
5-year growth assets 1%, earnings per share -28%, employment 24%
Solvency borrowing ratio = 48%, interest cover 1.5 times
Political donations 0
Charitable donations £325,839

Major developments
1946 formed as Metropolitan Estate and Property Corporation Ltd
1973 name changed to MEPC
1986 minority interest in Threadneedle Property Co Ltd
1987 bought Oldham Estate
1989 minority interest in Lansdown Estates Group Ltd
1993 rights issue raised £222 million
1994 acquired American Property Trust

Outlook
MEPC, the UK's second-largest property company, has acquired the unfortunate reputation of getting its timing wrong. Although this may be a rather sweeping judgement, it is certainly true that the company was caught out by the property crash of the early 1990s. It also has a track record of successfully purchasing assets but failing to redevelop these profitably.

The two developments which have caused MEPC the greatest problems during the years of recession have been those at Alban Gate in the City of London, and a shopping centre at Tunbridge Wells. Alban Gate, a massive development straddling London Wall near the Barbican, was until recently dubbed MEPC's 'pink elephant' by unkind critics, thanks to the predominant colour of its stonework and its conspicuous lack of tenants.

As the London property market recovered, Alban Gate became almost fully let, although some of the new tenants undoubtedly managed to negotiate good letting terms. Despite this, at the end of 1993 MEPC admitted it had taken 'substantial write-downs' on both Alban Gate and the Tunbridge Wells shopping centre. City analysts estimated the total write-down could be as much as £100 million. Coming on top of a £222 million rights issue which MEPC made in June 1993, it served to focus attention once more on the group's constrained cash flow.

MEPC's chief executive, James Tuckey, during his year in office as president of the British Property Federation for 1993, lobbied hard to get the government to scrap plans to abolish upward-only rent reviews. Mr Tuckey argues that tenants are no longer held tightly in the grip of unreasonable landlords because market conditions changed as a result of the over-supply of office space. Tenants, he has said, are now offered much more flexible terms, including shorter leases and relief from rent rises.

MEPC is one of several companies which maintains that the property cycle has turned, although it has to be said that the upturn has only just started to be reflected in the group's figures. Vacant properties only represented 4 per cent of the portfolio at the end of 1993, compared to 8 per cent the year before. Gearing was better, at 48 per cent for 1993, compared to 82 per cent for 1992, and cash balances were also much healthier, with over £200 million in the coffers, more than twice the amount than at the previous year end.

The task for MEPC, as it hangs on to the tailcoat of the property recovery, is to ensure that it does not come a cropper again when the sector takes its next nose dive. One of the main reasons MEPC was hit so badly was that it owned a great deal of office property in the City and in central London. So it has made a concerted effort to achieve a better balance between office, industrial and retail property, and also to buy assets in a greater variety of locations. At the end of 1993 MEPC completed the £115 million purchase (paid for mainly with shares rather than cash) for American Property Trust, a unit trust controlled by UK pension funds which owns two shopping malls in Los Angeles and Atlanta. Unfortunately it seems that the gift of poor timing has yet to desert MEPC: the Los Angeles mall was hit by the earthquake of January 1994, barely two months after the ink was dry on the deal. At least the insurers picked up most of the bill.

Shares
MEPC's shares, in common with those of most UK property companies, were very much at the mercy of speculative investors in the 1980s. Even the stock market crash failed to stop the relative rise in property company values, and stock market valuations did not peak until 1989.

MEPC, although the second-largest property company in Britain, proved a less safe investment than many of its smaller rivals when the recession hit. In 1987 it bought the Oldham Estates group, which had a solid portfolio of property, but the boardroom philosophy changed from playing the 'rent collector' to high-quality tenants to adding value to its buildings. The timing of the resulting development programme in the City of London was controversial and hurt the company's share rating in 1991/2.

However, the share price recovered sharply throughout 1992, and by the first part of 1993 stood at very nearly an all-time high once more. This perhaps reflected the stock market's enthusiasm for property generally rather than for MEPC in

MEPC

Share record

Return on shareholder's equity	%	4.08
5-year price high	p	587.0
5-year price low	p	199.6
Dividend yield	%	5.23
5-year high	%	13.01
5-year low	%	3.48
Price/earnings ratio		30.2
5-year high		30.2
5-year low		7.0

Share price performance (in pence)

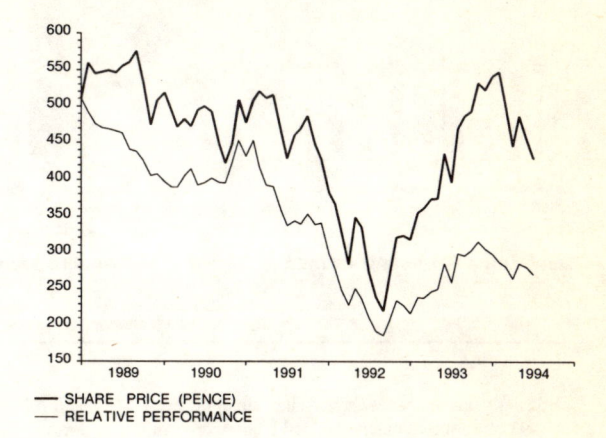

― SHARE PRICE (PENCE)
― RELATIVE PERFORMANCE

Financial record

		30/9/89	30/9/90	30/9/91	30/9/92	30/9/93
Total revenue	£	238,300	271,400	308,000	319,000	324,100
Pre-tax profit	£'000	127,570	149,800	143,800	109,600	94,200
Published retentions	£'000	34,000	42,500	36,100	13,500	-21,700
Earnings per share	p	26.93	31.40	30.54	23.55	19.42
Dividend per share	p	16.55	18.50	19.47	19.47	25.00
Fully diluted assets per share	£	8.56	7.69	5.89	4.50	4.74
Net debt/(cash)	£'000	898,400	1,077M	1,370M	1,228M	768,000
Shareholders' funds	£	2,849M	2,558M	1,969M	1,505M	1,616M
Rent as % assets	%	5.71	6.66	8.24	9.49	10.36
Return on capital	%	6.03	6.80	7.88	8.39	8.12
Return on shareholders' capital	%	3.12	4.06	5.15	5.20	4.08
Trading profit margin		69.02	72.03	72.14	67.30	65.54
Interest cover	%	1.94	1.82	1.64	1.46	1.55
Dividend cover		1.63	1.70	1.57	1.21	0.78
Income growth	%	9.46	13.89	13.49	3.86	1.31
Earnings growth	%	26.0	16.59	-2.73	-22.88	-17.54
Changes in assets	%	17.31	-1.36	-8.42	-10.85	-7.43
Number of employees		894	1,011	1,056	1,047	1,110

306 MEPC plc

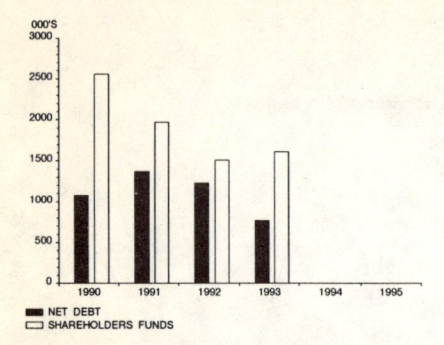

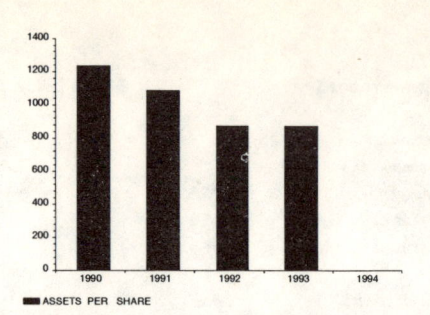

Debt and shareholders' funds

Assets per share

particular, and the latter's shares fell again at the end of 1993 when the company reported a sharp drop in net asset value. Subsequently the shares picked up again, following news that the group's finances – in particular its gearing – were looking solid.

Corporate conscience
Like most property companies, MEPC has a low ethical profile. It is not committed against ozone-depleting chemicals in its buildings, and is likewise implicated in tropical hardwoods, but otherwise does not trigger any negative ethical signals. Similarly, the company has few positive involvements. It is a member of Business in the Community, but other positive ethical policies appear to be absent.

Corporate governance
Separate Chairman and Chief Executive Y
Number of Directors 7
Number of Non-Executive Directors 4
(4 Independent Directors)
Insulated Directors None

Board Committees
Audit: Y   Remuneration: Y

Remuneration

Year end	31.09.91	31.09.92	31.09.93
Total board £M	1.93	1.29	1.31
% change	37	-33	1
Highest paid £	249,599	249,356	265,997
% change	9	-0.1	7

Board
Tuckey, James L *Chief Executive*
Watters, Iain R *Executive Director*
Beveridge, James A *Finance Director*
Field, Sir Malcolm *Independent Non-Executive*
Irvine, I A N *Indpendent Non-Executive*
Taylor, J F *Independent Non-Executive*
Lord Blakenham *Non-Executive Chairman*

This board is a model of balance, tilted towards the non-executives, who represent a strong team of working directors rather than the retired bankers or solicitors who sometimes occupy such seats.

MFI FURNITURE GROUP plc

Southon House, 333 The Hyde, Edgware Road, Colindale, London NW9 6TD
Tel: 0181 200 8000.
Chairman and chief executive Derek Hunt
Main brands Hygena, Schreiber
Size £604 million sales, £0.9 billion stock market value, 7,579 employees
5-year growth n/a
Solvency debt = 11% of shareholders' funds, interest cover 2 times
Political donations 0
Charitable donations £112,648

Major developments
1966 began as mail order business
1975 switch to cash and carry
1982 acquired Hygena brand name
1985 merged with ASDA
1987 management buyout
1992 joined the stock market

MFI

Share record

Return on shareholder's equity	%	22.73
5-year price high	p	183.0
5-year price low	p	91.0
Dividend yield	%	3.23
5-year high	%	5.49
5-year low	%	1.78
Price/earnings ratio		12.6
5-year high		38.4
5-year low		11.6

Share price performance (in pence)

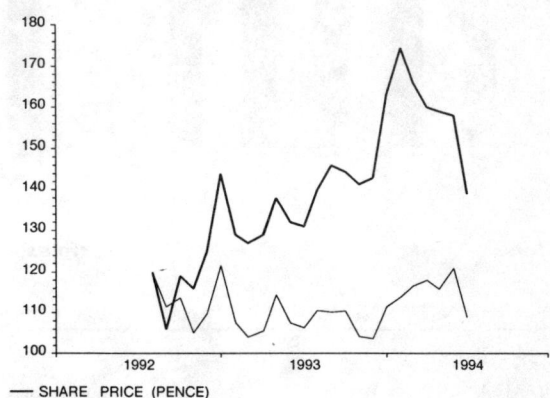

— SHARE PRICE (PENCE)
— RELATIVE PERFORMANCE

Financial record

		30/4/93
Total sales	£'000	603,900
Pre-tax profit	£'000	28,700
Published retentions	£'000	-6,900
Earnings per share	p	5.68
Dividend per share	p	3.75
Operating cash flow	£'000	-31,000
Net assets per share	p	37.23
Net debt/(cash)	£'000	67,000
Shareholders' funds	£'000	601,200
Return on capital	%	
Profit margin	%	4.50
Sales per employee	£	79.68
Interest cover		1.87
Dividend cover		1.51
Sales increase	%	
Earnings growth	%	
Investment x depreciation		1.13
Investment as % assets		9.66
Number of employees		7,579

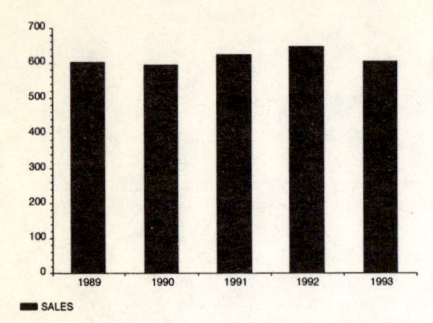

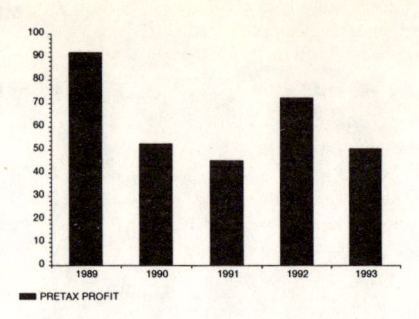

Sales

Profits

Outlook

Since it started life as a mail-order business in the mid-1960s, Mullard Furniture Industries has come a long way. No longer involved in mail order, it is now Britain's largest furniture retailer, and is known by the rather snappier title of 'MFI'.

The company was a pioneer in the market for self-assembly furniture – furniture that was cheap, reasonably cheerful and sold in an unstuffy manner. In the 1970s MFI moved from mail order to cash-and-carry retailing, creating one of the earliest chains of edge-of-town outlets. The next step was to become more vertically integrated, so MFI took over the Hygena brand name. Then, in 1985, came an episode which, in retrospect, was unfortunate: MFI was taken over by Asda. The rationale for the merger was never clear and in 1987 MFI was put up for auction.

The company was acquired by a team of long-serving managers, led by Derek Hunt. They paid a price which valued the whole group at £718 million and set themselves the target of returning to the stock market within three years. Huge amounts of debts were taken on by the buy-out team in order to finance the deal, and Asda held on to a 25 per cent shareholding.

Then the recession hit. MFI, like all furniture companies, suffered as a result of the drop in consumer spending and in particular as a result of plummeting sales of items related to house moving. Unlike Harris Queensway, MFI did not go under, but it had to fight for survival: as fast as the management team chipped away at costs, the recession chipped away at sales. In mid-1989 the company's 'like-for-like' sales (excluding the impact of store openings and closures) were running at around 14 per cent below the level of the year before. And eventually MFI had to concede that the three-year target for bringing the company back to the stock market had been over-optimistic.

Nevertheless, by 1992 the bluff Mr Hunt and his colleagues reckoned that MFI was strong enough to be floated. A price-tag of £669 million was put on the company, its 174 British superstores and 15 French outlets. The flotation, by normal stock market standards, was a flop. It came in July 1992, when the stock market was at a low ebb; more than half of the shares that were offered were not taken up, and had to be placed with institutional investors by underwriters.

But this tended to overshadow was still a pretty remarkable story. MFI operated in a sector which had been badly affected by recession, and since the buy-out from Asda it had been burdened with debt. The very fact that it had survived was an achievement. Derek Hunt and his colleagues were rewarded for their efforts with a total bonus of £11 million.

Since its return to the stock market, life has not been easy for MFI – nor for its staff. The company has shown a merciless determination to cut the number of employees: over 12 months to the end of November 1993 the group axed one in every seven jobs. Staff costs were cut by the best part of £2 million every month; operating profits went up by the same amount.

MFI is exactly the sort of company whose profitability should shoot up in response to an increase in retail spending: it is, in the parlance, highly geared to economic recovery. Even if the group's sales increase by 10 or 20 per cent, the cost of actually running the stores remains virtually unchanged: its extra gross profits (the difference between the price at which it buys and the price at which it sells) become extra net profits.

But the management has continued to operate the business in a way which assumes no help from the economy as a whole. Besides cutting staff, the company has also found that several of its existing stores can carry the full range of stock, but using only part of each building. Hence chunks of various MFI outlets have been separated off from the store itself and then leased out to other retailers: lease income such as this is now bringing in a useful £9 million or so a year. This typically canny response to hard times exemplifies the company's hard-nosed approach that has seen it through such a turbulent history.

Shares

When MFI returned to the stock market in July 1992, its shares fell. This was no reflection on the company itself, but simply a product of the stock market's weakness. Then MFI's sales in the few months after flotation failed to grow as they had done in the first part of the year. For investors, MFI was a disappointment initially. But as 1992 drew to a close – and as interest rates fell after Britain's exit from the ERM – the shares climbed strongly and moved above the price at which the company had been floated. The latter part of 1993 and early 1994 witnessed a new rise. City analysts upgraded their forecasts of the benefits that should accrue to MFI as they observed the company cashing in on increasing sales stemming from an improvement in the housing market. By mid-May 1994 the share price stood at 158p, against the 115p at which the company had been floated.

Corporate conscience

MFI raises only two ethical issues. It received two adverse judgements from the ASA in 1993, and its furniture uses tropical hardwoods. Positive indicators are also absent. The company has perhaps been too busy with its many transformations and appalling market conditions to worry sufficiently about corporate responsibility. It does not appear to have policies on such issues as equality and the environment, nor does it seem to be involved in community activity at a corporate level.

Corporate governance

Separate Chairman and Chief Executive N
Number of Directors 11
Number of Non-Executive Directors 4
(4 Independent Directors)
Insulated Directors None

Board Committees
Audit: Y   Remuneration: Y
Remuneration

Year end	25.04.92	24.04.93
Total board £M	1.30	1.83
% change		41
Highest paid £	232,000	334,000
% change		44

Board
Hunt, Derek *Chairman and Chief Executive*
O'Connell, John J *Executive Deputy Chairman*
Brock, David M *Executive Director*
Goodhew, Michael *Executive Director*
Love, David G *Executive Director*
Randall, John *Finance Director*
Tellett, Trevor J *Executive Director*
Baker, Mary *Independent Non-Executive Director*
Cook, Derek E *Independent Non-Executive*
Smith, Robert H *Ind. Non-Executive Director*
Whitney, Paul M *Ind. Non-Executive Director*

Surprisingly, for a new company coming to the stock market, MFI does not fully comply with Cadbury requirements. Derek Hunt, the kind of strong leader who needs a counterbalancing boardroom presence, remains both chairman and chief executive. While there are four independent non-executives, who staff the audit and remuneration committees, they are outnumbered by the executive directors. The first annual report did give full details of pay and bonuses, however, including a £10 million payment to top executives on flotation (which is not included in the above figures).

NEXT plc

Desford Road, Enderby, Leicester LE9 5AT
Tel: 01533 866411
Chairman Lord Wolfson of Sunningdale
Chief executive David Jones
No subsidiaries
Size £544 million sales, £930 stock market value, 9,415 employees
5-year growth sales -40%, earnings per share 538%, employment -44%
Solvency debt n/a, interest cover n/a
Political donations 0
Charitable donations £203,000

Major developments
1982 first Next shop opened
1984 George Davies appointed managing director
1986 company name changed from J Hepworth & Son merger with Grattan mail order
1987 acquired Combined English Stores for £325 million
1988 Next Directory launched, George Davies ousted, sold Salisburys, Zales, Allens chemists chain
1989 sold Biba in Germany, Eurocamp
1990 abandoned separate Next formats
1991 sold Grattan
1994 entered joint venture with Bath & Body Works

Outlook

Next is a little more than a decade old, yet in its short corporate life it has provided more thrills and spills for its investors than virtually any other retailer on the high street. There were times when the company seemed destined to conquer all; equally there were times when it seemed likely to go bust. In the end, it did neither, but is entering the second half of the 1990s as a retailer which appears at last to have discovered its role in the world.

NEXT plc

Share record

Return on shareholder's equity   %   26.42
5-year price high   p   252.0
5-year price low   p   12.5

Dividend yield   %   2.73
5-year high   %   28.80
5-year low   %   0.00

Price/earnings ratio   19.5
5-year high   41.4
5-year low   8.3

Share price performance (in pence)

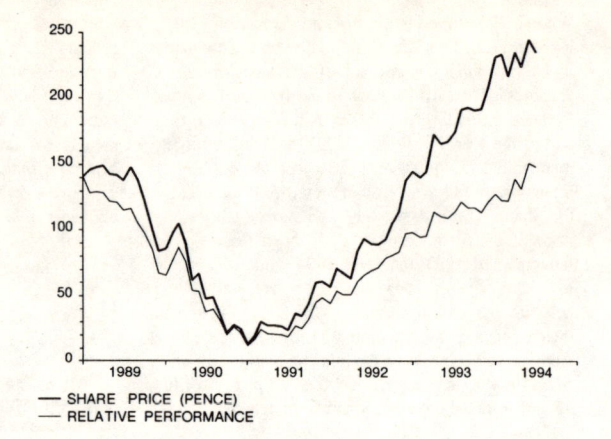

Financial record

		31/1/90	31/1/91	31/1/92	31/1/93	31/1/94
Total sales	£	903,300	877,900	462,000	484,700	544,200
Pre-tax profit	£'000	18,600	-7,200	12,500	36,200	73,500
Published retentions	£'000	10,400	-223M	8,600	27,400	43,700
Earnings per share	p	2.66	0.00	2.93	8.27	16.97
Dividend per share	p	4.70	0.70	1.50	2.50	5.50
Operating cash flow	£'000	-17,800	84,600	0	99,100	88,400
Net assets per share	p	150.15	97.87	53.06	57.50	68.63
Net debt/(cash)	£'000	141,700	490,500	89,200	-11,600	-87,800
Shareholders' funds	£'000	384,900	160,000	168,500	198,600	243,300
Return on capital	%	7.16	2.49	9.99	20.50	31.85
Profit margin	%	1.35	-0.84	2.62	7.16	12.95
Sales per employee	£	54.13	59.09	58.69	57.96	57.80
Interest cover		1.59	0.52	-10.00	-5.31	-9.52
Dividend cover		0.57	0.00	1.95	3.31	3.09
Sales increase	%	-16.63	-2.81	-47.37	4.91	12.28
Earnings growth	%	-77.51	-100.00	0.00	182.33	105.23
Investment x depreciation		0.90	0.37	0.00	0.31	1.09
Investment as % assets		14.97	6.64	0.00	9.88	21.76
Number of employees		16,688	14,857	7,872	8,363	9,415

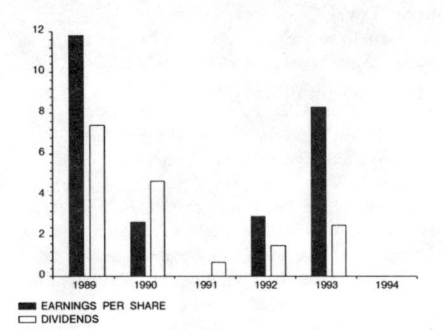

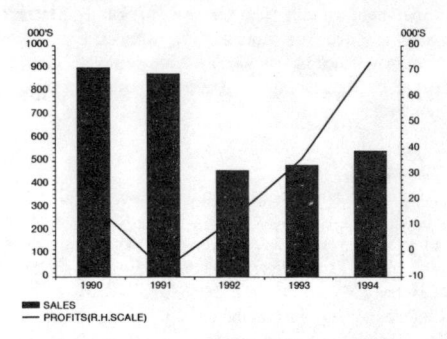

Earnings and dividends

Sales and profits

Next was the creation of two men: design guru Terence Conran, who had already established Habitat; and George Davies, who had cut his teeth in retailing with Littlewoods and then went on to join Pippa Dee, a company selling clothes on the Tupperware-party principle. They took over the old Hepworths and Kendalls chains and relaunched them as Next in 1982.

Next aimed to provide fashion-conscious women with clothes that were just a little bit sharper and sassier than the ranges on offer from Marks & Spencer and the existing high-street chains. And the formula worked. Next – helped, it must be said, by riding the extraordinary retail boom of the 1980s – prospered and grew.

In 1984 Next for Men was launched. A plethora of offshoots emerged over the next few years: Next to Nothing, Next Accessories, Next Interiors and Next Lingerie. The expansion continued at a breakneck pace: Davies dreamed up Next Too (selling casual clothes), Next Collection (more formal wear) and Next Boys and Girls.

In 1986 the company bought Grattan mail order and followed it in 1987 with the £325 million takeover of Combined English Stores, including Zales, Weir and Page. And in January 1988 the two sides of the business were combined in Next Directory, the mail-order operation for trendies which was launched amid a blaze of publicity and optimism.

Next and Mr Davies exuded self-confidence. They stood at the zenith of their fortunes. The company was valued by the stock market at nearly £1 billion. But the turning point came in 1988. As the year wore on, it became clear that many of the new shops that had been opened during Next's expansionary phase didn't actually make money: they might be stylish and refreshingly different, but they weren't profitable.

On 2 December 1988 Next was forced to issue a profit warning. Six days later George Davies and his wife Liz, who also sat on the board, were dismissed. Mr Davies's place as chief executive was taken by David Jones, a 45-year-old accountant who had joined the organisation with Grattan. Mr Jones criticised his predecessor for having too autocratic a style of management, and blamed him for having pressed ahead with Next's expansion when a cool-headed analysis would have shown that the new shops being opened were unlikely to make money.

The start of the Jones era was painful. Shops were closed and sold. Vast sums of money had to be set aside to cover redundancies, the severing of leases and write-downs on assets whose sale would realise less than they were worth in the company's books. The impact of writing down all the businesses being sold and closed was horrendous: in the financial year to the end of January 1991 the company recorded a loss of no less then £222 million. Next was valued at little more than £20 million.

Moreover, Next, like the other high-street chains, was beginning to feel the chill wind of the downturn in consumer spending. Most worrying of all, the company had issued bonds during its heyday which had to be repaid in 1992, and now faced the real threat of being unable to meet its liabilities. A long list of businesses were sold: most notably, Next shed Grattan, selling it to Otto Versand of Germany.

But after all the agonies, Next was left in 1994 with a pared-down operation of 300-odd shops selling clothes for both men and women, plus Next Directory. And by hammering away at the basics – being more careful about merchandise and ensuring that clothes were in stock in the right sizes and in the right colours – the company gradually started to recover. Sales per square foot, which is the acid test of retailing performance, climbed steadily from the £253 in 1990/91 to £411 in 1993/4. Earnings returned almost to the level reported at the peak of the Davies era.

The new Next management had shown itself determined not to become seduced by its own success: an experiment with the Next format in the United States is being tested only cautiously. No wonder: here is a company which has previously come perilously close to the edge of the abyss. It is an experience it does not wish to repeat.

Shares

Next investors have had an exciting time. In 1984 the shares were worth less than 100p; by the beginning of 1987 they were worth more than twice as much; and in the extraordinary months that led up to the October 1987 stock market crash Next became a darling of the City. Just as the retailer's confident modern style seemed to encapuslate everything about the 1980s, its shares were seen as the perfect yuppie investment: they peaked at 374p, just four weeks before the market collapsed.

Then one piece of bad news followed another. And as the awful price of clearing up the mess which the new management had inherited became apparent, the shares had few friends. As the deal to sell Grattan was being tied up, Next shares stood at 13p.

But since then, their recovery has been steady and sustained. Over the course of 1991 it became clear than the business was going to avoid bankruptcy. Over 1992, investors began to realise than the basic businesses that remained were actually quite profitable. And in 1994 they woke up to Next's potential for making serious money. By summer 1994 the shares were still a long way short of the sky-high levels they had reached in the feverish days of 1987. But people who had had the courage to buy at Next's nadir would have multiplied their money 18-fold.

Corporate conscience

Next's only ethical infringement is on advertising, where the ASA upheld one complaint in 1992. On the other hand, its only positive score is on equal opportunities. More than a fifth of UK managers are women, although only one per cent come from ethnic minorities. At least these things are regularly reviewed by the board.

Corporate governance

Separate Chairman and Chief Executive Y
Number of Directors 8
Number of Non-Executive Directors 4
(4 Independent directors)
Insulated Directors MD

Board Committees
Audit: Y   Remuneration: Y

Remuneration

Year end	31.1.92	31.1.93	31.1.94
Total board £M	0.8	0.8	1.1
% change		0	38
Highest paid £	268,159	274,201	374,882
% change		2	37

Board
Jones, David *Chief Executive*
Keens, David *Executive Director*
Harrison, Robert *Executive Director*
Varley, Andrew *Executive Director*
Burdus, Ann *Independent Non-Executive*
Mitchell-Innes, Alistair *Independent Non-Executive*
Stoddart, Michael *Independent Non-Executive*
Lord Wolfson *Non-Executive Chairman*

It might have been thought that Next's searing experience in the 1980s would have led it to adopt the strongest possible board membership and structures. That is not the case, however. The board has been strengthened slightly with the appointment of Ann Burdus, but Michael Stoddart has been a member of it since 1974, so cannot be expected to bring new insights or attitudes, although technically independent. Another digression from the Cadbury Code is the inclusion of David Jones on both audit and remuneration committees. Disclosure of pay has improved, and includes the fact that the maximum bonus is 50 per cent of salary. A tripled bonus was the main reason for the leap in pay of the highest paid director in 1993.

NFC plc

66 Chiltern Street, London W1M 1PR
Tel: 0171 317 0123
Chairman James Watson
Chief executive Peter Sherlock
Substantial shareholdings employees collectively 16.5%
Main brands and subsidiaries BRS, Exel, Lynx, National Carriers, Pickfords, Tankfreight
Size £1.9 billion sales, £1.3 billion stock market value, 32,800 employees
5-year growth sales 27%, earnings per share 50%, employment 3%
Solvency debt = 53% shareholders' funds, interest cover 7 times
Political donations 0
Charitable donations £466,000

Major developments
1981 formed as National Freight Consortium
1982 bought from government by management and employees
1989 became NFC plc
1990 bought Minuteman Delivery Systems
1991 bought Universal Terminal Warehouse Co (Texas); bought Bullens Ltd from Unigate
1992 sold Pickford Travel Services; bought Trammell Crow distribution

NFC

Share record

Return on shareholder's equity	%	25.14
5-year price high	p	287.0
5-year price low	p	102.5
Dividend yield	%	4.82
5-year high	%	6.49
5-year low	%	2.84
Price/earnings ratio		13.4
5-year high		25.5
5-year low		7.8

Share price performance (in pence)

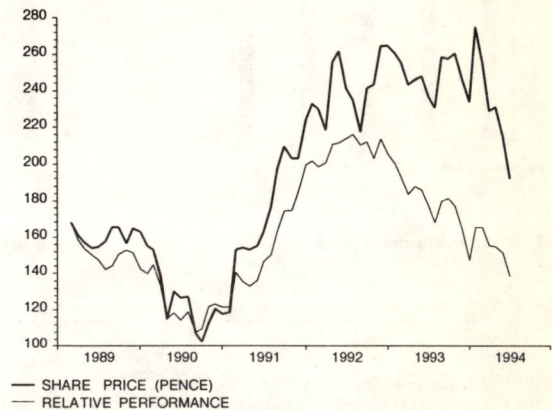

— SHARE PRICE (PENCE)
— RELATIVE PERFORMANCE

Financial record

		30/9/89	30/9/90	30/9/91	30/9/92	30/9/93
Total sales	£	1,494M	1,627M	1,664M	1,724M	1,902M
Pre-tax profit	£'000	80,000	83,600	88,600	97,100	105,000
Published retentions	£'000	36,600	43,300	36,500	45,200	51,900
Earnings per share	p	9.70	10.04	10.77	12.70	14.56
Dividend per share	p	4.79	5.41	5.99	6.27	6.71
Operating cash flow	£'000	40,300	15,800	44,200	14,800	19,100
Net assets per share	p	71.41	73.35	86.89	84.16	97.91
Net debt/(cash)	£'000	17,100	78,600	98,900	181,300	166,500
Shareholders' funds	£'000	327,800	331,100	336,100	331,500	312,900
Return on capital	%		23.24	21.29	22.71	24.46
Profit margin	%	5.23	5.10	5.30	5.66	5.52
Sales per employee	£	47.03	48.19	49.13	50.92	58.01
Interest cover		17.98	277.33	41.09	12.62	6.80
Dividend cover		2.02	1.86	1.80	2.02	2.17
Sales increase	%		8.91	2.26	3.61	10.31
Earnings growth	%		3.55	7.23	17.96	14.64
Investment x depreciation		0.89	1.10	0.87	1.09	0.96
Investment as % assets		7.62	8.03	7.95	10.02	11.06
Number of employees		31,763	33,761	33,861	33,850	32,780

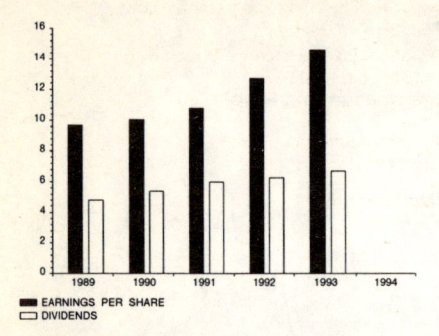

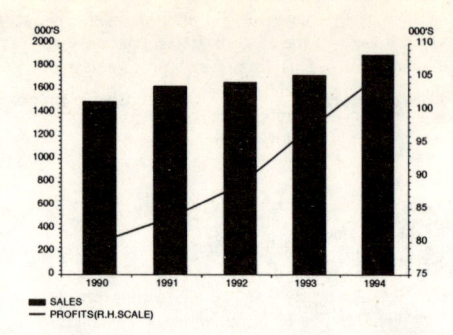

Earnings and dividends

Sales and profits

1993 sold Waste Management to Wessex Water
1994 abandoned attempt to sell Lynx parcels business

Outlook

NFC, the UK's biggest transport and distribution business, has undergone a metamorphosis since its £53 million employee-led buy-out from the government in 1982, and its former guise as the National Freight Corporation. The company, which joined the stock market in 1989, is now a substantial service business, and is a lone example of a major public UK company with significant employee ownership. Its management has demonstrated unusual skills in balancing the company's commitment to employees with its obligations to shareholders although its balance has been switching to the latter.

The transformation continues apace, and NFC has tried to avoid putting all its eggs in one geographical basket, turning itself into a broadly based international group in order to avoid over-dependence on the volatile UK economy. On the other hand, NFC has focused on two particular fields – transport and logistics. An important development in this process was the shedding of its waste-management business for £113 million to Wessex Waste Management. The well-timed sale halved the group's net debt and increased the scope for further expansion of its core distribution business.

Logistics – essentially the provision of sophisticated, reliable distribution for key corporate customers – has now replaced transport as the dominant side of NFC's operations, with expansion initially through major food-retailing customers such as Tesco and Sainsbury. Despite the recession, the group has managed to attract many new customers backed with long-term contracts, including Courtaulds's food packaging, and Norweb's consumer business, Somerfield (previously Gateway), chocolate manufacturer Terry's of York, Homepride and Dairy Crest. But the benefits of new accounts take time to filter through, with revenues not apparent for at least six months.

The former dominance of transport stemmed from the pre-flotation days, when the group was the road-freight arm of British Rail, incorporating such well-known brand names as Pickfords and BRS (formerly British Road Services). But the transport business was hit hard by the downturn in the economy, while the Pickfords removal business was also dented by the collapse in the housing market. In addition to slimming down the business, there has been significant cost-cutting and reorganisation at BRS, resulting in a substantial rise in profits, with changes also underway at the loss-making parcels division, Lynx.

After unsuccessful negotiations the company was forced to abandon plans to sell Lynx, which then started to show some recovery, and should eventually break even.

The ravages of the recession took their toll most visibly on the travel and property operations, with NFC eventually selling its retail chain of travel agents to Airtours in September 1992. The property business has also been slimmed down; Hyperion now acts mainly as a property provider to the main operating companies.

On the acquisitions trail, NFC has moved into the US and the Continent, boosting the proportion of its overseas earnings from virtually nothing to 40 per cent. In the first quarter of 1993 it actively pursued this policy by buying companies in France, Germany and Belgium.

NFC has shown that it is not afraid to take tough action when required, and the recession has prompted an inevitable spate of redundancies. But the group has survived the various world recessions in relatively good shape.

A three-part £45 million restructuring programme is intended to show financial benefits in 1995, and it is critical that managers deliver the benefits. Despite the misgivings of the Stock Exchange, the company originally set out its 'best view' prospects at the annual meeting, which is known as one of the liveliest events in the corporate calender because of the large number of employee shareholders.

Shares

NFC's flotation in 1989 caught the public's imagination, and during first-day dealings the shares jumped from 150p to nearly 280p before settling at 248p. Institutional buying of the shares in a very tight market forced them up to a premium rating. The onset of recession and a warning from the board about profits caused the rating to slip to a low point in 1990. The City revised its opinion the next year as it saw the transport side hold up well. Despite the economic gloom, the shares soared in 1991. By the end of that year they had doubled in value and the company joined the FTSE 100 index. The shares continued to outperform the market during 1992 but tailed off at the end of that year as investors became wary of NFC's rising debt. At the start of 1993 the rest of the market was re-rated and the group's relative worth sank, although it stood to be a major gainer from a recovery in the economy. The board's sale of the waste-management business was seen as a potential bonus. But this prac;tice of giving 'best estimates' was abandoned in 1993, with US legal requirements taking the blame. NFC is becoming less and less different. This drift caused a rumpus at the 1994 annual meeting when former chairman Sir Peter Thompson accused his successor of abandoning key principles.

Corporate conscience

Being partly a worker-owned company, NFC might be expected to be more conscientious than companies run on more conventional lines. It does pay more attention to small shareholders, revealing more about itself than do most companies, and it is perhaps more sensitive towards existing and former employees. Yet it lacks a decent equal opportunities or environmental policy, and has had various convictions sustained against it. BRS Northern was fined £2,000 for an offence under the Road Traffic (Carriage of Dangerous Substances, etc.) Regulations; and the group received 2 convictions for water pollution in 1991/2.

NFC is also implicated in the issues of alcohol and tobacco: Exel Logistics runs distribution services for various brewers in the UK and US, and in the United States Exel also distributes R J Reynolds tobacco products.

The company does have a strong commitment to community involvement, and set up the NFC Foundation, which receives one per cent of the group's profits, to administer the Social Responsibilities Programme.

Corporate governance

Separate Chairman and Chief Executive Y
Number of Directors 12
Number of Non-Executive Directors 6
(5 Independent Directors)
Insulated Directors None

Board Committees
Audit: Y   Remuneration: Y

Remuneration

Year end	30.09.91	30.09.92	2.10.93
Total board £M	1.30	1.60	1.9
% change	0	23	19
Highest paid £	205,077	230,804	254,618
% change	30	13	10

Board
Sherlock, Peter *Chief Executive*
Watson, James Kenneth *Executive Chairman*
Barr, Ian Cameron *Executive Director*
Olliver, Denis George *Executive Director*
Roberts, Graham Stanley *Executive Director*
Larman, Trevor George *Finance Director*
Fowler, Sir Norman *Independent Non-Executive*
Marin-Postel, Christine *Independent Non-Executive*
Menzies-Wilson, William *Ind. Non-Executive*
Robb, John Weddell *Independent Non-Executive*
Teare, Andrew Hubert *Independent Non-Executive*
Corrigan, Valerie Elizabeth *Non-Executive*

NFC pays greater heed than other companies to the interests of employees and other interest groups although the separate section of the directors' report devoted to 'people development' was abandoned in 1994. NFC has had an audit committee since 1982 so had no difficulty with Cadbury. The company still follows the common practice of giving directors three-year service contracts, which has been the cause of excessive 'golden handshakes' in some companies but gives a reasonable explanation of performance bonuses.

NORTHERN FOODS plc

Beverley House, St Stephens Square, Hull HU1 3XG
Tel: 01482 25432
Chairman and chief executive Christopher Haskins
Main brands and subsidiaries Bowyers, Dale Farm Foods, Express Dairy, Fox's biscuits, Northern Dairies, Palethorpes, Park Cakes, The Pizza Factory, Pork Farms
Size £2.0 billion sales, £1.2 billion stock market value, 30,200 employees
5-year growth sales 95%, earnings per share 53%, employment 35%

NORTHERN FOODS

Share record

Return on shareholder's equity	%	35.85
5-year price high	p	316.5
5-year price low	p	132.9
Dividend yield	%	5.26
5-year high	%	5.58
5-year low	%	3.32
Price/earnings ratio		11.4
5-year high		18.6
5-year low		10.8

Share price performance (in pence)

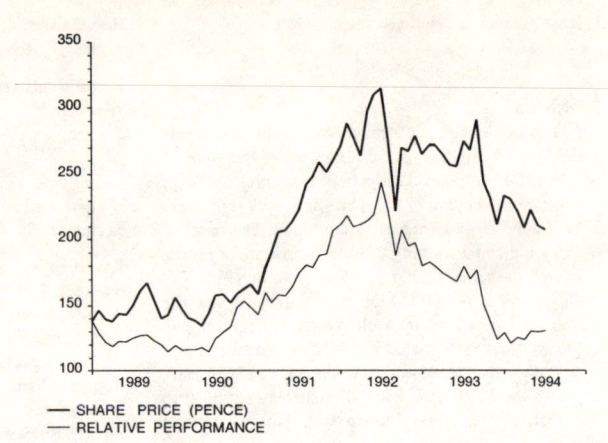

— SHARE PRICE (PENCE)
— RELATIVE PERFORMANCE

Financial record

		31/3/89	31/3/90	31/3/91	31/3/92	31/3/93
Total sales	£	1,041M	1,094M	1,187M	1,444M	2,026M
Pre-tax profit	£'000	85,500	90,200	105,400	126,200	153,200
Published retentions	£'000	26,600	31,200	45,900	51,900	66,200
Earnings per share	p	12.96	13.90	16.16	19.13	19.88
Dividend per share	p	5.32	5.91	6.86	7.88	8.40
Operating cash flow	£'000	13,200	23,100	81,200	6,500	16,600
Net assets per share	p	67.13	69.17	69.18	68.40	77.05
Net debt/(cash)	£'000	6,000	6,900	8,400	199,000	120,500
Shareholders' funds	£'000	296,300	314,200	305,400	277,000	321,100
Return on capital	%	28.65	29.23	34.34	41.26	46.60
Profit margin	%	8.21	8.24	8.88	8.74	7.51
Sales per employee	£	47.63	50.21	51.78	53.48	67.05
Interest cover		86.50	65.43	31.11	17.18	7.39
Dividend cover		2.43	2.35	2.36	2.43	2.37
Sales increase	%	2.17	5.10	8.46	21.67	40.29
Earnings growth	%	10.05	7.31	16.22	18.40	3.92
Investment x depreciation		2.20	2.28	1.72	1.98	1.60
Investment as % assets		18.71	19.01	14.44	14.64	14.69
Number of employees		21,864	21,795	22,924	27,002	30,219

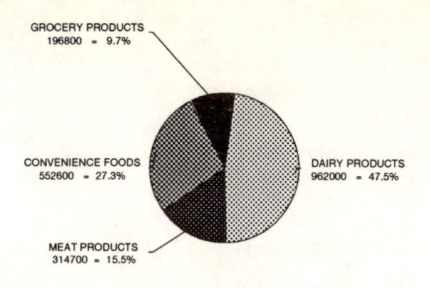

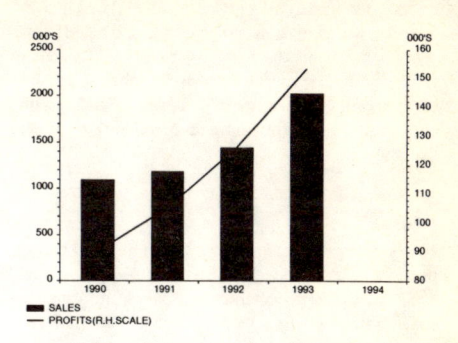

Sales analysis

- GROCERY PRODUCTS 196800 = 9.7%
- CONVENIENCE FOODS 552600 = 27.3%
- MEAT PRODUCTS 314700 = 15.5%
- DAIRY PRODUCTS 962000 = 47.5%

Sales and profits

(000'S) SALES / PROFITS(R.H.SCALE), 1990–1994

Solvency debt = 35% shareholders' funds, interest cover 7 times
Political donations 0
Charitable donations £542,998

Major developments
1949 formed as Northern Dairies
1950 became public
1973 name changed to Northern Foods
1979 bought Bluebird (US)
1982 bought Keystone Foods (US)
1983 sold Bluebird
1985 bought Bowyers
1986 sold Keystone
1989 bought Avana Meat Products
1991 bought Express Dairy and Kara Foods

Outlook
Like Asda, Northern Foods began life as a Yorkshire dairy company. But Asda opted to become a retailer, while Northern has grown by becoming a major supplier to the big retailers. It has also remained in the dairy business. Indeed, at the end of 1991 Northern bought Express Dairies from Grand Metropolitan, and early in 1993 it announced a plan to set up a joint venture with dairy farmers to cope with the privatisation of the Milk Marketing Board. Doorstep deliveries have progressively been franchised, freeing capital and management while retaining an interest in this business, but following the acquisition of Express Dairies, milk accounts for nearly half of group profits.

As with every other type of grocery, the supermarkets take an increasing share of milk sales. Yet Northern has proved adept at serving the supermarket groups not only with milk but, since the mid-1980s, with other products too. Unlike many food companies, Northern does not complain about the power of the supermarkets and the consequent squeeze on suppliers' margins. That is not only because this company is the largest food supplier to Marks & Spencer, but it is also the manufacturer of many of the fancy products on other supermarket shelves. Northern has profited mightily from the growth of the leading supermarket chains, and especially their success in selling 'added-value' items. 'Added value' can be applied to a multitude of products, from sandwiches, pies and quiches to classic prepared meals like chicken Kiev; and Northern supplies them all.

To some extent, most obviously in the case of quiches and trifles, these products are a clever means of using the milk – moving 'downstream', to use an analogy from the oil industry, from the basic commodity into end-use products (usually offering higher returns because of the added skill which brings the added value). But Northern has diversified into other product areas which also form the basis for some of its ready-made dishes, such as pies. In fact, as so often, diversification has been the group's least successful venture. Notably, its fashionable move into the US proved disastrous. Northern bought Bluebird, a pork processor, in 1979, and followed this up with the acquisition of Keystone Foods, a major supplier of hamburgers to McDonald's. Neither transaction proved successful, and Northern soon came back to Britain with its tail between its legs. Diversification in this country has been more rewarding, especially in the case of Fox's biscuits, but the addition of Bowyer's to Pork Farm never really worked out.

Yet by sticking to fresh foods, by working closely with the leading supermarkets, and by investing heavily to ensure quality, hygiene and productivity, Northern appears to have pulled off that most difficult trick – finding something to do with the excess cash flows from its core business, and doing it successfully. The price war between supermarkets has had a devastating effect on doorstep milk deliveries.

Like all food companies, it is under pressure to cut prices. But its largest single customer is Marks & Spencer, which remains aloof from the frenzied competition in the middle part of the market. The other challenge it faces is to demonstrate that it can do equally well in other countries besides Britain, with the rest of Europe now more favoured in this respect than the US.

Shares

Northern Foods, like all companies in the food industry, is a defensive stock and its decline in 1986 and 1987 relative to the market as a whole reflected to some extent the City's view that other shares showed better prospects in a bull market. It also reflected the view that the group was a little accident-prone, owing to its unsuccessful ventures in the US. During the market crash the shares outperformed the market, however, and they remained strong until late in 1988 when the scare over salmonella in eggs brought profits down.

A heavy capital-spending programme and the high price of pigs counted against the rating during 1989, but the following year the benefits came through as sales of prepared meals took off despite the recession. The company's reputation as a defensive stock became firmly established in 1990 and grew over the following year as profit growth was maintained while that of supposed rivals like Unigate fell. Its close association with the UK's main food retailers made all the difference. Northern's solid status was confirmed when it launched a rights issue in November 1991, as part of its Express Dairy deal, and the shares rose by 4 per cent.

The rating began to decline in mid-1992, after outperforming the food-manufacturing sector by 27 per cent over 12 months. It seemed that investors were worried that the rise had been overdone and a series of profit downgradings by analysts took the rating down. The shares fell steadily throughout 1993 as the intensity of the competition in the food-manufacturing industry became clear. Only in early 1994 did Northern's attraction – as a uniquely strong company, committed to innovation – come to be recognised by the market.

Corporate conscience

The management culture of Northern Foods is a mixture of left-leaning politics and gritty northern pragmatism that relegates concern for the environment and equal opportunities to the status of 'trends'. As a result, Northern Foods does not have a comprehensive policy on the environment, although it is a member of BITC and supports Opportunity 2000.

Northern Foods has had convictions for health and safety breaches and for water pollution. In addition, there are a large number of cases of discharge consents being exceeded, although most of these refer to Express Dairies before it was taken over.

While being 'clean' with regard to most other issues of conscience, the group's meat operations involve intensive farming, and Northern Foods has made no commitment to phasing out CFCs in refrigeration.

Corporate governance

Separate Chairman and Chief Executive N
Number of Directors 6
Number of Non-Executive Directors 3
(3 Independent Directors)
Insulated Directors None

Board Committees
Audit: Y   Remuneration: Y

Remuneration

Year end	31.03.91	31.03.92	31.03.93
Total board £M	0.50	0.50	0.50
% change		0	0
Highest paid £	154,602	181,275	185,086
% change		17	2

Haskins, Christopher *Chairman & Chief Executive*
Morgan, Michael *Executive Director*
Clark, Martin *Finance Director*
Edey, Russell *Independent Non-Executive*
Fry, Jonathan *Independent Non-Executive*
Howard, Brian *Independent Non-Executive*

Christopher Haskins has a good record at Northern Foods, but, with no separate chairman, there is a need for a strong, questioning boardroom presence to act as a counterbalance to him. At least half the small board are made up of independent directors. The company also has audit and remuneration committees and has abandoned the practice of insulating directors from re-election. Little effort is put into disclosure of directors' pay, however.

P&O plc

79 Pall Mall, London SW1Y 5EJ
Tel: 0171 930 4343
Chairman Lord Sterling of Plaistow
Managing director Sir Bruce MacPhail
Main subsidiaries Bovis, Earls Court & Olympia arenas, Ashby & Horner, Sterling Security Services
Size £5.7 billion sales, £4.0 billion stock market value, 51,800 employees
5-year growth sales 25%, earnings per share -63%, employment -20%
Solvency debt = 53% shareholders' funds, interest cover 3 times
Political donations £100,000 Conservative Party
Charitable donations £445,000

P&O

Share record

Return on shareholders' equity	%	6.47
5-year price high	p	741.0
5-year price low	p	304.0
Dividend yield	%	5.66
5-year high	%	13.38
5-year low	%	4.81
Price/earnings ratio		30.5
5-year high		33.3
5-year low		8.6

Share price performance (in pence)

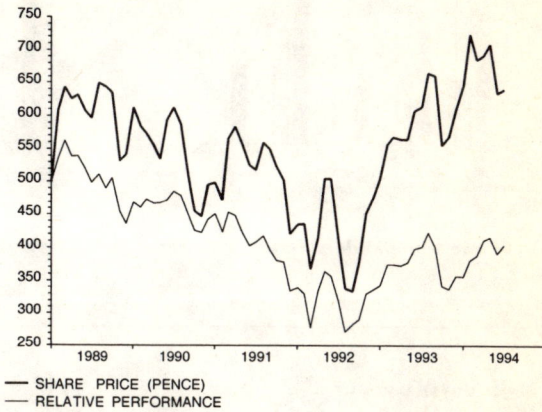

— SHARE PRICE (PENCE)
— RELATIVE PERFORMANCE

Financial record

		31/12/89	31/12/90	31/12/91	31/12/92	31/12/93
Total sales	£	4,578M	5,036M	4,897M	5,528M	5,746M
Pre-tax profit	£'000	376,900	261,300	217,400	208,900	260,200
Published retentions	£'000	76,600	35,400	14,800	13,300	221,600
Earnings per share	p	58.81	38.24	29.67	20.98	22.04
Dividend per share	p	27.81	28.76	30.50	30.50	30.50
Operating cash flow	£'000	-326M	100,500	-161M	-47,900	281,000
Net assets per share	p	777.76	729.33	747.77	709.12	782.13
Net debt/(cash)	£	1,351M	1,396M	1,070M	1,888M	1,406M
Shareholders' funds	£	1,911M	1,743M	2,273M	2,255M	2,677M
Return on capital	%	15.66	12.47	11.13	9.84	9.94
Profit margin	%	8.15	5.38	4.57	3.53	4.44
Sales per employee	£	71.07	67.12	69.34	77.72	111.02
Interest cover		6.00	3.21	2.77	2.44	2.86
Dividend cover		2.11	1.33	0.97	0.69	0.72
Sales increase	%	35.60	10.01	-2.76	12.89	3.94
Earnings growth	%	21.40	-34.98	-22.39	-29.30	5.05
Investment x depreciation		3.24	1.33	1.77	1.14	-0.26
Investment as % assets		15.69	6.46	8.75	5.65	-1.15
Number of employees		64,423	75,034	70,628	71,133	51,755

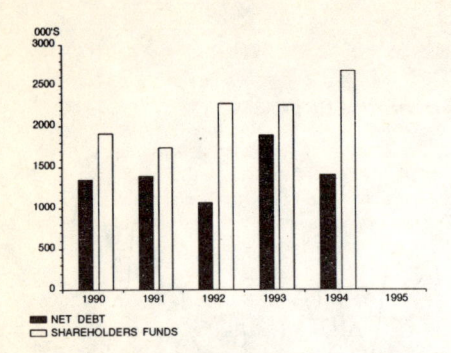

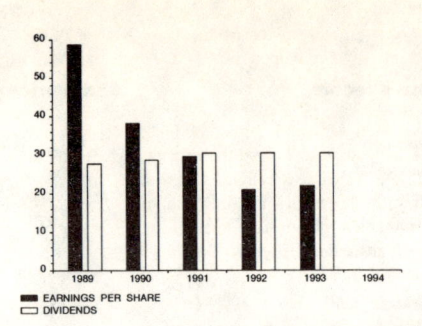

Debt and shareholders' funds

Earnings and dividends

Major developments
1840 formed by Royal Charter
1983 fought off bid from Trafalgar House
1985 merger with Sterling Guarantee Trust; sale of cross-Channel ferries to European Ferries
1989 bought Spring Grove Services
1990 bought Laing Properties
1991 sold Felixstowe Dock & Railway Co
1992 sold Plantation Management
1993 sold Spring Grove, Sutcliffe Catering and Buck & Hickman

Outlook
For many years shipping has not been a good business for anybody except a few eccentric entrepreneurs. In the early 1980s it threatened to throttle P&O, which had been the world's largest shipping line. The company faced a takeover by 1960s wheeler-dealer (now Sir) Nigel Broakes of Trafalgar House. Trafalgar's bid failed, but ironically P&O was effectively taken over by another 1960s entrepreneur, (now Lord) Jeffrey Sterling. Sadly, considering its great history, the company has become just another property and service conglomerate, and even more sadly, its major public connection with shipping in recent times was through the *Herald of Free Enterprise* tragedy in 1987 (when 192 people were killed as a cross-Channel ferry sank). The name remains, however, and at least the group has the satisfaction of being in better shape than Trafalgar, where Sir Nigel has been kicked upstairs to become president following the invasion by Hongkong Land.

P&O is so old that it was first incorporated (in 1840) by Royal Charter, since there was no Companies Act to govern incorporation at that time. The company grew with the Empire, but also shrank with it and with the decline of shipping as a means of transport after the Second World War. There were half-hearted attempts to diversify in the 1970s, including a flirtation with oil and the acquisition of the Bovis construction business which is still part of the group. Diversification was rather less successful than it had been at the other Inchcape family business (bearing the Inchcape name) and Trafalgar pounced in 1983 when Lord Inchcape had announced his retirement.

Jeffrey Sterling saved the group from Trafalgar, but only at the expense of merging it with his own Sterling Guarantee Trust (SGT). SGT had begun as an investment trust acquired from Slater Walker in the late 1960s, and pursued the then fashionable business of acquiring undervalued, property-based companies, in this case usually in the service sector. SGT shot Mr Sterling, as he then was, to prominence when he and his team took over and saved Town and City Properties, the developer of the Arndale shopping centres that had become caught up in the property collapse of the 1970s.

The merger of SGT with P&O in 1985 produced the basis of today's P&O. Subsequently the group has acquired the remainder of container company OCL and has expanded its property interests through a variety of deals, including the curious Pall Mall joint venture to buy Laing Properties. The cross-Channel ferry business was actually sold to European Ferries early in 1985, only for P&O to buy European Ferries in stages during the later 1980s.

Despite all this activity, P&O entered the 1990s with profits falling and debts rising along with major doubts about key parts of its empire. The cross-Channel ferry business faced the threat from Eurotunnel in the (rapidly shortening) medium term, and was repeatedly refused permission to make anti-competitive agreements with its cross-Channel rivals. The cruise market was suffering under the recession. Property and construction faced a crisis barely less severe than in the 1970s. And in housing, Bovis could not have been in a worse geographic or market position, concentrated as it was in the south east of the UK and the upper echelons of the market.

But what had been a geographic weakness in recession proved a boon for Bovis as the revival in the housing market helped profits to bounce back in 1993. Although P&O's hopes of rationalising the cross-Channel ferry market through mergers with rivals such as Sealink remain on hold, the absence of full-fire competition from the Channel Tunnel is providing a welcome breathing space which could well last until the peak tourist season of 1995. In spite of all this, there remains the uncomfortable feeling that the group could still benefit from the arrival of another Jeffrey Sterling.

Shares

The value of P&O's shares peaked relative to the rest of the market in 1986 and then declined until 1992, despite the strong increases in profit which marked the early part of that period and the attraction of a high yield. There were flurries of interest along the way, as in 1987 when the shares rose sharply after the group bought European Ferries and were boosted later that summer when it sold a stake in property group Stockley. Further expansion and steady growth in profits during 1988 helped the shares recover from the market crash but the rating weakened following investment in the cruise business that autumn through the £125 million purchase of Sitmar and the effects of a seamen's strike. The group's profits peaked in 1989, pushing the shares up once more, but the City slowly formed the view that it was under financial pressure and the rating flopped again. Neither the joint bid for Laing Properties nor the acquittal of the ferry business in the *Herald of Free Enterprise* case rallied the shares much in 1990. The deeply discounted rights issue in 1991 came hard on the heels of official denials that one was needed, and the rating plunged. It was only salvaged by the devaluation of the pound and interest rate cuts of 1992. These helped the shares outperform the all-share index by 23 per cent as the City acknowledged the one-off benefit to the balance sheet and profits. Improved profits and the absence of a much rumoured rights issue helped support the company's share price in early 1994.

Corporate conscience

P&O is a member of BITC, but does not make an outstanding contribution to the community. It does not have adequate equal opportunities and environmental policies, nor does it have a good record of employee relations.

European Ferries was on the receiving end of an adverse judgement by the ASA in 1992; there were 4 health and safety convictions in 1988–92, 2 of which were against Bovis Construction. And the John Forman subsidiary was convicted of water pollution in 1990, being fined £350. There has been only one example of exceeding discharge consents to water, at Pandoro in Newcastle-under-Lyme. But the building operations use tropical hardwoods, there is no commitment to phase out various uses of CFCs, and the group has some military involvement through Three Quays engineering services, Buck & Hickman machine tools and Bovis Construction. P&O also has limited dealings with countries which infringe human rights, and the group is involved in the sale of tobacco. All in all, the company gives little indication of recognising its corporate responsibilities. In his annual statement, chairman Lord Sterling does make passing reference to environmental policies, reporting an internal audit system and a commitment to 'best practice', but the report does not expand on this approach.

Corporate governance

Separate Chairman and Chief Executive Y
Number of Directors 13
Number of Non-Executive Directors 3
(2 Independent Directors)
Insulated Directors All execs

Board Committees
Audit: N   Remuneration: Y

Remuneration

Year end	31.12.91	31.12.92	31.12.93
Total board £M	3.16	3.07	3.40
% change	14	-3	10
Highest paid £	406,000	426,000	534,000
% change	4	5	25

Board
MacPhail, Sir Bruce *Managing Director*
Lord Sterling of Plaistow *Executive Chairman*
Crossman, J M *Executive Director*
Dunlop, G D S *Executive Director*
Harding, T J R *Executive Director*
Harris, T C *Executive Director*
Lampl, Sir Frank *Executive Director*
Morris, D E A *Executive Director*
Thomas, P *Executive Director*
Warner, P L *Executive Director*
Cazalet, Sir Peter *Independent Non-Executive*
Steele, J R *Independent Non-Executive*
Hambro, Charles E A *Non-Executive*

The P&O board is a model for reform – a model of a board that needs reforming, that is. In 1992 it did establish audit and remuneration committees; but with only two independent directors out of 13, especially with such a long-standing dominant duo at the top, it remains very unbalanced. P&O is also one of the companies which protects all its executive directors from re-election by shareholders, subjecting only the non-executives to such rigours. The annual report points out the inclusion of performance-related bonuses, but declines to explain the bases on which these are calculated. The company keeps its directors on service contracts of no more than 12 months, which is one of the few ways in which it steals a march on most of its competitors.

PEARSON plc

Millbank Tower, Millbank, London SW1P 4QZ
Tel: 0171 411 2000
Chairman and chief executive Viscount Blakenham
Substantial shareholdings Lazard Frères 9%, News Corporation 8%
Main brands and subsidiaries Alton Towers, BSkyB (16%), Chessington World of Adventures, *The Economist* (50%), *Financial Times*, Lazard Borthers (50%), Longman, Penguin Books, Madame Tussauds, Thames TV, Warwick Castle, Westminster Press, Yorkshire–Tyne Tees (14%)
Size £1.8 billion sales, £3.6 billion stock market value, 15,500 employees
5-year growth sales 28%, earnings per share -14%, employment -44%
Solvency debt n/a, interest cover 22 times
Political donations £25,000 Conservative Party, £5,000 Centre for Policy Studies
Charitable donations £1.27 million

Major developments
1897 formed as S Pearson & Son
1969 became public
1984 changed to Pearson plc
1988 sold oil drilling business; share swap with Elsevier
1989 bought the outstanding 33% of Les Echoes; sold 53.5% stake in Château Latour to Allied Lyons
1990 bought Alton Towers
1991 ended Elsevier engagement
1993 bought stake in Thames Television from Thorn-EMI; demerged Royal Doulton and Camco
1994 bought Software Toolworks

Outlook
It was in 1993 that Pearson finally shook off the tag of conglomerate, the business structure which went fatally out of vogue during the 1980s. Instead, the company decided it was to be termed a 'leisure and media' group, an announcement which could hardly have been more trendy. Despite deciding to demerge its oil services business, Camco, and the fine-china company Royal Doulton, Pearson could not, after more than a century with its fingers in a host of pies, bring itself into really tight focus. Hence the Lazard Brothers banking business remains on board

Despite this, Pearson now looks as single-minded as at any other time in its century-plus existence, ever since it sprang to life as a family-owned Yorkshire building group. From that base it grew well beyond its Yorkshire heritage, becoming involved in such projects as constructing the Blackwall tunnel under the Thames and similar structures in New York, as well as railways all over the world. Like many successful private businessmen, members of the Pearson family did not feel constrained to stick to what they knew. Quite the opposite, in fact: they moved into oil, merchant banking, publishing and engineering. (On the way there was also a brief period in the 1930s when the Cowdrays – as the family became, following the ennoblement of the first successful member of the family, who combined his business flair with being a Liberal MP – owned British Airways.) By the time Pearson became a public company in 1969, the third Lord Cowdray had added a touch of class to the rather prosaic activities, in the shape of Château Latour vineyards and Royal Doulton fine china. He also added the *Financial Times* to the Westminster Press local newspapers and moved into book publishing with interests in Penguin and Longman.

Pearson was only part-owner of many of these companies, which made for a particularly messy structure as a public company. But it was not until the 1980s that the tidying-up process began. First, the minority stakes in the publishing business, Pearson Longman, and the oil interests, were bought in. Then some of the less attractive businesses were sold, such as Fairey Engineering and Doulton Glass Industries. Finally, acquisitions were made in publishing and entertainment to give these businesses greater market presence, and especially greater presence worldwide. The US book publishing business Addison-Wesley is an example, as is the globalisation of the *Financial Times*.

The group's concentration on leisure and media has dramatically simplified its structure and placed the company right at the heart of one of the fastest-growing and most fashionable stock market sectors, even if its pursuit of acquisition targets has not smacked of ruthless decisiveness. But current chairman Lord Blakenham is no slave to fashion: for example, he resists the trend to split the roles of chairman and chief executive, and is one of the few in that position to argue coherently that his company is better the way it is. And while Pearson suffered during the recession, its record under the present family custodian has been good. The *Financial Times* remains not just an excellent newspaper but also an excellent business, and the group has resisted the temptation to waste money by trying to expand it madly, while steadily extending its geographic coverage with printing operations around the world. The other newspapers suffered from the slump in advertising, but better financial results are expected when the advertising business improves again, especially as a result of severe cost-cutting. In the entertainment sector Madame Tussaud's, Alton Towers, Chessington and Warwick Castle are a powerful combination. And Lazards remains a strong bank, even if Pearson owns only a part of it, and even though investment banking is notoriously volatile.

The group went through a curious episode in the late 1980s when it entered an arrangement (in 1988) with Dutch publisher Elsevier which looked like a prelude to merger. The deal fell apart early in 1991, however, apparently because the relative stock market valuations of the two groups made a full merger

PEARSON

Share record

Return on shareholders' equity	%	15.17
5-year price high	p	725.0
5-year price low	p	285.7
Dividend yield	%	2.55
5-year high	%	5.25
5-year low	%	2.07
Price/earnings ratio		24.4
5-year high		38.7
5-year low		8.4

Share price performance (in pence)

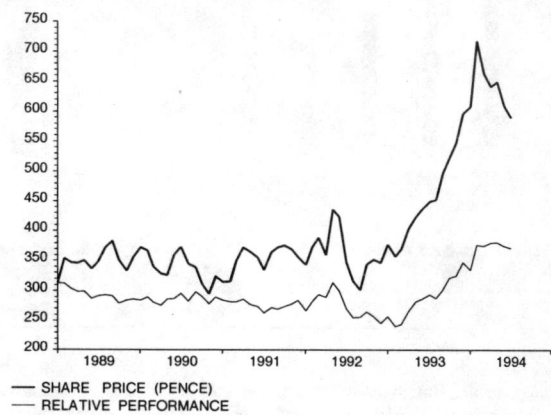

— SHARE PRICE (PENCE)
— RELATIVE PERFORMANCE

Financial record

		31/12/89	31/12/90	31/12/91	31/12/92	31/12/93
Total sales	£	1,460M	1,535M	1,600M	1,636M	1,870M
Pre-tax profit	£'000	238,900	214,700	162,200	142,000	221,200
Published retentions	£'000	220,400	55,000	72,800	39,800	-35,300
Earnings per share	p	30.25	26.25	19.88	14.61	26.15
Dividend per share	p	10.41	11.26	11.26	11.62	13.00
Operating cash flow	£'000	-12,900	-28,800	25,700	61,000	49,500
Net assets per share	p	200.17	212.45	225.09	263.58	256.26
Net debt/(cash)	£'000	358,800	400,600	98,500	110,900	-73,300
Shareholders' funds	£'000	649,200	705,800	975,400	1,068M	997,300
Return on capital	%	30.30	25.03	18.16	14.48	18.24
Profit margin	%	10.75	8.70	7.50	6.28	9.17
Sales per employee	£	52.30	52.20	56.17	58.49	120.54
Interest cover		7.58	5.22	6.71	8.34	22.02
Dividend cover		2.91	2.33	1.77	1.26	2.01
Sales increase	%	22.21	5.15	4.25	2.21	14.33
Earnings growth	%	24.86	-13.23	-24.26	-26.51	78.96
Investment x depreciation		1.61	2.08	1.50	0.93	0.89
Investment as % assets		13.11	15.67	12.95	8.21	11.76
Number of employees		27,915	29,410	28,492	27,966	15,514

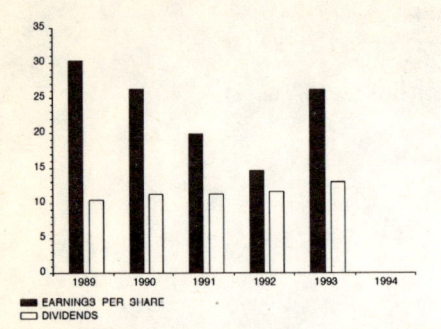

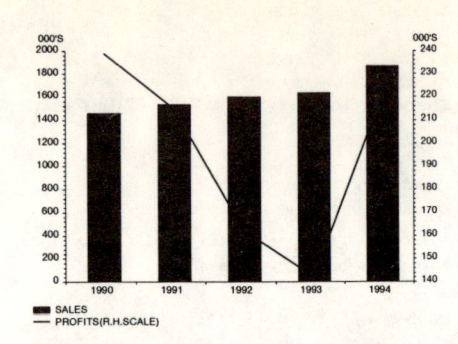

Earnings and dividends

Sales and profits

impossible. But at least the arrangement served a subsidiary purpose of fending off Rupert Murdoch's News International, which had built up a share stake in Pearson. And Elsevier went on to merge with Reed instead.

Pearson's wild card is BSkyB. As in the case of Granada, the move into satellite broadcasting represents a long-term diversification into new media (Pearson does also have a stake in Yorkshire Television and in 1993 bought the programme-maker Thames TV, but is clearly much less dependent than Granada on terrestrial transmission) and could prove highly profitable in the future. Although BSkyB represents a huge investment in the short term its recent profit performance – the surplus is up to about £4 million a week – indicates that it could be extremely lucrative in the longer term. Pearson retains its 14 per cent stake in Yorkshire – Tyne Tees which hit a dreadful patch in 1993 following the overselling of air time, but which is clearly one of the remaining cherries to be picked from the ITV tree. Pearson is limited to 20 per cent by law and faces the possibility that Granada might be a rival for Yorkshire's hand. But in a more relaxed regulatory climate a bid could not be ruled out.

Shares

For a conglomerate, Pearson was highly rated in 1986, but during 1987 the rest of the market began to lose interest in the shares until it was seen as a possible takeover target. The rating soared when Italian magnate Benedetti took a 4.9 per cent stake and would have gone even higher after Rupert Murdoch bought nearly 15 per cent of the shares, had not the market crash overtaken the speculators. The pot was brought back to the boil in 1988, though, by speculation that Reed might try to take the group over.

The deal with Elsevier finally killed off such talk (ironically, considering Reed's eventual merger with the Dutch group), and while the shares themselves stayed strong, they began to lose ground steadily relative to the market until 1990. Over that period the management tidied up the group's sprawling portfolio of interests, only to launch a £71.5 million share placing in 1990 to buy the Alton Towers theme park. The brief rise in the rating faded when Murdoch reduced his stake that autumn and dipped further in 1991 when Pearson talked of untying its deal with Elsevier. Further pressure came as provisions for the stake in BSkyB mounted, and the City worried about the effect of recession on all areas of the group.

After a roller coaster of a ride in 1992, the shares recovered in 1993, swept up by the enthusiasm for any stock to which the word 'media' could be loosely associated, and helped by a £100 million payout by BSkyB.

Corporate concience

Pearson's operations are relatively benign, so it is relatively free from black marks on issues of conscience. *The Economist* (50 per cent owned by Pearson) was subject to an adverse judgement by the ASA in 1991, and the group's newspapers do accept advertising for alcohol and a variety of other products which themselves would impinge on ethical concerns. Pearson is implicated marginally in repressive regimes, and a handful of its small black workforce was paid below a reasonable level in South Africa. An associated company also exceeded discharge levels to water on several occasions in 1990/91. Pearson's employment record has been marred by ruthless cost-cutting measures in the newspaper operations, and has little positive to commend it such as a vigorous equal opportunities policy. The group is a member of the Per Cent Club, though not BITC.

Corporate governance

Separate Chairman and Chief Executive N
Number of Directors 13
Number of Non-Executive Directors 8
(5 Independent Directors)
Insulated Directors All execs

Board Committees
Audit: Y   Remuneration: Y

Remuneration

Year end	31.12.91	31.12.92	31.12.93
Total board £M	1.44	1.55	2.39
% change		11	7	55
Highest paid £	266,000	299,000	453,000
% change		4	12	52

Board
Viscount Blakenham *Chairman & Chief Executive*
Barlow, Frank *Managing Director*
Burrell, Mark *Executive Director*
Veit, David *Executive Director*
Joll, James *Finance Director*
Gyllenhammar, Pehr *Independent Non-Executive*
Lewis, Gill M *Independent Non-Executive*
Mark, Reuben *Independent Non-Executive*
Sankey, Vernon L *Independent Non-Executive*
Stevenson, Dennis *Independent Non-Executive*
David-Weill, Michel *Non-Executive*
Haas, Jean-Claude *Non-Executive*
Hornby, Sir Simon *Non-Executive*

The company stands out for having the courage to transfer details of directors' pay and shareholdings from the accounts section into the main body of the annual report, alongside other biographical notes about directors. A five-year pay comparison is given and an ample policy statement provided for the basis on which directors' salaries are calculated. The aims of boardroom committees are generously detailed. Lord Blakenham does not agree with the principle of separating the roles of chairman and chief executive, marring otherwise exemplary adherence to standards of corporate governance.

PILKINGTON plc

Prescot Road, St Helens, Merseyside WA10 3TT
Tel: 01744 28882
Chairman Sir Antony Pilkington
Chief executive Roger Leverton
Main subsidiaries Triplex Safety glass
Size £2.7 billion sales, £1.4 billion stock market value, 41,100 employees
5-year growth sales -6%, earnings per share -93%, employment -32%

Solvency debt = 56% shareholders' funds, interest cover 1 time
Political donations 0
Charitable donations £766,000

Major developments
1826 formed as St Helens Crown Glass Co
1970 became public as Pilkington Brothers
1980 bought Flachglas in Germany
1986 took full control of Libby-Owens Ford
1987 fought off bid from BTR
1990 launched energy-saving K glass
1991 sold 50% of Pilkington Optronics to Thomson CSF; sold South African interests; set up European headquarters in Brussels
1993 took 40% stake in Polish glass business; sold Sola US spectacle lens business
1994 set up South American joint venture with Saint Gobain; announced flotation of Australian business

Outlook

At the beginning of 1987 a brilliant campaign by Pilkington's managers and workers persuaded one of Britain's most successful companies, BTR, to withdraw from a takeover bid for the St Helens-based glass-maker. Subsequent events may make BTR relieved that it was not responsible for facing the problems, but will also leave shareholders and workers wondering whether their loyalty was misplaced.

Only 5,000 jobs remain in St Helens, less than a third than during the peak of the 1970s and only about half as many as there were at the start of the First World War. Pilkington has always been a caring company, so such job losses have not been made lightly, and certainly not merely for the benefit of the shareholders. Indeed, shareholders have fared little better than the workers, seeing the final dividend cut at the end of 1991–2 and earnings virtually disappear.

The question is whether the company would have fared much better under BTR's control, and whether the more vicious cuts which BTR might have been expected to make, in order to benefit shareholders in the short term, would have been in the long-term interests of the company. BTR would have been unlikely to have instigated the unfortunate diversification into contact lenses and defence. But 'Pilks' (as the company is known) could reasonably argue that such diversification was made in response to shareholders' concerns about the cyclical nature of the core business in glass – action prompted by the BTR bid. More pertinently, BTR would almost certainly not have invested in UK 6, the sixth glass line which came into production in 1990 just as demand for glass was plummeting. It is a central tenet of BTR's approach that you should never get into a position where you are desperate for somebody's order: customers turned away are better than overcapacity.

The BTR approach to business, however, would never have produced Pilkington in the first place. The company, while in one respect a victim of its monopolistic position and family ownership or direction, is

PILKINGTON plc

Share record

Return on shareholder's equity	%	1.33
5-year price high	p	270.0
5-year price low	p	70.0
Dividend yield	%	2.76
5-year high	%	12.50
5-year low	%	1.55
Price/earnings ratio		61.6
5-year high		104.5
5-year low		5.4

Share price performance (in pence)

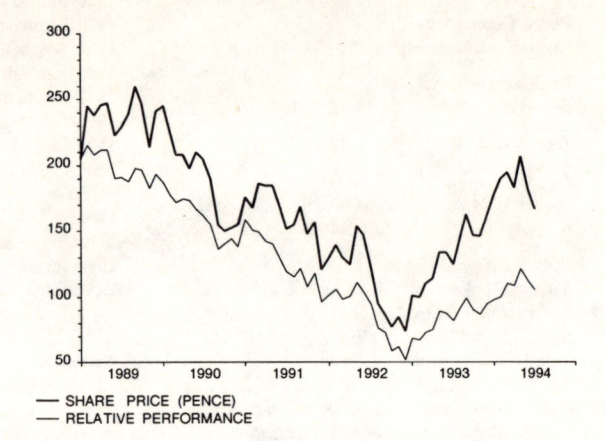

— SHARE PRICE (PENCE)
— RELATIVE PERFORMANCE

Financial record

		31/3/90	31/3/91	31/3/92	31/3/93	31/3/94
Total sales	£	2,915M	2,650M	2,611M	2,573M	2,737M
Pre-tax profit	£'000	323,400	169,300	100,100	73,200	72,400
Published retentions	£'000	100,600	-62,600	-20,100	-51,400	8,200
Earnings per share	p	25.81	10.19	4.24	1.58	1.68
Dividend per share	p	10.50	10.50	6.00	4.00	4.00
Operating cash flow	£'000	-21,700	-14,700	-124M	-53,300	132,000
Net assets per share	p	306.52	296.53	284.65	313.65	293.10
Net debt/(cash)	£'000	667,800	800,400	760,200	932,300	743,900
Shareholders' funds	£'000	1,044M	929,300	929,300	1,269M	1,311M
Return on capital	%	19.89	11.90	9.69	7.06	6.83
Profit margin	%	11.04	6.13	3.24	2.07	1.87
Sales per employee	£	48.14	44.83	48.53	59.97	66.60
Interest cover		4.74	2.67	1.70	1.52	1.34
Dividend cover		2.46	0.97	0.71	0.40	0.42
Sales increase	%	13.31	-9.11	-1.45	-1.45	6.41
Earnings growth	%	-7.49	-60.51	-58.39	-62.66	5.88
Investment x depreciation		1.58	1.82	0.90	0.68	0.68
Investment as % assets		13.79	14.61	7.81	5.61	6.45
Number of employees		60,550	59,100	53,800	42,900	41,100

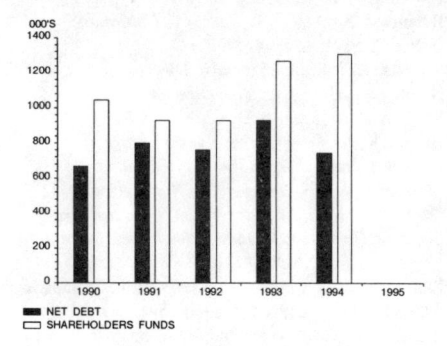

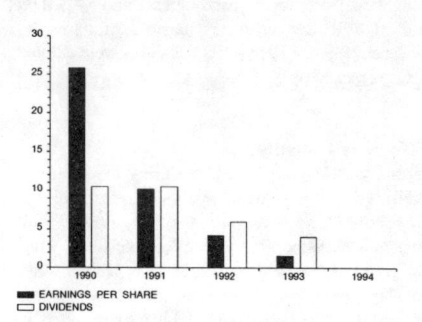

Debt and shareholders' funds

Earnings and dividends

also a symbol of risk-taking in new technology. Its early origins were as accidental as they are for most companies: stemming from a doctor who decided to concentrate on his wine and spirits business and thence moved into glass. But it was transformed from a run-of-the-mill 19th-century industrial manufacturer into the major supplier of glass in the UK, with Continental interests and worldwide exports, by a bold decision to invest in plate-glass production in the 1870s (a decision which almost triggered the flotation of Pilkington on the Stock Exchange a century earlier than eventually happened). Proving that such decisions can be highly risky, a similar choice to invest in new technology after the First World War turned out to be disastrous, but the modern group was built on the extremely expensive development of the float glass process in the 1950s.

Opportunism and luck have also played their part in Pilks's growth – in the early years when rival companies ran into difficulties for one reason or another, and, more recently, when it was able to acquire a presence in Germany (following the decision of French food and drink group BSN to get out of glass-making) and in the US (when Gulf & Western wanted to sell its stake in Libby-Owens-Ford). Such luck, combined with its private status until 1970, had caused the group to become arrogant and complacent, and suffer from the usual British malaise of being blinded by technology to the real requirements of the market. This left Pilks selling too much standard glass: a commodity product too readily substituted by that of foreign competitors (there have been no UK competitors for decades) and hence subject to continued pressures on margins.

The group sought to improve its strategic approach by appointing Roger Leverton as chief executive in 1992, as well as ending its attempt to smooth cyclicality through diversification.

Mr Leverton faced a tough task, not because of resistance to a market-led approach, but because of the nature of the business. Three-quarters of production goes to the construction and motor industries, which are inevitably cyclical. Producing glass is a capital-intensive and energy-intensive business: two factors which make life difficult for the company in 1990s Britain, and also make production volume a crucial factor in profitability. In addition, the recession left Pilks with mounting debts, which forced not only the cut in dividend but also the sale of spectacle-lens business Sola. Other moves to cut debt followed. The company announced plans to float its Australian offshoot. Roger Leverton set a target for the group: between 1993 and 1995 gearing should be cut to 50 per cent. And in 1994, at last, there were signs that demand for glass had stopped falling and prices were beginning to rise.

Shares

In 1987, following Pilkington's famous victory in seeing off the takeover bid from BTR, the company's rating subsequently dropped and the shares were held mainly for their yield rather than their prospects. The diversification programme that followed and that was supposed to free the group from dependency on the building cycle only left Pilkington with debt and made the City doubt the board's judgement. In 1989 expansion into Europe brought hopes of better profits, though the rating slipped again until 1991 when there was a slight rally as Pilkington raised cash from the sale of its South African operation. But not even the plan to switch European headquarters from St Helens to Brussels halted the slide for long.

The shares' reputation for their high yield took a knock in 1992 when there was a cut in the dividend for the first time in Pilkington's 22-year history as a public company. This gave a further twist to the downward spiral in the share rating. Since their peak in 1987 the shares had lost a staggering 75 per cent of their value relative to the market, giving pause for thought to those loyal shareholders who helped to fend off BTR. But the shares staged a strong recovery in late 1993 and early 1994 as debts were cut and earnings picked-up.

Corporate conscience

Despite huge employment cuts during the recession and the group's growing internationalisation, Pilkington just about retains the values of a responsible family company. Gone are the comfortable times when Sir Harry Pilkington initiated 'Sir Harry' days enabling employees to take a limited number of days off each year if they had a bit of a hangover, yet Pilks remains a good employer, even if it has not yet thoroughly embraced such 'modern' notions as equal opportunities. In keeping with its traditions, though, Pilkington is a member of BITC, and of the Per Cent Club. In fact it has a proud record of community support, especially in its St Helens home, where early attempts to offset the impact of 1970s unemployment formed a model for many job creation schemes and for BITC itself. The group continues this activity – for example, funding a science education scheme for primary schools in the area.

Pilkington's does have a comprehensive environment policy, as befits a major energy and mineral user. It has not been independently audited, but is committed to regular internal monitoring and review and has clear, quantified targets. The company does use CFCs, and is not committed to phasing them out, but on the other hand its water pollution record is relatively good. The group is a member of the British Nuclear Forum, however, and makes radiation shielding for nuclear power stations.

Pilkington's Visioncare contact lens company is implicated in animal testing. And the group has some operations in countries with poor human rights records, mainly India, Brazil, Mexico and Taiwan. It is also a military supplier, making submarine periscopes, helicopter and bomber windshields, and insulation for the Trident submarine.

Corporate governance

Separate Chairman and Chief Executive Y
Number of Directors 11
Number of Non-Executive Directors 5
(5 Independent Directors)
Insulated Directors All execs

Board Committees
Audit: Y Remuneration: Y

Remuneration

Year end	31.03.92	31.03.93	31.03.94
Total board £M	1.85	1.98	2.90
% change	-5	7	47
Highest paid £	335,278	347,318	445,630
% change		7	4	28

Board
Leverton, Roger *Chief Executive*
Pilkington, Sir Antony R *Executive Chairman*
Grunwell, Peter *Executive Director*
Nicholson, Sir Robin *Executive Director*
Nightingale, Glen *Executive Director*
Robb, Andrew *Finance Director*
Hurn, F Roger *Independent Non-Executive*
Kopper, Hilmar *Independent Non-Executive*
Macomber, John D *Independent Non-Executive*
Quinlan, Sir Michael *Independent Non-Executive*
Simpson, George *Independent Non-Executive*

Pilkington is a model of a responsible company which has long believed in good governance. Before the Cadbury Code was formed, the board had audit and remuneration committees staffed by what the company termed 'independent' directors (although the audit committee includes the managing director). And before the Cadbury Committee had finally reported, in June 1992, the Pilkington annual report included a statement from the independent directors signed by their senior member, Lord Croham, who explained the working of the board committees. The relevant accounts note explained that directors had received pay increases in line with inflation in 1991 and 1992, but the bonus scheme had not yielded any payments in those two years. The board has not yet plucked up courage to expose the executive directors to re-election by shareholders, and has now adopted the fashion for producing a glossy 'review' separately from the formal report and accounts, leaving the latter with no section on corporate governance.

THE RANK ORGANISATION plc

6 Connaught Place, London W2 2EZ
Tel: 0171 706 1111
Chairman Sir Leslie Fletcher
Chief executive Michael Gifford
Main brands and subsidiaries Associated Leisure amusement machines, Butlin's, Hard Rock Cafe, HavenWarner holidays, Mecca and Top Rank bingo, Odeon Cinemas, Pinewood Studios, Rank Xerox (49%), Ritzy, Fifth Avenue, Central Park night clubs, Shearings coach holidays, Universal Studios theme park (Florida) (50%)
Size £2.1 billion sales, £3.4 billion stock market value, 41,000 employees
5-year growth sales 93%, earnings per share -32%, employment 80%
Solvency debt = 64% shareholders' funds, interest cover 2 times
Political donations £25,000 Conservative Party
Charitable donations £278,344

THE RANK ORGANISATION

Share record

Return on shareholders' equity	%	11.65
5-year price high	p	445.2
5-year price low	p	180.4
Dividend yield	%	3.92
5-year high	%	9.16
5-year low	%	2.51
Price/earnings ratio		18.9
5-year high		26.5
5-year low		7.3

Share price performance (in pence)

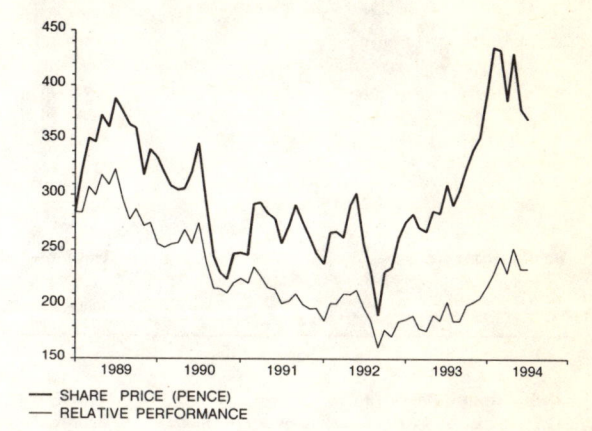

— SHARE PRICE (PENCE)
— RELATIVE PERFORMANCE

Financial record

		31/10/89	31/10/90	31/10/91	31/10/92	31/10/93
Total sales	£	1,093M	1,333M	2,114M	2,096M	2,107M
Pre-tax profit	£'000	266,600	301,200	251,800	238,200	274,600
Published retentions	£'000	119,100	75,600	22,600	20,800	141,400
Earnings per share	p	27.52	26.44	15.53	15.85	18.62
Dividend per share	p	11.58	12.40	12.40	12.40	12.40
Operating cash flow	£'000	-85,300	-38,200	15,500	-13,900	46,800
Net assets per share	p	288.27	387.34	331.39	326.28	319.23
Net debt/(cash)	£'000	466,900	710,600	960,800	999,300	955,300
Shareholders' funds	£	1,098M	1,713M	1,494M	1,383M	1,486M
Return on capital	%	21.84	16.90	13.86	13.48	14.90
Profit margin	%	9.46	10.05	4.43	4.40	5.31
Sales per employee	£	47.96	44.90	46.99	49.92	51.35
Interest cover		3.45	8.83	1.92	1.99	2.26
Dividend cover		2.38	2.13	1.25	1.28	1.50
Sales increase	%	32.63	21.97	58.59	-0.86	0.52
Earnings growth	%	1.60	-3.93	-41.27	2.07	17.44
Investment x depreciation		3.09	2.93	1.53	1.17	1.21
Investment as % assets		15.88	9.84	8.68	8.01	8.76
Number of employees		22,790	29,689	44,993	41,991	41,029

THE RANK ORGANISATION plc

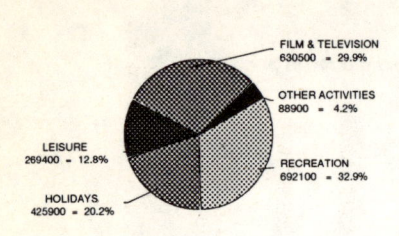

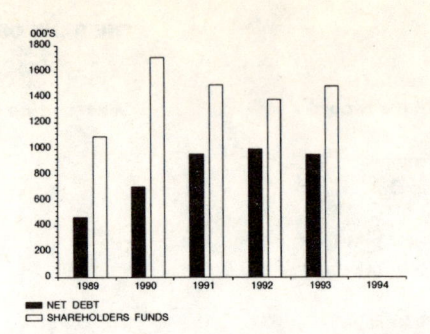

Profit analysis

- FILM & TELEVISION 630500 = 29.9%
- OTHER ACTIVITIES 88900 = 4.2%
- RECREATION 692100 = 32.9%
- HOLIDAYS 425900 = 20.2%
- LEISURE 269400 = 12.8%

Debt and shareholders' funds

(000's, 1989–1994: NET DEBT and SHAREHOLDERS FUNDS)

Major developments
1937 formed by J Arthur Rank as owner of Odeon theatre chain
1939 became public
1944 bought Pinewood Studios
1956 formed Rank Xerox as joint venture with Haloid Company
1961 opened first UK bingo club
1963 first hotels and motorway services
1969 reduced stake in Rank Xerox to 49%
1972 bought Butlins
1983 management shake-up
1986 bought Bingo and amusements centres from Ladbrokes
1988 bought Ahnert American Caravan Park Co
1989 invested £115m in Universal Studios theme park; bought 18 Pizza Piazza restaurants
1990 bought Mecca Leisure for £895m
1991 sold motorway services for £86m
1993 sold Prima Pasta and Pizza Piazza restaurants; sold Royal Lancaster hotel for £61m and 8 provincial hotels; Xerox reorganisation cost group £125m

Outlook
Two points stand out from an examination of Rank's business. First, the contribution to the group's profits made by the photocopier associate Rank Xerox is almost as much as all the managed businesses put together, far outstripping the contribution of even its largest operating division, Recreation. Second, the dismal performance of its film and television companies dragged down the group's profitability in recent years although 1993 saw some recovery.

Rank has spent years trying to sort out a muddle of many operating companies which has not been helped by the Xerox shareholding. The latest year's earnings per share was only just back above the 1986 level. Return on capital declined sharply in the late 1980s, not just because of recession and only improved marginally in 1993.

The presentation of the divisions brings a semblance of order to the muddle, although the distinction between 'Recreation' and 'Leisure' (the official titles for gambling and clubs) is fascinating, especially given that the other two divisions (Film and Television, and Holidays) could also be described by these names. Profits come mainly from half a dozen sub-divisions – Top Rank and Mecca bingo halls and the Rank cinema chain, Butlins, Haven UK and Shearings holidays and the Hard Rock Café chain. Some tidying up has been going on. For example, the motorway service operation has been sold, plus the cinema advertising business and troubled hotels.

The troubled video distribution operation in the US also went in 1994 after years of losses.

Yet Rank remains ensnared by attempts to escape its history as a downmarket leisure company. The present management was installed in 1983 to sort out the mess which had resulted from a first attempt at diversification. In the 1970s the group aimed to become a conglomerate, moving into completely unrelated areas such as investment property, home appliances and electronics. The results were disastrous, with profits plunging at the start of the 1980s, prompting major shareholders to force a change in top management. Michael Gifford and the late Sir Patrick Meaney cleared out most of the non-leisure businesses, but were less successful with their diversifications within the leisure industry.

The excessive debt that has taken its toll on the interest-cover figures stems from the acquisition of Mecca Leisure in 1990. This club and restaurant company had emerged as the result of an ambitious management buy-out from Grand Metropolitan; it was soon floated on the stock market, only to come a cropper with its over-ambitious acquisition of Pleasurama. Rank stepped in, but managed to pay far too much for Mecca, especially as the recession was already gathering pace.

One way of reducing those debts would be to sell the stake in Rank Xerox, but that is easier said than done. The shares would have to be bought by Xerox, which itself might find some difficulty raising the money at least until its own organisation is out of the way. In the meantime Rank will remain a curiosity for receiving around half its profits from such an investment, over which it has no control and little influence. On the other hand, swapping Rank Xerox shares for cash might set Rank off on the acquisition trail again.

Shares

Rank's listing throughout the 1980s as an industrial conglomerate, like Hanson or Trafalgar, was held responsible for the low rating of the shares, and the board campaigned for the company to be put into the more glamorous leisure sector. The industrial label did not prevent the shares being re-rated after the stock market crash of 1987, however, and a string of deals in the leisure business took the group closer to its goal, aided by rumours that Hanson was to bid for Xerox, to Rank's benefit, which caused the shares to peak in 1989.

In 1990, the board tapped the market with a £357 million rights issue without specifying a takeover deal, and the rating began a slide which continued, despite occasional rallies, for two years. Just as the board got its wish and the company was switched to the leisure sector, the stock market became uncertain about both the leisure sector and the group. The worries were confirmed that year when the board warned that economic pressures in the UK and US would affect the group.

The rating steadied in 1991 until it was hit by write-downs on its Mecca business. The retrenchment programme to deal with high debt took the shares upwards for a time but devaluation of the pound sent them plummeting to a new low. Late in 1992 the board renewed City confidence by issuing a positive statement on trading, and the stock market, scenting a recovery in the US and possibly the UK economies, re-rated the shares upwards. Analysts remained cautious about the group into 1993, saying that, with an upturn in the economy in view, there were better prospects for recovery in the leisure sector. But the prospects for Rank were enough to keep the shares advancing.

Corporate conscience

As a leisure company, Rank is not exposed to many issues of conscience. Surprisingly, it does have military connections and involvement with nuclear power. This is through Rank Brimar, which produces cathode-ray tubes for use in fighter aircraft, battle tanks and other military applications, as well as for nuclear research.

Other ethical issues are predictable, given the nature of group's businesses: it sells alcohol and tobacco and is involved in gambling through bingo clubs, casinos and through the manufacture, as well as distribution and operation, of slot-machines. The group's manufacturing activities use ozone-depleting chemicals, but the company has no record of water pollution or health and safety convictions. The holiday operations have suffered adverse ASA judgements, however.

Rank is a member of BITC, but the group does not evince the kind of enthusiasm for social, ethical, employment and environmental issues that is shown by its associate company Rank Xerox. Equal opportunities and environmental policies are notable for their absence rather than for their strength.

Corporate governance

Separate Chairman and Chief Executive Y
Number of Directors 12
Number of Non-Executive Directors 5
(1 Independent Directors)
Insulated Directors MD

Board Committees
Audit: Y   Remuneration: Y

Remuneration

Year end	31.10.91	31.10.92	31.10.93
Total board £	1.91	1.76	1.81
% change	29	-8	3
Highest paid £	309,000	316,000	337,336
% change	8	2	7

Board
Gifford, Michael *Chief Executive*
Crichton-Miller, Angus *Executive Director*
Daly, James *Executive Director*
Garrett, John *Executive Director*
North, Terence H *Executive Director*
Yates, Douglas M *Executive Director*
Turnbull, Nigel V *Finance Director*
Atterton, Dr David V *Non-Executive*
Jackaman, Michael C J *Non-Executive*
Fletcher, Sir Leslie *Non-Executive Chairman*
Stenham, Anthony W P *Non-Executive*
Harrison, James *Independent Non-Executive*

Rank has not been one of the most prominent supporters of the corporate governance revolution, but has nevertheless long had a separate chairman and chief executive, and significant non-executive representation on the board. In its 1991 annual report, published in early 1992, the company explained that the chairman's standing committee (consisting of the chairman and the non-executives) dealt with governance issues such as audit, appointments and remuneration, and it gave some details of directors' bonuses. This coverage was subsequently expanded, including in 1993 the full auditors' report on their corporate governance review.

RECKITT & COLMAN plc

1 Burlington Lane, London W4 2RW
Tel: 0181 994 6464
Chairman Sir Michael Colman
Chief executive Vernon Sankey
Main brands Airwick, Brasso, Cleen-o-Pine, Dettol, Disprin, Dettox, Gaviscon, Harpic, Haze, Immac, Lemsip, Robinson's drinks, Mr Sheen, Steradent, Veet, Windolene
Size £2.1 billion sales, £2.2 billion stock market value, 21,000 employees
5-year growth sales n/a, earnings per share n/a, employment -4.55%
Solvency debt = 83% shareholders' funds, interest cover 5 times
Political donations 0
Charitable donations £298,000

Major developments:
1954 created from merger of J & J Colman and Reckitt & Sons
1984 bought Airwick
1986 bought Durkee Famous Foods
1988 bought 66% of Aspro-Nicholas from Sara Lee Corp
1990 bought Boyle-Midway from American Home Product; sold fine art and graphic division
1991 sold Cherry Blossom shoe polish to Sara Lee
1992 sold US spice business
1994 sold industrial dyes business

Outlook
Reckitt & Colman is one of those long-established British companies which defies its Empire image. Quietly, without much fuss, and hence without burnishing this image, the company best known for products evoking the English village, such as Robinson's barley water and Brasso, has succeeded in becoming a global grocery group. It is not in the Procter & Gamble class, but with almost £2 billion in sales and over 20,000 employees, it is no minnow. Reckitt has long been an international company, although until the 1980s it focused largely on Commonwealth countries. A series of acquisitions in the United States has changed this, however, with accompanying European interests also boosting business on the Continent as well as in North America.

It has not all been plain sailing, though. The first attempts to expand the US business were disastrous, involving what was described as 'home leisure' products (basically knitting) and subsequently potato products such as instant mashed potato. The latter was not a sensible business to move into because it brought Reckitt up against the food giants, while the former had absolutely nothing to do with any of Reckitt's operations, although the purchase in the UK of artists' materials company Windsor & Newton illustrates the group's interest in diversification at that time.

Fortunately for Reckitt, none of these ventures was so costly as to break the company, so it had the opportunity to learn from these mistakes. Later purchases have been more fruitful. In 1984 air-freshener company Airwick was bought from Swiss chemicals group Ciba (then Ciba-Geigy). This acquisition was particularly useful to the group in the United States, where the brand was rather better known than Reckitt's own. Again in the US, Durkee Famous Foods was added in 1986, and four years later the group's biggest-ever acquisition came with the purchase of Boyle-Midway. This is not exactly a household name but the company owned well-known brands that included Immac depilatory products and other names famous in the US, such as Woolite carpet cleaner and Black Flag insecticides. Boyle-Midway was a US equivalent of Reckitt: a well-established operator with strong brands in small niches which are barely worth the giant grocery and household products groups attacking.

After a period of trouble in the US – in 1992 the company withdrew from the spice wars it had been waging with spice giant McCormick – Reckitt & Colman's ambition has been to increase the proportion of profits from America, an objective achieved in 1993 when 21 per cent of its £2.1 billion earnings (up from 16 per cent) came from this continent. Efforts to drive sales forward in faster-growing economies such as South America and south-east Asia have also borne fruit: these territories increased their share of earnings in 1993 from 16 to 20 per cent, despite Brazil's hyper-inflation.

Reckitt has been able to sustain such losses, and finance the string of acquisitions, because of its strong core business and especially the great cash flows associated with it. The group's profit retentions show, however, that it incurred substantial extraordinary costs over the years, which negated the strong growth in pre-tax profits.

The enormous figures showing return on capital and profit margin explain why Reckitt has been able to keep moving forwards, but they also raise the awkward question of how the group manages to make such huge returns. They certainly present a good argument for a secure home base and the ability to get away with what are euphemistically called 'premium prices' for steady-selling brands such as Lemsip, Dettol, Harpic, Windolene and, of course, Colman's mustard.

Shares
When Reckitt & Colman's shares hit the floor in the 1987 market crash, few analysts could have predicted that they would then steadily appreciate against the market as a whole for more than four years. During the Lawson boom the shares rose inexorably, while their status as a dependable stock with a solid yield seemed to be under threat only briefly in 1990, when the group bought Boyle-Midway in the US. But the City's doubts soon passed. The rise in the share rating continued throughout the UK's entry into the ERM and throughout the recession, reaching a peak

RECKITT & COLMAN

Share record

Return on shareholders' equity	%	1876.42
5-year price high	p	726.0
5-year price low	p	436.4
Dividend yield	%	3.68
5-year high	%	3.93
5-year low	%	2.50
Price/earnings ratio		13.5
5-year high		18.0
5-year low		11.4

Share price performance (in pence)

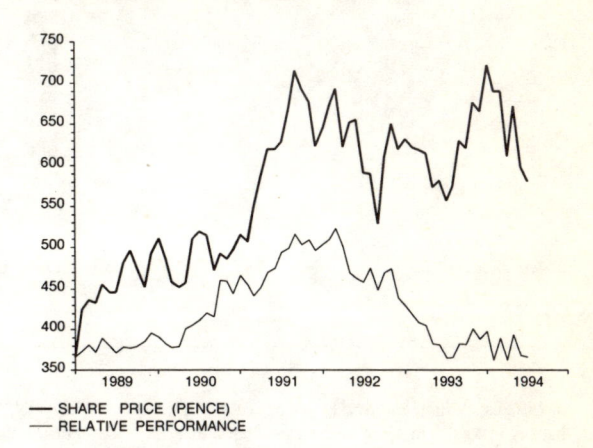

— SHARE PRICE (PENCE)
— RELATIVE PERFORMANCE

Financial record

		31/12/89	31/12/90	31/12/91	31/12/92	31/12/93
Total sales	£	1,566M	1,764M	1,987M	1,904M	2,096M
Pre-tax profit	£'000	211,600	233,430	249,140	215,450	256,980
Published retentions	£'000	78,580	79,660	85,030	33,480	102,870
Earnings per share	p	36.11	40.44	40.91	37.14	44.18
Dividend per share	p	11.90	13.60	15.10	16.20	17.55
Operating cash flow	£'000	48,240	156,880	116,190	104,200	147,710
Net assets per share	p	145.72	144.34	159.43	154.58	141.57
Net debt/(cash)	£'000	19,580	357,810	338,290	515,560	416,330
Shareholders' funds	£'000	591,590	435,240	518,780	617,830	704,230
Return on capital	%	47.65	53.69	56.43	49.46	58.15
Profit margin	%	13.31	13.19	12.50		12.26
Sales per employee	£	71.17	74.10	86.39	91.55	99.79
Interest cover		79.03	14.33	7.17	5.10	5.71
Dividend cover		3.03	2.97	2.71	2.30	2.52
Sales increase	%	12.32	12.64	12.66	-4.16	10.05
Earnings growth	%	9.51	12.00	1.16	-9.22	18.97
Investment x depreciation		1.48	1.22	1.00	0.98	1.05
Investment as % assets		15.84	14.18	12.92	12.04	14.31
Number of employees		22,000	23,800	23,000	20,800	21,000

334 RECKITT & COLMAN plc

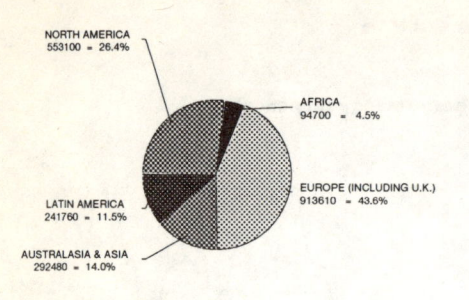

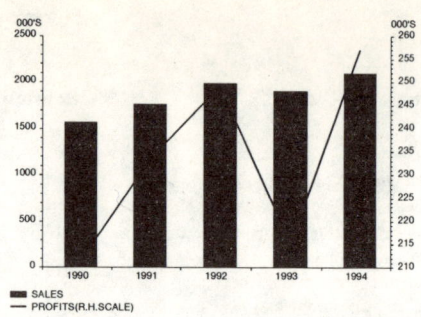

Sales analysis

NORTH AMERICA 553100 = 26.4%
AFRICA 94700 = 4.5%
EUROPE (INCLUDING U.K.) 913610 = 43.6%
LATIN AMERICA 241760 = 11.5%
AUSTRALASIA & ASIA 292480 = 14.0%

Sales and profits

SALES
PROFITS (R.H.SCALE)

---

in 1992 as the dividend rose by 11 per cent. The rating began to slip in 1992 as the City feared that the recession had to catch up with a group with two-thirds of its business in recession-hit countries. In 1993 the shares moved up (with erratic set-backs) to reflect the company's good cash flow, strong margins and brand position, coupled, increasingly, with a beneficial geographical spread. Although Reckitt & Colman has never set the stock market alight, the forecast yield on the shares for 1994 looked likely to be above the rate of inflation, at the very least.

Corporate conscience

Homely images of Colman's mustard obscure the fact that this is as much a chemical company as it is a food business. It is therefore exposed on the issue of animal testing, although the group has supported research into alternatives and says it has limited the extent of animal use in pharmaceuticals, and avoids it wherever possible elsewhere in the business.

The company belatedly became aware of its environmental impact at the end of the 1980s, as green consumerism began to have an effect on its sale of household products. Reckitt's response has been a thorough review of environmental issues, including independent audits of main sites, and the launch of an environmentally friendly range of household products under the Down To Earth brand name. This range is based on vegetable, rather than oil-based, cleaning agents and contains no phosphates, CFCs or other constituents which could have a significant environmental impact. The group has also moved towards greener packaging, using recycled materials where practicable, and making the packing itself recyclable. 'Green' audits of suppliers have also been undertaken. However, the company has on one occasion exceeded discharge consents in 1990/91, at its Colours factory in Hull, now sold.

Generally, Reckitt seems to retain the more caring attitude of the family company which it still is to some extent (with a Colman still at the head of the board). The group is not a member of BITC, however, but does contribute to specific ventures, especially in education. It does have a formal equal opportunities policy, which includes ethnic monitoring, and recruits a high proportion of female graduates. Reckitt is also highly unionised.

In South Africa, all its 400-plus black workers have been paid a reasonable wage. Elsewhere in the world, Reckitt has significant representation in Brazil, India, Mexico, Venezuela and Argentina. In 1986 it was accused of breaking the code on pharmaceutical marketing in Pakistan.

Corporate governance

Separate Chairman and Chief Executive Y
Number of Directors 12
Number of Non-Executive Directors 4
(4 Independent Directors)
Insulated Directors None

Board Committees
Audit: Y   Remuneration: Y

Remuneration

Year end	31.12.91	31.12.92	1.01.94
Total board £M	2.39	2.10	2.23
% change	28	-12	6
Highest paid £	374,937	372,958	421,939
% change	32	-0.5	13

Board
Sankey, Vernon L *Chief Executive*
Colman, Sir Michael J *Executive Chairman*
Brown, Colin C C *Executive Director*
de Mel, J C Lalith *Executive Director*

Foster, R Mark M *Executive Director*
Maydon, Peter J *Executive Director*
Turrel, Michael F *Executive Director*
Dobbie, Iain G *Finance Director*
Dalby, Alan J *Independent Non-Executive*
Hearne, Graham J *Independent Non-Executive*
Larréché, Prof. Jean-Claude *Ind. Non-Executive*
Valentine, Michael R *Independent Non-Executive*

In their review of 1992, Sir Michael Colman and Vernon Sankey acknowledged the Cadbury Report and said that the company had been run consistently with the spirit of the Cadbury Code for many years. The directors' formal report notes that the audit committee was set up in 1978, and consists of the four non-executives. There is also a salaries committee, which consists of three non-executives plus the chairman and chief executive, and a community affairs committee. Reckitt & Colman gives full explanations of directors' pay, including total board figures for pensions and benefits in kind as well as bonuses.

REDLAND plc

Redland House, Reigate, Surrey RH2 0SJ
Tel: 01737 242488
Chairman Sir Colin Corness
Chief executive Robert Napier
Size £2.2 billion sales, £2.7 billion stock market value, 21,400 employees
5-year growth sales 69%, earnings per share -58%, employment 8%
Solvency debt = 26% shareholders' funds, interest cover 7 times
Political donations 0
Charitable donations £517,000

Major developments
1919 company founded
1954 became public
1982 diversification into fuel distribution
1988 failed bid for Koppers
1989 pulled out of fuel distribution
1990 formed plasterboard joint venture with Lafarge Coppée
1992 bought Steetley; abandoned Lafarge Coppée joint venture
1993 sold Spanish business to Mihorco

Outlook
While most of the building and building-related industries were in a state of disintegration, in 1993 Redland was getting on with the business of preparing for the recovery. Its finances were not unaffected by the appalling impact of recession, and especially the impact on the building industry of inflated asset values and excessive debt. But Redland was fortunate (and/or far-sighted) in having substantial non-British interests, and clever currency deals, which helped to sustain it through the worst of the British slump.

Redland's expansion abroad pre-dates modern exhortations to join Europe and bears similarities to the RMC story. The company, which was set up just after the First World War to produce the concrete roof tiles for which it is famous, took a share stake in a German roof products company shortly after the Second World War (and the year before Redland became a public company in 1955). The success of this subsidiary, Braas, and the decline in the UK, resulted in almost half the group's profits stemming from Germany in 1991, the year before Redland's takeover of Steetley.

The acquisition of Steetley in 1992 increased the spread of Redland's interests – at an opportune time, considering Germany's slide into recession. Steetley had itself made several acquisitions in a dash for diversification away from its UK brick, aggregates and associated businesses. In particular, it brought to Redland a substantial position in the French aggregates industry as well as interests in Spain (which were soon sold) and Canada. The combination of the two groups leaves Redland reliant on no single country for a significant portion of profits. The UK is still the group's largest market, but sales in Germany, France and North America are substantial, and Redland has a base in the Middle and Far East as well as being represented throughout Europe and Scandinavia.

Diversification was one reason for the Steetley bid. But there was also a, rather more negative, British angle to the acquisition – the need to deal with overcapacity in the UK brick industry. Steetley had been the second largest brick producer in the UK, though a long way behind Hanson's joint Butterley/London Brick operation. All brick producers had suffered from the building slump, and combining two producers (even though Redland's brick interests were much smaller) gave the group the opportunity for 'rationalisation' – in other words, closing down kilns. Redland had already mothballed five plants; after combining with Steetley it closed these five as well as shutting six more (with great fairness: three from Redland and three from Steetley). The purchase of Steetley gave Redland a leg up the brick league table, presumably with at least some of the cost being dealt with in the takeover accounting rather than through its profits. As well as the benefit to the brick activities, Steetley also brought Redland reserves of aggregates in the UK – quarries, plants producing ready-mixed concrete and 'blacktop' for road and similar surfaces – a valuable asset, given the difficulty in gaining approval for new quarries.

The deal cost Redland £620 million, but it clearly had many advantages. The same has not always proved true for its corporate and strategic moves. In the late 1980s it made a disastrous attempt to enter the UK plasterboard market, followed by a swift

REDLAND

Share record

Return on shareholders' equity	%	9.03
5-year price high	p	650.1
5-year price low	p	304.5
Dividend yield	%	5.90
5-year high	%	10.95
5-year low	%	4.27
Price/earnings ratio		22.8
5-year high		27.7
5-year low		8.5

Share price performance (in pence)

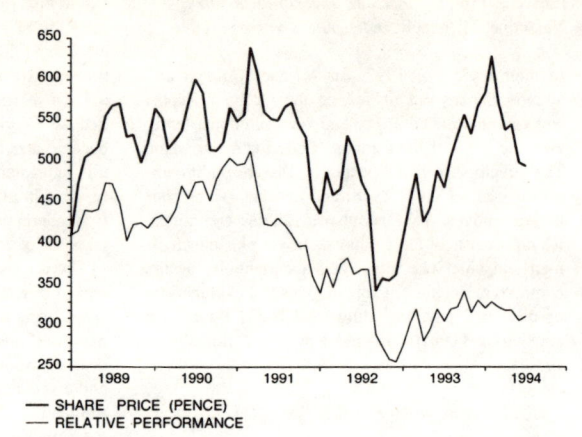

— SHARE PRICE (PENCE)
— RELATIVE PERFORMANCE

Financial record

		31/12/89	31/12/90	31/12/91	31/12/92	31/12/93
Total sales	£	1,310M	1,412M	1,299M	1,890M	2,216M
Pre-tax profit	£'000	245,100	244,400	186,000	221,500	267,300
Published retentions	£'000	103,700	64,100	12,100	-28,700	600
Earnings per share	p	54.39	47.55	29.97	22.88	22.67
Dividend per share	p	22.69	24.29	25.00	25.00	25.00
Operating cash flow	£'000	-137M	-47,800	-2,100	-16,100	250,200
Net total assets	£'000	536.80	578.60	580.69	564.57	485.81
Net debt/(cash)	£'000	252,300	345,300	131,300	663,700	383,700
Shareholders' funds	£'000	825,000	906,800	1,187M	1,408M	1,457M
Return on capital	%	21.81	18.11	13.41	13.06	13.71
Profit margin	%	16.22	15.28	13.19	10.94	10.53
Sales per employee	£	72.67	79.06	80.90	85.65	103.77
Interest cover		17.09	33.19	-427.25	8.83	7.34
Dividend cover		2.40	1.96	1.20	0.92	0.91
Sales increase	%	-24.24	7.76	-7.96	45.49	17.25
Earnings growth	%	9.51	-12.58	-36.97	-23.64	-0.94
Investment x depreciation		3.36	2.56	1.42	1.09	0.78
Investment as % assets		18.38	14.05	8.46	5.73	5.13
Number of employees		18,025	17,853	16,060	22,069	21,358

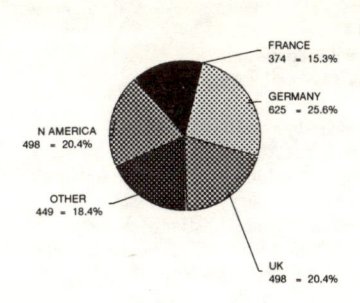

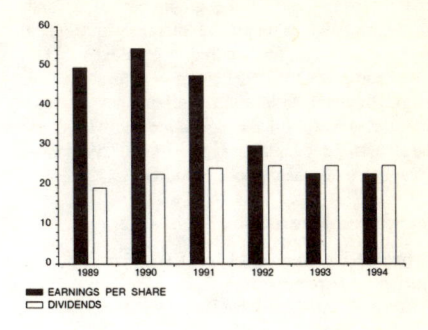

Sales analysis

Earnings and dividends

withdrawal in which the group sold its remaining 20 per cent share to the French partner, Lafarge Coppée, at the end of 1992. Previously, beginning in 1982, there was a doomed diversification into fuel distribution. This was also abandoned fairly quickly, by the end of 1989. A bid for Koppers in the US could also have been disastrous, had Redland won as the experience of Beazer, which did win, suggests. Beazer ended up being saved by Hanson.

These episodes show that Redland, unusually among large companies, has been prepared to admit when it is wrong. They do not necessarily demonstrate that the company has learned from its mistakes, although the emphasis now seems to be on geographical rather than product diversification. Redland's large share of its core roofing-tile market (virtually the whole market is divided between it and Marley) make diversification necessary, while helping to fund the mistakes. Perhaps now the group has finally done enough to escape this dominant past, and to move forwards to become a global building products company.

Shares

Redland's shares underperformed the stock market as a whole for most of the 1980s. The problem was that over the decade the board made acquisitions in Europe at a time when the UK building industry was expanding, and it often paid for these acquisitions by issuing new shares which lowered the value of those already in shareholders' hands. The group's rating suffered briefly in 1988 when it missed out on a counter bid for the US Koppers group. The shares began to rally the following year, reflecting the stock market's approval of a refocusing of the group's businesses into key areas.

In 1990 the share rating kept rising, reflecting how the overseas businesses were now seen as an advantage rather than a handicap as the UK boom was fading. The group was especially well regarded on account of its strength in German roof tiles at a time when the two Germanys were coming together. The following year the group brought out a deeply discounted rights issue in order to cut borrowings and fund acquisitions and this began a long fall to a trough in 1992, not helped by a realisation that the recession would be much more severe for builders than it had first thought.

There was a slight rally when Redland launched its bid for Steetley, but fears that the company would have to cut its dividend caused the shares to plunge later that year. In 1993 the market rally boosted the rating, based on hopes that a UK economic recovery would help the group and as cash came in from the sale of some Streetley companies. Analysts concluded that Redland was well diversified, and much better placed than most of its competitors, although the fact that its dividend would not be covered until 1995 limited the recovery.

Corporate conscience

Quarrying and manufacturing tiles or bricks clearly carry significant environmental risks, and while Redland has a comprehensive environmental policy, with specific responsibilities and regular monitoring, the group nevertheless has a poor water pollution record. Redland Clay Tiles was fined £400 in 1990 and £1,000 in 1991 for allowing clay pollution. There are several other examples of subsidiaries exceeding discharge consent levels, some relating to Steetley before it was taken over. The record has improved in recent years.

The group has also been convicted several times under health and safety laws. The largest fine was £1,750 for Redland Roof Tiles in Northampton in 1991. Otherwise the group seems to be an average employer. It does not have an adequate equal opportunities policy, nor is it highly unionised. The

338 REED ELSEVIER plc

company is a member of BITC, but its involvement in charities and the community seemed grudging until recently. In 1993 the group backed a fund-raising campaign in support of Shelter, with Redland promising to match funds raised by employees.

Redland raises two other issues of conscience. It is marginally involved in military affairs, having resurfaced the runways at RAF Honington and Alconbury; and an associated building supplier uses 2,500 tonnes a year of tropical hardwoods from Malaysia.

Corporate governance

Separate Chairman and Chief Executive Y
Number of Directors 10
Number of Non-Executive Directors 5
(3 Independent Directors)
Insulated Directors MD

Board Committees
Audit: Y   Remuneration: Y

Remuneration

Year end	31.12.91	31.12.92	31.12.93
Total board £M	1.67	1.72	1.62
% change	-2	3	-6
Highest paid £	258,633	299,354	311,467
% change	-0.2	16	4

Board
Napier, Robert S *Chief Executive*
Abbott, K A *Executive Director*
Johnson, P M *Executive Director*
Phillipson, G R *Executive Director*
Hewitt, Paul *Finance Director*
Biggam, Sir Robin A *Independent Non-Executive*
Browne, E J P *Independent Non-Executive*
Lord Kingsdown *Independent Non-Executive*
Pogue, R W *Non-Executive*
Corness, Sir Colin *Non-Executive Chairman*

The balance of the board is in favour of the non-executives, and the company is among the few to have a senior appointments committee in addition to remuneration and audit committees. Disclosure of directors' pay is adequate with brief explanation of bonus scheme targets.

REED ELSEVIER plc

Reed House, 6 Chesterfield Gardens,
London W1A 1EJ
Tel: 0171 499 4020
Joint chairmen Ian Irvine and Pierre Vinken
Main subsidiaries Butterworth, Cahners Publishing (USA), Elsevier Science Publishers, IPC Magazines, Pergamon Press, Official Airline Guides

Size £1.5 billion sales, £4.5 billion stock market value, employees n/a
5-year growth n/a
Solvency debt = 34% shareholders' funds, interest cover 14 times
Political donations 0
Charitable donations £400,000

Major developments
1903 formed as Albert E Reed and Co
1970 changed to Reed International after buying IPC
1981 bought The Berrows Organisation
1988 bought Octopus Publishing sold Crown Paints
1989 bought Independent Television Publications
1990 Reedpack packaging business sold
1991 bought Macmillan Directories
1992 merger with Elsevier
1993 sold stake in BSkyB

Outlook

Reed Elsevier was formerly Reed International in the UK and Elsevier in the Netherlands. But the merger of the two publishing groups was merely the culmination of some impressive corporate deal-making which, remarkably, seems to have avoided the huge number of traps which could have spelt disaster.

Reed International was a paper manufacturer which realised in the 1970s that paper manufacturing in the UK was not a good business to be in because paper could be produced more cheaply abroad. As a result, it embarked on a series of acquisitions which took it into many other markets, mostly related to paper, but not entirely. Crucially, as it later turned out, Reed bought IPC in 1970, which provided the publishing base for the future group. During the 1970s the company also moved into wallpaper, and hence paint and other DIY products.

The diversification programme almost bankrupted the group, forcing it to focus on its core business, thereby adopting a policy that was not to become a trend until the following decade. Former chairman Sir Alex Jarratt decided to concentrate on publishing, paper and paint. He sold or closed the printing businesses (including Odhams to Robert Maxwell), the Mirror Group national newspapers (also, fatefully, to Robert Maxwell), Spicer-Cowans paper merchants, plus Crown and Sanderson wallpaper companies. By the time Sir Alex retired in 1985, he believed that the process was more or less complete. And looking at a company such as Pearson, there is every reason to suppose that if it had stopped there, all would have been well. But his eventual successor, Peter Davis, went much further, selling Crown Paints (initially to Williams Holdings) as well as the paper and packaging interests, in order to concentrate entirely on publishing. Mr Davis also eventually decided not to stick with satellite television, selling out of BSkyB in 1993, although Reed Elsevier is supposedly committed to new forms of communication.

Reed International promised to spend the money raised from these sales to build an international

REED INTERNATIONAL

Share record

Return on shareholders' equity	%	-51.46
5-year price high	p	960.0
5-year price low	p	329.0
Dividend yield	%	2.97
5-year high	%	5.73
5-year low	%	2.28
Price/earnings ratio		23.7
5-year high		34.3
5-year low		10.1

Share price performance (in pence)

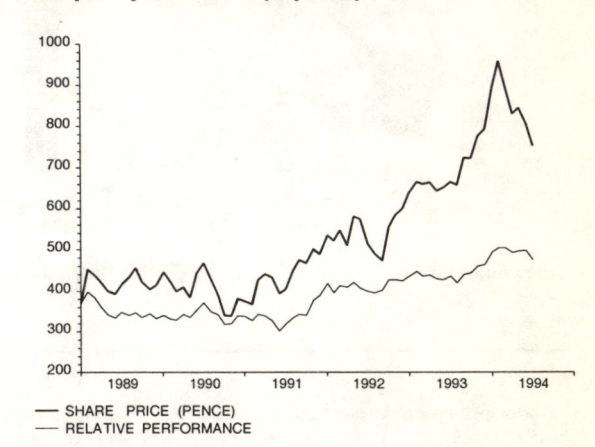

— SHARE PRICE (PENCE)
— RELATIVE PERFORMANCE

Financial record (for the UK quoted company until 1993)

		31/3/90	31/3/91	31/3/92	31/12/92 39 weeks	31/12/93
Total sales	£	1,578M	1,580M	1,631M	1,197M	1,479M
Pre-tax profit	£'000	276,300	221,800	231,600	137,100	274,000
Published retentions	£'000	133,600	53,200	74,000	2,400	91,800
Earnings per share	p	33.59	28.24	29.33	22.96	33.36
Dividend per share	p	14.00	15.00	16.00	12.75	18.75
Operating cash flow	£'000	119,200	34,700	136,000	46,500	95,300
Net assets per share	p	89.07	84.73	108.47	106.27	8.12
Net debt/(cash)	£'000	376,000	429,600	500,900	624,100	304,200
Shareholders' funds	£	1,374M	1,313M	1,370M	1,430M	906,700
Return on capital	%	53.46	59.74	57.30	32.51	98.40
Profit margin	%	17.02	13.55	13.84	10.86	18.02
Sales per employee	£	84.37	83.18	89.10	66.11	
Interest cover		74.75	8.90	6.71	5.19	13.58
Dividend cover		2.40	1.88	1.83	1.80	1.78
Sales increase	%	1.50	0.16	3.17	-26.61	23.61
Earnings growth	%	8.96	-15.93	3.87	-21.73	45.29
Investment x depreciation		-0.33	1.21	0.60	1.14	2.07
Investment as % assets		-6.83	23.58	12.84	17.50	34.85
Number of employees		18,700	19,000	18,300	18,100	

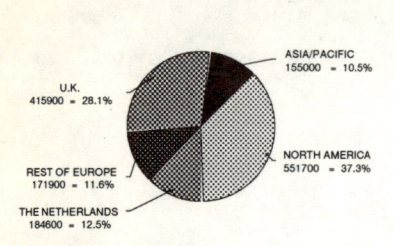

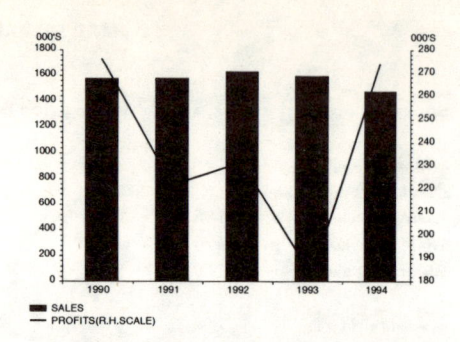

Sales analysis

Sales and profits

publishing company. Amongst other acquisitions, it bought Octopus Books (very expensively) and TV Times (questionably, just before the end of the listings monopoly) and various US interests, building on IPC's original stake in Cahners. But he did much more than these traditional deals, surprising the publishing world in 1992 with the Elsevier merger. Elsevier had recently ended a brief engagement with Pearson (see under Pearson), and ironically had just bought the basis of Robert Maxwell's empire, the Pergamon scientific publishing business. As a scientific publisher, Elsevier was a very similar operation to Pergamon, but had expanded ambitiously into other areas of publishing during the 1980s. The merger with Reed was almost upset by the currency turmoil in September 1992, and an adjustment eventually had to be made to the Elsevier share stake given to Reed in order to reflect the UK group's greater size. Originally Reed was to get 11.5 per cent of Elsevier, but this was slashed in half after the devaluation of sterling.

The merged group, Reed Elsevier, is one of the world's largest publishing operations. It is idiosyncratic as companies go, having no public shareholders itself but owned by two separately quoted companies – that is, Reed International and Elsevier. The merger of the two companies was certainly impressive in terms of its scale, although the benefit to shareholders took longer to emerge. The first full year's results were impressive, however, with a 30 per cent profits growth to £534 million, of which about £16 million came from acquisitions. These included primarily the $415 million purchase of Official Airline Guides, a healthy disdain for overpaying and its ability to rationalise effectively.

Takeovers are still clearly on the cards for Reed Elsevier, whose major hunting grounds are in the US and Europe and are expected to focus on areas such as legal and professional publishing. Despite local difficulties such as the recent rise in print prices, the merged group does control an empire with a good mix of high-margin growth businesses and lower-margin operations capable of benefiting from an upswing in advertising. Expectations for the combined are great – and therefore their ability to disappoint is commensurately large – but so far Reed Elsevier, whose merger cost £41 million to achieve, has shown an enviable focus and determination to build an operation with geographic and operational defensiveness as well as potential.

Shares

Reed International was regarded as a sleepy giant in the early 1980s but it became a stock market darling in 1985 when major predators like Hanson were said to be looking the group over and the board, headed by Peter Davis, was pushing through a major restructuring. The re-rating of the shares continued into the 1987 bull market when they peaked as a result of takeover rumours. The market crash brought a temporary pause, and while the rumours of takeover resurfaced the following year, the group's shares remained highly rated because of high earnings prospects.

The high point of 1988 came with the management buy-out of the packaging division, and the rating slipped during the Lawson boom as other companies proved a more attractive investment. The group had been highly acquisitive and profits were lower than predicted in 1989. By 1991 Reed had finished its transition into a pure publishing group and a series of market re-ratings reflected the benefits expected to accrue at a time when recession was hitting many other big companies. In early 1992 the rating levelled off as the City tried to assess the proposed merger with Elsevier, but by the end of the year the share price was up by 20 per cent. In 1993 shares hit a series of all-time peaks, but the group's potential to disappoint market expectations was demonstrated on the day of its healthy first-year results when investors meanly shaved 3 per cent off the price.

Corporate conscience

Having disposed of its manufacturing interests, Reed Elsevier avoids infringement of most ethical issues. It does have some dealings in the Third World and, through its magazine coverage and advertising, it is also indirectly implicated in sales of alcohol and tobacco, intensive farming and pesticides, together with the military, mining and nuclear industries. But there is no direct involvement in these industries or activities. Advertising has brought several complaints that were upheld by the ASA.

Reed does not operate a full equal opportunities policy, although it supports Opportunity 2000. It is a member of BITC and the Per Cent Club, and is a substantial donor to charities in the UK.

Corporate governance

Separate Chairman and Chief Executive Y
Number of Directors 20
Number of Non-Executive Directors 8
(5 Independent Directors)
Insulated Directors Ch, CE, JCE

Board Committees
Audit: Y   Remuneration: Y

Remuneration

Year end	31.12.92	31.12.93
Total board £M	5.20	7.20
% change		39
Highest paid £	493,000	637,000
% change		29

Board
Irvine, Ian *Executive Chairman*
Vinken, Pierre *Executive Chairman*
Alberti, Cornelis *Executive Director*
Bruggink, Herman *Executive Director*
Kels, James *Executive Director*
Krakoff, Robert *Executive Director*
Mellon, John *Executive Director*
Thomas, Ian *Executive Director*
Vlek, Paul *Executive Director*
Vollenhoven, Loek van *Executive Director*
Stapleton, Nigel *Finance Director*
Greener, Anthony *Independent Non-Executive*
Lewinton, Sir Christopher *Ind. Non-Executive*
Nelissen, Roelof *Independent Non-Executive*
Schuitemaker, Albert *Independent Non-Executive*
Webster, David *Independent Non-Executive*
Appel, Huib *Non-Executive*
Hamlyn, Paul *Non-Executive*
Vijver, Robert van de *Non-Executive*

Reed International is the legal UK entity, but for practical purposes the group operates as Reed Elsevier, which has its own board. Since the merger between the two companies, Reed and Elsevier, the group should have benefited from the best of both worlds: the Continental approach to governance, including a supervisory board, and the English emphasis on disclosure. The group has declined to introduce the supervisory board to its UK companies, however. It nevertheless has established board committees for remuneration and audit, though not nominations, and the separate UK company has its own governance structure as well. The Reed board stated as early as 1992 that it had complied with all the Cadbury proposals except for those still being finalised, and unusually included an auditor's concurrence with this statement. A very full directors' pay note in the annual report of Reed International details the workings of directors' bonus schemes and the amount of the bonuses and options, revealing that a ceiling is set for cash bonuses at 40 per cent of base salary.

RENTOKIL GROUP plc

Felcourt, East Grinstead, West Sussex RH19 2JY
Tel: 01342 833022
Chairman Henry King
Chief executive Clive Thompson
Major shareholders Sophus Berendsen of Denmark 52%
Size £588 million sales, £2.3 billion stock market value, 22,800 employees
5-year growth sales 111%, earnings per share 137%, employment 103%
Solvency debt n/a, interest cover n/a
Political donations 0
Charitable donations £25,000

Major developments
1927 formed as British Ratin Co
1957 merger with Rentokil
1960 name changed to Rentokil
1969 became public
1983 Clive Thompson appointed chief executive
1991 bought Calmic from Wellcome
1993 acquired Securiguard for £76m

Outlook

In the mid-1980s many companies achieved apparently impressive growth for a few years, only to stumble before long and reveal that the success had been based on accounting ingenuity, or external factors such as the consumer boom, or that the growth had been too rapid for management to cope with. Rentokil was one of those high-growth companies, but surprisingly, and rather mystifyingly, the figures remain spectacularly high.

RENTOKIL

Share record

Return on shareholders' equity	%	87.98
5-year price high	p	279.0
5-year price low	p	63.8
Dividend yield	%	1.50
5-year high	%	2.25
5-year low	%	1.02
Price/earnings ratio		24.6
5-year high		34.8
5-year low		14.7

Share price performance (in pence)

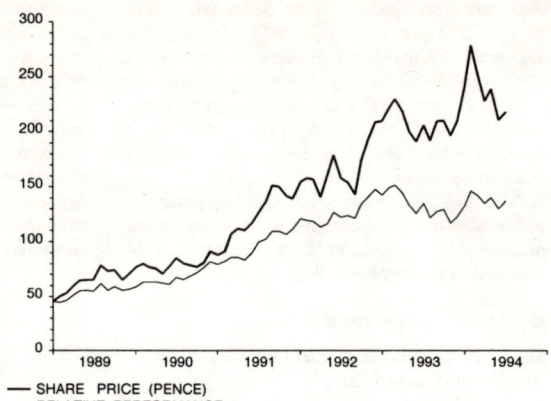

— SHARE PRICE (PENCE)
— RELATIVE PERFORMANCE

Financial record

		31/12/89	31/12/90	31/12/91	31/12/92	31/12/93
Total sales	£'000	279,275	309,117	388,972	465,962	588,100
Pre-tax profit	£'000	62,027	74,657	94,606	122,354	147,000
Published retentions	£'000	30,837	34,463	40,102	47,735	66,600
Earnings per share	p	4.05	4.92	6.23	7.97	9.63
Dividend per share	p	1.07	1.32	1.69	2.31	2.85
Operating cash flow	£'000	20,517	25,444	39,321	55,009	60,400
Net assets per share	p	10.35	11.44	12.28	16.61	13.10
Net debt/(cash)	£'000	-29,110	-31,097	-27,165	-60,192	-15,600
Shareholders' funds	£'000	94,878	105,236	113,524	283,219	346,000
Return on capital	%	73.39	71.98	85.34	89.71	103.73
Profit margin	%	22.21	24.15	24.32	26.10	24.76
Sales per employee	£	24.88	25.16	27.83	30.87	25.84
Interest cover		-24.79	-19.45	-57.87	-25.13	-47.53
Dividend cover		3.78	3.72	3.68	3.47	3.38
Sales increase	%	30.84	10.69	25.83	19.79	26.21
Earnings growth	%	23.55	21.44	26.79	27.89	20.78
Investment x depreciation		1.44	1.18	1.30	1.18	1.13
Investment as % assets		37.56	31.13	35.87	31.77	30.68
Number of employees		11,226	12,285	13,977	15,092	22,756

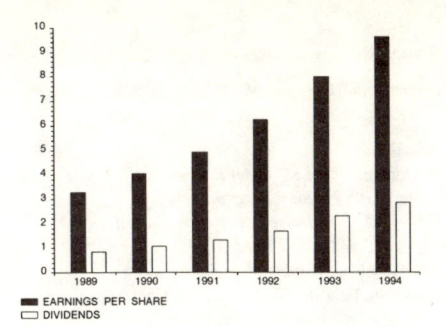

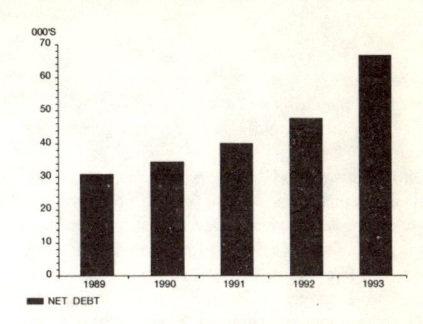

Earnings and dividends

Debt

In 1993, if you were to look at Rentokil's earnings growth of more than 20 per cent per annum, you would never know there had been a recession although the 20 per cent target has only just delivered in that year. The return on capital has been distorted by the many acquisition write-offs, but other figures remain impressive. And the investment figures show that even though the group uses few assets, it is not shy of building them up. Steady growth in employee numbers illustrates also that financial success has not been built on redundancy.

One of the secrets of Rentokil's success lies in the fact that it has remained consistently cash positive, maintaining sizeable cash balances despite a long string of small purchases. The group's monopoly in pest control (as determined by the Monopolies Commission in 1988, which promptly decided that nothing needed to be done about this unsatisfactory situation) partly accounts for this. But Rentokil is now much more than a pest-control company, and sustained success like this is not solely due to a dominant position in one market, nor is it simply financial. The pressure of a majority shareholder in the unusual shape of Danish company Sophus Berendsen may also have helped, but another factor must have been a clear, consistent strategy, and its determined implementation, for which the credit goes to chief executive Clive Thompson.

Mr Thompson is a chemist who learned marketing with the professionals at Shell, and came to Rentokil via Boots and Jeyes (now an independent company but then part of Cadbury Schweppes). He took over at Rentokil in 1982, when the company was involved primarily in wood treatment and pest control, reflecting its origins as a Danish-owned UK business selling rat poison, which merged with the wood-treatment company Rentokil in 1957. Under Mr Thompson, however, it has become a global supplier of a variety of services, mainly to business and mainly in the fields of health, safety and environmental improvement or protection. Thus the group has a medical service business handling needles, surgical instruments and waste, activities which have benefited from the need to stem the spread of Aids. Reacting to concern about about the prevalence of legionnaires' disease, it has diversified into water and ventilation systems, and provides filter systems to deal with cigarette smoke and other types of air pollution. Other services embraced by Rentokil are perhaps more mundane, such as office cleaning, the maintenance of office equipment and the provision of plants to office buildings, shopping centres and similar public areas.

Such activities have attracted a 'green' tag, although Rentokil is only an 'environmental' company in the loosest sense of the word. By the nature of its business, many of its activities are chemical-based, and the group has an historic association with Lindane, a particularly powerful insecticide used in wood treatment. Rentokil claims to be moving away from toxic chemicals where it can, but it will be a while before it can truly be regarded as environmentally friendly.

It may be a while, too, before Rentokil stops growing at such a high rate, although it is difficult to believe that such progress can be sustained, or indeed that the group will not follow the usual path of fast-expanding companies and suddenly come a cropper. Other groups such as BET and Granada have shown how easy it is to go wrong in the service sector. Rentokil succeeded through tight management and because it has not faced a huge acquisition – the kind of transaction that has tripped up many other companies. That acquisition-free record ended in 1993 with a successful hostile takeover bid for Securiguard, the service group which specialised in security services. That acquisition will help short-term earnings but could be more difficult to

344 REUTERS HOLDINGS plc

integrate and grow in the longer term. But Rentokil has defied the sceptics for so long that perhaps it will continue to do so.

Shares
Through all the thrills and spills of the late 1980s and early 1990s the Rentokil share price moved steadily upwards.

During this period investors and market traders were increasingly encouraged by the ability of the group's contract-based services to sustain growth in earnings per share. The rating rose most steeply with the onset of recession in late 1990 when defensive virtues were sought after. The rise continued into 1993 as the company continued to beat its 20 per cent growth target. But the shares dipped as the previous year's rise seemed overdone, and some wondered how much longer Rentokill could maintain its growth rate. The dip was only temporary, however, although it seems that the long advance is over for the time being, leaving the shares merely holding their ground.

Corporate conscience
With a name like 'Rentokil', this company clearly poses some ethical problems. Not only are some of its products tested on animals, their purpose is to destroy pests, and, as vigorous pesticides or insecticides, they have been accused of harming other organisms beyond their intended target. Rentokil sells a number of products containing ingredients which are on the government's Red List of dangerous substances, or have been banned in at least five countries: Amitrole, Gamma-HCH, Pentachlorophenol, and arsenic used in various wood treatments and weedkillers. Rentokil has stressed that it is researching into safer alternatives, however, including electronic means of deterring pests. It has also developed a comprehensive environmental policy and now makes great play of being an environmentally friendly company – on the grounds that many of its services improve the immediate physical environment, e.g. in offices where it services plants, washrooms and air-conditioning systems.

On other issues the group has an unexceptional record. The group supplies wood treatments to the military; it uses ozone-depleting chemicals in air conditioning; and has paid a handful of black workers in South Africa below reasonable levels. However, the company does have an adequate equal opportunities policy.

Corporate governance
Separate Chairman and Chief Executive Y
Number of Directors 6
Number of Non-Executive Directors 4
(1 Independent Director)
Insulated Directors All execs

Board Committees
Audit: Y   Remuneration: Y

Remuneration

Year end	31.12.91	31.12.92	31.12.93
Total board £M	1.24	1.42	1.38
% change	57	14	-2
Highest paid £	591,000	707,000	658,000
% change	98	20	-7

Board
Thompson, Clive M *Chief Executive*
Pearce, C T *Finance Director*
Heywood, D G *Independent Non-Executive*
King, H E St L *Non-Executive*
Koch-Nielsen, Robert *Non-Executive*
Werdelin, Hans K *Non-Executive Chairman*

This company has one of the smallest boards in the book, including only two executive directors both of whom are insulated from re-election. But with two of the non-executives being directors of the Danish majority owner, Sophus Berendsen, the independent representation is not high, either. Chairman David Newbigging made a brief and not very enthusiastic reference to the Cadbury Code in his statement on 1992, saying merely that the board had agreed to comply with the Code and already did so on most issues. In 1993 the directors made clear that they did not comply with the requirement for independent directors, but did not say whether they planned to change that position. On pay, where chief executive Clive Thompson ended 1992 with almost two and a half times his 1990 remuneration, the relevant note to the accounts gave the percentages of the total which were due to earnings under the terms of a 1988 scheme which pays out once earnings per share has grown by 10 per cent over the previous year's figure. This is a curious trigger point, given the group's target of 20 per cent growth.

REUTERS HOLDINGS plc

85 Fleet Street, London EC4P 4AJ
Tel: 0171 250 1122
Chairman Sir Christopher Hogg
Chief executive Peter Job
Substantial shareholdings Abu Dhabi Investment Authority 7.2%
Size £1.9 billion sales, £7.9 billion stock market value, 10,800 employees
5-year growth sales 58%, earnings per share 65%, employment 8%
Solvency debt n/a, interest cover 63 times
Political donations 0
Charitable donations £1,231,000

Major developments
1851 founded by Paul Julius Reuter

REUTERS HOLDINGS

Share record

Return on shareholders'
equity	%	41.07
5-year price high	p	539.8
5-year price low	p	140.8

Dividend yield	%	1.70
5-year high	%	3.27
5-year low	%	1.20

Price/earnings ratio		26.5
5-year high		31.2
5-year low		11.9

Share price performance (in pence)

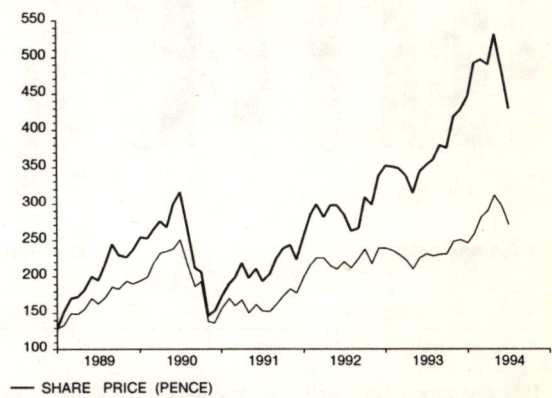

— SHARE PRICE (PENCE)
— RELATIVE PERFORMANCE

Financial record

		31/12/89	31/12/90	31/12/91	31/12/92	31/12/93
Total sales	£	1,187M	1,369M	1,467M	1,568M	1,874M
Pre-tax profit	£'000	283,100	320,100	340,300	383,200	440,000
Published retentions	£'000	126,600	144,200	158,100	146,400	194,000
Earnings per share	p	10.91	12.48	13.50	15.45	17.97
Dividend per share	p	3.25	3.75	4.25	5.30	6.50
Operating cash flow	£'000	7,600	180,100	275,000	200,800	131,000
Net assets per share	p	32.20	41.44	51.03	53.41	46.21
Net debt/(cash)	£'000	-37,300	-217M	-503M	-710M	-450M
Shareholders' funds	£'000	490,400	634,400	802,300	1,105M	960,000
Return on capital	%	62.43	52.98	44.37	43.93	53.39
Profit margin	%	24.00	23.25	23.19	24.42	23.48
Sales per employee	£	118.04	128.90	137.84	153.91	173.34
Interest cover		-16.18	-12.52	-6.82	-5.58	63.33
Dividend cover		3.36	3.33	3.18	2.91	2.76
Sales increase	%	18.30	15.34	7.13	6.89	19.55
Earnings growth	%	36.10	14.47	8.14	14.42	16.33
Investment x depreciation		1.69	1.34	0.77	1.04	1.28
Investment as % assets		38.39	35.46	30.55	39.24	47.21
Number of employees		10,055	10,621	10,640	10,185	10,811

REUTERS HOLDINGS plc

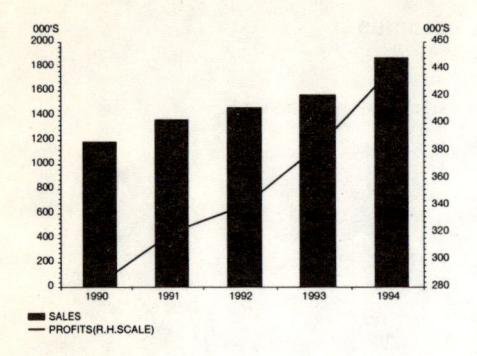

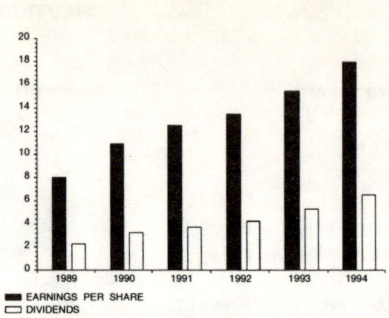

Sales and profits

Earnings and dividends

1859 first scoop: Napolean III's intervention in the Franco-Prussian war
1956 first to tell the world about Khrushchev's attack on Stalin
1964 moved into electronic technology
1984 public flotation
1987 bought Instinet Corp, I P Sharp Assoc
1989 launched Dealing-2000 computerised Forex dealing system
1992 took full control of Visnews
1993 bought Quotron

Outlook

Reuters began life in the mid 19th century as a provider of information to financial markets, and despite the huge changes and enormous growth which the company has experienced, that remains its job. It is still a news agency, and has recently moved with the times to include television within its ambit. But its main markets are financial, not media-based, and the main information it provides is financial data, not news reports, although news has been a crucial element of the Reuters service to financial clients.

Before telegraph links were completed in the 19th century, Julius Reuter used carrier pigeons to convey prices from the Brussels Stock Exchange to Aachen. In fact this was one of a series of short-lived ventures – the technology soon caught up with him when the telegraph line became fully operational. But he appears to have learned a lesson from this, and the success of Reuters lies in the way that it keeps abreast of technological development. The eventual basis of Mr Reuter's business was the communication of stock market prices between the London and Paris bourses in the 1850s, using the new technology of undersea cable. It was this service, on a rather grander scale, which pushed Reuters into computer technology when, in 1964, it licensed a US stock market information system. Six years later Reuters took the important step of adding news to its rather basic information service. The combination of prices and news remains the group's major contribution to the financial world, and its key competitive advantage.

Stock market services are now overshadowed by foreign exchange ('forex') products, however. Following the breakdown of fixed exchange rates in 1971, Reuters launched the Monitor system which provided currency dealers with information on exchange rates around the world. In 1981 the firm created an electronic market when it added a dealing system to the Monitor service. In 20 years the company had grown from a glorified news agency to become a substantial provider of electronic services. Moreover, the development of new products and services was demanding increasing amounts of investment, leading its newspaper owners to dream up the notion (curious at the time) of floating Reuters on the stock market in 1984. This provided two ironic touches: not only had the stock market given birth to and sustained the company which was now becoming part of it; the flotation of Reuters also provided many newspapers (including the *Guardian*) with the cash to modernise their own operations, just as Reuters's modernising move into electronics had required its flotation.

The group has been phenomenally successful since being cast off by its newspaper parents. Earnings growth slid gradually, to very low single figures in 1992, but then rose by 29 per cent in 1993. And during that period Reuters has maintained its heavy expenditure on developing new products, extended its geographic and service coverage, and built up substantial cash balances. Continuing volatility in foreign exchange markets, and notably the chaos caused by the ERM, has calmed fears that the group's forex base would be eroded by a return to something like

1960s-style stability. This may eventually happen, but, in the meantime, Reuters has finally managed to launch the Dealing 2000-2 automatic order matching system, which has enhanced its dominant position in the forex market.

This latest version of the Monitor forex system was much delayed. But, although delay is inevitable in the development of major electronic systems, there has been an important change of attitude at Reuters following the appointment of Peter Job as chief executive in 1991. He has been keen to attack the old arrogance and instil a concern for the customer and the product which the company badly needed in order to stave off attacks from smaller competitors.

Competitors abound, of course, and the latest technology which allows dealers to mix information from different suppliers makes it harder for Reuters to keep them at arm's length. Yet the company remains the world leader in forex, with little sign of a serious challenge to that position, and has a strong position in European equities markets. Its position in the United States was bolstered by the $80 million acquisition of Quotron, a loss-making offshoot of Citicorp. Continued innovation should keep Reuters ahead of its rivals – unless one of its mega-projects finally does turn very sour, or the group loses its chacteristic conservatism and blows its huge cash pile on a crazy acquisition.

Shares

Reuters's systems are used by traders on world markets, so its shares are peculiarly vulnerable to crashes and slumps in stock or money markets. During the bull market of 1987 the shares were well regarded, but after the crash that autumn they were downrated for a full year – the length of time it took to convince the City that the group could cut costs fast enough to keep profit moving. The re-rating that followed in 1989 was boosted by changes to the voting structure, which made the shares more attractive because they became more stable.

Growth in earnings per share of more than 29 per cent a year pushed the company's market rating upwards throughout 1990, helped by successes in the marketing of new trading systems. That summer it was the most highly rated stock on the Exchange, except for two oil companies, but then came news that orders for some of its systems had been cancelled and the shares crashed 42 per cent after a profit warning from the board. The group cut back on costs once again but the shares did not begin to rally until the US recession bottomed out and business confidence there was restored. This phase lasted for the early part of 1991 when another word of caution from the board kept the rating low for a while. The next year the shares outperformed the market as a whole once again as new systems gained approval and cash generation picked up. The shares were boosted in 1994 by a 23 per cent increase in the dividend and by the decision to split the shares into four, making them easier to market.

Corporate conscience

Reuters is still a young public company, and so has perhaps not yet come to terms with its responsibilities. It is a member of BITC and of the Per Cent Club, but that seems to be about as far as its commitment stretches. On the other hand, it is one of the 'cleanest' companies in this book. Indeed, it shares with Eurotunnel the distinction of having not a single black mark against it. Ethically minded investors do not (yet) consider an intricate involvement in the inner workings of the financial markets to be 'unsound', so on all other issues of conscience Reuters gets off scot-free.

Corporate governance

Separate Chairman and Chief Executive Y
Number of Directors 12
Number of Non-Executive Directors 7
(7 Independent Directors)
Insulated Directors None

Board Committees
Audit: Y Remuneration: Y

Remuneration

Year end	31.12.91	31.12.92	31.12.93
Total board £M	1.87	1.98	2.19
% change	-51	6	11
Highest paid £	376,000	396,000	435,000
% change	25	5	10

Board

Job, Peter *Chief Executive*
Ure, David *Executive Director*
Villeneuve, André *Executive Director*
Wood, Mark *Executive Director*
Rowley, Robert *Finance Director*
Bauman, Bob *Independent Non-Executive*
Giordano, Richard V *Independent Non-Executive*
Green, Michael P *Independent Non-Executive*
Gyllenhammar, Pehr *Independent Non-Executive*
Sinclair, Charles *Independent Non-Executive*
Snedden, David *Independent Non-Executive*
Hogg, Sir Christopher *Non-Executive Chairman*

Reuters's directors confidently asserted, in the annual report on 1992, that the company had complied with all aspects of the Cadbury Code, except those which the accountancy profession was still working on. And the company is certainly ahead of most, although as chairman Sir Christopher Hogg pointed out in his report, it needs to be, because of the protection from takeover afforded by the special Founders Share, designed to prevent the company's independence being compromised. The boardroom is balanced in favour of the non-executives, who are both powerful and formally independent. In a full note on executive pay, the company provides separate details for each executive director, an exact percentage for the bonus element and some details of how the bonus scheme works. It also reported that payments to five

348 RMC GROUP plc

executives not on the board were higher than for the highest-paid director. Top executives remain on three-year contracts.

RMC GROUP plc

RMC House, Coldharbour Lane, Thorpe, Egham, Surrey TW20 8TD
Tel: 01932 568833
Chairman Jim Owen
Managing Director Peter Young
Main brands and subsidiaries Atlas Aggregates, Bay 6, Butterley Aggregates, Durox, Great Mills, Hales Waste Control, Hall & Co, Hall Aggregates, No Frills
Size £3.2 billion sales, £1.9 billion stock market value, 28,600 employees
5-year growth sales 23%, earnings per share -47%, employment 7%
Solvency debt = 58% shareholders' funds, interest cover 4 times
Political donations 0
Charitable donations £43,000

Major developments
1930 built the first ready-mixed concrete plant in the UK
1952 UK company acquired by Ready Mixed Concrete of Australia
1955 opened first overseas plant, in Germany
1962 became public UK company
1963 moved into France and Israel
1968 merger with Hall & Ham River
1973 moved into Belgium
1976 moved into Spain
1979 acquired DIY companies; opened Thorpe Park leisure centre; moved into the US
1981 acquired 49% of RWK in West Germany
1982 name changed from Ready Mixed Concrete to RMC Group
1985 increased stake in RWK
1988 acquired Thos Ward Roadstone
1989 set up Hungarian joint venture
1990 moved into eastern Germany
1991 acquired majority stake in Ytong

Outlook
RMC is a remarkable company: its parentage is Australian; its business is now dominated by Germany; yet it is British. The Australian company 'reversed into' its UK equivalent in 1952, acquiring it and then moving itself to the UK.

How RMC established itself in Germany is even more curious. The story is that the Australian end of the business had to buy some plant from the US to satisfy the demands of an American customer, who then went bust as the plant was half way to Australia – in Hamburg. As a result, John Camden, who retired as chairman of the group in 1993, was despatched to Germany, where he established a German ready-mixed concrete business in 1955, at a time when it was likely to benefit greatly from the country's rebuilding after the Second World War. With the acquisitions of RWK and Ytong (which specialises in breeze blocks and similar aerated products) it has now grown to become the largest building materials company in Germany. That position was consolidated by the acquisition in 1990 of Rudersdorf Zement, one of the largest cement works in eastern Germany.

The result is that Germany now dominates the business: in 1993 it accounted for 43 per cent of sales and two-thirds of operating profits, despite the severe recession in Germany and despite continued development and diversification elsewhere in the group. The only risk – slight at present – is that the development of eastern Europe may result in cheaper products flooding into western Europe from Poland and other countries.

From the beginning of the 1960s RMC began to diversify both from its core business of ready-mixed concrete and from its bases in the UK and Germany. The process was helped by its flotation on the stock market in 1962. A move into aggregates had already begun in the UK in 1960, followed during that decade by expansion into Austria, France, Israel and Ireland. Geographical diversification continued in the 1970s, and in 1979 RMC made its first acquisitions in the US, also moving into DIY in the UK and opening the Thorpe Park leisure complex in a former gravel pit in Surrey.

In fact the group would have done better sticking to the building business which it knows best. Thorpe Park is sideshow (almost literally) which would be better owned by a leisure group, while RMC has found its Great Mills DIY chain to be one of the smaller players in a bitter battle dominated by B&Q and Texas Homecare. But, undismayed by the difficulties presented by such competition, the company launched a new format in 1991 aimed at the 'heavier' market of small builders and serious DIY workers. Bay 6, as it was termed, remained at an experimental level in 1994, however. Profits for 1993 from DIY, lesiure and the Halls builders' merchants chain came to only £16 million, well under a tenth of the total profits for the group.

Overall, however, RMC survived the recession remarkably well. It was helped by its aversion to price competition, a sentiment shared by other UK building companies and which has caused them to clash repeatedly with the fair-trading authorities over the years. And the group cleverly managed to avoid including the losses and debts of the eastern German acquisition in its accounts until the losses and debts had declined. When Readymix Berlin, as the eastern German company became called, was finally consolidated, it brought a bonus in tax concessions, which slashed RMC's tax charge.

RMC

Share record

Return on shareholder's equity	%	9.37
5-year price high	p	1075.0
5-year price low	p	384.0
Dividend yield	%	2.78
5-year high	%	6.94
5-year low	%	2.33
Price/earnings ratio		30.9
5-year high		46.6
5-year low		5.9

Share price performance (in pence)

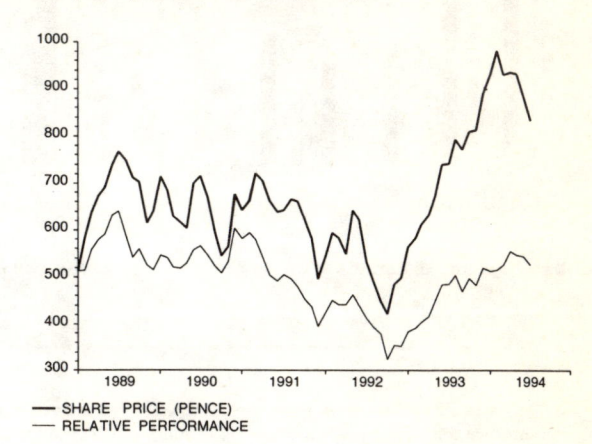

— SHARE PRICE (PENCE)
— RELATIVE PERFORMANCE

Financial record

		31/12/89	31/12/90	31/12/91	31/12/92	31/12/93
Total sales	£	2,571M	2,589M	2,798M	3,140M	3,170M
Pre-tax profit	£'000	247,500	216,200	167,400	166,600	177,100
Published retentions	£'000	125,300	75,500	31,100	21,800	35,900
Earnings per share	p	67.55	55.44	35.00	29.89	35.85
Dividend per share	p	18.00	19.30	20.00	20.00	21.00
Operating cash flow	£'000	3,900	-40,200	-25,300	47,100	10,900
Net assets per share	p	529.79	601.43	711.50	809.44	918.59
Net debt/(cash)	£'000	100,400	220,200	326,100	324,600	452,800
Shareholders' funds	£'000	593,700	630,900	695,000	761,400	780,500
Return on capital	%	29.36	22.07	16.42	14.20	13.37
Profit margin	%	9.44	8.19	5.74	4.86	4.84
Sales per employee	£	99.99	103.16	107.48	119.37	114.71
Interest cover		18.71	10.74	5.44	5.15	4.44
Dividend cover		3.75	2.87	1.75	1.49	1.71
Sales increase	%	24.49	0.72	8.05	12.24	0.95
Earnings growth	%	15.96	-17.93	-36.87	-14.60	19.94
Investment x depreciation		1.87	2.07	1.41	0.78	1.37
Investment as % assets		20.80	22.38	14.80	8.58	13.77
Number of employees		25,709	25,100	26,031	26,307	27,935

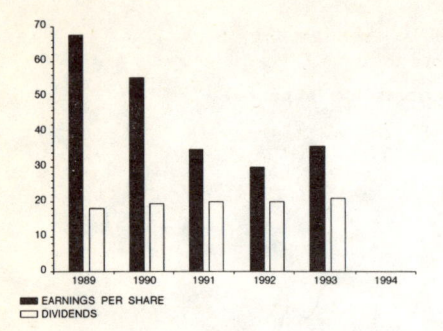

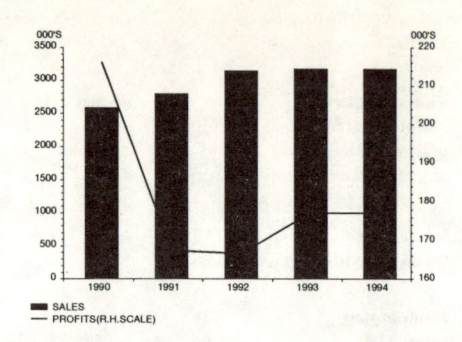

Earnings and dividends

Sales and profits

Thus it is difficult to assess the group's financial performance for the early 1990s. Reported earnings per share more than halved between 1989 and 1992, and debt levels rose substantially. But RMC managed net profits in each of the five years shown in the table (see Financial Record), and sustained relatively high levels of capital investment. By 1993, profits had started to grow again, although they were still well below the levels of the late 1980s.

Yet in 1994 the group seemed well placed to benefit from the economic recovery throughout Europe, despite changes among the senior management. Due to ill health, John Camden was forced to step down from the chair in 1993, taking instead the honorary position of president. But his successor, Jim Owen, was no stranger to the company, since he had stepped up from the post of managing director. It was a good time to be taking over, as business conditions were beginning to improve in most of RMC's markets, which might also help the newish 'broom' to sweep up some of the peripheral bits and pieces of the group.

Shares

In spite of the dominance of Germany in the company's business, RMC shares seem to have followed the UK building cycle. They rose steadily, compared to the market as a whole, reaching a peak in 1989, which had not been surpassed by the middle of 1994. The slide from that peak reached a low point towards the end of 1992, after which the share price recovered steadily. This was due in part to the continuing construction boom in eastern Germany, despite the deepening recession in the country as a whole, and to the anticipation of recovery in the UK. In 1994, when it transpired that recovery was going to be slower than expected, the outperformance came to an end and the shares began falling back again.

Corporate conscience

Despite the high-impact nature of its activities, and its experience in the more environmentally aware Germany, RMC came late to environmental concerns. Only in 1991 did the board form an environment committee in order to develop policy on such issues. This tardiness perhaps explains the group's poor record on environmental issues such as water pollution. Discharge consents were exceeded on 29 occasions in the year to March 1992, although this decreased to only 7 occasions in the following year. In addition, the group was fined a total of 7 times in 1990/91, the biggest penalty being a £1,500 fine on the ready-mixed concrete operations in the north west. North West Aggregates was fined £500 in 1991 for operating a roadstone coating plant without a proper registration certificate, while RMC Roadstone was fined £1,000 in 1992 for emitting excess quantities of grit and dust. The group has also been in the courts for breaches of health and safety laws, receiving four fines between 1990 and 1992.

These are the main ethical issues which the group contravenes, although RMC's presence in Israel could be said to count against it with regard to that country's infringement of human rights, and Great Mills sells products using tropical hardwoods. In other respects, RMC's conscience may be clouded by a continuing involvement in cartels in the UK. The cement and concrete industries have frequently fallen foul of fair-trading investigations: as long ago as 1978 the Restrictive Practices Court ordered RMC and other companies from entering into market-sharing and price-fixing agreements. Believing that these orders were being ignored, the Office of Fair Trading (OFT) began a lengthy investigation in 1985, and in 1990 RMC and three other companies were fined for operating a cartel in Oxfordshire. And later that year the group announced that it had uncovered restrictive agreements at nine of its British subsidiaries. In 1991 the director general of the OFT, Sir Gordon Borrie, warned the industry that companies could be in contempt of court if they persisted with their anti-competitive deals.

Corporate governance

Separate Chairman and Chief Executive Y
Number of Directors 9
Number of Non-Executive Directors 3
(3 Independent Directors)
Insulated directors MD

Board Committees
Audit: Y   Remuneration: Y

Remuneration

Year end	31.12.91	31.12.92	31.12.93
Total board £M	1.61	1.72	1.73
% change		7	0.5
Highest paid £	299,222	261,478	261,264
% change		-13	-0.1

Board
Owen, Jim *Executive Chairman*
Young, Peter *Managing Director*
Baumgarten, B B J *Executive Director*
Cooper, J B *Executive Director*
Jenkins, D W *Executive Director*
Walker, S R *Executive Director*
Fetcher, Sir Leslie *Independent Non-Executive*
Macfarlane, Sir Neil *Independent Non-Executive*
Mott, J C S *Independent Non-Executive*

RMC complies with the basic requirements of the Cadbury Code, but gives the impression that it does so with little enthusiasm, despite pointing out in its annual report for 1993 that aspects of the Code have been practiced at the company for years. The group has certainly not embraced greater openness with regard to directors' pay: there is no disclosure in the annual report of even the amount for directors' bonuses.

ROLLS-ROYCE plc

65 Buckingham Gate, London SW1E 6AT
Tel: 0171 222 9020
Chairman Sir Ralph Robins
Chief executive Dr Terry Harrison
Main subsidiaries NEI, Parsons Turbine Generators, Reyrolle
Size £3.5 billion sales, £2.4 billion stock market value, 49,200 employees
5-year growth sales 18%, earnings per share -74%, employment -11%
Solvency debt n/a, interest cover 6 times

Political donations £60,000 Conservative Party
Charitable donations £208,000

Major developments
1894 founded as F H Royce & Co
1904 began producing cars sold by C S Rolls & Co
1906 formed Rolls-Royce
1914 designed first aero-engine
1943 took over development of aero-engines from the Rover Co
1966 bought Bristol Siddeley engines
1971 receiver appointed and company nationalised
1973 Rolls-Royce Motors floated
1987 privatised
1989 bought Northern Engineering Industries (NEI)
1991 announced 10,000 job losses
1993 announced further 6000 job losses
1994 first flight of Trent engines

Outlook
Many people think that Rolls-Royce still makes expensive cars, but that no longer is the case. Mr Royce did indeed design and build exclusive cars for sale by Mr Rolls, and the two joined forces to float Rolls-Royce on the stock market in 1906. But eight years later the company produced its first aircraft engine, and it was aero-engines which drove the group forwards. They also drove it into bankruptcy in 1971, at which point the car business was separated, eventually to become part of Vickers.

Given the luxury carmaker's problems during the recession of the early 1990s, Rolls-Royce will not be sorry to have sold the business, but it has been keen to lessen its reliance on the volatile aircraft market since returning to the public stage in 1987. To that end, Rolls-Royce acquired industrial power-generation group NEI in 1989, and would like to see the two sides of the business on a roughly equal footing as regards turnover. Even with severe difficulties in the aerospace market, however, there is still some way to go towards that goal. Aero-engines remain the group's main focus of interest, although power operations showed their worth by keeping the group in profit (before exceptional provisions) during the aerospace slump of the early 1990s.

Since being rescued by the government in 1971, Rolls-Royce has made exceptional progress in aero-engines. The company crashed due to the exorbitant cost involved in entering the US passenger-jet market, which it had been squeezed out of by failing to recognise, or latch on to, the growing power of Boeing during the 1960s. It had minimal participation in the 707, and none at all in the 727, 737 and (initially) the 747. As a result, Rolls-Royce recognised in 1967 that unless it won orders from the US airframe manufacturers, it would be out of the aero-engine business by the mid-1970s. But the price extracted by Lockheed to take Rolls-Royce engines on its Tristar aircraft was crippling in both time and money. By 1971 it was clear that the price could not be met and the government, mindful of the company's importance in the military sphere, stepped in.

ROLLS-ROYCE plc

Share record

Return on shareholders' equity	%	4.90
5-year price high	p	226.6
5-year price low	p	89.7
Dividend yield	%	3.26
5-year high	%	10.51
5-year low	%	3.07
Price/earnings ratio		38.2
5-year high		40.6
5-year low		7.6

Share price performance (in pence)

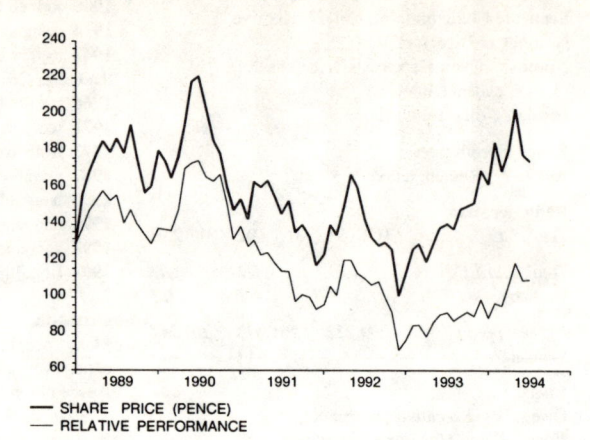

— SHARE PRICE (PENCE)
— RELATIVE PERFORMANCE

Financial record

		31/12/89	31/12/90	31/12/91	31/12/92	31/12/93
Total sales	£	2,962M	3,670M	3,515M	3,562M	3,518M
Pre-tax profit	£'000	237,000	226,000	109,000	84,000	76,000
Published retentions	£'000	125,000	65,000	-46,000	-250M	7,000
Earnings per share	p	21.09	16.89	8.31	6.56	5.39
Dividend per share	p	6.82	7.06	7.06	4.87	5.00
Operating cash flow	£'000	14,000	36,000	-58,000	82,000	60,000
Net assets per share	p	173.26	169.64	182.23	166.85	187.52
Net debt/(cash)	£'000	-175M	-126M	-15,000	-80,000	-442M
Shareholders' funds	£'000	1,126M	1,164M	1,122M	899,000	1,225M
Return on capital	%	18.73	16.67	9.22	7.70	6.16
Profit margin	%	8.00	6.10	2.93	2.19	1.82
Sales per employee	£	53.39	55.69	57.25	64.76	71.50
Interest cover		-15.36	28.25	6.65	5.00	5.95
Dividend cover		3.09	2.39	1.18	1.35	1.08
Sales increase	%	50.13	23.90	-4.22	1.34	-1.24
Earnings growth	%	-0.31	-19.89	-50.84	-21.05	-17.84
Investment x depreciation		1.91	1.41	1.69	1.10	1.09
Investment as % assets		15.96	14.35	14.98	13.04	12.93
Number of employees		55,475	65,900	61,400	55,000	49,200

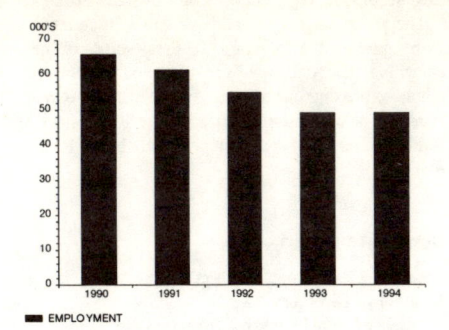

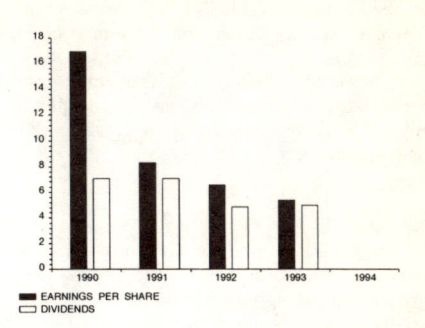

Employment

Earnings and dividends

The technology of Rolls-Royce engines was good, however. The RB211 was successfully completed, thanks to government funding, and derivatives of that engine have provided the basis for the group's success ever since. The 524 derivative was eventually adopted on the Boeing 747 and 767; the 535 earned the distinction of being the first non-US launch engine on a Boeing aircraft when it was chosen by British Airways (BA) for the 757 in 1978. Ironically, in the light of that, the latest version, known as the RB211-Trent, was rejected by BA in 1991 in favour of US General Electric (GE) engines for its Boeing 777 fleet, but this engine subsequently won substantial orders for the 777, and for the Airbus A330.

This is an exceptionally difficult market to compete in. There are only three major players – Pratt & Whitney being the third besides GE and Rolls-Royce – and a relatively small number of airlines, dominated by those in the US. The civil airline business is expected to experience continued long-term growth, but in the short term it suffered chaotic disruption in the early 1990s. The Gulf War, plus recession and the consequences of deregulation in the US, led to 1991 being the first year ever in which civil air traffic fell. The drop was soon reversed, but only at huge costs to the airlines. Meanwhile, a great backlog of aircraft orders had built up: orders placed in the good times of the late 1980s, which were turning into planes coming off the production lines just when airlines could least afford to pay for them. Cancellations and rescheduling grew, notably from GPA, the Irish finance group which had grabbed a tenth of the world aircraft market but then found itself in severe financial straits. On top of these difficulties, the aerospace industry had to deal with the decline in military spending as a consequence of recessionary pressures on governments and the collapse of the Soviet bloc which had previously provided an excuse for military spending.

Thus Rolls-Royce saw profits slide, and announced a series of job losses which collectively took 17,000 jobs out of the business in three years from 1989. And this was after a continuing process of job cuts which reduced the workforce from over 50,000 in the early 1980s to barely 40,000 before the NEI acquisition. At least the group was sensible enough to enter the recession with cash in the bank.

The long-term outlook for the industry remains optimistic, and this is a long-term business as the performance of the RB211 family has shown. But the long term depends on continued development of engines and variants to beat the competition, and that demands heavy expenditure in research and development. Sales are also increasingly dependent on clever financing – as BA's decision to opt for GE engines illustrated – which also requires subtantial resources. Rolls-Royce is smaller than its two rivals – Pratt & Whitney is part of United Technologies – so will inevitably find it harder to compete where scale is important. One answer is to share the cost and the risk of new projects, and Rolls-Royce has done that extensively. The V2500, used on many Airbus A320 planes, is the result of a joint venture with arch-rivals Pratt & Whitney, plus Japan Aero Engines, Daimler Benz subsidiary MTU, and Fiat. Financing the Trent involves partners to a lesser extent, with BMW having a 5 per cent stake, while similar quantities of shares are held by Japanese and French companies, and Rolls-Royce is also jointly developing a new, small engine with BMW.

These collaborations have helped give Rolls-Royce a comprehensive range of engines and gain a rising share of the market since the mid-1980s, as well as spreading the financing and the risk. The risks are still huge, however, in an incredibly difficult market. There are two saving graces: growing income from spares, and sterling devaluation. Spares provide Rolls-Royce with a lucrative and steady

354 ROLLS-ROYCE plc

stream of income following engine delivery – like razor companies making money from subsequent purchases of blades. And Rolls-Royce is a major beneficiary of sterling's devaluation, since most of its costs are in pounds, and most of its sales in dollars. On the down side, recovery in the civil airline business was predicted to occur later and later during the early 1990s, proving that nothing is certain in this high-stakes business.

Shares

The shares of Rolls-Royce have given investors a turbulent ride since flotation in 1987 at 170p, as they have fluctuated along with demand for air transport. The market crash of 1987 left them at 100p but a boom in engine orders then lifted them into 1988. The rise was consolidated in the following year when the expiry of the government's golden share, which effectively gave the government a veto over major changes, made the group excitingly vulnerable to a bid – though no bid actually materialised. But the link with NEI served only to cloud the picture, causing the shares to fall.

In 1990 the shares soared as a mystery buyer took a 3 per cent stake, and moved further ahead when the group linked with BMW in a joint venture. The shares peaked at 231p that summer as analysts talked about the group's rosy long-term prospects. But the weakness of the re-rating was exposed that autumn when a wave of selling sent the shares plummeting as a prelude to the real problem, a downturn in the airline business following the Gulf crisis. The shares likewise headed downwards throughout 1991 and 1992 despite a programme of severe cost-cutting. The shares were recommended by analysts in 1992 for their growth during a recovery, and job cuts helped them rally. But poor results that autumn sent them tumbling again towards a low of 92p.

The shares regained some altitude in the stock market rally of 1993, and analysts then simultaneously cut their profit forecasts and once again pointed to the group's long-term potential. The more positive view prevailed, with a continued rise into 1994.

Corporate conscience

Rolls-Royce is a major military and nuclear supplier, and is involved heavily in the power industry, but apart from these issues it raises few ethical or environmental concerns.

The group has a reasonable tradition as an employer, but has been forced to sack tens of thousands of staff in the last few years. It nevertheless retains a keen interest in training and development, but also remains a predominantly male preserve and has done little to change this. The group is a member of BITC, but its community record is not outstanding, especially considering how important it is in towns such as Derby. It has suffered health and safety convictions with the largest fine being £2,000, against the power company NEI. The group suffered one conviction for water pollution, Aldo being fined £1,000 in 1990. Despite this, it has a good record on trade effluent.

The group has only minor operations in countries with questionable regimes. It uses some ozone-damaging chemicals in solvent cleaners, but is committed to phasing out their use by 1996. Rolls-Royce is represented in South Africa, where it has paid a handful of its 1,500 or so black workers below a bare minimum.

Corporate governance

Separate Chairman and Chief Executive Y
Number of Directors 12
Number of Non-Executive Directors 4
(4 Independent Directors)
Insulated Directors None

Board Committees
Audit: Y   Remuneration: Y

Remuneration

Year end	31.12.91	31.12.92	31.12.93
Total board £M	1.54	1.56	1.85
% change	3	1	19
Highest paid £	256,000	278,000	308,000
% change	3	9	11

Board
Harrison, Dr Terence *Chief Executive*
Robins, Sir Ralph H *Executive Chairman*
Maudslay, Richard *Executive Director*
Miller, Stewart C *Executive Director*
Rose, John E V *Executive Director*
Sandford, John W *Executive Director*
Turner, Richard T *Executive Director*
Townsend, Michael *Finance Director*
Clark, John *Independent Non-Executive*
Higginson, Sir Gordon *Independent Non-Executive*
Mourgue, Harold G *Independent Non-Executive*
Nicholson, Sir Robin *Independent Non-Executive*

Rolls-Royce deserves praise for including some executive pay details in the short report for shareholders rather than confining these niceties, as do so many others, to the more densely worded official report and accounts. The group complies fully with Cadbury requirements, although the non-executives are heavily outnumbered; and pay details could be expanded.

ROTHMANS INTERNATIONAL plc

15 Hill Street, London W1X 7FB
Tel: 0171 491 4366
Chairman Lord Swaythling
Chief Executive William Ryan
Substantial shareholding Richemont AG 61%
Main brands Craven, Dunhill, Rothmans, Peter Stuyvesant
Size £6.9 billion sales, £2.7 billion stock market value, 20,000 employees
5-year growth sales 94%, earnings per share 116%, employment 47%
Solvency debt n/a, interest cover n/a
Political donations £100,000 Conservative Party
Charitable donations £385,000

Major developments
1972 Rothmans International created
1981 share stake sold to Philip Morris (US)
1987 sold interest in Rowenta-Werke; sold interest in Carling O'Keefe
1989 bought controlling stake in watchmaker Piaget and Baume et Mercier; Philip Morris sold stake back to Rupert family
1993 reconstruction separated Dunhill luxury products in Vendôme
1994 announced closure of factories in Berlin and the Hague

Outlook
Rothmans is a most un-British company, in almost every way. First, a majority of the shares are owned by a Swiss company representing the interests of the South African Rupert family. Second, and partly as a result of that, it is enmeshed in the kind of shareholding web more normally seen on the Continent. And third, most of its activities are carried on abroad.

The Rupert empire was founded in the 1940s, and Dr Anton Rupert soon expanded his pipe-tobacco business by taking on the South African concession. The business grew swiftly, and in 1972 the European, Canadian and Australasian tobacco interests were consolidated with Carreras in the UK company Rothmans International. During the 1980s it developed the luxury-goods side of Dunhill, and engaged in some contorted share-dealing which continued into the 1990s.

Rothmans's interests have for some time been intertwined with those of US tobacco giant Philip Morris. In 1981 the Rupert-family holding company, Rembrandt, sold half its shareholding in Rothmans to the maker of Marlboro. Philip Morris made the purchase partly to obstruct any attempt by its rival R J Reynolds (RJR) to achieve European expansion in this way, and partly because Philip Morris itself wished to use Rothmans to extend its European activities. The latter avenue was blocked by the European Community, however, when it decreed that the US group could exercise no more than 25 per cent of the voting shares. And the threat from RJR disappeared following its merger with Nabisco and subsequent hugely leveraged buy-out. In 1989 Philip Morris eventually sold the stake back to the Rupert family, which by this time had transferred its holding to the Swiss company Richemont. Philip Morris and Rothmans retain joint ventures in several countries, however, including Britain.

During the 1980s Rothmans also attempted to manage its businesses more actively. Some interests were sold, such as the Carling O'Keefe brewery stake held by the Canadian offshoot. Core interests were consolidated, as, for example, in the acquisition of Irish tobacco company P J Carroll. European manufacturing has been rationalised to take advantage of the greater flexibility following the creation of the EC single market. And like every other tobacco manufacturer, Rothmans has attempted to find something to soak up the huge cash flows cigarettes produce – by diversifying.

Some of this diversification was out of character, as exemplified by its brief ownership of electrical-goods maker Rowenta. But most focused on the luxury-goods business, built around the majority shareholding in Dunhill (like many of Rothmans's subsidiaries, a separately quoted company). Dunhill has virtually lost its connections with tobacco as it has grown from producing cigarette lighters to fashion and luggage, encompassing Montblanc pens and Chloé women's clothing as well as the Dunhill brand. Dunhill also owns half of the Cartier watch business, the remainder being owned by Richemont, thereby keeping everything in the family.

The 1980s were good years for the luxury-goods business, but that may not be the case in the 1990s. It is not so much recession in Europe and the US which matters, as the downturn in Japan. Half of Dunhill's sales are made in that country and in the rest of the Pacific rim, and much of its Western sales probably also end up there, in the hands of Japanese tourists.

Following more share shuffling in 1994 Dunhill is no longer so crucial to Rothmans. Richemont moved all its luxury products businesses into a new company, Vendôme, leaving Rothmans as a pure tobacco company. Shareholders received shares in each as awell as cash, with the added complication that Rothmans is now twin UK and Dutch companies. The new focus did not put off to a good start. Results for 1993 were hit by poor European sales, even though the company is not heavily exposed to European economies. Australia, Malaysia and Canada are the most important territories apart from Germany. As figures from other cigarette companies have shown, awareness among educated Westerners about the risk of cancer barely affects profits if advantage is taken of growing markets with lower health awareness and greater interest in Western brands. Rothmans is hampered a little, however, by the Englishness of brands such as Peter Stuyvesant, Dunhill and Rothmans. They seem to have less appeal than good old American brands such as Marlboro, Lucky Strike and Kent.

ROTHMANS INTERNATIONAL

Share record

Return on shareholder's equity	%	n/a
5-year price high	p	494.0
5-year price low	p	337.0
Dividend yield	%	4.48
5-year high	%	4.90
5-year low	%	3.17
Price/earnings ratio		11.2
5-year high		15.5
5-year low		10.3

Share price performance (in pence) from October 1993 when Rothmans shares were reorganised

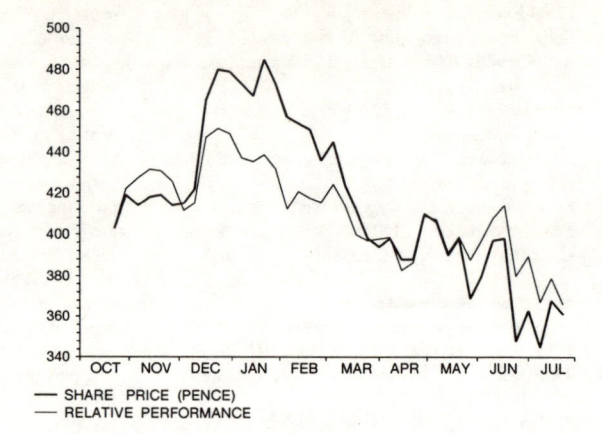

— SHARE PRICE (PENCE)
— RELATIVE PERFORMANCE

Financial record

		31/3/89	31/3/90	31/3/91	31/3/92	31/3/93
Total sales	£	1,304M	1,549M	5,698M	6,253M	6,893M
Pre-tax profit	£'000	327,300	405,600	542,500	593,900	636,200
Published retentions	£'000	136,000	154,300	190,800	208,100	230,100
Earnings per share	p	26.22	32.20	39.25	47.32	50.87
Dividend per share	p	6.15	7.70	9.25	10.25	11.50
Operating cash flow	£'000	73,600		187,200	82,800	197,000
Net assets per share	p	192.66	235.79	278.75	315.59	385.43
Net debt/(cash)	£	-457M	-505M	-700M	-752M	-1,006M
Shareholders' funds	£'000	761,500	904,900	962,300	1,146M	1,486M
Return on capital	%	29.74	31.55	35.37	33.12	29.84
Profit margin	%	16.82	16.98	8.19	8.19	8.04
Sales per employee	£	94.35	111.40	256.76	298.15	338.39
Interest cover		-7.67	-7.55	-9.35	-11.07	-9.86
Dividend cover		4.26	4.18	4.24	4.62	4.42
Sales increase	%	0.45	18.83	267.79	9.75	10.24
Earnings growth	%	19.47	22.82	21.89	20.56	7.50
Investment x depreciation		1.30		1.56	2.10	1.33
Investment as % assets		23.86		23.05	31.79	20.29
Number of employees		13,816	13,906	22,190	20,972	20,370

ROTHMANS INTERNATIONAL plc

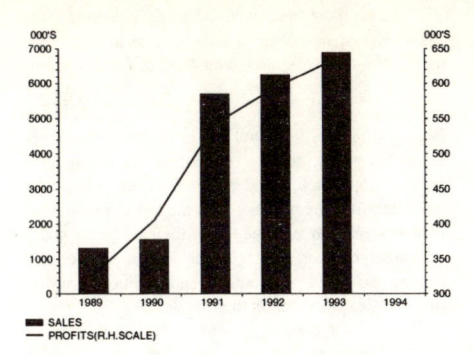

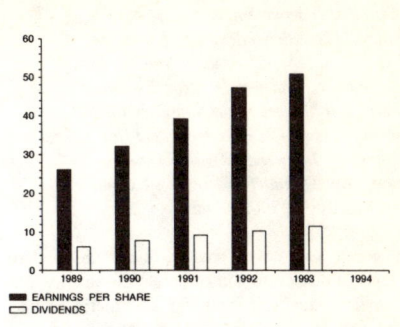

Sales and profits

Earnings and dividends

Rothmans has also seemed reluctant to venture seriously into the relatively uncharted territory of Eastern Europe, one of the great commercial opportunities (but also risks) for Western cigarette-makers. This cautious attitude may turn out to have been a sensible approach, if other companies come a cropper, but it is yet another trait which marks the group out from its British fellows, most of whom would have been only too happy to throw away millions on such a venture.

Shares

Rothmans appeared to be a classic defensive stock as its strong cash flows reaped good dividends for shareholders. The shares gained ground against the market as a whole through the crash of 1987; and as the company improved margins and pushed profits ahead, its rating soared until 1992. It was helped by Philip Morris's sale of a one-quarter stake in the group to South African interests in November 1989.

By June 1990 they had risen by 158 per cent against the market as a whole over a three-year period but after a temporary fall the advance continued, helped now by the takeover of P J Carroll. With the recession bearing down on the economy, the shares became a safe haven and shot upwards once more. A plateau was reached in the autumn of 1991 after the board warned that earnings growth was slowing. The shares held their value well until the middle of 1993. The new units issued as part of the restructuring initially rose against the market, but soon began to fall as the impact of slower European sales began to become apparent.

Corporate conscience

Rothmans's South African links have made it a target for anti-apartheid campaigners in the past, but the company's lack of direct involvement in South Africa actually leaves it officially uninvolved. Tobacco is therefore the main ethical issue: not just the production and sale of cigarettes and other products in the UK, but also tobacco marketing in the Third World. The group has subsidiaries or associates in places like Cameroon, Guinea, Turkey and Zaire; Carreras grows tobacco in Jamaica, while the group markets products in many countries throughout Africa, Latin America and south-east Asia.

Rothmans is notoriously uncommunicative, even to the extent of taking advantage in the past of a legal loophole to avoid making disclosures about employees in its annual report. It is therefore unlikely to be concerned about equal opportunities or other matters of employment. The company is a member of the Per Cent Club, but a substantial part of its donations go to the tobacco industry's Health Promotion Research Trust.

Corporate governance

Separate Chairman and Chief Executive Y
Number of Directors 14
Number of Non-Executive Directors 11
(9 Independent Directors)
Insulated Directors none

Board Committees
Audit: Y   Remuneration: Y

Remuneration

Year end	31.03.93	31.03.94
Total board £M	2.20	1.58
% change	-2	-18
Highest paid £	492,157	471,049
% change	14	-4

Board
Lord Swaythling *Executive Chairman*
Ryan, William P *Chief Executive Director*
Rupert, Johann P *Non-Executive Director*

THE RTZ CORPORATION plc

du Plessis, Jan P *Finance Director*
Baron de Staercke, Jacques *Ind. Non-Executive*
Craven, J A *Independent Non-Executive*
Crowley, L G *Independent Non-Executive*
Kelly, William M *Independent Non-Executive*
Mayo, John W *Independent Non-Executive*
Morgen, Kurt *Independent Non-Executive*
Stenham, Anthony W P *Independent Non-Executive*
Utz, John W *Independent Non-Executive*
Verloop, Ernst J *Independent Non-Executive*
Roux, Matthys J *Non-Executive*

The group has never seemed keen on modern concepts of disclosure and corporate governance, but nevertheless satisfies some important criteria, such as having two separate roles at the top of the company, although in the unconventional form of an executive chairman and executive deputy chairman. Rothmans also has audit and remuneration committees, although it did not comment on these in its 1992 report, nor on the payments to directors, except to disclose basic statutory information, and only regarding those directors working principally in the UK.

THE RTZ CORPORATION plc

6 St James's Square, London SW1Y 4LD
Tel: 0171 930 2399
Chairman Sir Derek Birkin
Chief executive Robert Wilson
Main subsidiaries Anglesey Aluminium, Borax Consolidated, CRA (Australia, 49%), Kennecott (US), Palabora Mining (39%), Rossing Uranium (41%)
Size £3.2 billion sales, £9 billion stock market value, 34,900 employees
5-year growth sales -34%, earnings per share -36%, employment -39%
Solvency debt = 12% shareholders' funds, interest cover 12 times
Political donations 0
Charitable donations £844,000

Major developments

1962 formed to acquire Consolidated Zinc Corp and Rio Tinto Co
1969 bought Pillar
1987 name changed to RTZ; acquired MK Electric
1988 bought Indal Ltd
1989 bought BP Minerals; sold RTZ Chemicals to Rhône Poulenc
1992 sold 51.5% stake in Rio Algom Ltd
1993 bought US coal interests; sold Pillar to Caradon
1994 bought COLONYO Coal company for £160m

Outlook

RTZ is, on most measures, the world's biggest mining group. It has come a long way in a short time since Rio Tinto merged with Consolidated Zinc in 1962. At that time the group was just another mining company, whose main claim to fame might have been giving Tiny Rowland one of the breaks he needed on his way to the top of Lonrho. But a combination of good luck, good political manoeuvring and good acquisitions has shot it to the top of the mining league – and hence to the top of the hate list of many a campaigner for the rights of indigenous peoples around the world, whose lives and traditions are disturbed by exploration on their lands.

The political connection was particularly important in developing and profiting from uranium, clearly a rather 'sensitive' mineral because of its military uses. The company's good luck stems partly from successful exploration, with uranium in Canada, Australia and Namibia, copper in South Africa, bauxite and iron in Australia. RTZ has also been lucky in that the right opportunities for acquisitions came along at the right time, and in that the occasional wrong acquisition has not broken the company bank.

The path to the top has not been smooth, despite the huge cash flows from successful developments in the 1960s. Like most groups, RTZ has not found it easy spending the money in the right way. Pillar, for example, was one of the 1960s star companies – an industrial company which RTZ bought in 1970 to boost UK earnings and to extend business away from commodity mining, especially into aluminium products. (In a similar vein, Everest double glazing was brought into RTZ for a while.) Tunnel Cement and Thomas Ward were acquired in the early 1980s, only to be sold a few years later as RTZ slimmed down its industrial interests. Pillar, too, suffered from the effects of the recession, which, together with the slimming-down process, caused its net income to be halved in 1992, at just £20 million out of a group total amounting to £348 million. It was finally sold to Caradon in 1993. RTZ also toyed for a while with becoming a general resources company. It built up chemical interests, and moved into oil and gas, opportunistically snapping up a quarter of Enterprise Oil when the privatisation flopped.

In the late 1980s RTZ decided to focus on mining again, and the group's luck returned when it took advantage of BP's need to sell mineral operations to buy back the shares unfortunately acquired by the Kuwait Investment Office (see under BP Outlook). RTZ's £2.4 billion deal with BP was described as a once-in-a-lifetime opportunity. Among other benefits, it brought to the group the huge Kennecott copper and gold operation in Utah, which accounts for approaching a third of group net income, and shot RTZ to a prominent position in the gold industry. Kennecott is rivalled in importance to the group only by CRA, the part-owned Australian associate of RTZ, and by RTZ Borax which had been the first addition to the newly merged Rio Tinto and Zinc, back in the 1960s.

THE RTZ CORPORATION

Share record

Return on shareholders' equity	%	13.64
5-year price high	p	897.0
5-year price low	p	395.0
Dividend yield	%	3.04
5-year high	%	6.58
5-year low	%	2.72
Price/earnings ratio		20.9
5-year high		24.9
5-year low		6.4

Share price performance (in pence)

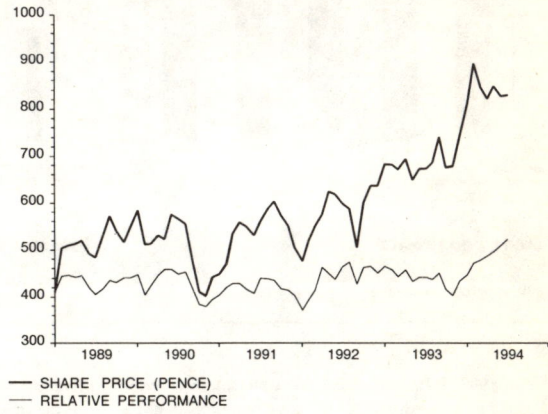

— SHARE PRICE (PENCE)
— RELATIVE PERFORMANCE

Financial record

		31/12/89	31/12/90	31/12/91	31/12/92	31/12/93
Total sales	£	4,832M	3,867M	3,552M	3,248M	3,184M
Pre-tax profit	£'000	1,104M	879,000	636,000	630,000	652,000
Published retentions	£'000	651,000	343,100	9,300	52,700	73,000
Earnings per share	p	63.11	43.01	29.29	46.03	40.36
Dividend per share	p	18.50	19.50	19.50	19.50	20.50
Operating cash flow	£'000					
Net assets per share	p	651.99	501.83	488.31	499.50	508.56
Net debt/(cash)	£'000	995,000	719,000	759,000	1,041M	384,000
Shareholders' funds	£	2,552M	3,758M	3,768M	2,899M	3,190M
Return on capital	%	28.94	19.73	16.07	14.86	14.33
Profit margin	%	15.83	16.21	11.01	10.96	10.58
Sales per employee	£	83.81	77.33	74.69	75.66	91.20
Interest cover		7.87	13.34	8.04	14.80	11.55
Dividend cover		3.41	2.21	1.50	2.37	1.97
Sales increase	%	23.40	-19.97	-8.15	-8.56	-1.97
Earnings growth	%	17.53	-31.85	-31.90	57.84	-12.70
Investment x depreciation						
Investment as % assets						
Number of employees		57,653	50,006	47,556	42,929	34,911

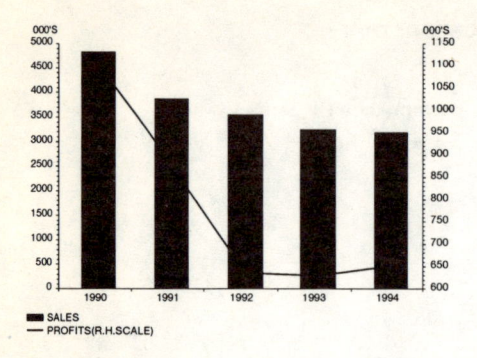

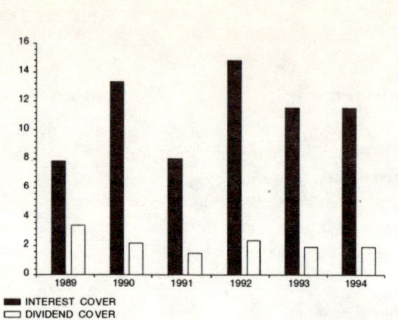

Sales and profits

Interest and dividend cover

In 1993 RTZ expanded its coal interests with acquisitions in the US, and was mentioned as a possible buyer of parts of British Coal despite the fact that its existing activities are primarily opencast, not deep, mining. Coal was clearly of increasing interest to RTZ, but the group's main interests remained chiefly in industrial and base metals, rather than in energy. Copper and gold are the most important metals, with the less glamorous but more stable iron ore also contributing a substantial portion of profits. Industrial minerals such as borates (used in soap and detergent) and titanium ore (for pigment, mainly in paint) represent the other major source of profits, as well as an area where RTZ has a dominant position worldwide.

Sheer size does not protect the group from the volatility of metal prices, however, and as a highly international company, RTZ is also heavily exposed to currency fluctuations. In 1993, these two factors almost cancelled each other out. Lower prices hit earnings by £122m, but currency added back £103m. A change of 10 cents in the traded price of copper affects RTZ earnings by £53 million, about twice as much as a $50 per ounce rise or fall in the gold price or a 5 per cent change in the dollar exchange rate. Like commodity prices, metal prices generally fell steadily as demand dropped due to world recession. Aluminium prices in particular have also been affected severely by higher exports from the former Comecon countries of Eastern Europe. Hence the group's earnings fell sharply from their 1989 peak. But RTZ's financial strength enabled it to keep investing during the recession, leaving it well placed for eventual recovery.

Shares

RTZ shares move in cycles linked to worldwide industrial production, and are additionally hit by currency fluctuations and world commodity prices.

Thus the share price rose with the economic growth of the mid-1980s, further helped by rising metal prices. Through the restructuring of 1988–93 the shares failed to make much impression on the market but also resisted the depressing impact of recession for most of the period. A rights issue in 1990 temporarily pulled the rating down but the continued benefits of the concentration on mining began to come through in 1990 and boosted the share prices once more. There was a weakening of the share price after the 1991 results, but by the spring of 1992 the market realised that cash flow was strong and the shares moved to new heights again. Hopes of a recovery kept the share rating high into 1993, and a move into coal mining in the United States was well received as a piece of good strategic thinking which saw the shares break out of their previous range in 1994.

Corporate conscience

Mining is inherently a dirty and disruptive business, and inevitably controversial. RTZ is unique, however, in the scale of antagonism which it has attracted back in the UK, rather than at its mining sites abroad, and in having prompted the formation of its very own pressure group, PARTIZANS (People Against RTZ and its Subsidiaries), which has been responsible for most of that domestic criticism. Since the 1970s PARTIZANS has logged RTZ's every move and dogged its development, relentlessly attacking every action which involves disruption to the environment and/or society of indigenous peoples around the world.

On one issue in particular, company and pressure group remain at loggerheads: RTZ (and other mining companies) is accused of digging up land belonging to native Americans, and thus breaching treaty rights. The miners argue that the US government has approved the sale of the land, whereas their opponents maintain that the government – and hence the miners – has illegally cheated the native Americans of their land rights. Similarly, in the 1970s RTZ was roundly criticised before the independence of Namibia from South Africa for not only maintaining a presence at the Rossing Uranium mine, but expanding it at a time when the United Nations was calling for withdrawal from the country. The group has also been accused of wrecking forest and causing wars through its activities in Papua New Guinea.

The group has recognised some of its past failings. Under the patient chairmanship of Sir Derek Birkin, its annual meetings are now more decorous than they were, for example in 1982, when protesters mounted the podium and the police were called. The group has completely reviewed its environmental policy to take account of a lack of coherence between one subsidiary and another and between those in different parts of the world. Unusually, a committee of non-executive directors monitors environmental affairs.

On other matters of conscience, the group is a small-scale military supplier of assorted parts and services; and as a uranium producer, it is heavily involved in the nuclear industry as well as having military connections. In South Africa it has paid some employees below a reasonable living wage.

On the plus side, RTZ is a member of BITC and the Per Cent Club, and is a large charitable donor in the UK.

Corporate governance

Separate Chairman and Chief Executive Y
Number of Directors 13
Number of Non-Executive Directors 6
(3 Independent Directors)
Insulated Directors Ch, CE

Board Committees
Audit: Y   Remuneration: Y

Remuneration
Year end	31.12.91	31.12.92	31.12.93
Total board £M	2.47	2.53	2.89
% change	14	2	14
Highest paid £	461,562	520,316	588,681
% change	2	13	13

Board
Wilson, Robert P *Chief Executive*
Birkin, Sir Derek *Non-Executive Chairman*
Adams, Robert *Executive Director*
Beals, George C *Executive Director*
Davis, Leon A *Executive Director*
Leslie, Jonathan *Executive Director*
Strachan, Ian C *Executive Director*
Bull, Christopher R H *Finance Director*
Giordano, Richard V *Ind. Non-Executive*
Lord Alexander of Weedon *Ind. Non-Executive*
Lord Armstrong of Ilminster *Ind. Non-Executive*
Henderson, Sir Denys *Non-Executive*
Jacomb, Sir Martin *Non-Executive*

SAATCHI & SAATCHI COMPANY plc   361

RTZ has a significant and strong non-executive contingent on the board. In addition to the audit and compensation committees, the company has committees for finance and general purposes as well as environmental issues. Details of directors' pay have been expanded.

SAATCHI & SAATCHI COMPANY plc

83-89 Whitfield Street, London W1A 4XA
Tel: 0171 436 4000
Chairman Maurice Saatchi
Chief executive Charles Scott
Main subsidiaries Bates Worldwide, BSB Dorland, Kobs & Draft Worldwide, Rowland Worldwide, Zenith Media
Size £4.3 billion sales, £315 million stock market value, 11,600 employees
5-year growth sales -2%, earnings per share -51%, employment -37%
Solvency debt n/a, interest cover 4 times
Political donations 0
Charitable donations £118,000

Major developments
1970 company founded
1975 became public
1981 bought Dorland
1982 bought Compton Communications (US)
1984 bought Hay Group (management consultancy)
1986 bought Ted Bates Advertising agency; bought Backer & Spielvogel; Martin Sorrell resigned to take over WPP
1987 abortive attempt to buy Midland Bank
1988 bought Gartner group and other consultancies
1990 Robert Louis-Dreyfus appointed chief executive; sold Gartner Group; sold Hay Group
1991 financial restructuring completed
1993 Charles Scott took over as chief executive; Charles Saatchi left the board.

Outlook
In 1979 Saatchi & Saatchi helped Margaret Thatcher win the general election with its 'Labour isn't working' poster. The advertising group was Mrs Thatcher's favourite for many years, repeating the success of its election performance in 1983 and 1987. So it is fitting, in a way, that the decline of Saatchi & Saatchi should have matched that of its most famous client.

Saatchi & Saatchi was a product of the times it helped to create. In 1979 it was a young but ambitious British advertising agency. The Saatchi brothers had only founded the business in 1970, and floated the company on the stock market in 1975. Billings in 1979 were £71 million, profits £2 million. There were fewer than 1,000 employees. In the mid-1980s it became, through a series of huge acquisitions, a

SAATCHI & SAATCHI

Share record

Return on shareholders' equity	%	-7.40
5-year price high	p	2684.9
5-year price low	p	88.9
Dividend yield	%	0.00
5-year high	%	n/a
5-year low	%	n/a
Price/earnings ratio		9.8
5-year high		109.2
5-year low		7.1

Share price performance (in pence)

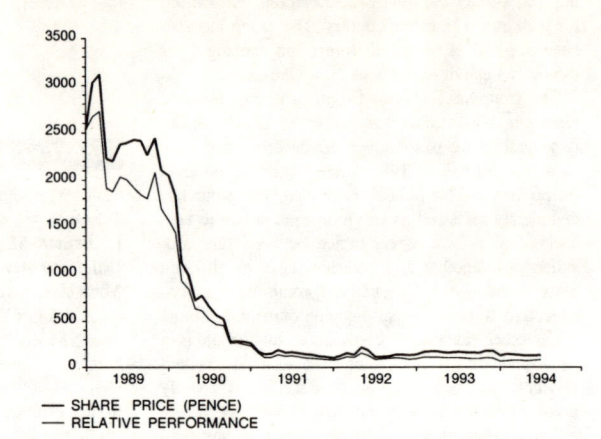

— SHARE PRICE (PENCE)
— RELATIVE PERFORMANCE

Financial record

		30/9/89	30/9/90	31/12/91 65 weeks	31/12/92	31/12/93
Total sales	£	4,364M	4,354M	5,073M	3,974M	4,279M
Pre-tax profit	£'000	64,400	38,400	-8,100	16,500	40,800
Published retentions	£'000	-72,700	-98,200	-76,900	-614M	7,300
Earnings per share	p	29.61	0.00	0.00	0.00	14.58
Dividend per share	p	69.14	0.00	0.00	0.00	0.00
Operating cash flow	£'000	-35,700	-5,800	-8,900	-5,100	19,000
Net assets per share	p	690.78	786.32	89.77	86.44	47.73
Net debt/(cash)	£'000	156,000	205,800	188,400	233,500	143,300
Shareholders' funds	£'000	170,400	-72,600	-217M	-205M	-134M
Return on capital	%	43.44	53.23	22.68	33.91	52.80
Profit margin	%	1.48	0.88	-0.16	0.42	0.95
Sales per employee	£	238.01	296.24	380.75	318.34	367.84
Interest cover		4.31	2.42	0.71	1.93	3.74
Dividend cover		0.43	0.00	0.00	0.00	0.00
Sales increase	%	14.96	-0.24	16.52	-21.67	7.69
Earnings growth	%	-88.42	-100.00	0.00	0.00	0.00
Investment × depreciation		1.84	0.82	0.73	0.64	0.60
Investment as % assets		27.23	13.52	18.36	11.24	13.23
Number of employees		18,336	14,696	13,323	12,482	11,633

Employment

Sales per employee

multinational service group, exemplifying the fashionable argument that Britain could and should become a nation of service rather than manufacturing industries. Saatchi & Saatchi moved into the United States with the purchase of Compton Communications in 1982, and shot to the top of the world league table in 1986 when it bought Ted Bates and Backer & Spielvogel. Together with a dramatic rise in money spent by companies on advertising during the mid-1980s boom, these takeovers turned the company into a stock market dream – a high-growth group in an expanding market. By 1987 billings were only just short of £4 billion, profits almost £118 million, and the group employed 16,000 people. Between 1981 and 1987 it raised earnings at a staggering compound rate of 38 per cent per annum.

But the year of Mrs Thatcher's last electoral triumph was also the last triumphant year for Saatchi & Saatchi. As with the British economy, the illusion of success was sustained for another year or so, partly by the takeover accounting. The buying went on, with an ill-thought-out and ill-fated move into mainstream management consultancy, and the crazy notion of making a bid for Midland Bank – probably the clearest sign that the Saatchi brothers had lost their touch. But growth did not continue. Sales and profits in 1988 were down, if only slightly. By March 1989 chairman Maurice Saatchi was forced to tell the annual meeting that all was not well. By the beginning of 1990 he had handed over executive responsibilities to Frenchman Robert Louis-Dreyfus, who left in March 1993 having saved the group from collapse.

Saatchi & Saatchi's traditionally strong cash flow suddenly turned negative in 1988. The following year there was a £214 million outflow, resulting in cash balances of £180 million in 1987 becoming net debts of £156 million just two years later. The outflow continued as the effect of faltering profits was exacerbated by the system of earn-outs by which the owners of acquired companies were paid, which prolonged the payments for years after the acquisitions had been made. Poor financial management did not help, allowing working capital and capital expenditure to continue careering out of control long after the good times had ended.

Overshadowing the growing débâcle was the nightmare of a special share issue made in 1988 when it had seemed inconceivable that the share price would plummet. When it did plunge, Saatchi & Saatchi faced the prospect of having to find £300 million to repay the debt which it had previously been expected would be converted into shares. Mr Louis-Dreyfus spent his first year fighting this crisis, by selling the management consultancies (which had been bought at the peak of the market and the peak of the acquisition folly) for whatever he could get, and by negotiating a refinancing which removed the disastrous convertible issue, though at the expense of hugely diluting existing shareholders' interests. He spent his second and third years hacking through the Saatchi jungle, dismissing people and cutting other costs where possible, and trying to create a foundation on which the group could grow.

That foundation was finally established, but it remains shelly. Saatchi group agencies have continued to win awards and pick up business, despite well-publicised losses of particular advertising accounts. The company is well represented around the globe, including the rest of Europe. But financially the picture has remained gloomy, to say the least. Matters were not improved in 1993 by an unusual £600 million rearrangement of goodwill previously written off following the acquisitions. But even without that, profits in 1992 and 1993 only recovered slowly. Average debts barely moved below £200 million. The situation should improve from 1993 onwards, but only slowly, unless the economies of the US and UK come to the rescue, which they singularly failed to do for Mr Louis-Dreyfus. There will be fewer redundancy expenses, and the saving made from those who have already gone will also help keep costs down. Costs will fall further, not least because new incentive schemes will replace high fixed salaries with bonuses. But progress is likely to be slow. Paying off debts will continue to be hampered by continuing payments on empty property well into the mid-1990s, even though that is not counted against profits because the payments have been provided for. In the longer term, the advertising market will presumably resume growth, but there are serious questions about whether traditional brand advertising will ever be the same again. It is a slow process and has tested the patience of chairman Maurice Saatchi who let it be known in 1993 that he was unimpressed with the rate of progress under Charles Scott. The company has survived. It remains to be seen whether both Maurice Saatchi and Charles Scott will do so.

Shares

Saatchi & Saatchi was one of the glamour stocks of the mid-1980s and its share graph stands as a monument to that hubristic decade. The shares soared from £1 in 1978 to £5.73 in 1986, and the company's rating against the market that year was also at its zenith. (Figures in the share price graph are not comparable because of the subsequent explosion of shares as part of the restructuring.) The acquisition of the Ted Bates agency that year sent the shares sliding in a prelude to the long-term problems that would follow. The trigger was finance director Martin Sorrell's departure to run the rival WPP Group, but the fall was a portent of much more significant events, and much worse to come.

The rating versus the market never recovered, although the 1987 bull market hauled the share price itself up once more. Then rumours about an attempt to take over Midland Bank and Hill Samuel started the shares downhill once more and the stock market crash of 1987 left them valued below £3. While there was a small recovery during the Lawson economic boom, the retreat was soon under way once more, the downward trend being assisted by an ill-timed rights issue in 1988 and a profit warning in early 1989.

Neither the brothers' plan to retrench by selling off bits of the empire, nor the hand-over of day-to-day management to Robert Louis-Dreyfus made much difference. Only the hope of a bid for the company supported the shares. The bottom eventually fell out of the stock after another profit warning in February 1990 brought the scale of the group's debt into focus. The shares were back to 1981 levels by the end of that year. The proposed reconstruction in 1991 made little impression on the shares, and while there was a small rise in 1992 when the group appeared to have ensured its survival and returned to profit, the rating against the market remained flat. In 1993 the shares edged back towards £2 as analysts recommended them on hopes of an economic recovery, but tumbled again as it became apparent that recovery would be more difficult than had been thought.

Corporate conscience

If ethical issues impinge at all upon advertisers, they must have a conscience about the products they help to sell – and some do, eschewing those areas they do not like. In this indirect sense, therefore, the Saatchi & Saatchi group is implicated in the sale of alcohol and tobacco, through clients such as Carlsberg-Tetley, BAT and Philip Morris; and in environmental matters through promoting cars for Toyota and Saab. The company's most famous client, the Conservative Party, might also count as an ethical issue to many readers.

Formally, however, this is a 'clean' company apart from a presence in countries raising human rights issues. It is a member of BITC and the Per Cent club. It operates in an industry where equal opportunities are rather more the norm than in most (and has a female executive board member in the form of finance director Wendy Smyth), and as far as employment conditions are concerned, the problem has been paying people too much, not too little.

Corporate governance

Separate Chairman and Chief Executive Y
Number of Directors 10
Number of Non-Executive Directors 6
(4 Independent Directors)
Insulated Directors None

Board Committees
Audit: Y   Remuneration: Y

Remuneration

Year end	31.12.91	31.12.92	31.12.93
Total board £	2.18	1.72	1.77
% change	-37	-21	3
Highest paid £	425,344	312,500	312,500
% change	-3	-27	–

Board
Scott, Charles *Chief Executive*
Saatchi, Maurice *Executive Chairman*
Sinclair, Jeremy *Executive Director*
Smyth, Wendy *Finance Director*
Cameron, Stuart *Independent Non-Executive*
Levitt, Prof. Theodore *Independent Non-Executive*
Russell, Thomas *Independent Non-Executive*
Gibson, Clive *Non-Executive*
Louis-Dreyfus, Robert *Non-Executive*
Walters, Sir Peter *Independent Non-Executive*

Once the failure of the Saatchi brothers' unrestrained reign had become apparent, chairman Maurice Saatchi was quick to adopt new notions of corporate governance, even before the Cadbury Committee reported for the first time. In his report on 1991, Mr Saatchi told shareholders that the newly strengthened non-executives had been formed into compensation and audit committees 'where they play a vital role in shaping corporate policy'. Part of that role was to draw up a new, long-term incentive programme for senior executives – a necessary development considering the high pay previously taken by the Saatchi brothers. From 1992, the company has made very full disclosure of directors' pay, pensions and share options, as well as US-style disclosure of payments to the chief executive and four highest-paid executives (which reveals that the heads of the advertising agency networks are paid more than the top directors). The addition of Sir Peter Watters has strengthened the non-executive team and the group is now a model of correct corporate governance, with a nominations committee as well as audit and compensation committees.

SEARS plc

40 Duke Street, London W1A 2HP
Tel: 0171 408 1180
Chairman Geoffrey Maitland-Smith
Chief executive Liam Strong
Main brands and subsidiaries Adams Childrenswear, British Shoe Corporation, Cable & Co, Curtess, Dolcis, Freeman Hardy Willis, Freemans, Millet's Leisure, Olympus Sport, Richards, Saxone, Selfridges, Miss Selfridge, Wallis Fashion Group, Warehouse
Size £2 billion sales, £1.8 billion stock market value, 40,700 employees
5-year growth sales -4%, earnings per share -40%, employment -22%
Solvency debt n/a, interest cover 18 times
Political donations £15,000 Conservative Party
Charitable donations £226,000

Major developments
1985 bought Foster Brothers Clothing
1986 bought Millet's Leisure Shops sold Sears Motors group
1987 sold US shoe interests
1988 sold Lewis's department stores
1988 bought Freemans mail order, Horne Brothers
1989 sold William Hill Organisation and Leisure Investments SA
1991 sold Horne Brothers
1992 sold Fosters; bought Richards from Storehouse; sold Galliford housebuilding
1993 sold stake in Aspreys

Outlook
Six decades after the late Charles Clore laid the foundations for Sears to grow into one of Britain's biggest retailing groups, the company has slimmed itself down.

It is certainly still large: its British Shoe Corporation offshoot, boasting names like Freeman Hardy Willis, Saxone and Dolcis, sells one-fifth of all the footwear bought in Britain. And Sears owns Freemans, Britain's third-largest mail-order retailing operation after GUS and Littlewoods. But the period from the mid-1980s has been characterised by a steady shedding of businesses as Sears has tried to focus on fewer areas. In 1987 it sold its American shoes business; the following year it disposed of the Lewis's (not to be confused with John Lewis) department-store chain to a group of managers. In 1989 the group collected £331 million from the sale of William Hill betting shops originally to Grand Metropolitan and thence to the doomed Brent Walker. More recently, the company pulled out of menswear retailing with the sale of Hornes, Fosters, Your Price and Dormie. And in 1993 Sears finally sold its housebuilding offshoot, Galliford. That left the group with its shoe shops, Freemans, the London department store Selfridges and chain stores selling clothes for women and children under names including Adams, Miss Selfridge, Warehouse, Richards and Wallis. Sears also owns the Olympus sportswear shops and Millets, and has a stake in a European shoes and sports retailing group, now known as Sears André.

That Sears was in need of a shake-up is beyond dispute. In 1988 it made profits of more than £270 million; in 1991 the surplus dropped below £100 million. It will be a long, hard haul to get back above the £200 million-a-year level. Shedding businesses was the relatively simple bit: the challenge now facing the company and its chief executive, Liam Strong, recruited in 1992 from British Airways, is improving returns from the sections that remain.

Part of the answer, having sold those businesses which are surplus to requirements, is to cut back the ones that Sears still owns. By 1995 there will be fewer than 900 shoe shops remaining, plus 200 or so concessions in other companies' outlets. That compares with more than 1,200 shoe shops, plus nearly 600 concessions, in 1992. This is not the first time the British Shoe Corporation empire has been cut: at its peak in the mid-1980s, it had around 2,500 shops. But Sears's supporters – or, more accurately, those who believe that the arrival of Mr Strong marked a genuine break with the somewhat lacklustre and sleepy management style of the last few years – are optimistic. Profits in 1992 were savaged largely by Sears having to set aside substantial sums to cover its 'restructuring' and make redundancy payments, but by 1994 it was clear that the underlying performance of all divisions was improving.

Making cuts will not be enough, of course: the shoe shops' problems were not simply a result of their being too numerous. They were badly managed, in the comprehensive sense of poor strategy, and poor or non-existent co-ordination between the different brands. British Shoe Corporation as a whole was also far too slow to recognise that consumers in the 1980s were becoming much keener on buying trainers like Reebok and Nike, and wanted fewer conventional shoes. And it had stuck far too long with the traditional, labour-intensive method of

SEARS

Share record

Return on shareholders' equity	%	7.07
5-year price high	p	136.0
5-year price low	p	58.0
Dividend yield	%	3.95
5-year high	%	12.31
5-year low	%	3.33
Price/earnings ratio		22.2
5-year high		30.8
5-year low		8.3

Share price performance (in pence)

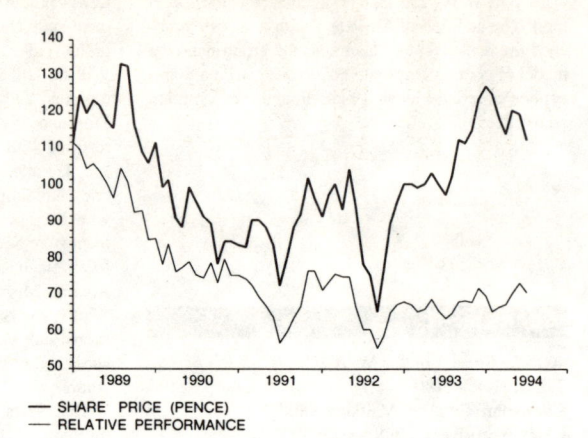

— SHARE PRICE (PENCE)
— RELATIVE PERFORMANCE

Financial record

		31/1/90	31/1/91	31/1/92	31/1/93	31/1/94
Total sales	£	2,092M	2,163M	1,979M	2,038M	2,016M
Pre-tax profit	£'000	195,500	127,800	96,300	89,000	124,400
Published retentions	£'000	86,200	18,400	-21,000	-123M	47,000
Earnings per share	p	8.71	6.32	3.99	3.09	5.25
Dividend per share	p	5.35	5.35	5.35	3.50	3.68
Operating cash flow	£'000	-36,500	186,300	-16,300	152,900	127,100
Net assets per share	p	105.08	103.89	104.91	86.60	87.85
Net debt/(cash)	£'000	182,000	177,100	152,800	47,200	-157M
Shareholders' funds	£	1,346M	1,298M	1,244M	1,088M	1,132M
Return on capital	%	13.87	10.73	8.15	8.66	10.94
Profit margin	%	9.07	5.57	4.06	3.78	5.90
Sales per employee	£	39.99	42.31	43.22	46.29	49.54
Interest cover		16.63	6.01	6.78	4.92	18.33
Dividend cover		1.63	1.18	0.75	0.88	1.43
Sales increase	%	-22.69	3.39	-8.49	2.96	-1.07
Earnings growth	%	-18.07	-27.46	-36.82	-22.49	69.60
Investment x depreciation		1.65	-0.79	0.50	-0.24	-0.06
Investment as % assets		6.84	-3.28	2.54	-1.30	-0.37
Number of employees		52,306	51,114	45,795	44,019	40,692

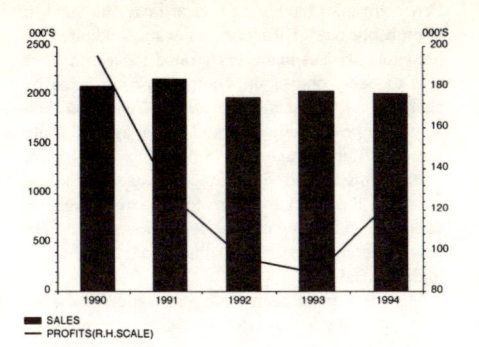

Sales and profits

Sales per employee

selling shoes. A self-service approach would be much more profitable, if it could be done properly, as trials revealed in 1993.

Good retailing should solve many of those problems, but Sears remains entrenched in sectors which promise relatively little growth – mail order as well as shoes.

Shares

Sears was supposed to be a defensive stock because it had a wide spread of interests, strong cash flow, low borrowings, and was supported by the value of its property assets. But it failed the test of recession, and even the shares' strong yield weakened in 1991.

The shares were at their strongest relative to the market as a whole in 1983 and have been slipping ever since. The basic share price peaked in the 1987 market boom when Australian entrepreneur Robert Holmes à Court revealed he had a small stake. The crash of that year caused the share rating to move up, as befits defensive company shares, a rise that was helped by the bid for mail-order house Freemans. But the decline resumed next year, until bid speculation sent the shares up once more that summer. Despite the speculation, all that materialised was the sale of the William Hill betting-shop chain in 1989, and the rating went down again. A recurring complaint in the City was that the group's results were not easy to analyse, especially because of difficulties in judging the benefits provided by profits in property. Partly because of this, and partly because the group was always seen as being slow to adapt to new developments in retailing, the shares did not gain from the Lawson boom. Indeed, they were soon caught by the downturn in consumer spending in 1990.

An upturn in the rating came in mid-1991, when doubts about the dividend being maintained were dispelled, but by 1992 the shares were down again and there were complaints that the group had lost its way.

By 1994, however, the shares had risen – both in terms of absolute price and as measured against the rest of the market.

Corporate conscience

As a huge shoe company, Sears must be anathema to vegans, even though less and less leather appears in shoe shops these days, replaced by more and more canvas and plastic. The group will also annoy animal-lovers by selling fox, mink, musquash and chinchilla in the form of fur coats at Selfridges, the only company in this book to be involved in the fur trade. In addition, branded cosmetics and toiletries may have been tested on animals. (Miss Selfridge's own brands are not tested on animals, however). On the environmental front, Selfridges also scores by selling fridges containing CFC-11 and CFC-12, which damage the ozone layer; tobacco, which damages people; and furniture including mahogany, which damages the world by depleting tropical forests (although the store says it aims to buy from suppliers who undertake reforestation).

Otherwise the group is exposed mainly on advertising, with one complaint upheld against (respectively) Freemans, Adams Childrenswear and British Shoe Corporation in the last few years. On the positive side, the group is a member of BITC, but that seems to be as far as its social and employment concerns formally extend.

Corporate governance

Separate Chairman and Chief Executive Y
Number of Directors 10
Number of Non-Executive Directors 4
(4 Independent Directors)
Insulated Directors None

Board Committees
Audit: Y   Remuneration: Y

SHELL TRANSPORT AND TRADING COMPANY plc

Remuneration

Year end	31.01.92	31.01.93	31.01.94
Total board £M	1.58	1.76	1.75
% change	35	11	-1
Highest paid £	266,464	325,000	493,000
% change	8	22	52

Board

Strong, Liam G *Chief Executive*
Maitland-Smith, Geoffrey *Executive Chairman*
Groom, Roger G *Executive Director*
Taylor, R *Executive Director*
Thomson, I *Executive Director*
Defty, D A *Finance Director*
Baroness O'Cathain *Independent Non-Executive*
Lord Tebbit *Independent Non-Executive*
Macdonald, D C *Independent Non-Executive*
Rankin, Sir Alick Michael *Ind. Non-Executive*

The board at Sears once appeared to be too cosy, bumbling along rather aimlessly and thus failing to protect and to capitalise upon its dominance of the shoe market. This all changed with the arrival of Liam Strong from British Airways. Several directors departed (with hefty pay-offs), and new directors gave the board a clearer purpose. It also acquired the structures of modern corporate governance, in the form of audit, remuneration and nominations committees, although the independent directors perhaps need strengthening in the same way that the executive team has been. Sears has begun to report greater detail of directors' pay, including the amounts of bonuses.

SHELL TRANSPORT AND TRADING COMPANY plc

Shell Centre, London SE1 7NA
Tel: 0171 934 1234
Chairman John Jennings
Managing director Mark Moody-Stuart
Size (Royal Dutch/Shell combined group) £33 billion sales, £24 billion stock market value, n/a employees
5-year growth sales 29%, earnings per share -37%, employment n/a
Solvency debt = 3% shareholders' funds, interest cover 51 times
Political donations 0
Charitable donations £41 million

Major developments

1897 Shell Transport and Trading formed
1907 alliance with Royal Dutch Petroleum Company
1985 bought out minority shareholding in Shell Oil (US)

Outlook

Few companies have such a clear image as Shell. It is probably one of the companies most admired by professionals and managers around the world. It is also probably one of the companies most hated by campaigners, especially because of its long history of opposing anti-apartheid action against South Africa. Both images are probably unjustified. The group has made its share of business blunders, although these often seem to be overlooked by admirers, and its reputation for ruthlessness is probably no more deserved than that of any other major multinational.

Shell is a giant even by the standards of the oil industry. Sales are dwarfed by the even more enormous Exxon, and by General Motors, but otherwise Shell is well up with the world leaders. It is easily the largest European business: in 1993 sales of £84 billion mean that Shell earns £160,000 a minute. At its peak in 1990 the group's £3 billion pre-tax profits exceeded the sales of half the companies in this book. Shell spends £6 billion a year on investment and exploration. Its chemical subsidiary alone is a huge enterprise, with its sales of £6 billion being about half the level of ICI's sales before the Zeneca split. It is also a huge mining company, operating mainly under the Billiton name, and concentrating primarily on aluminium.

Managing such a group is complex enough, but its structure adds complexity because, like Unilever and now Reed Elsevier, it is part British and part Dutch. The Royal Dutch Petroleum Company merged with Shell Transport and Trading in 1907, but, like Reed and Elsevier, the two companies kept their own separate identities. While the group is managed on a unified basis, shareholders own shares in either Royal Dutch or in Shell Transport (or both, if they wish). The stock market value for the group is the total value of both companies, although the group often appears smaller than it really is because in most UK contexts figures are quoted only for Shell Transport.

This history has made the group a true multinational – rootless, free to roam the world in search of oil and new markets, owing allegiance to no national flag and with a culture all its own. It has also left the group a more conservative and potentially inbred business than most of its rivals in the oil industry. Such conservatism with regard to financing has been beneficial in the early 1990s, enabling Shell to withstand the severe recession in the industry without experiencing the kind of traumas faced by BP. But it may also have made the group more reluctant than BP to slash costs in the face of poorer medium-term prospects than for many years.

Despite its size, Shell has suffered in the recession. Tax gains, asset sales and other non-trading items such as currencies flattered financial performance in 1992 and 1993. Full-year profits in 1993 rose by just 3 per cent to £3.23 billion after the group spent £500 million on restructuring, with the loss of 30 per cent

SHELL TRANSPORT AND TRADING COMPANY

Share record

Return on shareholders' equity	%	6.56
5-year price high	p	745.0
5-year price low	p	416.0
Dividend yield	%	4.23
5-year high	%	6.33
5-year low	%	3.84
Price/earnings ratio		22.0
5-year high		26.0
5-year low		10.1

Share price performance (in pence)

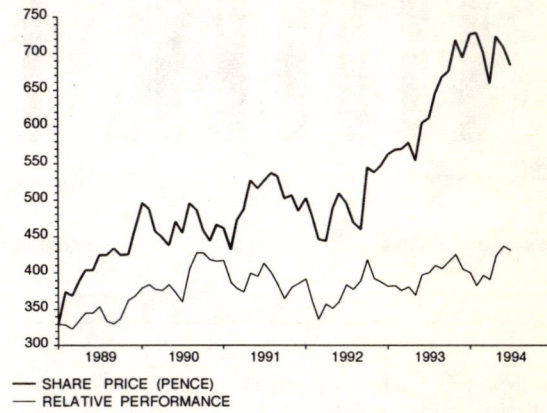

— SHARE PRICE (PENCE)
— RELATIVE PERFORMANCE

Financial record

		31/12/89	31/12/90	31/12/91	31/12/92	31/12/93
Total sales	£	25,912M	29,575M	29,774M	29,245M	33,499M
Pre-tax profit	£	2,793M	3,038M	2,048M	2,245M	2,245M
Published retentions	£'000	855,000	653,500	136,700	354,900	299,500
Earnings per share	p	45.41	42.45	19.76	30.75	28.48
Dividend per share	p	18.35	20.10	20.90	21.90	24.00
Operating cash flow	£'000	468,500	7,600	-287M		
Net assets per share	p	518.53	476.40	503.57	601.45	615.40
Net debt/(cash)	£'000	524,900	430,900	647,200	853,200	358,300
Shareholders' funds	£	11,984M	11,153M	11,561M	13,668M	14,027M
Return on capital	%	18.98	20.06	14.28	13.60	12.38
Profit margin	%	9.05	9.02	5.74	6.50	5.38
Sales per employee	£					
Interest cover		-14.56	-13,343	-64.99	-9.39	50.77
Dividend cover		2.47	2.11	0.95	1.40	1.19
Sales increase	%	16.04	14.14	0.67	-1.78	14.55
Earnings growth	%	45.71	-6.53	-53.45	55.60	-7.56
Investment x depreciation		1.33	1.56	1.45		
Investment as % assets		12.28	15.70	15.38		
Number of employees						

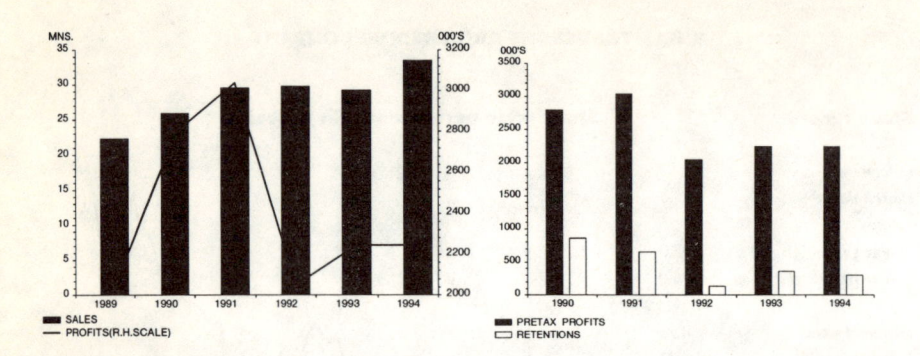

Sales and profits

Profits and retentions

of its workers. This helped spawn a £4.5 billion joint chemicals business with Montedison, the industrial arm of the collapsed Ferruzzi empire.

Shell remains a hugely strong company. It still has enormous cash flows and low debts, although ironically that will hamper its earnings recovery compared with more highly geared companies such as BP. It has strength in gas, notably in the Netherlands. Royal Dutch roots in the Far East also give it a potential advantage in the important markets of the Pacific, and have perhaps helped the group to contemplate risky ventures in areas such as China. And while its Mersey oil spill in 1989 resulted in unwelcome headlines as well as a hefty fine, it is trying to think seriously about environmentalism. Perhaps one day the two faulty impressions of the company will be replaced by a more accurate, single image.

Shares

While Shell's strong balance sheet has made it a core holding for institutions, the company's performance as a share has by no means been uneventful, especially when oil prices or currencies have moved suddenly.

The group's rating rose through 1986 as it recovered from the slump in oil prices, and it resisted the 1987 stock market crash in style. Investors found more exciting stocks during the ensuing boom, however, and the shares did not gain against the market as a whole until late in 1989. The immediate trigger for the re-rating which ensued in 1990 was a stronger oil price and sharply higher profits, but the shares continued to rise against the market when prices weakened again. What investors liked was the group's stability at a time when recession was setting in. The leap later that year was a bonus, when the Gulf crisis sent oil prices jumping and the rating reached a peak.

In 1991 the board embarked on an extensive investment programme of £12 billion a year with the aim of doubling the asset base in five years. Such a plan from a lesser company would have frightened shareholders but Shell's shares soon recovered. The following year the market began losing faith in oil companies as a safe haven from recession and put its money on shares supposedly poised to benefit from the expected economic recovery. Later, when the pound departed from the ERM, investors were worried about the group's ability to raise its dividend as there was a sudden currency drop against its Dutch twin company.

The rating soon recovered, however, and continued upwards in 1993, thanks to a better profits outlook and Shell's determination to improve margins.

Corporate conscience

Shell has emerged as one of the business world's most conscientious environmentalists, despite, or perhaps because of, its dependence on the environmentally damaging business of burning oil and gas. The wide reach of its operations also means that is in involved in virtually every area of ethical concern.

Taking these in alphabetical order: the group uses CFCs in manufacturing and refrigeration, but is committed to phasing them out: the volume used was reduced by half by the start of 1991, and is gradually being reduced to zero. The group is required by law to test rodenticides (made by Sorex) on animals, and various other chemicals such as detergents and anti-freeze also involve animal testing. Shell suffered 5 health and safety convictions in 1988–92, and its operations encompass a massive 64 countries where human rights are threatened.

Shell's military involvement includes the manufacture of camouflage fabrics by Don & Low, and solvents, resins and other products by Shell Chemicals, as well as the supply of fuel to the navy and air force. The group is a major miner, especially of coal in South Africa, Australia and the US, and gold in Australia, Ghana and Indonesia. The subsidiary British Lead Mills is also a member of the British Nuclear Forum and a supplier of casks for radioactive material.

Some of the group's pesticides have been implicated in health and safety incidents, and Shell was also accused in 1989 of infringing the international code of conduct on pesticide distribution.

Shell's insistence on remaining in South Africa, and its sanctions-busting activities in what was then Rhodesia, brought great opprobrium on its corporate head. But the group's employment record in South Africa is fairly good now. Of more than 2,000 black employees (about half its workforce), most were paid a reasonable wage.

Shell is even involved in tropical hardwood, because of tree clearance to build a pipeline in Gabon, for exploration in Colombia, and for mining gold and silver in Indonesia. The group is committed to making an assessment of environmental impact in such cases, however, and to minimising damage.

Concluding the alphabetical list, Shell has a number of water pollution cases. Shell UK was convicted twice in 1990 and 1991, with a fine of £1 million for a notorious oil spillage in the Mersey in 1989. There are also several examples of exceeeding discharge consent levels.

That is the (extensive) record, but it must be set in context, first of Shell's huge size, and secondly of its apparently sincere efforts to take its responsibilities seriously in various fields. In the UK Shell is a prominent member of BITC, and an enthusiastic supporter of the arts, charity and community organisations. It has developed powerful environmental and employment policies and has a tremendous reputation for staff training and development. The group remains hugely conservative, however, and for many years did not seem to have espoused equal opportunities with the energy which might have been expected. Very few senior managers are women or from ethnic minorities. Shell does now operate full equal opportunities monitoring. It has also introduced improved childcare policies, including career breaks for men as well as women, and Shell UK supports Opportunity 2000.

Corporate governance

Separate Chairman and Chief Executive Y
Number of Directors 11
Number of Non-Executive Directors 9
(6 Independent Directors)
Insulated Directors MD, all execs

Board Committees
Audit: Y   Remuneration: Y

Remuneration

Year end	31.12.91	31.12.92	31.12.93
Total board £M	1.32	1.67	1.73
% change	8	26	4
Highest paid £	515,604	606,680	512,714
% change	-3	18	-15

Board

Jennings, John *Executive Chairman*
Moody-Stuart, Mark *Managing Director*
Acland, Sir Antony *Independent Non-Executive*
Clark, Sir Robert *Independent Non-Executive*
Lord Armstrong of Ilminster *Independent Non-Executive*
O'Niell, Prof. R J *Independent Non-Executive*
Purves, Sir William *Independent Non-Executive*
Swire, Sir John *Independent Non-Executive*
Baxendell, Sir Peter *Non-Executive*
Holmes, Sir Peter *Non-Executive*
Thomson, William C *Non-Executive*

Shell's Anglo-Dutch nature results in some unusual elements of corporate governance, notably the fact that only the two top executive directors sit on the main board. Both are described as managing directors, while the senior of the two is also chairman of the board. In addition, a supervisory board exists, reflecting the Continental influence. The 1993 annual report made clear that the group complies with the Cadbury Code, and provided details of directors' pay and bonuses. Directors do not enjoy service contracts.

SIEBE plc

Saxon House, 2–4 Victoria Street, Windsor, Berkshire SL4 1EN
Tel: 01753 855411
Chairman Barrie Stephens
Chief Executive Allen Yurke
Main subsidiaries Comp-Air, Foxboro, James North, Ranco, Robertshaw, Tecalemit
Size £1.6 billion sales, £2.6 billion stock market value, 29,600 employees
5-year growth sales 33%, earnings per share 15%, employment -3%
Solvency debt = 66% shareholders' funds, interest cover 4 times
Political donations £20,000 Conservative Party
Charitable donations; £57,000

Major developments

1963 Barrie Stephens appointed chief executive
1983 bought Tecalemit
1985 bought Comp-Air
1986 bought Robertshaw

SIEBE

Share record

Return on shareholders' equity	%	19.73
5-year price high	p	627.0
5-year price low	p	121.8
Dividend yield	%	2.27
5-year high	%	8.10
5-year low	%	2.06
Price/earnings ratio		19.6
5-year high		22.9
5-year low		4.5

Share price performance (in pence)

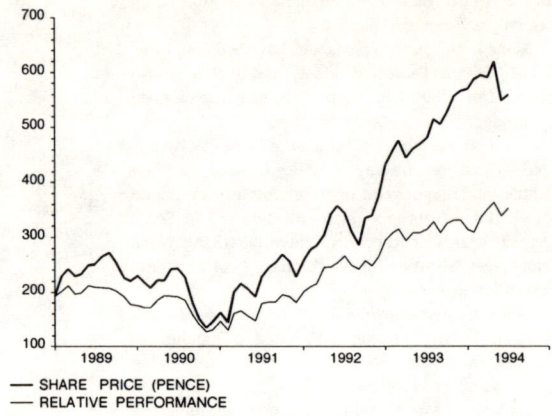

— SHARE PRICE (PENCE)
— RELATIVE PERFORMANCE

Financial record

		31/3/89	31/3/90	31/3/91	31/3/92	31/3/93
Total sales	£	1,215M	1,372M	1,481M	1,628M	1,619M
Pre-tax profit	£'000	152,500	181,300	159,100	169,600	185,100
Published retentions	£'000	73,300	77,300	57,200	57,000	66,800
Earnings per share	p	23.50	27.02	21.89	23.53	26.98
Dividend per share	p	5.61	7.40	8.13	8.95	9.86
Operating cash flow	£'000	25,600		-39,300	136,300	124,800
Net assets per share	p	200.70	220.02	295.19	268.61	346.43
Net debt/(cash)	£'000	228,000	230,400	629,100	562,000	531,400
Shareholders' funds	£'000	508,000	585,400	597,000	659,100	811,100
Return on capital	%	25.38	26.53	22.32	22.32	20.80
Profit margin	%	12.44	13.19	10.75	10.33	11.39
Sales per employee	£	39.78	44.22	45.21	50.97	54.60
Interest cover		8.59	8.45	3.92	3.48	4.24
Dividend cover		4.19	3.65	2.69	2.63	2.74
Sales increase	%	14.98	12.95	7.88	9.96	-0.58
Earnings growth	%	15.93	14.98	-19.00	7.51	14.65
Investment × depreciation		0.85	0.80	0.88	0.69	1.06
Investment as % assets		5.38	5.45	5.66	4.76	6.83
Number of employees		30,542	31,033	32,749	31,939	29,644

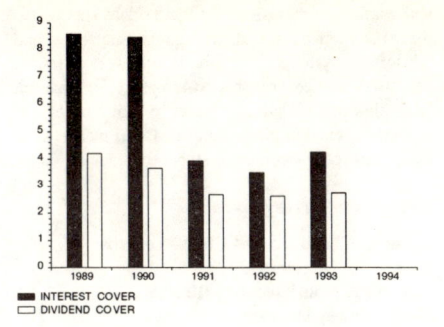

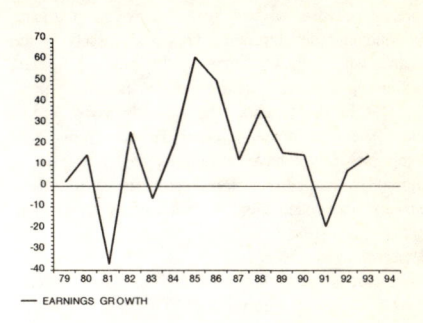

Interest and dividend cover

Earnings growth

1987 bought Ranco; bought Barber-Colman
1990 bought Foxboro
1993 rights issue raised £184m; bought Eckhardt, Germany

Outlook

So much of British manufacturing, and especially engineering, disappeared during the 1980s that Siebe is exceptional in having prospered. It has remained unashamedly a general engineering company, although it has concentrated increasingly on high technology, and in recent years its business has become dominated by control equipment.

The manner of Siebe's rise, and of the accounting behind that rise, tempers enthusiasm for the achievement, but there is no denying that Siebe has grown dramatically, has a global business which competes with the best, and runs the business tightly. The doubts arise partly because Siebe was one of the band of 1980s takeover merchants. The pace of takeovers made it difficult to make meaningful comparisons of performance from one year to the next, and the nature of takeover accounting made it easy for such companies to slide costs around the profit and loss account, thus enhancing their reported performance. In the case of Siebe, some of this is reflected in the trend of retentions, which looks on the surface to be excellent. And together with the goodwill write-offs following acquisitions, this explains why shareholders' funds grew more slowly than might have been expected, given the group's fondness for raising cash through rights issues. These factors make it difficult to assess the return on capital performance, which looks on the surface to be excellent. But the most worrying figures are probably those concerning investment. For a high-tech company, Siebe appears to invest very little, compared with its depreciation charge and with what is invested by other engineering companies. It is true that the depreciation figure is inflated by the annual write-off of research and development (whose capitalisation also has the effect of inflating profits), but that is not enough to explain the apparently low investment. The answer seems to be that much of the investment is paid for by selling assets.

Despite these doubts about the figures, Siebe is clearly more than a financial construction, otherwise it would not have survived the recession as well as it did. It is a tightly, almost ruthlessly, run group which can produce good figures partly because poor performers are not tolerated. Such businesses are sold or closed down, without much ceremony.

This approach stems from chairman and chief executive Barrie Stephens, a Welsh engineer who acquired it as a result of watching American companies in operation in the 1950s. He has applied it to Siebe since taking over as chief executive in 1963 (matching that other engineering company boss, Lord Weinstock, for length of tenure) when the company was called Siebe Gorman. It was then just about surviving by making diving equipment, but might well have gone under long before the 1980s. It survived thanks to radical staff cuts, which have continued to be implemented since the beginning of Mr Stephens's reign.

While Siebe's growth has been based firmly on acquisitions, there has been an element of luck too, especially when the purchase of Tecalemit in 1983 brought with it a couple of companies making controls. The operations took Mr Stephens's fancy, and he set about building this activity into the group's lead business. The move cost almost £1 billion, but with the purchase of Foxboro in 1990, it left Siebe able to challenge world leader Honeywell.

Siebe seems to have gained powerful positions in the United States and Europe, and shows much promise in Japan. It also seems to have survived the foolishly high debts taken on when it acquired

Foxboro, unlike many of its fellow buyers of the 1980s. (The figures are in fact worse than they appear because of the practice of capitalising research and development. This adds assets to the balance sheet, thus improving the gearing figures, and also improves interest cover by increasing profits.) Despite doubts about the methods Siebe used to attain such prominence, other British engineering companies might have something to learn from it, although perhaps the lesson is, since most of Siebe's business is outside the UK, not to rely on Britain.

Shares

Siebe grew steadily through the 1980s due to acquisitions financed by rights issues. This policy was not always popular with the stock market, and the rights issue which coincided with the 1987 stock market crash was particularly unfortunate. The group then abstained from share issues for a few years, and the profits made by the US deals financed by that issue helped the shares recover their rating against the rest of the market to the point where they entered the FTSE 100 index in 1989.

The shares promptly began to lose their shine as investors looked elsewhere in the face of recession. A steeper downturn started when the group became involved with the US Foxboro companies. The takeover deal was eventually struck in 1990 and the market concluded that the group's earnings would be diluted by it. The panic was short-lived, however, and good results at the end of that year brought a re-rating which was, if anything, enhanced by the onset of recession.

Despite the group's high gearing, its results were consistently good, and over 1992 and 1993 and into 1994 the strength of the US operations gave the shares a double boost. First the weak pound enhanced US profits, and secondly the US economy was recovering from recession while the UK was not.

Corporate conscience

Siebe is not the kind of company that feels the need to worry too much about its responsibilities beyond obeying the law, concentrating instead on extracting every extra ounce of performance from its subsidiaries. So it is no surprise that Siebe is not a member of BITC and that it does not have vigorous, public equal opportunities or environmental policies. What is perhaps surprising, given its size and type of operation, is that it also does not have any recent convictions under health and safety laws in 1988–92, nor is there any record of exceeding water pollution limits. Moreover, the group has commited itself to phasing out the use of CFCs and halons by 1996.

Siebe has a small presence in South Africa, where rather a large proportion of its black employees have been paid below even a minimum level. It is also involved in some countries with suspect regimes – Brazil, Mexico and Ghana.

But the main issues of conscience regarding the company are military and nuclear. The group is not a major Ministry of Defence contractor, but a number of subsidiaries do supply the military, including protection equipment for use in nuclear/biological/chemical warfare; compressors for the Trident submarine, the Australian navy and the Spanish air force; and lubrication systems for military vehicles. CompAir has also supplied compressed-air plant for Sizewell B, while other subsidiaries produce glove boxes and anti-contamination gloves, and Foxboro makes feedwater and reactor control systems for nuclear plants.

Corporate governance

Separate Chairman and Chief Executive Y
Number of Directors 9
Number of Non-Executive Directors 4
(4 Independent Directors)
Insulated Directors CE

Board Committees
Audit: Y   Remuneration: Y

Remuneration

Year end	31.03.91	31.04.92	31.04.93
Total board £M	1.10	1.40	1.90
% change		27	36
Highest paid £	476,858	537,481	620,643
% change		13	15

Board
Stephens, E B *Executive Chairman*
Yurko, A M *Chief Executive*
Mann, R *Finance Director*
Bonsey, C P *Executive Director*
Prohaska, J W *Executive Director*
Beck, Sir Philip *Independent Non-Executive*
Lloyd, Sir Richard Ernest *Ind. Non-Executive*
Lord Trefgarne *Independent Non-Executive*
Pybus, W B *Independent Non-Executive*

Barrie Stephens's length of tenure made him more powerful than most chief executives, and even after handing over the chief executive reins in 1993 there was clearly a need for a strong non-executive board presence. He did strengthen the non-executive contingent on the board in 1991 by appointing Lord Trefgarne and Sir Philip Beck – a necessary move considering that Bill Pybus was once chairman and has been a director since 1972, thus limiting his independence. Mr Pybus chairs the audit committee, while Sir Richard Lloyd chairs the appointments and remuneration committee. Details of directors' pay remain minimal, but the company does also reveal the numbers of highly paid executives who are not on the board.

SMITH & NEPHEW plc

2 Temple Place, Victoria Embankment,
London WC2R 3BP
Tel: 0171 836 7922
Chairman Eric Kinder
Chief executive John Robinson
Size £949 million sales, £1.5 billion stock market value, 13,100 employees
5-year growth sales 33%, earnings per share -5%, employment -9%
Solvency debt = 11% shareholders' funds, interest cover 325 times
Political donations 0
Charitable donations £1,126,000

Major developments
1937 formed
1986 bought Richards Medical company
1987 sold Anchor
1988 bought Albion Group (Simple range of toiletries); bought United Medical
1989 sold Avon Medical to Smiths Industries; bought Ioptex
1992 sold Nivea
1993 sold S&N plastics

Outlook

Smith & Nephew (S&N) is officially part of the pharmaceutical sector, but it is very unlike the drug companies – mainly because it does not make drugs (except for a generic drug manufacturing unit in the US). It is essentially a medical, rather than pharmaceutical, company (which perhaps helps to explain why the official title of the sector is 'health and household'). Smith & Nephew is Dr White's sanitary towels and Lil-lets tampons, cotton wool and Elastoplast, and, until 1993, Nivea skin-care products. But, more substantially, it is a supplier of medical and surgical products to hospitals. And this business is seen as its future – hence the scaling down of the consumer business, and hence the fact that this is one of the least well-known of Britain's top companies. (The group was also unsung as Britain's only domestic producer of denim – a legacy of its textile past – until the mills were closed in 1993.)

Nevertheless, S&N is a sizeable and very international business. Sales have stagnated in recent years, mainly because disposals have been made so that the company can consolidate on its professional healthcare products. On the other hand, the group trades throughout a wide area of the world. North America is by far the largest geographic region in which S&N does business, but the group also has a substantial market in Europe – indeed in 1992 numbers of Continental sales exceeded those in the UK, which contributed only a fifth of total sales.

The extent of dependence on North America is perhaps a little unfortunate at the time of a US presidential crusade to cut healthcare costs, but at least this is a problem S&N shares with the drug companies. Like the drug companies, it argues that in fact its products help to reduce costs, although it is unlikely to convince those charged with reducing the bills. S&N, along with the drug companies, maintains that innovative developments lead to less intrusive surgery, quicker recovery, easier home treatment, and hence to less time spent by patients in hospitals, which is the really expensive part of health care. And there is clearly some truth in this, considering, for example, developments in hip and other joint replacements – one of S&N's major businesses.

Prices are likely to remain under pressure in most major markets, however, even for innovative products which reduce hospitalisation. And much of S&N's business consists of fairly basic medical supplies, such as surgeons' gloves, bandages and dressings, which accounted for a third of total sales in 1992, while the more technologically advanced items, such as eye and ear implants and joint replacements, produced only about the same.

But it is easy to overdo the gloom surrounding pricing. As many drug companies have illustrated, it is possible to boost profits substantially without price increases so long as demand for the products is growing. Demand for medical and surgical products is likely to continue growing as the population of the developed world ages, and the countries of the less developed world become more able to afford better health care. The issue of ageing is of particular interest for S&N, because of its involvement in joint replacements. As well as hips, S&N produces shoulder systems and knee joints, likely to be in demand as the fitness craze of the 1980s brings its aftermath of repetitive-strain injuries, especially to knees.

Like many companies, S&N has struggled to find a role in the world. It has had its share of diversification for its own sake, leading it into dead-end acquisitions such as plastic products (an Australian manufacturer of ice cream tubs was sold in the spring of 1993). But during the 1980s the group identified a sensible core activity of supplying growth areas of the professional healthcare sector with increasingly specialist (and therefore more profitable) products. That strategy has been implemented without much fuss, but also without the financial disruption which often accompanies such 'refocusing'. It still has some way to go, assuming the remaining consumer businesses will eventually be sold, but by the start of 1993 S&N already had the fashionable combination of geographical spread and market focus which many companies crave. The rest is largely down to the power of the hospital buyers and their political masters.

Shares

Predictable, strong growth in earnings from well-established brands made the company a popular share to hold in the 1980s. But while the share price itself peaked in the speculative market of 1987, the rating versus the whole market did not. The group's defensive qualities caused the relative rating to rise

SMITH & NEPHEW plc

SMITH & NEPHEW

Share record

Return on shareholders' equity	%	30.48
5-year price high	p	170.0
5-year price low	p	90.0
Dividend yield	%	4.40
5-year high	%	6.30
5-year low	%	3.52
Price/earnings ratio		14.6
5-year high		20.1
5-year low		10.8

Share price performance (in pence)

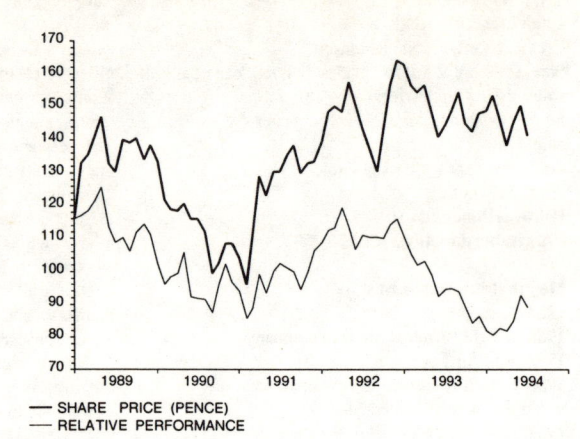

— SHARE PRICE (PENCE)
— RELATIVE PERFORMANCE

Financial record

		31/12/89	31/12/90	31/12/91	31/12/92	31/12/93
Total sales	£'000	710,100	729,700	791,700	857,700	948,700
Pre-tax profit	£'000	144,200	132,100	132,400	141,300	163,300
Published retentions	£'000	54,600	30,900	14,900	56,200	56,000
Earnings per share	p	10.12	9.09	8.42	8.96	9.54
Dividend per share	p	4.25	4.35	4.44	4.62	4.91
Operating cash flow	£'000	-15,200	86,200	37,500	4,300	
Net assets per share	p	42.33	42.55	41.94	42.12	44.50
Net debt/(cash)	£'000	158,600	83,700	67,800	42,700	39,100
Shareholders' funds	£'000	182,400	190,100	213,500	282,200	347,600
Return on capital	%	43.21	42.92	40.74	39.90	41.18
Profit margin	%	19.70	17.84	16.58	16.40	17.09
Sales per employee	£	49.30	51.47	57.10	63.13	72.43
Interest cover		10.39	8.59	16.01	59.63	325.20
Dividend cover		2.35	2.09	1.90	1.94	1.94
Sales increase	%	18.77	2.76	8.50	8.34	10.61
Earnings growth	%	10.00	-9.08	-7.41	6.39	6.57
Investment x depreciation		2.15	1.07	1.49	1.41	
Investment as % assets		21.63	13.58	19.18	18.94	
Number of employees		14,403	14,178	13,864	13,587	13,099

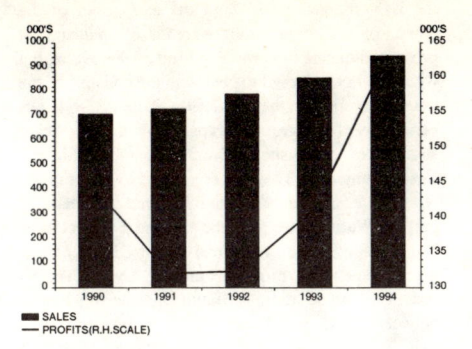

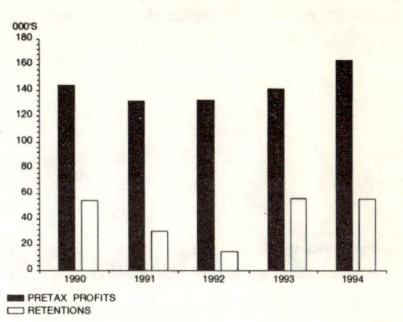

Sales and profits

Profits and retentions

during the market crash of that year, but by 1988 it was slipping once more, due to concern about weakening demand for some of the group's products. Reduced growth in earnings per share pushed the rating further down, until it hit the bottom in 1990. Then it picked up once again as investors turned to the relative safety of the shares with the onset of recession.

Smith & Nephew attempted to draw attention to the more interesting parts of its business in order to offset its image as a solid but dull investment, but in 1991 the market began questioning the prospects for the UK consumer and US lens business as profit growth faltered. Better sales figures for 1992 cheered investors and the rating relative to the sector consolidated for a time, only to start falling again towards the end of the year. The decline continued throughout 1993.

Corporate conscience

Despite being in the FTSE index, Smith & Nephew still behaves as though it were a semi-private company so far as its social responsibilities are concerned. The group is introspective, to the point of not even responding to EIRIS inquiries. It is therefore difficult to tell whether the company has adequate equal opportunities or environmental policies. But it does support Opportunity 2000 and has a reasonable record on charitable donations, including the Smith & Nephew Foundation which provides medical scholarships.

The group's operations seem relatively benign, however. It has one recent health and safety conviction – a fine of £2,000 in 1991 – but no record of water pollution. Some products do involve animal testing, but this has been reduced and the group supports FRAME (Fund for the Replacement of Animals in Medical Experiments), which researches alternatives. S&N has a marginal military connection, supplying cleaning materials for rifles. And it has paid over 100 of its 1,300-strong South African black workforce below even a basic minimum.

Corporate governance

Separate Chairman and Chief Executive Y
Number of Directors 11
Number of Non-Executive Directors 5
(4 Independent Directors)
Insulated Directors None
Board Committees
Audit: Y   Remuneration: Y
Remuneration

Year end	31.12.91	31.12.92	31.12.93
Total board £M	1.00	1.29	1.39
% change	10	29	8
Highest paid £	212,000	260,000	284,000
% change	18	23	13

Board
Robinson, John *Chief Executive*
Kinder, Eric *Executive Chairman*
Blair, Jack *Executive Director*
Fryer, Alan *Executive Director*
O'Donnell, Christopher *Executive Director*
Hooley, Peter *Finance Director*
Cleaver, Sir Anthony *Independent Non-Executive*
Kennedy, Sir Francis *Independent Non-Executive*
Lane, Dr Nancy J *Independent Non-Executive*
Pearse, Sir Brian *Independent Non-Executive*
Macpherson, Alastair *Non-Executive*

The company has recently paid more attention to the strength and balance of the board, appointing Midland Bank chief executive Sir Brian Pearse and IBM (UK) chairman Sir Anthony Cleaver as non-executives in February 1993, following Dr Nancy Lane in

1991. The non-executives now make up the audit and remuneration committees, and have divulged to shareholders a few more details about directors' pay than previously revealed.

W H SMITH GROUP plc

Strand House, 7 Holbein Place, London SW1W 8NR
Tel: 0171 730 1200
Chairman Jeremy Hardie
Chief executive Sir Malcolm Field
Substantial shareholding Smith family 51% B shares
Main subsidiaries Nice Day stationery, Our Price, Waterstone's, Do It All (50%), Virgin Megastores (50%)
Size £2.3 billion sales, £1.6 billion stock market value, 30,100 employees
5-year growth sales 19%, earnings per share 27%, employment -13%
Solvency debt = 18% shareholders' funds, interest cover 20 times
Political donations 0
Charitable donations £795,000

Major developments
1792 Henry Walton Smith opened a small news vendor's in London
1846 became W H Smith & Son
1848 first bookstall at Euston Station
1903 first overseas branch in Paris
1973 first W H Smith Travel Agency
1979 bought LCP Homecentres (Do It All)
1984 launched Screensport cable TV offshoot
1986 bought Paperchase; bought Our Price Music
1989 merged Do It All with Payless; bought Waterstone's booksellers
1990 bought Wall to Wall Music in USA
1991 W H Smith Television sold; W H Smith Travel sold
1992 bought 50% of Virgin retail
1994 put all Our Price stores into Virgin venture

Outlook
There are remarkable similarities between W H Smith and Boots, which made their partnership in the do-it-yourself chain Do It All appear at first to have been made in heaven. Both are long-established retailers which have struggled to escape their history in the fear that it is leading them nowhere. But, for both, the long-established high-street businesses have continued to be the best performers, while the new ventures have largely proved difficult, if not disastrous.

Do It All is a prime example. W H Smith entered the DIY market in 1979, in the early days of the 'shed' (out-of-town retail 'warehouse') industry. It prospered during the growth period of the 1980s, but when the boom turned to bust with the collapse of the housing market in the late 1980s, it found itself left behind by the aggressive expansionism and pricing strategy of Kingfisher's B&Q, and of Ladbroke's Texas Homecare. The answer seemed to be a merger with Payless, once Boots had acquired this chain as part of Ward White. But the merged business then had to cope with a dismal market for DIY, which is highly dependent on people moving house. And its task was made more difficult by the price war between B&Q and Texas, which it felt obliged to join, in order to maintain some semblance of market position.

Do It All was pinning its hopes on a recovery in the housing market, and on a new format. But the new format placed it in direct competition with B&Q in the 'serious' end of the market concerned with major projects, while Texas had slid into the softer, home adornment end. It was difficult to see Do It All winning against the might of B&Q, and the general consensus was that the chain needed heavy investment and drastic surgery, which might only be possible after W H Smith had sold out to Boots after the expiry of the standstill agreement between the two groups in 1994. One-third of all Do It All stores were sold in 1994, but the chain's future remains doubtful.

Do-it-yourself was by no means the first diversification to go wrong for W H Smith. A long flirtation with travel agencies (the first was opened in 1973) was finally abandoned in 1991. An even more eccentric move into cable and satellite television came a cropper at the same time. In the mid-1980s selling computers proved a very short-lived venture. And like most UK retailers, W H Smith has had its share of failures in the US.

Meanwhile, the prosaic news-wholesaling operation seems to have recovered satisfactorily from the upheavals in the newspaper distribution business. And the original chain of high-street newsagents-cum-general stores has continued to prosper, just as had Boots's chemist shops. ('Original' is not strictly correct – the shops were opened only in 1905 after the railway companies demanded exorbitant rent increases for Smith's station bookstalls.) A further similarity between W H Smith and Boots is that both companies got a little carried away in opening some over-large stores during the 1970s and early 1980s. But on the whole the format and merchandise was developed sensibly, and introducing electronic point-of-sale equipment helped to improve productivity and profitability quite dramatically.

One might well ask why such businesses wander into other areas, no matter how closely related, rather than sticking to what they do best. But not all the diversifications have been disastrous. The Waterstone's chain of bookshops appears successful, the only caveat being that W H Smith let their ex-employee Mr Waterstone set it up as his own busi-

W H SMITH GROUP

Share record

Return on shareholder's' equity	%	16.78
5-year price high	p	549.0
5-year price low	p	267.2
Dividend yield	%	3.91
5-year high	%	5.11
5-year low	%	3.26
Price/earnings ratio		18.0
5-year high		20.8
5-year low		10.3

Share price performance (in pence)

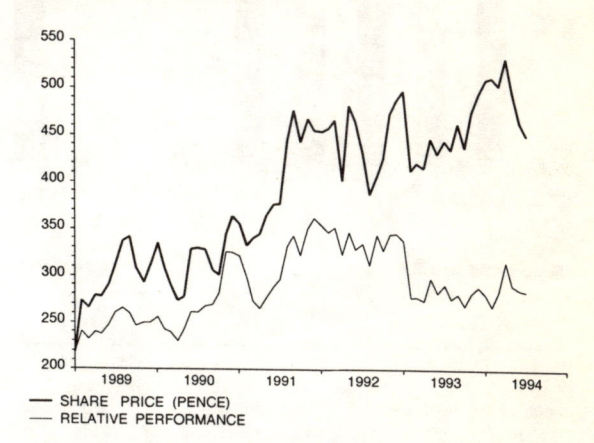

— SHARE PRICE (PENCE)
— RELATIVE PERFORMANCE

Financial record

		31/5/89	31/5/90	31/5/91	31/5/92	31/5/93
Total sales	£	1,941M	2,131M	1,971M	2,128M	2,312M
Pre-tax profit	£'000	84,100	86,000	89,000	113,000	113,900
Published retentions	£'000	77,200	62,000	18,400	45,100	45,600
Earnings per share	p	24.94	27.45	25.98	30.24	31.66
Dividend per share	p	9.85	10.90	12.29	13.40	14.20
Operating cash flow	£'000	-100	-36,400	94,600	12,900	-2,900
Net assets per share	p	193.21	233.41	219.57	210.42	206.96
Net debt/(cash)	£'000	121,700	220,500	231,900	85,200	86,000
Shareholders' funds	£'000	280,900	294,300	252,800	435,400	482,000
Return on capital	%	25.44	25.61	25.16	24.81	23.39
Profit margin	%	4.26	4.03	4.26	5.54	5.55
Sales per employee	£	56.20	60.65	65.39	72.57	76.83
Interest cover		8.15	4.29	3.77	33.82	19.83
Dividend cover		2.53	2.52	2.11	2.26	2.23
Sales increase	%	16.76	9.81	-7.52	7.96	8.66
Earnings growth	%	9.75	10.10	-5.37	16.42	4.69
Investment x depreciation		1.70	1.83	1.56	1.81	2.09
Investment as % assets		16.36	17.05	12.80	14.91	17.67
Number of employees		34,530	35,131	30,136	29,318	30,088

W H SMITH GROUP plc

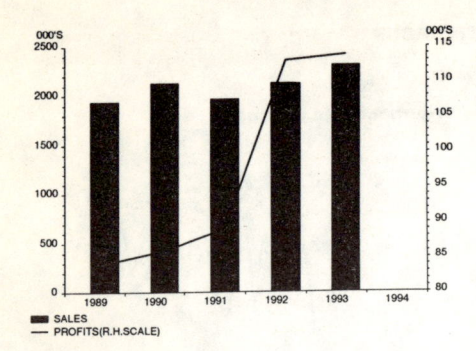

Sales and profits

Sales per employee

ness, before realising what a good idea it was and then buying it off him. Music shops, comprising Our Price and Virgin shops, and a joint venture with Virgin on Virgin megastores, suffered during the recession but may return to their former glory as the economy recovers, and if the group's campaign to get manufacturers to cut CD prices succeeds. An expansion of the Virgin joint venture to include all the Our Price outlets is seen as a prelude to a major mid-market push for this business. In addition, the latest attempts to introduce the right formula in the US, with music shops and hotel/airport W H Smith kiosks, should be more successful than previous endeavours in that country.

In the light of the group's less-than-illustrious diversification strategy, talk of expansion into China, to offset a low rate of high-street growth that is projected in Britain, looks to have all the potential for success of a Do It All. W H Smith's overseas performance, notably in the US, may not be a total failure but leaves the market nervous. China could be a winner, but it could combine all the attributes of DIY and America on a massive scale.

Shares

Unfashionable W H Smith underperformed the stock market in the expansionist era of 1986–7 as other high-street operations offered faster growth in share price. During the market crash of 1987 the group was regarded as a safe haven, an opinion which lasted into 1988, when the shares headed downwards. Analysts were concerned that the group's heavy capital expenditure programme would take years to pay off. A recovery began in 1989 when cost controls and increased sales volumes impressed investors who were then worrying about the performance of 1980s retail stars like Next and Burton.

The poor performance of the Do It All offshoot led to a weakening of the share rating at the end of 1989, but the recession encouraged investors to switch from vulnerable retailers and into W H Smith, regarded once more as a safe bet. There was additional excitement in 1990 over prospects for the investment in satellite television, but the shares fell back in 1991 when poor half-year results were followed by a cash call and withdrawal from both television and travel. But the group's defensive qualities saw the shares bounce back later that year as they gained 30 per cent against the market as a whole.

Worries about the performance of Do It All, coupled with concern about the impact of recession on retailers, hit W H Smith's shares during 1993. In the remedial action on the DIY business, shares continue to underperform the FTSE index, but they could be on their way up again if the company equalises voting rights between its A and B shares.

Corporate conscience

W H Smith retains some of the paternalist attitudes of its past as a family-run company. It takes its responsibilities seriously, both to employees and external interest groups. That does not mean it is free from involvement over ethical issues, but at least the group's top management is likely to acknowledge the existence of such concerns. In keeping with that approach, the group is a member of BITC and the Per Cent Club, and has adequate environmental and equal opportunities policies, as well as supporting Opportunity 2000. It has a good employment record so far as training and communication is concerned, but is not as enthusiastic as some companies regarding the monitoring and development of an equal opportunities strategy.

W H Smith has always taken community involvement seriously, and during 1992 launched a special campaign in conjunction with its 200th birthday. It contributed pound for pound to cash raised by staff, thus providing a total of £1 million for the Samaritans. Additional cash raised was used to create a W H Smith Charitable Trust, to be run by staff from throughout the group.

There are some negative points: Do It All uses tropical hardwoods – from Ghana, Malaysia and the Phillipines – in doors, toilet seats and garden furniture. The newsagents also sell magazines which would be considered by some people to include pornography, and the wholesale operation distributes such magazines. Finally, W H Smith has received an advertising complaint upheld by the ASA.

Corporate governance

Separate Chairman and Chief Executive Y
Number of Directors 12
Number of Non-Executive Directors 8
(7 Independent Directors)
Insulated Directors None

Board Committees

Audit: Y   Remuneration: Y
Remuneration

Year end	1.06.91	30.05.92	29.05.93
Total board £M	1.06	1.54	1.13
% change		45	-27
Highest paid £	206,000	323,000	264,000
% change		57	-18

Board

Field, Sir Malcolm *Chief Executive*
Roberts, David *Executive Director*
Troughton, Peter *Executive Director*
Napier, John *Finance Director*
Elson, Edward *Independent Non-Executive*
Lord Windlesham *Independent Non-Executive*
Morgan, Dr Janet P *Independent Non-Executive*
Orr, Michael *Independent Non-Executive*
Taylor, Martin *Independent Non-Executive*
Wilmot-Sitwell, Peter S *Independent Non-Executive*
Smith, Philip *Non-Executive*
Hardie, Jeremy *Non-Executive Chairman*

Like other long-established family companies (Sainsbury is a prime example), W H Smith takes its responsibilities seriously. This included establishing non-executive audit and remuneration committees before they were called for by the Cadbury Report, and publishing some details of bonus schemes. These committees have not prevented some rather wayward decisions from being made in recent years, although, with the retirement of Sir Simon Hornby, the company is now thought more likely to dismantle the restrictive voting structure of its 'A' and 'B' shares, which has helped maintain family control of the business. The wind of change can already be felt, with the appointment as chairman of Jeremy Hardie, the first head of the company not to come from its founding dynasty.

SMITHS INDUSTRIES plc

765 Finchley Road, London NW11 8DS
Tel: 0181 458 3232
Chairman and chief executive Roger Hurn
Main subsidiaries Avon Medical, Portex, Sims Medical Distribution, Vent-Axia
Size £726 million sales, £1.3 billion stock market value, 11,500 employees
5-year growth sales 3%, earnings per share 14%, employment -15%
Solvency debt n/a, interest cover n/a
Political donations 0
Charitable donations £600,000

Major developments
1914 formed as S Smith & Sons Motor Accessories
1965 changed to Smiths Industries
1987 bought Lear Siegler Avionics
1989 bought Avon Medical from Smith & Nephew; bought Aviation division of Louis Newmark
1991 bought Flexible Technologies (USA)
1992 bought H G Wallace; bought Vent-Axia group from APV

Outlook

Most companies which used to be major suppliers to UK car manufacturers made strenuous efforts during the 1980s to lessen their dependence on this customer market, which was apparently in terminal decline. Now that Japanese manufacturers Nissan, Toyota and Honda have revived the UK motor industry, this strategy does not seem quite so sensible as it once did, but the question is academic so far as Smiths Industries is concerned. This company went one better than the likes of GKN or Lucas, and abandoned the car industry altogether. In fact Smiths sold its last auto-component operations to Lucas in 1983, and GKN bought the distribution business the following year.

Smiths was able to do so partly because a background in clocks and instruments gave the company an early entrée into other markets. It began supplying instruments for aircraft during the First World War, and by the 1970s had a significant (though not enormous) aerospace business. The medical division had also been in place for some time, since the acquisition of Portland Plastics in 1950. So the group had less dependence on cars than most component suppliers, was generally in more specialist, high-tech businesses, and had sufficient other interests to form a base to replace its stake in the motor industry.

Another secret of the group's relative success is that, having escaped the clutches of the car industry, it was in no great hurry to find other businesses. The aerospace and medical interests, supplemented by a collection of general manufacturing businesses, were enough to be going on with. Perhaps more importantly, there was no new top management team desperate

SMITHS INDUSTRIES

Share record

Return on shareholders'' equity	%	30.43
5-year price high	p	526.0
5-year price low	p	186.0
Dividend yield	%	3.44
5-year high	%	6.63
5-year low	%	2.82
Price/earnings ratio		16.2
5-year high		19.4
5-year low		7.5

Share price performance (in pence)

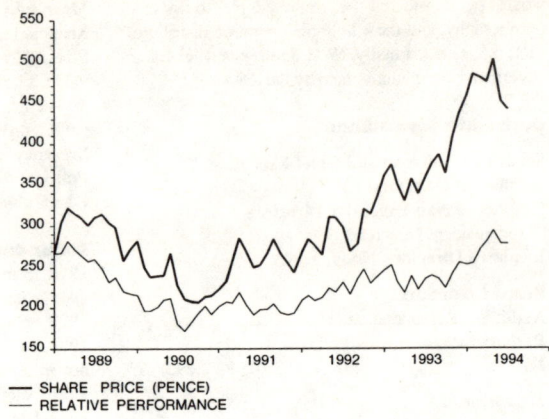

— SHARE PRICE (PENCE)
— RELATIVE PERFORMANCE

Financial record

		31/7/89	31/7/90	31/7/91	31/7/92	31/7/93
Total sales	£'000	704,900	673,000	655,500	635,300	725,800
Pre-tax profit	£'000	106,787	114,800	120,300	107,300	114,500
Published retentions	£'000	47,687	42,100	39,500	35,400	35,500
Earnings per share	p	23.77	25.84	27.61	25.01	27.06
Dividend per share	p	8.90	9.90	10.70	11.25	11.85
Operating cash flow	£'000	43,794	29,500	26,300	39,200	59,100
Net assets per share	p	101.74	112.93	114.40	122.11	124.32
Net debt/(cash)	£'000	-95,826	-115M	-79,100	-120M	-33,900
Shareholders' funds	£'000	273,191	300,400	309,300	330,000	266,700
Return on capital	%	37.09	38.28	37.49	32.57	33.54
Profit margin	%	15.15	17.06	18.35	16.83	15.69
Sales per employee	£	51.81	46.56	54.13	54.88	62.92
Interest cover		-7.96	-5.79	-6.16	-6.75	14.43
Dividend cover		2.67	2.61	2.58	2.23	2.28
Sales increase	%	5.78	-4.53	-2.60	-3.08	14.25
Earnings growth	%	13.34	8.70	6.87	-9.44	8.19
Investment x depreciation		1.10	1.02	1.19	1.19	1.19
Investment as % assets		17.34	16.82	19.24	20.53	20.55
Number of employees		13,606	14,453	12,109	11,576	11,535

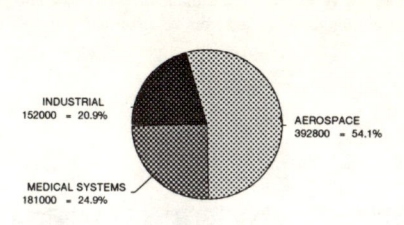

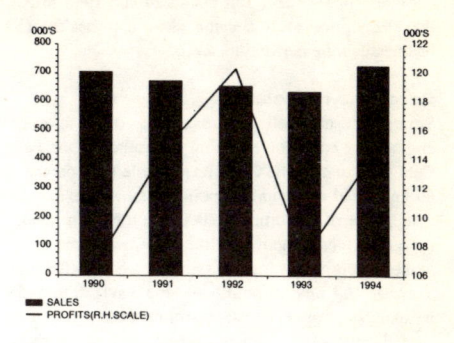

Profit analysis

INDUSTRIAL 152000 = 20.9%
MEDICAL SYSTEMS 181000 = 24.9%
AEROSPACE 392800 = 54.1%

Sales and profits

■ SALES
— PROFITS(R.H.SCALE)

---

to prove its corporate virility through takeovers and dramatic changes (as at TI, for example). Current boss Roger Hurn had been on the board since 1976 and became chief executive in 1981. Most of his top team have similarly long records of service. Moreover, their tenure has been characterised by patience – patience in waiting for the right opportunity for acquisition, and in not being sufficiently desperate to win a company that they paid wildly over the odds for it.

The right opportunity came in 1987 with the break-up of US engineering group Lear Siegler. Smiths paid $350 million for the avionics division (avionics being aviation electronics), a purchase that gave Smiths the presence in the US industry which it badly needed. Unfortunately it also increased the group's exposure to military work, just before the peace dividend led to the beginning of a long decline in military spending by many other Western governments.

That decline left Smiths needing to boost its other activities, and the acquisition of Intertech in 1992 helped to build up the medical division, which, despite a number of smaller acquisitions, had lagged behind the growth of aerospace during the 1980s, still relying substantially on its original business in plastic catheters, now known as Portex. There have also been some acquisitions to boost the industrial divisions, although these still have a miscellaneous appearance, rather than being a coherent collection of connected businesses.

Despite these purchases, the group's development has not been mainly concerned with corporate dealing. Like other engineering companies during the 1980s, it also focused on rationalisation, entailing job losses but creating more efficient manufacturing. Because of the cutbacks in military spending, this policy affected aerospace as much as the other activities: indeed Smiths was commendably early to see the need to rein in its aerospace activities as the end of the cold war upset traditional attitudes, and military budgets.

The group therefore moves forward with an interesting mix of businesses, in reasonable shape, and with a strong financial legacy from its years of cautious reorientation. It remains small in both its main markets, compared to most of its rivals, but many a small company has proved that it is possible to survive and grow in the shadow of the giants, while many a giant has shown that size is no protection from disaster.

Shares

The stock market's appreciation of Smiths Industries as a well-balanced and efficient investment peaked in 1986. The shares themselves did well in 1987 but other shares did better, causing the rating against the market as a whole to slip. Even key acquisitions, like that of Lear Siegler Avionics that July, had little impact. A more optimistic appreciation of the group's strength in earnings helped the rating recover by 1989, but a severe slide in the rating set in that summer as investors worried about the outlook for defence spending. The group won Eurofighter contracts in 1989 and 1990, but the rating did not move upwards again until mid-1990 when investors began to think that Smiths was not too greatly affected by defence cuts, had consistently good earnings, and would outperform its rivals. A steady re-rating set in, enlivened by jumps in the share price every time a big order was won.

By 1992 the company was established in City minds as a safe and predictable investment, although declining demand for aerospace and industrial products tended to offset this view. It had, however, become the star in its sector, eclipsing British Aerospace. By 1993 it seemed that the group's plan to expand its healthcare business could be an expensive option, and there was still little sign of an upturn in civil aerospace orders. But results in late 1993 lifted the share price as it became clear that healthcare businesses were performing well.

Corporate conscience

Smiths Industries belies its image as an old-fashioned engineering company by being a member of the Per Cent Club and of BITC, by its passable environmental and equal opportunities policies, as well as being a supporter of Opportunity 2000. On the other hand, the group has a significant military involvement. It makes displays and weapons aiming systems for the Tornado and other aircraft; warship navigation and weapon control systems; instrumentation for the EH101 helicopter; armoured-vehicle power distribution systems; cables and connectors for the Tomahawk cruise missile; and avionics for the F-15, F-16 and F/A-18 combat aircraft. Not surprisingly, Campaign Against the Arms Trade classifies the company as a major arms trader.

In its operations the group uses CFCs and is not yet committed to phasing them out. But it has a clean water pollution record and no recent health and safety convictions.

Corporate governance

Separate Chairman and Chief Executive N
Number of Directors 10
Number of Non-Executive Directors 5
(5 Independent Directors)
Insulated Directors None

Board Committees
Audit: Y   Remuneration: Y

Remuneration

Year end	3.08.91	3.08.92	31.07.93
Total board £M	1.35	1.29	1.53
% change	21	-4	19
Highest paid £	281,250	344,000	398,000
% change	23	22	16

Board
Hurn, F Roger *Chairman & Chief Executive*
Barber, Norman *Executive Director*
Kennedy, George *Executive Director*
Williams, Ron *Executive Director*
Taylor, Christopher *Finance Director*
Hamilton, Sir James *Independent Non-Executive*
Jarratt, Sir Alex *Independent Non-Executive*
Lyon, David *Independent Non-Executive*
Orrell-Jones, Keith *Independent Non-Executive*
Thompson, Sir Peter *Independent Non-Executive*

Roger Hurn's accession to the chairmanship on the completion of Sir Alex Jarratt's term of office in 1992 was a retrograde step since it combines the top two roles, and is only marginally excused by the fact that each of the three operating divisions has its own executive chairman. The board has a strong non-executive contingent, however, which makes up the audit committee and the appointments and remuneration committee (which also includes Mr Hurn). Yet these committees gave only minimal information on directors' pay in the 1992 annual report. The chairman is no longer insulated from re-election.

STOREHOUSE plc

The Heals Building, 196 Tottenham Court Road, London W1P 9LD
Tel: 0171 262 3456
Chairman Ian Hay Davison
Chief executive Keith Edelman
Main subsidiaries BhS, Blazer, Mothercare
Size £1.0 billion sales, £889 million stock market value, 18,100 employees
5-year growth sales -20%, earnings per share 172%, employment -40%
Solvency debt n/a, interest cover n/a
Political donations 0
Charitable donations £154,000

Major developments
1964 Habitat opened
1982 merged with Mothercare
1983 bought Richards; bought Heals
1986 became Storehouse after merger with British Home Stores
1988 launched Anonymous
1989 bought Blazer; sold stake in Savacentre to Sainsbury's
1990 sold Jacadi; Sir Terence Conran resigned; closed Anonymous; management buy-out of Heals; Conran Design Group sold; Conran Shop sold to Sir Terence Conran
1991 sold Mothercare overseas
1992 sold Habitat UK and France; sold Richards
1993 chief executive resigned and was replaced by Keith Edelman

Outlook

The story of Storehouse is about the building and the dismantling of an empire. At the start of 1983 the company which was to become Storehouse consisted of two businesses; ten years later it once again comprised two businesses. During the intervening decade it had grown dramatically and shrunk equally dramatically.

The company's genesis was in 1964 when the young Terence Conran opened his first branch of Habitat. The shop developed into a thriving chain and in 1982 merged with Mothercare; Heals and Richards were added in 1983. The deal that was intended to establish Storehouse as a force to be reckoned with came in 1986 when the company merged with British Home Stores (later to be renamed BhS). The idea

STOREHOUSE

Share record

Return on shareholders' equity	%	9.81
5-year price high	p	249.0
5-year price low	p	85.0
Dividend yield	%	3.21
5-year high	%	11.85
5-year low	%	2.51
Price/earnings ratio		19.8
5-year high		69.9
5-year low		14.2

Share price performance (in pence)

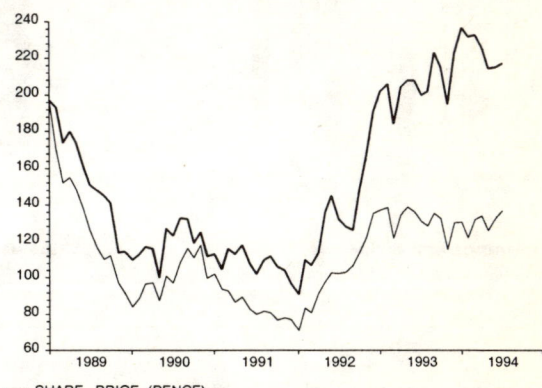

— SHARE PRICE (PENCE)
— RELATIVE PERFORMANCE

Financial record

		31/3/90	31/3/91	31/3/92	31/3/93	31/3/94
Total sales	£	1,310M	1,209M	1,180M	1,139M	1,046M
Pre-tax profit	£'000	28,700	21.800	16,184	47,800	68,800
Published retentions	£'000	-19,400	-27,600	-9,700	-20,200	17,200
Earnings per share	p	3.98	3.24	2.22	7.70	10.83
Dividend per share	p	5.00	5.00	5.00	5.00	5.50
Operating cash flow	£'000	96,800	57,500	-25,800	-51,800	25,900
Net assets per share	p	152.37	132.01	118.20	109.41	112.43
Net debt/(cash)	£'000	42,900	100	17,900	-24,400	-38,300
Shareholders' funds	£'000	484,800	453,200	438,300	423,900	446,400
Return on capital	%	8.86	6.33	4.79	11.98	15.43
Profit margin	%	2.04	1.70	0.96	3.75	6.58
Sales per employee	£	43.17	44.85	48.27	51.98	57.78
Interest cover		4.22	-17.64	-6.52	31.50	-27.67
Dividend cover		0.80	0.65	0.44	1.54	1.97
Sales increase	%	7.30	-7.76	-2.38	-3.43	-8.23
Earnings growth	%	-36.41	-18.64	-31.54	247.61	40.68
Investment x depreciation		-1.22	0.50	0.80	0.83	1.23
Investment as % assets		-13.26	5.28	8.61	10.29	9.72
Number of employees		30,352	26,945	24,440	21,916	18,095

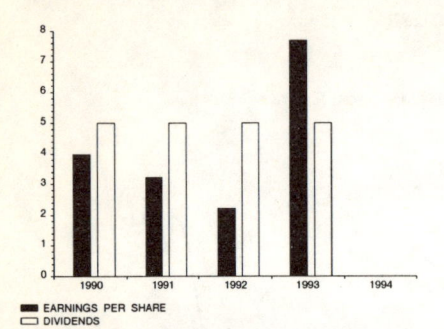

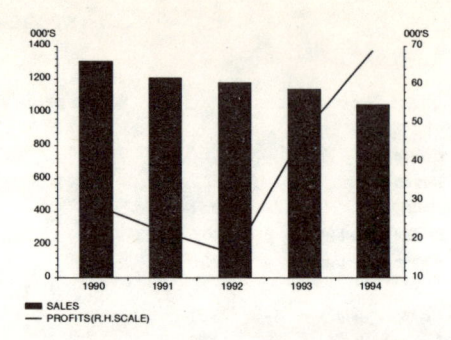

Earnings and dividends

Sales and profits

was simple: Conran believed that the application of his style to the dowdy but well-organised BhS could create a retail chain which was genuinely trendy and genuinely mass-market. The formula did not work, however.

Without doubt, BhS became more chic. But its established customers mistook that for its becoming more expensive. The chain, which had always struggled to match Marks & Spencer, lost further market share to its great rival and to groups like Next and Burton who were better at cashing in on the retail boom of the mid-1980s. In addition, Storehouse had fewer freehold sites than most of its competitors, so it suffered particularly badly from the sharp rise in shop rents between 1985 and 1989. And the company stumbled into some problems of its own making: Mothercare, for example, built a new warehouse which failed to deliver stock on time to the shops. Storehouse was slower than many of its rivals to exploit the potential of computerised tills which could monitor sales and ensure that new supplies were correctly ordered.

There were further acquisitions: Storehouse bought menswear chain Blazer in 1989 and the Jacardi children's clothing shops in 1989. But 1989 marked the turning point. By now the day-to-day running of the company had been handed over to Michael Julien, an accountant whose strengths lay in his traditional business values rather than in fashion-conscious retailing. He set about demolishing the house that Terence had built. Over the following three years Storehouse sold everything with the exception of BhS and Mothercare. In 1992, two years after Conran finally severed his links with the group he had founded, Storehouse even sold Habitat, on which the empire had been founded. The buyer was the foundation which controls Ikea, the Scandinavian retailer which arrived in Britain in the late 1980s and apparently succeeded where Habitat had failed – operating from edge-of-town warehouses selling smart furniture to young families.

Selling off the unwanted parts of Storehouse was painful: results in the early 1990s were characterised by a string of supposedly one-off 'restructuring costs' as staff were made redundant and leases were cut short. But by early 1993 the slimmed-down company at least looked a little more coherent. Under the leadership of American chief executive David Dworkin, BhS began to prosper. It cut more staff, tidied up its shops to give customers a better idea of what it was trying to concentrate on and made simple alterations such as changing the layout of its stores, turning unwanted stockroom space into selling areas.

The changes had a dramatic effect. In late 1992 BhS's sales were up by an underlying 10 per cent on a year earlier (ignoring the impact of changes in the structure of the group). The group then started to apply a similar strategy to the running of Mothercare. Unfortunately for the company, David Dworkin was lured back to the United States in early 1993, and Storehouse started looking for a successor – someone who would inherit a two-chain group very different from the rambling empire which Storehouse had become five years before. Keith Edelman was recruited from Carlton Communications in the summer of 1993. But there continued to be upheavals at the top of the organisation: Anne Iverson, who had helped revive Mothercare, left in 1994 – the tenth main-board director to quit in five years.

Shares

As a star of the 1980s retail boom Storehouse's rating against the market as a whole was at its height in 1986, although the shares themselves peaked in the 1987 bull market when the group was seen as ripe for a takeover. Trading problems became apparent at the time of an audacious bid from what was virtually a shell company, Benlox, in 1987. The stock market crashed, the bid failed, and by 1988 Storehouse's market value had halved to £1 billion.

The shares fell steadily until 1990, only perking up from time to time as takeover speculation surfaced. The main feature of this period was the weakening results. Even a stakebuilding exercise by Asher Edelman and a change of management could not stop the slide in the share price. By 1990 the company was seen as a better prospect during economic recovery than Next, though the shares were worth just 85p by December 1991 against a peak of 404p in 1987. The share rating did pick up swiftly that year despite a reduced dividend and acknowledgement that recovery was still some way off. Sir Terence Conran left the group, and restructuring gathered pace. Profits and the share price stayed low in 1991, but the following year there were signs of an improvement in the results just as chief executive Michael Julien left the board. The rise in 1992 was speeded by dismemberment of the group which was seen as helping to improve margins and sales growth. Storehouse participated in the recovery rally of 1993, but the shares dropped suddenly due to the news that David Dworkin was leaving as chief executive, then picked up towards the end of the year.

Corporate conscience

Storehouse's conscience is remarkably untroubled. It registers on only two of the EIRIS ethical criteria – advertising complaints and the use of ozone-depleting chemicals, with Mothercare having received an adverse judgement at the start of 1993. It does not sell any ethically sensitive products, and does not operate in ethically sensitive areas. Nor does it have any positive ethical attributes: no environmental or equal opportunities policies (although, until Anne Iverson's departure, there was one woman executive director); it has even been withdrawn from BITC and has stopped answering queries from EIRIS. For a group which needs all the customer goodwill it can get, that seems a rash, as well as retrogressive, step.

Corporate governance

Separate Chairman and Chief Executive Y
Number of Directors 7
Number of Non-Executive Directors 4
(4 Independent Directors)
Insulated directors Not known

Board Committees
Audit: Y   Remuneration: Y

Remuneration

Year end	31.03.92	31.03.93	02.04.94
Total board £M	1.77	4.77	1.33
% change		8	170	-72
Highest paid £M	0.41	3.29	0.61
% change		12	695	-82

Board

Edelman, Keith   *Chief Executive*
Bedford, Steve   *Executive Director*
Steele, Dick   *Finance Director*
Downes, Dr Margaret   *Independent Non-Executive*
Sorrell, Martin   *Independent Non-Executive*
Tagg, David E   *Independent Non-Executive*
Davison, Ian F Hay   *Non-Executive Chairman*

If ever a group needed a powerful board, Storehouse clearly does. Perhaps if it had included some wise non-executives in the 1980s, Sir Terence Conran's skills could have been channelled to better effect. Now the board is well-balanced, with a strong chairman and non-executive support, although that did not prevent an embarrassingly large payment being made to former chief executive David Dworkin on his premature departure. Keith Edelman's appointment as chief executive can only strengthen the board's resources, but the company badly needs to break the habit of losing directors. Disclosure of pay has improved dramatically, and includes the annualised equivalent of Keith Edelman's pay, which is shown in the table above.

TARMAC plc

Hilton Hall, Essington, Wolverhampton WV11 2BQ
Tel: 0902 307407
Chairman Sir John Banham
Chief executive Neville Simms
Main subsidiaries McLean Homes
Size £2.7 billion sales, £1.4 billion stock market value, 24,800 employees
5-year growth sales -22%, earnings per share -98%, employment -23%
Solvency debt = 17% shareholders' funds, interest cover 2 times
Political donations £12,500 Conservative Party
Charitable donations £168,000

Major developments

1984 joined in forming Channel Tunnel builders group
1988 bought Ruberoid plc
1989 bought Crown House Engineering Ltd
1992 sold Tarmac California, Briggs Oil, Bolton Brady; acquired PSA Projects from government
1993 restructured housing division; flotation of Ruberoid rights issue raised £215m; sold Econowaste

Outlook

In the spring of 1993 Tarmac reported a loss of £350 million. That included huge provisions which reflected the cost of escaping from the excesses of the 1980s, when Tarmac allowed ambition to outweigh caution.

Inextricably associated with the blacktop which gave the company its name, the group's chairman in

TARMAC plc

TARMAC

Share record

Return on shareholder's equity	%	0.47
5-year price high	p	305.5
5-year price low	p	51.2
Dividend yield	%	4.27
5-year high	%	15.46
5-year low	%	3.36
Price/earnings ratio		n/a
5-year high		n/a
5-year low		n/a

Share price performance (in pence)

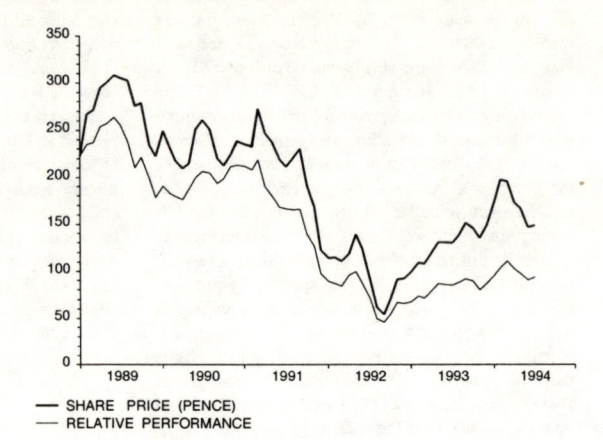

— SHARE PRICE (PENCE)
— RELATIVE PERFORMANCE

Financial record

		31/12/89	31/12/90	31/12/91	31/12/92	31/12/93
Total sales	£	3,409M	3,607M	3,225M	2,935M	2,669M
Pre-tax profit	£'000	359,200	185,800	28,200	-85,300	53,400
Published retentions	£'000	151,400	59,900	-38,600	-314M	-137M
Earnings per share	p	28.83	15.24	0.65	0.00	0.58
Dividend per share	p	10.87	10.87	5.32	5.32	5.50
Operating cash flow	£'000	7,300	-22,100	17,900	46,900	43,200
Net assets per share	p	287.65	286.43	265.32	241.52	212.46
Net debt/(cash)	£'000	456,400	409,300	452,600	472,500	188,400
Shareholders' funds	£'000	1,419M	1,600M	1,374M	1,021M	1,086M
Return on capital	%	24.38	12.43	4.38	-1.02	5.79
Profit margin	%	10.11	4.93	1.04	-2.81	1.94
Sales per employee	£	106.29	103.41	101.63	102.65	107.57
Interest cover		5.95	3.33	1.59	-0.4	2.31
Dividend cover		2.65	1.40	0.14	0.0	0.11
Sales increase	%	23.79	5.79	-10.58	-9.0	-9.05
Earnings growth	%	-10.90	-47.14	-95.73	-100.0	0.00
Investment x depreciation		1.67	1.62	0.59	0.25	0.35
Investment as % assets		6.91	7.27	2.99	1.44	2.10
Number of employees		32,073	34,876	31,734	28,590	24,814

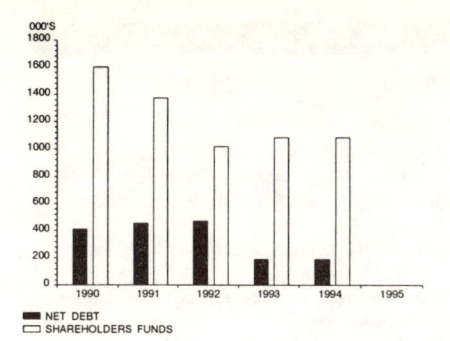

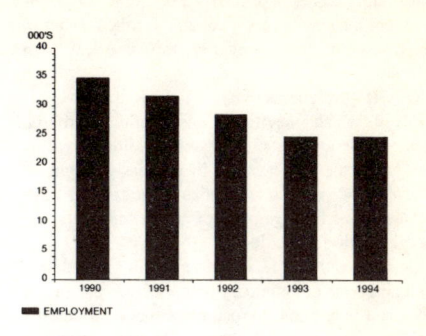

Debt and shareholders' funds

Employment

the 1980s, Sir Eric Pountain, was intent on building the UK's largest building and construction group. He achieved it, just in time to reap the whirlwind of the property and building collapse at the end of the 1980s. He had built Tarmac's housebuilding company, McLean Homes, to be the largest in the country, with a target of 15,000 completions a year. He had created a sizeable construction business, a web of property development interests, and a collection of industrial materials companies.

Neville Sims inherited the mess in 1992 and set about unwinding some of the worst involvements and scaling back the group's coverage. Hence the huge write-offs and provisions aginst the 1992 profits. Withdrawing from property was expected to cost £145 million, selling the industrial companies would incur a loss of £50 million, a further £72 million came from writing down housing land to sensible prices, while reorganisation and redundancy of the continuing businesses would cost a further £64 million.

Mr Sims decided to concentrate on just three businesses: housebuilding, construction, and quarrying. Other operations were sold where possible – Econowaste to the Hanson subsidiary ARC, readymix businesses in the US, and a number of Scottish quarries. Most substantially, the industrial operations were floated off as a separate public company in Ruberoid, raisinbg £60 million for Tarmac.

By the beginning of 1994 this strategy looked to be paying off. The disposals and rights issue had repaired the group's finances. Housing profits had begun to rise again and prospects for the other businesses were beginning to look up. But the profits had benefited from the previous year's provisions, and there were further huge write-offs which left another net loss for 1993. And even before interests costs and exceptional charges, the basic operating profit was barely ahead of the previous year's level.

At least things were moving in the right direction, however. The housing market stubbornly refused to take off, but another boom was probably the last thing that any builder needed. Construction seemed likely to be even more stubbornly stuck in the doldrums, while government anguish over the cost and environmental impact of its road-building programme suggested that there would be rather less business there than had seemed likely.

Tarmac remains Britain's biggest builder, but that remains an uncomfortable position.

Shares

Housebuilders were glamour stocks in the 1980s, and Tarmac was one of the most glamorous, especially once it managed to persuade investors that it was Britain's biggest housebuilder. By the time it did, however, the housing market was preparing to plunge, taking the shares with it. The slump began in 1989 and, after steadying in 1990 and 1991 as Tarmac's wide spread of activities temporarily seemed to offer some protection, continued with a vengeance in 1991 and 1992. Every time the worst seemed to be over, even worse news turned up, driving the shares even lower, to a nadir in autumn 1992.

Then, with the prospect of economic recovery and an improvement even in the hard-hit building sector, a muted recovery in the share price began. The appointment of Neville Sims, and his coherent strategy for rescuing the group from its troubles, encouraged investors, although by 1994 it had become apparent that there was still a long way to go and the road would be difficult, so the shares slipped back a little.

Corporate Conscience

Tarmac has attracted the wrath of roads protestors for its involvement in motorway building on Twyford Down and in Lancashire. The company has been criticised not only for building in sensitive areas – which it justifiably argues is primarily a decision of government, not the contractors – but also for the manner in which it, or its private security staff, has dealt with protestors.

This is just one activity in which the group is involved which inevitably raises ethical criteria. Quarrying is another major issue. Additionally Tarmac has some involvement in oppressive regimes, military and nuclear activities. The record also includes some infringements of health and safety and water pollution regulations.

On the positive side, the group promises (belatedly) a corporate environment policy before the end of 1994, and in response to road protestors it promised a panel of environmental experts. On the community front, it is a member of BITC.

Corporate governance

Separate Chairman and Chief Executive Y
Number of Directors 8
Number of Non-Executive Directors 4
(3 Independent Directors)
Insulated directors None

Board Committees
Audit: Y   Remuneration: Y

Remuneration

Year end	31.12.91	31.12.92	31.12.93
Total board £M	2.1	2.2	1.81
% change	12.1	1.2	-16
Highest paid £M	313,000	313,000	399,000
% change	0.6	0.6	27

Board
Simms, Neville I   *Chief Executive*
Lovering, John   *Executive Director*
McPherson, Ian G S   *Non-Executive Director*
Pickstock, Samuel F   *Executive Director*
Mason, Terence H   *Finance Director*
Brooke, Roger   *Independent Non-Executive*
Gill, Sir Anthony   *Independent Non-Executive*
Banham, Sir John   *Non-Executive Chairman*

Tarmac has the relevant structures, and since the board reorganisation in 1992 it has had a majority of non-executives and a non-executive chairman. The annual accounts give full explanation of directors' bonus schemes, which are based partly on annual performance and partly on three-year share price growth.

TATE & LYLE plc

Sugar Quay, Lower Thames Street,
London EC3R 6DQ
Tel: 0171 626 6525
Chairman and chief executive Neil Shaw
Main brands Mr Cube, Splenda, Stellar
Main subsidiaries Tunnel Refineries, United Molasses, A E Staley (US)
Size £3.7 billion sales, £1.5 billion stock market value, 15,800 employees
5-year growth sales 10%, earnings per share 18%, employment -15%
Solvency debt = 52% shareholders' funds, interest cover 5 times
Political donations £25,000 Conservative Party
Charitable donations £300,000

Major developments
1921 Tate & Lyle formed
1981 closed Liverpool sugar refinery
1984 bid for Brooke Bond beaten by Unilever
1987 Monopolies Commission blocked bid for Berisford
1988 bought A E Staley Manufacturing Co (USA); bought Amstar Sugar Corp; sold New York sugar refinery
1990 aborted second bid for Berisford; purchase of British Sugar blocked
1991 bought Bundaberg Sugar Company (Australia); launched Sucralose (synthetic sweetener)

Outlook
For decades Tate & Lyle was a comfortable old family business with a dominant position in a stable market. Then Britain joined the European Community and the sugar empire began to dissolve. The EC sugar regime discriminates against cane sugar (imported from tropical countries) in favour of the beet which is grown in Europe. Since Tate & Lyle's business was based on cane from the Commonwealth, the cosy company was thrown into turmoil. Unexpectedly, the group emerged from that trauma much stronger than it had been before. After toying with product diversification, it decided to focus on sugar and starch and has grown by spreading into other countries, building a sizeable business in the United States, extending the European base in Britain on to the Continent and establishing a presence elsewhere in the world.

The outcome might have been very different but for the presence of chief executive Neil Shaw, who led the group for most of the 1980s and into the 1990s, and but for the deep pocket of Unilever, which outbid Tate & Lyle in a contest for Brooke Bond in 1984. This was not the only takeover bid by Tate & Lyle to be thwarted; it made a series of unsuccessful assaults on British Sugar, the Silver Spoon company whose operations are based on beet. Tate & Lyle was one of several admirers interested in

TATE & LYLE

Share record

Return on shareholders' equity	%	23.42
5-year price high	p	466.0
5-year price low	p	233.0
Dividend yield	%	4.05
5-year high	%	5.38
5-year low	%	3.39
Price/earnings ratio		11.2
5-year high		16.7
5-year low		6.9

Share price performance (in pence)

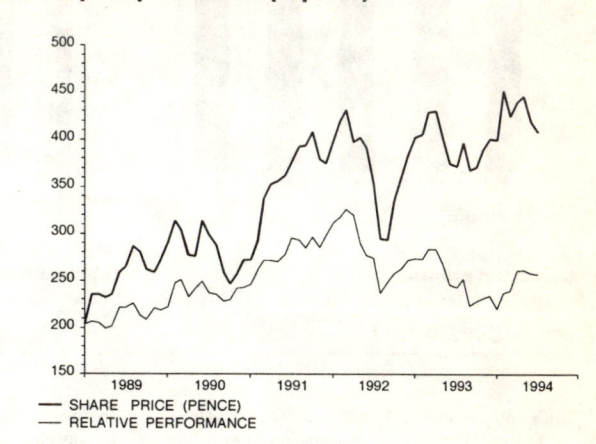

— SHARE PRICE (PENCE)
— RELATIVE PERFORMANCE

Financial record

		30/9/89	30/9/90	30/9/91	30/9/92	30/9/93
Total sales	£	3,360M	3,380M	3,221M	3,294M	3,698M
Pre-tax profit	£'000	199,000	218,600	234,600	190,000	223,800
Published retentions	£'000	69,100	128,600	91,900	59,300	88,900
Earnings per share	p	29.44	32.58	37.81	28.23	34.00
Dividend per share	p	9.00	10.00	11.20	12.00	13.00
Operating cash flow	£'000	54,400	140,700	-29,700	-50,800	118,200
Net assets per share	p	345.93	348.05	412.32	389.99	424.62
Net debt/(cash)	£'000	770,500	403,200	552,700	641,900	626,600
Shareholders' funds	£'000	820,500	907,000	1,063M	1,132M	1,217M
Return on capital	%	27.94	28.75	25.38	20.10	21.57
Profit margin	%	5.64	6.32	7.17	5.64	5.77
Sales per employee	£	180.64	202.73	199.34	193.72	233.55
Interest cover		3.68	4.49	5.56	4.79	5.49
Dividend cover		3.27	3.26	3.38	2.35	2.62
Sales increase	%	60.89	0.58	-4.69	2.26	12.27
Earnings growth	%	28.71	10.69	16.04	-25.33	20.43
Investment x depreciation		1.35	1.12	1.69	2.05	1.08
Investment as % assets		12.41	10.17	11.96	14.52	8.84
Number of employees		18,600	16,670	16,159	17,004	15,834

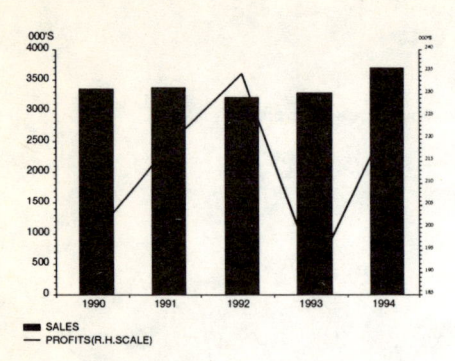

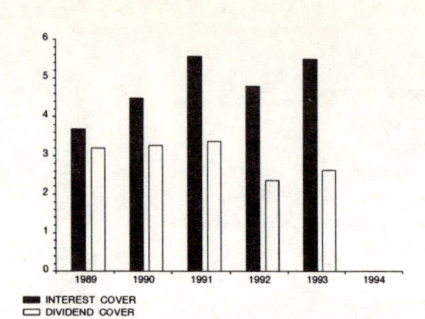

Sales and profits

Interest and dividend cover

British Sugar in the early 1980s, but was rebuffed by the Monopolies Commission – not surprisingly, since the combined companies would account for virtually all the UK sugar market. Unabashed, Tate & Lyle returned with bids for British Sugar's new owner, S & W Berisford, in 1987 and again in 1990. It also considered trying to buy the sugar company from the struggling Berisford in 1990, after abandoning plans for a full takeover. All this came to nought, however, with British Sugar eventually ending up in the hands of Associated British Foods.

Tate & Lyle had more success in the US, where it built up a diversified starch and sweetener business through a series of takeovers. Initially these were fairly small but in the late 1980s the group joined in the rush for making huge bids. The largest was the acquisition of Staley Continental in the US in 1988, which cost a net $1 billion even after various disposals. Staley had made a name for itself by extracting corn syrup from maize, and thereby cornering the lion's share of the market for non-diet soft-drink sweeteners. The addition of Staley gave the UK group a triple-pronged US business, in cane, beet and corn syrup, but it was further supplemented with another takeover. This time the victim was Amstar Sugar, the largest US cane refiner, otherwise known as Domino.

Mr Shaw's strategy has not been entirely acquisition-based, although there were other important deals such as Bundaberg in Australia and CST on the Continent. He has also ruthlessly pursued cost reduction in the UK business, controversially closing the Liverpool sugar refinery in 1981, for example.

In addition, Tate & Lyle has invested heavily in product development, which, on the face of it, seems strange for a company whose product seems as developed as it can ever be. Development has come through alternative carbohydrate products to sugar, notably the highly concentrated, sugar-based sweet-

ener Sucralose, known as Splenda, and a starch-based fat substitute sold as Stellar. These products have potential as diet-food ingredients in an age of calorie awareness, although there are doubts about that potential. The emergence of Sucralose was long delayed by the apparently interminable process of getting approval from the US Food and Drug Administration, despite having the backing of Johnson & Johnson, the US group which had been taken on by Tate & Lyle as a partner in the joint venture. By the mid-1990s, however, Splenda should make a significant contribution to Tate & Lyle's profits. Perhaps more significant, however, is the way in which this project illustrates how it is possible to develop specialist products for the food-manufacturing industry.

Although Tate & Lyle will remain essentially a commodities group for the foreseeable future, prone to swings in profit, it is regarded as more immune than some companies to retail-price pressure, and at least its business cycles follow a predictable pattern. Cash flow is regarded as good and the group benefits from being a world leader.

Shares

Tate & Lyle shed its image as a 'boring' defensive stock in 1987 when it first bid for S & W Berisford. The deal proved abortive but the shares rose against the market, and gained further after the 1987 crash because they were seen as a relatively safe haven. The next year Tate & Lyle embarked on a string of deals which caused the rating to be revised upwards, starting a trend which would continue until 1992. The only factor depressing the share price in 1989 was that high borrowings implied there would be a need for a rights issue. But the group did not make one, the profits from its acquisitions came through, and more deals were signalled. The shares then lost momentum as the group made a further bid for Berisford in 1990. Once again the deal fell through, and in 1991 Tate &

Lyle pressed on instead with overseas acquisitions. In a time of recession, investors were attracted to the company's strong cash flow and internal efficiency, as well as its claims to be more than a commodity business. There was also the prospect of long-term growth as the benefit of acquisitions and new products fed through, so the shares assumed a star rating.

They fell sharply in 1992, however, when the group reported the first fall in profits for 14 years and stated that US authorities had temporarily halted production of Sucralose. For the following two years the shares underperformed the market by 29 per cent, but by the start of 1994 were looking poised to gain from the economic recovery and analysts' support.

Corporate conscience

Since Neil Shaw is chairman of BITC, the group's commitment to community involvement can hardly be questioned. This is evident also from the company's annual report, which is one of a growing number which treat community and environmental affairs as a subject to be treated equally seriously as other aspects of the business.

Despite this, however, its conscience is not entirely untroubled. A subsidiary of the Australian associate, Bundaberg, makes rum; and the group is indirectly involved in alcohol production because some of its sales go to the brewing and distilling industry. It is also sometimes required by regulation to test products on animals. An associate has sugar estates in Zimbabwe – a country which offends ethical standards because it keeps prisoners of conscience – and a handful of the group's South African workers is paid below minimum living standards. These are all minor ethical transgressions, however, and the group's legal record is likewise only slightly blemished, with only one health and safety conviction. On the other hand, this incident entailed loss of life, and a fine of £100,000. The company has no convictions for water pollution, and only one parameter was exceeded (5 times) in 1990/91.

On the plus side, Tate & Lyle has a positive environmental record (if you are happy with its basic business of importing cash crops), operating a sound policy and having won some awards for development in the Third World. The group's employment record is marred by some serious disputes in the past, and its equal opportunity policies are inadequate, although the group does support Opportunity 2000 and Mr Shaw's conscientious approach includes a strong commitment to training and education.

Corporate governance

Separate Chairman and Chief Executive Y
Number of Directors 12
Number of Non-Executive Directors 8
(5 Independent Directors)
Insulated Directors None

Board Committees
Audit: Y   Remuneration: Y

Remuneration

Year end	30.09.91	30.09.92	25.09.93
Total board £M	2.14	3.22	4.40
% change	-26	50	38
Highest paid £	436,000	375,000	361,000
% change	-23	-14	-4

Board

Shaw, Neil M *Executive Chairman*
Mirsky, P J *Executive Director*
Walker, John *Executive Director*
Lewis, P S *Finance Director*
Hayes, Sir Brian *Independent Non-Executive*
Lady Prior *Independent Non-Executive*
Lord Walker *Independent Non-Executive*
Tate, H S *Independent Non-Executive*
Taylor, Jonathan F *Independent Non-Executive*
Callebaut, P M E *Non-Executive*
Powers, R M *Non-Executive*
Wilson, L R *Non-Executive*

The departure of chief executive Stephen Brown in March 1993, after only 11 months in the job, should have sounded alarm bells for Tate & Lyle investors, especially as a 'culture clash' was given by way of explanation, followed by forceful chairman Neil Shaw assuming Mr Brown's chief executive duties. Merging the top two roles was mitigated slightly by the creation of chief executives for the business divisions, and by the board including a majority of non-executives. The independent non-executives, on the other hand, feature too many titles and too few strong executives from other top companies. By mid-1993 the group had fallen into line with the Cadbury Report, however, and made improvements in the amount of disclosure in the annual report.

TAYLOR WOODROW plc

World Trade Centre, 1 St Katherine's Way, London E1 9TW
Tel: 0171 355 4848
Chairman Colin Parsons
Chief executive Anthony Palmer
Main subsidiaries Greenham, Myton, Taywood, Taymech
Size £1.1 billion sales, £602 million stock market value, 8,500 employees
5-year growth sales -11%, earnings per share -4%, employment -8%
Solvency debt = 23% shareholders' funds, interest cover 3 times
Political donations £91,000 Conservative Party
Charitable donations £127,000

TAYLOR WOODROW

Share record

Return on shareholder's equity	%	3.56
5-year price high	p	319.3
5-year price low	p	35.0
Dividend yield	%	1.30
5-year high	%	31.01
5-year low	%	0.69
Price/earnings ratio		28.5
5-year high		36.1
5-year low		14.0

Share price performance (in pence)

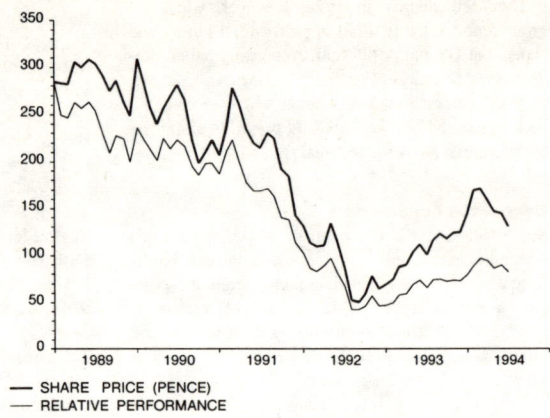

— SHARE PRICE (PENCE)
— RELATIVE PERFORMANCE

Financial record

		31/12/89	31/12/90	31/12/91	31/12/92	31/12/93
Total sales	£	1,285M	1,412M	1,395M	1,150M	1,150M
Pre-tax profit	£'000	69,700	48,300	-18,200	-71,600	33,400
Published retentions	£'000	40,500	24,000	-68,600	-93,800	10,800
Earnings per share	p	8.75	6.07	0.00	0.00	5.05
Dividend per share	p	8.68	9.16	9.50	1.00	1.50
Operating cash flow	£'000	-5,600	37,100		-42,600	120,400
Net assets per share	p	344.98	266.98	229.40	161.65	170.74
Net debt/(cash)	£'000	196,40	205,100	156,000	228,600	122,700
Shareholders' funds	£'000	857,300	677,600	677,000	525,000	531,300
Return on capital	%	8.71	7.14	0.48	-5.94	8.24
Profit margin	%	5.42	3.63	-1.32	-5.63	3.11
Sales per employee	£	139.69	156.24	156.97	112.04	135.99
Interest cover		4.52	1.68	-8.96	-2.77	3.22
Dividend cover		1.01	0.66	0.00	0.00	3.37
Sales increase	%	6.63	9.82	-1.21	-17.52	-0.04
Earnings growth	%	-41.70	-30.57	-100.00	0.00	0.00
Investment x depreciation		-2.77	-0.40	-0.34	-0.91	-3.86
Investment as % assets		-32.19	-4.62	-3.66	-14.26	-60.63
Number of employees		9,202	9,035	8,884	10,266	8,454

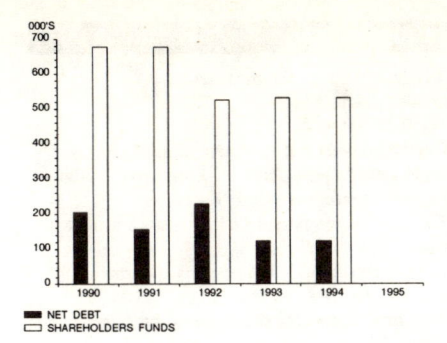

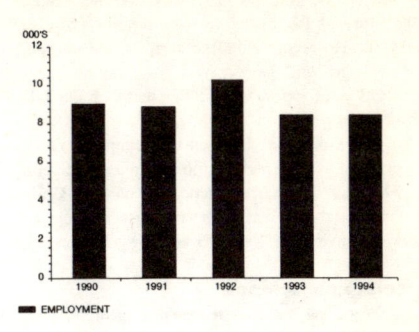

Debt and shareholders' funds

Employment

Major developments
1935 formed as Taylor Woodrow Estates
1943 changed to Taylor Woodrow Ltd
1984 joined Channel Tunnel builders group
1988 P&O built 10% share stake
1989 expanded property development interests; P&O shares
1991 bought stake in Y J Lovell

Outlook
Taylor Woodrow is a good example of a near-disaster turned overnight success. Badly hit by the 1990s property slump, this housebuilding, construction and property group bounced back into the black in 1993 with pre-tax profits of £30 million – against losses of £94 million in the previous year – leaving its critics dumbfounded. Colin Parsons, the group's chairman, attributed the turnaround to a solid, back-to-basics effort by the management team. Costs were slashed and the company continued to commit itself to a policy of not bidding for cut-throat contracting work, while maintaining its withdrawal from speculative development. All in all, Taylor Woodrow was very much the darling of City analysts in the spring of 1994, most of whom seemed to believe that its shares represented good value for at least the next year or so.

The group has dug its corporate fingers deep into several sectors. Its biggest area of activity remains property: at the end of 1993 it had nearly £500 million of investment properties, generating between them more than £40 million in income a year. This makes Taylor Woodrow one of the largest property companies in Britain. St Katherine's Dock in London is the group's single largest property asset, accounting for about half of the company's UK office portolio, but has lost almost half its value since 1989. Taylor Woodrow's property division has also extended its tentacles into Canada and the US, although exposure to the latter has been earmarked for reduction.

The company is also heavily involved in contracting and housing. Throughout 1993 Colin Parsons stuck to his guns and insisted that the group would not bid for contracting work that would not produce a profit. But the competition has been so fierce among contractors that this has proved a hard strategy to maintain, and a close analysis of the group's figures suggest that in reality Taylor Woodrow may not have implemented its policy quite as successfully as it would have observers believe.

Up to 85 per cent of the company's contracting work is in the UK, split between civil engineering and opencast coal mining, general building contracting, and management contracting, including work for the water companies. Although losses have forced the group to close its contracting businesses in Australia, Canada and the US, it operates in several other overseas areas, such as in Malaysia and Ghana.

As regards housing, the company appears to have stolen a march over many of its rivals. It started to expand its UK housebuilding activity in 1992, at a time when the sector looked moribund. This strategy has left it well placed to take advantage of the definite, if measured, return to health of the UK housing sector. The housing division is also actively buying and selling houses and plots of land in the US, Canada, Australia and Spain: in 1993 total sales worldwide stood at 2,769.

Although contracting, housing and property comprise the backbone of Taylor Woodrow, it also has a few small trading businesses. The main two are Greenham Trading, which operates in the UK, Denmark and Germany and acts as a wholesaler for equipment such as contractor tools, and Greenham Construction materials, which produces aggregates and block paving. The group's future rests on its core building business, however, and having survived the vicious recession of the early 1990s, the rest of the decade offers the prospect of steady recovery.

396   THORN EMI plc

Shares
Like most housebuilders, Taylor Woodrow basked in the glory of the boom days of home buying in the 1980s. However, after the turn of the decade, things changed and Taylor Woodrow was hit badly in the US even before it felt the teeth of the UK recession.

The shares dived in 1992 as the company, along with many of its key rivals, wallowed in a sea of debt. By 1994, thanks to the persistence of chairman Colin Parsons, plus the revival in the property market, the shares appeared once again to be rising inexorably.

Corporate conscience
Taylor Woodrow makes a reasonable effort to be a good corporate citizen, but infringes several ethical criteria by the nature of its business. It is a member of Business in the Community and has developed environmental policies. But the group's activities involve it in military and nuclear operations, quarrying and ozone-depleting chemicals. Unusually for a construction company, however, Taylor Woodrow has a clean health and safety record.

Corporate governance

Separate Chairman and Chief Executive Y
Number of Directors 11
Number of Non-Executive Directors 3
(3 Independent Directors)
Insulated Directors None

Board Committees
Audit: Y   Remuneration: Y

Remuneration
Year end	31.12.91	31.12.92	31.12.93
Total board £M	1.63	1.41	0.83
% change		-14	-11
Highest paid £	147,000	159,000	158,000
% change		8	-1

Board
Palmer, H Anthony *Chief Executive*
Parsons, Colin J *Executive Chairman*
Borwell, George B *Executive Director*
Egerton, K R *Executive Director*
Hedges, Peter *Executive Director*
Hogbin, Walter *Executive Director*
Smith, Robert G *Executive Director*
Green, David A *Finance Director*
Hambro, Charles E A *Independent Non-Executive*
McMahon, Sir Kit *Independent Non-Executive*
Russell, Sir George *Independent Non-Executive*

Recession, as well as the Cadbury Code, has helped this company come close to required standards of corporate governance. When Colin Parsons took over as chairman in 1992 he introduced several board changes, including the addition of a third non-executive director. The board has also been suitably tight-fisted over pay, considering its abysmal financial performance.

THORN-EMI plc
4 Tenterden Street, Hanover Square,
London W1A 2AY
Tel: 0171 355 4848

Chairman and chief executive Colin Southgate
Main subsidiaries Chrysalis, EMI, HMV, Radio Rentals, Rumbelows, Virgin Records
Size £4.5 billion sales, £4.6 billion stock market value, 49,400 employees
5-year growth sales 35%, earnings per share -19%, employment -24%
Solvency debt = 25% shareholders' funds, interest cover 10 times
Political donations 0
Charitable donations £3.5 million

Major developments
1928 formed as Electric Lamp Service Co
1980 became Thorn-EMI after merger
1982 bought Datasolve from BOC
1984 acquired the government's stake in Inmos
1988 bought Visionhire TV rental
1989 bought SBK Entertainment World Inc; bought 50% of Chrysalis Records; sold Inmos to SGS-Thomson
1990 bought music publisher Filmtrax
1991 sold Thorn Lighting to General Electric (USA); bought BET's stake in Thames TV; bought Virgin Music; sold Thorn-EMI Software; bought remaining 50% of Chrysalis Records
1992 Thames TV lost franchise
1993 sold stake in Thames Television to Pearson

Outlook
Thorn was an electrical conglomerate, a sort of mini GEC. EMI, of course, was a music business. Apart from the fact that electricity drives the machines that play the music, the main thing the two companies had in common when they merged in 1979 was an over-dependence on the UK. The last thing either company needed was to join forces with a business possessing a similar weakness.

For a while there was an attempt to build up the technology side of the merged group, using music as the cash source. But this foundered on the rock of the implacably unprofitable Inmos microchip business, while music made matters worse by declining rather than sustaining the rest of the group. Inmos brought down technology-lover Peter Laister and elevated Colin Southgate as chairman and chief executive, who ironically came from a technology-based background, joining the group with the acquisition of Datasolve from BOC in 1982. Mr Southgate has devoted his time at the top to reducing the Thorn element in the group and building up EMI.

The figures suggest that he has been extremely successful. Music now provides the majority of profits, and is highly international in nature, whereas

THORN-EMI

Share record

Return on shareholders' equity	%	258.03
5-year price high	p	1156.0
5-year price low	p	557.5
Dividend yield	%	3.99
5-year high	%	6.88
5-year low	%	3.46
Price/earnings ratio		19.7
5-year high		22.6
5-year low		8.7

Share price performance (in pence)

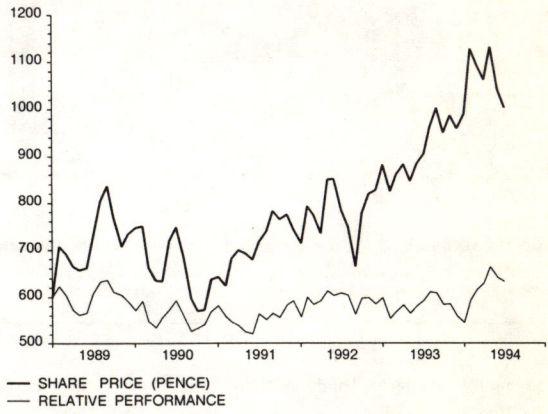

— SHARE PRICE (PENCE)
— RELATIVE PERFORMANCE

Financial record

		31/3/89	31/3/90	31/3/91	31/3/92	31/3/93
Total sales	£	3,291M	3,716M	3,660M	3,954M	4,452M
Pre-tax profit	£'000	289,100	317,500	258,700	255,300	341,800
Published retentions	£'000	96,400	147,800	15,600	-39,400	49,700
Earnings per share	p	60.02	66.38	53.76	46.82	48.92
Dividend per share	p	25.91	28.79	29.27	30.10	32.00
Operating cash flow	£'000	46,400	165,700	-8,100	76,100	61,500
Net assets per share	p	388.56	395.41	397.71	425.94	268.12
Net debt/(cash)	£'000	166,800	316,100	394,200	350,800	476,200
Shareholders' funds	£'000	590,000	1,297M	1,368M	1,370M	1,936M
Return on capital	%	30.48	34.24	28.33	25.79	33.70
Profit margin	%	8.08	7.99	6.74	6.21	7.22
Sales per employee	£	50.28	60.79	63.18	73.56	90.07
Interest cover		9.63	7.21	6.06	6.45	9.58
Dividend cover		2.32	2.31	1.84	1.56	1.53
Sales increase	%	7.75	12.91	-1.49	8.03	12.59
Earnings growth	%	17.16	10.58	-19.00	-12.92	4.50
Investment x depreciation		1.17	0.91	1.10	0.91	0.91
Investment as % assets		36.12	28.83	33.51	30.10	30.63
Number of employees		65,444	61,124	57,932	53,757	49,433

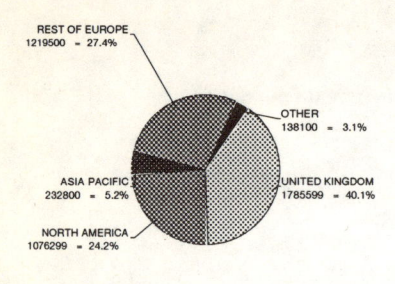

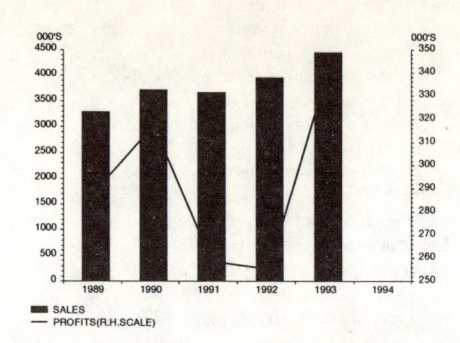

Sales analysis

- REST OF EUROPE 1219500 = 27.4%
- OTHER 138100 = 3.1%
- UNITED KINGDOM 1785599 = 40.1%
- ASIA PACIFIC 232800 = 5.2%
- NORTH AMERICA 1076299 = 24.2%

Sales and profits

SALES
PROFITS (R.H. SCALE)

---

technology contributes hardly anything. Most of the remainder of profits comes from the rental shops (DER and Radio Rentals in Britain, Rent-a-center in the US, and others around the world). The success has been a little haphazard, however. Attempts to sell defence electronics and lighting came to nothing, though the lamps business was eventually sold, leaving Thorn owning just the light fittings. Thorn-EMI's shareholding in Thames Television also has an erratic history. Having been blocked from selling its stake to Carlton in 1985 when that group was considered by the Independent Broadcasting Authority to be unsuitable, Thorn-EMI felt obliged in 1992 to buy out its ailing partner, BET, in the run-up to the new franchise awards, only to find Thames losing its slot – to Carlton – and leaving Thorn-EMI with a large share in an independent television production company. It was eventually relieved of this burden in 1993 when Pearson bought Thames.

Many sales did go through, however. During the 1980s the group bid farewell to Ferguson televisions, Kenwood kitchen equipment, and other famous brands such as Bendix, Parkinson Cowan and Tricity. Mr Southgate has even cut the umbilical cord and sold to its managers the software business from which he came. In addition, Thorn-EMI has stopped selling electrical equipment, through Rumbelows, with the chain being partly closed and partly converted to rental. The money has been spent largely on building up the music operation and internationalising the whole group. New labels have been acquired, including Chrysalis and Virgin (following repeated assertions by Richard Branson that his music business was not for sale).

As a result, Thorn-EMI has shot up the world music rankings, achieving the group's ambition of being among the top three operators in each of its markets. The same applies to rental, where it is market leader in the UK. Music and rental now constitute the core business of Thorn-EMI; a collection of other operations remain, but very much on sufferance, until somebody will offer enough to take them off the group's hands.

It is an interesting mix, with music becoming highly valued as an item of 'software' in the new electronic age. Music is potentially volatile, though, profits being dependent on the success of individual artists and albums in any one year. Rental, on the other hand, should be more stable, although this was not the case following the collapse of the consumer-spending boom in the late 1980s. The sad thing is, however, that neither Thorn nor EMI were aiming in this direction when they agreed to the merger, and each could probably have achieved something similar, with much less pain, by a different route. Speculation in 1994 suggested that a demerger might happen, which would take the group back to square one.

Shares

Thorn-EMI's shares enjoyed their highest rating in the early 1980s when the group was a diversified business. In 1985 problems with the Inmos microchip subsidiary and the consequent change of chairman and chief executive, which triggered a period of reorganisation and contraction that did not end until 1987, unsettled the stock market's view of the group. Early in 1989 the shares were finally re-rated as investors were encouraged by the purchase of a back catalogue of 'golden oldie' music which strengthened the entertainment side of the business and offset concerns about the rental and service businesses.

The shares soared in 1989 after the group sold off Inmos. But the rating against the market as a whole was uninspiring. Thorn-EMI failed to sell its defence businesses, though it did get rid of its consumer credit operation. Despite strong results, the rating did not rise throughout the following year as investors worried about internal changes at the group and its failure to sell the lighting division. The shares turned down after poor interim results, and early in 1991 the board issued a profit warning.

The bid for Thames Television did nothing to reduce investors' fears, and did little to clear up confusion about where the group was heading. However, Thorn-EMI remained strong financially, was standing up to recession well and its music business was gaining new fans in the market. The share rating picked up at the end of 1991 as investors took these factors into account, and in 1992 when the group took action over the troubled Rumbelows operation.

The shares fell suddenly in 1992 after the purchase of Virgin's music business, reflecting shareholders' concerns about the integration of the two. The shares then recovered in 1993 as investors became aware of the merits of a 'software catalogue' to complement the group's strong cash flow.

Corporate conscience

Thorn-EMI is most famous these days for its music, but the Thorn part of the business retains a significant military involvement (although negotiations to sell their businesses to the French company Thomson CSF were under way in June 1994), and that is the main ethical concern for the company.

Apart from these involvements, the company's record is reasonably clean. Like other international groups, Thorn-EMI has a presence in countries with questionable regimes, mainly India. And it uses ozone-depleting chemicals – CFCs in fridges and freezers, and as a solvent cleaner in manufacturing. Its water pollution record is clear, but there were 3 health and safety convictions in 1988–92, one of which was for Babcock Thorn, another for what is now GE-Thorn lamps. There were also 3 advertising complaints in 1991. A few of its black South African workforce are paid below reasonable levels.

Thorn-EMI's strongest suit ethically is on the social and employment front. The group is a big supporter of BITC, a member of the Per Cent Club, and hence a major donor to charities. It has an advanced environmental policy, including independent audit, and is more progressive than many groups on the issue of equal opportunities. Following a major internal survey of women in the group in 1989, a campaign was launched to correct previous weaknesses in the employment policy. There are several women directors of operating subsidiaries. The group now monitors disabled employees, in addition to women and those from ethnic minorities.

Corporate governance

Separate Chairman and Chief Executive N
Number of Directors 10
Number of Non-Executive Directors 6
(6 Independent Directors)
Insulated Directors MD

Board Committees
Audit: Y   Remuneration: Y

TI GROUP plc   399

Remuneration

Year end	31.03.92	31.03.93	31.03.94
Total board £M	5.40	7.04	9.34
% change	21	31	33
Highest paid £	419,749	702,759	584,977
% change	5	67	-18

Board
Southgate, Sir Colin G *Chairman & Chief Executive*
Fifield, James *Executive Director*
Metcalf, Michael *Executive Director*
Duffy, Simon *Finance Director*
Barnes, J D F *Independent Non-Executive*
Day, Sir Graham *Independent Non-Executive*
Einsmann, Dr Harald *Independent Non-Executive*
Lord Griffiths *Independent Non-Executive*
Nicoli, Eric *Independent Non-Executive*
Walters, Sir Peter *Independent Non-Executive*

Thorn-EMI combines the top two posts of chairman and chief executive, although it makes amends by having a powerful non-executive contingent which forms a majority of the board. The company has also been slow to adopt higher standards of disclosure, especially regarding the operation of the board and the constitution of non-executive committees. The 1993 annual report showed a great improvement, however, all the more necessary given the large payments to US music boss James Fifield – whose remuneration is not included in the table as he is not a UK director. In 1993 he received what amounted to £13 million in total.

TI GROUP plc

Lambourne Court, Abingdon Business Park,
Abingdon, Oxon OX14 1UH
Tel: 01235 555570
Chairman and chief executive Sir Christopher Lewinton
Main subsidiaries Bundy, John Crane, Dowty
Size £1.4 billion sales, £1.8 billion stock market value, 24,000 employees
5-year growth sales 50%, earnings per share -21%, employment 38%
Solvency debt = 15% shareholders' funds, interest cover 11 times
Political donations 0
Charitable donations £191,000

Major developments
1919 formed as Tube Investments
1982 changed to TI Group
1986 sold Russell Hobbs
1987 sold Raleigh Bicycles sold Creda and New World cookers, Parkray boilers; bought John Crane

TI GROUP

Share record

Return on shareholders' equity	%	30.38
5-year price high	p	451.0
5-year price low	p	185.0
Dividend yield	%	3.61
5-year high	%	6.58
5-year low	%	3.01
Price/earnings ratio		21.6
5-year high		28.4
5-year low		6.7

Share price performance (in pence)

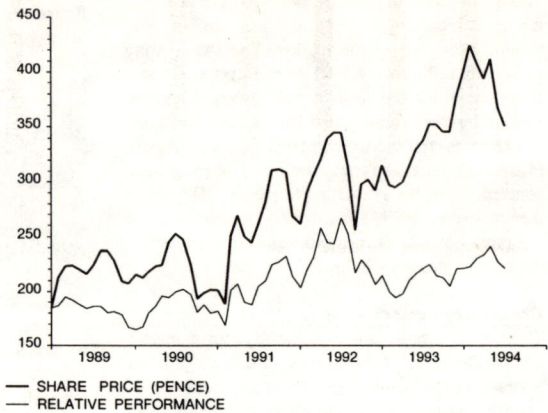

— SHARE PRICE (PENCE)
— RELATIVE PERFORMANCE

Financial record

		31/12/89	31/12/90	31/12/91	31/12/92	31/12/93
Total sales	£'000	926,900	893,600	899,500	1,149M	1,393M
Pre-tax profit	£'000	110,300	118,300	100,900	100,200	125,200
Published retentions	£'000	59,800	52,100	38,600	7,100	31,900
Earnings per share	p	22.77	24.39	21.05	18.79	18.08
Dividend per share	p	8.75	9.75	10.25	10.70	11.25
Operating cash flow	£'000	48,800	36,400	200	21,300	28,800
Net assets per share	p	120.26	117.31	127.60	220.23	159.89
Net debt/(cash)	£'000	-43,300	-50,000	38,800	242,700	191,000
Shareholders' funds	£'000	603,600	650,200	715,500	1,226M	1,259M
Return on capital	%	33.47	34.25	29.85	21.03	20.89
Profit margin	%	11.51	13.00	11.10	8.67	9.01
Sales per employee	£	53.27	52.56	52.60	53.46	58.03
Interest cover		-55.11	-9.36	-11.78	25.29	10.57
Dividend cover		2.60	2.50	2.05	1.76	1.61
Sales increase	%	-3.34	-3.59	0.66	27.77	21.19
Earnings growth	%	30.39	7.11	-13.70	-10.72	-3.81
Investment x depreciation		1.91	1.26	1.31	1.22	0.85
Investment as % assets		20.96	14.73	14.72	10.55	10.61
Number of employees		17,400	17,000	17,100	21,500	24,000

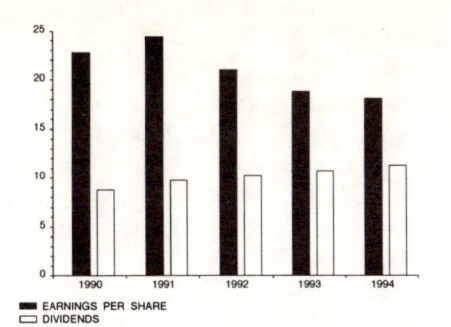

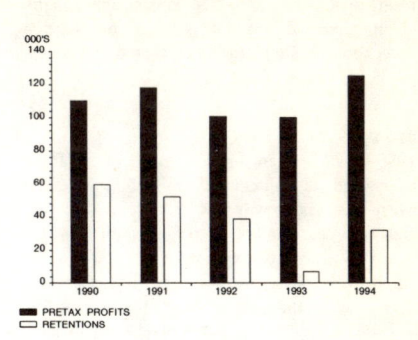

Earnings and dividends

Profits and retentions

1988 bought Bundy
1992 bought Dowty Group
1993 put Dowty landing gear business into joint venture with SNECMA, France

Outlook

Of all the British engineering companies stricken by the recession of 1980, TI superficially appeared to have the best prospects. Thanks to nationalisation, it had escaped from some of its steel-making activities, remaining in the ostensibly more promising areas of aluminium and specialised tubes. In addition, it had already moved into consumer businesses, notably Raleigh bicycles, Creda cookers and Russell Hobbs electrical equipment. In the event, however, TI was no better placed, and in some cases in a worse position, than Smiths Industries or Siebe. Despite a substantial departure from its pre-war status as the world leader in the manufacturing of precision steel tubes, TI was still considered to be a very British company: insular despite its exports, and with too much emphasis on production at the expense of concern for its customers and markets.

Sir Christopher Lewinton changed all that – a British American whose marketing background in the US giant Allegheny International (which once owned Wilkinson Sword) was about as far as you could get from that of the Midlands engineers who had run Tube Investments (as the company was known before the name was contracted to 'TI' in 1982). And under his direction, the group has been transformed in the same degree. It is now based on three acquisitions made since Sir Christopher's arrival in 1986, although tubes are still an important business. The consumer interests were quickly sold, including the troublesome Raleigh bicycle business, and most of the other operations have since followed suit, or are earmarked for eventual disposal.

The new TI has been built on the acquisition of specialist engineering companies John Crane (making seals for use mainly in the oil, motor, chemical and food-processing industries), Bundy (which is a US-based tube-maker) and Dowty, the ailing UK aerospace engineering company. Bundy's dealings with the US motor industry has meant that this sector remains an important customer for TI, though the group has sought to provide more 'added value', supplying assemblies rather than individual parts, for example, but which incorporate specialist components to assist the car assemblers, thereby enhancing the supplier's profitability.

The acquisition of Dowty in 1992 gave TI the third 'leg' which Sir Christopher had long craved. It also imparted to the group's existing aerospace interests the scale that they badly needed. In return, the application of TI management gave Dowty the direction and aggression which it had seemingly lacked as it meandered into computing rather than building on its key strengths. As with all acquirers, there have been questions about the extent to which TI's success since the mid-1980s has been due to its management and how much has been due to its accounting. TI certainly pushed acquisition accounting to its limits, and the retained-profit figures are also rather less impressive than the pre-tax profits or earnings per share, highlighting the extent of 'below-the-line' charges. TI is also unusual in its poor record of sales per employee.

The TI that was emerging from the recession of the early 1990s seemed in much better shape than its predecessor of a decade before. It is clearly a much more international operation now, although there is a long way to go in building up business in the Far East. It appears to be a more defensible business, in that its specialisms are more 'special', with more significant market positions than the likes of Creda or Raleigh. It may have been lucky

TI GROUP plc

to survive the 1980s, but now it seems capable of riding that luck during the 1990s, although by 1994 attention had begun to turn to the question of succession as Sir Christopher neared retirement.

Shares

In 1986 TI's low share price reflected potential for recovery and its vulnerability to a bid. By 1987 recovery was under way and the group was well enough regarded to allow it to raise cash from the market. Following the stock market collapse, the bid potential in the share price waned, but the group's status had sufficiently improved for the share rating against the rest of the market to rise through 1988 and 1989. In 1990 TI became that great rarity, an engineering company seen as a defensive stock in a recession. The rating grew in 1990 and strengthened further when the Mannesman group took a friendly shareholding. The cost of the group's restructuring was coming down and earnings had grown by 137 per cent since 1985. But there were still doubts and the recovery was reversed in the second half of 1990.

The next rise was more sustained, helped when the group turned predator. Investors were looking forward to TI reaping the benefit of the bid for Dowty, when the interim figures of August 1992 revealed that things would not go as smoothly as had been expected. The shares slipped until early 1993 and gained little in the 1993 market rally. Analysts predicted that Dowty would hold the group back for a time, but still considered the shares to be attractive in the longer term.

Corporate conscience

TI's military involvement, and especially exports, has been extended by the takeover of Dowty, which makes anti-submarine warfare equipment, hydraulics for the YF-22 advanced tactical fighter aircraft, equipment for the Sea King helicopter and the Tornado, and command systems for Trident submarines. TI's existing operations manufacture shaft seals for US navy ships, mortar barrels and other weapon casings. The group is also involved in the nuclear industry through Accles & Pollock, which makes cladding, pipes and tubing for power stations; John Crane, which produces seals for nuclear reactors; and an associated company, Norson Power, which makes manipulators to remove radioactive material.

On other issues of conscience, TI is an average company. It is a member of BITC and the Per Cent Club. It does not have adequate equal opportunities or environmental policies. It has some operations in companies with questionable regimes, such as India and Brazil, and has paid a handful of its small number of black workers in South Africa below a reasonable level. Like other manufacturers, it uses CFCs as solvent cleaners. TI has health and safety but no water pollution convictions.

Corporate governance

Separate Chairman and Chief Executive N
Number of Directors 13
Number of Non-Executive Directors 5
(4 Independent Directors)
Insulated Directors MD, JMD

Board Committees
Audit: Y   Remuneration: Y

Remuneration

Year end	31.12.91	31.12.92	31.12.93
Total board £M	1.80	1.81	2.70
% change	-21	1	49
Highest paid £	615,315	563,747	740,000
% change	-18	-8	31

Board
Lewinton, Sir Christopher *Chairman & Chief Executive*
Edwards, L Antony *Executive Director*
Fisher, Robert *Executive Director*
Potter, John *Executive Director*
Roe, James *Executive Director*
Saunders, Denis *Executive Director*
Sumner, Anthony J *Executive Director*
Walsh, Brian *Finance Director*
Chandler, Sir Colin *Independent Non-Executive*
Dieter, Dr Werner *Non-Executive*
Harris, John M *Independent Non-Executive*
Hignett, John M *Independent Non-Executive*
Lord Fanshawe of Richmond *Ind. Non-Executive*

In their report on 1992 the directors stated that they were satisfied that the company complied with all parts of the Cadbury Code, except those aspects for which guidance was still awaited, and that the auditors agreed with this view. While this might be true, the directors were not forthcoming about the manner in which they complied with the Code, nor how the combined role of chairman and chief executive fitted with Cadbury recommendations. Non-executive membership of three committees (organisation and remuneration, audit, and chairman's) was noted, but little information given on how these committees work or what their responsibilities are. The company did not move any further in the 1993 report. In pay, the relevant note to the accounts explained that executive directors are eligible for an annual bonus and a rolled-up, three-year payment, and reported the amounts earned under each, and the broad bases for the payments. It also noted that the chairmen (who was the highest paid director) did not receive an increase in base salary for 1994, after a £5000 increase in 1993.

TOMKINS plc

East Putney House, 84 Upper Richmond Road,
London SW15 2ST
Tel: 0181 871 9700.
Chairman Michael Moore
Chief executive Gregory Hutchings
Main subsidiaries Ferraris Piston Services, Firth Cleveland Engineering, Hattersley Newman Hender, Hattersley Heaton, Hayters, Murray Ohio (US), Pegler, Premier Screw and Repetition Co, Ranks Hovis McDougall, Shipman & Co, Smith & Wesson (US), Sunvic Controls, Totectors, Twiflex, Webb Fasteners
Size £2.1 billion sales, £2.5 billion stock market value, 30,500 employees
5-year growth sales 274%, earnings per share -3%, employment 208%
Solvency debt n/a, interest cover n/a
Political donations £42,000 Conservative Party
Charitable donations £483,789

Major developments
1925 company formed
1950 became public
1981 Greg Hutchings took over as chief executive
1984 bought Ferraris Piston Services
1985 bought Hayters
1986 bought GKN companies
1987 bought Pegler Hattersley
1988 bought Smith & Wesson
1989 bought Murray Ohio Manufacturing
1990 bought Philips Industries
1992 bought Ranks Hovis McDougall

Outlook

While it is difficult to warm to a man with a soulless approach to business and with an annual salary of £1 million, there can be no arguing with Greg Hutchings's record – up to 1994, at least. The chief executive of Tomkins, ably assisted by finance director Ian Duncan, has built a group with sales of £3 billion a year, assets of more than £1 billion, and a stock market value approaching £3 billion, through an icily efficient process of takeover, cost-cutting, cash management and vice-like control. From the decidedly flimsy foundations of a broken-down manufacturer of buckles, Tomkins has become a leading conglomerate that includes the famous brands of Rank Hovis McDougall (RHM), the no less famous guns of Smith & Wesson, in addition to lawnmowers, bath fittings, bikes and a variety of industrial products.

It has all seemed so easy since Mr Hutchings bought into F H Tomkins (as it then was) in 1981 – almost too easy. The company has grown largely as the result of acquisitions, which inevitably raises suspicions, given the lax nature of acquisition accounting in the 1980s. But Tomkins has not been afraid to sit back if the right target has not come along at the right price. Moreover, its accounting has always been much cleaner than most acquisitive companies, and unlike other conglomerates such as Williams Holdings or Hanson, it has not indulged in asset-trading.

Tomkins has often been likened to Hanson, principally because that is where Mr Hutchings learned his takeover trade. In fact Tomkins is much more similar to BTR in its disdain for asset-trading Hanson-style and more especially in its devotion to cash flow and return on capital, and the avoidance of market-share battles which might damage those idols. Like BTR, Tomkins has aimed to find poorly managed companies and make money by managing them well. It has become a cliché that such companies have good middle managers who have been stifled by bureaucracy and/or ineffective top management. Liberating those middle managers, giving them effective systems, the cash to invest and the financial incentives to perform to appropriate and demanding targets, is the classic Tomkins recipe for reaping the takeover rewards. It worked with tap and valve manufacturer Pegler Hattersley, the first audacious acquisition which brought Tomkins notoriety because the target was so much bigger than the bidder. And it appears to have worked with every other purchase, on both sides of the Atlantic, in boom and in bust.

Consistency is a watchword of Tomkins, but that does not protect it completely from disaster: takeovers are, by their nature, fraught with risk. Even on the agreed basis which Tomkins prefers – allowing much greater investigation of a company before it is acquired – unpleasant surprises can emerge. This has not happened yet, but it could do so in future. The takeover of RHM is particularly risky, because it leads the group into very different markets from those where it has proved itself. True, they are the low-tech, relatively stable businesses which Mr Hutchings likes, but RHM takes Tomkins into a number of areas for the first time: food; fast-moving consumer goods; commodity-related business; and markets dominated by powerful customers – the supermarket groups. These represent many new challenges for Tomkins, some of which may prove tougher than anticipated

There are two other potential weaknesses. First, Mr Hutchings refuses to buy businesses on the Continent, because of the social laws which make it more difficult to sack people than in the UK and the US. The acquisition in 1994 of two divisions – Outdoor Products and Dynamark Plastics – from US conglomerate Noma Industries for £77 million was another example of that strategy. But excluding such a large market seems dangerous. Second, the group's record of capital investment is questionable. Only rarely does Tomkins invest even as much as its depreciation charge, suggesting that it is not maintaining its capital base. Mr Hutchings might point out that the return on investment is more important than the amount of the investment, and that RHM is a case in point. But it is difficult to believe that a group which invests so little can maintain its size and performance in the long term.

TOMKINS

Share record

Return on shareholders' equity	%	13.45
5-year price high	p	282.0
5-year price low	p	94.5
Dividend yield	%	4.12
5-year high	%	6.29
5-year low	%	2.65
Price/earnings ratio		14.0
5-year high		21.0
5-year low		6.2

Share price performance (in pence)

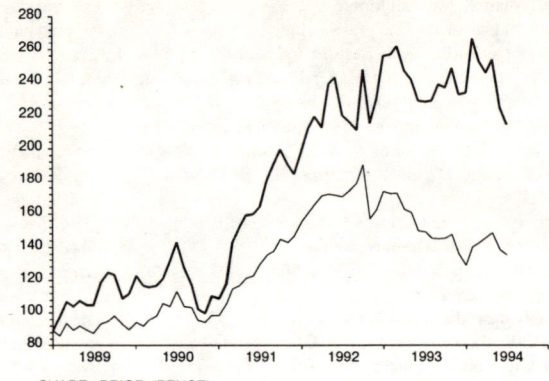

— SHARE PRICE (PENCE)
— RELATIVE PERFORMANCE

Financial record

		30/4/89	30/4/90	30/4/91	30/4/92	30/4/93
Total sales	£'000	550,437	720,456	1,039M	1,274M	2,060M
Pre-tax profit	£'000	65,106	77,062	112,098	130,578	160,400
Published retentions	£'000	28,331	33,051	42,351	52,659	42,400
Earnings per share	p	12.83	15.48	15.49	14.45	12.48
Dividend per share	p	2.92	4.00	4.75	5.47	6.35
Operating cash flow	£'000	-51,254	23,732	30,773	73,007	109,500
Net assets per share	p	113.98	136.27	99.13	90.10	121.03
Net debt/(cash)	£'000	22,981	-901	-53,419	-146M	-92,900
Shareholders' funds	£'000	179,111	216,400	390,120	449,829	802,000
Return on capital	%	32.46	27.25	31.12	29.23	23.00
Profit margin	%	10.79	9.88	10.26	9.76	7.55
Sales per employee	£	55.62	68.30	61.61	65.65	67.50
Interest cover		30.76	-70.87	-11.10	-12.44	-14.36
Dividend cover		4.40	3.87	3.26	2.64	1.97
Sales increase	%	76.24	30.89	44.22	22.63	61.64
Earnings growth	%	34.80	20.64	0.05	-6.73	-13.61
Investment x depreciation		0.98	1.19	0.72	0.80	0.99
Investment as % assets		12.48	18.30	9.11	12.48	7.91
Number of employees		9,897	10,549	16,865	19,407	30,511

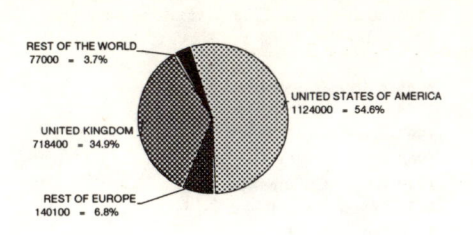

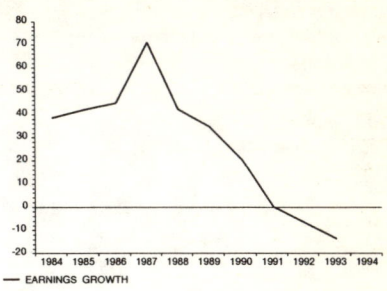

Profit analysis

REST OF THE WORLD 77000 = 3.7%
UNITED KINGDOM 718400 = 34.9%
REST OF EUROPE 140100 = 6.8%
UNITED STATES OF AMERICA 1124000 = 54.6%

Earnings

— EARNINGS GROWTH

Over the years Mr Hutchings has won more and more friends in the financial world as his record has become more impressive. There will always be the worry, however, that sooner or later even the fleetest runner might trip up.

Shares
A string of acquisitions through the early 1980s led up to the bold takeover of Pegler Hattersley in 1986 and caused shares in Tomkins to be highly rated, reflecting the optimistic atmosphere of the time. The market continued to shoot upwards in 1987, taking the shares with it, but they were slowing down relative to the market as a whole. The purchase of Smith & Wesson that summer and the market crash in the autumn left the rating back where it had been before the Pegler Hattersley acquisition.

During the ensuing boom the market preferred investing in companies closer to the consumer, and the rating went on shrinking through 1988, regardless of the purchase of Murray Ohio. Tomkins faced the problem of stock market scepticism regarding the whole group of acquisitive conglomerates and takeover accounting practices. Eventually analysts were able to distinguish between companies which managed good business performance and those which merely managed to present accounting numbers to that effect, and the relatively clean record of Tomkins helped to boost its market status. As recession set in during 1990, the shares also benefited from the opinion that the group's clutch of basic businesses were a safe bet.

While the rating slipped again at the time of the purchase of Philips Industries in 1990, the rise was resumed in 1991 and the group was praised for its tight management. The following year Tomkins won a place in the FTSE index, having outperformed the market by 45 per cent in 18 months. The rating slumped again when the group took over RHM in the autumn of 1992 and asked shareholders for cash for a diversification into food, which was seen as a much riskier project than its previous ventures. The stock market's recovery rally of 1993 failed to take shares in the company with it, but some analysts began to predict that Tomkins would once again outperform the market as it got to work on RHM. That hope was only just beginning to be reflected in the share price in early 1994.

Corporate conscience
Tomkins keeps such a tight rein on what it regards as shareholders' money that it is not prepared to pay people to worry about such trivia as group policies – or to answer queries from organisations such as EIRIS. Perhaps the company reasons that it is damned, anyway, so far as its ethics are concerned, because it owns the gunmaker Smith & Wesson. In fact that is not the only military connection: Twiflex makes disc brakes for the navy; Northern Rubber manufactures various products for the Tornado aircraft; and the Newman Hattersley subsidiary makes valves for the Canadian navy. Mainly through Hattersley there is also a nuclear connection, although Shiphan also supplies ball valves for waste handling at Sizewell B.

The acquisition of RHM has brought Tomkins into a number of new areas of ethical concern. These include animal testing and use of CFCs in connection with frozen foods. RHM had 3 convictions under health and safety laws in 1988–92, including a £6,000 fine under the Control of Substances Hazardous to Health Regulations 1988. Ledbury Preserves and RHM Foods were also fined for water pollution, and each had a few examples of exceeeding consent levels in 1990/91. RHM also makes a positive contribution to Tomkins, being a member of BITC and the Per Cent Club.

406 TRAFALGAR HOUSE plc

Corporate governance
Separate Chairman and Chief Executive Y
Number of Directors 7
Number of Non-Executive Directors 1
(1 Independent Director)
Insulated Directors MD

Board Committees
Audit: N   Remuneration: N

Remuneration

Year end	4.05.91	2.05.92	1.05.93
Total board £M	1.32	2.02	3.01
% change		53	36
Highest paid £M	0.65	1.17	1.20
% change		54	6

Board
Hutchings, Greg F   *Chief Executive*
Marchant, Richard N.   *Executive Director*
Muddimer, Robert M   *Executive Director*
Reading, Tony   *Executive Director*
Stark, J David S   *Executive Director*
Duncan, Ian A   *Finance Director*
Moore, Michael R N   *Non-Executive Chairman*

Tomkins has a separate chairman to keep an eye on chief executive Greg Hutchings, and did have long before the Cadbury Committee was formed. But that is as close as it gets to complying with the new spirit of corporate governance. Apart from the chairman, there are no other non-executive directors, hence no non-executive committees to scrutinise the actions of the board. The accounts reveal that the chief executive and finance director have a bonus scheme based on a combination of earnings and dividend growth and increase in the share price. Almost half of Mr Hutchings's £1 million remuneration comes from this incentive scheme. On the plus side, Tomkins is one of the few top companies whose directors do not have service contracts.

TRAFALGAR HOUSE plc
1 Berkeley Street, London W1A 1BY
Tel: 0171 493 5484
Chairman Simon Keswick
Chief executive Allan Gormly
Substantial shareholdings Hongkong Land 25%, Abu Dhabi Investment Authority 7.3%
Main subsidiaries John Brown, Cementation, Cleveland Structural Engineering, Cunard, Davy International, Ideal Homes, The Ritz Hotel, Scott Lithgow, Stafford Hotel, Trollope & Colls
Size £3.9 billion sales, £894 million stock market value, 35,900 employees

5-year growth sales 32%, earnings per share -91%, employment 24%
Solvency debt = 32% shareholders' funds, interest cover 2 times
Political donations £20,000 Conservative Party
Charitable donations £132,000

Major developments
1965 formed as Trafalgar House Investments Ltd
1967 bought Ideal Homes
1968 bought Trollope & Colls
1970 bought Cementation
1971 bought Cunard
1976 bought The Ritz
1982 bought Redpath Dorman Long; floated off Fleet Holdings (newspapers)
1986 bought John Brown Engineering
1987 bought Ellerman Lines
1989 bought Dukes Hotels; bought 40% of BREL
1991 bought Davy Corporation; sold Cunard Ellerman Cargo to P&O
1992 sold BREL stake; Hongkong Land took stake
1993 Sir Nigel Broakes and Sir Eric Parker stepped down

Outlook
Sir Nigel Broakes would have been the longest-serving boss in this book, had he not been kicked upstairs to become honorary president at the end of 1992. In retrospect it is surprising that he survived so long, as the semi-detached but nominal leader of a struggling conglomerate.

Sir Nigel was one of the earliest 'conglomerators'. One of the 1950s property men, he quickly moved into construction rather than the property-based businesses such as hotels (as in the case of Grand Met) or retailing (as with Sears). Trafalgar House was one of success stories of the 1960s, and continued to be much feared by potential targets during the 1970s despite some odd diversions such as the acquisition of Cunard, the Ritz and the *Express* newspaper group. By the time the 1980s dawned, however, Trafalgar was showing its age, and perhaps the inbred nature of its long-serving top management. (Sir Nigel's right-hand men – first Victor Matthews, then Eric Parker – were both old associates.) Sir Nigel himself seemed distracted by his role as chair of the London Docklands Development Corporation, and by other social and political activities.

During the 1980s Sir Eric Parker tried to push the group away from the basic, cut-throat construction business towards the more specialist and therefore more profitable technological end of the market, building huge bridges (such as that for the M25 over the Thames at Dartford) and chemical and steel plants. To this end, Trafalgar bought Redpath Dorman Long, Scott Lithgow and John Brown, in most cases taking advantage of the distressed state of these companies. But the final piece in this jigsaw – the purchase in 1991 of Davy Corporation, another great engineer fallen on hard times – proved to be the group's ultimate undoing.

TRAFALGAR HOUSE

Share record

Return on shareholders' equity	%	10.55
5-year price high	p	328.1
5-year price low	p	33.3
Dividend yield	%	3.05
5-year high	%	46.09
5-year low	%	2.81
Price/earnings ratio		9.7
5-year high		42.5
5-year low		3.7

Share price performance (in pence)

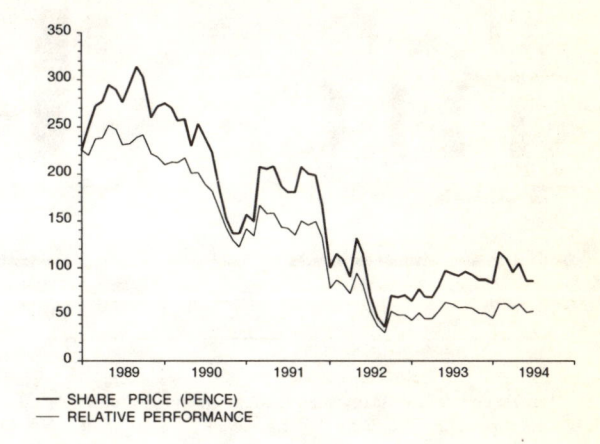

— SHARE PRICE (PENCE)
— RELATIVE PERFORMANCE

Financial record

		30/9/89	30/9/90	30/9/91	30/9/92	30/9/93
Total sales	£	2,932M	3,046M	3,202M	3,900M	3,879M
Pre-tax profit	£'000	266,200	157,800	123,100	62,500	50,100
Published retentions	£'000	101,100	-25,400	-44,400	-114M	-402M
Earnings per share	p	33.16	17.67	11.50	0.00	2.87
Dividend per share	p	13.85	14.48	14.81	4.93	2.90
Operating cash flow	£'000	94,100	70,400	80,600	-92,800	59,500
Net assets per share	p	218.21	218.47	200.42	169.67	152.17
Net debt/(cash)	£'000	334,200	308,700	179,400	279,400	251,600
Shareholders' funds	£'000	854,800	826,200	704,600	542,200	788,900
Return on capital	%	22.31	15.87	12.50	7.91	8.91
Profit margin	%	8.77	4.93	3.66	1.71	0.92
Sales per employee	£	100.74	105.29	99.66	98.23	107.91
Interest cover		13.59	3.42	4.39	8.02	1.82
Dividend cover		2.40	1.22	0.80	0.00	0.99
Sales increase	%	18.01	3.88	5.14	21.77	-0.52
Earnings growth	%	22.69	-46.88	-33.36	-100.00	0.00
Investment x depreciation		1.12	1.03	1.00	0.72	0.45
Investment as % assets		8.62	8.49	5.69	5.45	4.36
Number of employees		29,103	28,928	32,133	39,697	35,949

408 TRAFALGAR HOUSE plc

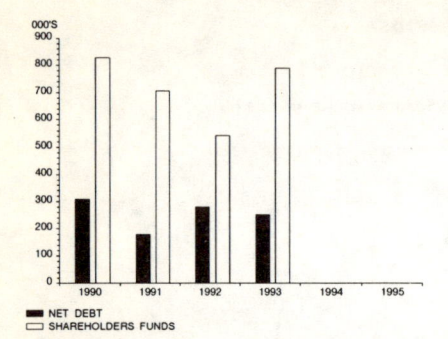

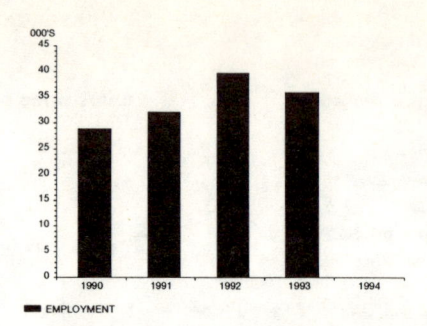

Debt and shareholders' funds

Employment

Davy's demise had finally been brought on by a contract to build a North Sea oil rig, taken on at ridiculously low cost because the company was so desperate for business, and which turned out to incur huge additional costs. Despite careful clauses in the purchase agreement, some of these extra costs eventually landed on Trafalgar, and reduced the potential purchase price paid to Davy shareholders. So both Davy and Trafalgar shareholders were unhappy. With recession and the Gulf War hitting most of the group's businesses in 1991, this was the worst possible time to encounter such a calamity. And matters seemed to be going from bad to worse. Involvement in buying the British Rail engineering company BREL was disastrous. Belated attempts to sell hotel assets, eventually including the Ritz, and to find a partner with whom to share the cruise business, came to nought. Despite a rights issue which raised additional cash at the time of the Davy deal, Trafalgar's balance sheet was becoming increasingly strained. Because of this, and perhaps because of worries about banking covenants, the group indulged in some over-optimistic accounting which eventually brought it into conflict with the accounting regulators, the Financial Reporting Review Panel. The FRRP came close to taking Trafalgar to court, but the company finally capitulated, adjusting its 1991 accounts to show a large loss instead of a profit.

But by this time Trafalgar was under attack. At the beginning of October 1992 Hongkong Land, the property arm of the gigantic Hong Kong group Jardine Matheson, snapped up 15 per cent of the shares. It then made an offer for a further 15 per cent, aimed at taking its holding up to the 30 per cent limit allowed without making a full takeover bid. Investors were not immediately interested in selling at what by then appeared to be a knock-down price, but Hongkong Land did build up to a 25 per cent shareholding over the next few months, and won two seats on the board as well as securing the effective retirement of both Sir Nigel and Sir Eric.

So Trafalgar, which has lived so well and for so long by the sword, has to all intents and purposes died by the sword. Even though Hongkong Land is in theory a minority shareholder, in practice the intruder calls the shots. This was emphasised in May 1993 when its chairman, Simon Keswick, took over as chairman of Trafalgar and his chief financial officer as finance director. Doubts about Hongkong Land's longer-term goals for Trafalgar were somewhat overshadowed towards the end of 1993 when it became clear that its intervention with giant banking group HSBC had staved off a potential financial crisis for the British company. Massive property write-downs, asset disposals and a £425 million rights issue seemed to have put Trafalgar back on track, however, even if the group's destination is still unclear.

Shares

A history of acquisition-led growth came to an end in the 1980s, leaving Trafalgar House's share rating heading inexorably downwards after reaching a pinnacle in 1985. The spike in the share price in 1987, along with the market boom, ended with the conjunction of a rights issue, a failed bid and the market crash. The rating rallied at the end of that year, while a clutch of unexciting bids in 1988 sent it down again. The shares held up during the consumer boom of the late 1980s, but by 1990 fears of massive property write-downs sent them plunging downwards.

Trafalgar House appeared to have confounded its critics at the end of 1990 when it maintained its final divided despite a steep fall in profits. The shares rallied and investors waited for the group to trade quietly through the recession. They were therefore rather unhappy in mid-1991 when the bid for Davy arrived, accompanied by a rights issue raising £310 million. Then they were shocked that December when the board warned that it might have to cut the interim dividend. The shares crashed and not even word that British Aerospace was considering a bid could pull them up.

When the board halved the dividend in 1992, the shares fell once more and by the autumn were back to levels last seen in the 1960s. Rescue of a kind came with the stakebuilding by Hongkong Land, which saw boardroom heads roll. Only then did the shares pick up a little, helped by Hongkong Land's fresh interest and despite terrible results. The new board further upset investors early in 1993 by making yet more provisions against falling property values and asking shareholders for £205 million through a distress rights issue in order to prevent the group from breaching its banking covenants. In the spring of 1993 analysts commented that, with the group facing negative cash flow, relatively high gearing and tough trading, investment in the company was not recommended. Having languished throughout much of 1993, coping with two rights issues and a great deal of bad news, the shares gained fresh vigour towards the end of the year, and although they had dropped down from their February peak, they reflected increasing market confidence in the spring of 1994.

Corporate conscience

There are several issues of conscience which touch Trafalgar House. For instance, the group has associates in Brazil and Argentina, whose human rights record leaves much to be desired, and in South Africa a number of black workers have been paid below the absolute minimum.

Many parts of the group are involved in military work, from Cementation building facilities for Trident submarines at Faslane, through Markham's torpedo tubes, to Trafalgar House Construction's work at Brize Norton RAF base. Export customers include Malaysia, where an arms training centre has been built, but where Trafalgar House lost a sizeable contract in 1994 because of the diplomatic row over the Pergau Dam affair. Trafalgar House Construction is also involved in mining, through its sand and gravel quarries, while a number of other subsidiaries supply the nuclear industry. Davy built a waste-treatment plant at Sizewell B, where Cleveland has also done some work, and the Offshore Construction Division has been involved with the Thorp reprocessing plant at Sellafield. The property and construction operations mean that the group is a user of tropical hardwoods, and of CFCs in insulation and air conditioning.

The company also has a poor record so far as regulation is concerned. Two advertising complaints were upheld against Cunard in 1991, and one against Ideal Homes. Group companies were convicted 9 times between 1988 and 1992 under health and safety laws, with Davy Mining being fined £10,000 in 1988. Cleveland Structural Engineering was fined £4,000 in 1991 for the illegal discharge of oil into water, although there were no other water pollution breaches throughout the group.

Trafalgar House can offer nothing in mitigation. It does not score on any of the positive criteria specified by EIRIS.

Corporate governance

Separate Chairman and Chief Executive Y
Number of Directors 15
Number of Non-Executive Directors 7
(3 Independent Directors)
Insulated Directors None

Board Committees
Audit: Y   Remuneration: Y

Remuneration

Year end	30.09.91	30.09.92	30.09.93
Total board £	2.50	2.59	2.7
% change		5	4	4
Highest paid £	432,000	452,000	353,000
% change		8	5	-22

Board

Gormly, Allan G *Chief Executive*
Clements, Alan *Executive Director*
Fletcher, John W S *Executive Director*
Fowler, Ian *Executive Director*
Myers, Barry *Executive Director*
Olsen, John *Executive Director*
Robinson, Ian *Executive Director*
Gawler, David *Finance Director*
Evans, Dick *Independent Non-Executive*
Howell, David A R *Independent Non-Executive*
Stenham, Cob *Independent Non-Executive*
Forster, Sir Archibald *Non-Executive*
Leach, Rodney *Non-Executive*
Powell, Sir Charles *Non-Executive*
Keswick, Simon *Non-Executive Chairman*

Trafalgar House makes an excellent case study in corporate governance. The company went into rapid decline towards the end of the long, apparently omnipotent, reign of Sir Nigel Broakes and Sir Eric Parker, and its accounting practices brought it into conflict with the FRRP. Then the conquest of the board by four Hongkong Land directors raised questions about how minority shareholders could be allowed to wield such power. The appointments and remuneration committee must certainly have been busy in 1992 and 1993 with the many comings and goings. The level of disclosure improved in the 1993 annual report, although there is still no detail of the workings of the various board committees and mention is made of a hefty £1.3 million compensation payment for loss of office. Despite the scant detail provided on directors' remuneration, it is at least gratifying to learn that Trafalgar paid no bonuses in 1992 or 1993.

UNILEVER plc

Unilever House, P O Box 68, Blackfriars,
London EC4P 4BQ
Tel: 0171 822 5252
Joint chairmen Michael Perry, Floris Maljers
Main brands Batchelor's, Bird's Eye, Blueband, Boursin, Brooke Bond, Calvin Klein perfume, Comfort, Domestos, Elida Gibbs, Elizabeth Arden, Elmlea, Fabergé, Flora, Krona, Lifebuoy, Lipton, Lux, Mattessons, Mentadent, Omo, Outline, Oxo, Pears, Persil, PG Tips, Ponds, Radion, Ragu, Red Mountain coffee, Rimmel, Signal, SR, Sunlight, Sunsilk, Surf, Timotei, Vaseline, Vesta, Wall's, John West, Mr Whippy, Wisk
Main subsidiaries Lever Brothers, National Starch and Chemical, Van den Berghs and Jurgens
Size £27.9 billion sales, £19.0 billion stock market value, 294,000 employees
5-year growth sales 29%, earnings per share 52%, employment -1%
Solvency debt = 29% shareholders' funds, interest cover 17 times
Political donations 0
Charitable donations £2 million

Major developments

1884 Lever & Co soap company formed to make Sunlight soap
1928 Margarine Union formed on merger of Van den Berghs and Jurgens
1929 merger of Lever Brothers and Margarine Union to create Unilever
1978 bought National Starch and Chemical
1984 bought Brooke Bond Oxo
1985 sold Mallinson-Denny, and Nairn
1986 bought Cheseborough-Pond's
1987 sold Stauffer Chemicals to ICI
1988 sold Thames Board
1989 bought Elizabeth Arden/Fabergé, Calvin Klein cosmetics
1990 sold Unimills
1992 sold BOCM-Silcock

Outlook

The European food industry has been quaking for some years at the prospect of US giant Philip Morris spending its huge cash flows from beer and tobacco to extend its European empire, following the purchase of Swiss confectioner Jacobs Suchard, and the subsequent addition of Terry's. But Unilever, just as big in the world's grocery markets, is as anxious to extend its food interests in the United States as Philip Morris is to build up its European business. Unilever's sales are comfortably exceeded by the Marlboro group, but excluding tobacco and non-grocery items, Unilever and Philip Morris are on a par, with Nestlé making it a threesome at the top of the tree with grocery sales of around $35 billion. Procter & Gamble, Unilever's arch-rival in the detergent and toiletries sector, trails in a poor fourth on this measure.

The scale of the group, and an introspective culture, have given Unilever the image of a slumbering giant, enmeshed in bureaucracy and slow to react to changing markets. This image, and the culture, have probably been reinforced by the group's curious Anglo-Dutch structure, which seems to have left Unilever with the humour of the Dutch and the gregariousness of the English. Like Royal Dutch/Shell Transport, and now Reed Elsevier, there are two separate companies, one quoted in Amsterdam and the other in London, although the group is run as a unified business, and agreements ensure that each set of shareholders has an equal claim on the company's equity and dividends. This is actually a hangover from British tax policy after the First World War, which penalised Dutch shareholders of Van den Bergh, one of the constituents of the group which was eventually formed in 1929 when Lever Brothers of the UK joined the recent merger of Van den Bergh with three Dutch companies to become Unilever.

Whatever the reason, Unilever has been slow to spot market changes, notably in food tastes and habits, where it ignored the growth of chilled (rather than frozen or ambient) foods for many years, as well as consumer pressure for 'purer' products without many of the additives traditionally used by the food manufacturers. Nor has the group been as tough as it might have been in improving manufacturing efficiency and cutting overheads. For example, a fundamental review of head office functions at the start of 1993 resulted in apparently superficial changes, rather than the substantial cuts in bureaucratic jobs which had been widely anticipated (although in total 9,000 jobs disappeared in 1992). In 1994 the company set aside £490 million to cover the cost of cutting a further 7,500 jobs.

Yet it could be argued that Unilever is a sufficiently profitable group that it does not need to risk the upheaval of sudden, large job cuts, with the consequent disruption and loss of staff morale. And there is another side to Unilever, as a long-term investor (see the investment statistics) and builder of strong market positions. It must also be said that the group has engaged in a substantial reorganisation of European production associated with the advent of the EC single market. And the slumbering-giant image does not fit with what amounts to corporate hyperactivity since the early 1980s.

A thorough review of the group in the early 1980s concluded (as in the case of so many other companies) that it should escape from the diversifications of the previous two decades, concentrate on its core business of groceries, with the exception of speciality chemicals (mainly flavours, fragrances and starch products), and aim to move into higher-margin businesses. As a result, the 1980s saw the sale of operations such as transport, advertising and packaging, but also a flood of acquisitions. From the start of 1984 to the end of 1992 Unilever bought 268

UNILEVER

Share record

Return on shareholders' equity	%	30.50
5-year price high	p	1248.0
5-year price low	p	589.0
Dividend yield	%	3.10
5-year high	%	3.79
5-year low	%	2.19
Price/earnings ratio		13.1
5-year high		19.3
5-year low		10.1

Share price performance (in pence)

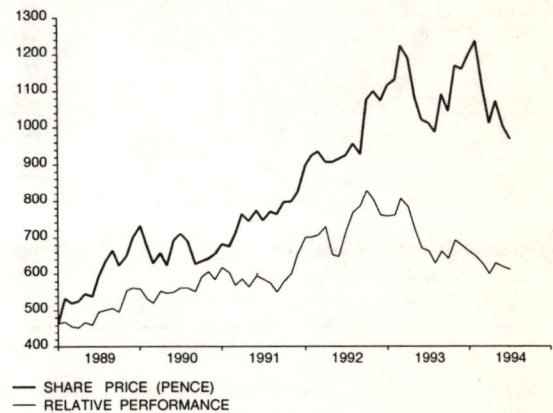

— SHARE PRICE (PENCE)
— RELATIVE PERFORMANCE

Financial record

		31/12/89	31/12/90	31/12/91	31/12/92	31/12/93
Total sales	£	21,521M	22,258M	23,163M	24,700M	27,863M
Pre-tax profit	£	1,700M	1,745M	1,832M	2,106M	2,352M
Published retentions	£'000	672,000	508,000	729,000	818,000	754,000
Earnings per share	p	55.78	60.24	64.57	71.55	84.89
Dividend per share	p	16.75	18.16	18.94	21.33	25.00
Operating cash flow	£'000	-719M	609,000	616,000	458,000	368,000
Net assets per share	p	371.55	394.98	422.06	500.36	524.91
Net debt/(cash)	£	2,280M	1,912M	1,512M	1,225M	1,356M
Shareholders' funds	£	2,767M	2,884M	3,488M	4,583M	4,703M
Return on capital	%	32.17	31.09	29.99	28.65	28.36
Profit margin	%	7.67	7.62	7.68	8.35	8.24
Sales per employee	£	72.71	73.95	77.73	86.06	94.77
Interest cover		7.48	5.99	7.32	15.05	17.34
Dividend cover		3.33	3.32	3.41	3.35	3.40
Sales increase	%	25.74	3.42	4.07	6.64	12.81
Earnings growth	%	29.54	8.00	7.18	10.81	18.64
Investment x depreciation		2.15	2.12	1.80	1.80	1.82
Investment as % assets		16.61	17.56	15.82	14.18	16.08
Number of employees		296,000	301,000	298,000	287,000	294,000

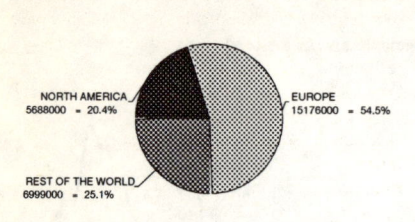

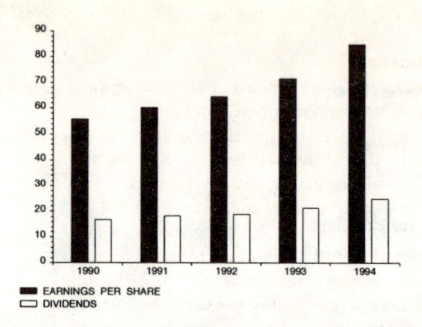

Geographical profit analysis

NORTH AMERICA 5688000 = 20.4%
EUROPE 15176000 = 54.5%
REST OF THE WORLD 6999000 = 25.1%

Earnings and dividends

■ EARNINGS PER SHARE
□ DIVIDENDS

companies and sold 149. Most of these deals were small, extending existing geographic or product coverage, for example in 1992 with the purchase of ice cream companies in Thailand, Hungary and Canada. The most important were the purchase in 1984 of Brooke Bond Oxo, the acquisition of Cheseborough-Pond's in 1986, and a major move into perfume three years later with the purchase of Elizabeth Arden/Fabergé.

The result of all this activity is a substantial increase in the proportion of sales and profits coming from North America, up from 13 per cent and 11 per cent respectively in 1981 to 21 per cent and 18 per cent in 1993. Following North American growth, virtually half of Unilever's sales and profits are estimated to come from the US, the UK and Germany. More dramatically, the proportion of sales and profits not in the four core businesses of food, detergents, toiletries and speciality chemicals has dwindled from a quarter of sales and 15 per cent of profits in 1981 to just 3 per cent of sales and 2 per cent of profits in 1993.

Food remains the group's main business, accounting for about half of its sales and profits, and it will become even more significant if Unilever manages to make a major takeover in the US. The division is divided into four product areas, the smallest of which is 'Professional Markets', being sales to caterers rather than end consumers. The other three areas are of roughly equal size: the original, margarine business, ice cream and tea (an interesting combination), and meal components, incorporating brands such as Birds Eye and Batchelors.

Most of these food areas are relatively low-growth, if not declining. But there are plenty of profitable opportunities within that general trend: in margarine, Unilever occupies huge market shares in most European markets, and low-fat spreads, for example, can command premium prices by substituting water for fat. (An illustration of Unilever's weakness in meeting new demands, however, is that Unigate's Gold leads the group's Delight in the low-fat market.) In the tea operation there is great hope for the marketing of tea as a soft drink, through a joint venture with Pepsi. Finally, Unilever has begun to come to terms with the age of the microwave, chilled food and healthier eating.

Detergents formed the other leg of the original group, and still represent an important operation for Unilever, with products such as Persil, Comfort and Domestos. In most countries Lever Brothers (the trading name for the detergents side of the business) is in fierce competition with Procter & Gamble in this business, and this competition proved suicidal in the US for both companies throughout the 1980s. But through heavy product development and promotion, Lever Brothers boosted its market share in the US dramatically, driving out some other competitors and moving towards the more profitable duopoly with P&G which endures in so many other countries.

The US has been the focus of the drive into 'personal products', as the group describes toiletries. The attraction of this market is its prospects of much higher growth, as well as higher margins, compared with food and detergents, and this may well lead Unilever to make further acquisitions in areas where it is under-represented, such as cosmetics. The group is not short of resources for making such acquisitions: it has been estimated that Unilever could comfortably spend £4 billion. The difficulty is more likely to be finding an appropriate target, especially because the company has traditionally avoided contested bids, and because one of the prime areas for expansion is Japan, where it is even harder to make such bids than in Germany or Switzerland. Meanwhile, as the company discovered in 1992, there is plenty scope for making many, smaller acquisitions, and for pressing on with improvements in efficiency.

The giant may creak a little with size, age, and culture, but it remains an extremely powerful competitor, able to challenge the likes even of Philip Morris.

Shares

During the 1980s Unilever's share value grew steadily as its margins improved following a £3.3 billion acquisition and disposal programme around the world. The shares fell back in the market crash of 1987, but the rating against the market as a whole recovered. It resumed an upward track in 1989, when it became clear that Unilever was more than just a defensive stock and analysts realised that it had above-average growth potential.

In 1990 the shares eased back down again as Unilever took another step in its restructuring, making a one-off charge to cover preparations for the European single market, at the same time as the recession slowed down profit growth and net debt rose to £3 billion. While the City remained convinced that the company was a good long-term investment, it found better short-term returns elsewhere. The shares were re-rated strongly at the end of that year, as the balance sheet recovered its strength, and improved further in both 1991 and 1992 because the results stood out in the recessionary times.

The 1993 bull market lifted the shares to a peak, but the rating slipped against the rest of the market as others were seen as offering more recovery potential. Disappointing profit figures in early 1994 sent the shares down again that year.

Corporate conscience

On paper, Unilever does have a strong environmental position. It has a comprehensive formal policy, has used independent audits and is committed to regular review of performance. Yet the group bitterly resisted attacks on its use of phosphates in detergents, and, as in other aspects of its business, has generally followed rather than led developments in packaging as well as product formulation. Once it does take something seriously, however, Unilever does a thorough and professional job, so while it has not been converted to environmentalism, it does now seem to see the need (or the advantage) in moving forward rapidly on issues like packaging. It has also made some commitment to eliminating CFCs, planning to use HFCs instead by 1996 at the latest.

On other environmental issues, UAC in Nigeria imports hardwoods from Taiwan as well as using local timber in its building operations, but there is a commitment to phase these out by the end of 1995. Back in the UK, the water pollution record is not good: there have been many examples of discharge consent levels being exceeded, with British Creameries at West Marton in Yorkshire having the worst record. Brooke Bond was convicted of pollution in 1991, receiving a £1,000 fine. Several Unilever companies test products on animals, but the group has reduced the use of animals and supports research into alternatives. It is also involved in meat processing, through Wall's bacon and ready-made meals.

As Britain's biggest consumer company, as well as the inheritor of Lord Leverhulme's philanthropic tradition, Unilever is committed to community support. It is a member of BITC and the Per Cent Club, a major contributor to charitable and community programmes, places employees on secondment and has a payroll-giving scheme. On the other hand, its consumer credentials were dented by 4 recent adverse advertising judgements: 2 for Lever Brothers in 1991 and 2 for Elida Gibbs in the following year.

Unilever is a responsible employer, with sound, though unexciting, equal opportunities policies, including support for Opportunity 2000 and high trade union representation. The group did suffer one health and safety conviction in 1991, however: Mattessons Wall's was fined £1,400 for offences under the Factories Act 1961.

This is a hugely international group, with significant operations in many countries with suspect regimes, including Chad, Indonesia, Malawi and Zaire. In South Africa, however, it paid all its 4,000 black employees above a reasonable level. There are a number of other ethical matters in which the group is marginally involved. Through UAC it has an interest in a Nigerian brewer; National Starch and Lever Industrial are small-scale suppliers to the Ministry of Defence; and the speciality chemical business makes pesticides.

Corporate governance

Separate Chairman and Chief Executive Y
Number of Directors 15
Number of Non-Executive Directors 0
(0 Independent Directors)
Insulated Directors None

Board Committees
Audit: N   Remuneration: Y

Remuneration

Year end	31.12.91	31.12.92	31.12.93
Total board £M	7.00	8.00	6.74
% change	17	14	-16
Highest paid £	688,793	695,102	705,781
% change	18	1	2

Board

Maljers, Floris *Executive Chairman*
Perry, Michael Sydney *Executive Chairman*
Anderson, Iain *Executive Director*
Brown, Roy *Executive Director*
Burgmans, Antony *Executive Director*
Butler, Clive *Executive Director*
FitzGerald, Niall *Executive Director*
Ganguly, Ashok *Executive Director*
Jemmett, Christopher *Executive Director*
Kemner, Alexander *Executive Director*
Miller Smith, Charles *Executive Director*
Muller, Okko *Executive Director*
Peelen, Jan *Executive Director*
Tabaksblat, Morris *Executive Director*
Eggerstedt, Hans *Finance Director*

UNITED BISCUITS (HOLDINGS) plc

A complicated system of governance exists, reflecting the company's Anglo-Dutch nature. There are two boards – executive and advisory – and while there are no independent directors on the executive board, 10 'advisory directors' sit on the advisory panel. Massive amounts of information are given in the annual report, though not in an easily digestible form.

UNITED BISCUITS (HOLDINGS) plc

Church Road, West Drayton, Middlesex UB7 7PR
Tel: 01895 432100
Chairman Sir Robert Clarke
Chief executive Eric Nicoli
Main brands Carr's, Crawford's, Hob Nobs, Hula Hoops, Jaffa Cakes, KP, McVitie's, McCoy's, Penguin, Ross Young's
Size £3.0 billion sales, £1.6 billion stock market value, 36,900 employees
5-year growth sales n/a, earnings per share n/a, employment -21%
Solvency debt = 25% shareholders' funds, interest cover 6 times
Political donations £40,000 Conservative Party
Charitable donations £745,000

Major developments

1948 formed from merger of McVitie & Price and Macfarlane Lang
1966 changed to United Biscuits (Holdings) following acquisition of Crawfords, Macdonalds
1970 bought Westimex (Belgium)
1974 bought Keebler
1979 bought Speciality brands
1982 bought Joseph Terrys (chocolate)
1986 proposed merger with Imperial blocked by Monopolies Commission
1988 bought Ross Young's; bought Callard & Bowser; sold Speciality brands
1989 Wimpy and Pizzaland restaurant businesses sold to Grand Met
1990 bought Verkade (Holland), Chocometz (France)
1993 sold Terrys

Outlook

Sir Hector Laing was an irrepressible believer in Britain and British business who longed to build a British food empire which could compete with the US giants in what he thought would be the key markets in the less developed countries of the world. Before his retirement in 1990 he did build an empire, based on a collection of Scottish biscuit-makers, including his own family company, but he somehow neglected to notice the importance of competing on the home ground of Europe before being able to win away from home.

His successors, cast in the less idiosyncratic (and therefore far less interesting) mould of professional managers, have turned their attention to correcting that myopia. It may be 10 years or more too late, but Europe seems to be the theme of the 1990s for United Biscuits (UB). A complementary theme, common to so many companies in this book, is a retreat from some peripheral product areas to concentrate on the main business of biscuits and snacks (and possibly frozen foods, although the centrality of this activity does seem to be open to question).

UB has an immensely strong UK base in biscuits and snacks. McVitie's has a dominant share of the UK biscuit market, thanks to the process of merger which would surely not have been allowed today by the Monopolies Commission. Not only does it have almost half the UK branded market, it also supplies a similar share of own-label products. And following Sir Hector's Scottish zeal for efficiency, the operations are renowned for their productivity. The figures show that UB has invested heavily, although critics might question whether that investment has paid adequate returns, especially looking at the relatively poor earnings growth during the 1980s. In the KP brand the group also has not only a strong product, but also a leading position in the UK snack market, especially in nuts.

Outside biscuits and snacks, and outside Britain, the story has not been so good. Ross Young's, the frozen-food business bought from Hanson as part of its break-up of Imperial Group, has never really fulfilled its potential. Moreover, it is faced with the might of Unilever (Birds Eye) and Nestlé (Findus) throughout Europe, and seems to have little hope of building a sizeable European frozen-food business. Perhaps frozen foods will eventually go the way of chocolate and restaurants: Terry's was sold in 1993; Pizzaland and Wimpy were sold to Grand Metropolitan (where they became, for the most part, Burger King) in 1989, many years after UB should have decided to concentrate on making food rather than selling it.

The group has not been entirely Anglo-centred. As long ago as 1974 it purchased Keebler, a mid-West biscuit company in the United States. Keebler has grown considerably and has a significant national position, but UB has found life tough all the same. First there were the 'cookie' wars with Procter & Gamble. The US giant eventually withdrew on financial grounds, but the battle had damaged Keebler's pocket, too, especially because of a hefty legal bill for a patent infringement case. Even then, Keebler was not out of trouble: its struggle with Nabisco to gain market supremacy hit the company's profits hard – a staggering 60 per cent fall in operating profit in 1992. The restructuring of Keebler accounted for most of the 1993 reorganisation charge of £120 million, but in 1994 the organisation was still in intensive care.

UB had also made some tentative steps on to the

UNITED BISCUITS (HOLDINGS)

Share record

Return on shareholders' equity	%	24.79
5-year price high	p	435.0
5-year price low	p	235.0
Dividend yield	%	6.19
5-year high	%	8.68
5-year low	%	3.98
Price/earnings ratio		12.7
5-year high		18.1
5-year low		8.2

Share price performance (in pence)

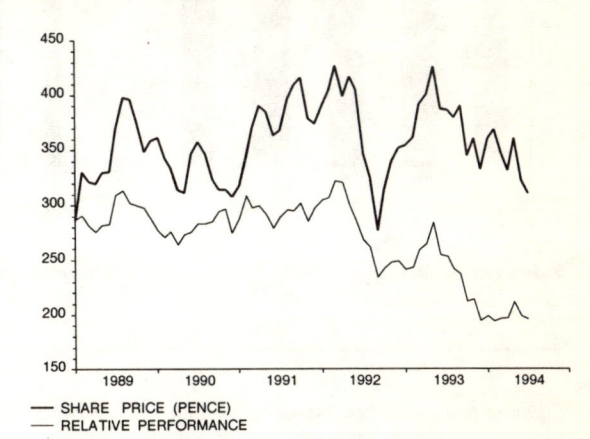

— SHARE PRICE (PENCE)
— RELATIVE PERFORMANCE

Financial record

		31/12/89	31/12/90	31/12/91	31/12/92	31/12/93
Total sales	£	2,458M	2,428M	2,661M	2,801M	3,049M
Pre-tax profit	£'000	186,500	199,000	211,400	173,700	181,800
Published retentions	£'000	143,800	55,600	58,400	34,800	-10,000
Earnings per share	p	28.28	28.77	30.21	24.34	24.24
Dividend per share	p	13.80	14.40	15.30	15.30	15.30
Operating cash flow	£'000	-26,700	19,100	-16,400	-46,600	700
Net assets per share	p	162.57	154.48	193.57	230.74	180.29
Net debt/(cash)	£'000	117,200	241,900	248,500	288,400	360,800
Shareholders' funds	£'000	603,400	842,900	985,700	1,172M	1,156M
Return on capital	%	33.24	32.16	31.44	21.37	21.65
Profit margin	%	7.62	8.18	7.92	6.20	5.96
Sales per employee	£	52.34	59.86	66.14	72.37	82.61
Interest cover		9.75	10.33	7.65	5.72	5.85
Dividend cover		2.05	2.00	1.97	1.59	1.58
Sales increase	%	13.51	-1.20	9.56	5.26	8.89
Earnings growth	%	5.16	1.72	5.03	-19.45	-0.38
Investment x depreciation		1.73	2.03	1.91	1.69	1.10
Investment as % assets		18.54	18.19	18.44	14.24	10.99
Number of employees		46,958	40,565	40,226	38,698	36,914

UNITED BISCUITS (HOLDINGS) plc

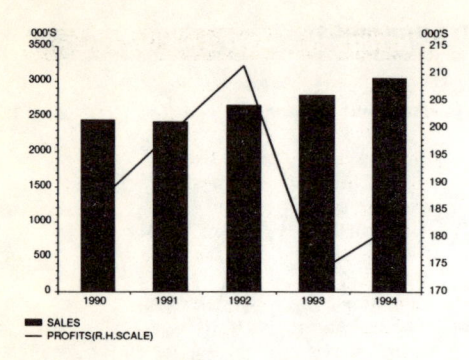

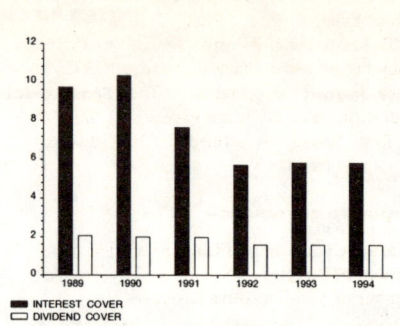

Sales and profits

Interest and dividend cover

Continent many years ago. Westimex, the Belgian Croky crisp company, was bought in 1970, and UB moved into Spain in 1973 with the acquisition of Ortiz. But this policy was largely neglected in the 1980s, owing perhaps to a preoccupation with the US and with new markets such as China and Brazil. Europe has returned to the top of the agenda in the 1990s, however, with a flurry of acquisitions to build up biscuit and snack-food businesses in Holland, Italy, Hungary and Scandinavia in order to create a web of interests across the Continent. The geographical spread of businesses is still patchy, but there is clearly the basis for a pan-European operation.

Up against the Goliaths of the food industry, the future for United Biscuits is likely to remain tough in both the US and Europe, helping to push thoughts of Third World markets to the back of the group's mind. But Sir Hector would no doubt argue that his company has proved time and again that it can defeat the giants, and with such a profitable UK base to build on, it will not be easily defeated by them.

Shares

The United Biscuits share price has risen entertainingly over the years, although the company's worth against the market as a whole peaked in 1981 and has fluctuated weakly ever since. The 1986 bull market found UB acting as a 'white knight' to try and save the Imperial Group from Hanson, which did not help its reputation in the City. The shares were taken higher by the market trend in 1987 but did not rise as fast as most, causing the rating to sink. The rating recovered during the market crash of that year as the food businesses were seen as a safe investment. Further improvement followed, reflecting heavy cost-cutting, but the spikes in its share price were based on rumours of stakebuilding in anticipation of a bid for UB, rather than a belief in the company itself. No bid came, but the rumours resurfaced in January 1989, and while the shares were pushed up by hopes of a bid, analysts became worried that the group would buy up Nabisco's European operations. In the event UB was pipped at the post and so prevented from overspending, but both the shares and their rating fell back.

From 1990 to 1992 the shares gained against the market as its food businesses were once again recognised for their defensive qualities during a recession. Safe dividends and steady growth saw the group through to 1992, but then the share price fell by 40 per cent due to reports of poor trading in the United States. When the panic was over, the shares did regain some of the ground lost. However, the market was by then looking for an upturn in the economy, and defensive shares like UB lost ground against shares in those companies expected to perform well during a recovery.

Having underperformed the market in 1992 and 1993, the City remained a little cautious about UB's shares, although the yield provided some support in early 1994. The weakness in the price was, however, expected to continue until UB offered some evidence that its confident trading talk had been translated into profits.

Corporate conscience

Sir Hector Laing, UB's former chairman, was a driving force behind BITC (and its chairman for many years), so there is no doubting this company's commitment to community involvement, and that applies also to its social responsibilities generally. While UB has had to close factories and lay off workers (most embarrassingly in Halifax, a BITC target town), the group attempts to behave responsibly to employees, as well as to other stakeholders. It has a good record on equal opportunities, with monitoring of ethnic minorities and women, and reasonable childcare provision, including paid paternity leave. The group also supports Opportunity 2000. There was one health and safety conviction in 1990, bringing a fine of £1,500 to Ross Young's.

UB has a comprehensive formal environmental policy but no commitment to phase out CFCs (used in the frozen-food operations). There was only a handful of water discharge excesses in the 1991/2, but Ross Young's was fined £250 for discharging ammonia solution.

Corporate governance

Separate Chairman and Chief Executive Y
Number of Directors 15
Number of Non-Executive Directors 9
(7 Independent Directors)
Insulated Directors None

Board Committees
Audit: Y   Remuneration: Y

Remuneration

Year end	31.12.91	31.12.92	1.1.94
Total board £M	2.74	2.17	2.70
% change		-33	-21	24
Highest paid £	425,000	451,000	452,000
% change		18	27	0.2

Board

Nicoli, E L *Chief Executive*
Clarke, Sir Robert C *Executive Chairman*
Chadbourne, Brian *Executive Director*
Hearn, David *Executive Director*
Stewart, D R J *Executive Director*
Warren, J A *Finance Director*
Fraser, Sir Charles *Independent Non-Executive*
Lady Howe *Independent Non-Executive*
Lord Prior *Independent Non-Executive*
Napier, Robert S *Independent Non-Executive*
Short, Colin M *Independent Non-Executive*
Spickschen, Thorlef *Independent Non-Executive*
van Schaik, Gerard *Independent Non-Executive*
Shaw, Neil M *Non-Executive*
Wyman, T H *Non-Executive*

The company prides itself on being a leader in issues of corporate governance – it was one of the first to install a majority of non-executives in the boardroom. The level of disclosure in the annual report is encouraging and in line with the group's assertion that corporate governance will increasingly be seen as a hallmark of successful companies. The company also offers shareholders comfort on the independence of its pension fund management and its attention to environmental issues.

UNITED NEWSPAPERS plc

Ludgate House, 245 Blackfriars Road,
London SE1 9UY
Tel: 0171 921 5000
Chairman Lord Stevens of Ludgate
Deputy Chairman Lord Ampthill
Managing Director Graham Wilson
Main brands *Daily Express, Daily Star, Daltons Weekly, Exchange & Mart, Sunday Express, Yorkshire Post*
Main subsidiaries Express Newspapers, Hong Kong International Trade Fair Group, Link House, Miller Freeman, Morgan-Grampian, United Provincial Newspapers
Size £908 million sales, £1.3 billion stock market value, 11,800 employees
5-year growth sales 13%, earnings per share 0.5%, employment -10%
Solvency debt n/a, interest cover 10 times
Political donations 34,000 Conservative Party
Charitable donations ££456,000

Major developments

1969 merger of Yorkshire Post Group and United Newspapers
1981 David Stevens (now Lord Stevens) became chairman
1984 bought Link House
1985 bought Fleet Holdings/Express Newspapers
1987 announced plans to quit Fleet Street
1989 rebuffed merger with the Telegraph Group
1992 closed *Punch* magazine
1993 sold Extel Financial
1994 bought Harmon Publishing

Outlook

Like many media groups, United Newspapers has an image problem. National newspapers are supposed to be glamorous, powerful institutions that pump out huge earnings. In reality, however, newspapers have a disproportionate tendency to perform badly in financial terms, and they are all on a steady downward trend.

So while United Newspapers has a wealth of media assets, it is the national titles which grab the City's attention, leaving a distinctly unhappy impression that this is a group making heavy weather of going nowhere. Yet it would be unfair to taint the company's entire history and prospects with the troubles of its national newspaper titles.

United Newspapers' current profile dates back to the 1970s, when David Stevens (now Lord Stevens) was put on to the board of United Newspapers in a non-executive capacity to look after Drayton Trust's investment in what was regarded as a sleepy regional newspaper company. This City businessman, with not a drop of printer's ink running in his veins, became chairman in early 1981, and it was in Octo-

UNITED NEWSPAPERS plc

Share record

Return on shareholder's equity	%	25.06
5-year price high	p	727.0
5-year price low	p	270.4
Dividend yield	%	5.00
5-year high	%	10.07
5-year low	%	3.70
Price/earnings ratio		15.4
5-year high		22.4
5-year low		7.5

Share price performance (in pence)

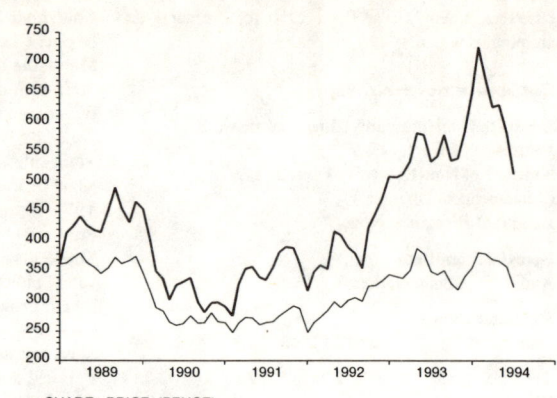

— SHARE PRICE (PENCE)
— RELATIVE PERFORMANCE

Financial record

		31/12/89	31/12/90	31/12/91	31/12/92	31/12/93
Total sales	£'000	801,618	829,120	812,598	831,508	980,466
Pre-tax profit	£'000	109,953	95,052	85,172	99,502	118,112
Published retentions	£'000	68,614	42,119	8,140	36,771	46,488
Earnings per share	p	35.60	29.63	26.05	33.54	35.76
Dividend per share	p	20.43	20.43	20.43	20.92	22.00
Operating cash flow	£'000	-52,668	59,050	14,079	24,767	65,057
Net assets per share	p	230.07	242.92	217.28	162.59	196.48
Net debt/(cash)	£'000	196,346	247,422	262,779	292,988	-20,099
Shareholders' funds	£'000	180,951	189,384	179,577	166,777	417,013
Return on capital	%	35.07	26.77	24.27	31.42	34.80
Profit margin	%	13.53	11.42	10.63	12.04	12.98
Sales per employee	£	61.18	66.08	67.63	70.10	76.69
Interest cover		7.23	4.31	4.06	5.44	10.27
Dividend cover		1.74	1.45	1.28	1.60	1.63
Sales increase	%	6.34	3.43	-1.99	2.33	9.26
Earnings growth	%	-1.29	-16.78	-12.05	28.73	6.60
Investment x depreciation		3.25	1.45	0.67		
Investment as % assets		29.82	12.86	6.33	9.04	6.81
Number of employees		12,102	12,548	12,015	11,862	11,846

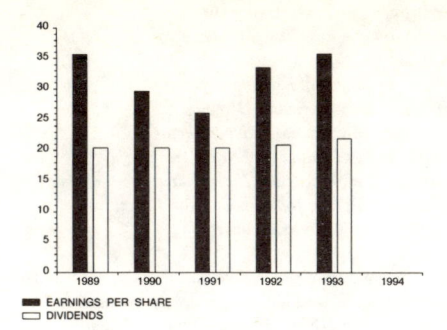

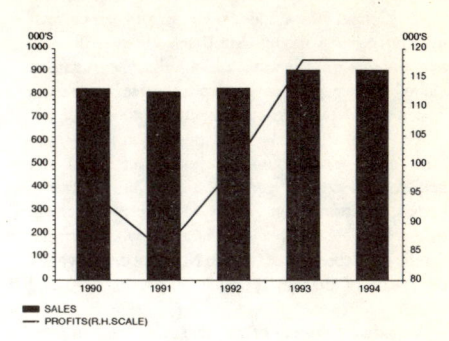

Earnings and dividends

Sales and profits

ber 1985 that United Newspapers paid £317 million for the former Beaverbrook Express newspaper empire, Fleet Holdings. This company had been going through a brief spell of independence after emerging from the property and shipping empire of Trafalgar House.

Although the price tag was considered generous, Stevens brought his financial experience to bear, cutting staff and costs and boosting profits. Unlike Murdoch's showdown at Wapping, however, it took Stevens several years to bring about the transformation to new technology. But while he was cutting costs, the national newspaper market was doing United Newspapers no favours. Against the background of gentle decline in the sector, the group's major titles, in the fiercely competitive mid-market, looked as though they had boarded a fast train to extinction.

The battle against the *Daily Mail* has lasted ever since the *Daily Express* was launched at the start of the century. And despite halcyon days at the time of the Second World War, when its circulation topped the 4 million mark, the *Express* has more recently been the loser: the paper's circulation fell from 1.9 million a day in December 1984 to just under 1.4 million by March 1994, while the *Sunday Express*, recently revamped as a tabloid under Eve Pollard, has drifted from almost 2.5 million a week to just 1.6 million. Likewise, circulation of the *arriviste Daily Star*, which flirted for a while in the 1980s with a 'tits and bums' format that would have shamed archrival the *Sun*, has dropped from 1.6 million to around 750,270.

Longer-term factors aside, the group's two daily titles have been affected by the price-cutting tactics of papers such as the *Sun* and *The Times*. Spending to promote the papers and introduce new sectors has also had to be kept high.

Although United Newspapers is now best known for its national titles, it is fortunately not entirely dependent on their performance for its own outlook. And having disposed of Extel Financial to Pearson for £73.5 million in late 1993 (ridding itself, in the process, of Stevens's most questionable purchase of recent years), the company now appears to be demonstrating an aplomb for acquisition, which is winning over some of its City critics.

After raising £190 million in a rights issue in mid-1993, the group splashed out $100 million on US periodical publisher Harmon in early 1994, a deal which won the company warm applause. A smaller (£24 million) acquisition of the Hong Kong International Trade Fair Group was further indication that United Newspapers has its eyes set on the Far East for acquisitional growth. Although these two deals increased group debt to about £100 million, the company still has significant fire power to mount takeovers, and these are widely expected to help the company meet market expectations for its future earnings growth.

Throughout 1993 the profit performance from the group's national newspapers as well as the recession-affected magazines and exhibitions division remained weak. Its regional newspapers, including titles such as the *Yorkshire Post*, produced about 23 per cent of the profits, while its advertising titles, most famously *Exchange & Mart*, accounted for about a quarter of the surplus. Margins on these latter two businesses were way ahead of anything achieved elsewhere within United Newspapers.

Shares

United Newspapers' performance figures have not encouraged investors to give the company's shares special treatment over the years. Profits in 1992 nudged only just above their 1988 level, although hopes of asset sales, rationalisation and favourable acquisitions helped the price to outstrip the FTSE 100 index before the profits improved in 1993.

420   VODAFONE GROUP plc

At the end of the 1980s speculation that a sizeable share stake had been amassed by *Daily Telegraph* owner Conrad Black added some fizz to the company's price, even though Mr Black claimed that his intentions were friendly, adding that he regarded United Newspapers as underpriced. He was, as it turned out, virtually alone in his thinking at the time.

After the 1989 takeover speculation, the share price dived for a couple of years from 1990, not helped in 1991 by general concern about media barons, following the death of Robert Maxwell. Investors were further discouraged when, in the depths of depression, United Newspapers unveiled two years of drastically lower profits in 1990 and 1991.

A gradual recovery of confidence in the company could be seen during 1992, culminating in significantly stronger market backing during 1993 and the early part of 1994, despite, or possibly because of, continued speculation that Lord Stevens was ready to sell the national newspaper titles, even though this former money man had clearly become a convert to lure of 'Fleet Street'.

Even a £190 million rights issue in July 1993 barely dented the rising share price, boosted by the £74 million disposal of what was left of the Extel Financial news service, and reflecting what the market judged to be astute acquisitions and an optimistic outlook.

Corporate conscience

This company is unusual in the two main ethical issues it raises: advertising complaints and pornography. Seven complaints against Express Newspapers were upheld by the ASA in the two years to the beginning of 1994. The pornography involvement stems from the *Daily Star*'s 'page 3 girl' and the group's printing of the *Daily* and *Sunday Sport*. These issues are balanced on the positive side by membership of BITC and the Per Cent Club, but the group does not have adequate public policies on the environment and equal opportunities.

Corporate governance

Separate Chairman and Chief Executive Y
Number of Directors 11
Number of Non-Executive Directors 4
(3 Independent Directors)
Insulated Directors Not known

Board Committees
Audit: Y   Remuneration: Y

Remuneration
Year end	31.12.92	31.12.93
Total board £M	2.10	2.40
% change		14
Highest paid £	400,840	436,776
% change		9

Board

Lord Stevens of Ludgate *Executive Chairman*
Wilson, Graham *Managing Director*
Cameron, Andrew *Executive Director*
Donaldson, Nigel *Executive Director*
Freeman, Marshall *Executive Director*
Stern, Charles *Executive Director*
Toulmin, Michael *Executive Director*
Bull, George *Independent Non-Executive*
Forster, Sir Archibald *Independent Non-Executive*
Pountain, Sir Eric *Independent Non-Executive*
Lord Ampthill *Non-Executive*

The recent drafting-in of non-executives to the boardroom has changed the corporate governance ambience at United Newspapers, whose chairman is not renowned for enthusiastic support for such modern notions and whose continued presence at the head of the company has been queried by some major shareholders after he was forced to stand down from the helm of fund management group Invesco MIM. The arrival of George Bull, Sir Archibald Forster and Sir Eric Pountain in 1992 and 1993 means the group can now operate non-executive remuneration, nominations and audit committees, although the company's annual report gives no detail of their workings.

VODAFONE GROUP plc

The Courtyard, 2-4 London Road, Newbury, Berkshire RG13 1LJ
Tel: 01635 33251
Chairman Sir Ernest Harrison
Chief executive Gerald Whent
Main subsidiaries Orbitel (50%), VHL Communications, Vodac, Vodapage Ltd, Vodata Ltd
Size £851 million sales, £5.7 billion stock market value, 3,100 employees
5-year growth sales 110%, earnings per share 92%, employment 91%
Solvency debt n/a, interest cover n/a
Political donations £50,000 Conservative Party
Charitable donations £106,500

Major developments
1982 won licence for second UK cellular network
1984 Vodafone incorporated as subsidiary of Racal Electronics
1985 service began
1988 became Racal Telecom, planned flotation announced
1991 demerged as Vodafone
1993 digital services Eurodigital and Metrodigital launched

VODAFONE GROUP

Share record

Return on shareholders' equity	%	36.54
5-year price high	p	631.0
5-year price low	p	230.0
Dividend yield	%	1.92
5-year high	%	2.69
5-year low	%	0.23
Price/earnings ratio		24.0
5-year high		75.2
5-year low		15.7

Share price performance (in pence)

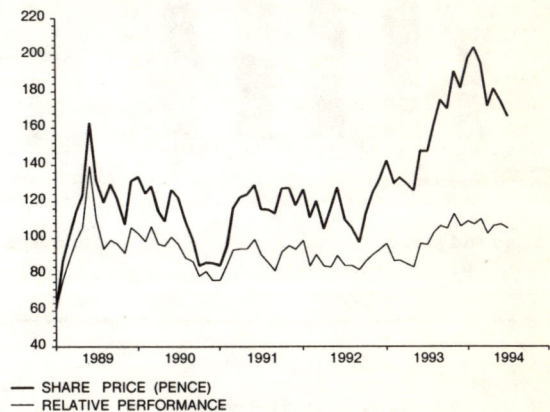

— SHARE PRICE (PENCE)
— RELATIVE PERFORMANCE

Financial record

		31/3/90	31/3/91	31/3/92	31/3/93	31/3/94
Total sales	£'000	405,778	536,838	585,337	664,100	850,529
Pre-tax profit	£'000	164,778	244,928	271,765	322,473	349,252
Published retentions	£'000	94,047	150,362	75,995	151,770	160,711
Earnings per share	p	11.85	16.88	18.37	21.96	22.75
Dividend per share	p	2.45	5.27	10.80	6.96	8.35
Operating cash flow	£'000	5,018	-5,150	92,408	161,408	108,274
Net assets per share	p	26.89	41.86	45.49	53,24	63.17
Net debt/(cash)	£'000	-2,588	-30,831	-64,761	-152M	-111M
Shareholders' funds	£'000	269,419	418,199	452,149	596,192	697,741
Return on capital	%	73.61	71.55	62.45	65.33	59.76
Profit margin	%	41.12	46.19	48.16	48.97	41.39
Sales per employee	£	249.25	220.56	273.27	284.65	272.87
Interest cover		-64.41	-101.29	-33.11	-20.65	-29.33
Dividend cover		4.84	3.20	1.70	3.16	2.72
Sales increase	%	68.98	32.30	9.03	13.46	28.07
Earnings growth	%	90.93	42.42	8.85	19.53	3.58
Investment x depreciation		4.83	2.91	0.91	1.51	1.65
Investment as % assets		47.86	35.19	13.54	23.07	24.64
Number of employees		1,628	2,434	2,142	2,333	3,117

VODAFONE GROUP plc

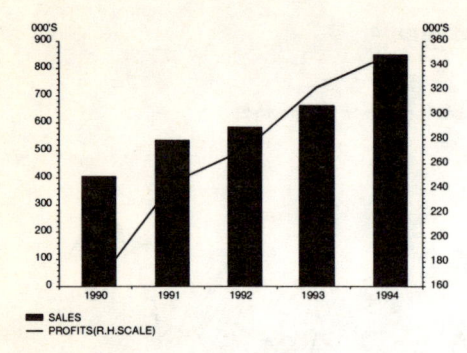

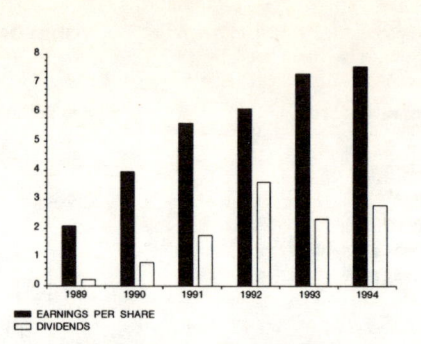

Sales and profits

Earnings and dividends

Outlook

Vodafone is the cuckoo which got thrown out of the nest when it grew too big, rather than throwing the rest of the family out. The government wanted a second mobile-phone network operator to compete with Cellnet – already 60 per cent owned by British Telecom. It invited applications and eventually awarded the licence in 1982 to the consortium led by the electronics group Racal.

The fledgling cellular-phone industry got off to a flying start in the City during the boom times of the late 1980s, as the mobile phone became as essential a piece of yuppie equipment as the Filofax, BMW or the Porsche. Vodafone, owned by Racal Telecom (part of the Racal group) flourished, and soon overtook Cellnet as the market leader, signing up its two hundred thousandth subscriber in July 1988, only three and a half years after its network first came into operation.

Racal Telecom was partially floated in 1988 and became self-financing. But the sale of this initial 20 per cent of the company was not without incident. Millicom, the US telecom group with a five per cent stake in Racal, campaigned for the complete sale of the telecom business, with 90 per cent of the shares going to existing Racal shareholders and the balance being sold to raise funds. Racal's chairman, Sir Ernest Harrison, who had built the company from a tiny radio business into one of Britain's top three international electronics groups, saw off Millicom's intervention after winning considerable backing from small shareholders.

Within a few years Racal's telecom business began to overshadow the rest of group. The parent group found that its own stock market value often fell below that of its 80 per cent stake in Racal Telecom, as a result of which Racal Telecom was demerged completely as a separate company called Vodafone in September 1991. It was big enough to join the FTSE share index immediately. Only 10 years after Racal first won its cellular-phone licence, and seven years after the Vodafone network became operational, Vodafone produced its 1991–2 results, which showed pre-tax profits of £272 million on a turnover of £585 million.

The rapid growth of the cellular-phone industry was helped by the decision to vary the American model in two significant ways. The introduction of a host of service providers to sell airtime to users on behalf of the two operators created intense competition, while the concept that the caller should pay for the calls – rather than the subscriber, who in the US paid for incoming and outgoing calls – encouraged people to give their numbers to others. By the end of 1994 there were expected to be nearly 3 million cellular-phone users in the UK, making it the largest market in Europe. Vodafone had 54 per cent of the market, with 1.4 million subscribers. Its network, which has cost over £800 million to build, covered 98 per cent of the population and 80 per cent of the land mass.

The first generation of mobile phones in the UK used analogue technology, where the signal is a continuous electrical wave which changes frequency and amplitude in order to convey speech. The next leap forward was to digital technology, which offers a broader and better-quality service. Here speech is converted to coded patterns of digital pulses which are sent down the line. It allows encryption, making mobile-phone calls secure from almost all but the most sophisticated eavesdroppers.

Vodafone has built a new digital network which covers about 90 per cent of the UK population. It is based on the GSM (Groupe Spécial Mobile) standard agreed by about 32 countries in Europe and the rest of the world. Subscribers to GSM networks will eventually be able to use their phones in any country with a GSM network, and still get billed at home.

In 1992 Vodaphone launched a downmarket, 'low user' version of its analogue service, called LowCall, in response to a similar move by its rival Cellnet. LowCall, with cheap handsets, low rental and relatively high call charges, also helped fill the gap before Vodafone's GSM network was fully up and running, and encouraged wider domestic use of the mobile phone.

Although Vodafone's cellular-phone operations account for the bulk of its business, a quarter stems from associated activities like data transmission over the phone networks, radio paging, packet radio (where data is converted into compressed digital pulses and sent over air waves), 'value-added' services like voice messaging and data transmission, and Orbitel, its 50:50 joint venture in making telecom equipment with Swedish group L M Ericsson. It also has 10 joint ventures overseas, building and running cellular networks in countries as varied as France, Hong Kong, Australia, South Africa and Greece.

Shares

After Racal floated off the first slice of Vodafone in 1988 at 170p, the shares soared to 519p in six months as the $6.5 billion bid by McCaw for LIN Broadcasting in the US put a sky-high price on cellular-phone systems. The shares later settled back to a steady trading range of between 320p and 400p. Uncertainty over the proposed break-up of Racal in 1990 led to a slump in Vodafone's shares, but when plans for a management buy-out at Racal were suspended later that year, the shares recovered. The rating against the market slipped in 1991 when the recession was seen to have affected mobile-phone sales, but that autumn the rest of Vodafone's shares were floated off and the old trading range was regained.

For a spell the shares were marked up on signs of an economic recovery, and fell back down again when one failed to appear. There was a mark-down in the summer of 1992 when a price war broke out among cellular-phone companies, but Vodafone's results that autumn were at the top end of analysts' forecasts and later the group won a licence for a network in Australia, both of which triggered a re-rating. This was compounded by hopes that the economy was about to recover, and the shares gained strongly in the 1983 market rally. Analysts remained confident of the group's prospects despite the new challenge from Mercury One-2-One and Hutchison Telecom's Orange mobile-phone services. Vodafone's profits for 1993/4 rose by 13 per cent, whereas its share price dipped in line with the downturn in the market in the first half of 1994.

Corporate conscience

As a relatively new public company, Vodafone is still putting in place some of the policies and practices established by other businesses, although it is comparatively untainted by serious issues of conscience. For instance, it pulled out of Mexico (regarded as having an oppressive regime) in 1993. It has infringed the advertising code, but has a clean record with regard to matters of health and safety and water pollution. Furthermore, it is publicly committed to a policy of not discriminating against the disabled, which applies to all areas of employment.

Corporate governance

Separate Chairman and Chief Executive Y
Number of Directors 9
Number of Non-Executive Directors 4
(3 Independent Directors)
Insulated Directors Not known

Board Committees
Audit: Y   Remuneration: Y

Remuneration

Year end	31.03.91	31.03.92	31.03.93
Total board £M	1.10	1.38	1.69
% change		25	23
Highest paid £	381,529	479,237	515,144
% change		26	8

Board

Whent, G A *Chief Executive*
Gent, C C *Executive Director*
Henning, David J *Executive Director*
Hydon, K J *Executive Director*
Peett, E J *Executive Director*
Barlow, Sir William *Independent Non-Executive*
Clark, Sir Robert *Independent Non-Executive*
Lomer, Geoffrey J *Independent Non-Executive*
Harrison, Sir Ernest *Non-Executive Chairman*

Since Sir Ernest Harrison is chairman of Vodafone, it is no surprise that the company's approach to corporate governance mirrors that of its once-parent Racal. Vodafone does have a higher proportion of independent directors on its board, in addition to audit and remuneration committees (although it would be easy to miss that fact without a very careful perusal of the annual report). The company gives no analysis at all of directors' pay, nor any mention of bonus schemes and service contracts.

S G WARBURG GROUP plc

1 Finsbury Avenue, London EC2M 2PA
Tel: 0171 606 1006
Chairman Sir David Scholey
Chief executive Lord Cairns
Main subsidiaries Mercury Asset Management (75%), Rowe & Pitman
Size £1.0 billion sales, £1.5 billion stock market value, 4,500 employees
5-year growth sales n/a, earnings per share nil, employment n/a

S G WARBURG plc

Share record

Return on shareholder's equity	%	n/a
5-year price high	p	1007.0
5-year price low	p	286.0
Dividend yield	%	3.97
5-year high	%	6.99
5-year low	%	2.45
Price/earnings ratio		8.4
5-year high		23.2
5-year low		8.1

Share price performance (in pence)

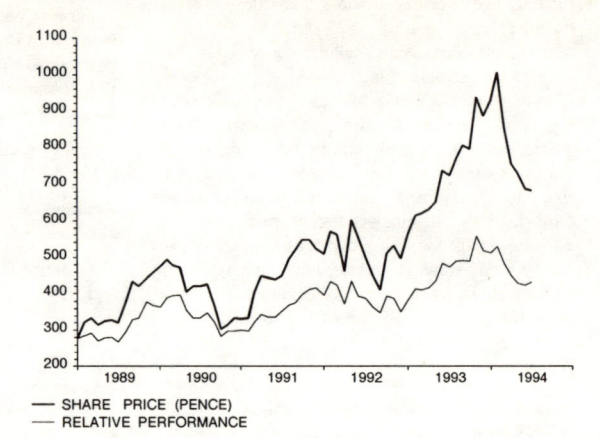

— SHARE PRICE (PENCE)
— RELATIVE PERFORMANCE

Financial record

		31/3/90	31/3/91	31/3/92	31/3/93	31/3/94
Gross profit	£'000					
Bad debt provision	£'000					
Pre-tax profit	£'000			166,300	148,200	297,000
Published retentions	£'000	80,600	48,400	63,700	43,100	130,800
Earnings per share	p	0.00	0.00	49.87	39.63	82.42
Dividend per share	p	15.00	16.00	18.00	19.00	22.00
Net assets per share	p	464.20	479.61	532.73	552.91	859.55
Shareholders' funds	£	689,200	719,900	838,600	889,400	1,007M
Return on long term capital	%					
Retern on shareholders' equity	%					
Pre-tax margin	%					
Operating profit per employee	£					
Free resources ratio	£	5.96	5.56	6.94	5.54	5.37
Dividend cover		0.00	0.00	2.77	2.09	3.75
Net income growth	%					
Earnings growth	%	0.00	0.00	0.00	-20.55	107.99
Total advances	£	2,016M	1,895M	1,642M	1,777M	4,994M
Customer deposits	£	5,267M	5,498M	4,881M	5,021M	7,057M
Number of employees						4,472

S G WARBURG plc

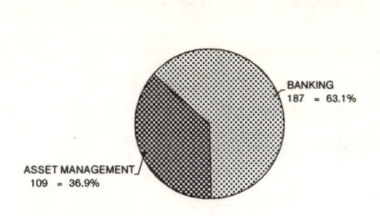

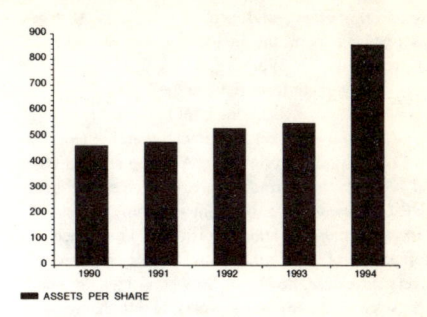

Sales analysis

BANKING 187 = 63.1%
ASSET MANAGEMENT 109 = 36.9%

Assets per share

ASSETS PER SHARE (1990–1994)

Solvency debt = 45% shareholders' funds, interest cover n/a
Political donations 0
Charitable donations £1.4 million

Major developments
1933 Siegmund Warburg came to London to set up the New Trading Company
1946 name changed to S G Warburg
1986 acquired stockbroker Rowe & Pitman and traders Ackroyd & Smithers
1987 quarter of Mercury Asset Management shares floated on the stock exchange
1994 Henry Grunfeld announced intention to step down as joint president

Outlook
Warburg has become Britain's premier merchant bank, or investment bank, as these institutions are now generally known, following the US terminology. This is a remarkable achievement, considering that the company began relatively recently in 1933, and that it was always considered an outsider in the closed City world where the pedigree of several other institutions stretched back centuries.

Siegmund Warburg and his partner, Henry Grunfeld, were regarded as outsiders only in London, where they arrived as refugees from Hitler's Germany. Warburg in particular was not new to the world of international business. The family bank in Hamburg, M M Warburg, was one of Germany's great private banks until the outbreak of the Second World War. The US branch of the empire was powerful both on Wall Street and due to its White House connections. Grunfeld was not so well connected, but his background in the family steel business was perhaps equally important when it came to creating the New Trading Company, as their business was first called – a little different from the run of stuffy City institutions which were its competitors.

Whatever the reason, S G Warburg has been credited with being instrumental in rebuilding London's financial standing after the war. Sir Siegmund, as he became in 1966, effectively invented the Eurodollar market (that is, dollar funds traded outside the US). Less felicitously, perhaps, he brought the concept of the hostile takeover to a London stock market which had been used only to agreed mergers and acquisitions.

The company also developed a culture unusual in the City. At Warburg there has always been an aversion to the kind of star status usually awarded key members of staff. In addition, a frugality has always applied – although that reputation has perhaps been dented by the huge bonuses paid to staff in 1994.

These differences may have been responsible for Warburg's much greater success than any other company in handling London's Big Bang, helped by the fact that it bought what were probably the best firms: stockbroker Rowe & Pitman; 'jobber' or market maker Ackroyd & Smithers; and the government stocks dealer Mullens. Whereas other banks have bought high-quality firms and found it difficult to integrate them into the organisation, Warburg, on the other hand, seems to have gone from strength to strength. That is partly because the group was not focused as exclusively on London as were some other houses. Even at the height of the 1980s stock market boom, Warburg was planning to become more internationally based.

Ironically, considering Siegmund Warburg's family connections, this policy proved to be one of his failures: he did not manage to integrate the US and German arms with his UK creation. But in the late 1980s and early 1990s his successors at Warburg have nevertheless built a substantial international network. The group is still overshadowed by the vast US banks, but it is one of the few European firms to be in a position to rival them. For example, in 1993 Warburg ranked third in the world with regard to giving advice on mergers and acquisitions, and Mercury Asset Management, the investment arm which is 75 per cent owned by Warburg, had a fifth of its funds under management from outside the UK.

Nevertheless, investment banks are ultimately at the mercy of the market to a much greater extent than most other kinds of company. A rising stock market and high levels of trading are good for the share-related business, as a buoyant economy boosts the market for mergers and acquisitions, and hence the profitability of investment banks. Their costs are relatively inflexible, however. So when times are good, profits soar, but investors worry about the sustainability of those profits.

Warburg has shown, however, that it can ride the cycle successfully. It survived the death of Sir Siegmund in 1982, and the decision by Henry Grunfeld to step down as president in 1994 on his 90th birthday (although he still went into work every day) will have caused little upset in the firm – Warburg long ago outgrew its founders. The question that remains is whether it can match its big US competitors.

Shares

Financial institutions are largely prey to the roller coaster of the financial markets, which can be seen very clearly in Warburg's share price chart. For almost two years after the stock market collapse in 1987, the group's shares fell (relative to the stock market) because the financial boom was over. Then there was a brief surge which soon collapsed in 1990, followed by another recovery. The fall from the peak at the beginning of 1992 was relatively modest, however, and was succeeded by a great surge that lasted until the beginning of 1994. This was based partly on optimism about financial prospects generally, and partly upon the recognition that Warburg had built up a sturdy intenational business. The next slide, at the start of 1994, was due to fears that the company had lost huge sums as a result of the collapse of the bond markets, but the slide was halted when the annual results revealed that losses had been much less than anticipated.

Corporate conscience

As a merchant bank, Warburg's exposure to most issues of conscience is via the companies that it serves. The nature of the merchant-banking business excludes such issues as water pollution and the production of alcohol or tobacco which affect manufacturing and service companies in other sectors. The ethics of banking are a subject of debate for some people. But the culture created by Siegmund Warburg and Henry Grunfeld causes Warburg to be generally regarded as having more integrity than most investment banks, and a serious sense of its responsibilities. It is a major donor to charities and a member of ABSA. Both Warburg and Mercury Asset Management are also members of BITC and the Per Cent Club, and the group makes no political donations.

Corporate governance
Separate Chairman and Chief Executive Y
Number of Directors 23
Number of Non-Executive Directors 8
(6 Independent Directors)
Insulated Directors None

Board Committees
Audit: Y   Remuneration: Y

Remuneration

Year end	31.3.92	31.3.93	31.3.94
Total board £M	7.69	5.65	10.74
% change		-27	90
Highest paid £M	1.00	0.51	1.52
% change		-49	197

Board
Scholey, Sir David *Executive Chairman*
Lord Cairns *Chief Executive*
Bass, P *Executive Director*
Gore, M B G *Executive Director*
Higgs, D A *Executive Director*
Mayo, J W *Executive Director*
Sargent, M C *Executive Director*
Stevenson, H A *Executive Director*
Twachtmann, P *Executive Director*
Verey, H N *Executive Director*
van der Wyck, H C *Executive Director*
von Simson, P *Executive Director*
Ward, R G *Executive Director*
Wyman, T H *Executive Director*
Leathes, S W *Finance Director*
Corness, Sir Colin *Independent Non-Executive*
Gough, C B *Independent Non-Executive*
Hurn, F R *Independent Non-Executive*
Rowland, J D *Independent Non-Executive*
Schinzler, Dr H-J *Independent Non-Executive*
van Vlissingen, P F *Independent Non-Executive*
Lewisohn, O M *Non-Executive*
Stancliffe, J C G *Non-Executive*

This huge board is a reflection of the nature of banking governance as well as the collegiate nature of Warburg in particular. It is difficult to believe that a board of such size can operate effectively as a decision-making body and as a check on the chairman and chief executive. The non-executives remain easily outnumbered, although more were included in 1993 and 1994. The annual report for 1994 provided a statement on corporate governance which explained the workings of the board and mentioned the existence of a board administration committee, consisting of the chief executive and five other executive directors. Warburg has made moves to comply with the Cadbury Code, but retains an executive director, John Mayo, as chairman of the audit committee, 'in view of his qualifications and experience in the law'. The 1994 annual report revealed that the enormous payments that year were largely due to bonuses stemming from the good trading conditions of 1993. But it also revealed that while the bonuses were decided by the non-executive appointments and compensation committee, there are no fixed formulae with which to arrive at the amount of bonus paid.

WILLIAMS HOLDINGS plc

Pentagon House, Sir Frank Whittle Road,
Derby DE2 4XA
Tel: 01332 202020
Chairman Nigel Rudd
Chief executive Roger Carr
Main brands and subsidiaries Amdega, Cuprinol, Hammerite, Heatrae-Sadia, Kidde-Graviner, Kidde Hartnell, Larch-Lap, Nutone, Polycell, Polyfilla, Rawlplug, Smallbone kitchens, Swish, Thorn fire protection, Valor, Vi-Spring, William Fairey, Yale
Size £1.2 billion sales, £2.1 billion stock market value, 14,900 employees
5-year growth sales 7%, earnings per share -33%, employment -14%
Solvency debt = 60% shareholders' funds, interest cover 9 times
Political donations £25,000 Conservative Party
Charitable donations £127,000

Major developments
1957 formed as W Williams & Sons
1982 takeover by Nigel Rudd and Brian McGowan
1984 bought H J B Jackson
1985 bought Duport, London & Midland Industrials, Fairey Engineering
1986 bid for McKechnie Brothers defeated
1987 bid for Norcros defeated
1988 bought Crown Paints and Polycell, Berger paints, Smallbone kitchens, Pilgrim House
1989 demerged Pendragon car dealership; bought Kidde fire-protection business
1990 sold Crown Berger to Nobel Industries (Sweden)
1991 bought Yale & Valor; lost hostile bid for Racal Electronics
1993 bought Thorn fire-extinguisher business; Brian McGowan retired; sold small engineering businesses to management for £140m
1994 rights issue raised £267m; bought Solvay woodcare division

Outlook
The trouble with being an acquisitive conglomerate is that failing to win a takeover battle tarnishes your reputation for an activity which is at the very core of your strategy. On the other hand, the price of the target company tends to escalate during a takeover battle, so that the successful bidder ends up paying far too much.

In some cases, that excessive purchase price can quickly be turned into a bargain by selling off parts of the acquired company at even more inflated prices: Hanson's dismemberment of Imperial Group was the classic example. Williams, on the other hand, is not as great an asset-trader as Hanson, though more so than BTR or Tomkins, and it has always been reluctant to pay such extreme prices as some of its fellow conglomerates. For an acquisitive conglomerate, it therefore has rather a bad record of making acquisitions, the most recent example of which was its defeat at the hands of Racal at the end of 1991.

In fact Williams has never won a contested takeover bid. During the 1980s, for instance, it failed in its attempt to win over shareholders of Norcros (who have probably lived to regret their decision) and McKechnie. The group's successes have been agreed deals. In the early 1980s, after accountants Nigel Rudd and Brian McGowan had bought into the ailing foundry company that it was then, Williams pounced mainly on clapped-out engineering companies, often buying them from parent groups keen to sell. That is a much better basis for getting a bargain, and so it proved with the purchase of Swish curtain-track company Duport, Pearson subsidiary Fairey Engineering, Crown and Berger paints (from Reed and Hoechst respectively) and Rawlplug, the fixings business. More recently, in 1991, Williams agreed a deal with Yale and Valor, the company that combined Valor gas fires and the US lock and building products group Yale and Nutone.

These acquisitions rocketed Williams up the corporate league table into the £1 billion sales category (compared with just £100 million in 1985). But in fact sales in 1992 were lower than they had been in 1989, because of the disposal of Crown Berger paints. The sale of this subsidiary proves that, while Williams is not primarily an asset-trader, it has no particular attachment to a business, even if it has only recently been acquired. Unlike most conglomerate bosses, though, Messrs Rudd and McGowan have a fondness for aquiring a disparate range of brands. The disposal of Crown Berger shows that this fondness does not extend to sentimentality – it is more a function of their belief in high margins, which tend to stem from products (usually brand names) with leading market positions.

For Williams, attention to margins seems to take precedence over return on capital, although this may be a consequence of takeover accounting, under which frequent write-offs reduce the capital part of the return-on-capital calculation. Apart from this minor deviation, Williams follows the familiar conglomerate path: tight cost and cash control, minimal overheads, and a determination to eradicate problems the minute they appear. One other difference, however, is an apparently greater willingness to invest, despite an insistence on very short pay-back periods.

The result of 10 years of stewardship by Messrs Rudd and McGowan was a tightly managed, fairly

WILLIAMS HOLDINGS

Share record

Return on shareholders' equity	%	446.26
5-year price high	p	412.9
5-year price low	p	180.8
Dividend yield	%	4.40
5-year high	%	8.56
5-year low	%	3.74
Price/earnings ratio		18.9
5-year high		24.3
5-year low		6.4

Share price performance (in pence)

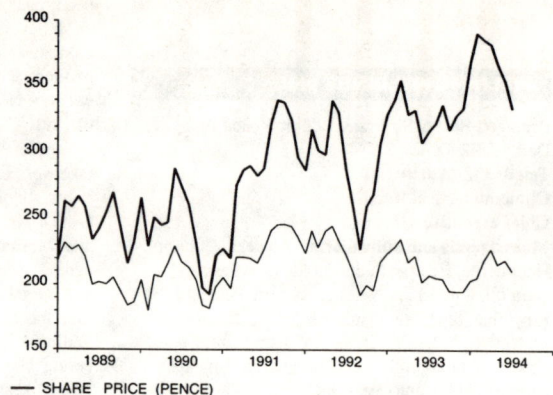

— SHARE PRICE (PENCE)
— RELATIVE PERFORMANCE

Financial record

		31/12/89	31/12/90	31/12/91	31/12/92	31/12/93
Total sales	£'000	1,134M	833,550	1,002M	1,035M	1,213M
Pre-tax profit	£'000	153,457	126,093	168,300	155,200	173,400
Published retentions	£'000	59,142	100,264	18,567	30,500	13,700
Earnings per share	p	29.32	22.15	22.35	17.65	19.55
Dividend per share	p	11.36	11.85	12.20	12.35	12.59
Operating cash flow	£'000	13,282	78,343	-8,304	-3,300	46,600
Net assets per share	p	127.58	111.18	123.53	140.38	131.20
Net debt/(cash)	£'000	137,301	4,627	115,923	150,200	192,800
Shareholders' funds	£'000	269,488	329,398	402,378	395,200	319,100
Return on capital	%	42.87	37.26	40.55	28.97	30.42
Profit margin	%	13.53	15.13	16.78	14.99	14.30
Sales per employee	£	65.70	62.82	67.15	70.74	81.32
Interest cover		10.46	13.19	18.97	9.13	9.14
Dividend cover		2.58	1.87	1.83	1.43	1.55
Sales increase	%	37.37	-26.51	20.18	3.36	17.11
Earnings growth	%	9.89	-24.47	0.90	-21.04	10.79
Investment x depreciation		2.09	1.34	1.13	1.04	0.95
Investment as % assets		17.17	12.18	8.67	9.17	9.37
Number of employees		17,263	13,269	14,917	14,636	14,912

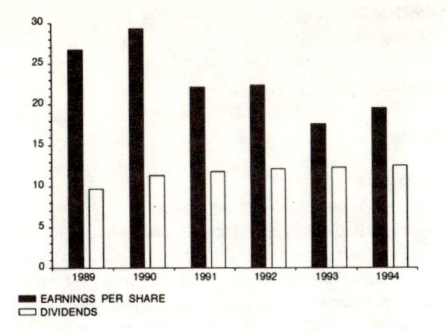

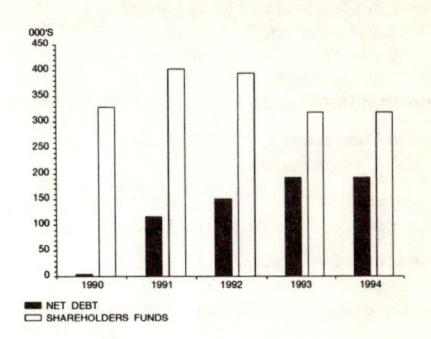

Earnings and dividends

Debt and shareholders' funds

diverse group. Interests include various aspects of building (Cuprinol, Polycell, Yale and Rawlplug, plus upmarket conservatories, garages and kitchens), fire and safety equipment (supplemented by the 1993 acquisition from Thorn of its portable fire extinguisher business), and a fairly random collection of engineering operations. There was a significant change in 1993, however. First, Brian McGowan announced he was going into semi-retirement and left the board. Second, Nigel Rudd announced a new strategy of abandoning conglomeracy, to concentrate instead on three core businesses – building products, security and fire protection. As a consequence, a collection of small engineering companies was sold to managers.

The transition was generally welcomed but left some observers still waiting to be convinced that Williams can deliver something more than the basic formula of cost-cutting, takeover-led growth.

Shares

The peak in the company's rating against the market in 1988 came after two years of hectic bid activity. Up to that time management could boast that it had not made a dud acquisition. The board kept interest in the group alive with bids and the odd divestment but got more excitement than it bargained for in December 1989 when the fraud squad was called in to investigate a share-ramping episode. This involved someone tricking *The Times* newspaper into running a false story about a takeover bid for Williams which briefly pushed the shares up by 25 per cent.

In 1990 the shares rallied as the group was expected to do well in the recession, but poor results that year sent the rating down again. In 1991 the bid for Yale and Valor was well received by the City. The management was cited by some as a model of how to conduct business during a recession, but when the bid for Racal failed, the rating dipped. In 1992 the shares fell as the board said it was no longer looking for a big acquisition, but by the end of the year the shares were being acquired for their recovery potential. The shares did well in the 1993 bull market as the devaluation of sterling made the US division in particular a good recovery prospect. But the improvement did not last and the shares' standing continued its erratic course into 1994 as investors waited to see the outcome of the new strategy.

Corporate conscience

Williams is often compared to Tomkins, and there are many similarities on issues of conscience as well as in other aspects of the two groups. Like Tomkins, Williams is not a member of BITC, does not have public policies covering equal opportunities and the environment, and did not respond to the EIRIS questionnaire. The group has made some concessions to its new-found big-company status, having made a commitment in 1989 to donate £500,000 over five years to the Prince's Youth Trust.

Otherwise its record is negative although there are no water pollution transgressions. Animal testing is involved in the manufacture of products from Cuprinol and Polycell; as well as being a user of CFCs, the group employs halons to a significant degree in its fire extinguisher businesses; and tropical hardwoods are implicated in Vi-Spring beds, Compton conservatories and Smallbone kitchens.

Williams also has a small interest in Brazil, but the main ethical concern regarding the company is a military one. Aerospace Forgings manufactures parts for military aircraft, while Fairey Engineering produces ammunition containers and makes military bridges and pontoons. The fire protection businesses also supply the military, and there is a small nuclear involvement as well.

GEORGE WIMPEY plc

Corporate governance

Separate Chairman and Chief Executive Y
Number of Directors 7
Number of Non-Executive Directors 4
(2 Independent Directors)
Insulated Directors MD

Board Committees
Audit: Y   Remuneration: Y

Remuneration

Year end	31.12.91	31.12.92	31.12.93
Total board £M	2.42	2.45	2.27
% change	27	1	-7
Highest paid £	645,000	670,000	690,000
% change	9	4	3

Board
Carr, Roger M *Chief Executive*
Rudd, A Nigel R *Executive Chairman*
Davies, Michael T *Executive Director*
Bishops, Sir Michael *Independent Non-Executive*
Rigg, J A *Independent Non-Executive*
Rowe-Ham, Sir David *Independent Non-Executive*
Rhodes, W W *Non-Executive*

Not a company which has ever paid too much attention to such things as corporate governance, Williams Holdings has come into line with most Cadbury requirements, although it does not have a Nominations Committee. The company gives the minimum information necessary on directors' pay, but was spared the need to explain bonus payments in 1993 by the fact that there were none.

GEORGE WIMPEY plc

27 Hammersmith Grove, London W6 7EN
Tel: 0181 748 2000
Chairman Sir John Quinton
Chief executive Joe Dwyer
Substantial shareholdings Grove Charity Management (family trusts) 5%
Size £1.6 billion sales, £595 million stock market value, 11,600 employees
5-year growth sales -23%, earnings per share -83%, employment -33%
Solvency debt = 1% shareholders' funds, interest cover 2 times
Political donations £20,000 Conservative Party
Charitable donations £100,000

Major developments
1979 became public
1984 joined in forming Channel Tunnel builders group; sold share in Euston Centre properties to British Land; sold 5% stake in Oldham Estates
1986 Grove trusts sold 16% shareholding
1989 expanded US quarrying
1991 sold Wimpey Waste to Wessex Waste Management
1992 sold stake in Little Britain London property development
1993 Grove trusts sold 29% shareholding

Outlook

George Wimpey is Britain's second-largest housebuilder. Badly hit, therefore, by the collapse in the housing market at the end of the 1980s, its management subsequently made substantial provisions that won the approval of City analysts. Values of the company's residential land and commercial activities had plummeted, along with its fortunes, and by the end of 1992 it was up to the group's forceful chief executive, Joe Dwyer, to take strong action.

By the end of 1993 Mr Dwyer's single-minded stance seemed to be paying off. A record loss of £112 million in 1992 was transformed into a profit of £25 million after the group sold 40 per cent more houses than in the previous year.

Wimpey is not just a UK housebuilder, although that does remain its largest area of operation. As well as building overseas, the group has also invested in minerals, construction and property. Its housing activities are concentrated in the UK and in North America, while its Homes division also operates in Europe and Australia, although the company has indicated it intends withdrawing from these areas in the long term. Profitablity in the housing division during 1994 will depend very much on what happens to house prices. While the company is achieving a respectable number of completions and sales, it is suffering slightly from depressed margins.

As regards construction, Wimpey, along with its rivals, has been battered by the longest and deepest recession since the war. In the spring of 1994 the situation was not looking any brighter, although there was some evidence from the Royal Institution of Chartered Surveyors and the Department of the Environment which suggested that the sector's fortunes might be improving.

In response to the sorry state of affairs in the UK construction industry, Wimpey has increasingly cast its eyes overseas. Most of its overseas work has historically been in the Middle East, but it has begun taking on more jobs in the Caribbean, Europe and the Far East.

The minerals businesses continue to be depressed in both the UK and the US. Capital expenditure has been promised in the hope of improving operations, but whether this will be effectively implemented has been questioned by some observers. As well as its minerals operations in the UK and North America, the company also owns a coastal quarry in southern Ireland and a business in the Czech Republic.

The property business has been substantially written down since 1991, with a further writedown of £15 million in 1993. At the end of that year

GEORGE WIMPEY

Share record

Return on shareholder's equity	%	2.84
5-year price high	p	274.5
5-year price low	p	65.0
Dividend yield	%	3.95
5-year high	%	18.18
5-year low	%	2.72
Price/earnings ratio		41.4
5-year high		99.3
5-year low		6.3

Share price performance (in pence)

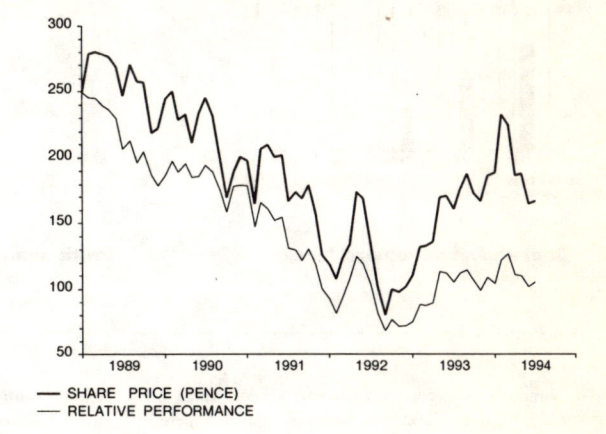

— SHARE PRICE (PENCE)
— RELATIVE PERFORMANCE

Financial record

		31/12/89	31/12/90	31/12/91	31/12/92	31/12/93
Total sales	£	2,008M	1,905M	1,690M	1,626M	1,555M
Pre-tax profit	£'000	124,500	9,500	-16,000	-103M	21,800
Published retentions	£'000	50,500	-26,100	-53,800	-135M	3,000
Earnings per share	p	26.33	0.41	0.00	0.00	4.57
Dividend per share	p	10.19	10.19	10.19	5.09	5.25
Operating cash flow	£'000	-134M	91,200	43,200	107,900	6,000
Net assets per share	p	378.95	341.39	321.86	270.45	235.41
Net debt/(cash)	£'000	382,200	305,400	206,400	122,700	5,900
Shareholders' funds	£'000	731,800	630,300	584,600	446,400	535,900
Return on capital	%	16.84	5.44	2.01	-8.20	5.98
Profit margin	%	6.11	0.54	-1.47	-6.24	1.65
Sales per employee	£	115.40	116.87	117.35	117.85	134.19
Interest cover		3.99	1.05	-0.04	-4.23	2.35
Dividend cover		2.61	0.00	0.00	0.00	0.87
Sales increase	%	18.54	-5.13	-11.29	-3.76	-4.37
Earnings growth	%	-19.25	-98.43	-100.00	0.00	0.00
Investment x depreciation		3.54	1.94	1.61	-2.33	0.83
Investment as % assets		34.10	20.76	12.24	-25.85	7.53
Number of employees		17,400	16,300	14,400	13,800	11,590

432 GEORGE WIMPEY plc

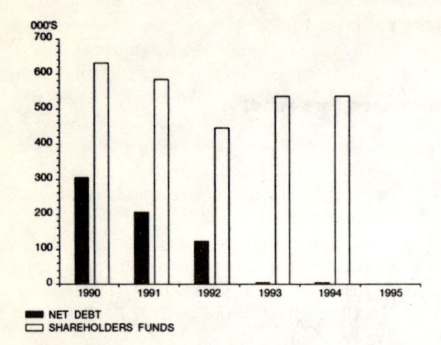

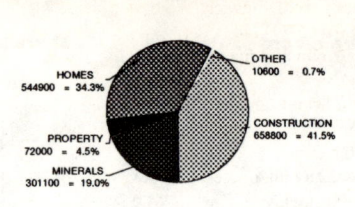

Debt and shareholders' funds

Profit analysis

Wimpey's property portfolio had a book value of £135 million. Further writedowns are considered unlikely.

Shares
The price of Wimpey's shares in the early 1990s reflects the fortunes of the housebuilding sector as a whole. From a high in the mid-1980s, the price fell steadily to hit rock bottom in 1992 after it became apparent that Wimpey had enormous debts, and losses to match. Since then the shares have risen again steadily and, despite its problems, the company has seemed to be pulling itself together. As a result, analysts pronouced that the shares will remain good value for a while to come, although they may change their mind if Wimpey's much lauded recovery goes into reverse.

Corporate consience
The company devoted three pages of its 1993 annual report to 'Quality, Training and Community', illustrating its commitment to increasing staff skills and monitoring its impact on the world. This is supported by proper environmental and equal-opportunities policies. Wimpey inevitably transgresses other criteria because it is involved in quarrying and some of its building activities have been on military and nuclear sites. It also uses ozone-depleting chemicals and tropical hardwoods and has suffered health and safety convictions in the UK. Some overseas operations are in countries with poor human rights records.

Corporate governance
Separate Chairman and Chief Executive Y
Number of Directors 11
Number of Non-Executive Directors 4
(4 Independent Directors)
Insulated Directors All execs

Board Committees
Audit: Y   Remuneration: Y

Remuneration

Year end	31.12.91	31.12.92	31.12.93
Total board £M	1.69	1.84	1.46
% change	53	9.0	-21
Highest paid £	207,000	229,000	265,000
% change	9	11	16

Board
Dwyer, J A *Chief Executive*
Andrew, Richard A *Executive Director*
Brant, D G *Executive Director*
Grey, R W *Executive Director*
Penton, D M *Executive Director*
Ross, T S *Executive Director*
Wood, R N A *Finance Director*
Curry, Peter A M *Independent Non-Executive*
Grassick, W P C *Independent Non-Executive*
Graves, Dr D J T *Independent Non-Executive*
Quinton, Sir John *Non-Executive Chairman*

The retirement of Wimpey veteran Sir Clifford Chetwood in 1993 and his replacement by ex-Barclays bank boss Sir John Quinton helped give the board more balance. It has also improved pay disclosure, although more details on pay consideration would be useful.

WOLSELEY plc

Vines Lane, Droitwich, Worcestershire WR9 8ND
Tel: 01905 794444
Chairman and managing director Jeremy Lancaster
Main brands and subsidiaries Builder Center, Controls Center, Drainage Center, Pipeline Center, Plumb Center
Size £2.5 billion sales, £2.3 stock market value, 16,300 employees
5-year growth sales 52%, earnings per share -12%, employment 9%
Solvency debt = 29% shareholders' funds, interest cover 11 times
Political donations 0
Charitable donations £27,000

Major developments

1982 went public; moved into US with purchase of Ferguson Enterprises
1985 bought Carolina distributor, US, for £55 millon
1986 bought Grovewood from BAT Industries for £109 million; name changed to Wolseley
1987 bought Familian Corp, US, for £61 million
1992 bought Brossette, France, for £95 million
1993 bought Erb Lumber, US, for £51 million
1994 bought OAG Group, Austria, for £57 million

Outlook

Wolseley seems not to have noticed that the 1980s are over. Having grown fast through acquisition almost from the moment it was floated on the stock exchange in 1982, the company has simply carried on in that groove. Surprisingly, unlike most other companies which attempted this, it has not yet tripped up. And, what is more, there appear to be a solid business, sensible management and sound principles behind its success.

Perhaps the difference is that this is an old family business with a long tradition of caution and frugality, rather than a management buyout with a tight deadline for coming to the stock market and feeling that it has something to prove after that. Wolseley-Hughes, as the group was called until 1986, was an engineering company with an agricultural background. It had been founded in 1889 as the Wolseley Sheep Shearing Machine Company but from agricultural equipment it moved into more mainstream manufacturing, and in particular radiators. In the 1960s it escaped from the cut-throat world of making central-heating radiators by turning its branch network into a distributor of central-heating equipment. That grew to encompass other plumbing supplies, and Plumb Center, still the basis of Wolseley's business in the UK, was born. Having built Plumb Center to be a leader in the UK, the group then set about doing exactly the same in the US, and, unusually, it succeeded – with Ferguson Enterprises.

Both these businesses were expanded fast in the 1980s. In the UK the Plumb Center chain doubled in size between 1985 and 1988, and Ferguson was not far behind in the US. But Wolseley avoided the common trap of 'gearing up' – that is, taking on a large amount of debt. So, unlike many of the 'boom' companies of the 1980s, this group entered the recession with relatively low levels of debt and hence interest.

It also managed to limit the fall in profits much better than many companies, especially considering its exposure to the housing market. Operating profits (before interest costs) fell from £127 million in 1989 to just under £90 million two years later. Nevertheless the relatively low interest cost and a policy of not issuing an over-high dividend meant that the dividend could be held at its previous level and still amount to only half the earnings per share. By 1992 not only did profits begin to rise once more but Wolseley also began to branch out again – this time on to the Continent with the purchase of the French company Brossette. By acquiring a business that was very similar to Wolseley, the group thus avoided the serious mistake of entering a new country with a new business. And by not buying a business that is in trouble, Wolseley also avoided the mistake of thinking one can turn round a struggling company.

It all seems a little too good to be true. Even the assortment of manufacturing businesses managed to maintain reasonable profit levels during the recession, despite the fact that it includes curiosities such as electrical fittings, aerial and satellite communication systems, and pump manufacturing. This division, too, has been expanded – surprisingly, given its lack of homogeneity and divergence from the rest of the group.

Expansion is once again the order of the day everywhere. Brossette had already moved into Belgium, and Wolseley is keen to expand further on the Continent. In the UK and the US it has already begun to benefit significantly from the economic recovery, and there seems no limit to the ambitions of Jeremy Lancaster, who joined the company in 1961, and took over as chairman from his father in 1976. If it were not for his down-to-earth common sense, it would be easy to attribute much of the group's success to the familiar pattern of acquisition-led growth financed by expensive shares and fuelled by acquisition accounting. But it is difficult to square this with a chairman who can say: 'If you have ideas above your station you're dead in the water. This is not a fancy business.' Such lack of grandeur suggests that Wolseley may scale greater heights yet.

Shares

Despite its solid progress through the late 1980s, Wolseley's shares actually slipped from a peak in 1986 and made little progress again, compared to the market as a whole, until 1990. Then investors began to believe that this company could not only survive the recession, despite the tribulations of others in the building-related sectors, but also prosper. There was a period of hesitation in the second half of 1992, when doubts set in about the move on to the

WOLSELEY plc

Share record

Return on shareholder's equity	%	18.41
5-year price high	p	975.0
5-year price low	p	235.0
Dividend yield	%	2.15
5-year high	%	6.41
5-year low	%	1.82
Price/earnings ratio		20.5
5-year high		29.0
5-year low		6.3

Share price performance (in pence)

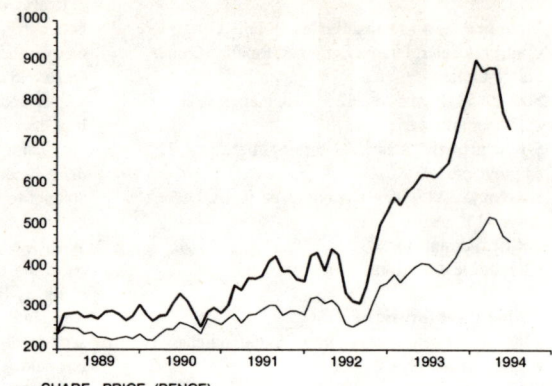

— SHARE PRICE (PENCE)
— RELATIVE PERFORMANCE

Financial record

		31/7/89	31/7/90	31/7/91	31/7/92	31/7/93
Total sales	£	1,644M	1,847M	1,738M	1,954M	2,491M
Pre-tax profit	£'000	117,597	118,537	89,373	90,259	119,116
Published retentions	£'000	54,711	52,521	23,751	29,432	46,398
Earnings per share	p	35.68	35.04	26.75	25.86	31.54
Dividend per share	p	11.00	12.10	12.10	12.55	13.95
Operating cash flow	£'000	1,883	7,046	21,474	40,452	39,486
Net assets per share	p	211.47	210.81	220.09	195.49	289.06
Net debt/(cash)	£'000	110,597	122,624	100,646	92,255	122,201
Shareholders' funds	£'000	301,561	316,674	349,824	242,176	423,011
Return on capital	%	32.41	29.57	21.84	23.46	26.62
Profit margin	%	7.15	6.42	5.14	4.62	4.78
Sales per employee	£	109.61	121.34	117.36	134.71	152.64
Interest cover		18.27	13.27	11.77	17.34	11.42
Dividend cover		3.24	2.90	2.21	2.06	2.26
Sales increase	%	28.44	12.36	-5.93	12.43	27.50
Earnings growth	%	18.31	-1.79	-23.66	-3.32	21.94
Investment x depreciation		1.53	1.21	0.84	0.59	0.76
Investment as % assets		22.44	18.95	15.10	11.47	12.84
Number of employees		14,998	15,223	14,806	14,502	16,318

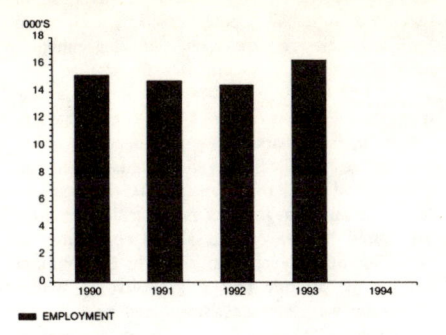

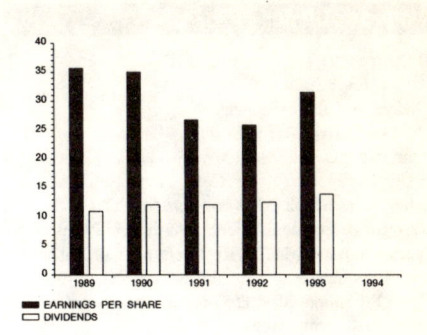

Employment

Earnings and dividends

Continent and the associated issue of yet more shares to finance the acquisition of Brossette. But then the shares' upward climb resumed, broken only by periods when the advance became too much for some investors, such as in the spring of 1994. The company remained well respected, however, although further progress of the share price was limited by the enormous surge which had taken place over the previous three years.

Corporate conscience
Wolseley manufactures and distributes products which impinge on ethical issues in a number of ways, although these are relatively minor and the group's conscience seems comparatively untroubled. Three small subsidiaries produce parts for military equipment, for example, and the group imports an estimated 5,000 cubic metres of tropical hardwood from Indonesia, Malaysia and the Philippines. It also received a couple of fines for health and safety breaches between April 1990 and March 1993. The US subsidiaries distribute insulation material inflated with CFCs, and air-conditioning equipment which uses similar ozone-depleting chemicals. These matters do not seem to be important to Wolseley, however. It has responded to EIRIS enquiries, but does not openly operate policies relating to equality of employment and the environment, nor does it appear to rate community involvement highly. (None of these matters were mentioned in the 1993 annual report.)

Corporate governance
Separate Chairman and Chief Executive N
Number of Directors 10
Number of Non-Executive Directors 2
(0 Independent Directors)
Insulated Directors MD

Board Committees
Audit: Y   Remuneration: Y

Remuneration

Year end	31.7.92	31.7.93
Total board £M	1.55	1.87
% change		21
Highest paid	222,143	258,977
% change		17

Board
Lancaster, Jeremy *Chairman & Managing Director*
Banks, C A *Executive Director*
Dibben, D A *Executive Director*
Ferris, W C *Executive Director*
Footman, J W *Executive Director*
Watson, J C *Executive Director*
Young, J W G *Executive Director*
Ireland, R *Finance Director*
Tucker, D L *Non-Executive Director*
Harford, Sir Timothy *Non-Exec Deputy Chairman*

Jeremy Lancaster clearly takes a dim view of the recommendations of the Cadbury Committee: in a section on corporate governance in the directors' report for 1993, the Code is described as being too prescriptive. Nevertheless, what the board describes as 'stewardship of the company' is an important attribute, and the auditors agree that Wolseley does actually comply with all the provisions of the Code except with regard to the number of non-executive directors. Three non-executives are required for the audit committee, while this company has only two. The statement on corporate governance suggested little readiness to make further appointments, only going so far as to say that 'changes will be made when appropriate and in the best interests of the group'.

WPP GROUP plc

27 Farm Street, London W1X 6RD
Tel: 0171 408 2204
Chairman Gordon Stevens
Chief executive Martin Sorrell
Main subsidiaries Alton Wire Products, Business Design Group, Carl Byoir, Coley Porter Bell, The Henley Centre, Hill and Knowlton, McColl Group, Millward Brown International, North Kent Plastic Cages, Ogilvy & Mather, Research International, J Walter Thompson
Size £1.4 billion sales, £557 million stock market value, 20,400 employees
5-year growth sales 42%, earnings per share -84%, employment 16%
Solvency debt = 12% shareholders' funds, interest cover 3 times
Political donations 0
Charitable donations £200,000

Major developments
1971 formed as Wire and Plastic Products
1986 became WPP Group after Martin Sorrell took control
1987 bought J Walter Thompson
1988 bought the Henley Centre for Forecasting
1989 bought the Ogilvy Group; bought Millward Brown plc
1991 sold stake in Abbott Mead Vickers; refinancing package agreed
1992 David Ogilvy retired; further refinancing and board changes
1993 rights issue to raise £88 million
1994 announced plans to float off market research business

Outlook
WPP overtook Saatchi & Saatchi as the world's largest advertising group in 1989, when it acquired Ogilvy & Mather to add to the J Walter Thompson empire bought two years previously. Then the group, run by former Saatchi finance director Martin Sorrell, mimicked his mentors' collapse. In September 1990 there was a dramatic slump in the share price as, first, the company warned that its profits would not be as great as had been anticipated and, second, investors realised the extent to which the ambitious group had become over-stretched. There followed months of negotiations with bankers to put in place new funding. But no sooner were the new arrangements in place than it became clear that these stop-gap measures would not be enough. More negotiations followed, resulting in a more susbtantial financial restructuring in 1992, which left the banks owning half the company.

It is a familiar tale of over-ambition and over-borrowing, but the speed of WPP's rise and fall, and the extent to which it copied the Saatchi story, is remarkable. In 1984 WPP was Wire and Plastic Products, one of those obscure companies occupying the nether regions of the stock market, which had no real reason to remain a public company – except to form a vehicle for some young, thrusting entrepreneur to make a quick entry into the market. And along came Mr Sorrell, intent on setting up a new type of marketing services group that concentrated on 'below-the-line' marketing – promotional activity, market research, direct sales and design – rather than conventional media advertising. Having created such a group through a series of small purchases, Mr Sorrell then saw the need and opportunity to move into mainstream advertising. His £277 million bid for the arthritic (but still creative) J Walter Thompson was audacious, since even after WPP's growth spurt, it was still small by comparison to JWT. But the bid came at just the right time, at the peak of the 1987 consumer and stock market booms. JWT put up little defence, and investors lapped up the huge share issue made to pay for the deal.

Things would probably have been fine if Mr Sorrell had been able to stop there. There was no difficulty slashing costs at the overblown US agency (a butler was reputedly employed to deliver peeled grapes to JWT boss Don Johnson). But WPP had gained a taste for making acquisitions and, like many such acquirers, ended up overreaching itself.

The purchase of Ogilvy & Mather proved to be the bid too far, landing the group with too much debt at a time when profits were falling. Like other advertising executives, Mr Sorrell had not expected decreasing profitability, believing the industry to be recession-proof. It was thought that, since the earlier recession of 1980–81, companies now recognised the importance of maintaining support for brands through the bad times, to make the good times even better. WPP went further, arguing that its customers for advertising were more heavily represented in packaged goods, rather than more volatile areas such as cars or electrical products. Its billings would therefore be less affected than those of other agencies. The group also pointed to its wide spread of marketing services, in addition to media advertising, and suggested this would offer further protection from recession.

It all sounded a little implausible at the time, and so it soon proved to be. Producers of packaged goods might maintain advertising levels, but with the price of advertising slots on television plummeting, companies obtained the same 'share of voice' for less money, which meant less commission for WPP. And recession took its toll on all areas of marketing, not just advertising.

WPP's troubles were compounded by the 'earn-out' formula for making acquisitions (brought with Mr Sorrell from Saatchi & Saatchi), which meant that long after a new subsidiary had stopped bringing in extra cash, the group was still having to pay the former owners of the company. And since some of these payments were in shares, the number of shares which had to be issued soared as the share price dived.

Like Saatchi & Saatchi, however, WPP survived and operating profits began to grow in 1992. A finan-

WPP GROUP

Share record

Return on shareholder's equity	%	-6.46
5-year price high	p	649.9
5-year price low	p	26.5
Dividend yield	%	1.17
5-year high	%	70.93
5-year low	%	0.00
Price/earnings ratio		10.7
5-year high		40.1
5-year low		0.4

Share price performance (in pence)

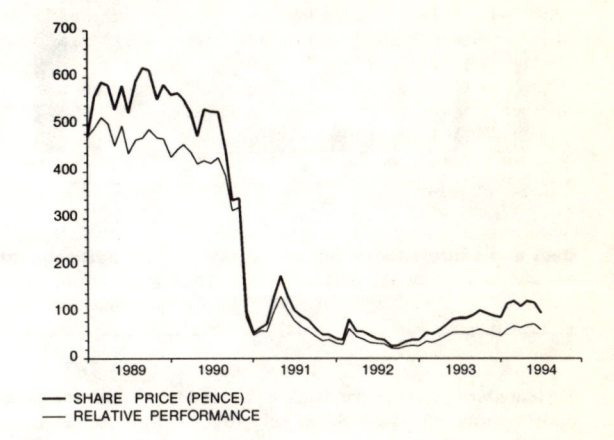

— SHARE PRICE (PENCE)
— RELATIVE PERFORMANCE

Financial record

		31/12/89	31/12/90	31/12/91	31/12/92	31/12/93
Total sales	£	1,005M	1,264M	1,204M	1,273M	1,431M
Pre-tax profit	£'000	75,039	90,014	40,150	53,751	79,457
Published retentions	£'000	19,875	32,920	13,407	-11,929	15,355
Earnings per share	p	62.34	67.23	0.00	2.27	10.04
Dividend per share	p	20.67	0.00	0.00	0.00	1.00
Operating cash flow	£'000	238,529	-26,551	n/a	23,283	100,389
Net assets per share	p	-184.52	15.36	27.50	3.71	-10.13
Net debt/(cash)	£'000	318,599	288,822	331,907	237,236	81,393
Shareholders' funds	£'000	455,400	585,788	576,981	603,460	667,290
Return on capital	%	-506.05	-365.32	828.04	277.48	1,890
Profit margin	%	7.32	6.91	3.01	3.81	5.03
Sales per employee	£	57.23	55.96	56.76	61.63	70.08
Interest cover		3.68	3.04	1.79	2.42	3.42
Dividend cover		3.02	0.00	0.00	0.00	10.05
Sales increase	%	83.77	25.72	-4.72	5.73	12.35
Earnings growth	%	34.44	7.85	-100.00	0.00	341.90
Investment x depreciation		1.07	0.90	0.65	0.83	0.89
Investment as % assets		13.49	16.85	12.64	12.96	17.36
Number of employees		17,568	22,590	21,218	20,664	20,416

WPP GROUP plc

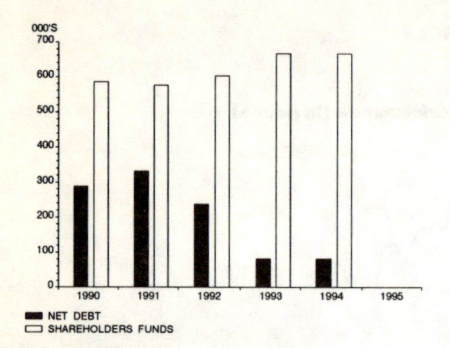

Debt and shareholders' funds

Sales and profits

cial restructuring cost millions to put in place and left the group with hefty debts. But in early 1994, after revealing another strong rise in profits, WPP said it would float off its market research business, which would cut its remaining £350 million debt by a third.

Shares
The booming market of 1987 saw a company which had been making shopping trolleys just two years earlier emerge as the vanquisher of J Walter Thompson, one of the world's biggest advertising agencies. Shares in WPP were at their peak when the bid was made, but the rights issue to pay for JWT flopped just before the stock market crash, causing the shares to fall from nearly £11 to just over £3 in the space of a few months.

The shares rallied in 1987 after an 800 per cent leap in profits, and enjoyed a good rating throughout the bid for Ogilvy & Mather and the economic boom. Yet the group seemed no sooner to have taken from Saatchi the poisoned chalice of being the world's number one agency, than it crashed. The rating had started to slip in 1990 as world economies headed into recession, but that September brought a frantic selling of the shares as rumours of financial difficulties reached the market. The shares lost two-thirds of their value in one week and the board issued a profit warning and said it needed talks with its bankers.

The next year there was a rally as hopes mounted for a rescue without a rights issue. The summer of 1991 brought a fresh fall as the group was pressured to refinance its $1 billion of debt. The crisis dragged on and the shares reached their low of 26.5p in 1992; then the situation was finally resolved as the refinancing went through later that year. WPP's shares rose steadily throughout 1993 and the early part of 1994, even though there was no expectation of a new advertising boom.

Corporate conscience
Like its rival in the advertising industry, Saatchi & Saathi, WPP has little direct involvement in areas which excite ethical interest. But like the Saatchi group, WPP does work for some companies and industries which raise issues of conscience, such as Rothmans and Seagram in tobacco and spirits.

Directly, however, it raises only two issues. WPP has operations in a variety of countries with oppressive regimes, and the group has a subsidiary called Refrigeration (Bournemouth) whose name indicates that it is a CFC user.

WPP does not have well-developed social policies, nor is the group a member of BITC, but the subsidiary agency J Walter Thompson is.

Corporate governance
Separate Chairman and Chief Executive Y
Number of Directors 10
Number of Non-Executive Directors 6
(6 Independent Directors)
Insulated Directors All execs

Board Committees
Audit: Y   Remuneration: Y

Remuneration
Year end	31.12.91	31.12.92	31.12.93
Total board £M	1.04	1.35	2.04
% change	-7	23	41
Highest paid £	508,000	510,000	956,000
% change	0.2	0.3	87

Board
Sorrell, Martin *Chief Executive*
Brooks, Brian J *Executive Director*
Sampson, Gordon C *Executive Director*
Lerwill, Robert *Finance Director*
Bullmore, J J D *Independent Non-Executive*

Jackson, John *Independent Non-Executive*
Judge, Paul R *Independent Non-Executive*
Morten, Stanley *Independent Non-Executive*
Quelch, Prof. John A *Independent Non-Executive*
Stevens, Gordon *Non-Executive Chairman*

The board was substantially strengthened in 1992, following the financial restructuring. The annual report for 1992 detailed the membership and workings of audit, compensation and remuneration committees, and asserted compliance with all finalised Cadbury proposals, yet the 1993 report virtually ignored this issue. Nevertheless, this is one of the best annual reports produced by any company in this book, in that it analyses and comments on the company's industrial prospects as well as providing the usual statutory information and publicity on the group. It is unfortunate, then, that the details of bonus and incentive payments are blurred, especially since the figures have been so high.

Analysis and tables

The information in this book provides a unique view of how big business in Britain coped with the worst recession since 1945. The financial records span the five years from 1989 to 1994, which for most companies were the beginning and end of the recession. And the analysis in this chapter shows how they coped not only at the beginning and end of that period but throughout it. Unlike most such analyses, what follows examines how companies performed in each of the five years.

It is not a pretty picture, despite the fact that these are the companies which remained Britain's largest at the end of the period, hence presenting a more optimistic picture than a review of all those which began the period in that elevated position.

Only 18 companies out of more than 100 companies for which five years' data is available managed to increase earnings per share in each of the five years. Astonishingly, only 36 increased sales in each year. Only 21 companies produced positive cash flows in each year and, not surprisingly, investment suffered: only 39 of the companies in this book invested more than their depreciation charge in all five years.

Cash crises are also reflected in the figures for interest and dividend cover. As many as 16 companies saw interest cover slide more than once during the period to less than three times, with Forte scooping the pool by achieving that in each of the five years. Reluctance to cut dividends also left 28 companies with uncovered dividends in more than one year.

In many cases, employment also suffered although, perhaps surprisingly, more than 50 companies ended the period employing more people than in 1989. For some, that was the result of takeovers which also boosted other figures. On the other hand, corporate reshaping cut back other companies, the demergers of Courtaulds and ICI being the most significant. Others had no such excuse for finishing the period smaller than when it began: a total of 20 companies had lower sales in the final year, a massive 56 reported lower earnings, although only 27 reduced their dividends below the level in the first year. Shareholders in 37 companies found either the asset backing for each share or the aggregate shareholders' funds lower at the end of 1993 than five years previously. Sometimes, as with Thorn-EMI and Granada, that was a reflection of the huge change in the nature of the group, but in the main these companies were the ones which have suffered most in the recession. They include several banks, insurance companies and builders, and other walking wounded such as British Aerospace, Saatchi & Saatchi, Forte and Burton.

This analysis illustrates the difficulty of interpreting financial data, and shows how dangerous it is to draw conclusions about company performance from single indicators. For example, huge write-offs which reduced the capital base meant that several hard-hit companies were among the few which managed to end the period with higher return on capital. On the other hand, some of the most successful companies, such as the supermarket chains, were among 35 which had negative cash flows in each year – in the case of the supermarkets, as a consequence of heavy investment.

A combination of indicators is therefore necessary to produce a rounded view of the overall winners and losers.

The following table (in alphabetical order) shows what can be regarded as the overall leaders, having met the five key criteria shown. It illustrates the amazing growth of the food retailers and those who supply them. Consistency is also a virtue: most of these companies also made this winning league last year, with Tesco the only one from 1993 which has not made it this time, due to a marginal decline in earnings per share in the year to February 1994.

Criteria (in each year): *growth in sales and in earnings, investment higher than depreciation, and positive retentions; plus higher employment at the end of the five years.*

Cadbury Schweppes
Glaxo
Kwik Save
William Morrison
Northern Foods
Rentokil
Rothmans
Sainsbury

At the other end of the scale is a collection of companies which have consistently struggled through this period. (Many others have struggled, but have slipped out of the catchment for this book.) There are two categories here. First, a trio of clear losers – which would have been a quartet had Saatchi & Saatchi not escaped the criteria of two years' fall in earnings because earnings disappeared completely after the first year, making further falls impossible. Consistency is again a factor, unfortunately, since all bar GKN also appeared in this league last year. There is hope, however, from the fact that another entrant last year, Royal Insurance, is now on the recovery path, although Costain provides a warning – it has slipped out of the book this year.

442 ANALYSIS AND TABLES

Criteria: *falling earnings in at least three years, investment below depreciation in more than one year, negative retentions in at least three years, lower assets per share and lower shareholders funds at the end of the period than at the beginning.*

GKN
Trafalgar House
Saatchi & Saatchi

The second caterory of losers are those which have shrunk dramatically. None of these companies were in the same table last year. In fact the three which were do not appear in this year's edition (Barratt Developments, Slough Estates and Vickers).

Criteria: *lower values at the end of the period than at the beginning for: assets per share, shareholders' funds, sales, earnings, dividends and employment.*

Forte
Saatchi & Saatchi
Sears
Tarmac
Taylor Woodrow
Wimpey

The final league table in this collection includes many from the previous list, highlighting the big spenders – not on investment, but in interest and dividend payments. These are the companies which have stretched their finances to the limit, but which, in the worst traditions of British business, have nevertheless continued to pay dividends at excessive rates. Of these companies, only Lonrho also appeared in this table last year.

Criteria: *interest cover below three time for more than one year, dividends below earnings for more than one year*

Burton
Forte
Ladbroke
Lonrho
Pilkington
Tarmac
Taylor Woodrow
Wimpey

The remaining tables focus on individual criteria rather than combinations of indicators. They show two important aspects of corporate governance, plus league tables based on the largest and smallest companies in the book, and the top and bottom on each of the key factors included as part of the reference data in the text for each company.

POLITICAL DONATIONS

1. Companies which stopped making such donations in the past year

Allied Domecq
Coats Viyella
General Accident
MEPC
Thames Water
TI
Rothmans

2. The top donors
(£ '000s)

115	**Hanson**
80	**Forte**
60	**Glaxo**
60	**Rolls-Royce**
50	**Scottish & Newcastle**
42	**Tomkins**
40	**United Biscuits**
35	**Guardian Insurance**
30	**Legal & General**
30	**Argyll Group**
30	**Whitbread**
28	**Inchcape**
25	**Dixons**
25	**GKN**
25	**Kingfisher**
25	**Lucas**
25	**Rank Organisation**
25	**Tate & Lyle**
25	**Williams Holdings**

THE LARGEST AND THE SMALLEST

1. Stock market value
(As at mid-July 1994. Note that figures for Shell and Unilever are for the combined group, not just for the UK quoted company)

Top 20

£ billions	company
62.2	**Royal Dutch/Shell**
30.1	**Unilever**
24.6	**British Telecom**
22.0	**BP**
19.5	**HSBC**
17.3	**Glaxo**
13.5	**BTR**
13.4	**BAT Industries**
13.0	**Hanson**
12.2	**British Gas**
11.9	**Marks & Spencer**
9.9	**SmithKline Beecham**
9.3	**Cable & Wireless**
9.0	**Barclays Bank**
9.0	**RTZ**
8.9	**Guinness**
8.9	**Grand Metropolitan**
7.9	**Reuters**
7.9	**National Westminster Bank**
7.6	**GEC**

Bottom 20

£ millions	company
877	**MAI**
846	**Southern Water**
840	**Welsh Water**
829	**Seeboard**
823	**Burton Group**
817	**Northern Electric**
816	**Kwik Save**
798	**MANWEB**
742	**Wessex Water**
727	**Dixons**
711	**South Western Electricity**
648	**South Wales Electricity**
645	**South West Water**
602	**Taylor Woodrow**
595	**Wimpey**
560	**Northern Ireland Electricity**
557	**WPP**
455	**Body Shop**
381	**Northumbrian Water**
315	**Saatchi & Saatchi**

2. Sales
(For banks, the figures are net interest plus other income, for insurance companies, total premium income.)

Top 20

£ billions	company
63.4	**Royal Dutch/Shell**
47.7	**BP**
27.9	**Unilever**
17.9	**BAT Industries**
13.7	**British Telecom**
10.8	**British Aerospace**
10.6	**ICI**
10.4	**British Gas**
9.8	**BTR**
9.8	**Hanson**
9.7	**Sainsbury**
8.6	**Tesco**
8.3	**Prudential**
8.1	**Grand Metropolitan**
8.0	**HSBC**
7.4	**Barclays Bank**
7.0	**National Westminster Bank**
6.3	**British Airways**
6.2	**SmithKline Beecham**
6.0	**Marks & Spencer**

Bottom 20

£ millions	company
892	**South Western Electricity**
851	**Vodafone**
792	**Scottish Hydro-Electric**
726	**Smiths Industries**
604	**MFI**
593	**De La Rue**
588	**Rentokil**
586	**South Wales Electricity**
583	**Anglian Water**
546	**Enterprise Oil**
544	**Next**
482	**Northern Ireland Electricity**
482	**Yorkshire Water**
382	**Welsh Water**
319	**Southern Water**
252	**Northumbrian Water**
206	**Wessex Water**
195	**Body Shop**
194	**South West Water**
147	**MAI**

444 ANALYSIS AND TABLES

GROWTH RATES

3. Number of employees
(Note that some figures may be total numbers, whether full-time or part-time, while others are full-time equivalent numbers)

Top 20
('000s)	company
294	Unilever
190	BAT Industries
156	British Telecom
130	Lonrho
130	BTR
127	Royal Dutch/Shell
120	Sainsbury
104	HSBC
101	BET
99	Barclays Bank
98	National Westminster Bank
97	British Aerospace
93	GEC
87	ICI
81	Bass
80	Boots
79	British Gas
78	Coats Viyella
73	BP
72	Kingfisher

Bottom 20
5.1	MAI
5.0	Welsh Water
4.8	PowerGen
4.7	Yorkshire Water
4.7	Northern Electric
4.6	MANWEB
4.5	S. G. Warburg
3.6	Scottish Hydro-Electric
3.5	Northern Ireland Electricity
3.4	Southern Water
3.2	South Wales Electricity
3.1	Vodafone
2.9	Northumbrian Water
2.6	South West Water
2.5	Body Shop
1.9	Wessex Water
1.5	Eurotunnel
1.1	MEPC
0.7	Enterprise Oil
0.5	Land Securities

1. Sales growth

Top 20
%	company
274	Tomkins
133	Caradon
131	Body Shop
124	Kwik Save
111	Rentokil
110	Vodafone
102	Cable & Wireless
99	Inchcape
98	Wm Morrison
95	Northern Foods
94	Carlton Communications
93	Rank Organisation
92	Glaxo
83	Severn Trent
76	Associated British Foods
71	J Sainsbury
70	Asda
70	De La Rue
69	Redland
67	MAI

Bottom 20
%	company
3.3	BET
3.0	Smiths Industries
-1.0	Granada
-1.9	Saatchi & Saatchi
-3.6	Sears
-4.4	GKN
-4.5	GEC
-6.1	Pilkington
-6.3	Reed International
-10.6	Taylor Woodrow
-11.8	Forte
-12.7	Grand Metropolitan
-18.0	British Steel
-19.3	ICI
-20.2	Storehouse
-20.5	Courtaulds
-21.7	Tarmac
-22.5	Wimpey
-34.1	RTZ
-39.8	Next

2. Earnings per share growth

Top 20

%	company
624	Guardian Insurance
538	Next
172	Storehouse
155	National Westminster Bank
153	Wm Morrison
138	Rentokil
137	Wellcome
124	De La Rue
108	Prudential
98	MAI
98	Body Shop
92	Vodafone
91	J. Sainsbury
79	Legal & General
77	Glaxo
76	Kwik Save
65	Reuters
64	General Accident
64	SmithKline Beecham
56	Tesco

Bottom 20

-58	Dixons
-58	Redland
-61	GKN
-61	Forte
-63	P & O
-65	Enterprise Oil
-67	Asda
-67	BICC
-70	Britsh Aerospace
-74	Rolls-Royce
-83	Wimpey
-84	WPP
-87	Lucas
-89	BET
-89	Burton
-91	British Steel
-91	Trafalgar House
-94	Pilkington
-98	Tarmac
-100	Fisons

3. Employment growth

Top 20

%	company
257	Eurotunnel
208	Tomkins
121	Kwik Save
103	Rentokil
94	Body Shop
94	Burmah Castrol
91	Vodafone
80	Rank Organisation
76	Enterprise Oil
69	Caradon
68	Wm Morrison
63	Carlton Communications
51	Bowater
48	Severn Trent
39	Glaxo
38	Northern Foods
38	TI Group
37	Asda
36	J Sainsbury
30	Guinness

Bottom 20

-23	TSB
-24	British Aerospace
-24	British Steel
-24	Thorn-EMI
-25	GKN
-31	De La Rue
-32	Pilkington
-33	Wimpey
-35	ICI
-36	GEC
-37	Saatchi & Saatchi
-37	British Telecom
-39	BP
-39	RTZ
-40	Storehouse
-43	Grand Metropolitan
-44	Next
-44	Pearson
-46	Forte
-66	Courtaulds

Index of brands and subsidiaries, and their parent companies

This index relates the main brands and subsidiaries of the companies covered in this book to their owners. It does not include all the names listed under the key reference data that precedes the Outlook for each company, only the most significant, and concentrates mainly on subsidiary companies rather than brand names.

Abekas Carlton Communications
Actifed Wellcome
Adams Childrenswear Sears
AEI Cables General Electric Company
Airwick Reckitt & Colman
Allied Bakeries Associated British Foods
Allied Dunbar BAT Industries
Alton Towers Pearson
Amdega Williams Holdings
Anglesey Aluminium RTZ
Anglia Television MAI
Ansells Allied Domecq
Aquafresh SmithKline Beecham
Aqua Libre Grand Metropolitan
ARC Hanson
Elizabeth Arden Unilever
Arlington Securities British Aerospace
Armitage Shanks Blue Circle
Artex BPB
Associated Asphalt English China Clays
Avery General Electric Company
Avon Medical Smiths Industries
AZT Wellcome

Backer Spielvogel Bates Saatchi & Saatchi
Baileys liqueur Grand Metropolitan
Balfour Beatty BICC
B&Q Kingfisher
Bassett's Cadbury Schweppes
Beazer Hanson
Beconase Glaxo
Becotide Glaxo
Beefeater gin Allied Domecq
Beefeater restaurants Whitbread
Bells whisky Guinness
BhS Storehouse
Biffa Waste Services Severn Trent
Birds Eye Unilever

Blue Band Unilever
Boddingtons Whitbread
Bovis P&O
Bowyers Northern Foods
British Gypsum BPB
British Linen Bank BPB
British Shoe Corporation Sears
British Sugar Associated British Foods
Britoil British Petroleum
Brooke Bond Unilever
John Brown Trafalgar House
BRS NFC
Brush Traction BTR
BSkyB Granada, Pearson
Builder Center Wolseley
Bundy TI
Burberrys Great Universal Stores
Burger King Grand Metropolitan
Butlin's Rank
Butterley Brick Hanson
Butterworth Reed Elsevier
Buxted Poultry Hillsdown

Canada Dry Cadbury Schweppes
Carl Byoir WPP
Carling Black Label Bass
Carlsberg-Tetley Allied Domecq
Carr's United Biscuits
Castrol Burmah Castrol
Catteau Tesco
Cementation Trafalgar House
Center Parcs Scottish & Newcastle
Central Television Carlton Communications
Chef & Brewer Scottish & Newcastle
Chloride Industrial Batteries BTR
Chrysalis Thorn-EMI
Cleanaway GKN
Cleveland Structural Engineering Trafalgar House
Coats Patons Coats Viyella
Comet Kingfisher
Comp-Air Siebe
Coral Bookmakers Bass
Courvoisier Allied Domecq
Coutts National Westminster Bank
Crawford's United Biscuits
John Crane TI
Creda General Electric Company
Crookes Healthcare Boots
Mr Cube Tate & Lyle
Cunard Trafalgar House

Cuprinol Williams Holdings
Currys Dixons
Curtess Sears

Davy International Trafalgar House
Debenhams Burton
Dettol Reckitt & Colman
A B Dick General Electric Company
Direct Line Insurance Royal Bank of Scotland
Disprin Reckitt & Colman
Do It All Boots, W H Smith
Dolcis Sears
Domestos Unilever
Dorothy Perkins Burton
Dorma Coats Viyella
Dowty TI
Dulux ICI
Dunlop BTR
Dunlopillo BTR

Eagle Star Insurance BAT Industries
Economist Pearson
Elastoplast Smith & Nephew
Elida Gibbs Unilever
Embassy Hanson
EMI Thorn-EMI
Everest MB-Caradon
Exel NFC
Express Dairy Northern Foods
Express Lifts General Electric Company

Fairclough Amec
Financial Times Pearson
Flora Unilever
Forward Trust HSBC
Foseco Burmah Castrol
Foxboro Siebe
Fox's biscuits Northern Foods
Freemans mail order Sears
Fry's Cadbury Schweppes

Gilbey's Gin Grand Metropolitan
Gilbarco General Electric Company
Golden Wonder Dalgety
Gordon's gin Guinness
GPT General Electric Company
Grandfield Rock Collins Saatchi & Saatchi
Great Mills Grand Metropolitan
Green Giant Grand Metropolitan
Greenaways Lonrho

INDEX OF BRANDS AND SUBSIDIARIES

Greenham Taylor Woodrow

Häagen-Dazs Grand Metropolitan
Hales Waste RMC
Happy Eater Forte
Hard Rock Café Rank
Harpic Reckitt & Colman
Harrison & Sons Lonrho
Harvester restaurants Forte
Hawker Siddeley BTR
Henley Centre WPP
Hill and Knowlton WPP
Hilton International Ladbroke
HMV Thorn-EMI
Holiday Inn Bass
Homebase J Sainsbury
Homepride Tomkins
Horlicks SmithKline Beecham
Hotpoint General Electric Company
Hygena MFI

Imigran Glaxo
Imperial Tobacco Hanson
Initial UK BET
Intal Fisons
International paint Courtaulds
IPC Reed Elsevier

Jacksons of Piccadilly Associated British Foods
Jaeger Coats Viyella
J&B whisky Grand Metropolitan

Kays Great Universal Stores
Kellock Holdings Bank of Scotland
Kennecott RTZ
Kentucky Fried Chicken Forte
Kingsmill Associated British Foods

Lemsip Reckitt & Colman
Lil-lets Smith & Nephew
Little Chef Forte
Lo-Cost Argyll
Lombard finance National Westminster Bank
London Brick Hanson
Longman Pearson
Lucozade SmithKline Beecham
LWT Granada Group

McCorquodale Bowater
McLean Homes Tarmac
McVitie's United Biscuits
Madame Tussauds Pearson
Mann Egerton Inchcape
Marconi General Electric Company
Marshall Ward Great Universal Stores
Mattessons Unilever
Mecca bingo Rank
Mercantile Credit Barclays
Mercury Asset Management S G Warburg
Mercury Communications Cable & Wireless
Meridian TV MAI

Metropole Hotels Lonrho
Midland Bank HSBC
Millet's Sears
Mira Caradon
Mirrlees Blackstone BTR
Mothercare Storehouse
Moving Picture Company Carlton Communications
Murphy's Stout Whitbread
Myson Blue Circle

National Carriers NFC
NEI Rolls-Royce
Northern Dairies Northern Foods
NOP MAI

Odeon Cinemas Rank
Ogilvy & Mather WPP
Oldham Batteries BTR
Omo Unilever
Olympus Sport Sears
Our Price W H Smith
Oxo Unilever

Palethorpes Northern Foods
Parsons Turbines Rolls-Royce
PC World Dixons
Penguin Books Pearson
Penguin biscuits United Biscuits
Pergamon Press Reed Elsevier
Persil Unilever
Peter Stuyvesant Rothmans
PG Tips Unilever
Phoenix Assurance Sun Alliance
Pickfords transport NFC
Pilkington's Tiles BTR
Pillar RTZ
Pillsbury Grand Metropolitan
Pinewood Studios Rank
Pizza Hut Whitbread
John Player Hanson
Plumb Centre Wolseley
Polycell Williams Holdings
Pontin's Scottish & Newcastle
Pork Farms Northern Foods
Portex Smiths Industries
Potterton Blue Circle
Presto Argyll
Principles Burton

Quantel Carlton Comminications
Quorn Zeneca

Rawlplug Williams Holdings
Rest Assured BTR
Retrovir Wellcome
Reyrolle Rolls-Royce
Ribena SmithKline Beecham
Robinson's Reckitt & Colman
Rockware BTR
Rossing Uranium RTZ
Ross Young's United Biscuits
Rowland Worldwide Saatchi & Saatchi
Royal Ordnance British Aerospace
Ryvita Associated British Foods

Safeguard Insurance MAI
Safeway Argyll
Sankey Vending GKN
Savacentre Sainsbury
Saxone Sears
Schreiber MFI
SCM Chemicals Hanson
Scotch House Great Universal Stores
Selfridges Sears
Shearings Rank
Shorrock BET
Silver Spoon sugar Associated British Foods
Simple soap Smith & Nephew
Skol Allied Domecq
Smirnoff Grand Metropolitan
Spring Grove Services Granada
Stelrad Caradon
Stones bitter Bass
Sunblest Associated British Foods
Superdrug Kingfisher
Sutcliffe Catering Granada
Swinton Insurance Sun Alliance
Swish Williams Holdings

Tagamet SmithKline Beecham
Teacher's whisky Allied Domecq
Tecalemit Siebe
Technicolor Carlton Communications
Tennant's Lager Bass
Tenormin Zeneca
Tetley bitter Allied Domecq
Tetley tea bags Allied Domecq
Texas Homecare Ladbroke
Thames TV Pearson
J Walter Thompson WPP
Thorn fire protection Williams Holdings
Tilade Fisons
Tileon BTR
Timotei Unilever
Tioxide ICI
Top Shop Burton
Trebor Cadbury Schweppes
Triplex Safety glass Pilkington
Trollope & Colls Trafalgar House
Tums SmithKline Beecham
Tunnel Refineries Tate & Lyle
R Twining & Co Associated British Foods
Twyfords Caradon
Ty-Phoo Hillsdown

UK Waste Management Wessex Water
Ulster Bank Nat West Bank
United Distillers Guinness
United Molasses Tate & Lyle
United Transport BET

Van Heusen Coats Viyella
Vantona Viyella Coats Viyella
Vaseline Unilever
Vent-Axia Smiths Industries

INDEX OF BRANDS AND SUBSIDIARIES

Ventolin   Glaxo
Vernons   Ladbroke
VG instruments   Fisons
Victoria Wine   Allied Domecq
Virgin Megastores   W H Smith
Virgin Records   Thorn-EMI

Wagon Finance   MAI
Wallace Evans   Welsh Water
Wallis   Sears
Wall's   Unilever
Waterstone's   W H Smith
Welcome Break   Forte
John West   Unilever
Westminster Press   Pearson
Wiggins Teape   Arjo Wiggins Appleton
Windolene   Reckitt & Colman
Woolworths   Kingfisher
Worthington beer   Bass

Yale   Williams Holdings
Yarrow Shipbuilders   General Electric Company
Youngers beer   Scottish & Newcastle

Zantac   Glaxo
Zenith Media   Saatchi & Saatchi
Zovirax   Wellcome

Glossary

(A word or phrase given in italics is defined under its own entry in this list.)

'A' and 'B' shares   See *Ordinary shares*.

ABSA   Association for Business Sponsorship of the Arts.

ACT (advance corporation tax)   Tax on *dividends*, which is deducted by a company from dividends paid to shareholders, and paid to the Inland Revenue. It is normally deductible from corporation tax on UK profits, but some companies with low UK earnings do not have enough UK tax to set ACT against. They therefore end up paying more tax than if all their earnings came from the UK. This problem affects companies such as British Petroleum which have a high proportion of overseas earnings.

ASA   Advertising Standards Authority: the watchdog which sets standards and considers complaints by the public about advertisements.

Assets   Land, property, stock, equipment or other valuable goods owned by a company. See *Current assets, Fixed assets, Intangible assets*.

Associate company   A company linked to but not controlled by another company, usually defined as having between 20 per cent and 50 per cent of its *shares* owned by the other company. The company which owns that proportion of the shares takes the same share of its *profits* and *assets* into its accounts.

Bad debt   A debt which a company has decided the customer is not going to pay. Usually a provision is made first, when the possibility of non-payment arises, before the debt is finally *written off*.

Balance sheet   The accounting statement which shows *assets*, liabilities and *capital* employed, in other words what the company owns and what it owes at a particular date.

Bear market/run   The opposite of *bull*, in stock market terms – a pessimistic view of a share price or of the market as a whole. Bear raid: a major selling exercise which drives down a company's *share* price.

Below the line   The line is that drawn at the calculation of *profit* or *earnings per share*. Before the clamp-down on creative accounting in 1992 and 1993, *extraordinary items* were shown below the line, so omitting large costs from the *earnings per share* calculation.

Big Bang   The shake-up of the stock market in 1986, which ended monopolistic practices, especially the separation between the market-makers (who make money, as in any market, from selling *shares* at a higher price than they were bought) and the stock brokers, whose income is in the form of a commission on share deals for clients. Big Bang brought many new entrants to the stock market, notably large banks, but resulted in overcapacity and heavy losses for many players.

BITC   Business in the Community: the organisation whose membership consists of companies committed to giving increased support to the communities in which they operate. See Commentary and Key, section on corporate conscience.

Black Monday   Monday 19 October 1987, when the UK stock market followed Wall Street in a precipitous crash. The *FTSE 100 index* fell from 2302 on the Friday evening to 1802 by Tuesday night. The threat of financial collapse encouraged governments to relax their financial stand, lowering interest rates more than they otherwise would, and further boosting the consumer boom of the late 1980s.

Black Wednesday   Wednesday 16 September 1992, when the UK withdrew from the European Exchange Rate Mechanism after failing to maintain the pound above its *ERM* base level. The government was subsequently able to reduce interest rates swiftly, since these no longer needed to be at a high level in order to support the pound.

Bull market/run   An optimistic view leading to a rising *share* price or market. See also *Bear market/run*.

Buy-in   In the context of *shares*, the purchase by a company of its own shares, which are subsequently cancelled, intended to enhance shareholder value if the company believes the shares can be bought at a price which will increase *earnings per share* for the remaining shares. In the context of corporate reconstruction, the introduction of a new management team to a business, with new finanace – similar to a buy-out except that the existing management is replaced.

Cadbury Committee   The committee set up to recommend improvements in corporate governance, which published the Cadbury Code in December 1992. See Commentary and Key, section on corporate governance.

Capital   The money invested in a company, described as capital employed in accounts. See *Working capital*.

Capital appreciation   In the context of *share* prices, the increase in the value of the share, which produces a *profit* when the shares are sold. This is usually the main gain to shareholder, rather than the income from six-monthly *dividends*.

scrip. (If the number of shares doubles, the share price will halve.) Scrip *dividends* are now offered increasingly as an alternative to taking the dividend as cash. This also helps solve some companies' tax problems.
Share   See *Ordinary shares, Preference shares.*
Share capital   *Capital* subscribed by shareholders. See *Equity.*
Shareholders' funds   The total of *capital* subscribed by shareholders and the *reserves* accumulated over the years.
Share swap   An agreement between two companies to buy each others' *shares* to create a mutual interest, e.g. Guinness/LVMH, and Midland Bank/HSBC before the takeover.
Solvency margin   For insurance companies, a measure of capital adequacy, being *shareholders' funds* as a percentage of premiums written.
Subsidiary   A company controlled by another, usually taken as having at least 50 per cent of its shares owned.
Turnover   Equivalent to sales or *revenue*. Also used as in *capital* turnover and stock turnover to indicate rate of use.
Working capital   *Capital* (i.e. money) tied up in a business to finance its trading. Equivalent to *current assets* less *current liabilities*. Often not adequately controlled, so adding to debts and interest costs. Hence a source of easy cash following a takeover by more effective management.
Write-down   Reduction in value, usually of property.
Write-off   A reduction in value, usually of property or similar *assets*, or, in the case of banks, of bad debts. Writing off the bad debts eliminates them from a company's balance sheet, but does not necessarily mean that the company has abandoned attempts to collect the debts.
Yield   See *Dividend yield.*

EIRIS

Where do you draw the line?

Exporting arms around the globe? Cutting corners on environmental protection? Marketing tobacco?

Different people emphasise different ethical concerns. But many now seek to reflect their beliefs in their investment decisions. When buying shares, unit trusts, personal pensions or endowment mortgages, they want to support companies they feel are doing good, and avoid those doing damage.

To do this you need accurate up-to-date facts and knowledge of the choices available and how to use them. That's where EIRIS (the Ethical Investment Research Service) comes in:

* Check your existing shares against your ethical criteria with our Portfolio Screen service. 1994 charges begin at £47 for individuals and small organisations.

* Keep up-to-date quarterly with "The Ethical Investor". 1994 Subscriptions are £12 for individuals, £24 for professionals and organisations.

* Find a financial adviser or fund manager from our free list of those using our services, or with experience in this field.

We look forward to helping you put your principles into practice

The Ethical Investment Research Service (EIRIS)
Freepost, London. SW8 1BR
tel: 071 735 1351